DK FRENCH DICTIONARY

FRENCH · ENGLISH
ENGLISH · FRENCH

D0042762

DK PUBLISHING, INC.

A DK PUBLISHING BOOK
www.dk.com

First American Edition, 1997

4 6 8 10 9 7 5

This book was originally published in the
DK Pockets series in 1999.

Published in the United States by
DK Publishing, Inc.
95 Madison Avenue
New York, New York 10016

ISBN 0–7894–2194–1

This edition revised by DK Publishing, Inc.

Printed and bound in Italy by Legoprint

THE IMITATED PRONUNCIATION

If the syllables given are pronounced as if they formed part of an English word, the speaker will probably be understood. However, the real sounds of the French language can be achieved by remembering a few simple rules:

r (italic) not to be pronounced at all.

ng (italic) not to be pronounced at all. It merely indicates that the preceding vowel has a nasal sound; ah*ng* is pronounced like **au** in "aunt", *ang* like **ang** in "fang," *ong* like **ong** in "wrong," and *ung* like **ung** in "lung."

r (bold type) pronounced more strongly than in English – rrroll it on the tongue.

sh (bold) like **s** in "measure."

eh like **e** in "bed."

er like **u** in "fur."

er (bold) is the same sound, but longer and with the **r** sounded.

er like **e** in "her." but more closed.

ah like **a** in "far." but shorter.

ai or ay like **ai** in "fair."

E, EE represent the sound of the French **u**: say "tree" with lips rounded as when whistling, and the terminal sound of **ee** is the one required.

oo like **oo** in "book," "look," "took."

There is practically **no stress** in French words; the same value should be given to all syllables.

LA PRONONCIATION FIGURÉE

Prononcer chaque syllabe comme si elle appartenait à un mot français, mais en tenant compte des indications suivantes:

a   a extrèmement bref. Dans certains mots (**have, had, has, man, hat** etc.), entre l'**a** de "bal" et l'**è** de "complète."

a, eu o son indistinct et sourd, analogue à celui d'**e** dans "me," "de," "que." Ce son est souvent indiqué par une apostrophe dans la prononciation figurée de certaines finales anglaises: **lesson,** less -'n.

o   son très bref, entre **eu** dans "fleur" et **a** dans "lac." Par exemple: **but,** botte (son presque comme "batte").

oa   désigne un son qu'on reproduira avec une exactitude suffisante en prononçant à peu près, et d'une seule émission de voix, comme **au** dans "laure," "Fauré."

r   à la fin d'un mot ou d'une syllabe, ne se fait sentir que très faiblement, à moins qu'il ne soit immédiatement suivi d'une voyelle.

h   cette lettre s'aspire toujours distinctement.

th   (dur=*ts*, et doux=*dz*). Prononcer *is* et *dz* en mettant le bout de la langue entre les dents comme lorsqu'on zézaie.

L'**e** muet à la fin d'une syllabe ne doit jamais se prononcer.

ACCENT TONIQUE

En anglais, l'accentuation d'une syllabe est donnée dans la prononciation figurée par le symbole ´ placé après la syllabe accentuée.

ABBREVIATIONS

a	adjective	poss	possessive
abbr	abbreviation	pp	past participle
adv	adverb	prep	preposition
art	article	pres part	present participle
auto	car	pron	pronoun
Brit	British	psych	psychology
chem	chemistry	refl	reflexive
com	commercial	s	singular
comput	computing	TM	trademark
conj	conjunction	v	verb
eccl	ecclesiastical	vulg	vulgar
f	feminine noun		
fam	familiar		
fin	financial		
fig	figurative sense		
geog	geographical		
hair	hairdressing		
inf	infinitive		
interj	interjection		
interrog	interrogative		
jur	legal		
m	masculine noun		
mech	mechanical		
med	medical		
mil	military		
mus	musical		
n	noun		
naut·	nautical		
num	numeral		
pers	persons		
phr	phrase		
pl	plural		
pop	popular		

ABRÉVIATIONS

abbr	abréviation	poss	possessif
adj	adjectif	pp	participe passé
adv	adverbe	prep	préposition
art	article	pres part	participe présent
auto	auto	pron	pronom
Brit	britanique	psych	psychologie
chem	chimie	refl	réflechi
com	commercial	s	singulier
comput	informatique	v	verbe
conj	conjonction	vulg	vulgaire
eccl	ecclésiastique	TM	marque déposée
f	nom féminin		
fam	familier		
fig	figuré		
fin	financier		
geog	géographique		
hair	coiffure		
inf	infinitif		
interj	interjection		
interrog	interrogatif		
jur	juridique		
m	nom masculin		
mech	mécanique		
med	médical		
mil	militaire		
mus	musical		
n	nom		
naut	nautique		
num	chiffre		
pers	personnes		
phr	expression		
pl	pluriel		
pop	populaire		

FRENCH · ENGLISH
FRANÇAIS · ANGLAIS

For an explanation
of the imitated
pronunciation please
read page 4.

à, ăh, *prep* to; at; in; within; on; by; for; from.

a, ăh, *v* has.

abaissement, ăh-bayss-mahng, *m* lowering; fall; diminution; disgrace.

abaisser, ăh-bayss-eh, *v* to lower; to pull down. **s'–,** to humble oneself; to stoop.

abandon, ăh-bahng-dong, *m* abandonment; desertion; ease. **àl'–,** neglected state.

abandonné, e, ăh-bahng-donn-eh, *pp* & *a* deserted; neglected; disused.

abandonner, ăh-bahng-donn-eh, *v* to abandon; to desert; to give up; to let go. **s'–,** to indulge (à, in); to let oneself go.

abasourdir, ăh-băh-zoohr-deer, *v* to stun.

abatage, abattage, ăh-băh-tăhsh, *m* cutting down; slaughter.

abâtardir, ăh-bah-tăhr-deer, *v* to debase. **s'–,** to degenerate.

abat-jour, ăh-băh-shoohr, *m* reflector; lampshade.

abattement, ăh-băht-mahng, *m* prostration.

abattis, ăh-băh-te, *m* felling; giblets.

abattoir, ăh-băh-to'ăhr, *m* slaughterhouse.

abattre, ăh-băh-tr, *v* to bring down; to cut down. **s'–,** to fall.

abattu, e, ăh-băh-tE, *pp* & *a* brought down; depressed.

abbaye, ăh-bay-yee, *f* abbey.

abbé, ăh-beh, *m* abbot; priest.

abbesse, ăh-bess, *f* abbess.

abcès, ăhb-say, *m* abscess.

abdiquer, ăhb-de-keh, *v* to abdicate.

abdomen, ăhb-doh-menn, *m* abdomen.

abeille, ăh-bay'e, *f* bee.

abhorrer, ăh-bor-eh, *v* to abhor; to loathe.

abîme, ăh-beem, *m* abyss.

abîmer, ăh-bee-meh, *v* to spoil; to damage.

abject, e, ăhb-sheckt, *a* base; mean.

abjection, ăhb-sheck-se-ong, *f* vileness.

abjurer, ăhb-shE-reh, *v* to renounce.

ablution, ăhb-lE-se-ong, *f* washing.

abnégation, ăhb-neh-găh-se-ong, *f* self-denial.

aboi, ăh-boăh, *m* **aboiement,** ăh-boăh-mahng, *m* bark; barking.

abois, ăh-boăh, *mpl* **aux abois,** oh-z'–, at bay; desperate situation.

abolir, ăh-bol-eer, *v* to abolish.

abominable,* ăh-bomm-e-năh-bl, *a* abominable.

abomination, ăh-bomm-e-năh-se-ong, *f* abomination.

abondamment, ăh-bong-dăh-mahng, *adv* plentifully.

abondant, e, ăh-bong-dahng, *a* abundant.

abonder, ăh-bong-deh, *v* to abound (**en,** in, with).

abonné, e, ăh-bonn-eh, *mf* subscriber.

abonnement, ăh-bonn-mahng, *m* subscription. **carte d'–,**kăhrt d–, season ticket.

abonner (s'–),săh-bonn-eh, *v* to subscribe.

abord, ăh-bor, *m* access. **d'–,** at first.

aborder, ăh-bor-deh, *v* to land; to approach; to accost; to tackle; to collide with.

aborti-f, ve, ăh-bor-tiff, *a* abortive.

aboucher, ăh-boo-sheh, *v* to bring together. **s'–,** to confer.

aboutir, ăh-boo-teer, *v* to end; to abut; to lead.

aboutissant, ăh-boo-tiss-ahng, *m* abuttal. **tenants et –s,** ter-nahng z'eh–, ins and outs.

aboyer, ăh-bo'ăh-yeh, *v* to bark.

abrégé, ăh-breh-**sheh,** *m* summary; synopsis.

abréger, ăh-breh-**sheh,** *v*

to shorten.

abreuver, ăh-brer-veh, *v* to water animals; (fig.) to soak. **s'–,** to drink plentifully.

abreuvoir, ăh-brer-vo'ăhr, *m* watering place.

abréviation, ăh-breh-ve-ah-se-ong, *f* abbreviation; shortening.

abri, ăh-bre, *m* shelter.

abricot, ăh-bre-ko, *m* apricot.

abriter, ăh-bre-teh, *v* to shelter.

abroger, ăh-bro-**sheh,** *v* to repeal.

abrupt, e,* ăh-brEpt, *a* abrupt; steep; rugged.

abrutir, ăh-brE-teer, *v* to stupefy. **s'–,** to make a beast of oneself.

absent, e, ăhb-sahng, *a* absent.

absenter(s'), săhb-sahng-teh, *v* to absent oneself.

abside, ăhb-seed, *f* apse.

absinthe, ăhb-sangt, *f* wormwood; absinth.

absolument, ăhb-sol-E-mahng, *adv* absolutely.

absolution, ăhb-sol-E-se-ong, *f* absolution; pardon.

absorber, ăhb-sor-beh, *v* to absorb; to engross.

absorption, ăhb-sorp-se-

ong, *f* absorption.

absoudre, ăhb-soo-dr, *v* to absolve.

abstenir(s'), săbhs-ter-neer, *v* to abstain.

abstinence, ăhbs-te-nahngss, *f* abstinence; fasting.

abstraire, ăhbs-trair, *v* to abstract.

abstrait, e,* ăhbs-tray, *a* abstract; abstruce; obscure.

absurde,* ăhbss-EErd, *a* absurd; silly.

absurdité, ăhbss-EEr-de-teh, *f* absurdity; nonsense.

abus, ăh-bE, *m* abuse.

abuser, ăh-bE-zeh, *v* to deceive; to abuse.

abusi-f, ve,* ăh-bE-ziff, *a* improper (use of word).

académie, ăh-kăh-deh-mee, *f* academy.

acajou, ăh-kăh-**shoo,** *m* mahogany.

acariâtre, ăh-kăh-re-ah-tr, *a* sour-tempered.

accablant, e, ăh-kăh-blahng, *a* overwhelming; oppressive; unbearable.

accablement, ăh-kăh-bler-mahng, *m* depression; dejection.

accabler, ăh-kăh-bleh, *v* to overwhelm;to crush; to overcome (**de,** with).

accaparer, ăh-kăh-păh-reh, *v* to monopolize; to forestall.

accéder, ăhck-seh-deh, *v* to accede; to comply (à, with).

accélérateur, ăhck-seh-leh-răh-ter, **m** accelerator.

accélérer, ăhck-seh-leh-reh, *v* to hasten.

accent, ăhck-sahng, *m* accent; tone; stress.

accentuer, ăhck-sahng-tE-eh, *v* to accentuate; to emphasize.

acceptation, ăhck-sehp-tăh-se-ong, *f* acceptance.

accepter, ăhck-sehp-teh, *v* to accept.

acception, ăhck-sehp-se-ong, *f* regard; meaning (of word).

accès, ăhck-say, *m* access; fit.

accessoire, ăhck-sess-o'ăhr *a* secondary; of minor interest.

accident, ăhck-se-dahng, *m* accident; mishap.

accidenté, e, ăhck-se-dahng-teh, *a* eventful; checkered; victim (of accident).

accise, ăhck-seez, *f* excise.

acclamer, ăh-klăh-meh, *v* to acclaim.

acclimater, ăh-kle-măh-teh, *v* to acclimatize.

accolade, ăh-kol-ăhd, *f* embrace.

accommodant, e, ăh-komm-odd-ahng, *a* easy to deal with.

accommodement, ăh-komm-odd-mahng, *m* settlement.

accommoder, ăh-komm-od-eh, *v* to suit; to do up (food); s' –à, to adapt oneself to; s' –de, to put up with.

accompagnement, ăh-kong-păhn'yer-mahng, *m* attendance; accessory; accompaniment.

accompagner, ăh-kong-păhn'yeh, *v* to accompany.

accompli, e, ăh-kong-ple, *pp & a* accomplished; thorough.

accomplissement, ăh-kong-pliss-mahng, *m* completion; fulfillment.

accord, ăh-kor, *m* agreement; consent; tuning; **d'–**, agreed; **tomber d' –**, tong-beh d–, to come to an agreement; **mettre d' –**, met-tr-d–, to conciliate.

accordage, ăh-kor-dăhsh, *m* tuning.

accorder, ăh-kor-deh, *v* to accord; to grant; to tune; to reconcile; s'–,to agree.

accoster, ăh-koss-teh, *v* to accost (a person); to come alongside.

accoter, ăh-kot-eh, *v* to stay; s' –,to lean.

accoucher, ăh-koo-sheh, *v* to give birth; to deliver a child.

accoucheur, ăh-koo-sher, *m* obstetrician.

accoucheuse, ăh-koo-sher-z, *f* midwife.

accouder (s'), săh-koo-deh, *v* to lean on one's elbow.

accoupler, ăh-koo-pleh, *v* to couple; to yoke; to pair.

accourir, ăh-koo-reer, *v* to run up; to hasten.

accoutrement, ăh-koo-trer-mahng, *m* garb.

accoutrer, ăh-koo-treh, *v* to rig out.

accoutumer, ăh-koo-tE-meh, *v* to accustom; s'–à, to get used to.

accréditer, ăh-kreh-de-teh, *v* to accredit; to credit.

accroc, ăh-kro, *m* tear; hitch.

accrocher, ăh-kro-sheh, *v* to hook on; to catch; s'–,to cling.

accroire, ăh-kro'ăhr, *v*

(used infinitive only and with **faire**), to make believe; **en faire –,** ahng fayr –, to impose (**à,** upon).

accroissement, ăh-kro'ahss-mahng, *m* increase.

accroître, ăh-kro'ăh-tr, *v* to increase; **s'–,**to grow.

accroupir, (s'), săh-kroo-peer, *v* to squat.

accru, e, ăh-krE, *pp* increased.

accueil, ăh-ker'e, *m* reception; welcome.

accueillir, ăh-ker-yeer, *v* to receive; to welcome.

accumulateur, ăh-kE-mE-lăh-ter, *m* accumulator; storage battery.

accumuler, ăh-kE-mE-leh, *v* to accumulate; to heap.

accusation, ăh-kE-zăh-se-ong, *f* accusation; charge.

accusé, e, ăh-kE-zeh, *mf* accused person; **–de réception,** – der reh-sep-se-ong, acknowledgment.

accuser, ăh-kE-zeh, *v* to accuse; to indict.

acerbe, ăh-sairb, *a* sour; harsh.

acéré, e, ăh-seh-reh, *a* sharp; steeled.

achalandé, e, ăh-shăh-lahng-deh, *a* well-stocked.

acharnement, ăh-shăhr-ner-mahng, *m* relentlessness; desperate eagerness.

acharner (s'), săh-shăhr-neh, *v* to be relentless; to persist in something.

achat, ăh-shăh, *m* purchase.

acheminement, ăsh-meen-mahng, *m* step.

acheminer, ăhsh-me-neh, *v* to dispatch; to convey; to route. **s'–,** to set out; to proceed.

acheter, ăhsh-teh, *v* to buy; **s'–,** to be bought; to be purchased.

acheteur, ăhsh-ter, *m* purchaser; buyer.

achever, ăhsh-veh, *v* to finish.

achoppement, ăh-shop-mahng, *m* stumbling; **pierre d'–,**pe'air d–, stumbling- block.

acide, ăh-seed, *m* acid; *a* sour; sharp.

acier, ăh-se-eh, *m* steel.

aciérie, ăh-se-eh-ree, *f* steelworks.

acné, ăhck-neh, *f* acne.

acolyte, ăh-kol-eet, *m* acolyte; accomplice.

acompte, ăh-kongt, *m*

installment; deposit.

à-côtés, ăh-koht-eh *mpl* perk.

acoustique, ăh-kooss-tick, *f* acoustics; *a* acoustic.

acquérir, ăh-keh-reer, *v* to acquire.

acquiescer, ăh-ke-ess-eh, *v* to acquiesce (**à, in**).

acquis, e, ăh-ke, *pp* acquired; *m* knowledge; experience.

acquisition, ăh-ke-ze-se-ong, *f* acquisition; purchase.

acquit, ăh-ke, *m* receipt; **– à caution,** – t'ah koh-se-ong, permit (customs).

acquittement, ăh-kit-mahng, *m* payment; acquittal; discharge.

acquitter, ăh-ke-teh, *v* to clear; to pay; to receipt; to acquit (an accused person); **s' –de,** to carry out.

âcre, ahkr, *a* acrid; sour.

âcreté, ah-krer-teh, *f* acridity; pungency.

acrimonie, ăh-kre-monn-ee, *f* acrimony.

acrobate, ăh-kro-baht, *mf* acrobat.

acrobatie, ăh-krob-ăh-see, *f* acrobatics.

acte, ăhckt, *m* act; action; deed; certificate; **faire – de,** fair – de, to show proof of.

ac-teur, -trice, ăhck-ter, *mf* actor; actress.

actif, ăhck-tiff, *m* assets.

acti-f, ve, * ăhck-tiff, *a* active.

action, ăhck-se-ong, *f* act; deed; share; *pl* stock.

actionnaire, ăhck-se-onn-air, *mf* shareholder.

actionner, ăhck-se-onn-eh, *v* to set in motion; to sue.

activer, ăhck-te-veh, *v* to urge on; to activate.

activité, ăhck-te-ve-teh, *f* activity.

actualité, ăhck-tE-ăh-lee-teh, *f* reality; event; **les-s,** leh z–, the news; newsreel.

actuel, le, * ăhck-tE-ell, *a* present; real.

acuité, ăh-kE-e-teh, *f* acuteness.

adage, ăh-dăhsh, *m* saying; adage.

adapter, ăh-dăhp-teh, *v* to adapt; to fit; to apply; **s'–,** to be suitable (**à,** for).

addition, ăh-de-se-ong, *f* addition; bill (restaurant).

additionnel, le, ăh-de-se-onn-ell, *a* additional.

adepte, ăh-dept, *a* adept.

adhérer, ăh-deh-reh, *v* to

adhere; to join (party).

adhésion, ăh-deh-se-ong, *f* adhesion; joining (of party).

adieu, ăh-de-er, *m* farewell; *adv* good-bye; farewell.

adjacent, ăhd-shăh-sahng, *a* adjacent; contiguous.

adjoindre, ăhd-sho'ang-dr, *v* to adjoin; **s'–,** to take as an associate; to join.

adjoint, ăhd-sho'ang, *m* assistant; deputy mayor.

adjudant, ăhd-shE-dahng, *m* adjutant.

adjudicataire, ăhd-shE-de-kăh-tair, *m* highest bidder.

adjugé! ăhd-shE-sheh, *pp* gone! (in auctions).

adjuger, ăhd-shE-sheh, *v* to award; to knock down (at auctions); **s'–,** to appropriate to one's use.

adjurer, ăhd-shE-reh, *v* to adjure; to beseech.

admettre, ăhd-met-tr, *v* to admit; to allow.

administrateur, ăhd-me-niss-trăh-ter, *m* administrator; manager; director; trustee.

administré, e, ăhd-me-niss-treh, *pp* & *n* administered; person under one's jurisdiction.

administrer, ăhd-me-niss-treh, *v* to administrate; to administer.

admira-teur, -trice, ăhd-me-răh-ter, *mf* admirer.

admirer, ăhd-me-reh, *v* to admire.

admission, ăhd-miss-e-ong, *f* admission; admittance.

admonester, ăhd-monn-ess-teh, *v* to reprimand.

admonition, ăhd-monn-e-se-ong, *f* warning.

adolescent, e, ăh-doll-ess-sahng, *mf* youth, lad; girl.

adonner (s'), săh-donn-eh, *v* to addict oneself to; to devote oneself to.

adopter, ăh-dop-teh, *v* to adopt.

adorable, ăh-do-răh-bl, *a* adorable; charming.

adora-teur, -trice, ăh-dor-ăh-ter, *mf* worshipper.

adorer, ăh-do-reh, *v* to adore; to be passionately fond of.

adosser, ăh-dohss-eh, *v* to lean (against).

adoucir, ăh-doo-seer, *v* to soften; **s'–,** to grow softer.

adoucissement, ăh-doo-siss-mahng, *m* softening; alleviation.

adresse, ăh-dress, *f*

address; skill.

adresser, ăh-dress-eh, *v* to
address; to direct; **s'-,**to
apply; to be directed.

adroit, e,* ăh-dro'ăh, *a*
handy; skillful; artful.

aduler, ăh-dE-leh, *v* to
fawn upon, to adulate.

adulte, ăh-dEElt, *a* adult;
grown-up.

adultère, ăh-dEEl-tair, *a*
and *n* adulterous;
adulterer; adultery.

advenir, ăhd-ver-neer,
impers v to happen; to
befall.

adversaire, ăhd-vair-sair,
m opponent; foe.

adverse, ăhd-vairss, *a*
adverse.

adversité, ăhd-vair-se-teh,
f misfortune; adversity.

aéré, e, ăh-eh-reh, *a* aired;
airy; aerated.

aérodrome, ăh-eh-ro-
drohm, *m* airfield;
airport.

aérogare, ăh-eh-ro-gahr, *f*
air terminal.

aéroport, ăh-eh-ro-por, *m*
airport.

affable,* ăh-făh-bl, *a*
affable.

affaiblir, ăh-fay-bleer, *v* to
weaken.

affaire, ăh-fair, *f* affair;
business; matter; thing;
action; work; scrape;

avoir –à, ăh-vo'ăhr –
ăh, *v* to have to do with;
faire des –s, fair day z'–,
to do business; **faire
l'–de,** fair l– der, to suit;
homme d'–s, omm d–,
businessman; **se tirer
d'–,**ser tereh d–, to get
out of a scrape; **j'en fais
mon –,**shahng fay monn
–, I take it upon myself.

affairé, e, ăh-fay-reh, *a*
busy.

affaissé, e, ăh-fess-eh, *pp*
sunk down; depressed.

affaisser (s'), săh-fess-eh,
v to sink; to flag.

affamé, e, ăh-făh-meh, *pp*
& *a* starved; starving.

affamer, ăh-făh-meh, *v* to
starve.

affectation, ăh-feck-tăh-
se-ong, *f* affectation;
simulation; assignment.

affecté, e, ăh-feck-teh, *a*
affected, conceited.

affecter, ăh-feck-teh, *v* to
feign; to set apart; to
allocate; **s'–,**to be
moved; affected.

affection, ăh-feck-se-ong, *f*
affection; fondness;
disease.

affectionner, ăh-feck-se-
onn-eh, *v* to be fond of.

afférent, e, ăh-feh-rahng,
a pertaining to.

affermer, ăh-fair-meh, *v*

to rent; to lease.

affermir, ăh-fair-meer, *v*
to strenghten.

afféterie, ăh-feh-tree, *f*
affectation.

affichage, ăh-fe-shăhsh, *m*
bill-posting.

affiche, ăh-feesh, *f*
placard; poster.

afficher, ăh-fe-sheh, *v* to
stick up; to make a show
of; to expose.

affiler, ăh-fe-leh, *v* to
sharpen.

affilié, e, ăh-fe-le-eh, *a*
affiliated.

affiner, ăh-fe-neh, *v* to
refine.

affirmer, ăh-feer-meh, *v*
to assert; to affirm.

affleurer, ăh-fler-reh, *v* to
level; to crop out.

affliger, ăh-fle-sheh, *v* to
afflict; to grieve.

affluent, ăh-flE-ahng, *m*
tributary; *a* affluent.

affluer, ăh-flE-eh, *v* to
flow; to run; to abound.

affolé, e, ăh-foll-eh, *a*
distracted; panic-
stricken; spinning
(compass).

affoler, ăh-foll-eh, *v* to
drive mad; to panic.

affranchi, e, ăh-frahng-
she, *pp* & *a* freed;
prepaid.

affranchir, ăh-frahng-sheer, v to free; to prepay; to stamp (letter).

affranchissement, ăh-frahng-shiss-mahng, m emancipation; prepayment; postage.

affréter, ăh-freh-teh, v to charter; to freight.

affreu-x, se, * ah-frer, a horrible; dreadful; hideous.

affriander, ăh-free-ahng-deh, v to attract; to entice.

affront, ăh-frong, m insult; disgrace.

affronter, ăh-frong-teh, v to confront; to dare; to face.

affubler, ăh-fE-bleh, v to muffle up; **s'–**, to rig oneself out.

affût, ăh-fE, m lying in wait (for game); carriage (gun); **être à l'–**, ay-tr ăh l–, to be on the watch (**de,** for).

affûter, ăh-fE-teh, v to sharpen.

afin, ăh-fang, conj **–de,** in order to; **–que,** in order that.

agacement, ăh-găhss-mahng, m annoyance.

agacer, ăh-găh-seh, v to set on edge; to irritate; to provoke; to tease.

agacerie, ăh-găhss-ree, f provocation; pl allurement.

âge, ahsh, m age; old age; period; generation.

âgé, e, ah-sheh, a aged; old.

agence, ăh-shahngss, f agency.

agencement, ăh-shahngss-mahng, m arrangement (of house); pl fittings; fixtures.

agenda, ăh-shang-dăh, m memorandum book; diary.

agenouiller (s'), săhsh-noo'e-yeh, v to kneel.

agent, ăh-shahng, m agent; middleman; policeman.

agent de voyages, ăh-shahng-der-vo'ăh-yăhsh m travel agent.

agglomérer (s'), săh-glomm-eh-reh, v to agglomerate.

aggravation, ăh-grăh-văh-se-ong, f aggravation; worsening.

aggraver, ăh-grăh-veh, v to aggravate; to make worse; to increase; **s'–**, to become worse.

agile, * ăh-shill, a nimble; quick.

agir, ăh-sheer, v to act; to do; to work; **de quoi**

s'agit-il? der kwăh săh-she-till? what is the matter? **il s'agit de ...,** ill săh-she der ... the matter, thing, or question is (about, to) ...

agiter, ăh-she-teh, v to agitate; to shake; to toss; to wave; **s'–**, to exert oneself; to fret; to swell; to get disturbed.

agneau, ăhn-yoh, m lamb.

agonie, ăh-gonn-ee, f death struggle; anguish; great pain. **à l'–**, ăh-l–, dying.

agonisant, ăh-gonn-e-zahng, a dying.

agrafe, ăh-grăhf, f hook; clasp; staple.

agrafeuse, ăh-grăh-ferz, f stapler.

agraire, ăh-grair, a agrarian.

agrandir, ăh-grahng-deer, v to enlarge; **s'–**, to become larger; to expand.

agrandissement, ăh-grahng-diss-mahng, m enlargement.

agréable, * ăh-greh-ăh-bl, a agreeable; pleasing; acceptable.

agréé, ăh-greh-eh, m solicitor; attorney.

agrégation, ăh-greh-găh-se-ong, f high level

competitive exam.

agrégé, ăh-greh-**sh**eh, *m* holder of the "agrégation."

agrément, ăh-greh-mah*ng*, *m* consent; favor; pleasure; *pl* charms.

agrès, ăh-gray, *m pl* rigging; tackle.

agresseur, ăh-grayss-**er**, *m* aggressor.

agreste, ăh-gresst, *a* rustic.

agricole, ăh-gre-kol, *a* agricultural.

agriculteur, ăh-gree-kEEl-ter, *m* agriculturist; farmer.

agripper, ăh-gre-peh, *v* to clutch.

aguerrir, ăh-ghay-reer, *v* to harden; to accustom; **s'–,** to become inured to war^. *a* hardened; accustomed.

aguets, ăh-ghay, *mpl* **aux –,** oh *z'*–, on the watch.

ahurir, ăh-E-reer, *v* to astound; to confuse.

ahurissement, ăh-E-riss-mah*ng*, *m* flurry; bewilderment.

aide, ayd, *m* helper; assistant.

aide, ayd, *f* help; assistance; **à l'–!** ăh l–! help!

aider, ay-deh, *v* to assist; to help.

aïe, ăh-e, *int* oh dear! oh! (pain).

aïeul, ăh-yerl, *m* grandfather; *f* **aïeule,** ăh-yerl, grandmother.

aïeux, ăh-yer, *mpl* ancestors; forefathers.

aigle, ay-gl, *m* eagle; lectern; *f* standard.

aiglon, ay-glong, *m* eaglet.

aigre,* ay-gr, *a* sour; acid; tart.

aigrefin, ay-grer-fang, *m* crook.

aigrelet, te, ay-grer-lay, *a* sourish.

aigrette, ay-grett, *f* egret; tuft.

aigreur, ay-grer, *f* sourness; acrimony; ill-feeling; spite.

aigrir, ay-greer, *v* to sour; to irritate; to envenom; **s'–,** to become sour; to become embittered.

aigu, ë, ay-ghE, *a* sharp; pointed; acute; shrill.

aiguille, ay-gwee-yer, *f* needle; hand (of clock, watch); index; spire; switch; point (rail).

aiguillette, ay-gwee-yet, *f* tag covering lace ends; slice of flesh.

aiguilleur, ay-gwee-yer, *m* point man.

aiguillon, ay-gwee-yong, *m* goad; sting; prickle;

thorn; spur.

aiguillonner, ay-gwee-yonn-eh, *v* to goad; to spur on.

aiguiser, ay-gwee-zeh, *v* to whet; to sharpen.

ail, ăh'e, *m* garlic.

aile, ayl, *f* wing; sail; aisle; flank (of army or fleet).

ailé, e, ay-leh, *a* winged.

aileron, ayl-rong, *m* pinion; small wing; fin.

ailette, ay-lehtt, *f* winglet.

ailleurs, ăh'e-yer, *adv* elsewhere; **d'–,** moreover.

aimable,* ay-măh-bl, *a* amiable; lovable; kind; pleasing.

aimant, ay-mah*ng*, *m* loadstone; magnet.

aimant, e, ay-mah*ng*, *a* loving; affectionate.

aimanter, ay-mah*ng*-teh, *v* to magnetize.

aimer, ay-meh, *v* to love; to like; to be fond of; to enjoy; **s'–,** to love each other.

aine, ayn, *f* groin.

aîné, e, ay-neh, *a & n* elder; eldest;

aînesse, ayness, *f* primogeniture; **droit d'–,** dro'ăh d–, birthright.

ainsi, ang-se, *adv & conj* so; thus; therefore,

–que, – ker, as well as; **–de suite, –** der sweet, so on; **–soit-il, –** so'ăh-till, amen!

air, air *m* air; wind; look; appearance; likeness; tune; **avoir l'air de,** ăh-vo'ăhr lair der, to look like; **en l'–,** ahng l–, in the air; upward; at random.

airain, ay-rang, *m* brass; **d'–,** d–, pitiless; hard.

aire, air, *f* area; threshing-floor; zone; aerie.

ais, ay, *m* plank; board.

aisance, ay-zahngss, *f* ease; comfort; competency; **être dans l'–,** ay-tr dahng l–, to be well off.

aise, ayz, *f* ease; comfort; enjoyment; **à l'–,** ăh l–, comfortable.

aise, ayz, *a* glad; pleased (**de,** of, with).

aisé, e,* ay-zeh, *a* easy; well-off.

aisselle, ayss-ell, *f* armpit.

ajonc, ăh-shong, *m* gorse.

ajourner, ăh-shoohr-neh, *v* to postpone; to put off; to defer; to summon; **s'–,** to adjourn.

ajouter, ăh-shoo-teh, *v* to add; **s'–,** to be added.

ajuster, ăh-shEEs-teh, *v* to adjust; to fit; to arrange; to reconcile; to aim at;

s'–, to be adjusted; adapted; to adapt oneself; to fit.

alanguir, ăh-lahng-gheer, *v* to make languid; to enfeeble; to weaken.

alarme, ăh-lăhrm, *f* alarm.

alarmer, ăh-lăhr-meh, *v* to alarm; **s'–,** to take fright.

albâtre, ăhl-bah-tr, *m* alabaster; snowy whiteness.

albumine, ăhl-bE-meen, *f* albumen.

alcali, ăhl-kăh-le, *m* alkali.

alcool, ăhl-kohl, *m* alcohol; spirits; *fam* booze.

alcoolisme, ăhl-koh-lissm, *m* alcoholism.

alcôve, ăhl-kohv, *f* alcove; recess.

alcyon, ăhl-se-ong, *m* kingfisher; halcyon.

aléa, ăh-leh-ăh, *m* risk; chance.

aléatoire, ăh-leh-ăh-to'ăhr, *a* risky; hazardous.

alêne, ăh-laynn, *f* awl.

alentour, ăh-lahng-toohr, *adv* around; about.

alentours, ăh-lahng-toohr, *mpl* neighborhood; surroundings; outskirts.

alerte, ăh-layrt, *f* alarm; alert.

alerte, ăh-layrt, *a* alert; sharp; quick; nimble.

algue, ăhl-gh, *f* alga; seaweed.

aliénable, ăh-le-eh-năh-bl, *a* transferable.

aliénation, ăh-le-eh-năh-se-ong, *f* transfer; estrangement; madness.

aliéné, e, ăh-le-eh-neh, *n* & *a* lunatic; mad(man).

aliéner, ăh-le-eh-neh, *v* to transfer; to alienate; to estrange.

aligner, ăh-leen-yeh, *v* to set in a line; **s'–,** to fall in.

aliment, ăh-le-mahng, *m* food.

alimentaire, ăh-le-mahng-tair, *a* dietary; nutritious; alimentary.

alinéa, ăh-le-neh-ăh, *m* paragraph.

alité, e, ăh-le-teh, *pp* & *a* laid up; bedridden.

aliter, ăh-le-teh, *v* to confine to bed; **s'–,** to take to one's bed.

allaiter, ăh-lay-teh, *v* to suckle; to nurse.

allant, ăh-lahng, *pres part* & *a* going; active; stirring.

allécher, ăh-leh-sheh, *v* to allure; to entice.

allée, ăh-leh, *f* going; alley; passage; lane;

path; **–s et venues,**
–z'eh ver-nE, going and
coming; running about.

allège, ăh-laysh, *f* lighter
(nav.); tender; sill
(window).

alléger, ăh-leh-sheh, *v* to
lighten; to unload; to
ease.

allègre, * ăhl-lay-gr, *a*
lively; cheerful.

allégresse, ăhl-leh-gress, *f*
cheerfulness; glee.

alléguer, ăhl-leh-gheh, *v*
to allege.

allemand, e, ăhl-mahng, *a*
& *n* German.

aller, ăh-leh, *v* to go; to
get on; to become; to fit;
to suit; **comment allez-
vous?** komm-ahng t'ăh-
leh voo? how are you?;
cet habit vous va bien,
set ăh-be voo văh b'ang,
this clothing suits you
(or fits you) well; **s'en –,**
sahng n'–, to go away.

aller, ăh-leh, *m* **billet
d'–et retour,** bee-yay
d–eh rer-toor, return
ticket.

allergie, ăh-lair-shee, *f*
allergy.

allergique, ăh-lair-shick, *a*
allergic.

alliage, ăh-le-ăhsh, *m*
alloy.

alliance, ăh-le-ahngss, *f*

alliance; match;
wedding ring.

allier, ăh-le-eh, *v* to ally;
to match; to blend; to
mix; to alloy; **s'–** to
combine; to unite (à,
with); to intermarry; to
harmonize with.

allô!, ăh-loh *int* hello (on
phone).

allocation, ăh-lock-ăh-se-
ong, *f* allowance; grant.

allocution, ăh-lock-E-se-
ong, *f* short speech.

allonge, ăh-longsh, *f*
(table); extension.

allonger, ăh-long-sheh, *v*
to lengthen; to prolong;
s'–, to grow longer; to
lie down.

allouer, ăh-loo-eh, *v* to
allow; to grant.

allumer, ăh-lE-meh, *v* to
light; to kindle; **s'–,** to
light up; to catch fire.

allumette, ăh-lE-mett, *f*
match.

allumeur, ăh-lE-mer, *m*
igniter; lamplighter.

allure, ăh-lEEr, *f* gait; pace;
manner; aspect.

allusion, ăhl-lE-ze-ong, *f*
allusion; **faire –à,** fayr –
ăh, to allude to.

aloi, ăh-lo'ăh, *m* **de bon –**
respectable; worthy; **de
mauvais –** unsavoury;
unworthy.

alors, ăh-lor, *adv* then; at
that time; in that case.

alouette, ăh-loo-ett, *f* lark.

alourdir, ăh-loor-deer, *v*
to render heavy; **s' –,** to
become heavy.

aloyau, ăh-lo'ăh-e-oh, *m*
sirloin.

alpestre, ăhl-pess-tr, *a*
Alpine.

alpinisme, ăhl-pe-nism *m*
mountaineering.

altérable, ăhl-teh-răh-bl, *a*
liable to change.

altérant, e, ăhl-teh-rahng,
a alterative; producing
thirst.

altération, ăhl-teh-răh-se-
ong, *f* change;
deterioration;
misrepresentation;
falsification; faltering.

altercation, ăhl-tayr-se-
ong, *f* wrangling.

altéré, e, ăhl-teh-reh, *a*
altered.

altérer, ăhl-teh-reh, *v* to
alter; to impair; to
debase; to misrepresent;
to falsify; **s'–,** to become
worse.

alternati-f, -ive, * ăhl-
tair-năh-tiff, *a*
alternative; alternating;
-ive, *nf* alternative.

alterner, ăhl-ter-neh, *v* to
alternate; to take turns.

altesse, ăhl-tess, *f*

highness (title).

altitude, ăhl-tee-tEEd, *f* altitude.

alto, ăhl-to, *m* tenor violin.

alun, ăh-lung, *m* alum.

alvéole, ăl-veh-ol, *f* cell; socket.

amabilité, ăh-măh-be-le-teh, *f* pleasantness; kindness.

amadouer, ăh-măh-doo-eh, *v* to coax.

amaigrir, ăh-may-greer, *v* to make thin; to emaciate.

amaigrissant, e ăh-may-gree-ssahng-té, *a* regime; cure; diet; **amaigrissement** *m* loss of weight.

amande, ăh-mahngd, *f* almond.

amandier, ăh-mahng-de-eh, *m* almond tree.

amant, e, ăh-mahng, *mf* lover; suitor; sweetheart.

amarrer, ăh-măh-reh, *v* to moor; to fasten; to lash.

amas, ăh-mah, *m* heap; pile; mass.

amasser, ăh-măhss-eh, *v* to amass; to heap up; **s'–,** to gather.

ama-teur, ăh-mahter, *a mf* amateur; lover; dilettante.

amazone, ăh-măh-zohn, *f*

amazon; female rider; riding-habit; *m* the Amazon river.

ambassade, ăhng-băhss-ăhd, *f* embassy.

ambassa-deur, -drice, ahng-băhss-ăh-der, *mf* ambassador; ambassadress.

ambiance, ahng-be-ahngss, *f* atmosphere (of surroundings, of environment, etc.).

ambiant, e, ahng-be-ahng, *a* surrounding; ambient.

ambigu, ë, ahng-be-ghE, *a* ambiguous; obscure.

ambitieu-x, se, * ahng-be-se-er, *a* ambitious; pretentious; *n* ambitious person.

ambition, ahng-be-se-ong, *f* ambition.

ambre, ahng-br, *m* amber.

ambulance, ahng-bE-lahngss, *f* ambulance.

ambulancier, ahng-bE-lahngss-e-eh, *m* ambulance man; orderly.

ambulant, e, ahng-bE-lahng, *a* itinerant; strolling; traveling (circus, etc.).

âme, ahmm, *f* soul; mind; spirit; life; feeling; ghost; heart; essence; core; creature; bore (of gun); valve.

améliorer, ăh-meh-le-o-reh, *v* to improve; to make better; **s'–,** to get better.

aménagement, ăh-meh-năhnsh, *m* fitting out; disposition; *pl* fittings; accommodation.

aménager, ăh-meh-năh-sheh, *v* to arrange.

amende, ăh-mahngd, *f* fine; penalty; costs; **–honorable,** –onn-or-ăh-bl, apology.

amendement, ăh-mahngd-mahng, *m* amendment; improvement.

amender, ăh-mahng-deh, *v* to improve.

amener, ăhm-neh, *v* to bring; to introduce; to bring in; on or about; **mandat d'–,** mahng-dăh d–, warrant for arrest; capias.

am-er, ère, * ăh-mair, *a* bitter.

américain, e, ăh-meh-re-kang, *a & mf* American.

amertume, ăh-mair-tEEm, *f* bitterness.

ameublement, ăh-mer-bler-mahng, *m* furniture.

ameuter, ăh-mer-teh, *v* to train to hunt together; to excite; to draw a crowd; **s'–,** to rebel; to riot.

ami, e, ăh-me, *mf* friend; **chambre d'** –, shahng-br d–, spare room; *a* friendly to; fond of.

amiable, ăh-me-ăh-bl, *a* amicable; **à l' –,** ăh l–, amicably; by private contract.

amiante, ah-me-ahngte, *f* asbestos.

amical, e, * ăh-me-kăhl, *a* friendly; kind.

amidon, ăh-me-dong, *m* starch.

amincir, ăh-mang-seer, *v* to make thinner; **s'–,** to become thinner.

amiral, ăh-me-răhl, *m* admiral; **contre –,** kong-tr' –, rear admiral.

amirauté, ăh-me-roh-teh, *f* admiralty.

amitié, ăh-me-te-eh, *f* friendship; *pl* kind regards; compliments; love.

ammoniaque, ăh-monn-e-ăhck, *f* ammonia.

amnésie, ăhm-neh-zee, *f* loss of memory; amnesia.

amnistie, ăhm-niss-tee, *f* amnesty.

amoindrir, ăh-mo'ang-dreer, *v* to diminish.

amollir, ăh-moll-eer, *v* to soften; to mollify; to enervate.

amonceler, ăh-mongss-leh, *v* to heap up.

amont, ăh-mong, *m* upriver; upstream; uphill.

amorce, ăh-morss, *f* bait; allurement; priming; cap.

amortir, ăh-mor-teer, *v* to deaden; to pay off; to redeem; **s'–,** to grow weak or faint.

amortissable, ăh-mor-tiss-ăh-bl, *a* redeemable.

amortissement, ăh-mor-tiss-mahng, *m* paying off; redemption; (wireless) damping.

amortisseur, ăh-mor-tiss-er, *m* shock absorber.

amour, ăh-moohr, *m* love; passion; **–propre,** – pro-pr, self-love; self-esteem.

amourette, ăh-moo-rett, *f* passing love affair.

amoureu-x, se, * ah-moo-rer, *a* in love; enamored.

amovible, ăh-mov-ee-bl, *a* removable.

ampère. ahng-pair, *m* ampere.

ampèremètre, ahng-pair-met-tr, *m* ammeter.

amphibie, ahng-fe-bee, *a* amphibious.

ample, * ahng-pl, *a* ample; spacious; large; copious.

ampleur, ahng-pler, *f* ampleness; largeness; fullness.

ampliation, ahng-ple-ăh-se-ong, *f* duplicate; true copy; **pour –,** poohr –, a true copy.

amplification, ahng-ple-fe-kăh-se-ong, *f* enlargement.

amplifier, ahng-ple-fe-eh, *v* to enlarge upon.

amplitude, ahng-ple-tEEd, *f* amplitude.

ampoule, ahng-pool, *f* blister; phial; (electric light) bulb.

ampoulé, e, ahng-pool-eh, *a* blistered; bombastic.

amputer, ahng-pE-teh, *v* to amputate.

amuser, ăh-mE-zeh, *v* to amuse; to entertain; to deceive; **s'–,** to enjoy oneself.

amuse-gueule, ăh-mEEz-gherl, *m* cocktail snack.

amygdale, ăh-meegh-dăhl, *f* tonsil.

an, ahng, *m* year, **jour de l'–,shoohr** der l–, New Year's day.

analogue ăh-năh-log, *a* analogous.

analyser, ăh-năh-le-zeh, *v* to analyze; to parse; to criticize.

ananas, ăh-năh-năh, *m* pineapple.

anarchie, ăh-năhr-shee, *f* anarchy.

anathème, ăh-năh-taym, *m* anathema.

ancêtre, ahng-say-tr, *m* ancestor.

anchois, ahng-sho'ăh, *m* anchovy.

ancien, ahng-se-ang, *m* elder; senior.

ancien, ne, * ahng-se-ang, *a* ancient; old; past; former; retired.

ancienneté, ahng-se-enn-teh, *f* antiquity; seniority; age.

ancre, ahng-kr, *f* anchor; **lever l'–,** ler-veh l–, to weigh anchor; **–de salut,** – der săh-lE, sheet anchor.

andouille, ahng-doo'e-yer, *f* chitterlings; idiot (familiar)

andouillette, ahng-doo'e-yette, *f* small sausage.

âne, ahn, *m* donkey; dunce.

anéantir, ăh-neh-ahng-teer, *v* to annihilate; to destroy; to tire out.

anéantissement, ăh-neh-ahng-tiss-mahng, *m* annihilation; utter exhaustion; self-humiliation.

anémie, ăh-neh-mee, *f* anemia.

ânerie, ahn-ree, *f* stupidity; gross ignorance; blunder.

anesthésie, ăh-ness-teh-ze, *f* anesthesia.

anesthésiste, ăh-ness-teh-zist, *m* anesthetist.

anévrisme, ăh-neh-vrissm, *m* aneurysm.

ange, ahngsh, *m* angel; **être a ux–s,** ay-tr oh z' –, to be overjoyed.

angine, ahng-sheen, *f* sore throat.

anglais, ahng-glay, *a* English (language); *n* English *m*.

angle, ahng-gl, *m* angle; corner.

Angleterre, ahng-gler-tair, *f* England.

angliciser, ahng-gle-se-zeh, *v* to anglicize.

anglicisme, ahng-gle-sissm, *m* anglicism.

angoisse, ahng-gwăhss, *f* anguish; pang.

anguille, ahng-ghee-yer, *f* eel; **–sous roche,** – soo rosh, a snake in the grass.

anicroche, ăh-ne-krosh, *f* hitch.

animal, ăh-ne-măhl, *n* & *a* animal; sensual; brutal.

animer, ăh-ne-meh, *v* to animate; to enliven; to

cheer; to excite; **s'–,** to become excited; warm; angry; to encourage each other.

anis, ăh-ne, *m* aniseed.

ankylose, ahng-ke-lohz, *f* stiffness.

anneau, ăh-noh, *m* ring.

année, ăh-neh, *f* year; crop; vintage.

annelé, e, ăhn-leh, *a* ringed.

annexe, ăh-nex, *f* annex; rider; schedule.

annihilation, ăhn-ne-ee-lăh-se-ong, *f* annihilation.

anniversaire, ăh-ne-vair-sair, *n* & *a* anniversary; birthday.

annonce, ăh-nongss, *f* announcement; advertisement.

annoncer, ăh-nong-seh, *v* to announce; to foretell; **s'–bien,** s– be-ang, to look promising.

annoter, ăhn-no-teh, *v* to annotate.

annuaire, ăh-nE-air, *m* yearbook; directory.

annulaire, ăhn-nE lair, *m* ring finger, *a* annular.

annulation, ăhn-nE-lăh-se-ong, *f* canceling.

annuler, ăhn-nE-leh, *v* to annul; to cancel.

anoblir, ăh-nob-leer, *v* to

ennoble.

anodin, e, ăh-nod-ang, *a* mild; unmeaning; painkiller.

anomalie, ăh-nomm-ăh-lee, *f* anomaly.

ânon, ah-no*ng*, *m* little donkey.

ânonner, ah-nonn-eh, *v* to falter; to mumble.

anonyme, * ăh-nonn-eem, *a* anonymous; **société –,** soss-e-eh-teh –, joint-stock company.

anormal, e, * ăh-nor-măhl, *a* abnormal.

anse, ah*ng*ss, *f* handle; creek.

antan, ah*ng*-tah*ng*, *m* yesteryear.

antécédent, ah*ng*-teh-seh-dah*ng*, *a* & *m* antecedent; previous.

antenne, ah*ng*-tenn, *f* antenna; feeler; horn; (wireless) aerial.

antérieur, e, * ah*ng*-teh-re-er, *a* former, past; front.

antériorité, ah*ng*-teh-re-o-re-teh, *f* priority.

anthère, ah*ng*-tair, *f* anther; tip.

anthropophage, ah*ng*-trop-of-ăhsh, *a* & *m* cannibal.

antibiotique, ah*ng*-te-be-oh-tick, *a* & *m*,

antibiotic.

anticonceptionnel, le ah*ng*-te-ko*ng*-sep-se-o*ng*-nell, *a* contraceptive.

antidérapant, ah*ng*-te-deh-răh-pah*ng*, *a* nonskid (tire).

antidote, ah*ng*-te-dott, *m* antidote.

antienne, ah*ng*-te-enn, *f* anthem.

antiquaire, ah*ng*-te-kair, *m* antique dealer; antiquarian.

antiquité, ah*ng*-te-ke-teh, *f* antiquity; *pl* antiques.

antiseptique, ah*ng*-te-sayp-tick, *a* & *m* antiseptic.

antre, ah*ng*-tr, *m* cave; den.

anxiété, ah*ng*k-se-eh-teh, *f* anxiety.

anxieu-x, se, * ah*ng*k-se-er, *a* anxious; uneasy.

août, ăh'oo, or oo, *m* August.

apaiser, ăh-pay-zeh, *v* to appease; **s' –,** to subside; to abate; to compose oneself.

apanage, ăh-păh-năhsh, *m* -appanage; attribute; lot.

aparté, ăh-păhr-teh, *m* words spoken aside.

apercevoir, ăh-pair-ser-vo'ăhr, *v* to perceive; **s'–**

(de or **que),** to notice.

aperçu, ăh-pair-SE, *m* glance; summary view.

apéritif, ăh-peh-re-tiff, *m* appetizer; aperitif.

aphte, ăhft, *m* mouth ulcer.

apitoyer, ăh-pe-to'ah-e-eh, *v* to move to compassion; **s' –,** to pity.

aplanir, ăh-plăh-neer, *v* to level; to smooth.

aplatir, ăh-plăh-teer, *v* to flatten.

aplomb, ăh-plo*ng*, *m* perpendicularity; self-possession; audacity; **d' –,** upright.

apogée, ăh-po-sheh, *m* apogee; greatest height; peak.

apologie, ăh-poll-o-shee, *f* apology; vindication.

apostat, ăh-poss-tăh, *m* apostate.

aposter, ăh-poss-teh, *v* to set on a watch.

apostolat, ăh-poss-toll-ăh, *m* apostleship.

apostrophe, ăh-poss-trof, *f* apostrophe; address; reproach.

apostropher, ăh-poss-trof-eh, *v* to address; to challenge.

apothicaire, ăh-po-te-kair, *m* apothecary; **compte d' –,** ko*ng*t d–, exorbitant bill.

apôtre, ăh-poh-tr, *m*
apostle.

apparaître, ăh-păh-ray-tr,
v to appear.

apparat, ăh-păh-răh, *m*
pomp; state; **d' –,**
formal.

appareil, ăh-păh-ray'e, *m*
preparation; display;
apparatus; appliance.

appareiller, ăh-păh-ray'e-
eh, *v* to match; to set
sail.

apparemment, ăh-păh-
răh-mahng, *adv*
apparently.

apparence, ăh-păh-
rahngss, *f* appearance.

apparent, e, ăh-păh-rahng,
a apparent.

apparenté, e, ăh-păh-
rahng-teh, *a* related.

apparition, ăh-păh-re-se-
ong, *f* appearance;
publication; ghost.

appartement, ăh-păhr-ter-
mahng, *m* apartment;
flat.

appartenir, ăh-păhr-ter-
neer, *v* to belong to; to
concern.

appas, ăh-pah, *mpl*
attractions; charms.

appât, ăh-pah, *m* bait;
allurement.

appauvrir, ăh-poh-vreer, *v*
to impoverish.

appel, ăh-pell, *m* call;
appeal; muster.

appeler, ăhp-leh, *v* to call;
to appeal; to name; **s' –,**
to be called.

appendice, ăh-pang-diss,
m appendix; appendage.

appendicite, ăh-pang-de-
sit, *f* appendicitis.

appesantir, ăh-per-zahng-
teer, *v* to make heavy; **s'
–,** to become heavy; to
dwell (**sur,** upon).

appesantissement, ăh-per-
zahng-tiss-mahng, *m*
heaviness; dullness.

appétissant, e, ăh-peh-
tiss-ahng, *a* appetizing;
tempting.

appétit, ăh-peh-te, *m*
appetite; hunger; **l'
–vient en mangeant,** l–
ve-ang t'ahng mahng-
shahng, the more one
has, the more one
wants.

applaudir, ăh-ploh-deer, *v*
to applaud; to
commend; **s'– (de,** on),
to congratulate oneself.

applaudissement, ăh-
ploh-diss-mahng, *m*
applause; cheering.

application, ăh-ple-kăh-
se-ong, *f* application;
attention; diligence;
appropriation.

applique, ăh-pleek, *f*

bracket.

appliqué, e, ăh-ple-keh,
pp & a applied; studious;
diligent.

appliquer, ăh-ple-keh, *v* to
apply; to lay on; to
adapt; to devote; **s' –,** to
be applied; to be
applicable to; to apply
oneself.

appoint, ăh-po'ang, *m*
balance; odd money.

appointements, ăh-
po'angt-mahng, *mpl*
salary.

apport, ăh-por, *m* share of
capital; *pl* vendor's
shares.

apporter, ăh-por-teh, *v* to
bring (something
portable).

apposer, ăh-poh-zeh, *v* to
affix; to append; to add.

apposition, ăh-poh-ze-se-
ong, *f* affixing;
apposition.

apprécier, ăh-preh-se-eh,
v to appreciate; to value.

appréhender, ăh-preh-
ahng-deh, *v* to
apprehend; to arrest; to
fear.

appréhension, ăh-preh-
ahng-se-ong, *f*
apprehension; fear.

apprendre, ăh-prahng-dr,
v to learn; to hear; to
teach; to inform.

apprenti, ăh-prahng-te, *m* apprentice; novice.

apprentissage, ăh-prahng-tiss-ăhsh, *m* apprenticeship.

apprêt, ăh-pray, *m* preparation; dressing of food; affectation.

appris, e, ăh-pre, *pp* learnt; taught; **malappris,** măh-lăh-pre, ill-bred.

apprivoiser, ăh-pre-vo'ăh-zeh, *v* to tame.

approba-teur, trice, ăh-pro-băh-ter, *mf* approver. *a* approving; of approval.

approbati-f, ve, * ăh-pro-băh-tiff, *a* approbatory; of approval.

approbation, ăh-pro-băh-se-ong, *f* approval.

approchant, e, ăh-pro-shahng, *a* near; like; approximate; *adv* thereabouts.

approche, ăh-prosh, *f* approach; access.

approcher, ăh-pro-sheh, *v* to approach; to bring near **s' –,** to come near.

approfondi, e, ăh-pro-fong-de, *a* profound; thorough.

approfondir, ăh-pro-fong-deer, *v* to deepen; to sift.

approprier, ăh-pro-pre-eh, *v* to appropriate; to adapt; to suit; **s' –,** to appropriate to oneself.

approuver, ăh-proo-veh, *v* to approve.

approvisionnement, ăh-pro-ve-ze-onn-mahng, *m* victual; supply; stores.

approvisionner, ăh-pro-ve-ze-onn-eh, *v* to provide; **s'–,** to provide oneself (**de,** with); to lay in store.

approximati-f, ve, * ăh-prock-se-măh-tiff, *a* approximate; rough.

appui, ăh-pwe, *m* support; sill.

appuyer, ăh-pwe-yeh, *v* to support; to prop; to insist; **s'–,** to lean; to rely (**sur,** on).

âpre, ah-pr, *a* rough; harsh; severe.

après, ăh-pray, *prep* after; *adv* afterwards; **d'–,** from, according to; **et–?**eh–? what then?

après-demain, ăh-prayd-mang, *adv* the day after tomorrow.

après-dîner, ăh-pray-de-neh, *m* after dinner.

après-midi, ăh-pray-me-de, *m & f* afternoon.

âpreté, ah-prer-teh, *f* roughness; harshness;

greediness.

apte, ăh-pt, *a* fit; capable; qualified (**à,** of, for).

aptitude, ăhp-te-tEEd, *f* aptitude; fitness (**à,** to; **pour,** for).

apurer, ăh-pE-reh, *v* to audit.

aquarelle, ăh-ko'ăh-rell, *f* watercolor.

aquarium, ăh-ko'ăh-re-omm, *m* aquarium.

aquatique, ăh-ko'ăh-tick, *a* aquatic.

aqueduc, ăhck-dEEk, *m* aqueduct.

aquilin, ăh-ke-lang, *a* aquiline.

aquilon, ăh-ke-long, *m* north wind; cold wind.

arable, ăh-răh-bl, *a* arable; tillable.

arachide, ăh-răh-sheed, *f* peanut.

araignée, ăh-rayn-yeh, *f* spider.

aratoire, ăh-răh-to'ăhr, *a* agricultural.

arbalète, ăhr-băh-lett, *f* crossbow.

arbitrage, ăhr-be-trăhsh, *m* arbitration.

arbitraire, * ăhr-be-trayr, *a* arbitrary; despotic.

arbitre, ăhr-bee-tr, *m* arbitrator; umpire; master; **libre –,** lee-br' –, free will.

arborer, ăhr-bor-eh, v to set up; to hoist; to don.

arbre, ăhr-br, m tree; shaft; axle.

arbrisseau, ăhr-bre-soh, m small tree.

arbuste, ăhr-bEEst, m shrub.

arc, ăhrk, m bow; arc; arch.

arcade, ăhr-kăhd, f row of arches; arcade.

arc-boutant, ăhrk-boo-tahng, m buttress.

arceau, ăhr-soh, m arch; vault.

arc-en-ciel, ăhr-kahng-se-ell, m rainbow.

archange, ăhr-kahngsh, m archangel.

arche, ăhrsh, f arch; ark.

archéologue, ăhr-keh-o-log, m archeologist.

archer, ăhr-sheh, m bowman.

archet, ăhr-shay, m bow, fiddlestick.

archevêque, ăhr-sher-vayk, m archbishop.

archidiacre, ăhr-she-de-ăh-kr, m archdeacon.

archiduc, ăhr-she-dEEk, m archduke.

archiduchesse, ăhr-she-dE-shess, f archduchess.

archipel, ăhr-she-pell, m archipelago.

architecte, ăhr-she-teckt, m architect.

architecture, ăhr-she-teck-tEEr, f architecture.

archives, ăhr-sheev, fpl archives;records; recording office.

arçon, ăhr-song, m saddlebow; **cheval d'–,** sher-văhl-d, vault; vaulting horse.

ardemment, ăhr-dăh-mahng, adv ardently; eagerly; passionately.

ardent, e, ăhr-dahng, a burning; glowing; eager.

ardeur, ăhr-der, f ardor; eagerness; heat; spirit.

ardoise, ăhr-do'ăhz, f slate.

ardoisière, ăhr-do'ăh-ze-air, f slate quarry.

ardu, e, ăhr-dE, a arduous; difficult.

are, ăhr, m (unit of land measure in the French metrical system, equal to 100 square meters, or 119.60 square yards).

arène, ăh-rain, f arena; ring.

arête, ăh-rayt, f fishbone; edge; ridge.

argent, ăhr-shahng, m silver; money; cash; **–comptant,** –kong-tahng, ready money;– **fou,–** foo, lots of money.

argenté, e, ăhr-shahng-teh, a silvered; silver-white.

argenter, ăhr-shahng-teh, v to plate.

argenterie, ăhr-shahng-tree, f silver plate; plate.

argille, ăhr-sheel, f clay.

argileu-x, se, ăhr-she-ler, a clayey.

argot, ăhr-gho, m slang.

arguer, ăhr-ghE-eh, v to argue; to infer.

argument, ăhr-ghE-mahng, m argument; reasoning; summary.

argumenter, ăhr-ghE-mahng-teh, v to argue; to infer (**de,** from).

argutie, ăhr-ghE-see, f quibble.

aride,* ăh-reed, a arid; dry; barren.

aridité, ăh-re-de-teh, f aridity; dryness; barrenness.

aristocratie, ăh-riss-to-krăh-see, f aristocracy.

arithmétique, ăh-reet-meh-tick, f arithmetic.

arlequin, ăhr-ler-kang, m harlequin.

arlequinade, ăhr-ler-ke-năhd, f harlequinade; buffoonery.

armateur, ăhr-măh-ter, m shipowner.

armature, ăhr-măh-tEEr, f ironwork; framework;

fittings.

arme, ăhrm, *f* weapon; arm; **maître d'–,** may-tr d–, fencing master; **faire des–s,** fair day z'–, to fence.

armée, ăhr-meh, *f* army; multitude.

armement, ăhr-mer-mahng, *m* armament.

armer, ăhr-meh, *v* to arm (**de,** with); to set against (**contre,** kong-tr); to cock; to equip; **s'–,** to arm oneself (**de,** with); to summon up.

armoire, ăhr-mo'ăhr, *f* cupboard; wardrobe.

armoiries, ăhr-mo'ăh-ree, *fpl* arms; coat of arms.

armorial, ăhr-mo-re-ăhl, *m* book of heraldry.

armure, ăhr-mEEr, *f* armor.

armurier, ăhr-mE-re-eh, *m* gunsmith; armorer.

arnica, ăhr-ne-kăh, *mf* arnica.

aromatiser, ăh-ro-măh-te-zeh, *v* to aromatize; to perfume.

arome, ăh-rohm, *m* aroma.

aronde, ăh-rongd, *f* (obs.) swallow; **en queue d'–,** ahng ker d–, dovetailed.

arpège, ăhr-paish, *m* arpeggio.

arpent, ăhr-pahng, *m* acre.

arpentage, ăhr-pahng-tăhsh, *m* land surveying.

arpenter, ăhr-pahng-teh, *v* to survey; to stride along.

arpenteur, ăhr-pahng-ter, *m* land surveyor.

arquer, ăhr-keh, *v* to arch; to bend; **s'–,** to become curved.

arrache-pied (d'), dăh-răhsh-pe-eh, *adv* at a stretch; without interruption.

arracher, ăh-răh-sheh, *v* to force out; to pull out; to pluck out; to snatch; to tear away; to wrest; **s'–,** to tear oneself, to break away (**à,** from).

arrangement, ăh-rahngsh-mahng, *m* arrangement; preparation; adjustment; accommodation.

arranger, ăh-rahng-sheh, *v* to arrange; to settle; to repair; to suit; to trim up; **s'–,** to make shift (**de,** with); to come to an arrangement (**avec,** with).

arrérages, ăh-reh-răhsh, *mpl* arrears.

arrestation, ăh-ress-tăh-se-ong, *f* arrest; custody.

arrêt, ăh-ray, *m* decree; stop; catch.

arrêt d'autobus, ăh-re-doh-toh-bEs, *m* bus stop.

arrêté, ăh-ray-teh, *m* decision; order, decree.

arrêter, ăh-ray-teh, *v* to stop; to detain; to restrain; to arrest; to fix; to resolve; to book; to engage; to conclude; **s'–,** to stop; to resolve (**à,** on).

arrhes, ăhr, *fpl* deposit (of money).

arrière, ăh-re-air, *m* back part; stern; *adv* behind; *interj* away! **en –,** ahng n' –, backward; **–pensée –** pahng-seh, *f* ulterior motive; **–plan, –** plahng, *m* background; **–saison, –** say-zong, *f* end of autumn; closing season.

arriéré, ăh-re-eh-reh, *m* arrears.

arriéré, e, ăh-re-eh-reh, *a* in arrears; backward (mentally).

arrimer, ăh-re-meh, *v* to stow.

arrimeur, ăh-re-mer, *m* stevedore.

arrivage, ăh-re-văhsh, *m* arrival (of cargo, goods).

arrivée, ăh-re-veh, *f* arrival.

arriver, ăh-re-veh, *v* to arrive (**à,** at); to come;

to reach; to occur; to succeed (**avec** with); to become of. **arrive que pourra,** ăh-reev ker poo-răh, happen what may.

arriviste, ăh-re-visst, *m* & *f* pushy person; climber (social).

arrogamment, ăh-ro-găh-mahng, *adv* arrogantly.

arrogance, ăh-ro-gahngss, *f* arrogance.

arrogant, e, ăh-ro-gahng, *a* arrogant; haughty.

arroger (s'), săh-ro-sheh, *v* to arrogate to oneself; to assume.

arrondir, ăh-rong-deer, *v* to round; **s' –,** to become round; to increase.

arrondissement, ăh-rong-diss-mahng, *m* rounding; administrative district; borough.

arrosage, ăh-ro-zăhsh, *m* watering.

arroser, ăh-ro-zeh, *v* to water; to sprinkle; to wet; to baste.

arrosoir, ăh-ro-zo'ăhr, *m* watering can; sprinkler.

arsenal, ăhr-ser-năhl, *m* arsenal; dockyard.

arsenic, ăhr-ser-nick, *m* arsenic.

art, ăhr, *m* art.

artère, ăhr-tair, *f* artery.

artériole, ăhr-teh-re-ol, *f* small artery.

artésien, ăhr-teh-ze-ang, *a* artesian.

arthrite, ăhr-treet, *f* arthritis.

artichaut, ăhr-te-shoh, *m* artichoke.

article, ăhr-tee-kl, *m* article; thing; paragraph; item; goods; **–de fond, –** der fong, leading article.

articulation, ăhr-te-kE-lăh-se-ong, *f* articulation; joint.

articulé, e, ăhr-te-kE-leh, *a* articulated.

articuler, ăhr-te-kE-leh, *v* to utter; to pronounce; to set forth.

artifice, ăhr-te- fiss, *m* contrivance; deceit; **feu d' –,** fer d –, fireworks.

artificiel, le, * ăhr-te-fe-se-ell, *a* artificial.

artificieu-x, se, * ăhr-te-fe-se-er, *a* artful.

artillerie, ăhr-tee-yer-ree, *f* artillery.

artilleur, ăhr-tee-yer, *m* artilleryman.

artisan, ăhr-te-zahng, *m* artisan; craftsman.

artiste, ăhr-tisst, *m* artist; actor; performer.

as, ahss, *m* ace; (fig.) one who excels in some part.

ascendance, ăhss-sahng-

dahngss, *f* ascending line; ascendancy.

ascendant, ăhss-sahng-dahng, *m* ascendancy; *pl* fore-fathers.

ascendant, e, ăhss-sahng-dahng, *a* ascending.

ascenseur, ăhss-sahng-ser, *m* lift; hoist; elevator.

ascension, ăhss-sahng-se-ong, *f* ascension; ascent; Ascension day.

ascète, ăhss-sett, *m* ascetic; hermit.

ascétisme, ăhss-seh-tism, *m* asceticism.

à sens unique, ăh-sahngss-E-neeck *a* one-way (*street*).

asile, ăh-zeel, *m* asylum; shelter; refuge; sanctuary.

aspect, ăhss-pay, *m* aspect; view; appearance.

asperge, ăhss-pairsh, *f* asparagus.

asperger, ăhss-pair-sheh, *v* to sprinkle (**de,** with).

aspérité, ăhss-peh-re-teh, *f* roughness.

aspersion, ăhss-pair-se-ong, *f* aspersion; sprinkling.

asphalte, ăhss-făhlt, *m* asphalt.

asphyxier, ăhss-feek-se-eh, *v* to asphyxiate; to suffocate.

aspic, ăhss-pick, *m* asp; spike lavender; cold meat in jelly.

aspirant, ăhss-pe-rahng, *m* candidate.

aspirant, e, ăhss-pe-rahng, *a* suction (pump, etc.).

aspirateur, ăhs-pe-răh-ter *m* vacuum cleaner.

aspiration, ăhss-pe-răh-se-ong, *f* inhalation; suction; (fig.) longing.

aspirer, ăhss-pe-reh, *v* to inhale; to exhaust; to suck up; (fig.) to long for.

aspirine, ăhss-pe-reen, *f* aspirin.

assaillant, e, ăhss-sah'e-ahng, *n & a* assailant.

assaillir, ăhss-sah'eer, *v* to assail; to attack.

assainir, ăhss-ay-neer, *v* to make healthy.

assaisonnement, ăhss-ay-zonn-mahng, *m* seasoning; salad dressing.

assaisonner, ăhss-ay-zonn-eh, *v* to season; to dress (salad).

assassin, ăhss-ăh-sang, *m* murderer.

assaut, ăhss-oh, *m* assault; attack; fencing match.

assemblage, ăhss-ahng-blăsh, *m* assemblage; gathering; medley; joining.

assemblée, ăhss-ahng-bleh, *f* assembly; congregation; party; meeting.

assembler, ăhss-ahng-bleh, *v* to collect; to convoke; to join together; **s'** –, to meet; **qui se ressemble s'assemble,** kee ser rerss-sahng-bl săhss-ahng-bl, birds of a feather flock together.

asséner, ăhss-eh-neh, *v* to strike; to deal (a blow).

assentiment, ăhss-ahng-te-mahng, *m* assent.

asseoir, ăhss-o'ăhr, *v* to seat; **s'** –, to sit down.

assermenter, ăhss-air-mahng-teh, *v* to swear in.

assertion, ăhss-air-se-ong, *f* assertion.

asservir, ăhss-air-veer, *v* to enslave; to subdue.

asservissement, ăhss-air-viss-mahng *m* enslavement; slavery.

assesseur, ăhss-ess-er, *m* assessor; assistant; judge.

assez, ăhss-eh, *adv* enough; fairly; rather.

assidu, e, ăhss-e-dE, *a* assiduous; diligent; attentive.

assiduité, ăhss-e-dwe-teh, *f* assiduity; regular attendance; *pl* assiduous attentions.

assidûment, ăhss-ahss-dE-mahng, *adv* assiduously; diligently.

assiégeant, e, ăhss-e-eh-shahng, *n & a* besieger.

assiéger, ăhss-e-eh-sheh, *v* to besiege; to dun (**de,** with).

assiette, ăhss-e-ett, *f* plate; situation; assessment.

assignable, ăhss-een-yăh-bl, *a* assignable.

assignation, ăhss-een-yăh-se-ong, *f* assignment; summons; writ; subpoena; appointment.

assigner, ăhss-een-yeh, *v* to assign; to allot; to summon; to appoint.

assimiler, ăhss-e-me-leh, *v* to assimilate (**to,** with).

assis, e, ăhss-e, *pp* seated.

assise, ăhss-eez, *f* course; layer; basis; foundation; *pl* assizes.

assistance, ăhss-iss-tahngss, *f* attendance; audience; help.

assistant, e, ăhss-iss-tahng *n & a* person present; helper; *pl* those present.

assister, ăhss-iss-teh, *v* to attend; to be present; to help.

association, ăhss-o-se-ăh-se-ong, *f* association;

partnership.

associé, e, ăhss-o-se-eh, *mf* associate; partner.

associer, ăhss-o-se-eh, *v* to associate; **s' –,** to join (**à, avec,** with); to enter into partnership; to share (**à,** in).

assombrir, ăhss-ong-breer, *v* to darken; **s' –,** to become gloomy.

assommant, e, ăhss-omm-ahng, *a* boring.

assommer, ăhss-omm-eh, *v* to knock down; to bore to death.

assommoir, ăhss-ommo'ăhr, *m* bludgeon; (fig.) sleazy bar.

assomption, ăhss-ongp-se-ong, *f* Assumption.

assortiment, ăhss-or-te-mahng, *m* assortment; set; stock; match.

assortir, ăhss-or-teer, *v* to assort; to stock; to match; **s' –,** to harmonize (**à, avec,** with).

assoupir, ăhss-oo-peer, *v* to make drowsy; to hush up **s' –,** to doze; to die away.

assoupissant, e, ăhss-oo-piss-ahng, *a* soporific.

assoupissement, ăhss-oo-piss-mahng, *m* drowsiness; indolence.

assouplir, ăhss-oo-pleer, *v* to make supple; **s' –,** to become supple.

assourdir, ăhss-oohr-deer, *v* to deafen; to muffle.

assourdissant, e, ăhss-oohr-diss-ahng, *a* deafening.

assouvir, ăhss-oo-veer, *v* to satiate; to glut.

assujettir, ăhss-E-**shayt**-eer, *v* to subdue; to bind; to fasten; **s'–,** to subject oneself.

assujettissement, ăhss-E-**shayt**-iss-mahng, *m* subjection.

assumer, ăhss-E-meh, *v* to assume.

assurance, ăhss-E-rahngss, *f* assurance; reliance; boldness; insurance.

assuré, e, ăhss-E-reh, *pp & a* assured; insured; secured; confident.

assurément, ăhss-E-reh-mahng, *adv* certainly; assuredly.

assurer, ăhss-E-reh, *v* to assure; to insure; to secure; to assert; **s'–,** to make sure (**de,** of; **que,** that).

assureur, ăhss-E -rer, *m* insurer; underwriter.

asthme, ăhssm, *m* asthma.

asticot, ăhss-te-ko, *m* maggot.

asticoter, ăhss-te-kot-eh, *v* (fam.) to worry; to tease.

astiquer, ăhss-te-keh, *v* to polish.

astral, e, ăhss-trăhl, *a* stellar; astral.

astre, ăhss-tr, *m* star.

astreindre, ăhss-trang-dr, *v* to subject; to compel.

astringent, e, ăhss-trang-shahng, *a* astringent.

astrologue, ăhss-troll-og, *m* astrologer.

astronome, ăhss-tronn-omm, *m* astronomer.

astuce, ăhss-tEEss, *f* cunning; astuteness; witticism.

astucieu-x, se,* ăhss-tE-se-er, *a* artful; crafty; witty.

atelier, ăh-ter-le-eh, *m* workshop; studio; gang; **chef d'–,** shayf d–, overseer.

à temps partiel, ăh-tahng-păhr-se-ell *a, adv* part-time.

atermoiement, ăh-tair-mo'ăh-mahng, *m* respite.

athée, ăh-teh, *m* atheist.

athlète, ăht-lett, *m* athlete; champion.

atlas, ăht-lăhss, *m* atlas.

atmosphère, ăht-moss-fair, *f* atmosphere.

atome, ăh-tom, *m* atom.

atomique, ăh-to-mick, *a*

atomic.

atomiseur, ăh-to-me-zer, *m* atomizer; spray.

atours, ăh-toohr, *mpl* attire; finery.

atout, ăh-too, *m* trump card.

âtre, ah-tr, *m* hearth.

atroce,* ăh-tross, *a* atrocious; heinous; excruciating.

atrocité, ăh-tross-e-teh, *f* atrocity; (archit.) eyesore.

atrophié, e, ăh-trof-e-eh, *a* wasted; withered.

attabler (s'), săh-tăh-bleh, *v* to sit down to table.

attachant, e, ăh-tăh-shahng, *a* engaging.

attache, ăh-tăhsh, *f* tie; bond; fastening; leash.

attaché, ăh-tăh-sheh, *m* attaché (of an embassy).

attaché, e, ăh-tăh-sheh, *pp* & *a* attached.

attachement, ăh-tăhsh-mahng, *m* affection.

attacher, ăh-tăh-sheh, *v* to attach; to fasten; to bind; to interest; to endear; **s'–,** to cling.

attaque, ăh-tăhck, *f* attack; fit; stroke.

attaquer, ăh-tăh-keh, *v* to attack; to begin; to sue; **s'–à,** to attack.

atteindre, ăh-tang-dr, *v* to

reach; to attain; to strike; to injure.

atteinte, ăh-tangt, *f* blow; injury; violation.

attelage, ăht-lăhsh, *m* team; harness; coupling.

atteler, ăht-leh, *v* to put to; to yoke.

attenant, e, ăht-nahng, *a* adjoining.

attendant (en), ahng n'ăh-tahng-dahng, *adv* meanwhile.

attendre, ăh-tahng-dr, *v* to wait for; to expect; to look forward to; **s'–à,** to expect; to rely upon.

attendrir, ăh-tahng-dreer, *v* to make tender; to move; **s'–,** to be moved.

attendrissement, ăh-tahng-driss-mahng, *m* emotion.

attendu, e, ăh-tahng-dE, *pp* expected; *prep* considering.

attentat, ăht-tahng-tăh, *m* criminal attempt; outrage.

attente, ăh-tahngt, *f* waiting; expectation.

attenter, ăh-tahng-teh, *v* to make a criminal attempt.

attenti-f, -ve,* ăh-tahng-tiff, *a* attentive.

attention, ăh-tahng-se-ong, *f* attention; care;

kindness.

atténuer, ăht-teh-nE-eh, *v* to weaken; to extenuate.

atterrer, ăh-tay-reh, *v* to throw down; to astound.

atterrir, ăh-tay-reer, *v* to land.

atterrissage, ăh-tay-riss-ăhsh, *m* landing.

attestation, ăh-tess-tăh-se-ong, *f* certificate; testimonial.

attester, ăh-tess-teh, *v* to attest; to take to witness.

attiédir, ăh-te-eh-deer, *v* to cool; **s'–,** to cool down.

attirail, ăh-te-rah'e, *m* apparatus; paraphernalia.

attirant, e, ăh-te-rahng, *a* attractive; alluring.

attirer, ăh-te-reh, *v* to attract; to draw; to bring on; **s'–,** to bring on oneself; to attract each other.

attiser, ăh-te-zeh, *v* to stir up; to poke.

attitré, e, ăh-te-treh, *a* regular; appointed; official.

attitude, ăh-te-tEEd, *f* attitude.

attouchement, ăh-toosh-mahng, *f* touch; feeling.

attraction, ăh-trăhck-se-ong, *f* attraction.

attrait, ăh-tray, *m* attraction; charm.

attrape, ăh-trăhp, *f* catch; trick; hoax; trap; **–nigaud**, – ne-goh, con game.

attraper, ăh-trăh-peh, *v* to entrap; to catch; to cheat; to get.

attrayant, e, ăh-tray'e-ahng, *a* attractive.

attribuer, ăht-tre-bE-eh, *v* to attribute; to assign; to impute; **s' –**, to claim.

attribution, ăht-tre-bE-se-ong, *f* attribution; prerogative.

attrister, ăh-triss-teh, *v* to sadden; **s' –**, to grieve.

attroupement, ăh-troop-mahng, *m* gathering; mob.

attrouper, ăh-troo-peh, *v* to assemble; **s' –**, to crowd.

au (*sing*), **aux** (*pl*), oh, contraction of **à le, à les.**

aubaine, oh-bayn, *f* windfall; godsend.

aube, ohb, *f* dawn.

aubépine, oh-beh-peen, *f* hawthorn.

auberge, oh-bairsh, *f* inn; **–de jeunesse**, der **sher**-ness, youth hostel.

aubergine, oh-bair-sheen,

f aubergine; eggplant.

aubergiste, oh-bair-**sh**isst, *m* innkeeper.

aucun, e, oh-kung, *a* any; no; none; *pron* anyone; no one.

aucunement, oh-kEEn-mahng, *adv* by no means; not at all.

audace, oh-dăhss, *f* audacity; insolence; daring.

audacieu-x, se*, oh-dăh-se-er, *a* audacious; impudent; bold.

au-dessous, oh-der-soo, *adv* below; underneath.

au-dessus, oh-der-sEE, *adv* above.

audience, oh-de-ahngss, *f* audience; hearing; court; sitting.

audiencier, oh-de-ahngss-e-eh, *m* usher; crier of a court.

audi-teur, trice, oh-de-ter, *mf* hearer.

auditi-f, ve, oh-de-tiff, *a* auditory.

audition, oh-de-se-ong, *f* hearing; audition.

auditoire, oh-de-to'ăhr, *m* audience.

au fond, oh-fong, *a* basically.

auge, ohsh, *f* trough; hod.

augmentation, og-mahng-tăh-se-ong, *f* increase;

rise.

augmenter, og-mahng-teh, *v* to increase; to raise; **s' –**, to increase.

augure, oh-ghEEr, *m* augury; omen; augur.

augurer, oh-ghE-reh, *v* to augur; to surmise.

auguste, oh-ghEEst, *a* august.

aujourd'hui, oh-shoohr-dwe, *adv* today; nowadays.

aumône, oh-mohn, *f* alms; charity.

aumônier, oh-moh-ne-eh, *m* chaplain.

aune, ohn, *m* alder; *f* ell.

auparavant, oh-păh-răh-vahng, *adv* before; previously; once; first.

auprès, oh-pray, *adv* near; close; hard by.

auprès de, oh-pray der, *prep* near; close to; in comparison with.

auréole, oh-reh-ol, *f* halo; glory; crown; nimbus.

auriculaire, oh-re-kE-lair, *m* the little finger; *a* auricular.

aurifère, oh-re-fair, *a* auriferous.

aurifier, oh-re-fe-eh, *v* to fill with gold.

aurore, oh-ror, *f* dawn.

ausculter, ohss-kEEl-teh, *v* to auscultate; to sound

the chest of.

auspice, oss-piss, *m* auspice.

aussi, ohss-e, *adv* too; also; likewise; so; as; as much. *conj* therefore; consequently; –...**que,** – ker, as...as.

aussitôt, ohss-e-toh, *adv* immediately; –**que,** – ker, as soon as.

austère,* ohss-tair, *a* stern; rigid.

autant, oh-tahng, *adv* as much; as many; so much; so many; **d'–mieux,** d– me-er, all the better; **d' –moins,** d– mo'*ang,* all the less; **d' –que,** d– ker, more especially as.

autel, oh-tell, *m* altar.

auteur, oh-ter, *m* author; writer; **droit d'–,** dro'ăh d–, copyright.

authenticité, oh-tahng-te-se-teh, *f* authenticity; genuineness.

autobiographe, oh-toh-be-oh-grăhf, *m* autobiographer.

autobiographie, oh-toh-be-oh-grăh-fee, *f* autobiography.

autobus, oh-toh-bEEs, *m* bus.

autocratie, oh-toh-krăh-sec, *f* autocracy.

autographe, oh-toh-grăhf, *m* autograph.

automate, oh-toh-măht, *m* automation.

automatique,* oh-toh-măh-tick, *a* automatic.

automne, oh-tonn, *m* autumn.

automobile, oh-toh-mo-beel, *f* car; *a* self-moving; **canot –,** kăh-no –, motorboat.

automobilisme, oh-toh-mo-be-lissm, *m* motoring.

automobiliste, oh-toh-mo-be-lisst, *mf* motorist.

autopsie, oh-top-see, *f* post-mortem examination; autopsy.

autorisation, oh-toh-re-zăh-se-ong, *f* authority; permission.

autoriser, oh-toh-re-zeh, *v* to authorize.

autorité, oh-toh-re-teh, *f* authority; power; control.

autoroute, oh-toh-root, *f* highway; freeway.

autoroute qui contourne, oh-toh-root-ke-kong-toohrn, *f auto* bypass.

autour, oh-toohr, *adv* round about.

autour de, oh-toohr *der,* *prep* around; about.

autre, oh-tr, *pron* another;

a other; different; **tout –,** too t'–, quite different; anybody else; **nous –s, vous –s,** noo z'–, voo z'–, we; you; ourselves; yourselves; **à d'– s,** ăhd d–, nonsense!

autrefois, oh-trer-fo'ăh, *adv* formerly.

autrement, oh-trer-mahng, *adv* otherwise.

autruche, oh-trEEsh, *f* ostrich.

autrui, oh-trwe, *pron* others.

auvent, oh-vahng, *m* pent-house; shed.

aux, oh, *m & fpl* to the; at the.

auxiliaire, ohk-se-le-air, *a & m* auxiliary.

aux seins nus, oh-sang-nE *a* topless.

aval, ăh-văhl, *m* guarantee; endorsement; lower part; **en –,** ahng n'–, down the river.

avaler, ăh-văh-leh, *v* to swallow; (fig.) to pocket.

avance, ăh-vahngss, *f* advance; money advanced; **d'–,** d–, beforehand.

avancement, ăh-vahngss-mahng, *m* progress; rise.

avancer, ăh-vahngss-eh, *v* to advance; to promote;

to hasten; to hold forth; to proceed; to progress; to be fast (clock); **s'–,** to come forward.

avanie, ăh-văh-nee, *f* outrage; affront.

avant, hă-vahng, *adv* far; deep; forward; *prep* before; *m* forepart; bow; **en –,** ahng n'–,in front; **–de** or **que,** before; **–> dernier, –** dair-ne-se-eh, last but one; **–hier, –** t'e-air, the day before yesterday; **–propos, –** pro-poh, foreword; **–> veille, –**vay'e, two days before.

avantage, ăh-vahng-tăhsh *m* advantage; benefit.

avantageu-x, se,* ăh-vahng-tăhsh-er, *a* advantageous.

avant-première, ăh-vahng-prer-me-air *f* preview.

avare, ăh-văhr, *m* miser; *a* avaricious.

avarice, ăh-văh-riss, *f* avarice.

avarie, ăh-văh-ree, *f* damage; average.

avarier, ăh-văh-re-eh, *v* to damage; to spoil; **s'–,** to get damaged.

avec, ăh-veck, *prep* with; by.

avenant, ăh—nahng, *m* additional clause (to an insurance policy).

avenant, e, ăhv-nahng, *a* prepossing; **à l'–,** ăh-l–l– in keeping with.

avènement, ăh-vane-mahng, *m* accession; coming.

avenir, ăhv-neer, *m* future; prospects; posterity; **à l' –,** ăhl–, in future.

avent, ăh-vahng, *m* advent.

aventure, ăh-vahng-tEEr, *f* adventure; love affair; **à l'–,** ăhl–, at random.

aventuré, e, ăh-vahng-tE-reh, *a* hazardous.

aventurer, ăh-vahng-tE-reh, *v* to venture; **s'–,** to take a chance.

aventureu-x, se,* ăh-vahng-tE-rer, *a* adventuresome.

aventuri-er, ère, ăh-vahng-tE-re-eh, *mf* adventurer; adventuress.

avenue, ăhv-nE, *f* avenue.

avérer, ăh-veh-reh, *v* to aver; **s'–,** to be proved.

averse, ăh-vairss, *f* heavy shower.

aversion, ăh-vair-se-ong, *f* dislike (**pour,** of, for).

averti, e, ăh-vair-te, *a* experienced, wide-awake.

avertir, ăh-vair-teer, *v* to warn; to inform.

avertissement, ăh-vair-tiss-mahng, *m* warning; notice; preface.

aveu, ăh-ver, *m* admission; avowal; confession; **homme sans–,** omm sahng z'–, vagabond.

aveugle, ăh-ver-gl, *a* blind.

aveuglément, ăh-ver-gleh,mahng, *adv* blindly; implicitly.

aveugler, ăh-ver-gleh, *v* to blind; **s'–,** to be blind (**sur,** to).

aveuglette, (à l'), ăh-lăh-ver-glett, *adv* in the dark; blindly.

aviateur, ăh-ve-ăh-ter, *m* airman.

aviation, ăh-ve-ăh-se-ong, *f* flying; Air Force.

avide,* ăh-veed, *a* greedy; eager.

avilir, ăh-ve-leer, *v* to degrade; **s'–,** to degrade oneself; to depreciate.

avilissement, ăh-ve-liss-mahng, *m* degradation; debasement.

avion, ăh-ve-ong, *m* airplane.

aviron, ăh-ve-rong, *m* oar; **l'–,** rowing (sport).

avis, ăh-ve, *m* opinion;

advice; caution; news.

avisé, e, ăh-ve-zeh, *a*
advised; wise;
circumspect.

aviser, ăh-ve-zeh, *v* to
perceive; to advise; to
see to it; **s'**–, to take it
into one's head (**de,** to).

aviver, ăh-ve-veh, *v* to
brighten; to quicken; to
polish.

avocat, ăh-vo-kăh, *m*
barrister; counsel;
lawyer.

avocat, ăh-vo-kăh, *m*
avocado.

avoine, ăh-vo'ăhn, *f* oats.

avoir, ăh-vo'ăhr, *v* to
have; to get; to be; *m*
property; **qu'avez-vous?**
kăh-veh voo? what is
the matter with you? **j'ai
chaud,** shay shoh, I am
warm; **il y a,** ill e ăh,
there is; there are; ago;
j'ai 20 ans, sheh-vang-
ahng, I am 20.

avoisiner, ăh-vo'ăh-ze-
neh, *v* to be near.

avortement, ăh-vor-ter-
mahng, *m* abortion.

avorter, ăh-vor-teh, *v* to
miscarry; **se faire** –, to
have an abortion.

avorton, ăh-vor-tong, *m*
abortive child or
animal.

avoué, ăh-voo-eh, *m*

solicitor; attorney.

avouer, ăh-voo-eh, *v* to
confess; to acknowledge.

avril, ăh-vreel, *m* April.

axe, ăhks, *m* axis; axle.

ayant-droit, ay-yahng-
dro'ăh, *m* rightful
owner; beneficiary.

azote, ăh-zot, *m* nitrogen.

azur, ăh-zEEr, *m* azure;
blue.

azyme, ăh-zeem, *a*
unleavened.

B

baba, băh-băh, *m* baba; spongy plum cake **–au rhum,** – oh romm, sponge cake moistened with rum syrup.

babillage, băh-bee-yăsh, *m* prattling.

babiller, băh-bee-yeh, *v* to prattle; to babble.

babine, băh-been, *f* lip of animal; chops (of animals).

babiole, băh-be-ol, *f* bauble; toy; knickknack.

bâbord, bah-bor, *m* port side.

babouin, băh-boo-ang, *m* baboon.

bac, băhck, *m* ferryboat.

baccalauréat, băh-kăh-loh-reh-ăh, *m* high school diploma.

bâche, bahsh, *f* canvas cover.

bachelier, băh-sher-le-eh, *m* one who has passed high school.

bachot, băh-sho, *m* "baccalauréat"; small boat.

bacille, băh-sill, *m* bacillus.

bâcler, bah-kleh, *v* to do hastily.

badaud, e, băh-doh, *mf* idler; saunterer.

badigeonner, băh-de-shonn-eh, *v* to whitewash; to paint.

badin, e, băh-dang, *a* & *mf* playful; joker.

badinage, băh-de-năhsh, *m* banter; lighthearted tone.

badiner, băh-de-neh, *v* to joke.

bafouer, băh-foo-eh, *v* to scoff at.

bagage, băh-găhsh, *m* luggage; **plier –,** ple-eh –, to pack up; to make off.

bagarre, băh-găhr, *f* fight; scuffle; brawl.

bagatelle, băh-găh-tell, *f* trifle; trinket.

bagne, băhn-yer, *m* convicts' prison.

bague, băhg, *f* ring.

baguette, băh-ghett, *f* wand; rod; stick; long stick of bread.

bah! băh, *interj* nonsense! pooh! indeed!

bahut, băh-E, *m* chest; cupboard.

bai, e, bay, *a* bay.

baie, bay, *f* bay; berry; opening.

baigner, bain-yeh, *v* to bathe; **se –,** to bathe.

baignoire, bain-yo'ăhr, *f* bathtub; (theater) box.

bail, bah'e, *m* lease; *pl* **baux,** boh.

bâillement, bah'e-mahng, *m* yawning; gaping.

bâiller, bah'e-eh, *v* to yawn; to gape.

bailleur, bah'e-er, *m* lessor.

bailli, bah'e-yee, *m* bailiff.

bâillon, bah'e-yong, *m* gag.

bâillonner, bah'e-yonn-eh, *v* to gag.

bain, bang, *m* bath; **salle de –,** săhl-der –, *f* bathroom.

bain-marie, bang-măh-ree, *m* double saucepan (cooking).

baïonnette, băh'e-onn-ett, *f* bayonet.

baiser, bay-zeh, *m* kiss.

baisse, bess, *f* fall; decline; drop.

baisser, bess-eh, *v* to lower; to let down; to decline; **se –,** to stoop.

bal, băhl, *m* ball.

balade, băh-lăhd, *f* stroll; ramble.

balader (se), ser băh-lăh-deh, *v* (fam.) to take a stroll.

baladin, băh-lăh-dang, *m* mountebank; buffoon.

balafre, băh-lăh-fr, *f* gash; scar.

balai, băh-lay, *m* broom; brush.

balance, băh-lahngss, *f* scale; pair of scales.

balancer, băh-lahng-seh, *v* to balance; to weigh; to hesitate; to swing; (fam.) to turn out; to dismiss.

balancier, băh-lahng-se-eh, *m* pendulum; pole; beam.

balançoire, băh-lahng-

so'ăhr, *f* seesaw; swing.

balayer, băh-lay-yeh, *v* to sweep.

balayures, băh-lay-yEEr, *fpl* sweepings.

balbutier, băhl-bE-se-eh, *v* to stammer; to mumble.

balcon, băhl-kong, *m* balcony.

baldaquin, băhl-dăh-kang, *m* canopy.

baleine, băh-lain, *f* whale.

baleinier, băh-lay-ne-eh, *m* whaler; **–de sauvetage, –** der sohv-t ăhsh, lifeboat.

balise, băh-leez, *f* beacon; buoy.

ballade, băh-lăhd, *f* ballad; ballade.

ballant, e, băh-lahng, *a* swinging; dangling.

balle, băhl, *f* ball; bullet; bale; **prendre la –au bond** prahng-dr lăh – oh bong, to seize the opportunity.

ballet, băh-lay, *m* ballet.

ballon, băh-long, *m* balloon; football.

ballot, băh-loh, *m* bale.

ballottage, băh-lot-ăhsh, *m* second ballot; shaking.

ballotter, băh-lot-eh, *v* to toss; to ballot.

balnéaire, băhl-neh-air, *a* bathing; **station –,** stăh-

se-ong –, seaside; health resort.

balourdise, băh-loohr-deez, *f* stupid thing; blunder.

balsamique, băhl-zăh-mick, *a* balsamic.

balustre, băh-lEEs-tr, *m* railing; balustrade.

bambin, e, bahng-bang, *mf* little child; tiny tot.

bambocheur, bahng-boh-sher, *m* debauchee.

bambou, bahng-boo, *m* bamboo.

ban, bahng, *m* proclamation; banishment.

banal, e,* băh-năhl, *a* commonplace; banal.

banane, băh-năhn, *f* banana.

banc, bahng, *m* bench.

bancal, e, bahng-kăhl, *a &* *n* bandy-legged.

bandage, bahng-dăhsh, *m* bandaging; truss; tire.

bande, bahngd, *f* strip; wrapper; gang; lot; tire.

bandeau, bahng-doh, *m* headband; bandage.

bandolette, bahngd-lett, *f* narrow band; small bandage.

bander, bahng-deh, *v* to bandage; to bind up; to stretch; to blindfold.

banderole, bahngd-rol, *f*

streamer.

bandit, bahng-de, *m* bandit.

bandoulière, bahng-doo-le-air, *f* shoulder belt; **en –,** ahng –, slung over the shoulder.

banlieue, bahng-le-er, *f* suburbs.

bannière, băh-ne-air, *f* banner; flag.

bannir, băh-neer, *v* to banish.

banque, bahngk, *f* bank; banking.

banqueroute, bahngk-root, *f* bankruptcy.

banquet, bahng-kay, *m* feast; banquet.

banquette, bahng-kett, *f* bench; seat.

banquier, bahng-ke-eh, *m* banker.

banquise, bahng-keez, *f* ice-shelf, -floe.

baptême, băh-taym, *m* baptism.

baptiser, băh-te-zeh, *v* to christen.

baquet, băh-kay, *m* tub; bucket.

baragouiner, băh-răh-gwee-neh, *v* to talk gibberish.

baraque, băh-răhck *f* shed; hovel; hut.

baratter, băh-răh-teh, *v* to churn.

barbare, băhr-băhr, *a* & *mf* barbarian; barbarous.

barbe, băhrb, *f* beard.

barbelé, băhr-ber-leh, *a* barbed; *m* barbed wire.

barbiche, băhr-beesh, *f* tuft of beard.

barbier, băhr-be-eh, *m* barber.

barboter, băhr-bot-eh, *v* to dabble; to paddle.

barbouiller, băhr-boo'e-yeh, *v* to daub; to scribble.

barbu, e, băhr-bE, *a* bearded.

barème, băh-raym, *m* scale of change.

barguigner, băhr-gheen-yeh, *v* to hum and haw; to hesitate.

baril, băh-re, *m* barrel; cask; keg.

bariolage, băh-re-o-lăhsh, *m* medley (of colors).

bariolé, băh-re-o-leh, *a* gaudy; of many colors.

baromètre, băh-roh-met-tr, *m* barometer.

baron, băh-rong, *m* baron; *f* **baronne,** băh-ronn.

baronnet, băh-ro-nay, *m* baronet.

baroque, băh-rock, *a* odd; baroque (style).

barque, băhrk, *f* boat.

barrage, băh-răhsh, *m* stoppage; dam; barrage.

barre, băhr, *f* bar; tiller; stroke.

barreau, băh-roh, *m* bar; law profession.

barrer, băh-reh, *v* to bar; to cross out.

barrette, băh-rehtt, *f* hair slide; barrette.

barrière, băh-re-air, *f* barrier; gate.

bas, bah, *adv* low down; *m* bottom; stocking.

bas, se,* bah, *a* low; mean; base.

basané, e, băh-zăh-neh, *a* sunburnt; swarthy.

bas-côté, băh-koh-teh, *m* aisle (side).

bascule, băhss-kEEl, *f* seesaw; weighing machine.

base, bahz, *f* basis; base.

baser, bah-zeh, *v* to base; to ground.

bas-fond, bah-fong, *m* low ground.

basque, băhsk, *f* flap (coat, etc.); *a* & *mf* Basque.

basse, bahss, *f* bass; violoncello.

basse-cour, bahss-koohr, *f* poultry yard.

bassesse, băhss-ess, *f* baseness; meanness.

bassin, băhss-ang, *m* basin; dock; pelvis.

bassiner, băhss-e-neh, *v* to

warm (a bed); to bathe (wound, etc.).

bassinoire, băhss-e-no'ăhr, *f* warming pan.

basson, bahss-ong, *m* bassoon.

baste! băhsst! *interj* pooh! bosh! nonsense!

bastingage, băhss-tang-găhsh, *m* netting.

bastringue, băhss-trang-gh, *m* sleazy dancing place.

bas-ventre, bah-vahng-tr, *m* lower abdomen.

bât, bah, *m* packsaddle.

bataille, băh-tah'e, *f* battle.

bataillon, băh-tah'e-ong, *m* battalion; host.

bâtard, e, bah-tăhr, *n & a* illegitimate; French loaf of bread.

bateau, băh-toh, *m* boat.

bateleur, băht-ler, *m* tumbler; buffoon.

batelier, băh-ter-le-eh, *m* boatman.

bâti, bah-te, *m* tacking; frame; *pp* built.

batifoler, băh-te-foll-eh, *v* to play; to romp.

bâtiment, bah-te-mahng, *m* building; ship.

bâtir, bah-teer, *v* to build; to erect.

bâtisse, bah-tiss, *f* building; masonry.

batiste, băh-tisst, *f* cambric; lawn.

bâton, bah-tong, *m* stick; club; **à –s rompus,** ăh–rong-pE, by fits and starts; **mettre des –s dans les roues,** met-tr day–dahng lay roo, to put a spoke in one's wheel.

bâtonner, bah-tonn-eh, *v* to cudgel.

battage, băh-tăhsh, *m* beating; churning; threshing.

battant, băh-tahng, *m* leaf (door); clapper (bell).

battant, e, băh-tahng, *a* beating; pelting.

battement, băht-mahng, *m* beat(ing); throb(bing); clapping.

batterie, băht-ree, *f* fight; battery; set; **–de cuisine,** –de kwee-zeen, kitchen utensils; percussion; drums.

battoir, băh-to'ăhr, *m* beater; paddle; bat.

battre, băh-tr, *v* to beat; to thrash; to coin; to churn; to thresh; to shuffle; **se–,** to fight.

baudet, boh-day, *m* donkey; sawhorse.

bauge, bohsh, *f* lair (of wild boar); dirty hovel; squirrel's nest.

baume, bohm, *m* balm; balsam.

bavard, e, băh-văhr, *mf* chatterbox; *a* talkative.

bavardage, băh-văhr-dăhsh, *m* chitchat.

bavarder, băh-văhr-deh, *v* to chatter.

baver, băh-veh, *v* to dribble.

bavoir, băh-vo'ăhr, *m* bib.

bazar, băh-zăhr, *m* bazaar.

béant, e, beh-ahng, *a* gaping; **bouche –e,** boosh –ahngt, agape.

béat, e,* beh-ăh, *a* sanctimonious; blissful.

beau, boh, *m* beautiful; beauty; fine weather.

beau (before vowel or a mute *h*: **bel,** bell), boh, *m*; **belle,*** bell, *f, a* beautiful; handsome; fine fair; **avoir–,** ăh-vo'ăhr–, to... in vain; **de plus belle,** with renewed ardor.

beaucoup, boh-koo, *adv* much; many; a great deal.

beau-fils, boh-fiss, *m* stepson; son-in-law.

beau-frère, boh-frair, *m* brother-in-law.

beau-père, boh-pair, *m* father-in-law; stepfather.

beauté, boh-teh, *f* beauty.

beaux-parents, boh-păhrah*ng*, *mpl* parents-in-law.

bébé, beh-beh, *m* baby.

bec, beck, *m* beak; snout.

bécarre, beh-kăhr, *m* natural (music).

bécasse, beh-kăhss, *f* woodcock.

bécassine, beh-kăhss-een, *f* snipe; silly girl.

bec-de-lièvre, beck der le-ay-vr, *m* harelip.

béchamel, beh-shăh-mell, *f* cream sauce.

bêche, baish, *f* spade.

bêcher, bay-sheh, *v* to dig.

becqueter, bayk-teh, *v* to peck; to kiss.

bedaine, ber-denn, *f* paunch; belly.

bedeau, ber-doh, *m* beadle.

bée, beh, *af* open; gaping; **bouche –**, boosh –, open-mouthed.

beffroi, beh-fro'ăh, *m* belfry.

bégayer, beh-ghay-yeh, *v* to stammer; to stutter.

bègue, baygh, *n* & *a* stammerer; stammering.

bégueule, beh-gherl, *f* haughty; prude.

beige, baish, *a* beige.

beignet, bayn-yay, *m* fritter.

bêler, bay-leh, *v* to bleat.

bélier, beh-le-eh, *m* ram; battering ram.

belle-fille, bell fee-ye, *f* daughter-in-law; stepdaughter.

belle-mère, bell mair, *f* mother-in-law; stepmother.

belle-soeur, bell ser, *f* sister-in-law.

belliqueu-x, se,* bell-le-ker, *a* warlike.

bémol, beh-mol, *m* flat (music).

bénédicité, beh-neh-de-se-teh, *m* grace before meals.

bénédiction, beh-neh-dick-se-ong, *f* blessing.

bénéfice, beh-neh-fiss, *m* benefit, profit; living.

benêt, ber-nay, *a* & *m* booby; simpleton; silly.

bénévole,* beh-neh-vol, *a* voluntary; unpaid.

béni, e, beh-ne, *a* blessed.

béni-n, gne, beh-nang, *a* benign; kind.

bénir, beh-neer, *v*, to bless.

bénitier, beh-ne-te-eh, *m* holy-water basin.

benzine, bang-zeen, *f* benzine.

béquille, beh-kee-ye, *f* crutch.

bercail, bair-kah'e, *m* (sing. only) sheepfold; fold.

berceau, bair-soh, *m* cradle; arbor; cradle vault.

bercer, bair-seh, *v* to rock; to lull; to delude.

berceuse, bair-ser*z*, *f* rocking chair; lullaby.

béret, beh-ray, *m* beret.

berge, bairsh, *f* steep bank of a river.

berg-er, ère, bair-sheh, *mf* shepherd.

bergère, bair-shair, *f* easy chair.

bergerie, bair-sher-ree, *f* sheepfold.

berlue, bair-lE, *f* dimness of sight; false vision.

berner, bair-neh, *v* to toss in a blanket; to fool.

besace, ber-zăhss, *f* beggar's bag.

besogne, ber-zon-yer, *f* work; task; labor.

besogneu-x, se, ber-zon-yer, *a* needy; necessitous.

besoin, ber-zo-ang, *m* need; want; necessity; **au –**, -oh –, in case of need.

bestial, e,* bess-te-ăhl, *a* beastly; brutish.

bestiaux, bess-te-oh, *mpl* cattle.

bétail, beh-tah'e, *m* cattle; livestock.

bête, bayt, *f* beast; animal;

a* stupid; **–noire, –no'ăhr,** aversion.

bêtise, bay-teez, *f* stupidity; stupid thing.

béton, beh-tong, *m* concrete.

betterave, bett-răhv, *f* beetroot.

beugler, ber-gleh, *v* to bellow; to bawl.

beurre, ber, *m* butter.

beurrer, ber-reh, *v* to butter.

bévue, beh-vE, *f* blunder; mistake.

biais, be-ay, *m* slant; expedient; **en –,** ahng–, on the cross.

biaiser, be-ay-zeh, *v* to slope; to shuffle.

bibelot, beeb-lo, *m* trinket; knicknack.

biberon, beeb-rong, *m* feeding bottle.

bible, bee-bl, *f* bible.

bibliophile, be-ble-off-eel, *m* lover of books.

bibliothécaire, be-ble-o-teh-kair, *m* librarian.

bibliothèque, be-ble-o-teck, *f* library; bookcase.

biche, bish, *f* hind; doe.

bicoque, be-kock, *f* paltry house; hut; hovel.

bicyclette, be-se-klett, *f* bicycle.

bidon, be-dong, *m* can.

bidonville, be-dong-veel,

m shantytown.

bielle, be-ell, *f* connectingrod.

bien, be-ang, *adv* well; quite; very; *m* good; property; welfare; **–que, –ker,** although; **tout va –,** too văh–, all is well.

bien-aimé, e, be-ang n'ay-meh, *a* beloved.

bien-être, be-ang n'ay-tr, *m* comfort; welfare.

bienfaisant, e, be-ang-fer-zahng, *a* kind; charitable.

bienfait, be-ang-fay, *m* kindness; favor; boon.

bienfai-teur, trice, be-ang-fay-ter, *mf* benefactor; benefactress.

bien-fonds, be-ang-fong, *m* real estate.

bienheureu-x, se, be-ang-ner,rer, *a* blessed; happy.

bienséance, be-ang-seh-ahngss, *f* decorum; propriety.

bientôt, be-ang-toh; *adv* soon; shortly.

bienveillance, be-ang-vay'e-yahngss, *f* kindness; goodwill.

bienveillant, e, be-ang-vay'e-yahng, *a* kind; benevolent.

bienvenu, e, be-angv-nEE, *a & n* welcome.

bienvenue, be-angv-nEE, *f*

welcome.

bière, be-air, *f* beer; coffin; bier.

biffer, be-feh, *v* to strike out; to cancel.

bifteck, beef-teck, *m* beefsteak.

bifurquer (se), ser be-fEEr-keh, *v* to fork.

bigarré, e, be-găh-reh, *a* motley; streaked.

bigorneau, be-gor-noh, *m* winkle (periwinkle).

bigot, e, be-gho, *mf* bigot; *a* bigoted.

bigoudi, be-goo-de, *m* curler (hair).

bijou, be-shoo, *m* jewel; trinket; (fig.) darling.

bijouterie, be-shoot-ree, *f* jewelry.

bijoutier, be-shoo-te-eh, *m* jeweler.

bikini, be-ke-ne, *m* bikini.

bilan, be-lahng, *m* balancesheet; schedule.

bile, beel, *f* bile; gall; anger.

bilieu-x, se, be-le-er, *a* bilious; irritable.

billard, bee-yăhr, *m* billiards; billiards room.

bille, bee-ye, *f* ball; marble; log.

billet, bee-yay, *m* bill; note; ticket; **–de banque,** – der bahngk, banknote; **–simple, –**

sang–pl, single ticket;
–d'aller et retour, –
dăh-leh-eh rer-toohr,
return ticket.

billevesée, bill-ver-zeh, *f*
nonsense.

billion, bill-e-*ong, m*
thousand millions.

billot, bee-yo, *m* block.

bimensuel, -le, be-măhng-
sE-ell, *a* bimonthly.

binette, be-nett, *f* hoe;
(pop.) face.

binocle, be-nock-kl, *m*
pince-nez.

biographie, be-og-răh-fee,
f biography.

bipède, be-payd, *a* & *m*
biped; two-legged.

biplan, be-plahng, *m*
biplane.

bique, bick, *f* nanny-goat.

bis, biss, *adv* twice; again;
encore!

bis, e, be, *a* brown.

bisaïeul, e, be-zăh-yerl, *mf*
great-grandfather; great-
grandmother.

biscornu, e, biss-kor-nE, *a*
odd; queer.

biscotte, biss-kot, *f* rusk.

biscuit, biss-kwe, *m*
biscuit.

bise, beez, *f* north wind;
cold blast; *fam* kiss.

biseau, be-zoh, *m* bevel.

bisque, beesk, *f* shellfish
soup; vexation.

bisquer, bees-keh, *v*
(fam.) to be vexed.

bisser, biss-eh, *v* to
encore.

bissextile, be-secks-teel, *af*
used only in **Année –,**
Leap Year.

bistré, e, biss-treh, *a*
tawny; swarthy.

bizarre,* be-zăhr, *a* odd;
whimsical; eccentric.

blafard, e, blăh-făhr, *a*
dim; wan; pale.

blague, blăhg, *f*
tobaccopouch; (fam.)
joke.

blaguer, blăh-gheh, *v*
(fam.) to joke; to hoax.

blaireau, blay-roh, *m*
badger; shaving brush.

blâme, blahm, *m* blame;
censure.

blâmer, blah-meh, *v* to
blame; to find fault
with.

blanc, blahng, *m* white;
white man; blank.

blan-c, che, *a* white;
clean; blank; pale; **nuit
blanche** nwe blahngsh,
sleepless night.

blanchaille, blahng-
shah'e, *f* whitebait.

blanchâtre, blahng-shah-
tr, *a* whitish.

blancheur, blahng-sher, *f*
whiteness.

blanchir, blahng-sheer, *v*

to whiten; to bleach; to
grow white.

blanchissage, blahng-
shiss-ăhsh, *m* washing.

blanchisserie, blahng-
shiss-re, *f* laundry;
laundering.

blanquette, blahng-kett, *f*
stew with white sauce.

blaser, blah-zeh, *v* to
blunt; to pall; **se–,** ser–,
to get tired of (**de**) to
become blasé.

blason, blah-zong, *m*
heraldry; coat-of-arms.

blasphème, blăhss-faym,
m blasphemy.

blé, bleh, *m* corn; wheat;
grain.

blême, blaym, *a* pallid;
ghastly; wan.

blémir, bleh-meer, *v* to
grow pale.

blessant, e, bless-ahng, *a*
offensive (**pour,** to);
hurtful.

blessé, bless-eh, *m*
wounded man; *pp* & *a*
wounded.

blesser, bless-eh, *v* to
wound; to hurt; to
injure; to offend; **se –,** to
hurt oneself; to be
offended (**de,** at, with).

blessure, bless-EEr, *f*
wound; injury.

blet, te, blay, *a* overripe.

bleu, e, bler, *a* blue; *m*

bruise.

bleuâtre, bler-ah-tr, *a* bluish.

bleuet, bluet, bler-ay, blE-ay, *m* cornflower.

bleuir, bler-eer, *v* to make blue; to turn blue.

blindé, blang-deh, *a* steelplated; ironclad.

bloc, block, *m* block; lump; log; **en –,** ahng –, in the lump.

blocus, block-EEss, *m* blockade.

blond, e, blong, *a* fair; light; blond.

bloquer, block-eh, *v* to blockade; to block up.

blottir (se), serblot-eer, *v* to crouch; to snuggle down.

blouse, blooz, *f* frock; smock-frock; pinafore; pocket (billiards).

blouser, bloo-zeh, *v* to dupe; **se –,** ser –, (fam.) to blunder.

bluette, blE-ayt, *f* spark; literary trifle.

boa, bo'ah, *m* boa; fur tippet.

bobard, bo-bahr, *m* (fam.) lie; fib.

bobine, bob-een, *f* bobbin; spool; reel; coil.

bobo, bob-o, *m* slight hurt.

bocage, bock-ăhsh, *m* grove; copse.

bocal, bock-ăhl, *m* glass bowl; wide-mouthed bottle.

bock, bock, *m* beerglass; glass of beer.

bœuf, berf, *m* bullock; beef.

bohémien, ne, bo-eh-me-ang, *mf* Bohemian; gypsy.

boire, bo'ăhr, *v* to drink; to soak up (paper, etc.).

bois, bo'ăh, *m* wood; timber; horns (deer).

boisé, e, bo'ăh-zeh, *a* wooded; wainscoted.

boiserie, bo'ăhz-ree, *f* wainscot.

boisseau, bo'ăhss-oh, *m* bushel.

boisson, bo'ăhss-ong, *f* drink; beverage; drinking.

boisson non alcoolisée, bo'ăhss-ong-ăhl-koll-e-seh *f* soft drink.

boîte, bo'ăht, *f* box; case; tin;**–aux lettres,** –oh lay-tr, mailbox; **–de vitesses,** –derve-tess, gearbox.

boiter, bo'ăh-teh, *v* to limp.

boiteu-x, -se, bo'ăh-ter, *mf* cripple; *a* lame; limping.

bol, boll, *m* bowl; basin.

bombance, bong-bahngss, *f* feasting.

bombarder, bong-băhr-deh, *v* to bombard.

bombe, bongb, *f* bomb; shell.

bomber, bong-beh, *v* to make convex; to bulge out.

bon, bong, *m* good; good quality; bond; order; check.

bon, ne, bong, *a* good; kind; advisable; right.

bonasse, bonn-ăhss, *a* meek.

bonbon, bong-bong, *m* sweet; candy.

bonbonnière, bong-bonn-e-air, *f* candy box.

bond, bong, *m* bound; leap; jump; **faire faux –,**fair foh –, to fail.

bonde, bongd, *f* bunghole; sluice; plughole.

bondir, bong-deer, *v* to bound; to spring; to skip.

bonheur, bonn-er *m* happiness; delight; luck.

bonhomie, bonn-omm-ee, *f* good nature; simplicity.

bonhomme, bonn-omm, *m* good-natured man; old man; fellow.

bonification, bonn-e-fe-kăh-se-ong, *f* improvement; allowance.

bonifier, bonn-e-fe-eh, v to improve.

boniment, bonn-e-mahng, m sales talk; tall story.

bonjour, bong- shoor, m good morning.

bonne, bonn, f maid.

bonnement, bonn-mahng, adv simply; plainly.

bonnet, bonn-ay, m cap; cup (bra); **gros –,** groh –, big wig; magnate.

bonneterie, bonn-tree, f hosiery.

bonnetier, bonn-te-eh, m hosier.

bonsoir, bong-so'ăhr, m good evening; good night.

bonté, bong-teh, f goodness; kindness (**pour,** to).

bord, bor, m border; edge; rim; side; bank; shore.

bordée, bor-deh, f volley; broadside.

border, bor-deh, v to border; to edge; to hem; to tuck up.

bordereau, bor-der-roh, m schedule; detailed account; memorandum.

bordure, bor-dEEr, f border; edge; curb.

bord du trottoir, bor-der-trot-o'ăhr m curb.

boréal, e, bor-eh-ăhl, a northern.

borgne, born-yer, a blind in one eye; (fig.) shady.

borne, born, f boundary; milestone; terminal.

borné, e, bor-neh, pp & a limited; narrow; shortsighted.

borner, bor-neh, v to bound; to limit; to confine.

bosquet, boss-kay, m grove; thicket.

bosse, boss, f hump; bump; embossment.

bosseler, boss-leh, v to emboss; to dent; to batter.

bossu, e, boss-E, mf hunchback; a hunchbacked.

bot, bo, n & a used only in **pied-bot,** pe-eh-bo, clubfoot; clubfooted.

botanique, bot-ăh-nick, f botany; a botanical.

botte, bott, f boot; high boot; bundle; hank; thrust; **à propos de –s,** ăh pro-poh de –, without any reason.

botter, bott-eh, v to help one with his boots; (fam) to suit; to boot; to kick.

bottier, bott-e-eh, m bootmaker.

bottin, bott-ang, m French Post-Office Directory; telephone directory.

bottine, bott-een, f half-boot; lady's boot; boot.

bouc, book, m goat; – **émissaire,** –eh-miss-air, scapegoat.

boucanier, boo-kăh-ne-eh, m buccaneer.

bouche, boosh, f mouth; opening.

bouchée, boo-sheh, f mouthful.

boucher, boo-sheh, v to stop; to obstruct; to cork.

bouch-er, èr, boo-sheh, mf butcher.

boucherie, boosh-ree, f butcher's shop or trade; shambles; slaughter.

bouchon, boo-shong, m cork; stopper.

boucle, boo-kl, f buckle; ring; curl; **–d'oreille,** –doh-ray'e, earring.

bouclé, e, boo-kleh, a curly.

boucle d'oreille, book-ler-do-ray'e, f earring.

boucler, boo-kleh, v to buckle; to ring; to curl.

bouclier, boo-kle-eh, m shield; buckler.

bouder, boo-deh, v to pout; to sulk.

boudin, boo-dang, m blood sausage.

boue, boo, f mud; mire;

dirt.

bouée, boo-eh, f buoy.

boueur, or **boueux,** boo-er, m garbage collector.

boueu-x, se, boo-er, a muddy.

bouffant, e, boo-fahng, a puffed; baggy.

bouffée, boo-feh, f puff; whiff.

bouffer, boo-feh, v to puff out; (pop) to eat greedily.

bouffi, e, boo-fe, pp & a puffed up; inflated; (**de,** with).

bouffon, boo-fong, m buffoon; jester.

bouffon, ne, boo-fong, a comical; droll.

bouge, boosh, m hovel; den; bulge.

bougeoir, boo-sho'ǎhr, m candlestick.

bouger, boo-sheh, v to stir; to budge; to move.

bougie, boo-shee, f candle; sparkplug.

bougonner, boo-ghonn-eh, v to grumble.

bougran, boo-grahng, m buckram.

bouillabaisse, boo'e-yǎh-bess, f highly seasoned fish soup.

bouillant, e, boo'e-yahng, a boiling; hot-tempered.

bouilli, e, –, boo'e-yee, a

boiled.

bouillie, boo'e-yee, f baby cereal; gruel.

bouillir, boo'e-yeer, v to boil.

bouilloire, boo'e-yo'ǎhr, f kettle.

bouillon, boo'e-yong, m broth; soup; stock; bubble.

bouillonner, boo'e-yonn-eh, v to bubble up; to boil.

bouillotte, boo'e-yot, f hot water bottle; bouillotte (card game).

boulangerie, boo-lahng-sh-ree, f bakery.

boule, bool, f ball.

bouleau, boo-loh, m birch tree.

boulet, boo-lay, m cannonball; shot; small ovoid coal.

boulette, boo-lett, f meatball; pellet; blunder.

boulevard, bool-vǎhr, m boulevard.

bouleversement, bool-vair-ser-mahng, m overthrow; confusion.

bouleverser, bool-vair-seh, v to overthrow; to upset.

boulier, boo-lee-eh, m abacus; scoring board.

boulon, boo-long, m bolt;

pin.

boulonner, boo-lonn-eh, v to bolt; (fam) to work hard.

bouquet, boo-kay, m bunch; nosegay; aroma; crowning piece; prawn.

bouquin, boo-kang, m (fam) book.

bouquiner, boo-ke-neh, v (fam) to read.

bouquiniste, boo-ke-nisst, m dealer in secondhand books.

bourbe, boohrb, f mud; mire; dirt.

bourbier, boohr-be-eh, m slough; mire.

bourde, boohrd, f fib; sham; (fam) mistake.

bourdon, boohr-dong, m bumblebee; great bell; drone bass.

bourdonner, boohr-donn-eh, v to hum; to buzz.

bourg, boohr, m market town; village.

bourgade, boohr-gǎhd, f small town or large village.

bourgeois, -e, boohr-sho'ǎh, mf citizen; middle-class man or woman; Bourgeois; **les petits –,** lay per te –, the lower middle class; master; a* citizenlike; middle-class; common.

bourgeoisie, boohr-sho'äh-zee, *f* middleclass.

bourgeon, boohr-shong, *m* bud; shoot; (fam.) pimple.

bourgeonner, boohr-shonn-eh, *v* to come into bud; (*fam*) to have pimples.

bourgogne, boohr-gonn-yer, *m* Burgundy wine.

bourrade, boo-rähd, *f* cuff; hard blow.

bourrasque, boo-rähsk, *f* gust of wind.

bourre, boohr, *f* flock; wadding.

bourreau, boo-roh, *m* executioner; tormentor.

bourrelet, boohr-lay, *m* pad; padding; cushion; (*fam*) rolls of fat.

bourrelier, boohr-le-eh, *m* harness-maker.

bourrer, boo-reh, *v* to stuff; to cram; (**de,** with); to thrash.

bourriche, boo-reesh, *f* basket; hamper.

bourru, e, boo-rE, *a* surly; rough.

bourse, boohrs, *f* purse; scholarship; stock exchange.

boursier, boohr-se-eh, *a & n* exhibitioner; speculator on the stock exchange.

boursoufler, boor-soo-ßeh, *v* to bloat; to puff up.

bousculer, boos-kE-leh, *v* to jostle; to hustle; to shove.

bouse, booz, *f* manure.

boussole, boo-sol, *f* compass.

bout, boo, *m* end; tip; à –, äh –, exhausted; **au –du compte,** oh – DE kongt, after all.

boutade, boo-tähd, *f* whim; freak; sally.

boute-en-train, boot-ahng-trang, *m* life and soul of a party.

bouteille, boo-tay'e, *f* bottle.

boutique, boo-teeck, *f* shop; boutique; store.

boutiqui-er, -ère, boo-te-ke-eh, *mf* storekeeper.

bouton, boo-tong, *m* bud; button; handle; knob; stud; pimple; –**de manchettes,** – der mahng-shett, *m* cufflink.

boutonner, boo-tonn-eh, *v* to button; to bud.

boutonnière, boo-tonn-e-air, *f* buttonhole.

bouture, bou-tEEr, *f* cutting (of plant).

bouvreuil, boo-vrer'e, *m* bullfinch.

boxe, box, *f* boxing.

boyau, bo'äh-yoh, *m* bowel; gut; hose; long narrow passage.

bracelet, brähss-lay, *m* bracelet.

braconnier, bräh-konn-e-eh, *m* poacher.

braguette, brah-ghett, *f* fly (of pants).

brailler, brah'e-yeh, *v* to bawl; to squall.

braire, brair, *v* to bray.

braise, brayz, *f* embers; live coals.

braisé, e, bray-zeh, *a* stewed; braised.

brancard, brahng-kähr, *m* stretcher; shaft.

brancardier, brahng-kähr-de-eh, *m* stretcher-bearer.

branche, brahngsh. *f* branch; bough; division.

brancher, brahng-sheh, *v* to branch; to plug in, to connect; to put through.

branchies, brahng-shee, *fpl* gills.

brandir, brahng-deer, *v* to brandish.

branlant, e, brahng-lahng, *a* shaking; tottering; loose.

branle, brangl, *m* swinging; impulse; motion; **donner le –,** donn-eh ler –, to set going.

branle-bas, brahngl-bah, *m* upset; clearing the decks for action.

branler, brahng-leh, *v* to swing; to totter; to be loose.

braquer, brăh-keh, *v* to aim (**sur,** at); to change direction (of car, etc.); (*fam*) to hold up a bank.

bras, brăh, *m* arm; handle; bracket; power; labor; **–dessus –dessous,** – der-sE – der-soo, arm in arm.

brasier, brăh-ze-eh, *m* red-hot coal-fire; brazier.

brassard, brăhss-ăhr, *m* armlet; armband.

brasse, brăhss, *f* fathom; stroke; breaststroke.

brassée, brăhss-eh, *f* armful; stroke.

brasser, brăhss-eh, *m* to brew; to concoct.

brasserie, brăhss-ree, *f* brewery; cafe; restaurant.

brasseur, brăhss-er, *m* brewer

bravade, brăh-văhd, *f* bravado; bluster.

brave,* brăhv, *a* brave; honest; good; smart; **un homme –,** ung n'omm –, a brave man; **un –homme,** ung – omm, a worthy man.

braver, brăh-veh, *v* to brave; to face; to dare.

bravoure, brăh-voohr, *f* bravery; courage; gallantry.

brebis, brer-be, *f* sheep; ewe;**– galeuse,** – găh-lerz, black sheep.

brèche, braysh, *f* breach; gap; notch.

bredouille, brer-doo'e-yer, *a* empty-handed; **être –,** to have failed.

bredouiller, brer-doo'e-yeh, *v* to mumble.

bref, brayf, *adv* briefly; in short; **bref, ève,** *a* brief; short.

breloque, brer-lock, *f* trinket; charm.

brème, braym, *f* bream.

bretelle, brer-tell, *f* strap; sling; *pl* suspenders.

breuvage, brer-văhsh, *m* drink; beverage.

brevet, brer-vay, *m* patent; licence; warrant; commission; diploma.

breveter, brerv-teh, *v* to patent; to grant a patent; to commission.

bréviaire, breh-ve-air, *m* breviary.

bribe, breeb, *f* scrap.

bric-à-brac, brick-ăh brăhk *m* junk.

bricole, bree-kol, *f* breast harness; *fpl* odds and ends; little bits; trifles.

bricoler, bree-ko-leh, *v* to put breast harness on horse; to do odd jobs; to putter about.

bricoleur, bree-ko-ler, *a* & *n* handy; handyman.

bride, breed, *f* bridle; reins; string (of bonnet, etc.); triple (crochet); **tourner –,** toohr-neh – to turn back.

brider, bre-deh, *v* to bridle; to restrain; to tie up.

brie, bree, *m* Brie cheese.

brièvement, bre-ayv-mahng, *adv* briefly.

brièveté, bre-ayv-teh, *f* briefness.

brigade, bre-găhd, *f* brigade; gang; **–de sûreté,** –der sEEr-teh, detective force.

brigadier, bre-găh-de-eh, *m* corporal; bombardier; sergeant; foreman.

brigand, bre-ghahng, *m* thief; robber.

brigue, breegh, *f* intrigue; cabal.

briguer, bre-gheh, *v* to aspire to; to solicit.

brillamment, bree-yăh-mahng, *adv* brilliantly.

brillant, e, bree-yahng, *a* bright; brilliant; shining. *n* brilliancy; shine;

diamond.

briller, bree-yeh, v to shine; to be conspicuous.

brimborion, brang-bo-re-ong, m bauble; trinket.

brimer, bree-meh, v to victimize; to persecute.

brin, brang, m bit; blade; sprig.

brioche, bre-osh, f bun.

brique, brick, f brick.

briquet, bre-kay, m cigarette lighter; **pierre à –,** pe-ayr ah–, f lighter flint.

briqueterie, brick-tree, f brickworks.

bris, bre, m wreck.

brisant, bre-zahng, m breaker; reef.

brise, breez, f breeze.

briser, bre-zeh, v to break; **se –,** to break up.

broc, brock, m jug; jar.

brocanter, brock-ahng-teh, v to deal in secondhand goods.

brocant-eur, -euse, brock-ahng-ter, mf secondhand storekeeper; broker.

brocard, brock-ăhr, m taunt; jeer; scoff.

brocart, brock-ăhr, m brocade.

broche, brosh, f spit; brooch.

broché, e, brosh-eh, pp & a paperback (books).

brochet, brosh-ay, m pike.

brochette, bro-shett, f skewer; small spit.

brochure, brosh-EEr, f pamphlet; brochure.

broder, brod-eh, v to embroider; (fig) to embellish (a story).

broderie, brod-ree, f embroidery; (fig) embellishment.

broiement, bro'ăh-mahng, m pounding; crushing.

broncher, brong-sheh, v to stumble; to trip; **sans –,** sahng –, without flinching.

bronches, brongsh, fpl bronchial tubes.

bronchite, brong-sheet, f bronchitis.

bronzage, brong-zăhsh m suntan.

bronze, brongz, m bronze.

bronzer, brong-zeh, v to bronze; to tan.

brosse, bross, f brush.

brosser, bross-eh, v to brush.

brou, broo, m husk; hull.

brouet, broo-ay, m thin broth.

brouette, broo-ett, f wheelbarrow; hand cart.

brouhaha, broo-ăh-ăh, m uproar; hubbub.

brouillamini, broo'e-yăh-me-ne, m (fam) confusion.

brouillard, broo'e-yăhr, m fog; haze.

brouille, broo'e-ye, f disagreement; quarrel.

brouiller, broo'e-yeh, v to mix up; to confuse; **se –,** to fall out; to quarrel.

brouillon, broo'e-yong, m rough draft; rough book.

brouillon, ne, broo'e-yong, n & a blundering; muddleheaded.

broussailles, broo-sah'e, fpl brushwood.

brouter, broo-teh, v to graze.

broyer, bro'ăh-yeh, v to pound; to crush.

bru, brE, f daughter-in-law.

bruine, brween, f drizzling rain.

bruire, brweer, v to rustle; to murmur.

bruissement, brweess-mahng, m rustling; rumbling.

bruit, brwee, m noise; din; rumor; sound.

brûlant, e, brE-lahng, a burning; scorching; fervent; impassioned.

brûle-pourpoint (à), ăh brEEl poohr-po'ang, adv point-blank.

brûler, brE-leh, v to burn;

to blow; to pass without stopping.

brûlure, brE-lEEr, *f* burn; scald.

brume, brEEm, *f* mist; haze.

brun, e, brung, brEEn, *a* & *n* brown; dusky; dark.

brunâtre, brE-nah-tr, *a* brownish.

brune, brEEn, *f* dusk; dark-complexioned woman.

brunir, brE-neer, *v* to brown; to burnish; to tan.

brusque,* brEEsk, *a* blunt; rough; abrupt; sudden.

brusquer, brEEss-keh, *v* to be blunt with; hurry on (with events).

brusquerie, brEEss-ker-ree, *f* bluntness; abruptness.

brut, e, brEt, *a* raw; rough; abrupt; coarse; gross.

brutal, e,* brE-tăhl, *a* brutal; brutish.

brutaliser, brE-tăhl-e-zeh, *v* to treat brutally; to bully.

brutalité, brE-tăhl-e-teh, *f* roughness; brutishness.

brute, brEt, *f* brute.

bruyamment, brE-yăh-mahng, *adv* noisily; loudly.

bruyant, e, brE-yahng, *a* noisy; loud.

bruyère, brE-yair, *f*

heather.

buanderie, bE-ahngd-ree, *f* laundry (place).

bûche, bEEsh, *f* log; (*fig*) blockhead; Christmas cake.

bûcher, bEE-sheh, *m* woodshed; funeral pyre; stake.

bûcheron, bEEsh-rong, *m* lumberjack; logger.

bûch-eur, -euse, BEE-sher, *mf* (*fam*) hard-working person.

budget, bEED-shay, *m* budget.

buée, bE-eh, *f* steam; vapor; blur.

buffet, bE-fay, *m* sideboard; buffet; refreshment cart.

buffle, bEE-ß *m* buffalo; buff-leather.

buis, bwe, *m* boxwood; box tree.

buisson, bwess-ong, *m* bush; thicket; **faire l'école buissonière,** fair leh-kol bwess-onn-e-air, to play truant.

bulle, bEEl, *f* bubble.

bulletin, bEEl-tang, *m* report; bulletin; ticket.

buraliste, bE-răh-lisst, *mf* tobacconist.

bureau, bE-roh, *m* office; desk; department.

bureaucrate, bE-roh-

krăht, *m* bureaucrat.

bureaucratie, bE-roh-krăhss-ee, *f* bureaucracy; (*fam*) red tape.

burette, bE-rayt, *f* cruet; oilcan.

burlesque, bEEr-lessk, *a* burlesque; ludicrous.

buse, bEEz, *f* buzzard; (*fig*) blockhead.

buste, bEEst, *m* bust.

but, bE, *m* mark; aim; goal; end; purpose.

buter, bE-teh, *v* to butt; to prop; to stumble; **se –,** ser –, to be bent (à, on).

buté, bE-teh, *a* fixed; obstinate.

butin, bE-tang, *m* plunder; booty.

butor, bE-tor, *m* (*fig*) lout.

butte, bEEt, *f* mound, knoll; **en –à,** ahng – ăh, exposed to.

buvable, bE-văh-bl, *a* drinkable.

buvard, bE-văhr, *m* blotting-pad; **papier –,** păh-pe-eh –, blotter.

buveu-r, -se, bE-ver, *mf* drinker.

ça, săh, *pron* contraction of **cela,** ser-lăh, that.

çà, săh, *adv* hither; **–et là,** – eh lăh, here and there.

cabale, kăh-băhl, *f* cabal.

cabane, kăh-băhnn, *f* hut; cabin.

cabanon, kăh-băh-nong, *m* cell; padded cell.

cabaret, kăh-băh-ray, *m* cabaret.

cabas, kăh-bah, *m* rush basket; shopping bag.

cabestan, kăh-bess-tahng, *m* capstan.

cabillaud, kăh-bee-yoh, *m* codfish (fresh).

cabine, kăh-been, *f* cabin; beach house; telephone booth.

cabinet, kăh-be-ney, *m* small room; closet; office; practice; bathroom; chambers; cabinet (pol.).

cabine téléphonique, kăh-been-teh-leh-fonn-eeck *f* pay-phone.

câble, kah-bl, *m* cable; rope.

câbler, kah-bleh, *v* to cable; to twist (strands).

câblogramme, kah-blo-grahmm, *m* cablegram.

caboche, kăh-bosh, *f* (*fam.*) head.

cabosser, kăh-bo-sseh, *v* to bump; to dent.

cabotage, kăh-bot-ăhsh, *m* coasting.

caboter, kăh-bot-eh, *v* to coast.

cabotin, kăh-bot-ang, *m* bad actor; show off.

cabrer (se), ser kăh-breh, *v* to rear; to fire up.

cabriole, kăh-bre-ol, *f* caper; leap; somersault.

cabriolet, kăh-bre-oll-ay, *m* convertible.

cacahuète, kăh-kăh-wait, *f* peanut.

cacao, kăh-kăh-o, *m* cocoa.

cacatoès, kăh-kăh-to'es, *m* cockatoo.

cachalot, kăh-shă-lo, *m* sperm-whale.

cache, kăhsh, *f* hiding-place; **cache-cache,** *m* hide-and-seek.

cache-nez, kăhsh-neh, *m* muffler; scarf.

cacher, kăh-sheh, *v* to hide; to conceal.

cachet, kăh-shay, *m* seal; style; tablet (med); fee (show bus).

cacheter, kăhsh-teh, *v* to seal (up).

cachette, kăh-shett, *f* hiding-place; **en –,** ahng –, secretly.

cachot, kăh-sho, *m* cell; dungeon; prison.

cachotterie, kăh-shot-ree, *f* little secret.

cadavre, kăh-dah-vr, *m* corpse; dead body.

cadeau, kăh-doh, *m* present; gift.

cadenas, kăhd-nah, *m* padlock.

cadenasser, kăhd-năhss-

eh, v to padlock.

cadence, käh-dahngss, f cadence; rhythm.

cadet, te, käh-day, a & n younger; least; youngest.

cadran, käh-drahng, m dial.

cadre, kah-dr, m frame; plan; managerial staff; staff.

cadrer, kah-dreh, v to conform; to tally.

cadu-c, que, käh-dEEk, a null and void.

cafard, käh-fähr, m cockroach; (fam) "the blues".

cafardage, käh-fähz-dähshe, m hypocrite.

cafarder, käh-fähr-deh, v to tattletale.

café, käh-feh, m coffee; coffeehouse; café; – **au lait,** – oh lay, coffee with milk, –**noir,** – no'ähr, black coffee.

cafetière, kähf-te-air, f coffeepot.

cage, kähsh, f cage; coop; frame.

cagneu-x, se, kähn-yer, a knock-kneed.

cagoule, käh-geol, f hood; balaclava.

cahier, käh-yeh, m notebook; workbook.

cahin-caha, käh-ang käh-äh, adv so-so; middling.

cahot, käh-o, m jolt; bump.

cahoter, käh-ot-eh, v to jolt; to bump along.

cahute, käh-EEt, f hut; hovel.

caille, kah'e, f quail.

cailler, kah'e-yeh, v to curdle; to clot.

caillot, kah'e-o, m clot.

caillou, kah'e-yoo, m pebble; flint; stone.

caisse, kess, f case; box; chest; cashregister; fund; checkout; (carriage) body; drum; –**d'épargne,** – deh-pährn'yer, savings bank.

caissi-er, ére, kess-e-eh, mf cashier.

cajoler, käh-sholl-eh, v to wheedle; to coax.

calamité, käh-läh-me-teh, f calamity.

calandre, käh-lahng-dr, f calender; mangle.

calcaire, kähl-kair, m limestone. a calcareous.

calciner, kähl-se-neh, v to calcine; to burn up.

calcul, kähl-kEEl, m calculation; arithmetic; calculus; stone (in bladder, etc.).

calculer, kähl-kE-leh, v to calculate; to reckon; to compute.

cale, kähl, f wedge; hold

(ship).

calé e, käh-leh, a wedged up; stalled; (fam.) learned.

caleçon, kähl-song, m men's pants; bathing trunks; leggings.

calembour, käh-lahng-boohr, m pun.

calembredaine, käh-lahng-brer-dayn, f joke; nonsense.

calendrier, käh-lahng-dre-eh, m calendar.

calepin, kähl-pang, m notebook.

caler, käh-leh, v to wedge up; to jam; to stall.

calfeutrer, kähl-fer-treh, v to stop up weatherstrip; **se –,** to to make oneself snug.

calibre, käh-lee-br, m caliber; size; diameter.

calice, käh-liss, m chalice; calyx.

calicot, käh-le-ko, m calico.

califourchon (à), äh käh-le-foohr-shong, adv astride.

câlin, e, kah-lang, a caressing; tender. m, cuddle.

câliner, kah-le-neh, v to caress; to fondle; to cuddle.

calleu-x, se, käh-ler, a

callous; horny.

calmant, kähl-mahng, m
sedative.

calmant, e, kǎhl-mahng, a
soothing.

calmar, kǎhl-mähr m
squid.

calme, kǎhlm, m calm;
stillness. a quiet; calm.

calmer, kǎhl-meh, v to
calm; to quiet; to still.

calomnie, kǎh-lomm-nee,
f calumny; slander.

calomnier, kǎh-lomm-ne-
yeh, v to calumniate; to
slander.

calorie, kǎh-lo-re, f
calorie.

calorifère, kǎh-lor-e-fair,
a heat-conveying. m
heating installation.

calorifuger, kǎh-lo-re-fE-
sheh, v to insulate.

calotte, kǎh-lott, f
skullcap; cap; (slang)
box on the ears;
priesthood; (fam.) slap.

calotter, kǎh-lott-eh, v to
box the ears of.

calque, kǎhlk, m tracing;
copy.

calquer, kǎhl-keh, v to
trace; to copy.

calvaire, kǎhl-vair, m
calvary; (fig.)
martyrdom.

calvitie, kǎhl-vee-see, f
baldness.

camarade, kǎh-mǎh-rǎhd,
m comrade; pal; friend.

camaraderie, kǎh-mǎh-
rǎhd-ree, f close
friendship; comradeship.

camard, e, kǎh-mǎhr, a
flat-nosed.

cambouis, kahng-boo-e, m
dirty oil or grease.

cambrer, kahng-breh, v to
bend; to arch; se –, ser
–, to arch one's back.

cambriolage, kahng-bre-
ol-ǎhsh, m burglary.

cambrioleur, kahng-bre-
ol-er, m burglar.

came, kǎhm, f cam; (fam.)
junk; drug; **arbre à –,**
ahr-br ǎh–, m camshaft.

camée, kǎh-meh, m
cameo.

camelote, kǎhm-lot, f
cheap goods; trash; stuff.

caméra, kǎh-meh-rǎh, f
movie camera.

camion, kǎh-me-ong, m
truck; wagon.

camionnage, kǎh-me-onn-
ǎhsh, m carting;
haulage.

camionnette, kǎh-me-
onn-ett, f van.

camisole, kǎh-me-zol, f
camisole; straitjacket.

camouflet, kǎh-moo-flay,
m affront; insult.

camoufler, kǎh-moo-fleh,
v to disguise; to

camouflage; **se –,** to
hide.

camp, kahng, m camp.

campagnard, e, kahng-
pǎhn-yǎhr, n & a
countryman;
countrywoman; rustic.

campagne, kahng-pǎhn-
yer, f country;
campaign.

campement, kahngp-
mahng, m encampment;
camping.

camper, kahng-peh, v to
camp.

camphre, kahng-fr, m
camphor.

camping, kahng-pee, m
camping; campground.

camus, e, kǎh-mE, a flat-
nosed.

canaille, kǎh-nah'e, f
scoundrel; crook.

canal, kǎh-nǎhl, m canal;
channel; pipe; conduit.

canapé, kǎh-nǎh-peh, m
sofa; open sandwich.

canard, kǎh-nǎhr, m duck;
drake; false news; rag
(newspaper).

cancan, kahng-kahng, m
cancan; (fam.) gossip.

cancaner, kahng-kǎh-neh,
v (fam.) to gossip.

cancer, kahng-sair, m
cancer.

cancéreu-x, se kahng-seh-
rer, a cancerous; n

cancer patient.

cancre, kahng-kr, *m* (*fig.*) dunce.

candélabre, kahng-deh-läh-br, *m* candelabra; streetlight.

candeur, kahng-der, *f* candor; frankness.

candidat, kahng-de-däh, *m* candidate.

candide, * kahng-deed, *a* candid; open; frank.

cane, kähn, *f* duck (female).

caneton, kähn-tong, *m* duckling.

canevas, kähn-vah, *m* canvas; sketch.

caniche, käh-neesh, *m* poodle.

canif, käh-niff, *m* penknife.

canin, käh-nang, *a* canine.

canine, käh-neen, *f* canine tooth.

caniveau, käh-ne-voh, *m* gutter.

canne, kähn, *f* cane; walking stick; rod.

cannelle, käh-nell, *f* cinnamon.

cannelure, kähn-lEEr, *f* groove.

canon, käh-nong, *m* cannon; gun.

canot, käh-no, *m* canoe; **–de sauvetage,** der sohvtahsh, lifeboat.

canotage, käh-not-ăhsh, *m* boating.

canotier, käh-not-e-eh, *m* oarsman; boater (hat).

cantaloup, kahng-täh-loo, *m* cantaloupe.

cantatrice, kahng-täh-triss, *f* professional singer; cantatrice.

cantharide, kahng-täh-reed, *f* Spanish fly.

cantine, kahng-teen, *f* canteen.

cantique, kahng-tick, *m* canticle; sacred song.

canton, kahng-tong, *m* subdistrict; canton.

cantonade, kahng-tonn-ăhd, *f* wings (theater); à **la –,** ăh lăh –, a way of speaking to everyone in general.

cantonnier, kahng-tonn-e-eh, *m* trackman.

canule, käh-nEEl, *f* cannula.

caoutchouc, käh-oot-shoo, *m* rubber; **bottes de –,** rubber boots.

cap, kähp, *m* cape.

capable, käh-päh-bl, *a* able; efficient; qualified.

capacité, käh-päh-se-teh, *f* capacity; capaciousness; qualification.

cape, kähp, *f* cape; cloak with a hood.

capitaine, käh-pe-tayn, *m* captain.

capital, e, käh-pe-tăhl, *a* capital; principal; chief.

capital, käh-pe-tăhl, *m* capital; stock.

capitale, käh-pe-tăhl, *f* capital (city).

capiteu-x, se, käh-pe-ter, *a* heady; strong (of wines).

capitonner, käh-pe-tonn-eh, *v* to stuff; to pad.

capituler, käh-pe-tE-leh, *v* to capitulate; to come to terms.

capon, käh-pong, *m* coward.

caporal, käh-por-ăhl, *m* corporal.

capote, käh-pot, *f* great coat; hooded cloak; hood (of car).

câpre, käh-pr, *f* caper.

caprice, käh-priss, *m* caprice; whim; fancy.

capsule, kähp-sEEl, *f* capsule; cap.

capter, kähp-teh, *v* to capture; to pick up.

captieu-x, se, * kähp-se-er, *a* captious.

capti-f, ve, kähp-tiff, *a* captive. *n* prisoner.

capture, kähp-tEEr, *f* capture; booty; arrest.

capturer, kähp-tE-reh, *v* to capture; to arrest.

capuchon, käh-pE-shong,

m hood; cover.

capucin, kăh-pE-sang, *m* capuchin; friar.

capucine, kăh-pE-seen, *f* nasturtium.

caque, kăhck, *f* keg; barrel.

caquet, kăh-kay, *m* cackle.

caqueter, kăhck-teh, *v* to cackle; to chatter.

car, kăhr, *conj* for; because; as.

car, kăhr, *m* bus.

carabine, kăh-răh-been, *f* rifle.

carabinier, kăh-răh-be-ne-eh, *m* rifleman.

caracoler, kăh-răh-koll-eh, *v* to wheel about; to prance.

caractère, kăh-răhck-tair, *m* character; temper; type; print.

carafe, kăh-răhf, *f* decanter; water bottle; carafe.

carafon, kăh-răh-fong, *m* small decanter.

carambolage, kăh-rahng-boh-lăhsh *m* pileup.

caramel, kăh-răh-mell, *m* burnt sugar; caramel; toffee.

carapace, kăh-răh-păhss, *f* carapace; shell.

carat, kăh-răh, *m* carat.

caravane, kăh-răh-văhn, *f* caravan.

carbonate, kăhr-bonn-ăht, *m* carbonate.

carbone, kăhr-bonn, *m* carbon.

carboniser, kăhr-bonn-e-zeh, *v* to carbonize; to char.

carburateur, kăhr-bE-rah-ter, *m* carburetor.

carbure, kăhr-bEEr, *m* carbide.

carcasse, kăhr-kăhss, *f* carcass; framework.

cardiaque, kăhr-de-ăhck, *a* & *mf* cardiac.

cardigan, kăhr-de-gahng, *m* cardigan.

cardinal, e, kăhr-de-năhl, *a* cardinal; principal; chief.

carême, kăh-raym, *m* Lent.

carence, kăh-rahngss, *f* deficiency; inadequacy.

carène, kăh-rain, *f* keel; bottom; careen.

caressant, e, kăh-rayss-ahng, *a* caressing; tender.

caresser, kăh-rayss-eh, *v* to caress; to stroke.

cargaison, kăhr-gay-zong, *f* cargo; freight.

cari, kăh-re *m* curry.

caricature, kăh-re-kăh-tEEr, *f* caricature.

carie, kăh-ree, *f* decay;
—**dentaire,** dahng-tair, —

dental decay; cavity.

carillon, kăh-ree-ong, *m* chime; peal.

carmin, kăhr-mang, *m* crimson.

carnage, kăhr-năhsh, *m* slaughter.

carnassier, kăhr-năhss-e-eh, *a* carnivorous.

carnaval, kăhr-năh-văhl, *m* carnival.

carnet, kăhr-nay, *m* note-book.

carnivore, kăhr-ne-vor, *a* carnivorous.

carotte, kăh-rot, *f* carrot.

carotter, kăh-rot-eh, *v* (*fam.*) to dupe; to cheat.

carpe, kăhrp, *f* carp.

carpette, kăhr-pett, *f* rug.

carré, kăh-reh, *m* square; landing.

carré, e, kăh-reh, *a* square; straight; peremptory.

carreau, kăh-roh, *m* square; pane; tile; diamonds (cards).

carrefour, kăhr-foohr, *m* crossroads.

carreler, kăhr-leh, *v* to pave with brick or tile.

carrément, kăh-reh-mahng, *adv* squarely; boldly; straightforwardly.

carrer, kăh-reh, *v* to square; **se** – to strut.

carrière, käh-re-air, *f*
quarry; career.

carriole, käh-re-ol, *f* light
covered cart.

carrosse, käh-ross, *m*
coach (horse-drawn).

carrosserie, käh-ross-re, *f*
body work (of car).

carrure, käh-rEEr, *f*
breadth of shoulders.

cartable, kähr-tabl, *m*
school bag.

carte, kährt, *f* card; ticket;
map; menu; **–blanche,**
blahngsh, full power.

carte des vins, kährt-er-
deh-vang *f* wine list.

carte routière, kähr-ter-
roo-te-air *m* road-map.

cartilage, kähr-te-lähsh,
m cartilage; (*fam.*)
gristle.

carton, kähr-tong, *m*
pasteboard; cardboard;
cartoon; hatbox;
bandbox; cardboard
box.

cartouche, kähr-toosh, *f*
cartridge; carton (of
cigarettes); refill.

cas, kah, *m* case; matter;
event; **en cas de,** ahng
kah der, in case of.

casani-er, ère, käh-zäh-
ne-eh, *a* home-loving.

cascadeur, kähss-käh-der,
m stuntman.

case, kahz, *f* hut; cabin;

pigeonhole; square (on
game board).

caser, kah-zeh, *v* to place;
to find a situation for.

caserne, käh-zairn, *f*
barracks.

casier, kah-ze-eh, *m*
pigeonhole; rack; filing
cabinet; **–judiciaire,**
–shE-de-se-air, police
record.

casque, kähssk, *m* helmet.

casquette, kähss-kett, *f*
cap.

cassant, e, kähss-ahng, *a*
brittle; blunt; sharp.

cassation, kähss-ah-se-
ong, *f* annulment;
quashing; appeal.

casse, kahss, *f* breakage.

casse-cou, kahss-koo, *m*
daredevil.

casse-noisettes, kahss-
no'äh-zett, *m*
nutcracker.

casse-tête, kahss-tayt, *m*
club; tomahawk; puzzle;
brainteaser.

casser, kahss-eh, *v* to
break; to crack; to
quash; to discharge.

casserole, kähss-rol *f*
saucepan; casserole.

cassette, kähss-ett, *f*
casket; cassette.

cassis, kahss-iss, *m* black
currant.

cassure, kahss-EEr, *f*

broken place; crack;
fracture.

caste, kähsst, *f* caste.

castor, kähss-tor, *m*
beaver.

casuel, käh-zE-ell, *m*
perquisites.

casuel, le,* käh-zE-ell, *a*
casual; accidental.

catalogue, käh-täh-log *m*
catalog; list.

cataplasme, käh-täh-
plähssm, *m* poultice.

catarrhe, käh-tähr, *m*
catarrh.

catastrophe, käh-tähss-
trof, *f* catastrophe.

catéchisme, käh-teh-
shissm, *m* catechism.

catégorie, käh-teh-go-re, *f*
category; order; class.

cathédrale, käh-teh-drähl,
f cathedral.

catholique, käh-toll-eeck,
a & *mf* Catholic.

cauchemar, kohsh-mähr,
m nightmare.

cause, kohz, *f* cause;
motive; case; trial; à
–de, äh – der, on
account of.

causer, koh-zeh, *v* to
cause; to chat.

causerie, kohz-ree, *f* talk;
chat; chattering.

causeuse, koh-zerz, *f*
settee.

caustique, kohss-tick, *a*

caustic.

cauteleu-x, se,* koht-ler, *a* cunning; crafty.

cautériser, koh-teh-re-zeh, *v* to cauterize; to burn.

caution, koh-se-ong, *f* bail; security; **sujet à —, SE-**shay t'ăh **—,** not to be trusted.

cautionnement, koh-se-onn-mahng, *m* bail; surety; security.

cautionner, koh-se-onn-eh, *v* to post bail for.

cavalerie, kăh-văhl-ree, *f* cavalry.

cavali-er, ère, kăh-văh-le-eh, *mf* horseman; horsewoman; rider; partner; *a* blunt, offhand.

cavalièrement, kăh-văh-le-air-mahng, *adv* bluntly; unceremoniously.

cave, kăhv, *f* cellar; vault; wine-cellar. *a* hollow.

caveau, kăh-voh, *m* cellar; vault.

caverne, kăh-vairn, *f* cavern; cave; den.

cavité, kăh-ve-teh, *f* cavity; hollow.

ce, cet, *m;* **cette,** *f* ser, sett, *a* this, that.

ceci, ser-se, *pron* this; this thing.

cécité, seh-se-teh, *f* blindness.

céder, seh-deh, *v* to yield; to give up; to hand over.

cédille, seh-dee-ye, *f* cedilla.

cèdre, say-dr, *m* cedar.

ceindre, sang-dr, *v* to enclose; to surround; to gird; to wreathe (**de,** with).

ceinture, sang-tEEr, *f* girdle; belt; waist; enclosure; zone; circle.

cela, ser-lăh, or slăh, *pron* that.

célèbre, seh-lay-br, *a* celebrated; famous.

célébrer, seh-leh-breh, *v* to celebrate.

celer, ser-leh, *v* to hide; to conceal (à, from).

céleri, seh-ler-re, *m* celery.

célérité, seh-leh-re-teh, *f* speed; swiftness.

céleste, seh-laist, *a* celestial, heavenly.

célibat, seh-le-băh, *m* celibacy.

célibataire, seh-le-băh-tair, *m* bachelor. *a* unmarried.

cellier, say-le-eh, *m* cellar; storeroom.

cellulaire, say-lE-lair, *a* cellular.

cellule, say-lEEl, *f* cell.

celui, *m* **celle,** *f* ser-lwe,

sell; *pron* he; she; him; her; the one; that.

cendre, sahng-dr, *f* ash; ashes; cinder.

cendré, e, sahng-dreh, *a* ash-colored.

cendrier, sahng-dre-eh, *m* ash-hole; ashtray.

cendrillon, sahng-dree-yong, *f* Cinderella.

cène, sayn, *f* Lord's Supper.

censé, e, sahng-seh, *a* reputed; supposed.

censeur, sahng-ser, *m* censor; critic.

censure, sahng-sEEr, *f* censorship; censure.

censurer, sahng-sE-reh, *v* to censure; to blame.

cent, sahng, *m & a* one hundred; hundred.

centaine, sahng-tain, *f* hundred; **une—,** EEn—, about a hundred.

centiare, sahng-te-ăhr *m* centiare (a square meter).

centième, sahng-te-aym, *m* the hundredth part; *a* hundredth.

centigrade, sahng-te-grăhd, *a* centigrade.

centigramme, sahng-te-grăhm, *m* centigram.

centime, sahng-teem, *m* one centime.

centimètre, sahng-te-may-tr, *m* centimeter; (*fam.*) tape measure; (hundredth part of a meter).

central, e, sahng-trähl, *a* central.

centralisation, sahng-trähle-zäh-se-ong, *f* centralization.

centre, sahng-tr, *m* center; middle.

centre de la ville, sahng-tr-der-läh-veel *m* town center.

centre de zone urbaine, sahng-tr-der-zohn-EEr-bayn *m* inner city.

centre-ville, sahng-tr-veel *m* town center.

centrifuge, sahng-tre-fEE sh, *a* centrifugal.

centupler, sahng-tE-pleh, *v* to increase a hundredfold.

cependant, ser-pahng, *adv* meanwhile; *conj* yet; however.

céramique, seh-räh-meek, *a* ceramic. *f* ceramics; pottery.

cerceau, sair-soh, *m* hoop.

cercle, sair-kl, *m* circle; ring; hoop; club.

cercueil, sair-ker-e, *m* coffin.

céréales, seh-reh-ähl, *fpl* cereals; corn crops.

cérébral, e, seh-reh-brähl, *a* cerebral.

cérémonial, seh-reh-monn-e-ähl, *m* ceremonial.

cérémonie, seh-reh-monn-ee, *f* ceremony.

cérémonieu-x, se,* seh-reh-monn-e-er, *a* ceremonious; formal.

cerf, sair, or sairf, *m* stag; deer; **–volant,** – voll-ahng, kite.

cerfeuil, sair-fer'e, *m* chervil.

cerise, ser-reez, *f* cherry.

cerisier, ser-re-ze-eh, *m* cherry tree.

cerneau, sair-noh, *m* green walnut.

cerné, e, sair-neh, *pp & a* surrounded; black-ringed (eyes).

cerner, sair-neh, *v* to surround; to trap.

certain, e,* sair-tang, *a* certain; sure; *pl* (before a noun) some.

certes, sairt, *adv* most certainly.

certificat, sair-te-fe-käh, *m* certificate; testimonial.

certifier, sair-te-fe-eh, *v* to certify; to testify.

certitude, sair-te-tEEd, *f* certitude; certainty; assurance.

cerveau, sair-voh, *m* brain; mind; intellect.

cervelas, sair-ver-lah, *m* sausage.

cervelle, sair-vell, *f* brains; head; intelligence.

ces, say (*pl* of **ce**), *mf a* these; those.

cessation, sess-äh-se-ong, *f* discontinuance.

cesse, sayss, *f* ceasing; respite.

cesser, sayss-eh, *v* to cease; to come to an end.

cessible, sayss-ee-bl, *a* transferable (*law*.).

cession, sayss-e-ong, *f* transfer (*law*.).

c'est-à-dire, sayt-ah-deer, *conj* that is to say.

chacal, shäh-kähl, *m* jackal.

chacun, e, shäh-kung, *pron* everyone; each; each one.

chafouin, e, shäh-foo-ang, *n & a* mean-looking; mean; sly-looking (person).

chagrin, shäh-grang, *m* grief; sorrow; trouble; shagreen (leather).

chagrin, e, shäh-grang, *a* sorrowful; gloomy; peevish.

chagrinant, e, shăh-gre-nahng, *a* grievous; sad; vexing.

chagriner, shăh-gre-neh, *v* to grieve; to vex.

chahut, shăh-EE, *m* rowdyism; noise; **faire du –,** fair dE –, to cause a rumpus; to cause an uproar.

chaîne, shain, *f* chain; line; *pl* fetters.

chaînon, shay-nong, *m* link (of chain).

chair, shair, *f* flesh; meat; pulp; **–de poule,** – der pool, goose-pimples.

chaire, shair, *f* pulpit; desk; professorship.

chaise, shayz, *f* chair; seat.

chaise longue, shayz longgh, *f* deck-chair; chaise-longue; couch.

chaland, shăh-lahng, *m* lighter; barge.

châle, shahl, *m* shawl.

chalet, shah-lay, *m* Swiss cottage; chalet.

chaleur, shăh-ler, *f* heat; warmth; zeal; heat (of animals).

chaleureu-x, se,* shăh-ler-rer, *a* warm; ardent.

chaloupe, shăh-loop, *f* rowboat; launch.

chalumeau, shăh-lE-moh, *m* reed; blowtorch.

chalut, shăh-lE, *m* trawl.

chalutier, shăh-lE-te-eh, *m* trawler.

chamailler (se), ser shăh-mah'e-yeh, *v* to squabble; to quarrel.

chambranle, shahng-brahngl, *m* door frame.

chambre, shahng-br, *f* bedroom; chamber.

chambre à un lit, chahng-brăh-ung-lee *f* single room.

chambrée, shahng-breh, *f* roomful.

chameau, shăh-moh, *m* camel.

chamelier, shăh-mer-le-eh, *m* camel driver.

chamois, shăh-mo'ăh, *m* chamois, wild goat; chamois leather; *a* buff.

champ, shahng, *m* field; ground; subject; scope; **sur le–,** sEEr ler –, immediately; **à tout bout de –,** ăh-too-boo der –, every moment.

champagne, shahng-păhn-yer, *m* champagne.

champêtre, shahng-pay-tr, *a* rural; rustic.

champignon, shahng-peen-yong, *m* mushroom.

champion, shahng-pe-ong, *m* champion.

chance, shahngss, *f* chance; luck.

chancelant, e, shahngss-lahng, *a* tottering.

chanceler, shahngss-leh, *v* to totter; to stagger.

chancelier, shahng-ser-le-eh, *m* chancellor.

chancellerie, shahng-sell-ree, *f* chancellory.

chanceu-x, se, shahng-ser, *a* lucky; risky.

chancre, shahng-kr, *m* canker.

chandeleur, shahngd-ler, *f* Candlemas.

chandelier, shahng-der-le'eh, *m* candlestick.

chandelle, shahng-dell, *f* candle.

change, shahngsh, *m* exchange; **agent de –,** ăh-shahng der –, stockbroker; exchange broker.

changeant, e, shahng-shahng, *a* changeable; fickle.

changement, shahngsh-mahng, *m* change; alteration.

changer, shahng-sheh, *v* to change; to alter; to exchange; to shift.

changeur, shahngsh-er, *m* moneychanger.

chanoine, shăh-no'ăhn, *m* canon.

chanson, shahng-so ng, *f* song; ballad.

chansonnette, shahng-sonn-ett, *f* simple song; ditty.

chansonnier, shahng-sonn-e-eh, *m* songwriter (*esp.* satirical); songbook.

chant, shahng, *m* singing; song; strain; canto.

chantage, shahng-tähsh, *m* blackmail.

chantant, e, shahng-tahng, *a* singing; tuneful.

chanter, shahng-teh, *v* to sing; to celebrate; (*fam.*) to say; **faire –, fair –,** to blackmail.

chanteu-r, se, shahng-ter, *mf* singer.

chantier, shahng-te-eh, *m* yard; lumberyard; dockyard; building site.

chantonner, shahng-tonn-eh, *v* to hum a tune.

chanvre, shahng-vr, *m* hemp.

chaos, käh-o, *m* chaos.

chape, shähp, *f* cope; cover.

chapeau, shäh-poh, *m* hat; bonnet; derby.

chapelain, shähp-lang, *m* chaplain.

chapelet, shähp-lay, *m* chaplet; rosary.

chapeli-er, ère, shäh-perle-eh, *mf* hatter.

chapelle, shäh-pell, *f* chapel.

chapellerie, shäh-pell-ree, *f* hatmaking; hat shop.

chapelure, shähp-lEEr, *f* bread crumbs.

chaperon, shähp-rong, *m* hood; chaperon.

chaperonner, shähp-ronn-eh, *v* to chaperon; to put a hood on.

chapiteau, shäh-pe-toh, *m* top; capital; crest; marquee.

chapitre, shäh-pe-tr, *m* chapter; heading.

chapitrer, shäh-pe-treh, *v* to lecture; to reprimand.

chapon, shäh-pong, *m* capon.

chaque, shähck, *a* each; every.

char, shähr, *m* car; chariot; hearse.

charabia, shäh-räh-be-äh, *m* gibberish.

charbon, shähr-bong, *m* coal; charcoal; carbuncle.

charbonnage, shähr-bonn-ähsh, *m* coal mine.

charbonner, shähr-bonn-eh, *v* to blacken; to char.

charbonneu-x, se, shähr-bonn-er, *a* coal-black; coal-like.

charbonnier, shähr-bonn-e-eh, *m* coal-man; charcoal-burner.

charcuterie, shähr-kEEt-ree, *f* delicatessen.

chardon, shähr-dong, *m* thistle.

chardonneret, shähr-donn-ray, *m* goldfinch.

charge, shährsh, *f* load; burden; expense; office; charge.

chargement, shähr-shermahng, *m* loading; cargo.

chargé, e, shähr-sheh, *pp* & *a* full; laden; heavy (of stomach); **–d'affaires,** – däh-fair, deputy ambassador.

charger, shähr-sheh, *v* to load; to charge; to entrust (**de,** with); **se –,** ser –, to take upon oneself.

chargeur, shähr-sher, *m* loader; shipper.

chariot, shäh-re-o, *m* wagon; cart; truck; carriage (of typewriter).

charitable,* shäh-re-tähbl, *a* charitable.

charité, shäh-re-teh, *f* charity; alms; benevolence.

charivari, shäh-re-väh-re, *m* hurly-burly; deafening noise.

charlatan, shähr-läh-

tahng, m quack;
charlatan.

charmant, e, shăhr-
mahng, a charming;
delightful.

charme, shăhrm, m
charm; spell; attraction.

charmer, shăhr-meh, v to
charm.

charmille, shăhr-mee-ye, f
arbor.

charnel, le, shăhr-nell, a
carnal; sensual.

charnière, shăhr-ne-air, f
hinge.

charnu, e, shăhr-nE, a
fleshy.

charogne, shăh-ronn-yer,
f carrion.

charpente, shăhr-pahngt, f
framework.

charpentier, shăhr-pahng-
te-eh, m carpenter.

charpie, shăhr-pee, f
shredded linen.

charretée, shăhr-teh, f
cartload.

charretier, shăhr-te-eh, m
carter.

charrette, shăh-rett, f cart.

charrier, shăh-re-eh, v to
cart; to drift; (fam.) to
poke fun at; to
exaggerate.

charroi, shăh-ro'ăh, m
carting.

charron, shăh-rong, m
wheelwright.

charrue, shăh-rE, f plow;
**mettre la – devant les
bœufs,** met-tr lăh–der-
vahng lay ber, to put the
cart before the horse.

charte, shăhrt, f charter.

chartreuse, shăhr-trerz, f
chartreuse (liqueur).

chas, shah, m eye of a
needle.

châsse, shahss, f shrine;
frame.

chasse, shahss, f chase;
hunting; shooting sport;
pursuit.

chasse-neige, shăhss-
naysh, m (inv in pl)
snowplow; stem
(skiing).

chasser, shăhss-eh, v to
hunt; to drive away; to
shoot; to discharge.

chasseur, shăhss-er, m
hunter; sportsman;
footman.

châssis, shahss-e, m frame;
sash; chassis.

chaste,* shăhsst, a chaste;
pure; modest.

chasteté, shăhss-ter-teh, f
chastity; purity.

chat, te, shăh, mf cat;
–huant, –E-ahng, m
tawny owl; brown owl.

châtaigne, shah-tain-yer, f
sweet chestnut.

châtain, e, shah-tang, a
chestnut.

château, shah-toh, m
castle; mansion.

châteaubriant, shah-toh-
bre-ahng m thick grilled
steak.

châtelain, e, shaht-lang,
mf owner of a manor or
castle.

châtier, shah-te-eh, v to
chastise; to punish; to
correct.

châtiment, shah-te-
mahng; m chastisement;
punishment.

chatoiement, shăh-to'ăh-
mahng, m glistening;
shimmer (colors).

chaton, shăh-tong, m
kitten; setting of stone.

chatouiller, shăh-too'e-
yeh, v to tickle.

chatouilleu-x, se, shăh-
too'e-yer, a ticklish;
touchy.

chatoyer, shăh-to'ăh-yeh,
v to glisten; to shimmer.

châtrer, shah-treh, v to
castrate; to prune.

chatterie, shăht-ree, f
usually pl coaxing way.

chaud, shoh, m heat;
warmth; **avoir –,** ăh-
vo'ăhr –, to be warm.

chaud, e,* a hot; warm;
new (of news).

chaudière, shoh-de-air, f
copper; boiler.

chaudron, shoh-drong, m

kettle; caldron; (*fam.*) bad piano.

chaudronnier, shoh-dronn-e-eh, *m* boilermaker; brazier.

chauffage, shoh-fāsh, *m* warming; heating; **–central,** – sahng-trăhl, *m* central heating.

chauffe, shohf, *f* heating; furnace.

chauffe-eau, shohf-oh, *m* water heater.

chauffer, shoh-feh, *v* to warm; to heat; to get hot.

chauffeur, shoh-fer, *m* chauffeur; stoker; driver.

chaume, shohm, *m* stubble; thatch.

chaumière, shoh-me-air, *f* thatched house; cottage.

chausse-pied, shohss-pe-eh, *m* shoehorn.

chaussée, shohss-eh, *f* road; pavement.

chausser, shohss-eh, *v* to put shoes or boots on; to supply with shoes or boots.

chaussette, shohss-ett, *f* sock.

chausson, shohss-ong, *m* slipper; babies' bootees; **–de dance,** der dahngss, ballet shoes.

chaussure, shohss-EEr, *f* shoes; footwear.

chauve, shohv, *a* bald.

chauve-souris, shohv-soo-re, *f* bat.

chauvin, e, shoh-vang, *mf* chauvinist.

chauvinisme, shoh-ve-nissm, *m* chauvinism.

chaux, shoh, *f* lime; **blanc de –,** blahng der –, whitewash.

chavirer, shăh-ve-reh, *v* to capsize.

chef, sheff.; *m* chef; chief; boss; **de son –,** der song –, on one's responsibility.

chef-d'œuvre, shay-der-vr, *m* masterpiece.

chef-lieu, sheff-le-er, *m* chief town (of country).

chemin, sher-mang, *m* way; road; path; **–de fer,** – der fair, railroad; **en –,** ahng –, on the way.

chemineau, sher-me-no, *m* tramp.

cheminée, sher-me-neh, *f* chimney; fireplace; mantel-piece; funnel.

cheminer, sher-me-neh, *v* to walk; to jog on.

cheminot, sher-me-no, *m* railroad worker.

chemise, sher-meez, *f* shirt; case; folder; **–de nuit,** – der nwee, nightdress.

chemisier, sher-me-ze-eh,

m shirtmaker; woman's blouse or shirt.

chenal, sher-năhl, *m* channel.

chenapan, sher-năh-pahng, *m* rascal.

chêne, shain, *m* oak.

chéneau, sheh-noh, *m* eaves; gutter.

chenet, sher-nay, *m* andiron.

chenil, sher-ne, *m* kennel.

chenille, sher-nee-ye, *f* caterpillar.

chèque, sheck, *m* check; **–barré,** – băh-reh, check for deposit only.

chèque de voyage, sheck-der-voăh-yăhsh *m* traveler's check.

cher, shair, *adv* dear; at a high price.

ch-er, ère,* shair, *a* dear; beloved; costly.

chercher, shair-sheh, *v* to seek; to look for; **envoyer –,** ahng-vo'ăh-yeh –, to send for.

chercheur, shair-sher, *m* seeker; inquirer.

chère, shair, *f* living; fare; cheer; **faire bonne –,** fair bonn –, to live well; to feast.

chéri, e, sheh-re, *a* darling; beloved; favorite. *m* dear one; dearest.

chérir, sheh-reer, *v* to cherish; to love.

cherté, shair-teh, *f* high price; dearness.

chérubin, sheh-rE-bang, *m* cherub.

chéti-f, ve,* sheh-tiff, *a* puny; paltry; weak.

cheval, sher-văhl, *m* horse; –vapeur, – văh-per, horsepower.

chevaleresque, sher-văhl-resk, *a* chivalrous.

chevalerie, sher-văhl-ree, *f* chivalry; knighthood.

chevalet, sher-văh-lay, *m* support; stand.

chevalier, sher-văh-le-eh, *m* knight; –d'industrie, –dang-dEEs-tree, wheeler-dealer.

chevaucher, sher-voh-sheh, *v* to ride; to overlap.

chevelu, e, sherv-lE, *a* hairy.

chevelure, sherv-lEEr, *f* head of hair.

chevet, sher-vay, *m* bolster; bedside.

cheveu, sher-ver, *m* hair (a single); les –x, lay –, the hair.

cheville, sher-vee-ye, *f* ankle; peg; pin; bolt.

chèvre, shay-vr, *f* nanny-goat; ménager la –et le chou, meh-năh-sheh

lăh – eh ler shoo, to run with the hare and hunt with the hounds.

chevreau, sher-vroh, *m* kid (goat).

chèvrefeuille, shay-vrer-fer'e, *m* honeysuckle.

chevrette, sher-vrett, *f* young doe; young nanny goat.

chevreuil, sher-vrer'e, *m* roe deer.

chevrier, sher-vre-eh, *m* goatherd.

chevron, sher-vrong, *m* rafter.

chevrotant, sher-vrot-ahng, *a* quivering; tremulous.

chevrotin, sher-vrot-ang, *m* kid leather.

chez, sheh, *prep* at; to; with; among; in; at or to the house of.

chic, sheeck, *m* stylishness; knack. *a* smart; stylish; (*fam.*) fine! a sport (of person).

chicane, she-kăhn, *f* chicanery; pettifogging.

chicaner, she-kăh-neh, *v* to quarrel with; to shuffle; to quibble.

chicanerie, she-kăhn-ree, *f* chicanery.

chiche,* sheesh, *a* stingy; *interj* I dare you!

chicorée, she-kor-eh, *f*

chicory; endive.

chicot, she-ko, *m* stump.

chien, she-ang, *m* dog; cock (gun).

chienne, she-enn, *f* bitch (dog).

chiffe, sheef, *f* flimsy stuff; weak man.

chiffon, she-fong, *m* rag; scrap; duster; *pl* finery.

chiffonné, e, she-fonn-eh, *pp & a* rumpled; of irregular but agreeable features.

chiffonner, she-fonn-eh, *v* to crumple; to vex.

chiffonnier, she-fonn-e-eh, *m* ragman; chiffonnier.

chiffre, shee-fr, *m* figure; number; total; cipher; en –s connus, ahng – konn-E, in plain figures; –d'affaires, – dăh-fair, turnover.

chiffrer, she-freh, *v* to cipher; to assess.

chignon, sheen-yong, *m* bun.

chimère, she-mair, *f* chimera; idle fancy.

chimérique, she-meh-reeck, *a* chimerical.

chimie, she-mee, *f* chemistry.

chimique,* she-meeck, *a* chemical.

chimiste, she-meesst, *m*

chemist (scientific).

chimpanzé, shang-pahng-zeh, *m* chimpanzee; chimp.

chinois sheeno'ǎh, *a* Chinese.

chiot sheo, *m* puppy.

chiper she-peh, *v* to steal.

chipie, she-pee, *f* shrew.

chipoter she-pot-eh, *v* to quibble; to nibble.

chique, sheeck, *f* wad of tobacco.

chiquenaude, sheeck-nohd, *f* flick of finger.

chiquer she-keh, *v* to chew (tobacco).

chirurgie, she-rEEr-shee, *f* surgery.

chirurgien, she-rEEr-she-ang, *m* surgeon.

chlore, klor, *m* chlorine.

chlorure, klor-EEr, *m* chloride.

choc, shock, *m* shock; collision; clash; knock.

chocolat, shock-oll-ǎh, *m* chocolate. *a* chocolate colored.

chœur, ker, *m* choir; chorus; chancel.

choir, sho'ǎhr, *v* to fall.

choisi, sho'ǎh-ze, *pp* & *a* chosen; selected; choice.

choisir, sho'ǎh-zeer, *v* to choose; to select (**dans, entre, parmi,** from).

choix, sho'ǎh, *m* choice;

selection; election.

choléra, koll-eh-rǎh, *m* cholera.

chômage, shoh-mǎhsh, *m* unemployment; time spent without work.

chômer, shoh-meh, *v* to stand idle; to be out of work.

chômeur, shoh-mer, *m* unemployed.

chopper, shop-eh, *v* to stumble; to trip up.

choquant, e, shock-ahng, *a* offensive (**pour,** to); shocking; unpleasant.

choquer, shock-eh, *v* to shock; to strike; to touch; to displease; **se –,** to take offense (**de,** at); to be shocked.

chose, shohz, *f* thing; matter; affair; **bien des – s à,** be-ang deh – ǎh, my best regards to.

chou, shoo, *m* cabbage; dear; pet;**– fleur,** –fler cauliflower.

choucroute, shoo-kroot, *f* sauerkraut.

chouette, shoo-ait, *f* owl; *a* (*fam.*) fantastic; great; marvelous.

choyer, sho'ǎh-yeh, *v* to fondle; to pet.

chrétien, ne,* kreh-te-ang, *a* & *mf* Christian.

chrétienté, kreh-te-ang-

teh, *f* Christendom.

christ, krisst, *m* Christ; crucifix.

christianisme, krisst-e-ǎh-nissm, *m* Christianity.

chrome, krohm, *m* chromium; chrome.

chronique, kronn-eeck, *f* chronicle. *a* chronic.

chronomètre, kronn-omm-ay-tr, *m* chronometer.

chrysalide, kre-zǎh-leed, *f* chrysalis.

chrysanthème, kre-zahng-taym, *m* chrysanthemum.

chuchoter, shE-shot-eh, *v* to whisper.

chut, shEEt, *interj* hush!

chute, shEEt, *f* fall; downfall; failure.

ci, se, *adv* here; this; **– joint,** –sho'ang, enclosed; **comme –, comme ça,** komm –, komm sǎh, so-so, middling.

cible, see-bl, *f* target.

ciboulette, se-boo-lett, *f* chives.

cicatrice, se-kǎh-triss, *f* scar.

cidre, see-dr, *m* cider.

Cie (for **Compagnie**), kong-pǎhn-yee, *f* "Co."

ciel, se-ell, *m* heaven; sky.

cierge, se-airsh, *m* altar

candle.

cigale, se-gähl, *f* cicada.

cigare, se-gähr, *m* cigar.

cigarette, se-gäh-rett, *f* cigarette.

cigogne, se-gonn-yer, *f* stork.

cigüe, se-ghE, *f* hemlock.

cil, seel, *m* eyelash.

cime, seem, *f* summit; top; crest.

ciment, se-mahng, *m* cement.

cimenter, se-mahng-teh, *v* to cement.

cimetière, seem-te-air, *m* cemetery; churchyard; graveyard.

cinéaste, se-neh-ähsst, *m* moviemaker.

cinéma, se-neh-măh, *m* movie theater; **faire du –,** fair dE **–,** to act in films.

cingler, sang-gleh, *v* to lash; to sail.

cinglé, sang-gleh, *a* (*fam.*) nuts; cracked.

cinq, sangk, *a* five.

cinquantaine, sang-kahng-tain, *f* about fifty.

cinquante, sang-kahngt, *a* fifty.

cinquantenaire, sang-kahngt-nair, *m* fiftieth anniversary.

cinquantième, sang-kahng-te-aym, *a* fiftieth.

cinquième, sang-ke-aym, *m* & *a* fifth.

cintre, sang-tr, *m* semicircle; arch; coat hanger.

cintré, e, sang-treh, *pp* & *a* arched; fitted (of coat, etc.).

cirage, se-răhsh, *m* polishing; shoe polish.

circoncire, seer-kong-seer, *v* to circumcise.

circoncision, seer-kong-se-ze-ong, *f* circumcision.

circonférence, seer-kong-feh-rahngss, *f* circumference.

circonflexe, seer-kong-flex, *a* circumflex.

circonscription, seer-kongss-krip-se-ong, *f* district.

circonscrire, seer-kongss-kreer, *v* to circumscribe.

circonspect, e, seer-kongss-peckt, or seer-kongss-pay, *a* circumspect; wary.

circonspection, seer-kongss-peck-se-ong, *f* cautiousness.

circonstance, seer-kongss-tahngss, *f* circumstance; occasion.

circonstancier, seer-kongss-tahng-se-eh, *v* to state fully.

circonvenir, seer-kongv-neer, *v* to circumvent; to deceive.

circonvoisin, seer-kong-vo'ăh-zang, *a* surrounding; neighboring.

circuit, seer-kwe, *m* circuit; roundabout way.

circulaire, seer-kE-lair, *f* circular. *a* circular.

circulation, seer-kE-läh-se-ong, *f* circulation; currency; traffic.

circuler, seer-kE-leh, *v* to circulate; to move.

cire, seer, *f* wax.

cirer, se-reh, *v* to wax; to polish (shoes, floors, etc.); to spread about.

cirque, seerk, *m* circus.

ciseau, se-zoh, *m* chisel; *pl* scissors; shears.

ciseler, seez-leh, *v* to carve; to chisel.

citadelle, se-tăh-dell, *f* citadel.

citadin, e, se-tăh-dang, *mf* townsman; townswoman.

citation, se-tăh-se-ong, *f* quotation; subpoena.

cité, se-teh, *f* city; town.

citer, se-teh, *v* to quote; to mention; to summon; to subpoena.

citerne, se-tairn, *f* cistern; tank; reservoir.

cithare, se-tăhr, *f* zither.

citoyen, ne, se-to'ăh-yang, *mf* & *a* citizen; freeman.

citrate, se-trăht, *m* citrate.

citron, se-trong, *m* lemon; citron. *a* lemon-colored.

citronade, si-tro-năhd, *f* lemonade.

citrouille, see-troo'e-yer, *f* pumpkin; gourd.

cive, seev, *fpl* chives.

civet, se-vay, *m* game stew; **– de lièvre,** – der le-ay-vr, rabbit stew.

civière, se-ve-air, *f* stretcher.

civil, se-vill, *m* civilian; layman.

civil, e,* se-vill, *a* polite; civil.

civilisation, se-ve-le-zăh-se-ong, *f* civilization.

civiliser, se-ve-le-zeh, *v* to civilize.

civilité, se-ve-le-teh, *f* civility.

civique, se-veeck, *a* civic.

civisme, seeveesm, *m* public responsibility; public-spiritedness.

clafoutis, klăh-footee, *m* dessert made with fruit and batter.

claie, klay, *f* hurdle; screen.

clair, klair, *m* light; light part.

clair, e,* klair, *a* clear; bright; light; evident.

claire-voie, klair-vo'ăh, *f* opening; lattice; skylight.

clairière, klai-re-air, *f* glade.

clairon, klai-rong, *m* clarion; bugle; bugler.

clairsemé, e, klair-ser-meh, *a* thinly sown; sparse; scattered.

clairvoyance, klair-vo'ăh-yahngss, *f* clairvoyance; clear-sightedness.

clairvoyant, e, klair-vo'ăh-yahng, *n* & *a* clear-sighted; judicious; clairvoyant.

clameur, klăh-mer, *f* clamor; outcry.

clan, klahng, *m* clan; clique.

clandestin, e,* klahng-dess-tang, *a* clandestine.

clapet, klăh-pay, *m* clapper; valve.

clapier, klăh-pe-eh, *m* burrow; warren; hutch.

clapoter, klăh-pot-eh, *v* to chop, to ripple.

clapotis, klăh-pot-e, *m* ripple; splashing.

clapper, klăh-peh, *v* to smack; to clack.

claque, klăhck, *m* opera hat; *f* slap; hired applauders.

claquemurer, klăhck-mE-reh, *v* to shut up; to confine.

claquer, klăh-keh, *v* to clap; to smack.

claqueur, klăh-ker, *m* hired applauder.

clarifier, klăh-re-fe-eh, *v* to clarify; **se –,** to make clear.

clarinette, klăh-re-nett, *f* clarinet.

clarté, klăhr-teh, *f* clearness; light; brightness.

classe, klahss, *f* class; order; rank; form; school; classroom.

classement, klahss-mahng, *m* classification; filing.

classeur, klăhss-er, *m* files; filing cabinet.

classifier, klăhss-e-fe-eh, *v* to classify.

classique, klăhss-eeck, *m* classic; *a* classical.

clause, klohz, *f* clause; condition.

claustration, klohs-trăh-se-ong, *f* cloistering; confinement.

clavecin, klăhv-sang, *m* harpsichord.

clavicule, klăh-ve-kEEl, *f* collarbone.

clavier, klăh-ve-eh, *m* keyboard.

clef, or **clè,** kleh, *f* key; wrench; lever; keystone.

fermer à –, fair-meh ăh –, to lock.

clémence, kleh-mahngss, f clemency; mercy.

clerc, klair, m clerk; cleric; scholar. **faire un pas de –,** fair ung pah der –, to blunder.

clergé, klair-sheh, m clergy.

clérical, e, kleh-re-kăhl, a clerical.

cliché, kle-sheh, m stereotype; negative (photo); stereotyped phrase.

client, e, kle-ahng, mf client; patient; customer.

clientèle, kle-ahng-tell, f clients; customers.

cligner, clignoter, kleen-yeh, kleen-yot-eh, v to wink; to blink; to flicker.

clignotant, kleen-yot-ahng, m turn signal.

climat, kle-măh, m climate; clime; atmosphere.

climatérique, kle-măh-teh-reeck, a climatic.

climatisé, kle-măh-te-zeh, a air-conditioned.

climatiseur, kle-măh-te-zer, m air conditioner.

clin d'œil, klang-der'e, m wink.

clinique, kle-neeck, f nursing home; clinic. a clinical.

clinquant, klang-kahng, m tinsel; glitter.

clique, kleeck, f gang; set; clan.

cliquetis, kleeck-te, m clank; clashing; jingle.

clivage, kle-văhsh, m cleavage.

clochard, klo-shar, m tramp; homeless.

cloaque, klo'ăhck, m sewer; cesspool.

cloche, klosh, f bell; dish cover; (fam.) idiot.

cloche-pied (à), ăh klosh-pe-eh, adv hopping on one leg.

clocher, klosh-eh, v to limp; to go wrong somewhere.

clocher, klosh-eh, v to steeple; church tower.

clocheton, klosh-tong, m pinnacle; turret.

clochette, klosh-ett, f small bell; bellflower; bluebell.

cloison, klo'ăh-zong, f partition.

cloître, klo'ăh-tr, m cloister; monastery.

clopin-clopant, klop-ang klop-ahng, adv hobbling along.

cloque, clock, f blister.

clos, e, klo, pp & a closed; finished.

cloque, klock, f blister.

clos, klo, m close; enclosure; vineyard.

clôture, kloh-tEEr, f enclosure; seclusion; closing.

clôturer, kloh-tE-reh, v to enclose; to close down.

clou, kloo, m nail; boil; chief attraction; **–de girofle,** – der she-rofl, clove.

clouer, kloo-eh, v to nail; to rivet; to clench.

clouter, kloo-teh, v to stud.

clown, kloon, m clown.

club, klEEb, m club.

clystère, kliss-tair, m enema.

coacquéreur, ko'ăh-keh-rer, m joint purchaser.

coadministrateur, ko'ăhd-me-niss-trăh-ter, m codirector.

coaguler, ko'ăh-ghE-leh, v to coagulate; **se –,** to curdle.

coaliser (se), ser ko'ăh-le-zeh, v to unite; to form a coalition.

coasser, ko'ăhss-eh, v to croak.

coassocié, e, ko'ăh-soss-e-eh, mf co-partner.

cocagne (pays de), pay-

yee der kock-ăhn-yer, *m*
land of plenty; **mât de –,**
mah der –, greasy pole.
cocarde, kock-ăhrd, *f*
cockade.
cocasse, kock-ăhss, *a*
funny; droll.
coccinelle, kock-se-nell, *f*
ladybug.
coche, kosh, *m* coach;
barge; *f* notch; sow.
cocher, kosh-eh, *m*
coachman; driver.
cochon, kosh-ong, *m* hog;
pig; porker; swine; pork;
–de lait, – der lay,
sucking pig; **–d'Inde,** –
dangd, guinea pig.
cochonnerie, kosh-onn-
ree, dirtiness; indecent
action or language;
(*fam.*) dirty trick.
coco, kock-o, *m* coconut;
(*fam.*) pet.
cocon, kock-ong, *m*
cocoon.
cocotier, kock-ot-e-eh, *m*
coconut palm.
cocotte, kock-ot, *f*
stewpan; darling; child's
word for chicken;
–minute, – me-nEEt,
pressure cooker.
code, kod, *m* code; law.
coefficient, ko-eh-fe-se-
ahng, *m* coefficient.
coercition, ko-air-se-se-
ong, *f* coercion.

cœur, ker, *m* heart; soul;
love; courage; core;
avoir mal au –, ăh-
vo'ăhr măhl oh –, to
feel sick.
coffre, kofr, *m* trunk;
chest; box; **–fort,** – for,
safe.
coffrer, kof-reh, *v* (*fam.*)
to lock up.
coffret, kof-ray, *m* small
chest; jewelry box.
cognac, kon-yăhck, *m*
brandy.
cognée, kon-yeh, *f*
hatchet.
cogner, kon-yeh, *v* to
knock; to strike; to drive
in.
cohérent, e, ko-eh-rahng,
a coherent.
cohéritier, ko-eh-re-te-eh,
mf jointheir.
cohésion, ko-eh-ze-ong, *f*
cohesion.
cohue, koE, *f* crowd; mob;
rout; uproar.
coi, coite, *f* ko'ăh, ko'ăht,
a quiet; still.
coiffe, ko'ăhf, *f* headdress.
coiffer, ko'ăhf-eh, *v* to put
on the head. **se –,** to
brush one's hair; to
comb.
coiffeur, -euse, ko'ăhf-er,
mf hairdresser.
coiffeuse, ko'ăh-ferz,
dressing table.

coiffure, ko'ăhf-EEr, *f*
headdress; hairstyle;
hairdo.
coin, ko-ang, *m* corner;
angle; wedge.
coincer, ko-ang-seh, *v* to
wedge up; to jam.
coïncider, ko-ang-se-deh,
v to coincide.
coing, ko-ang, *m* quince.
col, kol, *m* collar; neck;
pass.
colère, koll-air, *f* anger;
wrath; ire.
colérique, koll-eh-reeck, *a*
angry; irascible.
colibri, koll-e-bre, *m*
hummingbird.
colifichet, koll-e-fe-shay,
m knickknack; trinket;
bauble.
colimaçon, koll-e-măh-
song, *m* snail.
colin-maillard, koll-ang-
mah'e-yăhr, *m*
blindman's buff.
colique, koll-eeck, *f* pain
in the stomach; stomach
cramp.
colis, koll-e, *m* package;
parcel.
collabora-teur, trice, kol-
lăh-bor-ăh-ter, *mf*
collaborator; assistant;
contributor.
collaborer, kol-lăh-bor-
eh, *v* to work together.
collage, koll-ăhsh, *m*

sticking; pasting; gluing.

collant, e, koll-ahng, *a*
sticking; tight; *m* pair of
tights.

collation, koll-ăh-se-ong, *f*
collation; light meal.

collationner, koll-ăh-se-
onn-eh, *v* to collate; to
compare; to lunch.

colle, kol, *f* paste; glue;
size.

collecte, koll-leckt, *f*
collection.

collecti-f, ve,* koll-leck-
teeff, *a* collective.

collectionner, koll-leck-
se-onn-eh, *v* to collect.

collège, koll-aysh, *m*
school; junior high
school.

collégien, koll-eh-she-
ang, *m* schoolboy;
collegian.

collégiennne , koll-eh-
she-angn *f* schoolgirl.

coller, koll-eh, *v* to stick;
to glue; to adhere.

collet, koll-ay, *m* collar;
snare; **–monté,** – mong-
teh, strait-laced.

colleur, koll-er, *m*
paperhanger.

collier, koll-e-eh, *m* collar;
necklace; ring.

colline, koll-een, *f* hill;
hillock.

colloque, koll-lock, *m*
colloquium; conference.

collusoire, koll-LE-zo'ăhr,
a collusive.

colombe, koll-ongb, *f*
dove.

colombier, koll-ong-be-eh,
m dovecote; pigeonhole.

colon, koll-ong, *m*
colonist; planter.

côlon, kohll-ong, *m* colon.

colonel, koll-onn-ell, *m*
colonel.

colonie, koll-onn-ee, *f*
colony; settlement.

colonnade, koll-onn-ăhd,
f colonnade.

colonne, koll-onn, *f*
column; pillar;
–vertébrale, – vair-teh-
brăhl, spine; backbone.

coloquinte, koll-ock-angt,
f bitter apple.

colorer, koll-or-eh, *v* to
color; to stain.

coloris, koll-or-e, *m*
coloring; hue.

colosse, koll-oss, *m*
colossus; giant.

colporter, koll-por-teh, *v*
to hawk about; to spread
(news).

colporteur, koll-por-ter,
m peddler; hawker.

combat, kong-băh, *m*
fight; battle; contest;
hors de –, or der –,
disabled.

combattre, kong-băh-tr, *v*
to fight; to contest; to

contend (**contre,** with).

combien, kong-be-ang, *adv*
how much; how many;
how; **–de temps,** – der
tahng, how long?

combinaison, kong-be-
nay-zong, *f* combination;
slip; contrivance.

combinaison de plongée,
kong-be-nay-zong-der-
plong-sheh *f* wetsuit.

combine, kong-been, *f*
(*fam.*) scheme;
arrangement; fiddle.

combiner, kong-be-neh, *v*
to combine; to contrive.

comble, kong-bl, *m*
heaping (measure);
summit; acme; *pl* gables;
de fond en –, der fong
t'ahng –, from top to
bottom; **pour –de,**
poohr – der, to crown;
to complete.

comble, kong-bl, *a*
crowded; full; heaped
up.

combler, kong-bleh, *v* to
fill; to heap; to cover; to
overwhelm (**de,** with);
to fulfill.

combustible, kong-bEEs-
tee-bl, *m* fuel; *a*
combustible.

comédie, komm-eh-dee, *f*
comedy; play; theater.

comédien, ne, komm-eh-
de-ang, *mf* actor; actress;

comedian.

comestible, komm-ess-tee-bl, *a* edible.

comestibles, komm-ess-tee-bl, *mpl* provisions; food.

comète, komm-ett, *f* comet.

comice, komm-iss, *m* agricultural or electoral meeting.

comique, komm-eeck, *m* comic actor; comic art; *a* comic; comical.

comité, komm-e-teh, *m* board; committee.

commandant, komm-ahng-dah*ng*, *m* commander; major; commanding officer.

commande, komm-ahngd, *f* order.

commander, komm-ahng-deh, *v* to command; to order; to overlook.

commanditaire, komm-ahng-de-tair, *m* silent partner.

commandite, komm-ahng-deet, *f* limited partnership.

comme, komm, *adv* as; like; as if; almost; how; *conj* as; since; because.

commençant, e, komm-ahng-sahng, *mf* beginner.

commencement, komm-ahngss-mahng, *m* beginning.

commencer, komm-ahngss-eh, *v* to begin.

comment, komm-ahng, *adv* how; why! what! –**donc!** – dong! to be sure!

commentaire, komm-mahng-tair, *m* commentary; comment; remark.

commenter, komm-ahng-teh, *v* to comment; to criticize; to pass remarks.

commerçant, komm-air-sahng, *m* trader; tradesman; dealer. *a* commercial; business.

commerce, komm-airss, *m* trade; business.

commère, komm-air, *f* gossip; busybody.

commettre, komm-et-tr, *v* to commit; to entrust; to appoint; to make (a mistake).

commis, komm-e, *m* clerk; shop assistant; –**voyageur**, –vo'äh-yäh-sher, commercial traveler.

commissaire, komm-iss-air, *m* commissioner; commissary; steward; superintendent (police); –**priseur**, – pre-zer,

auctioneer.

commissariat, komm-iss-säh-re-äh, *m* station (police).

commission, komm-iss-e-ong, *f* commission; message; errand; committee; commission agency; –**ner** *v* to commission.

commissionnaire, komm-iss-e-onn-air, *m* agent; porter; messenger; broker.

commode, komm-odd, *f* chest of drawers. *a* convenient; suitable; handy.

commodité, komm-odd-e-teh, *f* convenience.

commotion, komm-moss-e-ong, *f* disturbance; concussion.

commun, komm-ung, *m* generality; commonplace; lower class; domestic servant; *pl* domestic offices.

commun, e, komm-ung, komm-EEn, *a* common; ordinary; trivial; vulgar.

communal, e, komm-E-nähl, *a* communal.

communauté, komm-E-noh-teh, *f* community; convent; corporation.

commune, komm-EEn, *f* commune; parish.

communément, komm-E-neh-mahng, *adv* commonly.

communicant, e, komm-E-ne-kahng, *a* communicating.

communication, komm-E-ne-kăh-se-ong, *f* communication; message; cognizance; telephone call.

communier, komm-E-ne-eh, *v* to receive the sacrament.

communion, komm-E-ne-ong, *f* communion; sacrament; fellowship.

communiqué, komm-E-ne-keh, *m* official statement.

communiquer, komm-E-ne-keh, *v* to communicate; to impart; to infuse.

compact, e, kong-păhckt, *a* compact; dense.

compagne, kong-păhn-yer, *f* female companion; mate; partner; playmate.

compagnie, kong-păhn-yee, *f* company; society; companionship; **fausser –,** foh-seh –, to sneak away from someone.

compagnon, kong-păhn-yong, *m* companion; partner; mate; playmate.

comparable, kong-păh-

răh-bl, *a* comparable.

comparaison, kong-păh-ray-zong, *f* comparison.

comparaître, kong-păh-ray-tr, *v* to appear (in court).

comparant, kong-păh-rahng, *a* appearing (in court).

comparer, kong-păh-reh, *v* to compare.

compartiment, kong-păhr-te-mahng, *m* compartment; division.

comparution, kong-păh-rE-se-ong, *f* appearance (in court).

compas, kong-pah, *m* compass; compasses.

compassé, e, kong-păhss-eh, *a* formal; stiff.

compasser, kong-păhss-eh, *v* to measure; to regulate; to lay out.

compassion, kong-păhss-e-ong, *f* compassion; pity.

compatible, kong-păhstee-bl, *a* compatible.

compatir, kong-pah-teer, *v* to sympathize (à, with).

compatissant, kong-pah-tiss-ahng, *a* compassionate.

compatriote, kong-păh-tre-ot, *mf* fellow-countryman, fellow-countrywoman.

compenser, kong-pahng-seh, *v* to compensate.

compère, kong-pair, *m* announcer (theater); accomplice; chum.

compétence, kong-peh-tahngss, *f* competence; jurisdiction.

compétent, e, kong-peh-tahng; *a* competent; suitable.

compéti-teur, trice, kong-peh-te-ter, *mf* competitor.

compétition, kong-peh-te-se-ong, *f* competition; rivalry; contest.

compilateur, kong-pe-lăh-ter, *m* compiler.

compiler, kong-pe-leh, to compile.

complainte, kong-plangt, *f* lament; ballad.

complaire (à), kong-plair ăh, *v* to please; **se –,** to delight (à, dans, in).

complaisamment, kong-play-zăh-mahng, *adv* obligingly.

complaisance, kong-play-zahngss, *f* obligingness; kindness; complacency.

complaisant, kong-play-zahng, *m* flatterer.

complaisant, e, kong-play-zahng, *a* obliging; kind.

complément, kong-pleh-mahng, *m* complement;

object (grammar); remainder.

complet, kong-play, *m* full number; suit (of clothes).

compl-et, ète,* kong-play, *a* complete; full; utter.

compléter, kong-pleh-teh, *v* to complete; to make complete.

complexe, kong-plex, *a* complex; complicated.

complexion, kong-plex-e-ong, *f* constitution; disposition.

complexité kong-plex-e-teh, *f* complexity.

complication, kong-ple-kăh-se-ong, *f* complication.

complice, kong-pliss, *mf & a* accomplice; corespondent.

compliment, kong-ple-mahng, *m* compliment; *pl* congratulations.

complimenter, kong-ple-mahng-teh, *v* to congratulate.

compliqué, e, kong-ple-keh, *a* complicated.

compliquer, kong-ple-keh, *v* to complicate.

complot, kong-plo, *m* plot; conspiracy; scheme.

comploter, kong-plot-eh, *v* to plot.

comporter, kong-por-teh, *v* to permit; to admit; to comprise; **se –,** to behave.

composé, kong-poz-eh, *m* compound.

composé, e, kong-poz-eh, *a* composed; compound.

composer, kong-poz-eh, *v* to compose; to compound; to settle.

composi-teur, trice, kong-poz-e-ter, *m* composer; compositor.

composition, kong-poz-e-se-ong, *f* composition; agreement; examination; essay; **de bonne–,** der bonn –, easy to deal with.

compote, kong-pot, *f* stewed fruit; **en –,** ahng –, stewed; (*fig.*) bruised.

compréhensible, kong-preh-ahng-see-bl, *a* understandable.

compréhensi-f, ve, kong-preh-ahng-siff, *a* comprehensive.

compréhension, kong-preh-ahng-se-ong, *f* comprehension.

comprendre, kong-prahng-dr, *v* to understand; to include.

compression, kong-press-e-ong, *f* compression.

comprimé, kong-pre-meh, *m* tablet.

comprimé, e, kong-pre-meh, *pp & a* compressed.

comprimer, kong-pre-meh, *v* to compress; to condense; to restrain.

compris, e, kong-pre, *pp & a* understood; included; **y –, e –,** including; **non –,** nong –, excluding.

compromettant, e, kong-promm-ett-ahng, *a* compromising.

compromettre, kong-promm-et-tr, *v* to compromise; to imperil.

compromis, kong-promm-e, *m* compromise.

comptabilité, kong-tăh-be-le-teh, *f* accountancy; bookkeeping; accounts; accountant's office.

comptable, kong-tăh-bl, *m* accountant; expert – ecks-pair –,*m* licensed accountant. *a* accountable; responsible.

comptant, kong-tahng, *a* ready (money); cash; **au – oh –,** for cash.

compte, kongt, *m* account; reckoning; amount; right number; **en fin de –,** ahng fangd –, after all; **se rendre –de,** ser rahng-dr –, to realize.

compte en banque, kongt-ăhng-băhngk, *m* bank account.

compter, kong-teh, *v* to count; to reckon; to intend; to rely.

compte-rendu, kongt rahng-dE, *m* account; report; minutes (of meeting).

compteur, kong-ter, *m* speedometer; meter; recorder.

comptoir, kong-to'ăhr, *m* counter; trading syndicate branch; bar.

compulser, kong-pEEl-seh, *v* to examine (documents, etc).

compulsi-f, ve, kong-pEEl-seef, *a* psych compulsive.

comte, kongt, *m* count; earl.

comté, kong-teh, *m* county; earldom.

concasser, kong-kăhss-seh, *v* to pound; to crush.

concave, kong-kăhv, *a* concave.

concéder, kong-seh-deh, *v* to concede; to grant; to allow.

concentration, kong-sahng-trăh-se-ong, *f* concentration.

concentré, kong-sahng-treh, *m* extract; concentration.

concentrer, kong-sahng-treh, *v* to concentrate; to hold back (feelings).

conception, kong-sep-se-ong, *f* conception; thought.

concernant, kong-sair-nahng, *prep* relating to.

concerner, kong-sair-neh, *v* to concern; to belong to.

concert, kong-sair, *m* concert; concord; **de –,** der–. in concert; jointly.

concerter, kong-sair-teh, *v* to concert; to contrive; **se–,** to plan together.

concession, kong-sess-e-ong, *f* concession; grant; claim.

concessionnaire, kong-sess-e-onn-air, *m* concessionnaire; contractor; grantee.

concevable, kongss-văh-bl, *a* conceivable.

concevoir, kongss-vo'ăhr, *v* to conceive; to understand; to imagine.

concierge, kong-se-airsh, *mf* concierge; janitor; doorman.

conciergerie, kong-se-air-sher-ree, *m* janitor's lodge.

conciliable, kong-se-le-ăh-bl, *a* reconcilable.

conciliabule, kong-se-le-

ăh-bEEl, *m* secret assembly; secret meeting.

conciliant, e, kong-se-le-ahng, *a* conciliatory.

concilia-teur, trice, kong-se-le-ăh-ter, *mf* & *a* peacemaker; conciliator; conciliatory.

concilier, kong-se-le-eh, *v* to reconcile; **se –,** to win over.

concis, e, kong-se, *a* concise; brief.

concision, kong-se-ze-ong, *f* conciseness.

concitoyen, ne, kong-se-to'ăh-yang, *mf* fellow citizen.

conclave, kong-klăv, *m* conclave.

concluant, e, kong-klE-ahng, *a* conclusive.

conclure, kong-klEEr, *v* to conclude; to close; to infer; to prove; to move.

conclusi-f, ve, * kong-klE-zeeff, *a* conclusive.

conclusion, kong-klE-ze-ong, *f* conclusion; inference; motion; verdict.

concombre, kong-kong-br, *m* cucumber.

concordance, kong-kor-dahngss, *f* agreement; concord; concordance (Bible).

concorder, kong-kor-deh, v to live in agreement; to agree; to compound.

concourir, kong-koo-reer, v to concur; to converge; to compete; to cooperate.

concours, kong-koohr, m cooperation; concourse; competition; meeting.

concre-t, ète, kong-kray, a concrete.

concupiscence, kong-kEpiss-ahngss, f concupiscence; sexual desire.

concurremment, kong-kEEr-răh-mahng, adv concurrently; in competition.

concurrence, kong-kEErrahngss, f competition; concurrence; **jusqu'à –de,** shEEs-kăh – der, to the amount of.

concurrent, e, kong-kEErrahng, mf competitor.

condamnable, kong-dăhnăh-bl, a reprehensible; condemnable.

condamnation, kong-dăhnăh-se-ong, f condemnation; sentence; conviction.

condamné, e, kong-dăhneh, pp & mf condemned; convict.

condamner, kong-dăh-

neh, v to condemn; to convict; to sentence; to block up.

condenser, kong-dahngseh, v to condense.

condescendance, kong-dess-sahng-dahngss, f condescension.

condescendre, kong-desssahng-dr, v to condescend; to yield; to comply.

condiment, kong-demahng, m condiment.

condisciple, kong-de-seepl, m schoolmate.

condition, kong-de-seong, f condition; position; term.

conditionnel, le, * kongde-se-onn-ell, a conditional.

conditionner, kong-de-seonn-eh, v to condition; **air conditionné, air** kong-de-se-onn-eh, airconditioned.

condoléance, kong-dolleh-ahngss, f condolence.

conduc-teur, trice, kongdEEk-ter, mf conductor; leader; guide; driver. a conducting; leading.

conduire, kong-dweer, v to conduct; to lead; to guide; to drive; to steer; to carry; to manage; **se –,** to behave.

conduit, kong-dwe, m pipe; tube; way.

conduite, kong-dweet, f conduct; behavior; management; care; driving; channel; **changer de –,** shahngsheh der –, to turn a new leaf.

cône, kohn, m cone.

confection, kong-feck-seong, f making; manufacture; clothing industry; **–neur,** m readymade manufacturer; maker.

confédération, kong-feh-deh-răh-se-ong f confederacy.

confédéré e, kong-feh-deh-reh, a confederate.

confédérer, kong-feh-deh-reh, v to unite.

conférence, kong-feh-rahngss, f lecture; conference; **maître de –s,** may-tr der –, college professor.

conférencier, kong-feh-rahng-se-eh, m lecturer.

conférer, kong-feh-reh, v to confer (à, upon); to grant; to compare; to consult together.

confesser, kong-fayss-eh, v to confess; to acknowledge.

confession, kong-fayss-e-ong, f confession.

confiance, kong-fe-ahngss, f confidence; trust; reliance.

confiant, e, kong-fe-ahng, a confident; confiding; assured.

confiemment, kong-fe-däh-mahng, adv in confidence.

confidence, kong-fe-dahngss, f confidence; secret.

confidentiel, le, * kong-fe-dahng-se-ell, a confidential.

confier, kong-fe-eh; v to confide; to entrust; se –, to confide (à, in).

confiner, kong-fe-neh, v to confine; to border upon.

confins, kong-fang, mpl confines; borders.

confire, kong-feer, v to preserve; to pickle.

confirmati-f, ve, kong-feer-mäh-teeff, a confirmatory.

confirmer, kong-feer-meh, v to confirm; se –, ser–, to be confirmed.

confiscation, kong-fiss-käh-se-ong, f confiscation; forfeiture.

confiserie, kong-feez-ree, f confectionery; preserving; candy store.

confiseur, kong-fe-zer, m confectioner.

confisquer, kong-fiss-keh, v to confiscate.

confit, kong-fe, a preserved; candied.

confiture, kong-fe-tEEr, f preserves; jam.

conflagration, kong-flähgräh-se-ong, f conflagration.

conflit, kong-fle, m conflict; clash.

confluent, kong-flE-ahng, m confluence.

confondre, kong-fong-dr, v to confound; to confuse; to overwhelm; se–,ser–, to become indistinct; to be mistaken.

conformation, kong-formäh-se-ong, f conformation.

conforme, kong-form, a in accordance; conformable; consistent (à, with); pour copie–, poohr kop-e –, certified copy.

conformément, kong-formeh-mahng, adv in accordance (à, with).

conformer, kong-for-meh, v to conform; se–, ser–, to comply (à, with).

conformité, kong-for-meteh, f conformity.

confort, kong-for, m comfort; ease.

confortable, * kong-fortäh-bl, a comfortable; easy.

conforter, kong-for-teh, v to comfort; to strengthen.

confraternité, kong-frähtair-ne-teh, f brotherhood.

confrère, kong-frair, m colleague; fellow member (of profession, etc.); brother.

confronter, kong-frongteh, v to confront; to compare.

confus, e, kong-fE, a confused; embarrassed; overwhelmed.

confusion, kong-fE-ze-ong, f confusion; disorder; trouble; shame.

congé, kong-sheh, m leave; resignation; dismissal; holiday.

congédier, kong-sheh-deeh, v to discharge; to dismiss; to pay off.

congélateur, kong-shehläh-ter, m deep-freeze machine.

congélation, kong-shehläh-se-ong, f freezing.

congeler, kongsh-leh, v to congeal; to freeze.

congestion, kong-shess-teong, f congestion.

congre, kong-gr, *m* conger eel.

congrégation, kong-greh-gäh-se-ong, *f* congregation.

congrés, kong-gray, *m* congress.

conique, koh-neeck, *a* conic; conical.

conjecturer, kong-sheck-tE-reh, *v* to conjecture; to surmise; to guess.

conjoindre, kong-sho'ang-dr, *v* to join; to unite.

conjoint, e, * kongsho'ang, *pp* & *a* joined; united; **–s,** *mpl* husband and wife.

conjonction, kong-shongk-se-ong, *f* conjunction; union.

conjugaison, kong-shE-gay-zong, *f* conjugation.

conjugal, e, * kong-shE-gähl, *a* conjugal; married.

conjuguer, kong-shE-gheh, *v* to conjugate.

conjuration, kong-shE-räh-se-ong, *f* conspiracy; entreaty (in *pl*).

conjuré, kong-shE-reh, *m* conspirator, plotter.

conjurer, kong-shE-reh, *v* to conspire; to implore; to ward off.

connaissance, konn-ayss-ahngss, *f* knowledge; acquaintance; senses; learning; **sans –,** sahng–, unconscious.

connaisseur, konn-ess-er, *m* connoisseur.

connaître, konn-ay-tr, *v* to know; to be acquainted with; to be aware of; **se – (à** or **en),** to be a good judge (of); **chiffres connus,** shee-fr konn-E, plain figures.

connexe, konn-ecks, *a* connected (**à,** with).

connexion, konn-eck-se-ong, *f* connection.

connivence, konn-ne-vahngss, *f* connivance.

conquérant, kong-keh-rahng, *m* conqueror.

conquérant, e, kong-keh-rahng, *a* conquering.

conquérir, kong-keh-reer, *v* to conquer; to gain.

conquête, kong-kayt, *f* conquest.

consacrer, kong-säh-kreh, *v* to consecrate; to devote.

conscience, kong-se-ahngss, *f* conscience; conscientiousness; consciousness; awareness.

conscription, kongs-krip-se-ong, *f* conscription.

conscrit, kongs-kre, *m* conscript.

consécration, kong-seh-kräh-se-ong, *f* consecration; dedication.

consécuti-f, ve, * kong-seh-kE-teeff, *a* consecutive.

conseil, kong-say'e, *m* advice; council; counsel; adviser; **–d'administration,** –dähd-me-niss-träh-se-ong, board of directors; **–de guerre, –** der ghair, court-martial.

conseiller, kong-say'e-eh, *m* councillor; adviser.

conseiller, kong-say'e-eh, *v* to advise; to counsel.

consentement, kong-sahngt-mahng, *m* consent; assent.

consentir, kong-sahng-teer, *v* to consent; to agree.

conséquemment, kong-seh-käh-mahng, *adv* consequently; accordingly.

conséquence, kong-seh-kahngss, *f* consequence; inference; importance; **en –,** ahng –, consequently; **sans –,** sahng –, immaterial.

conséquent, e, kong-seh-kahng, *a* consequent; consistent; **par –,** pähr

–, in consequence.

conserva-teur, trice, kong-sair-väh-ter, *mf & a* guardian; keeper; commissioner; preservative; conservative.

conservation, kong-sair-väh-se-ong, *f* preservation; guardianship; registration (mortgages).

conservatoire, kong-sair-väh-to'ähr, *m* conservatory; museum; music school.

conserve, kong-sairv, *f* preserve; pickled food; tinned food.

conserver, kong-sair-veh, *v* to preserve; to conserve (food); to take care of; to retain.

considérable,* kong-se-deh-räh-bl, *a* considerable.

considération, kong-se-deh-räh-se-ong, *f* consideration; regard; esteem; **en – de,** ahng – der, out of regard for.

considérer, kong-se-deh-reh, *v* to consider; to examine; to value; to regard.

consignataire, kong-seen-yäh-tair, *m* consignee; trustee.

consignation, kong-seen-yäh-se-ong, *f* consignment; deposit.

consigne, kong-seen-yer, *f* orders; checkroom; confinement.

consigner, kong-seen-yeh, *v* to deposit; to record; to confine.

consistance, kong-siss-tahngss, *f* firmness; consistency; stability; credit.

consister, kong-siss-teh, *v* to consist (**à, dans,** of).

consolation, kong-soll-äh-se-ong, *f* consolation; comfort.

console, kong-sol, *f* bracket; console.

consoler, kong-soll-eh, *v* to console; to comfort.

consomma-teur, trice, kong-somm-äh-ter, *mf* consumer; customer.

consommation, kong-somm-äh-se-ong, *f* consummation; consumption; a drink (in café, etc).

consommé, kong-somm-eh, *m* stock; clear soup; consommé.

consommer, kong-somm-eh, *v* to consume; to complete.

consomption, kong-songp-se-ong, *f* consumption.

consonne, kong-sonn, *f* consonant.

conspirateur, kongs-pe-räh-ter, *m* conspirator.

conspiration, kongs-pe-räh-se-ong, *f* conspiracy; plot.

conspirer, kongs-pe-reh, *v* to conspire.

conspuer, kongs-pE-eh, *v* to hoot; to hiss.

constamment, kongs-täh-mahng, *adv* constantly.

constance, kongs-tangss, *f* constancy; persistence.

constant, e, kongs-tahng, *a* constant; steadfast.

constatation, kongs-täh-täh-se-ong, *f* establishment (of fact, etc.); certified statement.

constater, kongs-täh-teh, *v* to ascertain; to prove; to state; to report.

constellation, kongs-tell-läh-se-ong, *f* constellation.

consternation, kongs-tair-näh-se-ong, *f* consternation.

consterné, e, kongs-tair-neh, *a* dismayed.

consterner, kongs-tair-neh, *v* to dismay.

constipation, kongs-te-päh-se-ong, *f* constipation.

constipé, e, kongs-te-peh, *a* constipated.

constituant, e, kongs-te-tE-ahng, *a* constituent.

constituer, kongs-te-tE-eh, *v* to constitute; to appoint; to assign; **se –prisonnier,** ser – pre-zonne-eh, to give oneself up.

constitution, kongs-te-tE-se-ong, *f* constitution; composition.

constitutionnel, le, kongs-te-tE-se-onn-ell, *a* constitutional.

constricteur, kongs-trick-ter, *m* constrictor.

constructeur, kongs-trEEk-ter, *m* builder; **–mécanicien,** – meh-käh-ne-se-ang, engineer.

construction, kongs-trEEk-se-ong, *f* construction; building; structure.

construire, kongs-trE-eer, *v* to construct; to build; to construe.

consul, kong-sEEl, *m* consul.

consulaire, kong-sE-lair, *a* consular.

consulat, kong-sE-läh, *m* consulate.

consultant, kong-sEEl-tahng, *a* consulting; **médecin –,** mehd-sang –, consulting physician.

consultation, kong-sEEl-täh-se-ong, *f* consultation.

consulter, kong-sEEl-teh, *v* to consult; to refer to; to give consultations; **se–,** to consider.

consumer, kong-sE-meh, *v* to consume; to destroy; to squander.

contact, kong-tǎhckt, *m* contact; touch; connection.

contagieu-x, se, kong-tǎh-she-er, *a* contagious; infectious; catching.

contagion, kong-tǎh-she-ong, *f* contagion; infection.

contaminer, kong-tǎh-me-neh, *v* to contaminate.

conte, kongt, *m* tale; story; **–à dormir debout,** –ǎh-dor-meer der-boo, cock and bull story; **–de fées,** – der feh, fairy tale.

contemplation, kong-tahng-plǎh-se-ong, *f* contemplation; meditation.

contempler, kong-tahng pleh, *v* to contemplate; to meditate.

contemporain, e, kong-tahng-por-ang, *a* contemporary.

contenance, kongt-nahngss, *f* countenance; look; capacity.

contenir, kongt-neer, *v* to hold; to contain; to restrain.

content, kong-tahng, *a* contented; satisfied; pleased.

contentement, kong-tahngt-mahng, *m* satisfaction.

contenter, kong-tahng-teh, *v* to satisfy; to please.

contentieux, kong-tahng-se-er, *m* disputed claims; legal business. *a* in dispute; litigious.

contenu, kongt-nE, *m* contents; subject.

conter, kong-teh, *v* to tell; to relate; **en – (à),** to tell a tall story.

contestable, kong-tess-tǎh-bl, *a* debatable; questionable.

contestation, kong-tess-tǎh-se-ong, *f* contest; dispute.

contester, kong-tess-teh, *v* to contest; to dispute.

conteu-r, se, kong-ter, *mf* storyteller.

contexte, kong-text, *m* context.

contexture, kong-tex-tEEr, *f* contexture; structure.

contigu, ë, kong-te-ghE, *a* adjoining; contiguous.

contiguité, kong-te-gwe-teh, f contiguity.

continent, kong-te-nahng, m continent.

continental, e, kong-te-nahng-tăhl, a continental.

contingent, kong-tang-shahng, m share; proportion; quota.

contingent, e, kong-tang-shahng, a contingent.

continu,* e, kong-te-nE, a continued; continuous.

continuel, le, * kong-te-nE-ell, a continual.

continuer, kong-te-nE-eh, v to continue; to go on.

continuité, kong-te-nwe-teh, f continuity.

contondant, e, kong-tong-dahng, a blunt.

contorsion, kong-tor-se-ong, f contortion.

contour, kong-toohr, m outline; circuit.

contourner, kong-toohr-neh, v to outline; to distort; to twist; to go round.

contractant, e, kong-trăhck-tahng, mf & a contracting party; contracting.

contracter, kong-trăck-teh, v to contract; to acquire; to catch; **se –,** to shrink; to be

contracted.

contradictoire, kong-trăh-dick-to'ăhr, a contradictory.

contraindre, kong-trang-dr, v to constrain; to compel; **–en justice,** –ahng shEEs-teess, to sue.

contraint, e, kong-trang, a constrained; unnatural.

contrainte, kong-trangt, f compulsion; restraint.

contraire, kong-trair, a & n contrary; reverse; **au –,** oh –, on the contrary; on the other hand.

contrariant, e, kong-trăh-re-ahng, a vexing; provoking.

contrariété, kong-trăh-re-eh-teh, f contrariness; annoyance.

contraste, kong-trăhst, m contrast; opposition.

contrat, kong-trăh, m contract; deed; agreement; indenture; covenant.

contravention, kong-trăh-vahng-se-ong, f offense; breach of regulations; fine.

contre, kong-tr, prep against; versus; near. adv **par –,** păhr –, on the other hand. m opposite side.

contre-amiral, kong-trăh-me-răhl, m rear admiral.

contrebalancer, kong-trer-băh-lahng-seh, v to counterbalance.

contrebande, kong-trer-bahngd, f smuggling; smuggled goods.

contrebandier, kong-trer-bahng-de-eh, m smuggler.

contrebas (en), ahng kong-trer-bah, adv downwards; at lower level.

contrebasse, kong-trer-bahss, f double bass.

contrecarrer, kong-trer-kăh-reh, v to thwart.

contrecœur (à), ăh kong-trer-ker, adv reluctantly.

contrecoup, kong-trer-koo, m rebound; consequence.

contredire, kong-trer-deer, v to contradict.

contredit (sans), sahng kong-trer-de, adv unquestionably.

contrée, kong-treh, f country; region; district; land.

contre-épreuve, kongtr-eh-prerv, f countercheck.

contrefaçon, kong-trer-făh-song, f forgery; counterfeit; piracy;

infringement.

contrefacteur, kong-trer-făhck-**ter,** *m* forger; counterfeiter.

contrefaire, kong-trer-fair, *v* to counterfeit; to imitate; to mimic; to disguise; to infringe.

contrefait, kong-trer-fay, *pp* & *a* counterfeited; deformed.

contrefort, kong-trer-for, *m* buttress; spur; stiffener.

contre-jour (à), ăh kong-trer-shoohr, *adv* in a false light.

contremaître, kong-trer-may-tr, *m* foreman.

contremander, kong-trer-mahng-deh, *v* to countermand.

contremarque, kong-trer-măhrk, *f* check.

contrepartie, kong-trer-păhr-tee, *f* counterpart; opposite view.

contre-pied, kong-trer-pe-eh, *m* contrary; reverse.

contrepoids, kong-trer-po'ăh, *m* counterbalance.

contrepoil (à), ăh kong-trer-po'ăhl, *adv* against the grain; the wrong way.

contrepoint, kong-trer-po'ang, *m* counterpoint.

contrepoison, kong-trer-po'ăh-zong, *m* antidote.

contresens, kong-trer-sahngss, *m* misinterpretation; wrong way.

contresigner, kong-trer-seen-yeh, *v* to countersign.

contretemps, kong-trer-tahng, *m* mishap; disappointment; out of time; à –, ăh –, inopportunely.

contre-torpilleur, kong-trer-tor-pee-yer, *m* destroyer.

contrevenant, e, kong-trerv-nahng, *m* offender.

contrevenir, kong-trerv-neer, *v* to infringe; to transgress.

contrevent, kong-trer-vahng, *m* shutter.

contre-vérité, kong-trer-veh-re-teh, *f* falsehood; irony; satire.

contribuable, kong-tre-bE-ăh-bl, *m* taxpayer; *a* tax-paying.

contribuer, kong-tre-bE-eh, *v* to contribute; to be conducive.

contribution, kong-tre-bE-ong, *f* contribution; tax; rate; part.

contrister, kong-triss-teh, *v* to grieve; to sadden.

contrit, e, kong-tre, *a* contrite; penitent.

contrôle, kong-trohl, *m* register; list; checking; censure; control.

contrôler, kong-troh-leh, *v* to inspect; to control; to verify; to monitor; **se** –, to control oneself.

contrôleu-r, se, kong-troh-ler, *mf* inspector; ticket collector.

controuvé, e, kong-troo-veh, *pp* & *a* invented; false.

controverse, kong-trov-airs, *f* controversy.

contumace, kong-tE-măhss, *f* contumacy; default. *m* defaulter. *a* rebellious.

contusion, kong-tE-ze-ong, *f* bruise.

convaincant, e, kong-vang-kahng, *a* convincing.

convaincre, kong-vang-kr, *v* to convince; to convict.

convaincu, e, kong-vang-kE, *pp* & *a* convinced; convicted.

convalescence, kong-văh-layss-ahngss, *f* convalescence.

convenable, * kongv-năh-bl, *a* proper; fit; suitable.

convenance, kongv-nahngss, f fitness; convenience; pl good manners; propriety.

convenir, kongv-neer, v to agree (**avec,** with; **de,** on); to acknowledge; to suit; to be agreeable to.

convention, kong-vahng-se-ong, f convention; agreement; condition.

conventionnel, le, * kong-vahng-se-onn-ell, a conventional.

convenu, kongv-nE, pp agreed.

converger, kong-vair-sheh, v to converge.

conversation, kong-vair-săh-se-ong, f conversation.

converser, kong-vair-seh, v to converse; to talk.

conversion, kong-vair-se-ong, f conversion.

converti, e, kong-vair-te, mf & a convert; converted.

convertir, kong-vair-teer, v to convert; to turn; **se –,** to become converted (**à,** to).

convexe, kong-vex, a convex.

conviction, kong-vick-se-ong, f conviction; convincing proof.

convier, kong-ve-eh, v to invite; to prompt.

convive, kong-veev, m guest (at meal).

convocation, kong-vock-ăh-se-ong, f convocation; requisition; summons.

convoi, kong-vo'ăh, m funeral procession; train; convoy.

convoiter, kong-vo'ăh-teh, v to covet.

convoitise, kong-vo'ăh-teez, f covetousness.

convoquer, kong-vock-eh, v to convoke; to call; to summon.

convulsion, kong-vEEl-se-ong, f convulsion.

convulsi-f, ve, * kong-vEEl-seef, a convulsive.

coopéra-teur, trice, ko-op-eh-răh-ter, mf cooperator.

coopérer, ko-op-eh-reh, v to cooperate.

coordonner, ko-or-donn-eh, v to arrange; to coordinate.

copain, kop-ang, m chum.

copeau, kop-oh, m chip; shaving.

copie, kopee, f copy; manuscript; reproduction; imitation.

copier, kop-e-eh, v to copy; to imitate; to mimic.

copieu-x, se, * kop-e-er, a copious; plentiful.

copropriétaire, kop-rop-re-eh-tair, m joint-owner; co-owner.

coq, kock, m cock; cockerel; weathercock; **–à l'âne,** – ăh lahn, abrupt change of subject.

coque, kock, f shell; cockle; hull.

coquelicot, kock-le-ko, m poppy.

coqueluche, kock-lEEsh, f whooping cough; favorite (person); idol.

coquerico, kock-re-ko, m cock-a-doodle-doo.

coquet, te, * kock-ay, a flirtatious; elegant.

coquetier, kock-te-eh, m eggcup; egg merchant.

coquetterie, kock-ett-ree, f coquetry; flirtation; stylishness (in dress).

coquillage, kock-ee-yăhsh, m empty shell; shellfish.

coquille, kock-ee-ye, f shell.

coquin, e, kock-ang, a rogue; rascal; (fam) naughty.

coquinerie, kock-een-ree, f mischievousness; roguishness.

cor, kor, m horn; corn (on the foot).

corail, kor-ah'e, *m* coral.

coran, kor-ahng, *m* Koran.

corbeau, kor-boh, *m* raven; crow.

corbeille, kor-bay'e, *f* basket; wedding presents; flowerbed; – **à papier**, – ăh pah-pe-eh, wastepaper basket.

corbillard, kor-bee-yăhr, *m* hearse.

cordage, kor-dăhsh, *m* rope.

corde, kord, *f* string; cord; rope; **la –sensible**, lăh – sahng-see-bl, the tender spot; **tenir la –**, ter-neer lăh –, to have the best chance.

cordeau, kor-doh, *m* line; cord.

corder, kor-deh, *v* to string; to twist.

cordial, e, * kor-de-ăhl, *a* hearty.

cordon, kor-dong, *m* twist; string; cord; **–bleu**, –bler, first-rate cook.

cordonnerie, kor-donn-ree, *f* shoemaking; shoemaker's.

cordonnet, kor-donn-ay, *m* twist; small string; braid.

cordonnier, kor-donn-e-eh, *m* cobbler.

coriace, kor-e-ăhss, *a* tough (of meat, etc);

(*fam*) hard (person).

cormoran, kor-mor-ahng, *m* cormorant.

cornaline, kor-năh-leen, *f* cornelian stone.

corne, korn, *f* horn; feeler (of snail); dog-ear (book page).

corneille, kor-nay'e, *f* crow.

cornemuse, kor-ner-mEEz, *f* bagpipe.

cornet, kor-nay, *m* horn; cornet; ice cream cone.

corniche, kor-neesh, *f* cornice; ledge (of rock).

cornichon, kor-ne-shong, *m* gherkin; pickle; ninny (person).

cornu, e, kor-nE, *a* horned.

corollaire, kor-oll-lair, *m* corollary.

corps, kor, *m* body; corps; corpse; substance.

corpulent, e, kor-pE-lahng, *a* stout; corpulent.

correct, e, * kor-reckt, *a* correct; proper.

correcteur, kor-reck-ter, *m* proofreader.

correction, kor-reck-se-ong, *f* correction; accuracy; correctness; punishment.

corrélati-f, ve,* kor-reh-lăh-teeff, *a* correlative.

correspondance, kor-ress-pong-dahngss, *f* correspondence; connection (between trains); **petite –**, per-teet –, personal column.

correspondant, e, kor-ress-pong-dahng, *mf* & *a* correspondent; pen pal; guardian; corresponding.

corridor, kor-e-dor, *m* corridor; passage; hallway.

corrigé, kor-e-sheh, *m* corrected version.

corriger, kor-e-sheh, *v* to correct; to grade; to chastise.

corroboration, kor-rob-or-ăh-se-ong, *f* strengthening.

corroder, kor-rod-eh, *v* to corrode.

corrompre, kor-ong-pr, *v* to corrupt; to bribe.

corrompu, e, kor-ong-pE, *pp* & *a* corrupted; bribed; putrid.

corrup-teur, trice, kor-EEp-ter, *mf* & *a* corrupter; corrupting; briber.

corruptible, kor-EEp-tee-bl *a* corruptible.

corruption, kor-EEp-se-ong, *f* corruption.

corsage, kor-săsh, *m* bodice.

corsé, e, kor-seh, *a* full-bodied.

corser, kor-seh, *v* to give volume to; *(fig)* to thicken.

corset, kor-say, *m* corset.

cortège, kor-taysh, *m* procession; retinue.

corvée, kor-veh, *f* chore; drudgery; unpleasant job.

coryphée, kor-e-feh, *m* leader; chief.

cosaque, koz-ăhck, *m* cossack; brutal man.

cosmétique, koss-meh-teeck, *m* & *a* cosmetic.

cosmique, koss-meeck, *a* cosmic.

cosmopolite, koss-mop-oll-eet, *mf* & *a* cosmopolitan.

cosse, koss, *f* shell; husk; pod.

cossu, e, koss-E, *a* opulent; well-off.

costume, koss-tEEm, *m* costume; suit (man's); **grand –**, grahng –, full dress.

costumier, koss-tE-me-eh, *m* costumier; wardrobe master or mistress.

cote, kot, *f* mark; share; quota.

côte, koht, *f* rib; hill; coast; shore; **–à–, –ăh–,** side by side.

côté, koht-eh, *m* side; way; part; direction; **à –,** ăh –, near; **de ce –,** der ser –, this way; **mauvais –,** moh-vay –, wrong side.

coteau, kot-oh, *m* hillside; slope.

côtelette, koht-lett, *f* cutlet; chop.

coter, kot-eh, *v* to assess; to quote; to number.

coterie, kot-ree, *f* set; circle; clique.

côtier, koh-te-eh, *m* coasting vessel. *a* coasting; coastal.

cotillon, kot-ee-yong, *m* petticoat; cotillon.

cotisation, kot-e-zăh-se-ong, *f* contribution; subscription.

cotiser, kot-e-zeh, *v* to rate; **se–,** to club together; to open a subscription.

coton, kot-ong, *m* cotton; down; cotton thread.

cotonnade, kot-onn-ăhd, *f* cotton fabric; cotton goods.

côtoyer, koh-to'ăh-yeh, *v* to skirt; to border on.

cottage, kot-ăhsh, *m* cottage.

cou, koo, *m* neck.

couard, koo-ăhr, *mf* & *a* coward; cowardly.

couchant, koo-shahng, *m* sunset; west; decline. *a* setting.

couche, koosh, *f* couch; bed; layer; confinement; diaper.

couché, koo-sheh, *pp* & *a* lying down; in bed.

couche-culotte, koosh-kE-lot, *f* disposable diaper.

coucher, koo-sheh, *m* bedtime; sunset.

coucher, koo-sheh, *v* to lay down; to put to bed; **se–** to go to bed.

couchette, koo-shett, *f* crib; berth; sleeper (on trains, etc.).

couci-couça, koo-se-koo-sah, *adv (fam)* so-so.

coucou, koo-koo, *m* cuckoo; cuckoo clock; cowslip; peek-a-boo!.

coude, kood, *m* elbow; bend; angle.

coudée, kood-eh, *f* **–s franches, –** frahngsh, elbow room.

cou-de-pied, kood-pe-eh, *m* instep.

coudoyer, koo-do'ăh-yeh, *v* to elbow; to jostle.

coudre, koo-dr, *v* to sew; to stitch; to tack.

couenne, koo-ăhn, *f* rind (of bacon).

couette, ko'ett, *f* comforter.

coulage, koo-lăhsh, *m*
leakage; pouring;
casting.

coulant, e, koo-lahng, *a*
flowing; running; fluent;
accommodating
(person).

coulée, koo-leh, *f* flow;
casting.

couler, koo-leh, *v* to flow;
to glide; to run (of
liquid); to cast; to sink.

couleur, koo-ler, *f* color;
paint; suit (cards).

couleuvre, koo-ler-vr, *f*
grass snake; (*fig*) bitter
pill.

coulis, koo-le, *m* jelly;
meat or vegetable broth;
puree. *a* vent –, vahng –,
draft.

coulisse, koo-leess, *f*
groove; slide; wing of
theater; unofficial stock
market.

couloir, koo-lo'ăhr, *m*
passage; corridor; lobby.

coup, koo, *m* blow; stroke;
hit; kick; knock; rap;
thrust; cast; cut; stab;
lash; wound; shot;
report; toll; beat; clap;
peal; throw; haul; event;
deed; outburst; trick.

coupable, koo-păh-bl, *mf*
& *a* culprit; guilty.

coupage, koo-păhsh, *m*
mixing; diluting;

cutting.

coupant, e, koo-pahng, *a*
cutting; sharp.

coup de soleil, koo-der-
soll-a'ye *m* sunburn.

coup de téléphone, koo-
oder-teh-leh-fonn *m*
telephone call.

coupe, koop, *f* cut; cup;
section.

couper, koo-peh, *v* to cut;
to mix; to dilute; to cut
off.

couperet, koop-ray, *m*
chopper; knife (for
meat).

couperose, koop-rohz, *f*
copperas; blotchiness (of
complexion).

coupeur, koo-per, *m*
cutter.

couplage, koo-plăhsh, *m*
coupling; connecting.

couple, koo-pl, *m* pair;
couple; brace.

coupler, koo-pleh, *v* to
couple.

couplet, koo-play, *m* verse;
stanza.

coupole, koo-pol, *f*
cupola.

coupon, koo-pong, *m*
remnant; short length;
coupon; ticket.

coupure, koo-pEEr, *f* cut;
suppression; bill; note;
cutting.

cour, koohr, *f* yard; court;

courtship.

courage, koo-răhsh, *m*
courage; guts.

courageu-x, se,* koo-
răhsh-er, *a* courageous;
spirited; brave.

couramment, koo-răh-
mahng, *adv* fluently;
generally.

courant, koo-rahng, *m*
current; stream; course;
au–de, oh – der,
conversant with; **mettre
au–** met-tr-oh–, to
inform; *a* current;
running; ordinary;
present.

courbature, koohr-băh-
tEEr, *f* stiffness in the
joints; ache.

courbaturé, koohr-băh-tE-
reh, *a* stiff; aching.

courbe, koohrb, *f* curve;
bend; curb.

courbé, koohr-beh, *pp* &
a curved; bent; crooked.

courbette, koohr-bett, *f*
servile bow; cringing.

courbure, koohr-bEEr, *f*
curvature; bend.

coureur, koo-rer, *m*
runner; racer; (*fam*)
womanizer; *a* running.

courge, koohrsh, *f* squash.

courgette, koohrsh-ett, *f*
zucchini.

courir, koo-reer, *v* to run;
to hunt; to flow.

courlis, koohr-le, *m*
curlew.

couronne, koo-ronn, *f*
crown; coronet; wreath.

couronné, koo-ronn-eh,
pp & *a* crowned;
rewarded with a prize.

couronnement, koo-ronn-
mahng, *m* coronation;
crowning.

courrier, koo-re-eh, *m*
courier; mail; post;
messenger.

courrier électronique,
koo-re-eh-eh-leck-tro-
neeck, *m* e-mail.

courroie, koo-ro'ăh, *f*
strap; belt.

courroucer, koo-roo-seh,
v to irritate; to incense.

courroux, koo-roo, *m*
wrath.

cours, koohrs, *m* course;
flow; vent; currency;
market price; course (of
lectures, etc.); lesson.

course, koohrs, *f* running;
run; race; drive; errand;
pl shopping.

coursier, koohr-se-eh, *m*
steed.

court, e, koohr, *a* short;
limited; *m* court.

courtage, koohr-tăhsh, *m*
brokerage.

courtaud, e, koohr-toh, *a*
thickset.

court-circuit, koohr-seer-

kwe, *m* short circuit.

court de tennis, koor-der-
teh-neess *m* **tennis
court.**

courtepointe, koohr-ter-
po'angt, *f* quilt.

courtier, koohr-te-eh, *m*
broker.

courtisan, koohr-te-zahng,
m courtier.

courtiser, koohr-te-zeh, *v*
to court.

courtois, e, * koohr-to'ăh,
a courteous.

courtoisie, koohr-to'ăh-
zee, *f* courtesy.

couru, e, koo-rE, *pp* & *a*
run; sought after;
popular; (*fam*) dead
certainty.

cousin, koo-zang, *m* gnat.

cousin, e, koo-zang, *mf*
cousin.

coussin, kooss-ang, *m*
cushion; bolster.

coussinet, kooss-e-nay, *m*
pad; small cushion;
bearing.

cousu, e, koo-zE, *pp*
sewed; sewn.

coût, koo, *m* cost;
expense; charge.

coûtant, koo-tahng, *a* used
only in à **prix** –, ăh pre
–, at cost.

couteau, koh-toh, *m*
knife.

coutelas, koot-lah, *m*

cutlass; knife (kitchen).

coutellerie, koo-tell-ree, *f*
cutlery (industry).

coûter, koo-teh, *v* to cost.

coûteu-x, se, * koo-ter, *a*
expensive.

coutil, koo-te, *m* ticking
twill.

coutume, koo-tEEm, *f*
custom; practice.

coutumier, koo-tEE-me-
eh, *a* customary; usual.

couture, koo-tEE, *f* seam;
needlework; sewing.

couturi-er, ère, koo-tE-re-
eh, *mf* dressmaker.

couvée, koo-veh, *f* covey;
brood.

couvent, koo-vahng, *m*
convent.

couver, koo-veh, *v* to
brood; to sit on; to
hatch; to smolder; **–des
yeux,** – day z'e-er, to
look fondly on.

couvercle, koo-vair-kl, *m*
cover; lid; cap.

couvert, koo-vair, *m* place
setting; cover charge (in
restaurant); cover;
shelter; **mettre le** –,
met-tr ler –, to set the
table.

couvert, koo-vair, *a*
covered; overcast
(weather); clad.

couverture, koo-vair-tEEr,
f cover; blanket; rug;

security.

couvre-chef, koo-vrer-sheff, *m* hat; (*fam*) cap .

couvre-feu, koo-vrer-fer, *m* curfew.

couvre-lit, koo-vrer-le, *m* bedspread.

couvreur, koo-vrer, *m* roofer.

couvrir, koo-vreer, *v* to cover (**de,** with); to conceal; to screen; **se –,** to put one's hat on; to clothe oneself.

crabe, krahb, *m* crab.

crachat, krăh-shăh, *m* saliva; spit.

craché, krăh-sheh, *pp* & *a*; **tout –,** too –, the spitting image of.

cracher, krăh-sheh, *v* to spit; (*fam*) to cough up.

crachoir, krăh-sho'ăhr, *m* spittoon.

craie, kray, *f* chalk.

craindre, krang-dr, *v* to fear; to dread.

crainte, krangt, *f* fear; dread.

**crainti-f, ve, ** * **krang-teeff, *a* timorous; fearful.

cramoisi, e, krăh-mo'ăh-ze, *a* crimson.

crampe, krahngp, *f* cramp.

crampon, krahng-pong, *m* clamp; stud; crampon; (*fam*) bore.

cramponner, krahng-ponn-eh, *v* to cramp; **se – à,** to cling to.

cran, krahng, *m* notch; cog; peg; (*fam*) pluck.

crâne, krahn, *m* skull; *a* plucky; swaggering.

crânerie, krahn-ree, *f* pluck; swagger.

crapaud, krăh-poh, *m* toad.

crapule, krăh-pEEl, *f* debauchery; (*fam*) crook.

crapuleu-x, se, krăh-pE-ler, *a* villainous; dishonest.

craque, krăhck, *f* (*fam*) fib.

craquer; krăhck-leh, *v* to crack.

craquement, krăhck-mahng, *m* cracking; crackling.

craquer, krăh-keh, to crack; to crackle.

crasse, krăhss, *f* dirt; filth; stinginess. *a* gross; crass.

crasseu-x, se, krăhss-er, *a* filthy; nasty; sordid.

cratère, krăh-tair, *m* crater.

cravache, krăh-văhsh, *f* riding crop.

cravate, krăh-văht, *f* necktie.

crayeu-x, se, kray-e-er, *a* chalky.

crayon, kray-yong, *m* pencil.

crayonner, kray-yonn-eh, *v* to sketch; to draw.

créance, kre-ahngss, *f* credit; trust; right to a debt; credence.

créancier, kreh-ahngss-e-eh, *m* creditor.

créateur, kreh-ăh-ter, *m* creator; maker; *a* creative.

création, kreh-ăh-se-ong, *f* creation; production.

créature, kreh-ăh-tEEr, *f* creature.

crécelle, kreh-sell, *f* rattle.

crèche, kraysh, *f* crib; manger; nursery.

crédence, kreh-dahngss, *f* sideboard.

crédit, kreh-de, *m* credit; trust; loan; influence; esteem.

créditer, kreh-de-teh, *v* to credit (**de,** with).

credo, kreh-do, *m* creed; belief.

crédule, kreh-dEEl, *a* credulous.

crédulité, kreh-dE-le-teh, *f* credulity.

créer, kreh-eh, *v* to create; to invent; to establish.

crémaillère, kreh-mah'e-air, *f* rack; (*fam*) **pendre la –,** pahng-dr lăh –, to have a housewarming.

crémation, kreh-măh-se-ong, *f* cremation.

crème, kraym, *f* cream; custard; best.

crèmerie, krehm-ree, *f* creamery; dairy.

crémi-er, ère, kreh-me-eh, *mf* dairyman; dairywoman.

créneau, kreh-noh, *m* battlement.

crénelé, e, krehn-leh, *a* notched; crenellated.

créneler, krehn-leh, *v* to cog; to mill.

crénelure, krehn-lEEr, *f* indentation.

crêpe, krayp, *m* crepe; mourning veil. *f* pancake.

crêper, kray-peh, *v* to frizz; to crisp.

crépi, kreh-pe, *m* roughcast.

crépir, kreh-peer, *v* to roughcast; to crimp.

crépine, kreh-peen, *f* fringe (on upholstery).

crépiter, kreh-pe-teh, *v* to crackle.

crépu, e, kreh-pE, *a* woolly; fuzzy.

crépuscule, kreh-pEEss-kEEl, *m* twilight; decline.

cresson, krehss-ong, *m* cress; watercress.

crétacé, e, kreh-tähss-eh, *a* cretaceous.

crête, krayt, *f* crest; top; ridge; comb (of a cock).

crétin, kreh-tang, *m* idiot.

crétinisme, kreh-te-nissm, *m* idiocy.

cretonne, krer-tonn, *f* cretonne.

creuser, krer-zeh, *v* to dig; to hollow; to scoop out; to fathom.

creuset, krer-zay, *m* crucible; (*fam*) test.

creux, krer, *m* hollow cavity; bass voice.

creu-x, se, krer, *a* hollow; empty; unsubstantial; off-peak.

crevaison, krer-veh-zong, *f* puncture; bursting.

crevasse, krer-vähss, *f* crevice; chink; crack.

crève-cœur, krayv-ker, *m* heartbreaking thing.

crever, krer-veh, *v* to burst; to pierce; to puncture; **se –,** to burst.

crevette, krer-vett, *f* shrimp; prawn.

cri, kre, *m* cry; shout; shriek; scream; clamor; **le dernier –,** ler dair-ne-eh –, the latest fashion.

criailler, kree-ah'e-yeh, *v* to bawl.

criant, e, kree-ahng, *a* crying; glaring.

criard, e, kree-ähr, *a* clamorous; shrill; loud; gaudy.

crible, kree-bl, *m* sieve; riddle.

cribler, kree-bleh, *v* to sift; to riddle; to pierce with holes.

cric, kre, *m* jack (car).

cricket, kre-kay, *m* cricket (game).

cri-cri, kre-kre, *m* cricket (insect).

criée, kree-eh, *f* auction.

crier, kree-eh, *v* to cry; to shout; to shriek; to proclaim.

crieur, kree-er, *m* crier; auctioneer; town-crier.

crime, kreem, *m* crime.

criminalité, kre-me-näh-le-teh, *f* criminality.

criminel, le, kre-me-nell, *mf* & *a** criminal; culprit.

crin, krang, *m* horsehair; **les –s,** lay –, mane and tail.

crinière, kre-ne-air, *f* mane; (*fam*) thick head of hair.

crique, kreeck, *f* creek; cove.

criquet, kre-kay, *m* locust; (*fam*) cricket.

crise, kreez, *f* crisis; fit; attack.

crisper, kriss-peh, *v* to shrivel; to clench; to irritate; **se –,** to contract.

crisser, kriss-eh, *v* to grate; to grind.

cristal, kriss-tăhl, *m* crystal; cut-glass.

cristallin, kriss-tăh-lang, *a* crystalline.

cristalliser, kriss-tăh-le-zeh, *v* to crystallize.

critérium, kre-teh-re-omm, *m* criterion.

critique, kre-teeck, *m* critic; *f* criticism; censure; *a** critical.

critiquer, kre-te-keh, *v* to criticize.

croasser, kro'ăhss-eh, *v* to croak; to caw.

croc, kro, *m* hook; canine tooth; tusk; fang.

croche, krosh, *f* quaver; eigth (*mus*).

crochet, krosh-ay, *m* hook; picklock; clasp; bend; crochet.

crocheter, krosh-teh, *v* to pick (a lock).

crochu, e, krosh-E, *a* hooked; crooked.

crocodile, krock-odd-eell, *m* crocodile.

crocus, krock-EEss, *m* crocus; saffron.

croire, kro'ăhr, *v* to believe; to think; to trust to.

croisade, kro'ăh-zăhd, *f* crusade.

croisé, kro'ăh-zeh, *m* crusader; twill; *pp* & *a* crossed; double-breasted.

croisée, kro'ăh-zeh, *f* crossing; casement window; transept.

croisement, kro'ăhz-mahng, *m* crossing.

croiser, kro'ăh-zeh, *v* to cross; to interbreed (animal); to cruise.

croiseur, kro'ăh-zer, *m* cruiser.

croisière, kro'ăh-ze-air, *f* cruise.

croissance, krwăhss-ahngss, *f* growth; increase.

croissant, krwăhss-ahng, *m* crescent; French crescent roll.

croissant, e, krwăhss-ahng, *a* growing.

croître, kro'ah-tr, *v* to grow; to increase; to lengthen.

croix, kro'ăh, *f* cross.

croquant, krock-ahng, *m* (*fam*) peasant; poor wretch; *a* crisp.

croque-mitaine, krock-me-tain, *m* (*fam*) bogeyman.

croque-mort, krock-mor, *m* pallbearer.

croquer, krock-eh, *v* to crunch; to munch; to sketch.

croquette, krock-ett, *f* croquette.

croquis, krock-e, *m* sketch; outline.

crosse, kross, *f* crosier; butt-end; hockey sticks.

crotte, krot, *f* dung; dropping of animal dirt.

crotté, e, krot-eh, *a* dirty; muddy.

crotter, krot-eh, *v* to dirty.

crottin, krot-ang, *m* horse or sheep dung.

croulant, e, kroo-lahng, *a* sinking; tottering; tumbledown.

crouler, kroo-leh, *v* to fall; to sink; to crumble.

croup, kroop, *m* croup.

croupe, kroop, *f* rump; buttocks.

croupier, kroo-pe-eh, *m* croupier.

croupière, kroo-pe-air, *f* crupper.

croupion, kroo-pe-ong, *m* rump; butt; (*fam*) pope's nose.

croupir, kroo-peer, *v* to stagnate; to wallow.

croupissant, e, kroo-piss-ahng, *a* stagnating; putrescent.

croustillant, e, krooss-tee-yahng, *a* crisp.

croûte, kroot, *f* crust; scab; (*fam*) daub; old fogy; **casser une –,**

kăhss-ehEEn –, to take a snack.

croûton, kroo-tong, *m* crust end; crouton.

croyable, kro'ăh-yăh-bl, *a* credible; likely.

croyance, kro'ăh-yahngss, *f* belief; creed; faith.

croyant, e, kro'ăh-yahng, *mf* believer; *pl* the faithful.

cru, krE, *m* vineyards; vintage.

cru, e, krE, *a* raw; crude; coarse.

cruauté, krE-oh-teh, *f* cruelty.

cruche, krEEsh, *f* pitcher; blockhead.

cruchon, krE-shong, *m* jug; stone bottle.

crucial, e, krE-se-ăhl, *a* cross-shaped; crucial; fundamental.

crucifier, krE-se-fe-eh, *v* to crucify.

crucifix, krE-se-fe, *m* crucifix.

crudité, krE-de-teh, *f* crudity; crudeness; rawness; coarseness.

crue, krEE, *f* rise; swelling; flood.

cruel, le,* krE-ell, *a* cruel; sore; annoying.

crûment, krEE-mahng, *adv* bluntly.

crustacé, krEEss-tăhss-eh,

m & a crustacean; crustaceous.

crypte, kree-pt, *f* crypt.

cubage, kE-băhsh, *m* cubic measurement; cubage.

cube, kEEb, *m* cube; toy building block; *a* cubic.

cueillette, ker'e-yett, *f* picking; gathering; mixed cargo.

cueillir, ker'e-yeer, *v* to gather; to pick; to pluck.

cuiller or **cuillère,** kwee-yair, *f* spoon.

cuillerée, kwee-yer-reh, *f* spoonful.

cuir, kweer, *m* skin; hide; leather.

cuirasse, kwee-răhss, *f* breast plate; armor-plating.

cuirassé, kwee-răhss-eh, *m* battleship.

cuirassé, e, kwee-răhss-eh, *a* armored.

cuirassier, kwee-răhss-e-eh, *m* cuirassier.

cuire, kweer, *v* to cook; to bake; to roast; to stew; to smart.

cuisant, e, kwee-zahng, *a* sharp; acute; burning.

cuisine, kwee-zeen, *f* kitchen; cooking; cookery.

cuisiner, kwee-ze-neh, *v* to cook; (*fam*) to concoct (scheme, etc).

cuisini-er, ère, kwee-ze-ne-eh, *mf* cook; *f* stove.

cuisse, kweess, *f* thigh; leg of bird.

cuisson, kweess-ong, *f* cooking; baking; firing (of bricks, etc); smarting.

cuissot, kweess-o, *m* haunch.

cuit, e, kwee, *pp & a* cooked; done; drunk; done for.

cuivre, kwee-vr, *m* copper; –jaune, –shohn, brass.

cuivreu-x, se, kwee-vrer, *a* coppery.

cul, kE, *m* (vulgar, except in compounds), bottom; back; rump.

culbute, kEEl-bEEt, *f* somersault; fall; tumble; failure; ruin.

culbuter, kEEl-bE-teh, *v* to topple over; to tumble down.

culinaire, kE-le-nair, *a* culinary.

culminant, e, kEEl-me-nahng, *a* highest; prominent.

culot, kE-lo, *m* bottom; plug; (*fam*) cheek; [to have a] lot of nerve.

culotte, kE-lot, *f* buttock (of beef); underpants; pants; breeches.

culotter, kE-lot-eh, *v* to

breech.

culpabilité, kEEl-păh-be-le-teh, *f* guilt.

culte, kEElt, *m* worship; creed; cult; veneration.

cultivateur, kEEl-te-văh-ter, *m* grower; agriculturist; farmer.

cultiver, kEEl-te-veh, *v* to cultivate.

culture, kEEl-tEEr, *f* cultivation; culture.

cumuler, kE-mE-leh, *v* to hold several offices; to cumulate.

cupide, kE-peed, *a* covetous; greedy.

curage, kE-răsh, *m* picking (of teeth); clearing; cleaning.

curatelle, kE-răh-tell, *f* guardianship; trusteeship.

cura-teur, trice, kE-răh-ter, *mf* guardian; curator; trustee.

cure, kEEr, *f* cure; treatment; living; vicarage; parish.

curé, kE-reh, *m* priest.

cure-dent, kEEr-dahng, *m* toothpick.

curer, kE-reh, *v* to pick (teeth, etc) to clean out.

curieux, kE-re-er, *m* inquisitive person; bystander; curious thing

or fact.

curieu-x, se,* kE-re-er, *a* curious; inquisitive; singular.

curiosité, kE-re-ohz-e-teh, *f* curiosity; inquisitiveness; curio.

cutané, e, kE-tăh-neh, *a* cutaneous.

cuve, kEEv, *f* vat; tub; copper.

cuvée, kE-veh, *f* vatful; **bonne –,** bon –, quality.

cuver, kE-veh, *v* to ferment; to settle; – **son vin,** – song vang, to sleep oneself sober.

cuvette, kE-vett, *f* basin; washing-up bowl.

cuvier, kE-ve-eh, *m* wash-tub.

cyanure, se-ăh-nEEr, *m* cyanide.

cycle, see-kl, *m* cycle.

cycliste, see-kleest, *mf* cyclist.

cygne, seen-yer, *m* swan.

cylindre, se-lang-dr, *m* cylinder; roller.

cymbale, sang-băhl, *f* cymbal.

cynique, se-neeck, *m* cynic; *a** cynical.

cynisme, se-nissm, *m* cynicism.

cyprès, se-pray, *m* cypress.

cytise, se-teez, *m* laburnum.

dactylographe, dăhck-te-log-răhf, *mf* & *a* typist.

dactylographie, dăhck-te-log-răh-fee, *f* typing.

dada, dăh-dăh, *m* hobbyhorse; hobby; pet subject.

dadais, dăh-day, *m* ninny; simpleton.

dague, dăhg, *f* dagger.

daigner, dayn-yeh, *v* to deign.

daim, dang, *m* deer; buck; suede.

dais, day, *m* canopy.

dalle, dăhl, *f* flagstone; slab.

daltonisme, dăhl-tonn-issm, *m* color-blindness.

damas, dăh-mah, *m* damask.

dame, dăhm, *f* lady; queen (cards); a king in checkers; *pl* game of checkers.

dame! dăhm! *interj* why! well! indeed!

damer, dăh-meh, *v* to crown (in checkers); *(fam)* –le pion à, – ler pe-ong ăh, to outdo.

damier, dăh-me-eh, *m* checkerboard.

damner, dah-neh, *v* to damn.

dandiner (se), ser dahng-de-neh, *v* to waddle; to strut.

danger, dahng- sheh, *m* danger.

dangereu-x, se,* dahng-sher-rer, *a* dangerous.

dans, dahng, *prep* in, into; within; according to.

danse, dahngss, *f* dance; dancing.

danseu-r, se, dahng-ser, *mf* dancer.

dard, dăhr, *m* dart; sting.

darder, dăhr-deh, *v* to dart; to shoot; to beam.

darne, dăhrn, *f* fish steak.

dartre, dăhr-tr, *f* sore.

date, dăht, *f* date.

dater, dăh-teh, *v* to date.

datif, dăh-tiff, *m* dative.

datte, dăht, *f* (fruit) date.

dattier, dăh-te-eh, *m* date tree.

daube, dohb, *f* stew.

dauber, doh-beh, *v* to cuff; to jeer; to stew.

dauphin, doh-fang, *m* dolphin.

davantage, dăh-vahng-tăhsh, *adv* more.

de, der, *prep* of; from; out of; by; with; as; than; to; upon; since; some; any.

dé, deh, *m* thimble; die.

débâcle, deh-bah-kl, *f* breaking up; downfall.

déballage, deh-băh-lăhsh, *m* unpacking; *(fam)* show-down.

déballer, deh-băh-leh, *v* to unpack.

débandade, deh-bahng-dăhd, *f* stampede; à la –,ăh lăh –, helter-skelter.

débander, deh-bahng-deh, *v* to unbend; to disband; se–, to disband; to disperse; to run away.

débaptiser, deh-băh-te-zeh, *v* to change the name of.

débarbouiller, deh-băhr-boo'e-yeh, *v* to wash the face of; to clean; **se** –, to wash one's face; to extricate oneself.

débarcadère, deh-băhr-kăh-dair, *m* wharf; pier.

débarder, deh-băhr-deh, *v* to unload.

débardeur, deh-băhr-der, *m* longshoreman.

débarquement, deh-băhr-ker-mahng, *m* landing; arrival; unloading.

débarquer, deh-băhr-keh, *v* to land; to disembark; to unload.

débarras, deh-băh-răh, *m* riddance; junk closet; **bon** –! **bong** –! good riddance! **chambre de** –, shahng-br der –, storeroom.

débarrasser, deh-băh-răhss-eh, *v* to clear; to rid; **se** –, to get rid (**de**, of).

débat, deh-băh, *m* debate; *pl* pleadings; trial; case.

débattre, deh-băh-tr, *v* to debate; to discuss; **se** –, to struggle.

débauche, deh-bohsh, *f* debauch; debauchery.

débaucher, deh-boh-sheh, *v* to debauch; to entice away; **se** –, to go astray.

débile,* deh-beell, *a* weak; feeble.

débilité, deh-be-le-teh, *f* stupidity; weakness.

débiliter, deh-be-le-teh, *v* to weaken.

débine, deh-been, *f* (*fam*) destitution; straits; **il est tombé dans la** –, il ay tongbeh dahng lă–, he has fallen into poverty.

débiner, deh-be-neh, *v* (*fam*) to disparage; **se** –, to make off; to run away.

débit, deh-be, *m* sale; market; retail store; flow; utterance; output; delivery.

débit, deh-be, *m* debit.

débitant, deh-be-tahng, *m* dealer.

débiter, deh-be-teh, *v* to retail; to sell; to cut up; to recite; to debit (**de**, with).

débi-teur, trice, deh-be-ter, *mf* & *a* debtors .

déblai, deh-blay, *m* excavation; clearing; *pl* rubble.

déblatérer, deh-blăh-teh-reh, *v* to rail at.

déblayer, deh-blay-yeh, *v* to clear away.

débloquer, deh-block-eh,

v to raise the blockade of; to free.

déboire, deh-bo'ăhr, *m* vexation; disappointment.

déboiser, deh-bo'ăh-zeh, *v* to deforest.

déboîter, deh-bo'ăh-teh, *v* to dislocate; to disconnect.

de bonne réputation, der-bong-reh-pE-tăh-se-ong *a* reputable.

débonnaire, deh-bonn-air, *a* good-natured; meek; gentle.

débordement, deh-bor-der-mahng, *m* overflowing; (*fam*) dissoluteness.

déborder, deh-bor-deh, *v* to overflow; to project; to untuck.

débotter, deh-bot-eh, *v* to pull boots off; **au** –, oh –, immediately on arrival.

débouché, deh-boo-sheh, *m* outlet; market; issue.

déboucher, deh-boo-sheh, *v* to open; to uncork; to unblock; to emerge; to run into.

déboucler, deh-boo-kleh, *v* to unbuckle; to uncurl.

débourber, deh-boohr-beh, *v* to clean; to extricate from the mud.

déboursés, débours, deh-boohr-seh, deh-boohr, *mpl* expenses; disbursements.

débourser, deh-boohr-seh, *v* to disburse; to lay out.

debout, der-boo, *adv* upright; standing.

débouter, deh-boo-teh, *v* to dismiss.

déboutonner, deh-boo-tonn-eh, *v* to unbutton.

débraillé, e, deh-brah'e-yeh, *a* untidy; disarrayed.

débrayage, deh-bre-yash, *m* disengaging (of clutch); declutching.

débrayer, deh-bray-yeh, to declutch; to disengage.

débrider, deh-bre-deh, *v* to unbridle; to stop; **sans –,** without stopping.

débris, deh-bre, *m* remains; debris; rubbish.

débrouillard, e, deh-broo'e-yăhr, *mf & a* (*fam*) resourceful; capable.

débrouiller, deh-broo'e-yeh, *v* to disentangle; to unravel; **se –,** to cope.

début, deh-bE, *m* beginning; first appearance; lead.

débutant, e, deh-bE-tahng, *mf & a* beginner;

performer appearing for the first time.

débuter, deh-bE-teh, *v* to begin; to make one's first appearance.

deçà, der-săh, *adv* on this side.

décacheter, deh-kăhsh-teh, *v* to unseal.

décadence, deh-kăh-dahngss, *f* decay; decline.

décaisser, deh-kayss-eh, *v* to unpack; to disburse.

décaler, deh-cah-leh, *v* to unwedge; to alter (time); to displace.

décalquer, deh-kăhl-keh, *v* to transfer a tracing; to trace.

décamper, deh-kahng-peh, *v* to move off; to bolt.

décanter, deh-kahng-teh, *v* to decant.

décapiter, deh-kăh-pe-teh, *v* to behead.

décéder, deh-seh-deh, *v* to die; to decease.

déceler, dehss-leh, *v* to discover; to detect; to guess.

décembre, deh-sahng-br, *m* December.

décemment, deh-săh-mahng, *adv* decently.

décence, deh-sahngss, *f* decency; propriety.

décent, e, deh-sahng, *a*

decent; becoming; proper.

déception, deh-sep-se-ong, *f* disappointment; setback.

décerner, deh-sair-neh, *v* to award; to issue (writ, etc.)

décès, deh-say, *m* death; decease.

décevant, deh-ser-vahng, *a* misleading; disappointing.

décevoir, deh-ser-vo'ăhr, *v* to disappoint.

déchaîné, deh-shay-neh, *pp & a* unchained; furious; mad.

déchaîner, deh-shay-neh, *v* to unchain; to let loose.

déchanter, deh-shahng-teh, *v* to become disillusioned.

décharge, deh-shăhrsh, *f* discharge; discharging; unloading; acquittal; **à –, ăh –,** for the defense.

décharger deh-shăhr-sheh, *v* to unload; to relieve; to clear.

déchargeur, deh-shăhr-sher, *m* longshoreman.

décharné, e, deh-shăhr-neh, *a* emaciated.

déchaussé, e, deh-shohss-eh, *pp & a* barefooted; shrinking (of gums).

dèche, daysh, *f (pop)*
destitution.
déchéance, deh-sheh-
ahngss, *f* forfeiture;
downfall.
déchet, deh-shay, *m* waste;
loss.
décheveler, deh-sherv-leh,
v to dishevel; to tousle.
déchiffrer, deh-she-freh, *v*
to decipher; to sight-
read (music).
déchiqueter, deh-shick-
teh, *v* to cut up; to slash;
to tear.
déchirant, e, deh-she-
rahng, *a* piercing;
heartrending.
déchirement, deh-sheer-
mahng, *m* tearing;
anguish; excruciating
pain.
déchirer, deh-she-reh, *v* to
tear; to rend; to break.
déchirure, deh-she-rEEr, *f*
tear; rip.
déchoir, deh-sho'ǎhr, *v* to
fall; to decline; to decay.
décidé, e, deh-se-deh, *pp*
& *a* decided;
determined.
décidément, deh-se-deh-
mahng, *adv* decidedly.
décider, deh-se-deh, *v* to
decide; to determine; to
persuade; **se –,** to make
up one's mind.
décimal, deh-se-mahl, *a*

decimal.
décimale, deh-se-mahl, *f*
decimal (fraction).
décisi-f, ve,* deh-se-zeeff,
a decisive.
décision, deh-se-ze-ong, *f*
decision; resolution.
déclamer, deh-klǎh-meh,
v to declaim; to recite.
déclaration, deh-klǎh-rǎh-
se-ong, *f* declaration;
affidavit.
déclarer, deh-klǎh-reh, *v*
to declare; to proclaim;
to certify.
déclassé, e, deh-klǎhss-eh,
mf & *a* one who has lost
social position.
déclencher, deh-klahng-
sheh, *v* to unlock; to
disconnect; *(fam)* to
launch; to set in
motion.
déclinaison, deh-kle-nay-
zong, *f* declination (of
compass, star, etc);
declension.
décliner, deh-kle-neh, *v* to
decline; to deviate.
déclivité, deh-kle-ve-teh,
f declivity.
déclouer, deh-kloo-eh, *v*
to pry open.
décocher, deh-kosh-eh, *v*
to shoot; to let fly.
décoiffer, deh-ko'ǎh-feh, *v*
to take off hat; to
disarrange hair.

décollage, deh-ko-lash, *m*
unsticking; takeoff (of
plane).
décoller, deh-koll-eh, *v* to
unstick; to take off (of
plane).
décolleté, deh-koll-teh, *a*
low-cut; low-necked. *m*
neckline.
décolorer, deh-koll-or-eh,
v to discolor; to bleach.
décombres, deh-kong-br,
mpl rubbish.
décommander, deh-
komm-ahng-deh, *v* to
countermand; to cancel.
décomposer, deh-kong-
poz-eh, *v* to decompose.
décomposition, deh-kong-
poz-e-se-ong, *f*
decomposition;
discomposure; analyzing.
décompte, deh-kongt, *m*
deduction;
disappointment.
décompter, deh-kong-teh,
v to deduct; to be
disappointed.
déconcerter, deh-kong-
sair-teh, *v* to disconcert;
to confuse; to baffle.
décongeler, deh-kong-
sher-leh, to thaw; to
defrost (food).
déconseiller, deh-kong-
say'e-yeh, *v* to advise
against.
déconsidérer, deh-kong-

se-deh-reh, *v* to discredit.

décontenancer, deh-kongt-nahngss-eh, *v* to disconcert; to unsettle.

décontracté, deh-kong-trahck-teh, *a* relaxed.

décontracter (se), ser deh-kong-trahck-teh, *v* to relax.

déconvenue, deh-kongv-nE, *f* mishap; ill luck; disappointment.

décor, deh-kor, *m* decoration; *pl* stage-scenery.

décorateur, deh-kor-ăh-ter, *m* decorator; set designer.

décoration, deh-kor-ăh-se-ong, *f* decoration; medal.

décoré, e, deh-kor-eh, *a* decorated; wearing a decoration.

décorer, deh-kor-eh, *v* to embellish; to confer a decoration on.

découcher, deh-koo-sheh, *v* to sleep out; to stay out all night.

découdre, deh-koo-dr, *v* to unstitch.

découler, deh-koo-leh, *v* to drop; to trickle; to follow (**de,** from).

découper, deh-koo-peh, *v* to cut up; to cut out; to carve.

découplé, deh-koo-pleh, *pp* & *a* uncoupled; **bien** –, be-ang –, strapping.

découpure, deh-koo-pEEr, *f* workmanship; indentations.

décourageant, deh-koo-rah-shahng, *a* discouraging; disheartening.

découragement, deh-koo-răhsh-mahng, *m* discouragement; despondency.

décourager, deh-koo-răh-sheh, *v* to discourage; to deter; **se** –, to lose heart.

décousu, e, deh-koo-zE, *pp* & *a* unsewed; unconnected; desultory.

découvert, deh-koo-vair, *m* deficit; overdraft.

découvert, e, deh-koo-vair, *pp* & *a* uncovered; open; **à** –, ăh –, openly; unsecured; exposed.

découverte, deh-koo-vairt, *f* discovery.

découvrir, deh-koo-vreer, *v* to uncover; to discover; to unmask; to find out; **se** –, to take off one's hat; to come to light; to clear up (weather).

décrasser, deh-krăhss-eh, *v* to clean; to get dirt off.

décréditer, deh-kreh-de-teh, *v* to discredit.

décrépit, e, deh-kreh-pe, *a* decrepit; senile.

décret, deh-kray, *m* decree; order.

décréter, deh-kreh-teh, *v* to decree.

décrier, deh-kre-eh, *v* to run down; to decry.

décrire, deh-kreer, *v* to describe.

décrocher, deh-krosh-eh, *v* to unhook; to take off.

décroissance, deh-kro'ăhss-ahngss, *f* decrease.

décroître, deh-kro'ăh-tr, *v* to decrease; to diminish.

décrotter, deh-krot-eh, *v* to clean mud off (boots, etc); to brush.

décrottoir, deh-krot-o ăhr, *m* scraper.

déçu, e, deh-sE, *pp* & *a* disappointed.

décupler, deh-kE-pleh, *v* to increase tenfold.

dédaigner, deh-dayn-yeh, *v* to disdain.

dédaigneu-x, se,* deh-dayn-yer, *a* disdainful; scornful.

dédain, deh-dahng, *m* disdain; scorn.

dedans, der-dahng, *adv* inside; in; in it; in them.

m inside; interior.

dédicace, deh-de-kähss, *f*
dedication.

dédier, deh-de-eh, *v* to
dedicate.

dédire, deh-deer, *v* to
retract a statement.

dédit, deh-de, *m* forfeit.

dédommagement, deh-
domm-ähsh-mah*ng*, *m*
compensation;
indemnification.

dédommager deh-domm-
äh-sheh, *v* to
compensate; (**de,** for).

dédouaner, deh-doo-ah-
neh, *v* to clear; to clear
through customs.

dédoubler, deh-doo-bleh,
v to take the lining out
of; to diminish by half;
to divide in two.

déduction, dah-dEEk-se-
o*ng*, *f* deduction;
inference; **–faite de, –**
fayt der, after deducting.

déduire, deh-dweer, *v* to
deduct; to deduce; to
infer.

déesse, deh-ess, *f* goddess.

défaillance, deh-fah'e-
yah*ng*ss, *f* faintness;
faltering; failing.

défaillir, deh-fah'e-yeer, *v*
to faint; to falter; to fail.

défaire, deh-fair, *v* to
undo; to break; to
defeat; **se –de,** to get rid

of.

défait, e, deh-fay, *pp* & *a*
undone; defeated;
meager.

défaite, deh-fayt, *f* defeat;
pretext.

défalcation, deh-fähl-käh-
se-o*ng*, *f* deduction.

défalquer, deh-fähl-keh *v*
to deduct.

défaut, deh-foh, *m* defect;
fault; default; **à –de,** äh
– der, for want of; **faire
–, fair –,** to fail; to be
missing.

défaveur, deh-fäh-ver, *f*
disgrace; disfavor.

défavorable, * deh-fäh-
vor-äh-bl, *a* unfavorable.

défecti-f, ve, deh-feck-
teeff, *a* defective.

défection, deh-feck-se-
o*ng*, *f* desertion;
disloyalty.

défectueu-x, se, * deh-
feck-tE- er, *a* defective;
faulty.

défectuosité, deh-feck-tE-
oz-e-teh, *f* defect;
blemish; flaw.

défendre, deh-fah*ng*-dr, *v*
to defend; to forbid.

défense, deh-fah*ng*ss, *f*
defense; prohibition; *pl*
tusks.

défenseur, deh-fah*ng*-ser,

m defender.

défensi-f, ve, * deh-fah*ng*-
seeff, *a* defensive.

déférence, deh-feh-
rah*ng*ss, *f* deference.

déférer, deh-feh-reh, *v* to
bestow; to bring before;
to comply (**à,** with); to
defer; to tender (oath).

déferler, deh-fair-leh, *v* to
unfurl; to break.

défi, deh-fe, *m* defiance;
challenge.

défiance, deh-fe-ah*ng*ss, *f*
distrust; diffidence.

défiant, e, deh-fe-ah*ng*, *a*
distrustful; suspicious.

déficeler, deh-fiss-leh, *v* to
untie.

défier, deh-fe-eh, *v* to
challenge; to defy; **se –**
(**de**), to mistrust.

défigurer, deh-fe-ghE-reh,
v to disfigure.

défilé, deh-fe-leh, *m*
straight; march past.

défini, e, deh-fe-ne, *pp* &
a defined; definite;
precise.

définir, deh-fe-neer, *v* to
define.

définissable, deh-fe-niss-
äh-bl, *a* definable.

définiti-f, ve, * deh-fe-ne-
teeff, *a* definitive;
positive; **en –ve,** ah*ng* –,
finally.

définition, deh-fe-ne-se-ong, f definition; clue (of crossword puzzle).

défoncer, deh-fongss-eh, v to smash in; to break up.

déformer, deh-for-meh, v to put out of shape; to distort.

défraîchi, e, deh-fray-she, a no longer fresh; tatty.

défrayer, deh-fray-yeh, v to defray the expense of.

défricher, deh-fre-sheh, v to clear; to reclaim (of land).

défroque, deh-frock, f cast-off clothes (usu in pl; of monk, etc).

défroqué, deh-frock-eh, a & m unfrocked (priest, etc); ex-priest.

défunt, e, deh-fung, a deceased.

dégagé, e, deh-gäh-sheh, pp & a redeemed; free; easy; offhand.

dégager, deh-gäh-sheh, v to redeem; to clear; to release.

dégaine, deh-gain, f ungainliness; awkward gait.

dégainer, deh-gay-neh, v to unsheathe.

dégarnir, deh-gähr-neer, v to strip; to dismantle; se –de, to part with.

dégât, deh-gah, m damage; havoc; waste.

dégel, deh-**sh**ell, m thaw.

dégénérer, deh-**sh**eh-neh-reh, v to degenerate.

dégingandé, e, deh-shang-gahng-deh, a & mf ungainly; disjointed.

dégivrer, deh-she-vreh, v to deice; to defrost.

dégivreur, deh-she-vrer, m defroster.

dégommer, deh-gomm-eh, v to ungum; (fam) to give the sack to.

dégonfler, deh-gong-fleh, v to reduce; to bring down; to deflate; se –, to collapse (tire, balloon, etc); (fam) to get into a funk.

dégorger, deh-gor-sheh, v to disgorge; to clear; to scour.

dégourdi, e, deh-goohr-de, a sharp; acute (of person).

dégourdir, deh-goohr-deer, v to revive; to stretch; to sharpen; se –, to get sharp.

dégoût, deh-goo, m dislike; disgust; loathing.

dégoûtant, e, deh-goo-tahng, a sickening; disgusting.

dégoûté, e, deh-goo-teh, pp & a disgusted; fastidious; squeamish.

dégoutter, deh-goot-eh, v

to drip; to trickle.

dégrader, deh-gräh-deh, v to degrade; to debase; to damage.

dégrafer, deh-gräh-feh, v to unhook; to unclasp.

dégraisser, deh-grayss-eh, v to scour; to clean; to remove the grease from; to skim fat off; to dry clean.

degré, der-greh, m degree; step; stage.

dégringoler, deh-grang-goll-eh, v to tumble down.

dégriser, deh-gre-zeh, v to sober up.

dégrossir, deh-gross-eer, v to smooth rough edges of.

déguenillé, e, deh-gher-nee-yeh, a ragged.

déguerpir, deh-gair-peer, v to pack off; to clear out quickly.

déguisement, deh-gheez-mahng, m disguise.

déguiser, deh-ghee-zeh, v to disguise; to conceal.

déguster, deh-ghEEs-teh, v to taste; to sample; to eat or drink with relish.

déhanché, e, deh-ahng-sheh, a swaying; ungainly.

dehors, der-or, adv without; outside; m outside; exterior;

appearances.

déjà, deh-**shäh,** *adv* already; yet; then; before; as far back as; to begin with.

déjeuner, deh-**sher**-neh, *m* lunch; **petit –,** per-te –, breakfast.

déjeuner, deh-**sher**-neh, *v* to breakfast; to lunch.

déjouer deh-**shoo**-eh, *v* to foil; to outsmart; to thwart.

déjuger (se), ser deh-**shE-sheh,** *v* to change one's opinion.

delà der-**läh,** *prep* beyond; on the other side of; farther than; **au –de** oh – der beyond.

délabré, e, deh-läh-breh, *a* tattered; dilapidated; in ruins.

délabrement, deh-läh-brer-mahng, *m* ruin; decay; dilapidation.

délai, deh-lay, *m* interval; delay; **dans un –de,** dahng z'ung – der, within.

délaissement, deh-layss-mahng, *m* abandonment; relinquishment.

délaisser, deh-layss-eh, *v* to forsake; to abandon.

délassement, deh-lähss-mahng, *m* relaxation;

rest.

déla-teur, trice, deh-läh-ter, *mf* informer; spy.

délation, deh-läh-se-ong, *f* information; denunciation.

délayer, deh-lay-yeh, *v* to mix with water; to thin out; to spin out.

délecter (se), ser deh-leck-teh, *v* to delight (à, in).

délégation, deh-leh-gäh-se-ong, *f* delegation; assignment; proxy.

délégué, deh-leh-gheh, *m* delegate; deputy; union representative.

déléguer, deh-leh-gheh, *v* to delegate; to assign.

délétère, deh-leh-tair, *a* deleterious.

délibérément, deh-le-beh-reh-mahng, *adv* deliberately.

délibérer, deh-le-beh-reh, *v* to deliberate; to resolve.

délicat, e, * deh-le-käh, *a* delicate; dainty; scrupulous; tricky; difficult.

délicatesse, deh-le-käh-tess, *f* delicacy; nicety; scrupulousness.

délicieu-x, se, * deh-le-se-er, *a* delicious; delightful.

délictueu-x, se, deh-lick-tE- er, *a* unlawful; offensive; felonious.

délié, deh-le-eh, *pp* & *a* untied; loose; easy; slender; sharp.

délier, deh-le-eh, *v* to untie; to unbind; to release; to absolve.

délimiter, deh-le-me-teh, *v* to fix the limits of.

délinquant, deh-lang-kahng, *m* offender; delinquent.

délirant, e, deh-le-rahng, *a* delirious; frenzied; rapturous.

délire, deh-leer, *m* delirium; frenzy.

délit, deh-le, *m* misdemeanor; offense; **en flagrant –,** ahng fläh-grahng –, in the very act; **le corps du –,** ler kor dE –, the charge.

délivrance, deh-le-vrahngss, *f* deliverance; release; rescue; confinement.

délivrer, deh-le-vreh, *v* to deliver; to rid; to release; to set free.

déloger, deh-losh-eh, *v* to dislodge; to turn out; (*fam*) to clear out; **–sans tambour ni trompette, –** sahng tahng-boohr ne trong-payt, to steal away.

déloyal, e, * deh-lo'ăh-yăhl, *a* disloyal; dishonest; unfair.

déloyauté, deh-lo'ăh-yoh-teh, *f* dishonesty.

déluge, deh-lEE **sh,** *m* flood.

déluré, e, deh-lE-reh, *a* sharp; resourceful; sassy.

demain, der-mang, *adv* tomorrow; **après –,** ăh-pray –, the day after tomorrow.

démancher, deh-mahng-sheh, *v* to take the handle off; to dislocate.

demande, der-mahngd, *f* question; request; prayer; *pl* inquiries; orders.

demander, der-mahng-deh, *v* to ask; to beg; to claim; to want; to demand; to require; **se –,** to wonder.

demand-eur, eresse, der-mahng-der, *mf* plaintiff; applicant.

démangeaison, deh-mahng- **sh**ay-zong, *f* itching; longing.

démanger, deh-mahng-sheh, *v* to itch; to long.

démantibuler, deh-mahng-te-bE-leh, *v* to put out of order.

démaquillant, deh-măh-kee-yahng, *m* cleansing cream; makeup remover.

démaquiller, deh-măh-kee-yeh, *v* to remove makeup.

démarche, deh-mahrsh, *f* gait; walk; step; measure; attempt.

démarquer, deh-măhr-keh, *v* to unmark; to mark down (goods).

démarrage, deh-măh-răhsh, *m* unmooring; start.

démarrer, deh-măh-reh, *v* to start up; to cast off.

démarreur, deh-mah-rer, *m* starter (in car).

démasquer, deh-măhss-keh, *v* to unmask; to show up.

démêlé, deh-may-leh, *m* (usu *pl*) dispute; differences.

démêler, deh-may-leh, *v* to disentangle.

démêloir, deh-may-lo'ăhr, *m* large-tooth comb.

démembrer, deh-mahng-breh, *v* to dismember.

déménagement, deh-meh-năhsh-mahng, *m* removal. *v* moving.

déménager, deh-meh-năh-sheh, *v* to remove; to move (house).

démence, deh-mahngss, *f* madness; insanity.

démener (se), ser deh-mer-neh, *v* to struggle.

démenti, deh-mahng-te, *m* flat denial.

démentir, deh-mahng-teer, *v* to deny; to contradict.

démérite, deh-meh-reet, *m* demerit.

démériter, deh-meh-re-teh, *v* to deserve censure.

démesuré, e, deh-mer-ZEE-reh, *a* immoderate; excessive.

démettre, deh-met-tr, *v* to dislocate; to dismiss; **se –,** to resign.

démeubler, deh-mer-bleh, *v* to unfurnish.

demeurant, der-mer-rahng, *pp* residing; **au –,** oh –, after all; nevertheless.

demeure, der-mer, *f* residence; **à –,** ăh –, fixed; **mettre en –,** met-tr'ahng –, to call upon; to summon; **péril en la –,** peh-reel ahng lăh –, danger in delay.

demeurer, der-mer-reh, *v* to reside; to live; to stay; to stand; **en –là,** ahng –lăh, to go no farther.

demi, der-me, *m & a* half; (*fam*) a glass of beer.

démission, deh-miss-e-ong, *f* resignation;

donner sa démission, donn-eh säh –, to give one's resignation.

démobiliser, deh-mob-e-le-zeh, v to demobilize.

démocratie, deh-mock-räh-see, f democracy.

démodé, e, deh-mod-eh, a old-fashioned.

demoiselle, der-mo'äh-zell, f young lady; single woman; **–d'honneur, –** donn-**er**, bridesmaid.

démolir, deh-moll-eer, v to pull down.

démon, deh-mong, m demon; devil; an imp (of child).

démonétiser, deh-monn-eh-te-zeh, v to demonetize.

démoniaque, deh-monn-e-ähck, a demonic.

démonstration, deh-mongss-träh-se-ong, f demonstration.

démontable, deh-mong-täh-bl, a that can be dismantled.

démonter, deh-mong-teh, v to dismount; to take apart; to put out; se –, to lose face.

démontrer, deh-mong-treh, v to demonstrate; to prove.

démoraliser, deh-mor-äh-le-zeh, v to demoralize.

démordre, deh-mor-dr, v to let go; to desist.

démouler, deh-moo-leh, v to remove from mold.

démunir (se), ser deh-mE-neer, v to part (de, with).

dénaturé, e, deh-näh-tE-reh, pp & a altered; distorted; unnatural; depraved.

dénégation, deh-neh-gäh-se-ong, f denial.

dénicher, deh-ne-sheh, v to take out of its nest; to find out.

dénier, deh-ne-eh, v to deny.

dénigrer, deh-ne-greh, v to disparage.

dénombrement, deh-nong-brer-mahng, m numbering; enumeration; census.

dénommer, deh-nomm-eh, v to name.

dénoncer, deh-nongss-eh, v to denounce.

dénonciateur, deh-nongss-e-äh-ter, m informer.

dénoter, deh-not-eh, v to denote; to show.

dénouement, deh-noo-mahng, m outcome; issue; end; ending.

dénouer, deh-noo-eh, v to untie; to undo; to unravel; to loose; to

solve.

denrée, dahng-reh, f ware; provision; pl produce; commodities; **–s alimentaires, –** äh-le-mahngt-air, food products.

dense, dahngss, a dense.

densité, dahng-se-teh, f thickness; density.

dent, dahng, f tooth; notch; cog; prong.

dentaire, dahng-tair, a dental.

dentelé, e, dahngt-leh, a indented; notched; jagged.

dentelle, dahng-tell, f lace; lacework.

dentier, dahng-te-eh, m denture.

dentifrice, dahng-te-freess, m toothpaste.

dentiste, dahng-teesst, m dentist.

dentition, dahng-te-se-ong, f teeth; dentition.

dénuder, deh-nE-deh, v to denude; to strip.

dénué, e, deh-nE-eh, pp & a destitute; devoid of.

de nuit, der-nwee a, train overnight train.

dénûment, deh-nEE-mahng, m destitution; penury.

déodorant, deh-oh-doh-rahng, m deodorant.

dépannage, deh-pah-nash, *m* road repairs; repair service.

dépanner, deh-pah-neh, *v* to repair (broken-down cars); (*fam*) to help out.

dépaqueter, deh-păhck-teh, *v* to unpack.

dépareillé, e, deh-păh-ray'e-yeh, *pp* & *a* unmatched; odd; incomplete.

déparer, deh-păh-reh, *v* to strip; to disfigure; to spoil the look of.

départ, deh-păhr, *m* departure.

département, deh-păhr-ter-mahng, *m* department; county.

départir, deh-păhr-teer, *v* to allot; to bestow; **se –de,** to give up.

dépasser, deh-păhss-eh, *v* to pass; to go beyond; to exceed; to outrun; to rise above.

dépayser, deh-pay-yee-zeh, *v* to send from home.

dépaysé, deh-pay-yee-zeh, *a* out of one's element; **se sentir –,** not to feel at home.

dépêche, deh-paysh, *f* despatch; telegram.

dépêcher, deh-pay-sheh, *v* to dispatch; **se –,** to

make haste.

dépeindre, deh-pang-dr, *v* to depict.

dépendance, deh-pahng-dahngss, *f* dependence; dependency; *pl* out buildings.

dépendre, deh-pahng-dr, *v* to depend; to result; to belong to; to unhang.

dépens, deh-pahng, *mpl* expenses (legal), costs; **au –de,** at the expense of.

dépense, deh-pahngss, *f* expense; expenditure.

dépenser, deh-pahngss-eh, *v* to spend (money or time).

dépensi-er, iére, deh-pahngss-e-eh, *mf* spendthrift; *a* extravagant; prodigal.

déperdition, deh-pair-de-se-ong, *f* loss; waste.

dépérir, deh-peh-reer, *v* to fade away.

dépêtrer, deh-pay-treh, *v* to disentangle; to extricate.

dépeupler, deh-per-pleh, *v* to depopulate.

dépister, deh-piss-teh, *v* to track; to throw off the scent.

dépit, deh-pe, *m* spite; resentment; vexation; **en –de,** ahng – der, in

spite of.

dépiter, deh-pe-teh, *v* to vex; to spite.

déplacé, e, deh-plăhss-eh, *pp* & *a* in the wrong place; improper; uncalled for; displaced (of person).

déplacement, deh-plăhss-mahng, *m* removal; change of place; **frais de –,** fray der –, traveling expenses.

déplacer, deh-plăhss-eh, *v* to displace **se –,** to move; to travel.

déplaire, deh-plair, *v* to displease; to offend; **se –à,** to dislike (a place, etc).

déplaisant, e, deh-play-zahng, *a* disagreeable; unpleasant.

déplier, deh-ple-eh, *v* to unfold.

déplisser, deh-pliss-eh, *v* to unpleat.

déploiement, deh-plo'ăh-mahng, *m* unfolding; display.

déplorer, deh-plor-eh, *v* to deplore.

déployer, deh-plo'ăh-yeh, *v* to unfold; to display; to exert; to deploy.

déplumer, deh-plE-meh, *v* to pluck; to pick.

déporté, deh-por-teh, *m*

& *a* deported; transported convict.

déportements, deh-por-ter-mah*ng*, *mpl* misconduct.

déporter, deh-por-teh, *v* to deport; to transport.

déposant, deh-poh-zah*ng*, *m* depositor; witness.

déposer, deh-poh-zeh, *v* to deposit; to put down; to lodge; to give evidence; to depose; to leave; **marque –ée,** mahrk –, registered trademark.

dépositaire, deh-poh-ze-tair, *m* depositary; trustee.

déposition, deh-poh-ze-se-ong, *f* evidence.

déposséder, deh-poss-eh-deh, *v* to dispossess.

dépôt, deh-poh, *m* deposit; depositing; trust; store; warehouse; jail; sediment.

dépouille, deh-poo'e-ye, *f* skin; remains; *pl* spoils.

dépouillement, deh-poo'e-yer-mah*ng*, *m* deprivation; stripping; abstract; perusal; counting.

dépouiller, deh-poo'e-yeh, *v* to deprive; to strip; to skin.

dépourvoir, deh-poohr-vo'ăhr, *v* to leave

unprovided for; to strip.

dépourvu, e, deh-poohr-VE, *pp* & *a* destitute; unprovided; **au –,** oh –, unprepared.

dépraver, deh-prăh-veh, *v* to deprave.

déprécier, deh-preh-se-eh, *v* to depreciate; to undervalue.

dépression, deh-preh-se-ong, *f* depression; dejection; **–nerveuse, –** nair-verz, nervous breakdown.

déprimé, e, deh-pre-meh, *a* depressed.

déprimer, deh-pre-meh, *v* to depress; to disparage.

depuis, der-pwe, *adv* & *prep* since; ever since; from; **–peu, –** per, lately; **–quand? –** kah*ng*, how long?

député, deh-pE-teh, *m* representative; member of the French Parliament.

députer, deh-pE-teh, *v* to send; to delegate.

déraciner, deh-răh-se-neh, *v* to uproot.

déraillement, deh-rah'e-mah*ng*, *m* derailment.

dérailler, deh-rah'e-yeh, *v* to derail.

déraisonnable, deh-ray-zonn-ăh-bl, *a*

unreasonable.

déraisonner, deh-ray-zonn-eh, *v* to rave; to talk nonsense.

dérangement, deh-rah*ng* sh-mah*ng*, *m* derangement; disturbance; trouble; disorder; upset.

déranger, deh-rahng-sheh, *v* to displace; to put out of order; to disturb; to upset; **se –,** to put oneself out.

déraper, deh-răh-peh, *v* to trip; to skid.

déréglé, e, deh-reh-gleh, *pp* & *a* put out of order; irregular; disorderly; dissolute.

déréglement, deh-ray-gler-mah*ng*, *m* disorder; irregularity; dissoluteness.

dérégler, deh-reh-gleh, *v* to unsettle; to put out of order; **se –,** to get out of order; to lead a disorderly life.

dérider, deh-re-deh, *v* to unwrinkle; to cheer; **se – to** brighten up.

dérision, deh-re-ze-ong, *f* derision; mockery.

dérisoire, * deh-re-zo'ăhr, *a* derisive.

dérive, deh-reev, *f* drift; leeway; **à la –,** ăh lăh –, adrift.

dériver, deh-re-veh, *v* to drift; to come from.

derni-er, ère, dair-ne-eh, *a* last; latter; utmost; final; youngest; latest.

dernièrement, dair-ne-air-mahng, *adv* lately.

dérobé, e, deh-rob-eh, *pp* & *a* stolen; concealed; **à la dérobée,** ăh lăh–, stealthily.

dérober, deh-rob-eh, *v* to steal; to rob; to hide; to shield; **se –,** to steal away; to shun.

dérouiller, deh-roo'e-yeh, *v* to rub the rust off; **se –,** to polish up (a subject).

dérouler, deh-roo-leh, *v* to unroll.

déroute, deh-root, *f* rout; disorder.

dérouter, deh-root-eh, *v* to lead astray; to baffle; to divert.

derrière, dayr-e-air, *adv* & *prep* behind; at the back.

derrière, dayr-e-air, *m* back; hindquarters; (*fam*) bottom; rear.

dès, day, *prep* from; since; on; even; in; **–que, –ker,** as soon as.

désabuser, deh-zăh-bE-zeh, *v* to disillusion.

désaccord, deh-zăh-kor, *m* disagreement; discord.

désaccorder, deh-zăh-kor-deh, *v* to put out of tune; to set at variance.

désaccoutumer, deh-zăh-koo-tE-meh, *v* to cause to lose a habit.

désaffection, deh-zăh-feck-se-ong, *f* disaffection.

désagréable, * deh-zah-greh-ăhbl, *a* disagreeable; unpleasant.

désagréger, deh-zăh-greh-sheh, *v* to disintegrate.

désagrément, deh-zăh-greh-mahng, *m* unpleasantness; inconvenience; defect; nuisance.

désaltérer, deh-zăhl-teh-reh, *v* to quench the thirst of.

désapproba-teur, trice, deh-zăh-prob-ăh-ter, *a* disapproving.

désapprouver, deh-zăh-proo-veh, *v* to disapprove of.

désarmer, deh-zăhr-meh, *v* to disarm; to appease.

désarroi, deh-zăh-ro'ăh, *m* disarray; confusion.

désastre, deh-zăhss-tr, *m* disaster.

désavantage, deh-zăh-vahng-tăhsh, *m* disadvantage.

désaveu, deh-zăh-ver, *m* disavowal.

désaveugler, deh-zăh-ver-gleh, *v* to disabuse.

désavouer, deh-zăh-voo-eh, *v* to disavow; to disown.

desceller, deh-sell-eh, *v* to unseal.

descendance, deh-sahng-dahngss, *f* descent; lineage.

descendre, deh-sahng-dr, *v* to descend; to come or go down; to dismount; to alight; to stop or stay; to put up (at hotel, etc); to search; to take down.

descente, deh-sahngt, *f* descent; taking down; rupture; run (skiing).

description, dehss-kreep-se-ong, *f* description.

désembarquer, deh-zahng-băhr-keh, *v* to disembark; to land.

désemparer, deh-zahng-păh-reh, *v* to quit; to disable; **sans –,** sahng –, without stopping.

désenchanter, deh-zahng-shahng-teh, *v* to disenchant; to disillusion.

désenfler, deh-zahng-fleh, *v* to become less swollen.

désennuyer, deh-zahng-nwe-yeh, v to amuse; to enliven.

déséquilibré, e, deh-zeh-ke-le-breh, a mentally unbalanced; out of balance.

désert, deh-zair, m wilderness; desert.

déserter, deh-zair-teh, v to desert; to forsake.

désespéré, e, deh-zess-peh-reh, mf & a desperate; desperado.

désespérer, deh-zess-peh-reh, v to despair.

désespoir, deh-zess-po'ăhr, m despair.

déshabiller, deh-zăh-bee-yeh, v to undress.

déshabituer, deh-zăh-be-tE-eh, v to disaccustom.

déshériter, deh-zeh-re-teh, v to disinherit.

des heures creuses, deh-zer-krerz a off-peak (time).

déshonnête, deh-zonn-ayt, a indecent; immodest.

déshonneur, deh-zonn-er, m dishonor; disgrace.

déshonorer, deh-zonn-or-eh, v to dishonor; to disgrace.

désignation, deh-zeen-yăh-se-ong, f designation; indication; nomination.

désigner, deh-zeen-yeh, v to point out; to denote; to appoint.

désillusion, deh-zill-lE-ze-ong, f disillusion.

désinfecter, deh-zang-feck-teh, v to disinfect.

désintéressement, deh-zang-teh-ress-mahng, m disinterestedness.

désintéresser, deh-zang-teh-ress-eh, v to indemnify; **se –,** to lose interest.

désintéressé, deh-zang-teh-ress-eh, a not involved; unbiased; unselfish.

désinvolte, deh-zang-vollt, a casual, free and easy.

désinvolture, deh-zang-voll-tEer, f free and easy manner.

désir, deh-zeer, m desire; wish.

désirer, deh-ze-reh, v to desire; to wish.

désister (se), ser deh-ziss-teh, v to desist; to waive.

désobéir, deh-zob-eh-eer, v to disobey.

désobéissance, deh-zob-eh-iss-ahngss, f disobedience.

désobligeance, deh-zob-le-shahngss, f unkindness.

désobliger, deh-zob-le-sheh, v to disoblige.

désœuvré, e, deh-zer-vreh, a idle.

désolant, e, deh-zoll-ahng, a distressing; grievous; very annoying.

désolation, deh-zoll-ăh-se-ong, f grief; desolateness.

désoler, deh-zoll-eh, v to distress; **se –,** to lament; to grieve.

désopilant, e, deh-zop-e-lahng, a funny; laughable.

désopiler (se – la rate), ser deh-zop-ee-leh lăh răht, (fam) to laugh immoderately.

désordonné, e, deh-zor-donn-eh, pp & a disorderly; untidy.

désordre, deh-zor-dr, m disorder; disturbance; licentiousness.

désorienter, deh-zor-e-ahng-teh, v to put out; to bewilder.

désormais, deh-zor-may, adv henceforth.

désosser, deh-zohss-eh, v to bone.

dessaisir, deh-say-zeer, v to dispossess; **se –,** to part (de, with).

dessaler, deh-săh-leh, v to remove salt; to soak; to capsize.

dessécher, deh-seh-sheh, *v* to dry up.

dessein, deh-sang, *m* design; plan.

desserrer, deh-say-reh, *v* to loosen.

dessert, deh-sair, *m* dessert.

desservant, deh-sair,-vahng, *m* officiating priest or clergyman.

desservir, deh-sair, *v* to clear the table; to play a dirty trick on; to officiate; to serve (of trains, etc.)

dessiller (les yeux), deh-see-yeh lay ze'er, *v* to open someone's eyes.

dessin, deh-sang, *m* drawing; design; pattern.

dessinateur, deh-se-näh-ter, *m* drawer; sketcher.

dessiner, deh-se-neh, *v* to draw; to sketch; to outline; **se –,** to become perceptible.

dessous, der-soo, *m* underpart; disadvantage; worst.

dessous, der-soo, *adv* & *prep* under; underneath.

dessus, der-sE, *adv* & *prep* on; above; uppermost; upon; over.

dessus, der-sE, *m* upper part; top; right side; advantage.

destin, dess-tang, *m* destiny; fate; lot.

destinataire, dess-te-näh-tair, *m* receiver; consignee; addressee.

destination, dess-te-näh-se-ong, *f* destination; object; end.

destinée, dess-te-neh, *f* destiny; fate.

destiner, dess-te-neh, *v* to destine; to intend; to fate.

destitué, e, dess-te-tE-eh, *pp* & *a* dismissed; devoid.

destituer, dess-te-tE-eh, *v* to dismiss.

destitution, dess-te-tE-se-ong, *f* dismissal; removal.

destruction, dess-trEEk-se-ong, *f* destruction.

désuétude, deh-sE-eh-tEEd, *f* disuse.

désunion, deh-zE-ne-ong, *f* separation; disunion.

désunir, deh-zE-neer, *v* to separate; to disunite.

détaché, e, deh-täh-sheh, *pp* & *a* detached; unconnected; indifferent; disinterested.

détachement, deh-tähsh-mahng, *m* detachment; indifference.

détacher, deh-täh-sheh, *v*

to untie; to detach; to undo; to separate; **se –,** to break away (**de,** from).

détail, deh-tah'e, *m* detail; particulars; trifle; retail.

détailler, deh-tah'e-yeh, *v* to cut up; to sell retail; to relate in detail.

déteindre, deh-tang-dr, *v* to take the color out of; to discolor; to fade; to run (of color).

détendre, deh-tahng-dr, *v* to unbend; to relax; to slacken.

détendu, e, deh-tahng-dEE, *a* slack; relaxed.

détenir, deh-ter-neer, *v* to detain; to keep back.

détente, deh-tahngt, *f* relaxation; slackening; expansion; trigger.

déten-teur, trice, deh-tahng-ter, *mf* holder.

détention, deh-tahng-se-ong, *f* detention; imprisonment.

détenu, deh-ter-nE, *m* prisoner.

détériorer, deh-teh-re-or-eh, *v* to damage; to impair; to deface.

déterminé, e, deh-tair-me-neh, *pp* & *a* determined; resolute.

déterminer, deh-tair-me-neh, *v* to determine; to

decide; to bring on; **se –**, to resolve.

déterrer, deh-tay-reh, *v* to dig up; to unearth; to discover.

détester, deh-tess-teh, *v* to detest; to hate; to abhor.

détoner, deh-tonn-eh, *v* to detonate; to explode.

détonner, deh-tonn-eh, *v* to be out of tune; to clash.

détordre, deh-tor-dr, *v* to untwist.

détour, deh-toohr, *m* turn; bend; winding; wile; roundabout way; subterfuge; **sans –**, sahng –, straightforward.

détourné, e, deh-toohr-neh, *pp* & *a* out of the way; embezzled.

détournement, deh-toohr-ner-mahng, *m* turning aside; embezzlement; abduction; hijacking.

détourner, deh-toohr-neh, *v* to lead astray; to turn away; to avert; to divert; to deter; to embezzle; to abduct; to hijack.

détracteur, deh-trähck-ter, *m* slanderer.

détraquer, deh-träh-keh, *v* to put out of order.

détrempe, deh-trahngp, *f*

distemper.

détremper, deh-trahng-peh, *v* to water; to dilute; to soften.

détresse, deh-trayss, *f* distress.

détriment, deh-tre-mahng, *m* detriment; prejudice.

détritus, deh-tre-tEEss, *m* detritus; garbage.

détroit, deh-tro'äh, *m* strait; straits; pass.

détromper, deh-trong-peh, *v* to disabuse; to correct someone's mistake.

détrôner, deh-troh-neh, *v* to dethrone.

détrousser, deh-trooss-eh, *v* to rob; to untuck.

détruire, deh-trweer, *v* to destroy.

dette, dett, *f* debt.

deuil, der, e, *m* mourning; sorrow; grief; **personnes en –**, pairsonn ahng, mourners.

deux, der, *m* & *a* two; both; second (the).

deuxième,* der-ze-aym, *a* &*m* second.

dévaler, deh-väh-leh, *v* to descend; to rush down.

dévaliser, deh-väh-le-zeh, *v* to rob; to plunder.

devancer, der-vahng-seh, *v* to get ahead of; to outrun; to precede; to anticipate.

devanci-er, ère, der-vahng-se-eh, *mf* predecessor.

devant, der-vahng, *prep* & *adv* before; opposite; in front; ahead; *m* front; forepart; **aller au –de**, äh-leh oh – der, to go to meet.

devanture, der-vahng-tEEr, *f* front; facade.

dévaster, deh-vähss-teh, *v* to devastate.

déveine, deh-vain, *f* bad luck.

développement, deh-ver-lop-mahng, *m* unfolding; development; growth.

développer, deh-ver-lop-eh, *v* to unfold; to develop; to expand; to explain; **se –**, to spread out.

devenir, derv-neer, *v* to become.

dévergondage, deh-vair-gong-däsh, *m* shamelessness; licentiousness.

dévergondé, e, deh-vair-gong-deh, *a* openly profligate.

dévergonder (se) ser deh-vair-gong-deh, *v* to lose all sense of shame.

déverser, deh-vair-seh, *v* to incline; to pour; to throw.

dévêtir, deh-vay-teer, *v* to undress.

déviation, deh-ve-a-se-ong, deviation.

dévider, deh-ve-deh, *v* to wind; to reel.

dévier, deh-ve-eh, *v* to deviate.

deviner, der-ve-neh, *v* to guess.

devinette, der-ve-nett, *f* puzzle; riddle.

devis, der-ve, *m* estimate.

dévisager, deh-ve-zăh-sheh, *v* to stare at.

devise, der-veez, *v* device; motto; currency.

deviser, der-ve-zeh, *v* to chat.

dévisser, deh-viss-eh, *v* to unscrew.

dévoiler, deh-vo'ăh-leh, *v* to unveil; to reveal.

devoir, der-vo'ăhr, *v* to owe; to be bound to; to have to; **je crois –,**sher kro'ăh –, I think it my duty to.

devoir, der-vo'ăhr, *m* duty; task; exercise; *pl* homework; **se mettre en –de,** ser met-tr'ahng– der, to set about.

dévorant, e, deh-vor-ahng, *a* devouring; ravenous; burning.

dévorer, deh-vor-eh, *v* to devour.

dévot, e, * deh-vo, *a & mf* devout; pious person.

dévotion, deh-vos-e-ong, *f* devotion; piety.

dévoué, e, deh-voo-eh, *pp & a* devoted; loving; **votre tout –,** vot-rer too –, sincerely yours.

dévouement, deh-voo-mahng, *m* devotedness; self-sacrifice.

dévouer, deh-voo-eh, *v* to devote.

dévoyé, e, deh-vo'ăh-yeh, *pp & a* misled; astray.

dextérité, decks-teh-re-teh, *f* dexterity; skill.

d'habitude, dăh-be-tEEd *a* **usually.**

diabète, de-ăh-bett, *m* diabetes.

diable, de-ăh-bl, *m* devil; mischievous child; **tirer le –par la queue,** te-reh ler – păhr lăh ker, to struggle hard for a living; **un bon –,** ung bong –, not a bad fellow.

diablement, de-ăh-bler-mahng, *adv (fam)* fiendishly; devilishly.

diabolique, * de-ăh-boll-eeck, *a* diabolical.

diacre, de-ăh-kr, *m* deacon.

diagnostic, de-ăhg-noss-teeck, *m* diagnosis.

diagonal, e,* de-ăh-gonn-ăhl, *a* diagonal.

diagnostique, de-ăhg-noss-teeck, *a* diagnostic.

dialecte, de-ăh-leckt, *m* dialect.

dialogue, de-ăh-log, *m* dialogue.

diamant, de-ăh-mahng, *m* diamond.

diamètre, de-ăh-met-tr, *m* diameter.

diapason, de-ăh-păh-zong, *m* pitch; tuning fork.

diaphane, de-ăh-făhn, *a* transparent.

diapositive, de-ah-poh-ze-teev, *f* transparency (photo).

diarrhée, de-ăh-reh, *f* diarrhea.

dictateur, dick-tăh-ter, *m* dictator.

dictature, dick-tăh-tEEr, *f* dictatorship.

dictée, dick-teh, *f* dictation.

dicter, dick-teh, *v* to dictate.

dictionnaire, dicks-e-onn-air, *m* dictionary.

dicton, dick-tong, *m* saying.

dièse, de-ayz, *m* sharp (music).

diète, de-ett, *f* diet.

dieu, de-er, *m* God.

diffamant, e, de-făh-mahng, *a* defamatory.

diffamation, de-făh-măh-se-ong, *f* libel; slander.

diffamer, de-făh-meh, *v* to defame; to slander.

différence, de-feh-rahngss, *f* difference.

différencier, de-feh-rahng-se-eh, *v* to distinguish.

différend, de-feh-rahng, *m* difference; dispute.

différent, de-feh-rahng, *a* different; unlike; various.

différentiel, le, de-feh-rahng-se-ell, *mf* & *a* differential.

différer, de-feh-reh, *v* to defer; to postpone; to differ (**de**, from).

difficile, * de-fe-seell, *a* difficult; particular; (*fam*) choosy.

difficulté, de-fe-kEEl-teh, *f* difficulty; obstacle; objection.

difforme, de-form, *a* deformed; ugly.

difformité, de-for-me-teh, *f* deformity.

diffus, e, de-fE, *a* diffuse; prolix.

diffuser, de-fE-zeh, *v* to diffuse; to broadcast.

diffusion, de-fE-ze-ong, *f* diffusion; diffuseness; **radio** –, răh-de-o –, broadcasting.

digérer, de-sheh-reh, *v* to assimilate; to digest.

digestion, de-shess-te-ong, *f* digestion.

digital, e, de-she-tăhl, *a* digital.

digitale, de-she-tăhl, *f* foxglove.

digne, * deen-yer, *a* worthy; deserving; dignified.

dignité, deen-yee-teh, *f* dignity; title; stateliness.

digue, deeg, *f* dike; dam; embankment.

dilapider, de-lăh-pe-deh, *v* to dilapidate; to squander.

dilater, de-lăh-teh, *v* to dilate; to enlarge.

dilatoire, de-lăh-to'ăhr, *a* dilatory.

dilemme, de-lemm, *m* dilemma.

diligence, de-le-shahngss, *f* diligence; speed; stage-coach.

diluer, de-lE-eh, *v* to dilute; to water down.

dimanche, de-mahngsh, *m* Sunday.

dimension, de-mahng-se-ong, *f* dimension; size; measurement.

diminuer, de-me-nE-eh, *v* to diminish; to lessen; to abate.

diminution, de-me-nE-se-ong, *f* decrease; abatement.

dinde, dangd, *f* female turkey.

dindon, dang-dong, *m* turkey-cock; (*fig*) goose.

dindonneau, dang-donn-o, *m* young turkey.

dîner, de-neh, *v* to dine.

dîner, de-neh, *m* dinner.

dînette, de-nett, *f* informal meal; doll's tea party.

diocèse, de-oss-ayz, *m* diocese.

diplomate, de-plomm-ăht, *m* diplomat.

diplomatie, de-plomm-ăh-see, *f* diplomacy.

diplômé, de-ploh-meh, *mf* & *a* graduate.

dire, deer, *v* to say; to tell; to speak; **dites donc!** deet dong, that's enough!

dire, deer, *m* saying; statement.

direct, e, * de-reckt, *a* direct; straight; through express (of train); live (of television).

direc-teur, trice, de-reck-ter, *mf* director; manager; headmaster; headmistress; principal.

direction, de-reck-se-ong, *f* management; manager's office; steering; direction.

dirigeable, de-re-shäh-bl, *m* dirigible; *a* manageable.

diriger, de-re-sheh, *v* to direct; to manage; to run; to guide; se –, to go (**vers, sur,** towards).

discerner, diss-air-neh, *v* to discern; to distinguish.

disciple, diss-ee-pl, *m* disciple; follower.

discipline, diss-e-pleen, *f* discipline.

discontinuer, diss-kongte-nE-eh, *v* to discontinue.

disconvenance, disskongv-nahngss, *f* unsuitableness; incongruity; disproportion.

discorde, diss-kord, *f* discord; disagreement.

discourir, diss-koo-reer, *v* to converse.

discours, diss-koohr, *m* conversation; speech; lecture; talk.

discourtois, e, * disskoohr-to'äh, *a* discourteous.

discrédit, diss-kreh-de, *m* discredit; disrepute.

discréditer, diss-kreh-deteh, *v* to discredit.

discr-et, ète, * diss-kray, *a* discreet; quiet.

discrétion, diss-kreh-seong, *f* discretion.

disculper, diss-kEEl-peh, *v* to exonerate.

discussion, diss-kEEsse-ong, *f* discussion; debate; dispute.

discuter, diss-kE-teh, *v* to discuss; to debate.

disert, e, de-zair, *a* fluent; eloquent.

disette, de-zett, *f* dearth; scarcity.

disgrâce, diss-grahss, *f* disgrace; misfortune.

disgracié, e, diss-grähss-eeh, *pp & a* unfortunate; out of favor.

disgracier, diss-grähss-eeh, *v* to put out of favor.

disgracieu-x, se, * dissgrähss-e-er, *a* ungraceful.

disjoindre, diss-sho-angdr, *v* to disjoint; to separate.

disloquer, diss-lock-eh, *v* to dislocate.

disparaître, diss-päh-raytr, *v* to disappear.

disparate, diss-päh-räht, *f* incongruity; *a* incongruous; dissimilar.

disparition, diss-päh-rese-ong, *f* disappearance.

disparu, e, diss-päh-rE, *pp & a* disappeared; missing.

dispensaire, diss-pahngsair, *m* clinic; outpatients' department (of hospital).

dispense, diss-pahngss, *f* dispensation; exemption; license.

disperser, diss-pair-seh, *v* to scatter; to disperse.

disponibilité, diss-ponn-ebe-le-teh, *f* availability; *pl* funds available.

disponible, diss-ponn-eebl, *a* disposable; available; disengaged.

dispos, diss-poh, *a* active; nimble; lively.

disposé, e, diss-poz-eh, *pp & a* disposed; inclined; willing.

disposer, diss-poz-eh, *v* to dispose; to have at command; to induce.

dispositif, diss-poz-e-tiff, *m* purview (law); contrivance (technology); apparatus.

disposition, diss-poz-e-seong, *f* arrangement; frame of mind; tendency; aptitude.

disproportionné e, dissprop-or-se-onn-eh, *a* disproportionate.

dispute, diss-pEEt, *f* dispute; quarrel.

disputer, diss-pE-teh, *v* to dispute; se –, to quarrel;

to vie.

disque, deesk, *m* disk; record.

dissemblable, diss-sahng-blãh-bl, *a* dissimilar.

dissension, diss-sahng-se-ong, *f* dissension.

dissentiment, diss-sahng-te-mahng, *m* dissent.

disséquer, diss-seh-keh, *v* to dissect.

dissertation, de-sair-tãh-se-ong, *f* dissertation; essay.

dissident, diss-se-dahng, *m* dissenter.

dissimulé, e, diss-se-mE-leh, *pp* & *a* dissembled; dissembling; deceptive.

dissimuler, diss-se-mE-leh, *v* to dissimulate; to conceal; to pretend ignorance of.

dissiper, diss-se-peh, *v* to dissipate; to waste; to dispel; **se** –, to vanish; to misbehave (at school).

dissolu, e, diss-soll-E, *a* dissolute.

dissoluble, diss-soll-EE-bl, *a* dissolvable; soluble.

dissolvant, diss-soll-vahng, *m* & *a* solvent; nail-polish remover.

dissoudre, diss-soo-dr, *v* to dissolve.

dissuader, diss-sE-ãh-deh,

v to dissuade.

distance, diss-tahngss, *f* distance.

distancer, diss-tahngss-eh, *v* to distance.

distant, e, diss-tahng, *a* distant; remote.

distendre, diss-tahng-dr, *v* to distend.

distillerie, diss-till-ree, *f* distillery.

distinct, e,* diss-tang-kt, *a* distinct.

distinction, diss-tangk-se-ong, *f* distinction; refinement.

distingué, e, diss-tang-gheh, *a* distinguished; refined.

distinguer, diss-tang-gheh, *v* to distinguish; to perceive.

distraction, diss-trãhck-se-ong, *n* inattention; absence of mind; absentmindedness; amusement.

distraire, diss-trayr, *v* to distract; to separate; to amuse.

distrait, e,* diss-tray, *a* inattentive; absentminded; scatterbrained.

distribuer, diss-tre-bE-eh, *v* to distribute.

distributeur, diss-tre-bE-ter, *m* deliverer;

distributor; –**automatique,** – oh-tomm-ãh-teeck –, vending machine.

distributeur automatique de billets, diss-tre-bE-ter-oh-toh-mãh-teeck-der-bee-yay, *m* automatic teller machine.

distribution, diss-tre-bE-se-ong, *f* distribution; delivery; handling.

dit, dee, *m* saying.

dit, e, dee, *pp* & *a* told; agreed; alias; **autrement** –, oh-trer-mahng–, in other words.

dito, de-to, *adv* ditto.

divaguer, de-vãh-gheh, *v* to wander; to ramble.

divan, de-vahng, *m* divan; sofa; couch.

diverger, de-vair-sheh, *v* to diverge.

divers, de-vair, *mpl* sundries.

divers, e, de-vair, *a* different; various; several; varied.

divertir, de-vair-teer, *v* to amuse; to divert.

divertissant, e, de-vair-tiss-ahng, *a* entertaining.

divertissement, de-vair-tiss-mahng, *m* amusement; entertainment.

dividende, de-ve-dahng d, *m* dividend.

divin, e,* de-vang, *a* divine; heavenly; exquisite.

diviniser, de-ve-ne-zeh, *v* to deify.

diviser, de-ve-zeh, *v* to divide.

divisionnaire, de-ve-ze-onn-air, *a* divisional; of a division.

divorce, de-vorss, *m* divorce; separation.

divulguer, de-vEEl-gheh, *v* to divulge.

dix, deess, (before a consonant, dee), *m & a* ten; tenth.

dixième, de-ze-aym, *m & a* tenth.

dizaine, de-zain, *f* ten; about ten.

do, do, *m* the note C.

docile,* doss-eell, *a* docile; tractable.

docteur, dock-ter, *m* doctor.

doctorat, dock-tor-ăh, *m* doctorate.

doctrine, dock-treen, *f* doctrine.

document, dock-E-mahng, *m* document.

documentaire, dock-E-mahng-tair, *m & a* documentary.

documenter, dock-E-mahng-teh, *v* to document.

dodo, dod-o, *m* sleep (in baby talk); **aller faire –,** ăh-leh-fair–, to go to bye bye.

dodu, e, dod-E, *a* plump.

dogmatiser, dog-măh-te-zeh, *v* to dogmatize.

dogme, dogm, *m* dogma.

dogue, dog, *m* large watchdog.

doigt, do'ăh, *m* finger; **à deux –s de,** ăh der – der, within an inch of.

doigter, doigté, do'ăh-teh, *m* fingering; tact.

doit, do'ăh, *m* debit.

doléance, doll-eh-ahngss, *f* complaint; grievance.

dolent, e, doll-ahng, *a* doleful; painful.

domaine, domm-ain, *m* domain; estate; property; (*fam*) province; sphere.

dôme, dohm, *m* dome; canopy.

domesticité, domm-ess-te-se-teh, *f* servants; domesticity.

domestique, domm-ess-teeck, *mf & a* servant; domestic; private; tame.

domicile, domm-e-seell, *m* domicile; residence; home.

domicilié, e, domm-e-se-

le-eh, *pp & a* domiciled; resident.

dominant, e, domm-e-nahng, *a* dominant; ruling; prevailing.

dominer, domm-e-neh, *v* to rule; to domineer; to govern; to overlook.

dominical, e, domm-e-ne-kăhl, *a* a dominical **oraison –e,** or-ay-zong –, the Lord's Prayer.

dommage, domm-ăhsh, *m* damage; loss; **c'est – say –,** it is a pity.

dompter, dong-teh, *v* to tame; to subdue.

dompteu-r, se, dong-ter, *mf* trainer (of animals).

don, dong, *m* gift; present; talent.

dona-teur, trice, donn-ăh-ter, *mf* donor.

donc, dong (and dongk at the beginning of a sentence and before a vowel), *conj* then; therefore.

donjon, dong- shong, *m* dungeon; keep; turret.

donne, donn, *f* deal (cards).

donnée, donn-eh, *f* notion; *pl* data.

donner, donn-eh, *v* to give; to strike; to look; to shine; to yield (of trees, etc); to deal; to

charge; **s'en –**, sahng –;
to enjoy oneself.

dont, dong, *pron* whose; of
whom; from whom; by
whom; of which; with
whom or which.

doré, e, dor-eh, *pp* & *a*
gilded; gilt; golden.

dorénavant, dor-eh-näh-
vahng, *adv* henceforth.

dorer, dor-eh, *v* to gild; to
glaze (pastry).

dorloter, dor-lot-eh, *v* to
coddle; to pamper.

dormant, e, dor-mahng, *a*
sleeping; dormant; dull.

dormeur, dor-mer, *m*
sleeper.

dormir, dor-meer, *v* to
sleep; to be dormant.

dorsal, e, dor-sähl, *a*
dorsal.

dortoir, dor-to'ăhr, *m*
dormitory.

dorure, dor-EEr, *f* gilding;
glaze (of pastry).

dos, doh, *m* back.

dosage, doh-zăhsh, *m*
dosage.

dose, dohz, *f* dose.

doser, doh-zeh, *v* to dose.

dossier, doh-se-eh,, *m*
back (of chair, etc)
brief; file of notes,
dossier.

dot, dott, *f* dowry;
marriage settlement.

dotal, e, dot-ăhl, *a* of the

dowry.

doter, dot-eh, *v* to endow
(**de,** with).

douairière, doo-ay-re-air,
f & *a* dowager.

douane, doo-ăhn, *f*
customs.

douanier, doo-ăh-ne-eh,
m customs officer.

doublage, doo-blăhsh, *m*
doubling; dubbing
(film).

double,* doo-bl, *a* double;
m duplicate; replica;
double.

doubler, doo-bleh, *v* to
double; to line (**de,**
with); to dub (film); to
understudy; to pass (on
road).

doublure, doo-blEEr, *f*
lining; substitute.

douceâtre, dooss-ah-tr, *a*
sweetish.

douceur, dooss-er, *f*
sweetness; softness;
charm; gentleness; *pl*
sweets; pleasant things.

douche, doosh, *f* shower.

doué, doo-eh, *a* gifted.

douer, doo-eh, *v* to endow
(with qualities).

douille, doo-ye, *f* socket
(electricity).

douillet, te,* doo'e-yay, *a*
delicate; tender.

douleur, doo-ler, *f* pain;
grief; sorrow.

douloureu-x, se,* doo-
loo-rer, *a* painful;
mournful; grievous.

doute, doot, *m* doubt.

douter, doo-teh, *v* to
doubt; **se –**, to suspect;
to have some notion (**de**
or **que,** of or that).

douteu-x, se,* doo-ter, *a*
doubtful; questionable.

douve, doov, *f* trench;
moat; open ditch.

dou-x, ce,* doo, dooss, *a*
sweet; soft; kind; gentle;
smooth; mild.

douzaine, doo-zain, *f*
dozen.

douze, dooz, *a* twelve;
twelfth (the).

douzième, doo-ze-aym, *mf*
& *a* twelfth.

doyen, do'ah-yang, *m*
dean; senior; elder.

dragée, drăh-sheh, *f*
sugared almond; sugar-
coated pill.

dragon, drăh-gong, *m*
dragon; termagant;
dragoon.

draguer, drăh-gheh, *v* to
dredge.

drainer, dray-neh, *v* to
drain.

dramaturge, drăh-măh-
tEEsh, *mf* dramatist;
playwright.

drame, drăhm, *m* drama;
(*fam*) catastrophe.

drap, drăh, *m* cloth; sheet.

drapeau, drăh-poh, *m* flag; colors; **sous les – x,** soo lay –, in the army.

draper, drăh-peh, *v* to cover with cloth; **se–,** to drape; to wrap oneself up.

draperie, drăhp-ree, *f* drapery; cloth manufacturer.

drapier, drăh-pe-eh, *m* draper; clothier.

dressage, dress-ăhsh, *m* training.

dresser, dress-eh, *v* to erect; to pitch; to lay out; to train; **se –,** to stand up.

dressoir, dress-o'ăhr, *m* sideboard; dresser.

drogue, drog, *f* drug; (*fam*) garbage.

droguer, drogh-eh, *v* to drug; **se –,** to take drugs.

droguiste, drogh-eesst, *m* druggist; retailer in chemicals.

droit, dro'ăh, *m* right; authority; law; title;duuty; tax; franchise; **faire son –,** fair *song –,* to study law; **qui de –,** ke der –, those whom it may concern.

droit, e, dro'ăh, *adv* straight; directly; **tout –,** too –, straight on. *a*

straight; right; erect; straightforward; righteous.

droite, dro'ăht, *f* right hand; right side.

droiture, dro'ăh-tEEr, *f* straightforwardness.

drôle, drohl, *m* rogue; scamp. *a* * funny; queer.

dru, e, drE, *adv* thick; hard. *a* fledged; dense; close; thick.

du, dE, contraction of **de le.**

dû, dE, *pp & a* owed; been obliged.

duc, dEEk, *m* duke.

duché, dE-sheh, *m* dukedom; duchy.

duchesse, dE-shess, *f* duchess.

duel, dE-ell, *m* duel.

dûment, dE-mahng, *adv* duly.

dune, dEEn, *f* dune.

d'une nuit, dEn-nwee *a,* *stay* overnight stay.

duo, dE-o, *m* duet.

dupe, dEEp, *f* dupe.

duper, dE-peh, *v* to dupe.

duperie, dEp-ree, *f* trickery.

duplicata, dE-ple-kăh-tăh, *m* duplicate.

duplicité, dE-ple-se-teh, *f* duplicity; double-dealing.

duquel, dE-kell, *pron*

contraction of **de lequel;** whose; from whom; of which; from which.

dur, dEEr, *m* hardness; (*fam*) tough guy.

dur, e, * dEEr, *a* hard; harsh; rough; stiff.

durable, dE-răh-bl, *a* lasting.

durant, dE-rahng, *prep* during.

durcir, dEEr-seer, *v* to harden; to set.

durcissement, dEEr-siss-mahng, *m* hardening.

durée, dE-reh, *f* duration.

durer, dEE-reh, *v* to last; to hold out.

dureté, dEEr-teh, *f* hardness; harshness.

duvet, dE-vay, *m* down.

dynamite, de-năh-meet, *f* dynamite.

E

eau, oh, *f* water; rain; **–de vie,** –der vee, spirit; brandy.

ébahir (s'), seh-băh-eer, *v* to be amazed (**de,** at).

ébats, eh-băh, *mpl* frolics.

ébattre (s'), seh-băh-tr, *v* to frolic.

ébauche, eh-bohsh, *f* sketch; outline.

ébaucher, eh-boh-sheh, *v* to sketch; to roughcast.

ébène, eh-bain, *f* ebony.

ébéniste, eh-beh-neesst, *m* cabinetmaker.

éblouir, eh-bloo-eer, *v* to dazzle.

éblouissement, eh-bloo-iss-mahng, *m* dazzling; dizziness.

éboulement, eh-bool-mahng, *m* falling rocks; crumbling.

ébouriffé, e, eh-boo-re-feh, *a* disheveled; tousled (hair); flurried.

ébranlement, eh-brahngl-mahng, *m* shaking; commotion.

ébranler, eh-brahng-leh, *v* to shake; to disturb; to put in motion; s' –, to totter; to begin to move.

ébrécher, eh-breh-sheh, *v* to notch; to indent; to chip.

ébruiter, eh-brwe-teh, *v* to divulge; s' –, to become known.

ébullition, eh-bE-le-se-ong, *f* boiling.

écaille, eh-kah'e, *f* scale; tortoiseshell.

écailler, eh-kah'e-eh, *v* to scale; to open (of shellfish).

écarlate, eh-kăhr-lăht, *a* & *f* scarlet.

écarquiller, eh-kăhr-kee-yeh, *v* to open wide (eyes); to straddle.

écart, eh-kăhr, *m* step aside; separation; digression; discrepancy; error, *m adv phr* à l'–, ah l'–, aside.

écarté, eh-kăhr-teh, *a* remote; lonely.

écartement, eh-kăhr-ter-mahng, spacing; putting aside.

écarter, eh-kăhr-teh, *v* to separate; to keep off; s'–, to deviate; to move aside.

ecclésiastique, eh-kleh-ze-ăhss-teeck, *m* clergyman. *a* ecclesiastical.

écervelé, e, eh-sair-ver-leh, *a* harebrained.

échafaud, eh-shăh-foh, *m* scaffolding; stage; scaffold.

échafaudage, eh-shăh-foh-dăhsh, *m* scaffolding; building up.

échafauder, eh-shăh-foh-deh, *v* to erect scaffolding; to pile up.

échalote, eh-shăh-lot, *f* shallot.

échancrer, eh-shahng-kreh, *v* to indent; to

hollow out.

échange, eh-shahngsh, *m* exchange; barter; **libre –** lee-br z'–, free trade.

échanger, eh-sahng-sheh, *v* to exchange.

échantillon, eh-shahng-tee-yong, *m* sample; pattern.

échappatoire, eh-shăh-pah-to'ăhr, *f* evasion; loophole.

échappée, eh-shăh-peh, *f* escapade; vista.

échappement, eh-shăhp-mahng, *m* escape; leakage; exhaust.

échapper, eh-shăh-peh, *v* to escape; to avoid; to slip; **s'–,** to steal away.

écharde, eh-shahrd, *f* splinter.

écharpe, eh-shăhrp, *f* scarf; sling; sash; **en –** ahng n'–, slanting.

écharper, eh-shăhr-peh, *v* to cut to pieces.

échasse, eh-shăhss, *f* stilt.

échassier, eh-shăhss-e-eh, *m* wading bird.

échauder, eh-shoh-deh, *v* to scald.

échauffement, eh-shohf-mahng, *m* heating; over-heating; overexcitement.

échauffer, eh-shoh-feh, *v* to heat; to overheat; to excite.

échauffourée, eh-shoh-foo-reh, *f* skirmish; fray.

échéance, eh-sheh-ahngss, *f* falling due; expiration; maturity.

échéant, eh-sheh-ahng, *pp* falling due; occurring; **le cas –,** ler kah z'–, should it so happen.

échec, eh-shayk, *m* check; failure; blow; *pl* chess; chessmen.

échelle, eh-shell, *f* ladder; steps; scale.

échelon, ehsh-long, *m* rung; step; degree.

échelonner, ehsh-lonn-eh, *v* to stagger; to arrange by degrees; to space out.

écheveau, ehsh-voh, *m* hank; skein.

échevelé, e, eh-sherv-leh, *a* disheveled.

échine, eh-sheen, *f* spine; backbone.

échiner, eh-she-neh, *v* to work to death.

échiquier, eh-she-ke-eh, *m* chessboard.

écho, eh-ko, *m* echo.

échoir, eh-sho'ăhr, *v* to fall due; to fall to the lot of.

échoppe, eh-shop, *f* stall.

échouer, eh-shoo-eh, *v* to run aground; to fail.

échu, e, eh-shE, *pp* fallen

due; outstanding.

éclabousser, eh-klăh-booss-eh, *v* to splash.

éclair, eh-klayr, *m* lightning; flash; éclair.

éclairage, eh-klay-răhsh, *m* lighting; illumination.

éclaircie, eh-klayr-see, *f* clearing; glade opening.

éclaircir, eh-klayr-seer, *v* to clear up; to elucidate.

éclairer, eh-klay-reh, *v* to light; to enlighten.

éclaireur, eh-klay-rer, *m* scout.

éclat, eh-klăh, *m* splinter; explosion; clap; splendor; uproar; scandal.

éclatant, e, eh-klăh-tahng, *a* bright; brilliant; resounding; flagrant; loud.

éclater, eh-klăh-teh, *v* to burst; to explode; to shine; **– de rire,** d-reer, to burst out laughing.

éclisse, eh-kleess, *f* wedge; splint.

éclopé, e, eh-klop-eh, *a* lame; cripple.

éclore, eh-klor, *v* to hatch; to dawn; to open.

éclosion, eh-kloh-ze-ong, *f* hatching; opening.

écluse, eh-klEEz, *f* lock.

écœurer, eh-ker-reh, *v* to sicken.

école, eh-kol, *f* school.

écoli-er, ère, eh-koll-e-eh, *mf* schoolboy; schoolgirl.

éconduire, eh-kong-dweer, *v* to get rid of; to deny.

économat, eh-konn-omm-ăh, *m* treasureship; bursar's office.

économe, eh-konn-omm, *m* steward; bursar; *a* economical; saving.

économie, eh-konn-omm-ee, *f* economy; saving; *pl* savings.

économique,* eh-konn-omm-eeck, *a* economic(al).

économiser, eh-konn-omm-e-zeh, *v* to economize; to save.

économiste, eh-konn-omm-eesst, *m* economist.

écorce, eh-korss, *f* bark; rind; peel; skin; outside.

écorcher, eh-kor-sheh, *v* to skin; to graze; to fleece.

écorchure, eh-kor-shEEr, *f* graze.

écosser, eh-koss-eh, *v* to shell; to hull.

écot, eh-ko, *m* share; quota; reckoning.

écoulement, eh-kool-mahng, *m* flow; drainage; turnover.

écouler, eh-koo-leh, *v* to flow out; to elapse; to sell off.

écoute, eh-koot, *f* listening place; wiretapping.

écouter, eh-koo-teh, *v* to listen; to pay attention to.

écouteu-r, se, eh-koo-ter, *mf* listener; *m* receiver (telephone); earphone.

écran, eh-krahng, *m* screen; smokescreen.

écrasant, e, eh-kräh-zahng, *a* crushing; overwhelming.

écraser, eh-kräh-zeh, *v* to crush; to overwhelm; to run over.

écrémer, eh-kreh-meh, *v* to skim.

écrevisse, eh-krer-veess, *f* crayfish.

écrier (s'), seh-kre-eh, *v* to exclaim.

écrin, eh-krang, *m* box; case; casket.

écrire, eh-kreer, *v* to write.

écriteau, eh-kre-toh, *m* board.

écriture, eh-kre-tEEr, *f* writing; handwriting; scripture; *pl* accounts.

écrivain, eh-kre-vang, *m* writer; author.

écrou, eh-kroo, *m* screwnut.

écrouer, eh-kroo-eh, *v* to put in jail.

écroulement, eh-krool-mahng, *m* falling down; collapse; ruin.

écrouler (s'), seh-kroo-leh, *v* to fall down; to collapse.

écru, e, eh-krE, *a* unbleached; raw.

écueil, eh-ker'e, *m* rock; reef; stumbling block.

écuelle, eh-kE-ell, *f* bowl.

écume, eh-kEEm, *f* foam; froth; scum.

écumer, eh-kE-meh, *v* to skim; to foam.

écureuil, eh-kE-rer'e, *m* squirrel.

écurie, eh-kE-ree, *f* stable; stud.

écusson, eh-kEEss-ong, *m* coat of arms.

écuyer, eh-kwee-yeh, *m* squire; riding master; rider.

édenté, e, eh-dahng-teh, *a* toothless.

édicter, eh-dick-teh, *v* to decree; to exact.

édification, eh-de-fe-kăh-se-ong, *f* edification; building.

édifice, eh-de-feess, *m* building; structure.

édifier, eh-de-fe-eh, *v* to

edify; to erect; to enlighten.

édit, eh-de, m edict; decree.

éditer, eh-de-teh, v to publish; to edit.

éditeur, eh-de-ter, m publisher.

édition, eh-de-se-ong, f edition; publishing.

édredon, eh-drer-dong, m eiderdown.

éducation, eh-dE-kăh-se-ong, f education; breeding; training.

éduquer, eh-dE-keh, v to educate; to bring up.

effacer, eh-făhss-eh, v to efface; to rub out; to wipe out; to eclipse.

effaré, e, eh-făh-reh, pp & a scared.

effaroucher, eh-făh-roo-sheh, v to scare away; **s'–,** to take fright at.

effectif, eh-fehck-teeff, m strength; size; number of.

effecti-f, ve, eh-fehck-teeff, a effective; actual.

effectivement, eh-fehck-teev-mahng, adv effectively; actually; that is so.

effectuer, eh-fehck-tE-eh, v to effect; to carry out.

efféminé, e, eh-feh-me-neh, a effeminate.

effervescence, eh-fair-vayss-ahngss, f effervescence; excitement.

effet, eh-fay, m effect; impression; bill; pl goods; effects; bills.

effeuiller, eh-fer'e-yeh, v to strip off leaves or petals.

efficace,* eh-fe-kăhss, a efficacious; effective.

effilé, e, eh-fe-leh, a slender; slim; sharp; frayed.

efflanqué, e, eh-flahng-keh, a lean; thin; lank.

effleurer, eh-fler-reh, v to skim; to touch slightly; to glance over.

effluve, eh-flEEv, m effluvium; smell.

effondrement, eh-fong-drer-mahng, m falling down; collapse.

effondrer (s'), seh-fong-dreh, v to fall down; to collapse.

efforcer (s'), seh-for-seh, v to strive; to endeavor.

effort, eh-for, m effort; endeavor; strain; exertion.

effrayant, e, eh-fray-yahng, a dreadful; frightful; (fam) awful.

effrayer, eh-fray-yeh, v to frighten.

effréné, e, eh-freh-neh, a unbridled; unrestrained.

effriter (s'), seh-fre-teh, v to crumble away.

effroi, eh-fro'ăh, m fright; terror.

effronté, e, eh-frong-teh, a impudent.

effrontément, eh-frong-teh-mahng, adv impudently.

effronterie, eh-frongt-ree, f impudence; insolence.

effroyable,* eh-fro'ăh-yăh-bl, a frightful; (fam) tremendous.

effusion, eh-fE-ze-ong, f effusion; overflowing; shedding.

égal, e, eh-găhl, a equal; even; like; same; level; **cela m'est –,** slăh may t' –, it is all the same to me.

également, eh-găhl-mahng, adv equally; alike; both; likewise; also.

égaler, eh-găh-leh, v to equal; to match.

égaliser, eh-găh-le-zeh, v to equalize; to level; to smooth.

égalitaire, eh-găh-le-tair, a leveling.

égalité, eh-găh-le-teh, f evenness; equality; uniformity; deuce (in tennis).

égard, eh-găhr, *m* regard; respect; consideration.

égaré, e, eh-găh-reh, *a* stray; bewildered; out of the way; erring.

égarement, eh-găhr-mahng, *m* distraction; misconduct; wandering.

égarer, eh-găh-reh, *v* to mislead; to mislay; to bewilder; **s'–,** to lose one's way.

égayer, eh-gay-yeh, *v* to enliven; to cheer up.

églantine, eh-glahng-teen, *f* sweetbriar; dog rose.

église, eh-gleez, *f* church.

egoïsme, eh-go-issm, *m* selfishness.

égoïste, eh-go-isst, *m* selfish person; egoist. *a* selfish.

égorger, eh-gor-sheh, *v* to cut the throat of; to kill.

égosiller (s'), seh-goz-ee-yeh, *v* to make oneself hoarse.

égout, eh-ghoo, *m* drain; sewer; drip.

égoutter, eh-ghoot-eh, *v* to drain; to drip.

égratigner, eh-grăh-teen-yeh, *v* to scratch.

égrener, eh-grer-neh, *v* to pick.

éjaculer, eh-shah-kEE-leh, *v* to ejaculate.

éjecter, eh-sheck-teh, *v* to eject.

élaborer, eh-lăh-bor-eh, *v* to elaborate; to work out.

élaguer, eh-lăh-gheh, *v* to lop; to prune.

élan, eh-lahng, *m* spring; start; dash; impetus.

élancé, e, eh-lahngss-eh, *a* slender; slim.

élancer, eh-lahngss-eh, *v* to dart; **s'–,** to rush.

élargir, eh-lăhr-sheer, *v* to widen; to extend; to release.

élastique, eh-lăhss-teeck, *a* & *m* elastic; springy.

électeur, eh-leck-ter, *m* elector.

élection, eh-leck-se-ong, *f* election; polling.

électricien, eh-leck-tre-se-ang, *m* electrician.

électricité, eh-leck-tre-se-teh, *f* electricity.

électriser, eh-leck-tre-zeh, *v* to electrify.

électrophone, eh-leck-tro-fon, *m* record player.

élégamment, eh-leh-găh-mahng, *adv* elegantly.

élégance, eh-leh-gahngss, *f* elegance.

élégie, eh-leh-shee, *f* elegy.

élément, eh-leh-mahng, *m* element; unit (of

furniture).

élémentaire, eh-leh-mahng-tair, *a* elementary; rudimentary.

éléphant, h-leh-fahng, *m* elephant.

élevage, ehl-văhsh, *m* breeding; animal husbandry.

élévation, eh-leh-văh-se-ong, *f* elevation; raising; rise.

élève eh-layv, *mf* pupil; scholar; student; *f* breeding (of cattle).

élevé, e, ehl-veh, *pp* & *a* raised; lofty; brought up; bred.

élever, ehl-veh, *v* to raise; to build; to extol; to bring up; **s' –,** to rise; to amount.

élider, eh-le-deh, *v* to omit; to cut off.

éliminer, eh-le-me-neh, *v* to eliminate; to get rid of.

élire, eh-leer, *v* to elect; to choose.

élision, eh-le-ze-ong, *f* omission.

élite, eh-leet, *f* pick; elite.

elle, ell, *pron* she; her; it; **elles,** they; them.

ellipse, eh-lips, *f* ellipsis; ellipse.

éloge, eh-losh, *m* praise;

commendation.

élogieu-x, se,* eh-losh-er-er, *a* eulogistic.

éloigné, e, eh-lo'ăhn-yeh, *a* removed; distant; out of the way; disinclined.

éloignement, eh-lo'ăhn-yer-mahng, *m* distance; absence; aversion.

éloigner, eh-lo'ăhn-yeh, *v* to remove; to keep away; to delay; to estrange.

éloquemment, en-lock-ăh-mahng, *adv* eloquently.

éloquence, eh-lock-ahngss, *f* eloquence.

élu, e, eh-lE, *pp* & *a* elected.

éluder, eh lE deh, *v* to elude; to evade.

émail, eh-mah'e, *m* enamel; glaze; *pl* **émaux,** ehmoh.

émaner, eh-măh-neh, *v* to emanate.

émarger, eh-măhr-sheh, *v* to annotate; to draw a salary.

emballage, ah-ng-băh-lăhsh, *m* packing; wrapping.

emballer, ahng-băh-leh, *v* to pack; to pack up; to wrap; **s'–,** to bolt; (*fam*) to get carried away (excitement, anger, etc).

embarcadère, ahng-băhr-kăh-dair, *m* pier; departure platform.

embarcation, ahng-băhr-kăh se-ong, *f* small boat; craft.

embarquer, ahng-băhr-keh, *v* to embark; to ship; to board (a plane).

embarras, ahng-băh-răh, *m* encumbrance; difficulty; perplexity; embarrassment; fuss.

embarrassant, ahng-băh-răhss-ahng, *a* cumbersome; awkward; embarrassing.

embarrasser, ahng-băh-răhss-eh, *v* to encumber; to perplex; to embarrass.

embaucher, ahng-boh-sheh, *v* to hire; to engage; to enlist; to entice away.

embaumer, ahng-boh-meh, *v* to perfume; to embalm.

embellir, ahng-bay-leer, *v* to embellish; to improve (in looks).

embêtant, e, ahng-bay-tahng *a* (*fam*) annoying; bothering.

embêter, ahng-bay-teh, *v* (*fam*) to bother; to bore; **s'–,** to be bored.

embêtement, ahng-bayt-mahng, *m* bother;

trouble.

emblée (d'), dahng-bleh, *adv* at the first attempt.

emblème, ahng-blaym, *m* emblem; badge.

emboîter, ahng-bo'ah-teh, *v* to encase; to interlock.

embolie, ahng-bo-le, *f* embolism; blood clot.

embonpoint, ahng-bong-po'ang, *m* plumpness.

embouchure, ahng-boo-shEEr, *f* mouth; mouthpiece.

embourber (s'), sahng-boohr-beh, *v* to get stuck in the mud; (*fam*) to become involved in trouble.

embouteillage, ahng-boo-tay-yăhsh, *m* bottling; traffic congestion.

embranchement, ahng-brahngsh-mahng, *m* branching-fork (classification); junction; branch-line.

embrancher (s'), sahng-brahng-sheh, *v* to branch off.

embrasé, e, ahng-brăh-zeh, *pp* & *a* in flames; burning.

embraser, ahng-brăh-zeh, *v* to set on fire; to kindle.

embrasser, ahng-brăhss-ɛh, *v* to embrace; to kiss.

embrasure, ahng-brăh-zEEr, *f* door-frame; window frame; opening.

embrayage, ahng-bray-yash, *m* clutch.

embrayer, ahng-bray-yeh, *v* to engage the clutch.

embrouillé, e, ahng-broo'e-yeh, *pp* & *a* entangled; intricate.

embrouiller, ahng-broo'e-yeh, *v* to tangle; to confuse.

embrumé, e, ahng-brEmeh *a* foggy; misty.

embryon, ahng-bree-yong, *m* embryo.

embûche, ahng-bEEsh, *f* snare; trap.

embuscade, ahng-bEsskăhd, *f* ambush.

émeraude, ehm-rohd, *f* emerald.

émeri, ehm-re, *m* emery.

émerveiller, ehm-mairvay'e-yeh, *v* to astonish; to fill with wonder.

émétique, eh-meh-teeck, *m* emetic.

émet-teur, trice, *m* transmitter. *a* transmitting; broadcasting.

émettre, eh-met-tr, *v* to issue; to express; to broadcast.

émeute, eh-mert, *f* riot; disturbance; outbreak.

émietter, eh-me-ayt-eh, *v* to crumble.

émigrer, eh-me-greh, *v* to emigrate.

émincé, eh-mang-seh, *m* thin slices of meat.

éminemment, eh-me-năhmahng, *adv* eminently.

éminence, eh-me-nahngss, *f* eminence.

émissaire, eh-miss-air, *m* emissary.

émission, eh-miss-e-ong, *f* issue; uttering; transmission; program (radio).

emmagasiner, ahng-măhgăh-ze-neh, *v* to store.

emmancher, ahng-mahngsheh, *v* to put a handle on; to haft; to begin; **s'–,** to fit together.

emmêler, ahng-may-leh, *v* to entangle.

emménager, ahng-mehnăh-sheh, *v* to move in.

emmener, ahngm-neh, *v* to take away; to lead away.

emmitoufler, ahng-metoo-fleh, *v* to wrap up.

émoi, eh-mo'ăh, *m* agitation; anxiety; flurry; emotion.

émolument, eh-moll-Emahng, *m* emolument; gain; profit; *pl* salary; fees.

émotion, eh-mohss-e-ong, *f* emotion.

émousser, eh-mooss-eh, *v* to blunt; to dull.

émouvant, e, eh-moo-vahng, *a* touching; stirring.

émouvoir, eh-moo-vo'ăhr, *v* to move; to stir up; to rouse; to affect.

empailler, ahng-pah'e-yeh, *v* to pack in straw; to stuff (animals).

empaqueter, ahng-păhckteh, *v* to pack up.

emparer (s'), sahng-păhreh, *v* to take possession.

empêché, e, ahng-paysheh, *pp* & *a* prevented; embarrassed; in a difficulty.

empêchement, ahngpaysh-mahng, *m* impediment; hindrance; obstacle.

empêcher, ahng-pay-sheh, *v* to prevent; to hinder; to keep from.

empereur, ahngp-rer, *m* emperor.

empeser, ahng-per-zeh, *v* to starch.

empester, ahng-pess-teh, *v* to infect; to stink.

empêtrer, ahng-pay-treh, *v* to entangle.

emphase, ahng-fahz, *f* emphasis; bombast;

pomposity.

emphatique,* ahng-fãh-teeck, *a* emphatic; bombastic.

empierrer, ahng-pe-ay-reh, *v* to gravel; to pave.

empiéter, ahng-pe-eh-teh, *v* to encroach; to trespass.

empiler, ahng-pe-leh, *v* to pile up; to stack.

empire, ahng-peer, *m* empire; rule; control.

empirer, ahng-pe-reh, *v* to make worse; to get worse.

emplacement, ahng-plãhss-mahng, *m* site; place.

emplâtre, ahng-plah-tr, *m* plaster; helpless person.

emplette, ahng-plett, *f* purchase.

emplir, ahng-pleer, *v* to fill up (**de,** with).

emploi, ahng-plo'ãh, *m* employment; use; occupation; situation.

employé, e, ahng-plo'ãh-yeh, *m* employee; clerk.

employer, ahng-plo'ãh-yeh, *v* to employ; to use.

employeur, ahng-plo'ãh-yer, *m* employer.

empocher, ahng-posh-eh, *v* to pocket.

empoigner, ahng-po'ãhn-yeh, *v* to grasp; to arrest.

empois, ahng-po'ãh, *m* starch.

empoisonner, ahng-po'ãh-zonn-eh, *v* to poison; to infect; (*fam*) to annoy; to irritate.

emporté, e, ahng-por-teh, *a* quick-tempered.

emportement, ahng-por-ter-mahng, *m* transport; outburst; fit.

emporter, ahng-por-teh, *v* to carry away; **s'–,** to lose one's temper.

empourprer (s'), sahng-poohr-preh, *v* to flush; to turn red.

empreinte, ahng-prangt, *f* impress; mark; stamp; print; **–digitale,** – de-she-tãhl, fingerprint.

empressé, e, ahng-press-eh, *a* eager; assiduous; obliging.

empressement, ahng-press-mahng, *m* earnestness; assiduous attention.

empresser (s'), sahng-press-eh, *v* to hasten (**de,** to).

emprisonner, ahng-pre-zonn-eh, *v* to imprison.

emprunt, ahng-prung, *m* loan; borrowing.

emprunté, e, ahng-prung-teh, *pp & a* borrowed;

self-conscious.

emprunter, ahng-prung-teh, *v* to borrow.

ému, e, eh-mE, *pp & a* moved (by emotion).

émule, eh-mEEl, *m* rival; competitor.

en, ahng, *pron* some; any; of it; of them; of, from or about him, her, it; there. *prep* in; into; within; at; in the; like a; by; while.

en avoir marre (de), ahng-ãh-vo'ãhr-mãhr-der, *v* fed-up (with).

en boîte, ahng-bo'ãht *a* canned.

encadrer, ahng-kãh-dreh, *v* to frame; to encircle.

encaisse, ahng-kayss, *f* cash in hand; cash balance.

encaissé, ahng-kayss-eh, *a* embanked.

encaissement, ahng-kayss-mahng, *m* packing; payment; cashing; embankment.

encaisser, ahng-kayss-eh, *v* to pack; to collect; to receive; to embank.

en-cas, ahng-kah, *m* snack.

encastrer, ahng-kãhss-treh, *v* to fit in; to embed.

encaustique, ahng-kohs-

teeck, *f* wax polish;
furniture polish.

encaver, ahng-kăh-veh, *v*
to store in a cellar.

enceinte, ahng-sangt, *f*
enclosure; precincts. *a*
pregnant.

encens, ahng-sahng, *m*
incense; (*fam*) praise;
flattery.

encenser, ahng-sahngsss-
eh, *v* to flatter.

enchaînement, ahng-
shain-mahng, *m*
chaining up; train (of
events).

enchaîner, ahng-shay-neh,
v to chain up; to fetter;
to connect.

enchanté, ahng-shahng-
teh, *pp* & *a* enchanted;
spellbound; delighted.

enchantement, ahng-
shahngt-mahng, *m*
enchantment; spell;
delight.

enchanter, ahng-shahng-
teh, *v* to enchant; to
delight; to charm.

enchant-eur, eresse,
ahng-shahng-**ter**, *mf*
enchanter; *a*
bewitching; enchanting.

enchâsser, ahng-shahss-
eh, *v* to enshrine; to set.

enchère, ahng-shair, *f*
bidding; auction.

enchérir, ahng-sheh-reer,

v to outbid.

enchevêtrer, ahngsh-vay-
treh, *v* to entangle.

enclaver, ahng-klăh-veh, *v*
to enclose; to wedge in.

enclin, e, ahng-klang, *a*
inclined; prone.

enclore, ahng-klor, *v* to
enclose; to fence in.

enclos, ahng-kloh, *m*
enclosure; pen; paddock.

enclume, ahng-klEEm, *f*
anvil.

encoche, ahng-kosh, *f*
notch.

encoignure, ahng-konn-
yEEr, *f* corner; corner
cupboard.

encolure, ahng-koll-EEr, *f*
neckline.

encombrement, ahng-
kong-brer-mahng, *m*
obstruction; traffic jam.

encombrer, ahng-kong-
breh, *v* to encumber; to
obstruct; to crowd.

en conserve, ahng-kong-
sairv *a* canned.

encontre (à l'– de), ăh
lahng-kong-trer der, *prep*
against; contrary to.

encore, ahng-kor, *adv* still;
again; yet; **pas–,**păh z' –,
not yet.

encourager, ahng-koo-
răh-sheh, *v* to
encourage.

encourir, ahng-koo-reer, *v*

to incur.

encre, ahng-kr, *f* ink.

encrier, ahng-kre-eh, *m*
inkstand.

encroûté, e, ahng-kroo-
teh, *a* to be a stick in
the mud; to be stuck in
a rut.

encyclopédie, ahng-se-
klop-eh-dee, *f*
encyclopedia.

en désordre, ahng-deh-
zor-dr *a* messy.

endetter, ahng-day-teh, *v*
to get (a person) into
debt; s'–, to run into
debt.

endiablé, ahng-de-ăh-
bleh, *pp* & *a* furious;
wicked; reckless.

endiguer, ahng-de-gheh, *v*
to dam in; to bank up.

endimancher (s'), sahng-
de-mahng-sheh, *v* to put
on one's Sunday best.

endoctriner, ahng-dockt-
tre-neh, *v* to gain over.

endolori, e, ahng-doll-or-
e, *a* aching; tender.

endommager, ahng-
domm-ăh-sheh, *v* to
damage.

endormi, e, ahng-dor-me,
pp & *a* gone to sleep;
sleeping; sleepy;
sluggish; numb.

endormir, ahng-dor-meer,
v to put to sleep; to lull;

endos, endossement, ahng-doh, ahng-dohss-mahng, m endorsement.

endosser, ahng-dohss-eh, v to put on; to endorse.

endroit, ahng-dro'ăh, m place; spot; right side.

enduire, ahng-dweer, v to coat.

enduit, ahng-dwe, m coat; layer.

endurant, e, ahng-dE-rahng, a enduring; patient; tolerant.

endurcir, ahng-dEEr-seer, v to harden; to inure.

endurcissement, ahng-dEEr-siss-mahng, m hardening; toughness.

endurer, anhg-dEEr-eh, v to bear; to endure.

énergie, eh-nair-shee, f energy; force.

énergique,* eh-nair-sheeck; a energetic.

énergumène, eh-nair-ghE-main, m fanatic; frantic person.

énervant, eh-nair-vahng, a (fam) aggravating; irritating.

énerver, eh-nair-veh, v to get on one's nerves.

enfance, ahng-fahngss, f childhood; infancy.

(fam) to deceive; **s'–,** to fall asleep; to lie idle.

enfant, ahng-fahng, mf child; infant.

enfanter, ahng-fahng-teh, v to give birth to.

enfantillage, ahng-fahng-tee-yăhsh, m childishness.

enfantin, e, ahng-fahng-tang, a childish.

enfariner, ahng-făh-re-neh, v to flour.

enfer, ahng-fair, m hell.

enfermer, ahng-fair-meh, v to shut in; to lock up; to enclose.

enfilade, ahng-fe-lăhd, f row; line; long string.

enfiler, ahng-fe-leh, v to thread; to string; to run through.

enfin, ahng-fang, adv at last; finally; in short; on the whole; after all.

enflammer, ahng-flăh-meh, v to set on fire; to rouse.

enfler, ahng-fleh, v to swell; to inflate; to puff up.

enfoncé, ahng-fong-seh, pp & a smashed in; sunk; done for.

enfoncer, ahng-fong-seh, v to sink into; to drive in; to smash; to surpass.

enfouir, ahng-foo-eer, v to bury; to hide in the ground.

enfourcher, ahng-foohr-sheh, v to straddle; to mount; to get on.

enfreindre, ahng-frang-dr, v to infringe.

enfuir (s'), sahng-fweer, v to run away; to vanish; to leak.

enfumer, ang-fE-meh, v to smoke out.

engagement, ahng-gahsh-mahng m engagement; contract; agreement; commitment.

engager, ahng-găh-sheh, v to engage; to pawn; to invite; to hire; **s'–,** to enlist; to undertake.

engelure, ahngsh-lEEr, f frostbite.

engendrer, ahng-shahng-dreh, v to beget; to engender; to father.

engin, ahng-shang, m engine; machine; tackle.

englober, ahng-glob-eh, v to lump together; to unite.

engloutir, ahng-gloo-teer, v to swallow up; to engulf.

engloutissement, ahng-gloo-tiss-mahng, m swallowing up; sinking.

engorger, ahng-gor-sheh, v to obstruct; to block up.

engouement, ahng-goomahng, *m* infatuation.

engouffrer, ahng-goo-freh, *v* to wolf down; to cram in.

engourdi, e, ahng-goohr-de, *pp* & *a* numbed; dull; torpid.

engrais, ahng-gray, *m* manure.

engraisser, ahng-grayss-eh, *v* to fatten; to fertilize.

engrener, ahng-grer-neh, *v* to throw into gear.

engueuler, ahng-gher-leh, *v* (*fam*) to scold; to blow up; to abuse.

enhardir, ahng-ăhr-deer, *v* to embolden.

énigme, eh-neegm, *f* enigma; riddle.

enivrer, ahng-ne-vrehh, *v* to intoxicate; to enrapture; **s'–,** to get drunk.

enjamber, ahng-shahng-beh, *v* to stride over.

enjeu, ahng-sher, *m* stake.

enjoindre, ahng-sho'ang-dr, *v* to enjoin; to order.

enjôler, ahng-shoh-leh, *v* to wheedle.

enjoliver, ahng-sholl-e-veh, *v* to embellish.

enjoué, e, ahng-shoo-eh, *a* playful; lively; sprightly.

enlacer, ahng-lăhss-eh, *v* to lace; to entwine; to interweave; to clasp; to

embrace.

enlaidir, ahng-lay-deer, *v* to disfigure; to grow ugly.

enlèvement, ahng-layv-mahng, *m* carrying away; removal; kidnapping.

enlever, ahng-l-veh, *v* to lift; to take away; to run away with; to collect; to kidnap; **s'–,** to rise; to come off; to be sold.

ennemi, ain-me, *m* enemy.

ennemi, e, ain-me, *a* hostile; adverse.

ennoblir, ahng-nob-leer, *v* to ennoble.

ennui, ahng-nwe, *m* tediousness; boredom; annoyance.

ennuyer, ahng-nwee-yeh, *v* to worry; to tire; to annoy; to bore; **s'–,** to feel bored.

ennuyeux-x, se,* ahng-nwee-yer, *a* tiresome; annoying; vexing; bothering.

énoncer, eh-nong-seh, *v* to state; to articulate.

enorgueillir (s'), sahng-nor-gher-yeer, *v* to be proud.

énorme, eh-norm, *a* enormous; huge.

énormément, eh-nor-meh-mahng, *adv* enormously; (*fam*)

tremendously.

en phase terminale, ahng-fåhz-tair-me-nähl *a med* terminal illness.

en poudre, ahng-poo-dr, *a* dehydrated (milk, eggs, etc).

enquérir (s'), sahng-keh-reer, *v* to inquire.

enquête, ahng-kayt, *f* inquiry; inquest.

enraciner, ahng-răhss-e-neh, *v* to root.

enragé, e, ahng-răh-**sheh**, *a* mad; enraged; furious; desperate.

enrager, ahng-răh-sheh, *v* to be mad; to be in a rage; **faire –,** fair –, to drive mad.

enrayer, ahng-ray-yeh, *v* to stop; to jam; to check.

enregistrement, ahng-rer-shiss-trer-mahng, *m* registration; entry; recording (record, etc).

enregistrer, ahng-rer-shiss-treh, *v* to register; to record.

enrhumer (s'), sahng-rE-meh, *v* to catch a cold.

enrichi, e, ahng-re-she, *a* & *mf* upstart.

enrichir, ahng-re-sheer, *v* to enrich; to embellish.

enrôler, ahng-roh-leh, *v* to enroll; to enlist.

enroué, e, ahng-roo-eh, *a* hoarse.

enrouler, ahng-roo-leh, *v* to roll up.

ensanglanter, ahng-sahng-glahng-teh, *v* to stain with blood.

enseigne, ahng-sayn-yer, *m* ensign; midshipman; junior lieutenant; *f* neon sign; *pl* (flag) colors.

enseignement, ahng-sayn-yer-mahng, *m* teaching; instruction; tuition; education.

enseigner, ahng-sayn-yeh, *v* to teach; to inform; to direct.

ensemble, ahng-sahng-bl, *m* whole; ensemble; mass; general appearance; harmony; *adv* together; at the same time.

ensevelir, ahng-serv-leer, *v* to shroud; to bury.

ensoleillé, ahng-soll-ay-yeh, *a* sunny; sunlit.

ensorceler, ahng-sor-ser-leh, *v* to bewitch.

ensuite, ahng-sweet, *adv* afterwards; after; then; next.

ensuivre (s'), sahng-swee-vr, *v* to follow; to ensue.

entailler, ahng-tah'e-yeh, *v* to notch.

entamer, ahng-tăh-meh, *v*

to make the first cut in; to begin.

entasser, ahng-tăhss-eh, *v* to pile up; to stack.

entendement, ahng-tahngd-mahng *m* understanding; sense; judgment.

entendre, ahng-tahng-dr, *v* to hear; to understand; to mean; **bien entendu,** be-ang n'ahng-tahng-dE, of course.

entente, ahng-tahngt, *f* understanding; sense; meaning.

enterrement, ahng-tair-mahng, *m* burial; funeral.

enterrer, ahng-tay-reh, *v* to bury; (*fam*) to outlive.

en-tête, ahng-tayt, *m* heading.

entêté, e, ahng-tay-teh, *a* obstinate; stubborn.

entêter, ahng-tay-teh, *v* to make giddy; **s'–,** to be obstinate.

enthousiasme, ahng-too-ze-ăhssm, *m* enthusiasm.

entier, ahng-te-eh, *m* entirety; whole.

enti-er, ère,* ahng-te-eh, *a* whole; perfect; full.

entonner, ahng-tonn-eh, *v* to strike up.

entonnoir, ahng-tonn-

o'ăhr, *m* funnel.

entorse, ahng-torss, *f* sprain; strain; twist.

entortiller, ahng-tor-tee-yeh, *v* to twist; to wind; to entangle; to get round.

entourage, ahng-too-răhsh, *m* environment; setting; circle.

entourer, ahng-too-reh, *v* to surround (**de,** with).

entracte, ahng-trăhckt, *m* intermission.

entraider (s'), sahng-tray-deh, *v* to help one another.

entrailles, ahng-trah'e, *fpl* entrails; bowels; feelings.

entrain, ahng-trang, *m* spirits; life; animation.

entraînant, e, ahng-tray-nahng, *a* captivating; winning.

entraînement, ahng-train-mahng, *m* force; impulse; sway; training; coaching.

entraîner, ahng-tray-neh, *v* to carry away; to attract; to involve; to bring about; to train.

entraîneur, ahng-tray-ner, *m* trainer; coach.

entrant, ahng-trahng, *m* person coming in. *a* coming in; entering.

entrave, ahng-trăhv, *f* impediment; *pl* fetters.

entre, ahng-tr, *prep* between; among; into; in.

entrebâiller, ahng-trer-bah'e-yeh, *v* to half-open; to set ajar.

entrechoquer (s'), sahng-trer-shock-eh, *v* to clash.

entrecôte, ahng-trer-koht, *f* steak (from ribs).

entrecouper, ahng-trer-koo-peh, *v* to intercept; to intersect.

entrecroiser (s'), sahng-trer-kro'ăh-zeh, *v* to intertwine.

entre-deux, ahng-trer-der, *m* space between; insertion.

entrée, ahng-treh, *f* entrance; admission; beginning; entry; entrée.

entrefaites, ahng-trer-fayt, *fpl* **sur ces** –, SEEr say z' –, meanwhile.

entrelacement, ahng-trer-lăhss-mahng, *m* intertwining.

entrelardé, e, ahng-trer-lăhr-deh, *pp* & *a* interlarded; streaky.

entremêler, ahng-trer-may-leh, *v* to intermingle; **s'** –, to interpose.

entremets. ahng-trer-may, *m* sweet; dessert.

entremetteur, ahng-trer-met-er, *m* go-between.

entremettre (s'), sahng-trer-met-tr, *v* to intervene.

entrepont, ahng-trer-pong, *m* steerage.

entreposer, ahng-trer-poh-zeh, *v* to store; to put in warehouse.

entrepôt, ahng-trer-poh, *m* warehouse.

entreprenant, e, ahng-trer-prer-nahng, *a* enterprising; pushing; bold; venturous.

entreprendre, ahng-trer-prahng-dr, *v* to undertake; to contract for; to attempt.

entrepreneur, ahng-trer-prer-ner, *m* contractor; builder; **–de pompes funèbres,** – der pongp fɛ-nay-br, undertaker.

entreprise, ahng-trer-preez, *f* enterprise; undertaking; contract; attempt.

entrer, ahng-treh, *v* to enter (**dans, en,** into); to begin; to bring in; **faire** –, fair –, to show in.

entresol, ahng-trer-sol, *m* mezzanine.

entretenir, ahng-trert-neer, *v* to keep up; to maintain; to cherish; **s'** –, to converse; to keep fit.

entretien, ahng-trer-te-ang, *m* upkeep; maintenance; conversation; interview.

entrevoir, ahng-trer-vo'ăhr, *v* to have a glimpse of; to foresee.

entrevue, ahng-trer-vɛ, *f* interview.

entrouvert, e, ahng-troo-vair, *a* ajar; half-open.

entrouvrir, ahng-troo-vreer, *v* to half-open.

énumérer, eh-nɛ-meh-reh, *v* to enumerate.

envahir, ahng-văh-eer, *v* to invade; to encroach on; to overrun.

enveloppe, ahngv-lop, *f* wrapper; cover; envelope.

envelopper, ahngv-lop-eh, *v* to envelop; to wrap up; to cover.

envenimer, ahngv-ne-meh, *v* to poison; **s'** –, to fester.

envergure, ahng-vair-ghɛɛr, *f* span; width.

envers, ahng-vair, *prep* towards; to; *m* wrong side; **à l'** –, ăh l'–, inside out.

envi (à l'), ăh lahng-ve, *adv* in emulation (**de,** of).

envie, ahng-vee, *f* envy; inclination; wish.

envier, ahng-ve-eh, *v* to envy; to long for.

environ, ahng-ve-rong, *adv* about; *pl* environs; surroundings; outskirts; vicinity.

environner, ahng-ve-ronn-eh, *v* to surround.

envisager, ahng-ve-zăh-sheh, *v* to look at; to face; to consider.

envoi, ahng-vo'ăh, *m* sending; dispatch; consignment; goods; parcel; remittance.

envoler (s'), sahng-voll-eh, *v* to fly away.

envoyé, ahng-vo'ăh-yeh, *m* messenger; envoy.

envoyer, ahng-vo'ăh-yeh, *v* to send; to forward; to dispatch.

envoyer par télécopie, ahng-vo'ăh-yeh-păhr-teh-leh-ko-pee, *v* to fax.

épagneul, eh-păhn-yerl, *m* spaniel.

épais, se, eh-pay, *a* thick.

épaisseur, eh-payss-er, *f* thickness.

épaissir, eh-payss-eer, *v* to thicken.

épanchement, eh-pahngsh-mahng, *m* effusion; discharge.

épancher, eh-pahng-sheh, *v* to pour out; to vent; **s'** –, to overflow; to open one's heart.

épandre, eh-pahng-dr, *v* to spread; to scatter.

épanouir (s'), seh-păh-noo-eer, *v* to bloom; to open up; to light up.

épargne, eh-păhrn-yer, *f* economy; saving.

épargner, eh-păhrn-yeh, *v* to save; to spare; to have mercy on.

éparpiller, eh-păhr-pee-yeh, *v* to scatter.

épars, e, eh-păhr, *a* scattered; disheveled.

épatant, e, eh-păh-tahng, *a* (*fam*) wonderful; super; great.

épater, eh-păh-teh, *v* to flatten; (*fam*) to amaze.

épaule, eh-pohl, *f* shoulder.

épave, eh-păhv, *f* wreck; waif; remnant.

épée, eh-peh, *f* sword.

épeler, eh-pleh, *v* to spell (word).

éperdu, e, * eh-pair-dE, *a* distracted; aghast; desperate.

éperlan, eh-pair-lahng, *m* smelt.

éperon, eh-prong, *m* spur;

buttress.

épervier, eh-pair-ve-eh, *m* hawk; casting net.

épi, eh-pe, *m* ear; spike; cluster.

épice, eh-peess, *f* spice; **pain d'** –, pang d –, gingerbread

épicerie, eh-peess-ree, *f* grocery; grocer's store.

épici-er, ère, eh-peess-e-eh, *mf* grocer.

épidémie, eh-pe-deh-mee, *f* epidemic.

épiderme, eh-pe-dairm, *m* epidermis.

épier, eh-pe-eh, *v* to spy; to watch.

épiler, eh-pe-leh, *v* to remove superfluous hair; to pluck (eyebrows).

épiloguer, eh-pe-logh-eh, *v* to carp.

épinards, eh-pe-năhr, *mpl* spinach.

épine, eh-peen, *f* thorn; spine.

épineu-x, se, eh-pe-ner, *a* thorny; prickly; ticklish.

épingle, eh-pang-gl, *f* pin; clothespin; **–de sûreté,** – der sEEr-teh, safety pin.

épingler, eh-pang-gleh, *v* to pin; to fasten with a pin.

épisode, eh-pe-zod, *m* episode.

épître, eh-pee-tr, *f* epistle.

éploré, e, eh-plor-eh, *a* in tears; weeping.

éplucher, eh-plE-sheh, *v* to pick; to peel; (*fam*) to examine.

épointer, eh-po'ang-teh, *v* to blunt.

éponge, eh-pongsh, *f* sponge.

éponger, eh-pong-sheh, *v* to sponge up; to mop.

épopée, eh-pop-eh, *f* epic poem.

époque, eh-pock, *f* epoch; time; date; period.

épouse, eh-pooz, *f* wife; spouse.

épouser, eh-poo-zeh, *v* to marry; to take up.

épousseter, eh-pooss-teh, *v* to dust.

épouvantable, * eh-poo-vahng-tăh-bl, *a* frightful; terrible.

épouvantail, eh-poo-vahng-tah'e, *m* scarecrow; (*fam*) bogeyman.

épouvante, eh-poo-vahngt, *f* fright; terror.

épouvanter, eh-poo-vahng-teh, *v* to frighten; to terrify.

époux, eh-poo, *m* husband; spouse; *pl* married couple.

éprendre (s'), seh-prahng-dr, *v* to fall in love (**de,** with).

épreuve, eh-prerv, *f* trial; test; proof; print (photo).

épris, e, eh-pre, *pp* & *a* taken; smitten.

éprouver, eh-proo-veh, *v* to try; to experience; to feel.

épuisement, eh-pweez-mahng, *m* draining; exhaustion.

épuisé, eh-pwee-zeh, *a* exhausted; tired out.

épuiser, eh-pwee-zeh, *v* to drain; to exhaust; to use up.

épurer, eh-pe-reh, *v* to purify; to refine.

équateur, eh-kwăh-ter, *m* equator.

équerre, eh-kair, *f* square set.

équestre, eh-kess-tr, *a* equestrian.

équilibre, eh-ke-lee-br, *m* equilibrium; poise; balance.

équipage, eh-ke-păhsh, *m* equipage; equipment; carriage; crew.

équipe, eh-keep, *f* gang; team; set; crew.

équipée, eh-ke-peh, *f* prank; lark.

équiper, eh-ke-peh, *v* to equip; to fit out.

équipement, eh-keep-mahng, *m* equipment; supplies; outfit.

équitable, * eh-ke-tăh-bl, *a* equitable; fair.

équitation, eh-ke-tăh-se-ong, *f* riding.

équité, eh-ke-teh, *f* equity.

équivalent, e, eh-ke-văh-lahng, *a* & *m* equivalent.

équivoque, eh-ke-vock, *f* ambiguity. *a* equivocal; dubious.

érable, eh-răh-bl, *m* maple.

éraflure, eh-răh-flEEr, *f* slight scratch.

éraillé, e, eh-rah'e-eh, *pp* & *a* frayed; bloodshot; hoarse.

ère, air, *f* era; epoch.

érection, eh-reck-se-ong, *f* raising; erection.

éreinté, e, eh-rang-teh, *a* tired out; harassed.

éreinter, eh-rang-teh, *v* to break the back of (horse); to exhaust; to criticize; **s'–,** to tire oneself out.

ergot, air-go, *m* spur (of cock, etc).

ermite, air-meet, *m* hermit.

errant, e, air-rahng, *a* wandering; roaming.

errer, air-reh, *v* to wander; to stray; to err.

erreur, air-rer, f error; mistake.

erroné, e, * air-ronn-eh, a erroneous.

escabeau, ess-kăh-boh, m stool; steps.

escadre, ess-kăh-dr, f squadron.

escadron, ess-kăh-drong, m squadron; **chef d'–,** shaif d–, major.

escalade, ess-kăh-lăhd, f scaling; climb.

escale, ess-kăhl, f port of call; stop over; touch down.

escalier, ess-kăh-le-eh, m stairs; staircase; steps.

escalope, ess-kăh-lop, f thin slice of meat (usually veal); escalope.

escamoter, ess-kăh-mot-eh, v to juggle; to filch.

escapade, ess-kăh-păhd, f prank; escapade.

escargot, ess-kăhr-go, m snail.

escarpé, e, ess-kăhr-peh, a steep; abrupt.

esclaffer (s'), sess-clăh-feh, v to shake with laughter.

esclandre, ess-klahng-dr, m scandal; scene.

esclavage, ess-klăh-văhsh, m slavery.

esclave, ess-klăhv, mf slave; a slavish.

escompte, ess-kongt, m discount; rebate.

escompter, ess-kong-teh, v to discount; (fam) to expect.

escorter, ess-kor-teh, v to escort; to convoy; to accompany.

escouade, ess-koo-ăhd, f squad; gang.

escrime, ess-kreem, f fencing.

escrimer (s'), sess-kree-meh, v to endeavor; to try hard.

escroc, ess-kro, m swindler; crook.

escroquer, ess-krock-eh, v to swindle.

espace, ess-păhss, m space; room; infinity; vacancy.

espacer, ess-păhss-eh, v to space; to leave space between.

espadrille, ess-păh-dree-ye, f canvas shoe with rope sole.

espagnol, e, ess-păhn-yol, a & mf Spanish; Spaniard; m Spanish.

espalier, ess-păh-le-eh, m espalier.

espèce, ess-payss, f species; kind; sort; case; pl specie.

espérance, ess-peh-rahngss, f hope; expectation.

espérer, ess-peh-reh, v to hope; to expect; to trust.

espiègle, ess-pe-ay-gl, a frolicsome; mischievous.

espion, ess-pe-ong, m spy.

espoir, ess-po'ahr, m hope; expectation.

esprit, ess-pre, m spirit; soul; ghost; mind; intellect; wit; feeling.

esquif, ess-keeff, m skiff.

esquinter, ess-kang-teh, v (fam) to exhaust; to smash; to ruin; to spoil.

esquisse, ess-keess, f sketch; outline.

esquiver, ess-ke-veh, v to avoid; to elude; **s'–,** to slip away.

essai, eh-say, m trial; attempt; essay; try; **coup d'–,** koo d–, first attempt.

essaim, eh-sang, m swarm; host.

essayer, eh-say-yeh, v to try; to try on; to attempt; **s'–,** to try one's skill (**à, dans,** at).

essence, eh-sahngss, f gasoline; spirits; essence.

essentiel, eh-sahng-se-ell, m main thing.

essentiel, le, * eh-sahng-se-ell, a essential.

essieu, eh-se-er, m axletree; axle.

essor, eh-sor, m flight;

scope; play; impulse.

essorer, eh-sor-eh, *v* to wring (clothes); to squeeze.

essoreuse, eh-sor-erz, *f* spin-dryer.

essouffler, eh-soo-fleh, *v* to make breathless.

essuie-glace, eh-swee-glähss, *m* wiper.

essuie-mains, eh-swee-mang, *m* hand towel.

essuyer, eh-swee-yeh, *v* to wipe; to dry; to sustain; to go through.

est, esst, *m* east.

estampe, ess-tahngp, *f* print; engraving.

estampille, ess-tahng-pee-ye, *f* stamp; mark; trademark.

estimation, ess-tee-mäh-se-ong, *f* estimate; valuation.

estime, ess-teem, *f* esteem; regard.

estimer, ess-tee-meh, *v* to estimate; to consider.

estomac, ess-tomm-äh, *m* stomach.

estrade, ess-trähd, *f* platform.

estragon, ess-träh-gong, *m* tarragon.

estropier, ess-trop-e-eh, *v* to cripple; to maim.

esturgeon, ess-tEEr-shong, *m* sturgeon.

et, eh, *conj* and.

étable, eh-täh-bl, *f* stable; cowshed. *m* bench.

établi, e, eh-täh-ble, *pp* & *a* established.

établir, eh-täh-bleer, *v* to establish; to set; to institute; to prove.

établissement, eh-täh-bliss-mahng, *m* establishment; institution; setting up.

étage, eh-tähsh, *m* story; floor.

étagère, eh-täh-shair, *f* set of shelves; shelf.

étai, eh-tay, *m* stay; prop.

étain, eh-tang, *m* tin; pewter.

étalage, eh-täh-lähsh, *m* window display.

étaler, eh-täh-leh, *v* to display; to spread out; to lay out; **s'–,** to sprawl; to show off; to fall down.

étalon, eh-täh-long, *m* stallion; standard (of weights etc).

étamine, eh-täh-meen, *f* sieve; stamen.

étanche, eh-tahngsh, *a* watertight.

étancher, eh-tahng-sheh, *v* to staunch; to make water-tight; to stop; to quench.

étang, eh-tahng, *m* pond; pool.

étape, eh-tähp, *f* stopover; stage.

état, eh-täh, *m* state; plight; profession; trade; list; statement; nation.

état-major, eh-täh mäh-shor, *m* staff; headquarters.

étau, eh-toh, *m* vice.

étayer, eh-tay-yeh, *v* to prop up.

été, eh-teh, *m* summer.

éteindre, eh-tang-dr, *v* to extinguish; to turn off (light, etc); **s'–,** to die out.

éteint, e, eh-tang, *pp* & *a* put out; extinct; faint.

étendard, eh-tahng-dähr, *m* standard; flag.

étendre, eh-tahng-dr, *v* to extend; to spread; to stretch; to expand; **s'–,** to reach; to expatiate.

étendu, e, eh-tahng-dE, *pp* & *a* extended; spread; extensive.

étendue, eh-tahng-dEE, *f* extent.

éternel, le, * eh-tair-nell, *a* eternal; unending.

éternuer, eh-tair-nE-eh, *v* to sneeze.

éther, eh-tair, *m* ether.

étinceler, eh-tangss-leh, *v* to sparkle; to gleam.

étincelle, eh-tang-sell, *f* spark.

étioler (s'), seh-te-oll-eh, to grow emaciated.

étique, eh-teeck, *a* lean; hectic; emaciated.

étiquette, eh-te-kett, *f* label; tag; etiquette; ceremony.

étirer, eh-te-reh, *v* to stretch; to draw.

étoffe, eh-tof, *f* stuff; cloth; material.

étoile, eh-to'ăhl, *f* star; asterisk.

étole, eh-tol, *f* stole.

étonnant, eh-tonn-ahng, *a* astonishing; wonderful; surprising.

étonner, eh-tonn-eh, *v* to astonish; to astound; to surprise.

étouffer, eh-too-feh, *v* to suffocate; to stifle; to smother; to choke; to hush up.

étourderie, eh-toohr-der-ree, *f* thoughtlessness; blunder.

étourdi, e, eh-toohr-de, *pp* & *a* heedless; scatterbrained; giddy.

étourdir, eh-toohr-deer, *v* to stun; to deafen; **s'–,** to escape from oneself.

étourdissant, e, eh-toohr-diss-ahng, *a* deafening.

étourdissement, eh-toohr-diss-mahng, *m* giddiness; stupefaction.

étourneau, eh-toohr-noh, *m* starling; scatterbrain.

étrange, * eh-trahng**sh**, *a* strange; odd; queer.

étranger, eh-trahng-sheh, *m* stranger; foreigner; foreign countries; **à l'–,** ăh l'–, abroad.

étrang-er, ère, eh-trahng-**sheh**, *a* strange; foreign.

étranglé, eh-trahng-gleh, *pp* & *a* strangled; narrow; tight.

étrangler, eh-trahng-gleh, *v* to strangle; to compress.

être, ay-tr, *v* to be; to exist; to belong; *m* being; existence; individual.

étreindre, eh-trang-dr, *v* to bind; to clasp; to grasp.

étreinte, eh-trangt, *f* fastening; grasp; embrace.

étrenne, eh-trenn, *f* (usually *pl*) New Year's gifts.

étrier, eh-tre-yeh, *m* stirrup; **le coup de l'–,** ler koo der l'–, stirrup cup.

étrille, eh-tree-ye, *f* currycomb.

étriqué, e, eh-tre-keh, *a* tight; skimpy.

étroit, e, * eh-tro'ăh, *a* narrow; tight; close; strict; **à l'–,** ăh l–, cramped.

étroitesse, eh-tro'ăh-tess, *f* narrowness; tightness; closeness.

étude, eh-tEEd, *f* study; chambers; practice; survey; **faire ses –s à,** fair seh zeh-tEEd-ăh, to be educated at.

étudiant, eh-tE-de-ahng, *m* student.

étudier, eh-tE-de-eh, *v* to study; to observe; **s'–,** to endeavor (**à,** to).

étui, eh-twee, *m* case; box; sheath.

étuvée, eh-tE-veh, *f* braised; **à l'–,** ăhl –, steamed.

eucharistie, er-kăh-riss-tee, *f* Eucharist.

euphonie, er-fon-ee, *f* euphony.

euh! er, *interj* hum! well!

eux, er, *pron* them; they.

évacuer, eh-văh-kE-eh, *v* to evacuate; to vacate.

évader (s'), seh-văh-deh, *v* to escape; to get away.

évaluer, eh-văh-lE-eh, *v* to value; to estimate.

évangile, eh-vahng-sheel, *m* Gospel.

évanouir (s'), seh-văh-noo-eer, *v* to faint; to vanish.

évanouissement, eh-văh-noo-iss-mahng, *m* fainting; swoon.

évaporer (s'), seh-văh-por-eh, *v* to evaporate.

évasé, e, eh-vah-zeh, *pp & a* widened.

évasi-f, ve,* eh-vah-zeeff, *a* evasive.

évasion, eh-vah-se-ong, *f* escape; flight.

éveil, eh-vay'e, *m* awakening; warning; **en –,** ahng n'–, on the alert.

éveillé, e, eh-vay'e-yeh, *pp & a* awakened; wide awake; vigilant; alert.

éveiller, eh-vay'e-yeh, *v* to awaken.

événement, eh-venn-mahng, *m* event; occurrence; issue.

éventail, eh-vahng-tah'e, *m* fan.

éventer, eh-vahng-teh, *v* to fan; to air; to make flat; **s' –,** to go flat.

éventrer, eh-vahng-treh, *v* to rip up; to disembowel.

éventualité, eh-vahng-tE-ăh-le-teh, *f* contingency; possibility.

éventuel, le,* eh-vahng-tE-ell, *a* contingent; possible; eventual.

évêque, eh-vayk, *m* bishop.

évertuer (s'), seh-vair-tE-eh, *v* to exert oneself; to do one's utmost.

évidemment, eh-ve-dăh-mahng, *adv* evidently; obviously.

évidence, eh-ve-dahngss, *f* evidence.

évident, e, eh-ve-dahng, *a* evident; clear.

évider, eh-ve-deh, *v* to scoop out.

évier, eh-ve-eh, *m* sink.

évincer, eh-vang-seh, *v* to turn out; to oust.

éviter, eh-ve-teh, *v* to avoid; to dodge.

évolué, eh-vol-E-eh, *a* advanced;developed.

évolution, eh-voll-E-se-ong, *f* evolution.

évoquer, eh-vock-eh, *v* to conjure up; to call up.

exact, e,* egg-zăhckt, *a* exact; accurate; true; punctual.

exaction, egg-zăhck-se-ong, *f* extortion.

exactitude, egg-zăhck-te-tEEd, *f* exactness; accuracy; punctuality.

exagérer, egg-zăh-**sheh**-reh, *v* to exaggerate; to go too far.

exalté, e, egg-zăhl-teh, *pp & a* exalted; elated; enthusiastic; fanatic.

exalter, egg-zăhl-teh, *v* to glorify; to praise; to excite.

examen, egg-zăh-mang, *m* examination; scrutiny.

examinateur, egg-zăh-me-năh-ter, *m* examiner.

examiner, egg-zăh-me-neh, *v* to examine; to inquire into.

exaspérer, egg-zăhss-peh-reh, *v* to exasperate; to provoke.

exaucer, egg-zoh-seh, *v* to hear; to grant.

excédent, eck-seh-dahng, *m* surplus; excess.

excéder, eck-seh-deh, *v* to exceed; to exasperate.

excellemment, eck-say-lăh-mahng, *adv* excellently.

excellence, eck-say-lahngss, *f* excellence.

excellent, e, eck-say-lahng, *a* excellent.

exceller, eck-say-leh, *v* to excel.

excentrique,* eck-sahng-treeck, *a* eccentric.

excepté, eck-sayp-teh, *prep* except.

excepter, eck-sayp-teh, *v* to except.

exception, eck-sayp-se-ong, *f* exception.

excès, eck-say, *m* excess.

excessi-f, ve,* eck-sayss-eeff, *a* excessive;

exorbitant.

excitant, e, eck-se-tahng, *a* exciting; stimulating.

excitation, eck-se-tăh-se-ong, *f* excitement.

exciter, eck-se-teh, *v* to excite; to rouse.

exclamer (s'–), secks-klăh-meh, *v* to exclaim.

exclure, ecks-klEEr, *v* to exclude.

exclusi-f, ve,* ecks-klE-zeeff, *a* exclusive.

exclusivité, ecks-klE-ze-ve-teh, *f* exclusiveness; sole rights.

excommunier, ecks-komm-E-ne-eh, *v* to excommunicate.

excroissance, ecks-kro'ăh-sahngss, *f* excrescence; growth.

excursion, ecks-kEEr-se-ong, *f* excursion; tour; outing.

excuse, ecks-kEEz, *f* excuse; *pl* apology.

excuser, ecks-kE-zeh, *v* to excuse; **s'–,** to apologize; to decline (offer, etc).

exécrer, ecks-eh-kreh, *v* to loathe.

exécutant, egg-zeh-kE-tahng, *m* performer.

exécuter, egg-zeh-kE-teh, *v* to execute; to perform; to carry out; to distrain; **s'–,** to yield.

exécution, egg-zeh-kE-se-ong, *f* execution; performance; distraint.

exemplaire, egg-zahng-plair, *m* copy. *a* exemplary.

exemple, egg-zahng-pl, *m* example; instance; copy; **par –,** păhr –, for instance; *interj* really!

exempt, e, egg-zahng, *a* exempt; exempted; free.

exempter, egg-zahng-teh, *v* to exempt; to dispense.

exercer, egg-zair-seh, *v* to exercise; to train; to practice; to follow (a profession).

exercice, egg-zair-seess, *m* exercise; practice; fiscal year; drill.

exhaler, egg-zăh-leh, *v* to exhale; to vent.

exhausser, egg-zohss-eh, *v* to raise.

exhiber, egg-ze-beh, *v* to exhibit; to show.

exhorter, egg-zor-teh, *v* to exhort.

exhumer, egg-zE-meh, *v* to exhume; to bring to light.

exigeant, e, egg-ze-shahng, *pp* & *a* exacting; hard to please.

exigence, egg-ze-shahngss, *f* exigency; demand.

exiger, egg-ze-sheh, *v* to exact; to demand; to insist upon.

exigu, ë, egg-ze-ghE, *a* scanty; small; slender.

exiguité, egg-ze-ghE-e-teh, *f* scantiness.

exil, egg-zeel, *m* exile.

exiler, egg-ze-leh, *v* to exile; to banish.

existence, egg-ziss-tahngss, *f* existence; life; stock in hand.

exister, egg-ziss-teh, *v* to exist; to live.

exode, egg-zod, *m* exodus.

exonérer, egg-zonn-eh-reh, *v* to exonerate.

exorbitant, e, egg-zor-be-tahng, *a* exorbitant.

exorciser, egg-zor-se-zeh, *v* to exorcise.

expansi-f, ve, ecks-păhng-seeff, *a* expansive; exuberant; effusive.

expédient, ecks-peh-de-ahng, *m* resource; *a* expedient; advisable.

expédier, ecks-peh-de-eh, *v* to post; to expedite; to dispatch; to draw up.

expéditeur, ecks-peh-de-ter, *m* sender; shipper; forwarding agent.

expéditi-f, ve, ecks-peh-de-teeff, *a* expeditious.

expédition, ecks-peh-de-se-ong, *f* expedition;

forwarding; consignment; copy.

expérience, ecks-peh-re-ahngss, f experience; experiment.

expérimenter, ecks-peh-re-mahng-teh, v to experiment; to try; to test.

expert, ecks-pair, m expert; specialist; surveyor. a skilled; -- **comptable,** – kong-tăh-bl, m certified accountant.

expertise, ecks-pair-teez, f valuation; survey.

expier, ecks-pe-eh, v to atone for.

expirer, ecks-pe-reh, v to expire; to breathe out; to die.

explicati-f, ve, ecks-ple-kăh-teeff, a explanatory.

explication, ecks-ple-kăh-se-ong, f explanation.

expliquer, ecks-ple-keh, v to explain; to construe; to account for.

exploit, ecks-plo'ăh, m deed; feat; writ.

exploitation, ecks-plo'ăh-tăh-se-ong, f working; cultivation; exploitation.

exploiter, ecks-plo'ăh-teh, v to work; to cultivate; to turn to account; to take advantage of.

exploiteur, ecks-plo'ăh-ter, m exploit; exploiter; (fam) swindler.

explorer, ecks-plor-eh, v to explore.

exploser, ecks-plo-zeh, v to explode; to blow up.

explosion, ecks-plo-ze-ong, f explosion; outbreak.

exportation, ecks-por-tăh-se-ong, f export.

exporter, ecks-por-teh, v to export.

exposant, ecks-po-zahng, m exhibitor; petitioner.

exposé, ecks-po-zeh, m statement; account.

exposer, ecks-po-zeh, v to expose; to exhibit; to explain.

exposition, ecks-po-ze-se-ong, f exposure; exhibition; statement.

exprès, ecks-pray, adv on purpose.

exprès, ecks-pray, a & m special delivery.

expr-ès, esse, ecks-pray, a express; explicit.

express, ecks-press, m express train. a express.

expression, ecks-prayss-e-ong, f expression; utterance; expressiveness.

exprimer, ecks-pre-meh, v to squeeze out; to express; **s' –,** to express oneself.

expulser, ecks-pEEl-seh, v to expel; to turn out.

exquis, e,* ecks-ke, a exquisite.

extase, ecks-tahz, f ecstasy.

extasier (s'), secks-tah-ze-eh, v to be enraptured.

exténuer, ecks-teh-nE-eh, v to extenuate; to exhaust.

extérieur, ecks-teh-re-er, m exterior; outside.

extérieur, e,* ecks-teh-re-er, a external; outward; foreign.

exterminer, ecks-tair-me-neh, v to destroy.

externe, ecks-tairn, m day student; non-resident medical student. a external.

extincteur, ecks-tangk-ter, m fire extinguisher.

extinction, ecks-tangk-se-ong, f extinction; suppression; paying off.

extirper, ecks-teer-peh, v to root out.

extorquer, ecks-tor-keh, v to extort.

extra, ecks-trăh, m extra. a inv extra special; first class.

extrader, ecks-trăh-deh, v to extradite.

extraire, ecks-trair, *v* to
  extract.

extrait, ecks-tray, *m*
  extract; abstract;
  certificate.

extraordinaire,* ecks-
  träh-or-de-nair, *a*
  unusual; extraordinary.

extravagant, ecks-träh-
  väh-gah*ng*, *a*
  extravagant; eccentric.

extrême,* ecks-traym, *a*
  extreme; utmost. *m*
  extreme limit.

extrémité, ecks-treh-me-
  teh, *f* extremity; end;
  last moments.

fable, făh-bl, *f* fable; story.

fabricant, făh bre-kah*n*g, *m* manufacturer.

fabrication, făh-bre-kăh-se-ong, *f* manufacturing; production.

fabrique, făh-breeck, *f* factory.

fabriquer, făh-bre-keh, *v* to manufacture; to make; to forge.

fabuleu-x, se,* făh-bE-ler, *a* fabulous.

façade, făhss-ăhd, *f* front; facade.

face, făhss, *f* face (of something); front; aspect; side; **en –,** ah*n*g –, opposite.

facétie, făh-seh-see, *f* facetiousness; jest.

facétieu-x, se,* făh-seh-se-er, *a* jocular.

fâché, fah-sheh, *a* sorry (**de,** for); angry (**contre,** with); on bad terms (**avec,** with).

fâcher, fah-sheh, *v* to offend; to grieve; to anger; **se –,** to take offense; to get angry.

fâcheu-x, se,* fah-sher, *a* grievous; troublesome; annoying; unfortunate.

facile,* făh-seell, *a* easy; fluent; ready.

facilité, făh-se-le-teh, *f* ease; fluency; readiness; *pl* abilities.

faciliter, făh-se-le-teh, *v* to facilitate.

façon, făh-song, *f* making; make; shape; manner; *pl* affectation.

façonner, făh-sonn-eh, *v* to shape; to form.

facteur, făhck-ter, *m* maker (of musical instruments); mailman; agent; factor.

factice, făhck-teess, *a* artificial.

factieu-x, se,* făhck-se-er, *a* factious; seditious.

factionnaire, făhck-se-onn-air, *m* sentry.

facture, făhck-tEEr, *f* invoice; bill.

facultati-f, ve,* făh-kEEl-tah-teeff, *a* optional.

faculté, făh-kEEl-teh, *f* faculty; power; right.

fadaise, făh-dayz, *f* drivel; nonsense.

fade, făhd, *a* insipid; flat; dull.

fagot, făh-go, *m* faggot; bundle.

fagoter, făh-got-eh, *v* to bundle up; to rig out; **se –,** to dress in a slovenly way.

faible, fay-bl, *m* weak spot; partiality. *a** weak; feeble; poor.

faiblesse, fay-bless, *f* weakness; deficiency; indulgence; fainting fit.

faiblir, fay-bleer, *v* to weaken; to relax.

faïence, făh-yah*n*gss, *f* earthenware; crockery.

failli, fah'e-yee, *pp & a* fallen; bankrupt.

faillir, fah'e-yeer, *v* to err; to fail.

faillite, fah'e-yeet, *f* failure; bankruptcy; **faire – faire –,** to go bankrupt.

faim, fang, *f* hunger.

fainéant, e, fay-ney-ahng, *mf* & *a* idler; slothful.

faire, fair, *v* to make; to do; to be; to form; to arrange.

faire du jogging, fair-der-dsho-geng *v* jog.

faire-part, fair-par, *m* death notice; wedding announcement.

faisable, fer-zăh-bl, *a* feasible.

faisan, fer-zahng, *m* pheasant.

faisandé, e, fer-zahng-deh, *a* bad (flavor); gamy.

faisceau, fayss-oh, *m* bundle; pile.

faiseur, fer-zer, *m* maker; doer; jobber; fussy person.

fait, fay, *pp* & *a* made; done; full-grown; accustomed; dressed up; **c'est bien –,** say be-ang –, serve (him, her, them, you, us, etc) right.

fait, fay, *m* fact; act; deed; doing; making; feat; **–s divers, – de-vair,**

miscellaneous news.

faîte, fayt, *m* summit; ridge.

faix, fay, *m* burden.

falaise, făh-layz, *f* cliff.

fallacieu-x, se,* făhl-lăh-se-er, *a* fallacious.

falloir, făh-lo'ăhr, *v* to be necessary; must; to be obliged; should; ought; to want; **il faut que je ...,** ill foh ker sher ..., I must; **il me faut,** ill mer foh, I want.

falot, făh-lo, *m* lantern.

falot, e, făh-lo, *a* colorless (pers); wan.

falsifier, făhl-se-fe-eh, *v* to counterfeit; to adulterate.

famé, e, făh-meh, *a* famed; **bien –,** be-ang –, of good repute.

famélique, făh-meh-leeck, *a* starving.

fameu-x, se,* făh-mer, *a* famous; first-rate.

familiariser, făh-me-le-ăhr-re-zeh, *v* to familiarize.

familier, făh-me-le-eh, *m* intimate; conversant (with, avec).

famili-er, ère,* făh-me-le-eh, *a* familiar.

famille, făh-mee-ye, *f* family; household.

famine, făh-meen, *f* famine; starvation.

fan, făhn, *mf* fan.

fanal, făh-năhl, *m* lantern; beacon.

fanatisme, făh-năh-tissm, *m* fanaticism.

faner, făh-neh, *v* to make hay; to wither; **se –,** to fade away.

faneur, făh-ner, *m* haymaker.

fanfare, fahng-făhr, *f* flourish (of trumpets); brass band.

fanfaron, fahng-făh-rong, *m* boaster; blusterer.

fange, fahngsh, *f* mire; mud; dirt.

fanion, fah-ne-ong, *m* flag.

fantaisie, fahng-tay-zee, *f* imagination; whim.

fantasque, fahng-tăhsk, *a* odd; whimsical.

fantassin, fahng-tăhss-ang, *m* infantryman.

fantastique,* fahng-tass-teeck, *a* fantastic.

fantôme, fahng-tohm, *m* phantom; specter; ghost.

faon, fahng, *m* fawn.

farce, făhrss, *f* stuffing; farce; practical joke.

farcir, făhr-seer, *v* to stuff; to cram.

fard, făhr, *m* paint; rouge.

fardeau, făhr-doh, *m* burden; load.

farder, făhrdeh, *v* to paint; to make up.

farfouiller, făhr-foo-yeh, v to rummage.

farine, făh-reen, f flour; meal.

farineu-x, se, făh-re-ner, a floury.

farouche, făh-roosh, a wild; fierce; sullen; shy.

fascicule, făhss-se-kEEl, m part; installment; booklet.

fasciner, făhss-se-neh, v to fascinate.

fastidieu-x, se,* făhss-te-de-er, a tedious.

fastueu-x, se,* făhss-tE-er, a pompous; ostentatious.

fatal, e,* făh-tăhl, a fatal; inevitable.

fatalisme, făh-tăh-lissm, m fatalism.

fatigant, e, făh-te-ghahng, a tiring; tedious.

fatigue, făh-teegh, f fatigue; stress; wear and tear.

fatiguer, făh-te-gheh, v to tire out; to annoy.

fatras, făh-trah, m clutter; hodgepodge.

fatuité, făh-tE-e-teh, f conceit.

faubourg, foh-boohr, m outskirt; suburb; quarter.

fauché, foh-sheh, a broke.

faucher, foh-sheh, v to mow; to cut; to reap (field, corn, etc); to mow down.

faucille, foh-see-ye, f sickle.

faucon, foh-kong, m falcon.

faufiler, foh-fe-leh, v to tack; to baste; to insert; **se –**, to creep in.

faune, fohn, f fauna.

faussaire, fohss-air, m forger.

fausser, fohss-eh, v to bend; to strain; to pervert; to falsify; to be out of tune; to distort; to sneak away.

fausset, fohss-ay, m spigot; falsetto.

fausseté, fohss-teh, f falseness; falsehood; insincerity.

faute, foht, f fault; error, mistake; lack; **–de, –der**, for want of.

fauteuil, foh-ter'e, m armchair; orchestra seat; rocking chair; wheelchair.

fauti-f, ve,* foh-teeff, a faulty; guilty.

fauve, fohv, m fawn color; wild beast; a tawny, buff.

fauvette, foh-vett, f warbler.

faux, foh, adv falsely; m falsehood; imitation; forgery.

fau-x, sse,* foh, a false; sham; base; bad; imitated.

faux, foh, f scythe.

faux-fuyant, foh-fwee-yahng, m evasion; subterfuge.

faveur, făh-ver, f favor; interest.

favorable,* făh-vor-ăh-bl, a favorable.

favori, te, făh-vor-e, a & mf favorite.

favoris, făh-vor-e, mpl sideburns.

favoriser, făh-vor-e-zeh, v to favor; to befriend; to aid.

fébrile, feh-breell, a feverish.

fécond, e, feh-kong, a fecund; fruitful; productive; teeming.

féconder, feh-kong-deh, v to fertilize.

fédéré, feh-deh-reh, a federated.

fée, feh, f fairy.

féerie, feh-ree, f fairytale; enchantment.

féerique, feh-reeck, a magical; enchanting.

feindre, fang-dr, v to feign; to pretend.

feint, e, fang, pp & a feigned; pretended; mock.

feinte, fangt, f pretense;

sham; dodge.

fêler, fay-leh, v to crack (glass, etc).

félicitation, feh-le-se-tăh-se-ong, f congratulation.

félicité, feh-le-se-teh, f happiness.

féliciter, feh-le-se-teh, v to congratulate; **se –,** to be pleased (**de,** with).

félin, e, feh-lang, a feline.

félon, feh-long, m traitor. a felonious; traitorous.

félonie, feh-lonn-ee, f treason.

félure, fay-lEEr, f crack; split.

femelle, fer-mell, f & a female.

féminin, feh-me-nang, m feminine gender.

féminin, e, feh-me-nang, a feminine; womanly.

femme, făhmm, f woman; wife; **–de chambre, –** der shahng-br, chambermaid; **–de charge, –** der shăhrsh, housekeeper; **–de ménage, –** der meh-năhsh, cleaning woman.

fémur, feh-mEEr, m thighbone; femur.

fenaison, fer-nay-zong, f haymaking.

fendre, fahng-dr, v to cleave; to split; to crack; to break through; **se –,**

to split; to lunge; to "fork out".

fendu, e, fahng-dE, pp & a slit; cracked.

fenêtre, fer-nay-tr, f window.

fente, fahngt, f split, crack; slot.

fer, fair, m iron; horseshoe; sword; pl fetters.

fer-blanc, fair-blahng, m tin plate.

ferblanterie, fair-blahngt-ree, f platemaking.

férié, e, feh-re-eh, a **jour –,shoohr –,** holiday (general); bank holiday.

fermage, fair-măhsh, m tenant farming.

ferme, fairm, f farm; farmhouse; farming.

ferme, fairm, adv firmly; hard. a* firm; steady; strong; stiff.

ferment, fair-mahng, m leaven; ferment.

fermenter, fair-mahng-teh, v to ferment; to rise.

fermer, fair-meh, v to shut; to close; **–à clef, –** ăh kleh, to lock.

fermeté, fair-mer-teh, f firmness; steadfastness; strength.

fermeture, fair-mer-tEEr, f closing; shutting.

fermeture éclair, fair-mer-tEEr eh-klayr, f zipper.

fermi-er, ére, fair-me-eh, mf farmer.

fermoir, fair-mo'ăhr, m clasp.

féroce,* feh-ross, a ferocious; wild; very strict.

ferraille, fay-rah'e f scrap iron; old iron.

ferrailleur, fay-rah'e-yer, m scrap-iron dealer.

ferré, e, fay-reh, pp & a iron-shod; versed; skilled.

ferrer, fay-reh, v to bind with iron; to shoe; to metal.

ferrure, fay-rEEr, f metal hiñge; horseshoes.

fertile, fayr-teel, a fertile; productive; eventful.

fervent, e, fair-vahng, a fervent.

ferveur, fair-ver, f fervor.

fesse, fayss, f buttock; bottom.

fessée, fayss-eh, f spanking.

fesser, fayss-eh, v to spank.

festin, fayss-tang, m feast; banquet.

feston, fayss-tong, m festoon.

fête, fayt, f feast; festivity; festival; saint's day;

birthday; holiday.

fêter, fay-teh, v to celebrate; to observe as a holiday; to welcome.

fétide, feh-teed, a fetid.

feu, fer, m fire; fireplace; passion; **–d'artifice, –** dǎhr-te-fiss, fireworks.

feu, e, fer, a late; deceased.

feuillage, fer'e-yǎhsh, m foliage.

feuille, fer'e, f leaf; sheet; paper.

feuilleter, fer'e-yer-teh, v to leaf through; to run through; to make puff pastry.

feuilleton, fer'e-yer-tong, m serial installment; literary or scientific article; installment.

feutre, fer-tr, m felt; felt hat.

fève, fayv, f bean.

février, feh-vre-eh, m February.

fiacre, fe-ǎh-kr, m horse-drawn carriage.

fiançailles, fe-ahng-sah'e, fpl betrothal; engagement.

fiancé, e, fe-ahng-seh, mf fiancé; fiancée.

fiancer (se), ser fe-ahng-seh, v to become engaged.

fibre, fee-br, f fiber;

feeling; constitution.

ficeler, fis-leh, v to tie up.

ficelle, fe-sell, f string; twine; (fam) dodge; trick; long thin loaf of bread.

fiche, feesh, f label; slip; index card; peg.

ficher, fee-sheh, v to drive in; to fix; to put; to give; **se –**, (fam) not to care less (**de**, about).

fichu, fee-shE, m small shawl; scarf.

fichu, e, fee-shE, a (pop) wretched; got up; done for.

ficti-f, ve,* fick-teeff, a fictitious.

fiction, fick-se-ong, f invention; fiction.

fidèle,* fe-dell, a faithful; true; exact; m believer.

fidélité, fe-deh-le-teh, f fidelity; loyalty.

fiel, fe-ell, m gall; bitterness; hatred.

fiente, fe-ahngt, f droppings.

fier (se), ser fe-eh, v to trust; to count on.

fi-er, ère,* fe-air, a proud; haughty.

fierté, fe-air-teh, f pride; dignity.

fièvre, fe-ay-vr, f fever; restlessness; excitement; **avoir de la –**, ǎh-vo'ǎhr

der lǎh –, to have a temperature.

fifre, fee-fr, m fife player.

figer, fe-sheh, v to congeal; to curdle.

figue, feeg, f fig.

figuier, fe-ghe-eh, m fig tree.

figurant, fe-ghE-rahng, m walk-on actor; extra.

figure, fe-ghEEr, f figure; form; face; countenance.

figuré, e, fe-ghE-reh, a figurative.

figurer, fe-ghE-reh, v to figure; to represent; **se –**, to imagine.

fil, feel, m thread; yarn; wire; edge; grain; current.

filament, fe-lǎh-mahng, m filament; thread; string.

filandreu-x, se, fe-lahng-drer, a stringy; tough; longwinded.

filant, e, fe-lahng, a shooting (stars).

file, feel, f file; row; line.

filer, fe-leh, v to spin; to shadow; to run; to slip away; pay out.

filet, fe-lay, m thread; net; snare; fillet; trickle.

filial, e,* fe-le-ǎhl, a filial.

filiale, fe-le-ǎhl, f subsidiary company.

filigrane, fe-le-grǎhn, m filigree; watermark.

fille, fee-ye, *f* girl; maid; daughter; servant; **petite –,** per-teet –, granddaughter.

filleul, e fee-yerl, *mf* godson; goddaughter.

film, feelm, *m* film; movie.

filon, fe-long, *m* lode; vein.

filou, fe-loo, *m* pickpocket; crook; cheat.

filouter, fe-loo-teh, *v* to cheat.

fils, feess, *m* son; **petit –,** per-te –, grandson.

filtre, feel-tr, *m* filter; percolator; **bout –,** boo –, filter-tip.

filtrer, feel-treh, *v* to filter; to strain.

fin, fang, *f* end; close; aim; purpose.

fin, e,* fang, *a* fine; thin; refined; sly; sharp (financier).

final, e,* fe-nähl, *a* final.

finance, fe-nahngss, *f* finance.

financer, fe-nahngss-eh, *v* to lay out money.

financier, fe-nahngss-e-eh, *m* financier.

financi-er, ère,* fe-nahngss-e-eh, *a* financial.

finaud, e, fe-noh, *a* cunning.

finesse, fe-ness, *f* fineness; nicety; delicacy; acuteness.

fini, fe-ne, *m* finish.

fini, e, fe-ne, *pp & a* finished; consummate; finite.

finir, fe-neer, *v* to finish; to put an end to.

fiole, fe-ol, *f* phial; flask.

firmament, feer-mäh-mahng, *m* firmament.

fisc, feessk, *m* treasury; IRS.

fissure, feess-EEr, *f* fissure; crack.

fixation, feek-säh-se-ong, *f* fastening.

fixe,* feeks, *a* steady; firm; regular.

fixer, feek-seh, *v* to fix; to determine; to set.

fixité, feek-se-teh, *f* unchangeableness; stability.

flacon, fläh-kong, *m* flask; small bottle; perfume bottle.

flageoler, fläh-sholl-eh, *v* to shake; to tremble.

flageolet, fläh-sholl-ay, *m* flageolet; small kidney bean.

flagrant, e, fläh-grahng, *a* flagrant; **en –délit,** ahng – deh-le, in the very act.

flair, flayr, *m* scent; flair.

flamant, fläh-mahng, *m* flamingo.

flambeau, flahng-boh, *m* torch; light.

flamber, flahng-beh, *v* to flame; to singe; to blaze.

flamboyer, flahng-bo'äh-e-eh, *v* to flare up; to glow.

flamme, flähmm, *f* flame.

flammèche, fläh-maish, *f* spark; flake.

flan, flahng, *m* custard tart; flan.

flanc, flahng, *m* flank; side.

flancher, flahng-sheh, *v* to flinch; to give in.

flâner, flah-neh, *v* to lounge; to hang about.

flanquer, flahng-keh, *v* to flank; to throw; to hit.

flaque, flähck, *f* puddle.

flasque, flähssk, *a* flabby; weak.

flatter, fläh-teh, *v* to flatter; to pat; to fawn upon.

flatteu-r, se,* fläh-ter, *mf* flatterer. *a* flattering.

flatuosité, fläh-tE-o-ze-teh, *f* flatulency.

fléau, fleh-oh, *m* scourge; curse; beam; bar.

flèche, flaish, *f* arrow; beam; spire.

fléchir, fleh-sheer, *v* to bend; to give way; to bow; to fall.

fléchissement, fleh-shiss-

mahng, *m* bending;
giving way.

flegme, flegm, *m*
composure; impassivity.

flemme, flem, *f* laziness.

flétrir, fleh-treer, *v* to
wither; to fade; to
brand; **se –,** to fade.

flétrissure, fleh-triss-EEr, *f*
withering; stigma.

fleur, fler, *f* flower;
blossom; prime; **à –de,**
ăh – der, on the surface
of.

fleurette, fler-rett, *f* small
flower; sweet nonsense.

fleurir, fler-reer, *v* to
flower; to bloom; to
thrive; to adorn with
flowers.

fleuve, flerv, *m* river.

flexion, fleck-se-ong, *f*
bending.

flirter, fleer-teh, *v* to flirt.

flocon, flock-ong, *m* flake;
flock.

floraison, flor-ay-zong, *f*
flowering; blooming.

florissant, e, flor-iss-ahng,
a flourishing.

flot, flo, *m* wave; stream;
crowd; floating.

flottant, e, flot-ahng, *a*
floating; wavering.

flotte, flot, *f* fleet; float;
(*fam*) water; rain.

flotter, flot-eh, *v* to float;
to waft; to waver; (*fam*)

to rain.

flou, e, floo, *a* hazy.

fluctuer, flEEk-tE-eh, *v* to
fluctuate.

fluet, te, flE-ay, *a* slender;
thin.

fluide, flE-eed, *m* & *a*
fluid.

flûte, flEEt, *f* flute; long
loaf of bread; tall
champagne glass.

flux, flE, *m* flux; flow.

fluxion, flEEk-se-ong, *f*
inflammation; swelling.

foi, fo'ăh, *f* faith; trust;
belief.

foie, fo'ăh, *m* liver.

foin, fo'ang, *m* hay.

foire, fo'ăhr, *f* fair.

fois, fo'ăh, *f* time;
occasion; **une –,**EEn –,
once; **à la –,** ăh lăh –, at
once; both.

foison, fo'ăh-zong, *f*
plenty; **à –,** ăh –,
abundantly.

foisonner, fo'ăh-zonn-eh,
v to abound.

fol, fol, *a* (see **fou**).

folâtre, foll-ah-tr, *a*
playful; frolicsome.

folâtrer, foll-ah-treh, *v* to
play around.

folie, foll-ee, *f* madness;
extravagance; mania.

folio, foll-e-o, *m* folio.

folle, fol, *f* (see **fou**).

follet, foll-ay, *a* merry; **feu**

–, fer –, will o' the wisp.

foncé, e, fong-seh, *a* dark
(color).

foncer, fong-seh, *v* to
deepen; to sink; to dash;
to rush (**sur,** at).

foncier, ère, fong-se-eh, *a*
landed; thorough;
fundamental.

foncièrement, fong-se-air-
mahng, *adv* thoroughly;
fundamentally.

fonction, fongk-se-ong, *f*
function; *pl* office;
duties.

fonctionnaire, fongk-se-
onn-air, *m* official; civil
servant.

fonctionner, fongk-se-
onn-eh, *v* to work; to
function.

fond, fong, *m* bottom;
foundation; depth;
ground; substance; **à –,**
ăh –, thoroughly.

fondamental, e,* fong-
dăh-mahng-tăhl, *a*
fundamental.

fondant, fong-dahng, *m*
fondant candy.

fondant, e, fong-dahng, *a*
melting.

fonda-teur, trice, fong-
dăh-ter, *mf* & *a* founder.

fondé, e, fong-deh, *pp* & *a*
founded; justified; **–de
pouvoir,** – der poo-
vo'ăhr, proxy.

fondement, fongd-mahng, *m* foundation; ground.

fonder, fong-deh, *v* to found; to build; to establish; **se –,** to be based on; to rely.

fonderie, fongd-ree, *f* foundry.

fondeur, fong-der, *m* founder.

fondre, fong-dr, *v* to melt; to cast; to disappear; to pounce.

fondrière, fong-dree-air, *f* quagmire; bog.

fonds, fong, *m* land; property; fund; funds; cash; *pl* securities; **–de commerce,** – der komm-airss, business.

fontaine, fong-tain, *f* fountain; spring; cistern.

fonte, fongt, *f* melting; casting; cast iron; holster.

fonts, fong, *mpl* font; **–baptismaux,** – bah-tiss-moh, christening font.

football, footbähl; *m* soccer.

for, for, *m* **–intérieur,** – ang-teh-re-er, conscience.

forain, e, for-ang, *a* foreign; traveling (of theater, fair, etc).

forban, for-bahng, *m* pirate.

forçat, for-săh, *m* convict.

force, forss, *a* plenty of. *f* strength; power.

forcé, e, for-seh, *pp* & *a* forced; **travaux –s,** trăh-voh –, penal servitude.

forcément, for-seh-mahng, *adv* forcibly; necessarily.

forcené, e, for-ser-neh, *mf* & *a* mad; furious.

forcer, for-seh, *v* to force; to break open; to compel.

forer, for-eh, *v* to bore; to drill.

forestier, for-ayss-te-eh, *m* forester.

foret, for-ay, *m* drill; borer.

forêt, for ay, *f* forest.

forfait, for-fay, *m* crime; forfeit; contract; **à –,** ăh –, by contract.

forfanterie, for-fahngt-ree, *f* bragging.

forge, forsh, *f* forge; ironworks.

forger, for-sheh, *v* to forge; to hammer; to make up; **se –,** to earn.

forgeron, for-sher-rong, *m* blacksmith.

formaliser (se), ser for-măh-le-zeh, to take offense (**de,** at).

formalité, for-măh-le-teh, *f* formality; ceremony.

format, for-măh, *m* size.

formation, fo-măh-se-ong, *f* formation; structure.

forme, form, *f* form; shape; mold; *pl* manners.

formel, le,* for-mell, *a* formal; express.

former, for-meh, *v* to form; to train; **se –,** to take form.

formidable, for-me-dăhbl, *a* fearsome; (*fam*) tremendous.

formulaire, for-mE-lair, *m* form.

formule, for-mEEl, *f* formula; prescription; form.

formuler, for-mE-leh, *v* to draw up.

fort, for, *adv* very; extremely. *m* strongest part; thickest; height; fort; forte.

fort, e,* for, *a* strong; stout; clever; thick; loud; severe; hard.

forteresse, fort-rayss, *f* fortress.

fortifiant, e, for-te-fe-ahng, *a* strengthening; tonic.

fortifier, for-te-fe-eh, *v* to strengthen; to fortify.

fortuit, e,* for-twee, *a* accidental; fortuitous.

fortune, for-tEEn, *f* fortune; chance; luck.

fortuné, e, for-tE-neh, *a*

fortunate; well-off.

fosse, fohss, *f* pit; hole; grave.

fossé, fohss-eh, *m* ditch.

fossette, fohss-ett, *f* dimple.

fossile, foss-eell, *m* & *a* fossil.

fossoyeur, fohss-o'ăh-yer, *m* gravedigger.

fou, folle, foo, fol, *mf* lunatic; fool; bishop (chess); *a* * crazy; mad; foolish. (Before a masculine noun beginning with a vowel or **h** mute, the masculine is **fol,** fol, instead of **fou**).

foudre, foo-dr, *f* lightning; thunderbolt; thunder; **coup de –,** coo der –, love at first sight.

foudroyant, e, foo-dro'ăh-yahng, *a* crushing; startling.

foudroyé, foo-dro'ăh-yeh, *pp* & *a* thunderstruck.

foudroyer, e, foo-dro'ăh-yeh, *v* to strike by lightning.

fouet, foo-ay, *m* whip; flogging.

fouetter, foo-ay-teh, *v* to whip; to flog; to lash; to whisk.

fougère, foo-shair, *f* fern.

fougue, foogh, *f* fire; impetuosity; spirit.

fouille, foo'e-ye, *f* excavation; digging.

fouiller, foo'e-yeh, *v* to excavate; to dig; to search; to rummage.

fouillis, foo'e-yee, *m* confusion; jumble.

fouine, foo-een, *f* marten.

foulant, e, foo-lahng, *a* pressing.

foulard, foo-lăhr, *m* silk handkerchief.

foule, fool, *f* crowd; throng; mob.

fouler, foo-leh, *v* to press; to tread; to trample; to sprain.

foulure, foo-lEEr, *f* sprain.

four, foohr, *m* oven; kiln; furnace; (*fig*) failure.

fourbe, foohrb, *m* cheat; *a* tricky; deceitful.

fourberie, foohr-ber-ree, *f* cheat; trickery.

fourbir, foohr-beer, *v* to furbish.

fourbu, e, foohr-bE, *a* foundered; tired out.

fourche, foohrsh, *f* fork; pitchfork.

fourcher, foohr-sheh, *v* to branch off; to dig with pitchfork.

fourchette, foohr-shett, *f* fork (utensil); wishbone.

fourchu, e, foohr-shE, *a* forked; split.

fourgon, foohr-gong, *m* van; wagon; hearse.

fourgonner, foohr-gonn-eh, *v* to poke; to rake.

fourmi, foohr-me, *f* ant; **avoir des –s,** ah-vo'ăhr deh –, to have pins and needles in one's legs.

fourmilière, foohr-me-le-air, *f* anthill.

fourmiller, foohr-mee-yeh, *v* to teem; to swarm (**de,** with).

fourneau, foohr-noh, *m* stove; furnace; boiler.

fournée, foohr-neh, *f* ovenful; batch; lot.

fourni, e, foohr-ne, *pp* & *a* furnished; thick.

fournir, foohr-neer, *v* to supply; to provide; to stock.

fournisseur, foohr-niss-er, *m* supplier; tradesman.

fourniture, foohr-ne-tEEr, *f* supply; *pl* fittings; supplies.

fourrage, foo-răhsh, *m* fodder.

fourré, foo-reh, *m* thicket.

fourré, foo-reh, *a* lined; fur-lined; filled (of chocolates, etc).

fourreau, foo-roh, *m* sheath; scabbard; cover; tight-fitting dress.

fourrer, foo-reh, *v* to stuff; to cram; to line with fur.

fourreur, foo-**rer,** *m*
 furrier.
fourrière, foo-re-**air,** *f*
 pound.
fourrure, foo-**rEEr,** *f* fur.
fourvoyer, foohr-vo'ăh-
 yeh, *v* to lead astray.
foyer, fo'ăh-yeh, *m*
 hearth; home; center;
 foyer.
frac, frăhck, *m* tailcoat.
fracas, frăh-kah, *m* noise;
 din; crash; roar; fuss.
fracasser, frăh-kăhss-eh, *v*
 to shatter; to smash.
fraction, frăhck-se-ong, *f*
 fraction.
fractionner, frăhck-se-
 onn-eh, *v* to divide into
 fractions.
fracture, frăhck-tEEr, *f*
 fracture; breaking.
fracturer, frăhck-tE-reh, *v*
 to fracture; to break.
fragile,* frăh-sheel, *a*
 fragile; brittle; frail.
fragilité, frăh-she-le-teh, *f*
 brittleness; frailty.
fragment, frăhg-mahng, *m*
 fragment; piece; scrap.
frai, fray, *m* spawn;
 spawning.
fraîcheur, fray-sher, *f*
 freshness.
fraîchir, fray-sheer, *v* to
 freshen.
frais, fray, *mpl* expenses;
 charges; efforts.

frais, fraîche,* fray;
 fraysh, *a* fresh; cool;
 new.
fraise, frayz, *f* strawberry.
framboise, frahng-bo'ăhz, *f*
 raspberry.
franc, frahng, *m* franc.
franc, franche,* frahng,
 frahngsh, *a* free; open;
 frank; genuine.
français, e, frahng-sseh, *a*
 French. *mf* Frenchman;
 Frenchwoman; *m*
 French language.
franchir, frahng-sheer, *v*
 to clear; to leap over; to
 overstep; to overcome.
franchise, frahng-sheez, *f*
 freedom; openness;
 exemption.
franciser, frahng-se-zeh, *v*
 to gallicize.
franco, frahng-ko, *adv* free
 of charge; paid.
frange, frahngsh, *f* fringe.
franglais, frahng-gleh, *m*
 mixture of French and
 English.
franquette, frahng-kett, *f*;
 à la bonne –, ăh lăh
 bonn –, without
 ceremony.
frappant, e, frăh-pahng, *a*
 striking.
frapper, frăh-peh, *v* to
 strike; to knock; to rap;
 to ice; **se –,** to get
 flustered.

fraternel, le,* frăh-tair-
 nell, *a* brotherly;
 fraternal.
fraterniser, frăh-tair-ne-
 zeh, *v* to fraternize.
fraternité, frăh-tair-ne-
 teh, *f* brotherhood;
 fraternity.
fraude, frohd, *f* fraud;
 deceit; smuggling.
frauder, froh-deh, *v* to
 defraud; to smuggle.
frauduleu-x, se,* froh-dE-
 ler, *a* fraudulent.
frayer, fray-yeh, *v* to open
 up; to clear a path; to
 spawn.
frayeur, fray-yer, *f* fright;
 dread; terror.
fredaine, frer-dayn, *f*
 prank; escapade.
fredonner, frer-donn-eh, *v*
 to hum.
frégate, freh-găht, *f*
 frigate; frigate bird.
frein, frang, *m* bit; bridle;
 brake; check.
freiner, freh-neh, *v* to
 brake; to put on the
 brakes.
frelater frer-lăh-teh, *v* to
 adulterate.
frêle, frail, *a* weak; frail.
frelon, frer-long, *m*
 hornet; drone.
frémir, freh-meer, *v* to
 shudder; to tremble; to
 rustle; to simmer.

frémissement, freh-miss-mahng, *m* shuddering; quivering; rustling.

frêne, frain, *m* ash tree.

frénésie, freh-neh-zee, *f* frenzy.

frénétique,* freh-neh-teeck, *a* frantic.

fréquemment, freh-kăh-mahng, *adv* frequently.

fréquence, freh-kahngss, *f* frequency; quickness.

fréquent, e, freh-kahng, *a* frequent.

fréquenter, freh-kahng-teh, *v* to frequent; to associate with.

frère, frair, *m* brother; friar.

fresque, fressk, *f* fresco.

fret, fray, *m* freight; chartering.

fréter, freh-teh, *v* to charter; to freight.

frétiller, freh-tee-yeh, *v* to frisk; to wriggle; to quiver.

freux, frer, *m* rook.

friable, fre-ăh-bl, *a* crumbly.

friand, e, fre-ahng, *a* fond of delicacies.

friandise, fre-ahng-deez, *f* delicacy; tidbit.

fricandeau, fre-kahng-doh, *m* larded veal.

fricassée, fre-kăhss-eh, *f* fricassée.

fricasser, fre-kăhss-eh, *v* to fricassee; (*pop*) to fritter away.

friche, freesh, *f* wasteland.

fricot, fre-ko, *m* (*pop*) stew.

fricoter fre-kot-eh, *v* (*pop*) to cook.

friction, frick-se-ong, *f* friction; rub down.

frictionner, frick-se-onn-eh, *v* to rub.

frigidaire, fre-she-dair, *m* refrigerator.

frigide, fre-sheed, *a* frigid.

frigorifier, fre-gor-e-fe-eh, *v* to chill; to refrigerate.

frileu-x, se,* fre-ler, *a* chilly; sensitive to cold.

frime, freem, *f* sham.

frimousse, fre-mooss, *f* (*fam*) face.

fringale, frang-găhl, *f* sudden hunger.

fringant, e, frang-ghang, *a* frisky; smart; lively.

fripé, e, fre-peh, *pp* & *a* rumpled.

friper, fre-peh, *v* to rumple; to crease.

fripi-er, ère, fre-pe-eh, *mf* secondhand clothes dealer.

fripon, ne, fre-pong, *mf* & *a* rogue; rascal; mischievous; roguish.

frire, freer, *v* to fry.

frise, freez, *f* frieze.

friser, free-zeh, *v* to curl; to touch; to skim; to border upon.

frisson, friss-ong, *m* shiver; shudder; thrill.

frissonner, friss-onn-eh, *v* to shiver; to quiver; to shudder.

frit, e, free, *pp* & *a* fried; (*pop*) done for; squandered.

friture, free-tEEr, *f* frying; dripping; fried fish; crackling noises (of telephone, etc.).

frivole, free-vol, *a* frivolous.

froc, frock, *m* frock (of monk, etc).

froid, fro'ăh, *m* cold; coldness.

froid, e,* fro'ăh, *a* cold; cool; indifferent.

froideur, fro'ăh-der, *f* coldness; coolness; indifference.

froissement, fro'ăhss-mahng, *m* bruising; rumpling; offense.

froisser, fro'ăhss-eh, *v* to rumple; to offend; se –, to take offense (**de,** at).

frôlement, frohl-mahng, *m* light rubbing or touching.

frôler, froh-leh, *v* to touch slightly; to graze.

fromage, from-ăhsh, *m*

cheese.

froment, from-ahng, *m* wheat.

froncer, frongss-eh, *v* to pucker; to frown; to gather.

fronde, frongd, *f* sling; catapult.

fronder, frongd-eh, *v* to jeer at.

front, frong, *m* forehead; brow; impudence; front; **faire–, fair–,** to face.

frontière, frong-te-air, *f* frontier; border.

fronton, frong-tong, *m* pediment.

frottement, frot-mahng, *m* rubbing; friction.

frotter, frot-eh, *v* to rub; to polish.

frottoir, frot-o'ăhr, *m* rubbing cloth; scrubbing brush.

frou-frou, froo-froo, *m* rustling.

frousse, froos, *f* (*fam*) fear; **avoir la –,** ăh-vo'ăhr-lăh –, to be scared.

fructifier, frEEk-te-fe-eh, *v* to bear fruit.

fructueu-x, se,* frEEk-tE-er, *a* fruitful; profitable.

frugal, e,* frE-ghăl, *a* frugal.

fruit, frwee, *m* fruit; offspring; profit.

fruiti-er, ère, frwee-te-eh,

mf fruitseller. *a* fruit-bearing.

frusques, frEEsk, *fpl* (*fam*) clothes; effects; gear.

fruste, frEEst, *a* crude; defaced.

frustrer, frEEs-treh, *v* to frustrate; to defraud.

fugiti-f, ve, fE- she-teeff, *a* fugitive; transient.

fugue, fEEgh, *f* fugue; spree.

fuir, fweer, *v* to flee; to shun; to leak; to escape.

fuite, fweet, *f* flight; escape; evasion; leakage.

fulgurant, e, fEEl-ghE-rahng, *a* flashing.

fumée, fE-meh, *f* smoke; fume.

fumer, fE-meh, *v* to smoke; to steam; to fertilize.

fumet, fE-may, *m* pleasant smell of cooking; scent; bouquet.

fumier, fE-me-eh, *m* manure; manure heap.

fumiger, fE-me-sheh, *v* to fumigate.

fumiste, fE-meesst, *m* heating engineer; (*fam*) lazy person; fraud.

fumivore, fE-me-vor, *a* smoke-absorbing.

fumoir, fE-mo'ăhr, *m* smokehouse.

funambule, fe-nahng-bEEl,

m tightrope walker.

funèbre, fE-nay-br, *a* funeral; mournful; dismal.

funérailles, fE-neh-rah'e, *fpl* funeral.

funeste, fE-naysst *a* fatal; disastrous.

funiculaire, fE-ne-kE-lair, *m* & *a* funicular.

fur, fEer, *m* **au –et à mesure,** oh – eh ăh merzEEr, in proportion; gradually as.

furet, fE-ray, *m* ferret.

fureter, fEer-teh, *v* to ferret out; to rummage.

fureur, fE-rer, *f* fury; rage; mania; **faire–,** fair – to be all the rage.

furibond, e, fE-re-bong, *a* furious.

furie, fE-ree, *f* fury; rage.

furieu-x, se,* fE-re-er, *a* furious; mad; raging.

furoncle, fE-rong-kl, *m* boil.

furti-f, ve,* fEEr-teeff, *a* furtive; stealthy.

fusain, fE-zang, *m* spindle tree; charcoal pencil.

fuseau, fE-zoh, *m* spindle; taper; *pl* skiing pants.

fusée, fE-zeh, *f* fuse; rocket.

fuselage, fEEz-lăhsh, *m* fuselage; body.

fuselé, e, fEEz-leh, *a*

tapering.

fusible, fE-zee-bl, *a* fusible.

fusible, fE-zee-bl, *m* fuse.

fusil, fE-ze, *m* rifle; gun.

fusillade, fE-zee-yăhd, *f* rifle fire; fusillade; shooting; execution.

fusiller, fe-zee-yeh, *v* to shoot.

fusion, fE-ze-ong, *f* fusion; melting; amalgamation.

fusionner, fE-ze-onn-eh, *v* to amalgamate.

fût, fE, *m* cask; stock; shaft.

futaille, fE-tah'e, *f* cask; barrel.

futé, e, fE-teh, *a* sly; cunning; crafty.

futile,* fE-teel, *a* futile; frivolous.

futilité, fE-te-le-teh, *f* futility; frivolousness.

futur, e, fE-tEER, *m* future; future tense; **(fam)** *mf* intended (husband, wife); *a* future; the life to come.

fuyant, e, fwee-yahng, *a* fleeting; fleeing; receding.

fuyard, e, fwee-yăhr *mf* runaway; *a* runaway; fugitive.

gabarit, găh-băh-re, *m* template; gauge; size.

gâcher, gah-sheh, *v* to mix; to make a mess of; to spoil.

gâchette, gah-sheh-t, *f* trigger.

gâchis, gah-she, *m* slush; mess; confusion; waste.

gadget, gah-dshe-t, *m* gadget; gimmick.

gaffe, găhf, *f* boathook; (*fam*) blunder; **faire une – fair** EEn –, to put one's foot in it; (*fam*) **faire –**, to be careful.

gage, găhsh, *m* pledge; pawn; forfeit; *pl* wages.

gager, găh-sheh, to bet.

gageure, găh-sh EEr, *f* wager; the impossible.

gagnant, gah-nee-ahng, *a* winning; *mf* winner.

gagne-pain, găhn-yer-pang, *m* livelihood.

gagner, găhn-yeh, *v* to earn; to win; to persuade; **se –**, to be catching.

gai, e, gheh, *a* gay; lively; cheerful.

gaiement, gheh-mahng, *adv* gaily.

gaieté, gheh-teh, *f* gaiety; cheerfulness.

gaillard, e, gah'e-yăhr, *a* lively; strong; free. *m* chap.

gain, ghang, *m* gain; profit; advantage.

gaine, ghain, *f* sheath; case; corset; girdle.

galamment, găh-lăh-mahng, *adv* courteously.

galant, găh-lahng, *m* lover; ladies' man; wooer.

galant, e, găh-lahng, *a* courteous; polite; worthy.

galanterie, găh-lahngt-ree, *f* love affair; politeness.

galbe, găhlb, *m* curve; contour.

gale, găhl, *f* mange.

galère, găh-lair, *f* galley; *pl* penal servitude.

galerie, găhl-ree, *f* gallery; spectators.

galet, găh-lay, *m* pebble; shingle.

galetas, găhl-tah, *m* attic.

galette, găh-lett, *f* pancake; biscuit; (*slang*) cash.

galeu-x, se, găh-ler, *a* scabby; mangy.

gallicisme, găhl-le-sissm, *m* French idiom.

galoche, găh-losh, *f* galosh; clog.

galon, găh-long, *m* braid; *pl* stripes.

galop, găh-lo, *m* gallop; great haste; scolding.

galoper, găh-lop-eh, *v* to gallop; to run on.

galopin, găh-lop-ang, *m* urchin; rogue.

gambader, gahng-băh-deh, *v* to leap; to skip.

gamelle, găh-mell, *f* lunch box.

gamin, e, găh-mang, *mf* kid; youngster.

gamme, găhm, f gamut; scale.

ganglion, gahng-gle-ong, m ganglion.

ganse, ghahngss, f cord; braid.

gant, ghahng, m glove; **–de toilette**, – der to'ǎhlett, washcloth.

garage, găh-rǎhsh, m garage.

garant, e, găh-rahng, mf guarantor; surety; bail.

garantie, găh-rahng-tee, f guarantee; warranty; safeguard.

garantir, găh-rahng-teer, v to guarantee; to secure; to protect.

garçon, găhr-song, m boy; lad; bachelor; waiter.

garçonnière, găhr-sonn-e-air, f bachelor's apartment.

garde, găhrd, m guard; watchman; warden.

garde, găhrd, f guard; care; keeping; watch; protection; nurse.

garder, găhr deh, v to guard; to watch; to look after; to keep.

gardien, ne, găhr-de-ang, mf guardian; keeper; trustee.

gare, găhr, f station; terminus.

gare! găhr, interj look out!

garenne, găh-rain, f warren.

garer, găh-reh, v to park (car); to shunt; **se –**, to get out of the way.

gargarisme, găhr-găh-reessm, m gargle.

garnement, găhr-ner-mahng, m scamp; rascal.

garnir, găhr-neer, v to furnish (**de**, with); to adorn; to line; to decorate; to garnish.

garnison, găhr-ne-zong, f garrison.

garniture, găhr-ne-tEEr, f set; trimming; ornaments; garnishing.

garrot, găh-roh, m tourniquet.

garrotter, găh-rott-eh, v to tie down; to garrote.

gars, gah, m lad.

gaspiller, găhss-pee-yeh, v to squander; to waste.

gastronome, găhss-tronn-omm, m gourmet.

gâteau, gah-toh, m cake; **petit—**, pertee—, cookie.

gâter, gah-teh, v to spoil; to damage; to spoil (person).

gauche, gohsh, f left side. a left; clumsy.

gauchement, gohsh-mahng, adv awkwardly.

gauch-er, ère, goh-sheh, a left-handed.

gaucherie, gohsh-ree, f awkwardness.

gaufre, ghoh-fr, f wafer; waffle.

gaule, gohl, f long pole; switch.

gave, găhv, m stream; torrent.

gaver, gahv-eh, v to cram (with food); to stuff.

gavroche, găh-vrosh, m street urchin.

gaz, gahz, m gas; gaslight.

gaze, gahz, f gauze.

gazeu-x, se, gah-zer, a sparkling; fizzy.

gazon, gah-zong, m grass; turf; green.

gazouiller, găh-zoo'e-yeh, v to warble; to chirp.

geai, shay, m jay.

géant, e, sheh-ahng, mf & a giant; giantess; gigantic.

geindre, shang-dr, v to whimper; to whine.

gel, shehl, m frost; freezing.

gelée, sher-leh, f frost; jelly.

geler, sher-leh, v to freeze.

gémir, sheh-meer, v to groan; to lament; to grieve.

gémissement, sheh-miss-mahng, m groan; lamentation.

gemme, shaym, f gem. a
sel –, sell –, rock salt.

gênant, e, shay-nahng, a
troublesome; awkward;
embarrassing.

gencive, shahng-seev, f
gum.

gendarme, shahng-dăhrm,
m policeman.

gendre, shahng-dr, m son-
in-law.

gêne, shayn, f hindrance;
embarrassment; want.

gêner, shay-neh, v to
hinder; to
inconvenience; **se –,** to
put oneself out.

général, e,* sheh-neh-
răhl, a & mf general;
dress rehearsal.

générale, sheh-neh-răhl, f
alarm.

généreu-x, se,* sheh-neh-
rer, a generous.

générosité, sheh-neh-roz-
e-teh, f generosity.

genèse, sher-nayz, f
genesis; birth; origin.

genêt, sher-nay, m broom.

génial, e,* sheh-ne-ăhl, a
inspired; full of genius.

génie, sheh-nee, m genius;
spirit; engineers.

genièvre, sher-ne-ay-vr, m
juniper; gin.

génisse, sheh-neess, f
heifer.

génitif, sheh-ne-teeff, m
genitive case.

genou, sher-noo, m knee.

genre, shahng r, m kind;
species; gender; manner.

gens, shahng, mf pl
people; men; servants.

gent, shahng, f brood;
race; tribe.

gentil, le, shahng-tee, a
nice; kind; good.

gentilhomme, shahng-tee-
yomm, m nobleman;
gentleman.

gentillesse, shahng-tee-
yess, f kindness.

gentiment, shahng-te-
mahng, adv nicely.

géographie, sheh-ogh-răh-
fee, f geography.

geôli-er, ère, shoh-le-eh,
mf jailer.

géologue, sheh-oll-ogh, m
geologist.

géométrie, sheh-omm-eh-
tree, f geometry.

gérance, sheh-rahngss, f
management.

gérant, e, sheh-rahng, mf
manager.

gerbe, shairb, f sheaf;
bundle; bunch.

gercé, shair-seh, a
chapped.

gerçure, shair-sEEr, f
crack; chap (of hands).

gérer, sheh-reh, v to
manage; to run.

germain, e, shair-mang, a
German; first (first
cousin).

germe, shairm, m germ;
shoot; seed.

gérondif, sheh-rong-deeff,
m gerund.

gésier, sheh-ze-eh, m
gizzard.

geste, shesst, m gesture;
motion; sign.

gesticuler, shess-te-kE-leh,
v to gesticulate.

gestion, shess-te-ong, f
management;
administration.

gibecière, sheeb-se-air, f
shoulder bag.

gibelotte, sheeb-lot, f
rabbit stewed in wine.

gibet, shee-bay, m gallows.

gibier, she-be-eh, m game
(birds, animals).

giboulée, she-boo-leh, f
sudden shower.

giboyeu-x, se, she-bo'ah-
yer, a well stocked with
game.

gicler, she-kleh, v to spurt
out.

gifle, shee-fl, f slap in the
face.

gigantesque, she-gahng-
tayssk, a gigantic.

gigot, she-go, m leg of
lamb.

gigoter, she-got-eh, v to
kick about.

gilet, she-lay, m vest.

gingembre, shang-shahng-br, *m* ginger.

girafe, she-rähf, *f* giraffe.

girofle, she-rofl, *m* clove.

giroflée, she-rof-leh, *f* gilly flower; wallflower.

girouette, she-roo-ayt, *f* vane; weathercock.

gisant, she-zahng, *a* lying.

gisement, sheez-mahng, *m* layer; deposit; stratum.

gît, she, *v* lies; **ci –,** **se –,** here lies.

gîte, sheet, *m* shelter; lair; leg of beef.

givre, shee-vr, *m* frost.

glabre, glah-br, *a* clean-shaven.

glace, glähss, *f* ice; icecream; mirror; car window.

glacé, e, glähss-eh, *pp* & *a* frozen; icy; glazed.

glacial, e, glähss-e-ähl, *a* icy; freezing.

glacière, glähss-e-air, *f* cold room; refrigerator.

glaçon, glähss-ong, *m* icicle; ice cube.

glaïeul, glah-yerl, *m* gladiolus; iris.

glaise, glayz, *f* clay.

glaive, glayv, *m* sword.

gland, glahng, *m* acorn; tassel.

glaner, gläh-neh, *v* to glean.

glapir, gläh-peer, *v* to yelp.

glas, glah, *m* knell; toll.

glissant, e, gliss-ahng, *a* slippery; sliding.

glisser, gliss-eh, *v* to slip; to slide; to glide; to touch lightly; **se –,** to creep.

globe, glob, *m* globe; ball; orb.

gloire, glo'ähr, *f* glory; pride; halo.

glorieu-x, se, * glor-e-er, *a* glorious; vain-glorious.

glorifier, glor-e-fe-eh, *v* to glorify; **se –,** to glory (**de,** in).

gloser, glohz-eh, *v* to gloss; to criticise.

glousser, glooss-eh, *v* to cluck.

glouton, ne, gloo-tong, *mf* glutton; *a* gluttonous.

glu, glE, *f* birdlime.

gluant, e, glE-ahng, *a* sticky; slimy.

glycine, glee-seen, *f* wisteria.

gober, gob-eh, *v* to gulp down; to swallow; (*fam*) to believe anything; to adore (someone).

gobeu-r, se, gob-er, *mf* simpleton; credulous person.

godet, god-ay, *m* saucer (for painters); bowl.

godiche, godichon, ne, god-eesh, god-e-shong, *mf* & *a* simpleton; awkward.

goéland, gweh-lahng, *m* seagull.

goélette, gweh-lett, *f* schooner.

gogo, gogh-o, *adv phr fam*; **à –, äh –,** in abundance.

goguenard, e, gog-nähr, *mf* & *a* jeering; sarcastic person.

goinfre, gwang-fr, *m* (*fam*) guzzler.

golf, golf, *m* golf; golfcourse.

golfe, golf, *m* gulf.

gomme, gomm, *f* gum; rubber.

gond, gong, *m* hinge.

gondole, gong-dol, *f* gondola.

gondoler, gong-do-leh, *v* to warp; to buckle; **se –,** (slang) to shake wiht laughter.

gonfler, gong-fleh, *v* to swell; to inflate.

gorge, gorsh, *f* throat; breast; pass; groove.

gorgée, gor-sheh, *f* mouthful; gulp; sip.

gorger, gor-sheh, *v* to gorge; to cram.

gosier, goz-e-eh, *m* throat; gullet.

gosse, goss, *m* (*fam*) kid; youngster.

goudron, goo-drong, m tar.

gouffre, goo-fr, m gulf; abyss.

goujat, goo-shǎh, m boor.

goulot, goo-lo, m neck (of a bottle).

goulu, e, goo-lE, mf & a glutton; greedy.

goulûment, goo-lEE-mahng, adv greedily.

gourd, e, goohr, a numb.

gourde, goohrd, f gourd; flask; (fam) fool.

gourdin, goohr-dang, m cudgel.

gourer (se), ser goohr-eh, v (fam) to be mistaken.

gourmand, e, goohr-mahng, mf & a being fond of (food); greedy.

gourmandise, goohr-mahng-deez, f love of food; pl delicacies.

gourmé, e, goohr-meh, pp & a stiff; starched.

gourmet, goohr-may, m epicure; gourmet.

gousse, gooss, f pod; husk; shell; clove.

goût, goo, m taste; flavor; liking; style.

goûter, goo-teh, v to taste; to relish; to try. m afternoon tea.

goutte, goot, f drop; sip.

gouttière, goo-te-air, f gutter; drainpipe.

gouvernail, goo-vair-nah'e, m rudder; helm.

gouvernant, goo-vair-nahng, m ruler.

gouvernante, goo-vair-nahngt, f governess; housekeeper.

gouverne, goo-vairn, f guidance; rule of conduct.

gouvernement, goo-vair-ner-mahng, m government; management.

gouverneur, goo-vair-ner, m governor; tutor.

grabat, grǎh-bǎh, m pallet.

grâce, grahss, f grace; mercy; thanks; charm.

gracier, grǎh-se-eh, v to pardon.

gracieu-x, se,* grǎh-se-er, a gracious; kind; courteous; pleasant; grateful.

grade, grǎhd, m grade; rank; degree.

gradé, grǎh-deh, m noncommissioned officer.

gradin, grǎh-dang, m tier; step.

gradué, grǎh-dE-eh, m graduate.

graduel, le,* grǎh-dE-ell, a gradual.

grain, grang, m grain; corn; squall.

graine, grayn, f seed; berry; grain.

graissage, grayss-ǎsh, m greasing; lubrication.

graisse, grayss, f grease; fat; drippings.

graisser, grayss-eh, v to grease.

graisseu-x, se, grayss-er, a greasy.

grammaire, grǎh-mair, f grammar.

grammatical, e,* grǎh-mǎh-te-kǎhl, a grammatical.

gramme, grǎhm, m gram.

grand, grahng, m grown-up.

grand, e,* grahng, a great; big; tall; grown-up; much.

grandeur, grahng-der, f greatness; size; magnitude; dignity.

grandiose, grahng-de-ohz, m grandeur. a grand.

grandir, grahng-deer, v to grow; to increase; to exaggerate.

grand magasin, grahng-mǎh-gǎh-zang, m department store.

grand-mère, grahng-mair, f grandmother.

grand-oncle, grahng-t'ong-kl, m great-uncle.

grand-père, grahng-pair, m grandfather.

grandroute, grahng-root, f

highway; main road.

grand-tante, grahng-tahngt, *f* great-aunt.

grange, grahngsh, *f* barn.

granit, grăh-neet, or grăh-nee, *m* granite.

granule, grăh-nEEl, *m* granule.

graphique, grăh-feeck, *m* graph; diagram. *a** graphic.

graphite, grăh-feet, *m* graphite.

grappe, grăhp, *f* bunch; cluster.

grappin, grăh-pang, *m* hook; grappling iron.

gras, grah, *m* fat part; (legs) calf; fat (on meat).

gras, se, grah, *a* fat; plump; greasy; rich.

grassement, grahss-mahng, *adv* plentifully.

grasseyer, grăhss-ay-yeh, *v* to roll one's r's.

grassouillet, te, grăhss-oo'e-yay, *a* plump; chubby.

gratification, grăh-te-fe-kăh-se-ong, *f* bonus.

gratifier, grăh-te-fe-eh, *v* to favor; to confer; to bestow.

gratin, grăh-tang, *m* burnt part; **au –,** oh –, (cooked) with breadcrumbs.

gratis, grăh-tiss, *adv* gratis.

gratitude, grăh-te-tEEd, *f* gratitude.

gratte-ciel, grăht-se-ell, *m* skyscraper.

gratter, grăh-teh, *v* to scratch; to scrape.

grattoir, grăh-to'ăhr, *m* scraper.

gratuit, e,* grăh-twee, *a* gratuitous; free.

gratuité, grăh-twee-teh, *f* gratuitousness.

grave,* grăhv, *a* grave; serious; deep.

gravelle, grăh-vell, *f* stones (in bladder, etc).

gravelure, grăhv-lEEr, *f* obscenity.

graver, grăh-veh, *v* to engrave.

graveur, grăh-ver, *m* engraver; etcher.

gravier, grăh-ve-eh, *m* gravel; grit.

gravir, grăh-veer, *v* to climb.

gravité, grăh-ve-teh, *f* gravity; weight; sedateness; seriousness.

graviter, grăh-ve-teh, *v* to gravitate.

gravure, grăh-vEEr, *f* engraving; print.

gré, greh, *m* will; liking; thankfulness.

gredin, e, grer-dang, *mf* villain; scoundrel.

gréer, greh-eh, *v* to rig.

greffe, grayf, *m* clerk's office.

greffe, grayf, *f* graft; grafting.

greffier, gray-fe-eh, *m* registrar.

grêle, grayl, *f* hail; *a* slender; slim.

grêlon, gray-long, *m* hailstone.

grelot, grer-lo, *m* small round bell.

grelotter, grer-lot-eh, *v* to shiver.

grenade, grer-năhd, *f* grenade; pomegranate.

grenadier, grer-năh-de-eh, *m* grenadier; pomegranate tree.

grenadine, grer-năh-deen, *f* pomegranate syrup; grenadine.

grenat, grer-năh, *m* garnet; *a* garnet-red.

grenier, grer-ne-eh, *m* attic; granary.

grenouille, grer-noo'e-ye, *f* frog.

grenu, e, grer-nE, *a* grainy; clotted (oil).

grès, gray, *m* sandstone; stoneware.

grève, grayv, *f* strand; beach; strike.

grever, grer-veh, *v* to burden.

gréviste, greh-veesst, *m*

striker.

gribouiller, gre-boo'e-yeh, v to scrawl; to scribble.

grief, gree-eff, m grievance; ground for complaint.

grièvement, gree-ayv-mahng, adv severely; grievously.

griffe, greeff, f claw; clutch; signature; stamp.

griffer, greeff-eh, v to scratch.

griffonner, greeff-onn-eh, v to scribble.

grignoter, green-yot-eh, v to nibble.

grigou, gre-goo, m miser; skinflint.

gril, gree, m grid; grill.

grillade, gree-yăhd, f grilling; grilled meat.

grillage, gree-yăhsh, m grilling; latticework; iron-railing; grate.

grille, gree-ye, f iron gate; railing.

griller, gree-yeh, v to grill; to toast.

grillon, gree-yong, m cricket.

grimace, gree-măhss, f grimace; wry face.

grimper, grang-peh, v to climb; to creep up.

grincement, grangss-mahng, m gnashing; grating; grinding (of teeth).

grincer, grang-seh, v to grate; to gnash; to creak.

grincheu-x, se,* grang-sher, a grumpy; bad-tempered.

gringalet, grang-găh-lay, m thin man.

grippe, greep, f influenza.

gripper, greep-eh, v to gripe; to clutch; to snatch up.

grippe-sou, greep-soo, m skinflint; miser.

gris, gre, m gray.

gris, e, gre, a gray; dull.

grisâtre, gre-zah-tr, a grayish.

griser, gre-zeh, v (fam) to make tipsy; to excite.

grisonner, gre-zonn-eh, v to go gray.

grive, greev, f thrush.

grogner, gronn-yeh, v to grunt; to growl; to grumble.

grognon, gronn-yong, a & mf (f inv) grumpy; grumbler.

groin, grwang, m snout.

grommeler, gromm-leh, v to grumble; to mutter.

grondement, grongd-mahng, m growling; snarl; rumbling.

gronder, grong-deh, v to growl; to roar; to rumble; to scold.

gros, groh, m main part; bulk.

gros, groh, adv much; a great deal; en –, wholesale.

gros, se,* groh, a big; large; fat; coarse; pregnant.

groseille, groh-zay'e, f currant; –à maquereau, – ăh măhck-roh, gooseberry.

grossesse, gross-ayss, f pregnancy.

grosseur, gross-er, f size; tumor.

grossi-er, ère,* gross-eh, a coarse; rough; vulgar.

grossièreté, gross-e-air-teh, f coarseness; rudeness; rude thing.

grossir, gross-eer, v to enlarge; to put on weight.

grossissant, e, gross-iss-ahng, a magnifying.

grotesque, grot-essk, m grotesque. a* grotesque; absurd.

grotte, grot, f grotto.

grouiller, groo'e-yeh, v to stir; to swarm; to rumble.

groupe, groop, m group; clump; cluster.

groupement, groop-mahng, m group.

grouper, groo-peh, v to

group.

gruau, grE-oh, *m* wheat flour; oatmeal;.

grue, grE, *f* crane.

grumeau, grE-moh, *m* clot; lump; curd.

gruyère, grE-yair, *m* Gruyère cheese.

guenille, gher-nee-ye, *f* rag; tattered garment.

guenon, gher-nong, *f* female monkey; ugly woman.

guêpe, ghayp, *f* wasp.

guêpier, ghay-pe-eh, *m* wasps' nest.

guère (ne...), ner ...ghair, *adv* hardly; not much.

guéret, gheh-ray, *m* fallow land.

guéridon, gheh-re-dong, *m* small pedestal table.

guérir, gheh-reer, *v* to cure; to heal; to recover.

guérison, gheh-re-zong, *f* cure; recovery.

guerre, ghair, *f* war; strife.

guerri-er, ère, ghair-e-eh, *mf* warrior. *a* warlike.

guerroyer, ghair-o'ăh-yeh, *v* to wage war.

guet, gay, *m* watch; **au –,** oh –, on the watch.

guet-apens, gay t'ăh-pahng, *m* ambush; trap.

guetter, ghay-teh, *v* to watch for; to look for.

gueule, gherl, *f* mouth (of animal); jaws; (*pop*) mug; **avoir la –de bois,** ăh-vo'ăhr lah – der bo'ăh, to have a hangover.

gueuler, gher-leh, *v (fam)* to bawl.

gueu-x, se, gher, *a* beggarly; wretched. *mf* beggar; tramp.

gui, ghe, *m* mistletoe.

guichet, ghe-shay, *m* wicket; booking office; box office.

guide, gheed, *m* guide; guidebook; *f* rein.

guider, ghe-deh, *v* to guide.

guidon, ghe-dong, *m* handlebar.

guigne, gheen-yer, *f* black cherry; bad luck.

guignol, gheen-yol, *m* puppet show.

guillemet, gheel-may, *m* inverted comma.

guillotine, ghee-yot-een, *f* guillotine.

guimauve, ghe-mohv, *f* marshmallow.

guindé, e, ghang-deh, *pp* & *a* hoisted; strained; stiff.

guinée, ghe-neh, *f* guinea.

guinguette, ghang-gayt, *f* open air café; dance hall.

guirlande, gheer-lahngd, *f* garland; wreath.

guise, gheez, *f* fancy; **à la –,** ah teh, as you please.

guitare, ghe-tăhr, *f* guitar.

gymnase, sheem-nahz, *m* gymnasium.

gymnaste, shem-năhs-t, *mf* gymnast.

gymnastique, shem-nahs-tik, *f* physical education; gymnastics.

gynécologue, shee-nehck-o-log, *mf* gynecologist.

There is no liaison with or elision before words marked thus; §

§ha! ăh, *interj* ha! ah!

habile,* ăh-beell, *a* clever; qualified.

habileté, ăh-beell-teh, *f* ability; cleverness.

habillement, ăh-bee-yer-mahng, *m* clothing; dress; suit of clothes.

habiller, ăh-bee-yeh, *v* to dress.

habit, ăh-be, *m* coat; dress-coat; *pl* clothes.

habitant, e, ăh-be-tahng, *mf* inhabitant; resident; inmate.

habitation, ăh-be-tăh-se-ong, *f* dwelling; house.

habiter, ăh-be-teh, *v* to inhabit; to live in; to reside.

habitude, ăh-be-tEEd, *f* habit; use; practice.

habitué, e, ăh-be-tE-eh, *mf* regular customer.

habituel, le,* ăh-be-tE-ell, *a* customary.

habituer, ăh-be-tE-eh, *v* to accustom; to inure.

§hache, ăhsh, *f* ax; hatchet.

§hacher, ăh-sheh, *v* to chop; to cut to pieces; to mince (meat, etc).

§hachette, ăh-shett, *f* hatchet.

§hachis, ăh-she, *m* hash; minced meat.

§hagard, e, ăh-găhr, *a* haggard.

§haie, ay, *f* hedge; line; row.

§haillon, ah'e-yong, *m* rag; tatter.

§haine, ain, *f* hatred; hate; spite.

§haineu-x, se,* ay-ner, *a* hateful; spiteful.

§haïr, ăh'e-eer, *v* to hate.

§haïssable, ăh-eess-ăh-bl, *a* odious; hateful.

§halage, ah-lăhsh, *m* towing.

§hâlé, e, ah-leh, *a* sunburnt.

haleine, ăh-lain, *f* breath; wind.

§haler, ah-leh, *v* to tow; to brown; to tan.

§haleter, ăhl-teh, *v* to pant.

§halle, ăhl, *f* market; marketplace.

§hallebarde, ăhl-băhrd, **il pleut des –,** ill pler day –, it rains cats and dogs.

§hallier, ăh-le-eh, *m* thicket.

hallucination, ăhl-lE-se-năh-se-ong, *f* hallucination.

§halte, ăhlt, *f* halt; stop; haltingplace; **–là! –** lăh, stop!

§haltère, ăhl-tair, *f* barbell.

§hamac, ăh-măhck, *m* hammock.

§hameau, ăh-moh, *m* hamlet.

hameçon, ăhm-song, *m* fishhook; (*fig*) bait.

§hampe, ahngp, *f* staff; handle.

§hanche, ahngsh, *f* hip; haunch.

§hangar, ahng-găhr, *m* shed; hangar.

§hanneton, ahn-tong, *m* bug.

§hanter, ahng-teh, *v* to frequent; to haunt.

§happer, ăh-peh, *v* to snap up; to snatch; to catch.

§harangue, ăh-rahng-gh, *f* harangue; address; speech.

§haras, ăh-rah, *m* stud farm.

§harasser, ăh-răhss-eh, *v* to tire out.

§harceler, ăhr-ser-leh, *v* to harass.

§harde, ăhrd, *f* leash; *pl* old clothes.

§hardi, e, ăhr-de, *a* bold; impudent.

§hardiment, ăhr-de-mahng, *adv* boldly.

§hardiesse, ăhr-de-ess, *f* boldness; assurance; impudence.

§hareng, ăh-rahng, *m* herring.

§hargneu-x, se, ăhrn-yer, *a* surly; peevish.

§haricot, ăh-re-ko, *m* kidney bean; –vert, – vair, French bean.

harmonie, ăhr-monn-ee, *f* harmony; harmonics.

harmonieu-x, se,* ăhr-monn-e-er, *a* harmonious.

§harnachement, ăhr-năhsh-mahng, *m* harnessing; harness.

§harnais, ăhr-nay, *m* harness.

§haro, ăh-ro, *m* outcry.

harpagon, ăhr-păh-gong, *m* (*fam*) miser.

§harpe, ăhrp, *f* harp.

§harpon, ăhr-pong, *m* harpoon.

§hasard, ăh-zăhr, *m* luck; chance; risk.

§hasardeu-x, se,* ăh-zăhr-der, *a* hazardous; unsafe.

§hâte, aht, *f* haste; hurry.

§hâter, ah-teh, *v* to hasten; to urge on; to expedite.

§hâti-f, ve,* ah-teeff, *a* forward; early; hasty.

§hausse, ohss, *f* block; rise.

§hausser, ohss-eh, *v* to arise; to lift; to increase; to advance; –les épaules, – leh zeh-pohl, to shrug one's shoulders.

§haussier, ohss-e-eh, *m* bull (stock exchange).

§haut, oh, *m* height; summit.

§haut, oh, *adv* high up;

loudly.

§haut, e,* oh, *a* high; lofty; tall; erect.

§hautain, e,* oh-tang, *a* haughty.

§hautbois, oh-bo'ăh, *m* oboe.

§hauteur, oh-ter, *f* height; eminence; haughtiness.

§haut-parleur, oh-pahr-ler, *m* loudspeaker; amplifier.

§havane, ăh-văhn, *m* Havana cigar.

§hâve, ahv, *a* wan; emaciated.

§havre, ah-vr, *m* harbor.

§havresac, ah-vrer-săhck, *m* knapsack.

§hé! eh, *interj* hey! well! stop it! I say!

hebdomadaire, ehb-domm-ăh-dair, *a* weekly; (*fam*) weekly paper.

héberger, eh-bair-sheh, *v* to lodge; to offer a home to.

hébété, e, eh-beh-teh, *a* dazed; vacant.

hébreu, eh-brer, *m & a* Hebrew.

hectare, eck-tăhr, *m* hectare.

§hein! ang, *interj* eh? what?

hélas! eh-lăhss, *interj* unfortunately!

§héler, eh-leh, v to hail.

hélice, eh-leess, f propeller; screw.

hélicoptère, eh-li-cop-tair, m helicopter.

hémisphère, eh-miss-fair, m hemisphere.

hémorragie, eh-mor-ăh-shee, f hemorrhage.

hémorroïdes, eh-mor-o-eed, fpl hemorrhoids.

§hennir, ăh-neer or eh-neer, v to neigh.

herbage, air-băhsh, m grass; pasture.

herbe, airb, f grass; herb; weed.

herboriste, air-bor-eest, f herbalist.

§hère, air, m wretch; poor devil.

héréditaire, eh-reh de-tair, a hereditary.

hérédité, eh-reh-de-teh, f heredity.

hérésie, eh-reh-zee, f heresy.

§hérisser, eh-riss-eh, v to bristle up; **se –,** to stand on end (of hair).

§hérisson, eh-riss-ong, m hedgehog.

héritage, eh-re-tăhsh, m inheritance; heritage.

hériter, eh-re-teh, v to inherit; to get.

hériti-er, ère, eh-re-te-eh, mf heir; heiress.

hermétique,* air-meh-teeck, a hermetic.

hermine, air-meen, f ermine.

§hernie, air-nee, f hernia; rupture.

héroïne, eh-ro-een, f heroine; heroin.

héroïque,* eh-ro-eeck, a heroic.

§héron, eh-rong, m heron.

§héros, eh-ro, m hero.

§herse, airss, f harrow.

hésiter, eh-ze-teh, v to hesitate.

hétéroclite, eh-teh-rock-leett, a heterogeneous; assorted.

§hêtre, ay-tr, m beech tree.

heure, er, f hour; time; moment; o'clock.

heureu-x, se,* er- rer, a happy; lucky; successful; favorable; blessed.

§heurt, er, m shock; blow.

§heurter, er-teh, v to knock; to jostle; to offend.

hiberner, e-bair-neh, v to hibernate.

§hibou, e-boo, m owl.

§hic, eeck, m (fam) rub; difficulty.

§hideu-x, se,* e-der, a hideous.

hier, e-air, adv yesterday.

hilarité, e-lăh-re-teh, f hilarity; mirth.

hippique, ip-peeck, a of horses; racing.

hippocampe, ip-pock-ahngp, m seahorse.

hippodrome, ip-pod-romm, m racecourse.

hirondelle, e-rong-dell, f swallow.

§hisser, iss-eh, v to hoist.

histoire, iss-to'ăhr, f history; story; tale; fib; **faire des –s,** fair deh-z –, to make a fuss.

historien, iss-tor-e-ang, m historian.

historique,* iss-tor-eeck, a historical.

hiver, e-vair, m winter.

hiverner, e-vair-neh, v to winter; to go into winter quarters.

§hocher, osh-eh, v to shake; to toss; to nod.

§hochet, osh-eh, m child's rattle.

§holà! oll-ăh, interj hey!

§homard, omm-ăhr, m lobster.

homicide, omm-ee-seed, m murder; mf murderer; a murderous.

hommage, omm-ăhsh, m homage; token; pl respects.

homme, omm, m man; (fam) husband.

homosexuel, le, ommo-

secks-Eel, *a* & *m*
homosexual.

honnête, onn-ayt, *m*
honesty; *a** honest;
decent; respectable.

honnêteté, onn-ayt-teh, *f*
honesty; decency.

honneur, onn-er, *m*
honor; credit; respect.

honorable,* onn-or-ăh-bl,
a honorable;
respectable; proper;
creditable.

honoraire, onn-or-air, *a*
honorary.

honoraires, onn-or-air,
mpl fee; fees.

honorer, onn-or-eh, *v* to
honor (**de,** with).

honorifique, onn-or-e-
feeck, *a* honorary.

§honte, ongt, *f* shame;
disgrace; scandal.

§honteu-x, se,* ong-ter, *a*
shameful; ashamed;
bashful.

hôpital, op-e-tăhl, *m*
hospital.

§hoquet, ock-ay, *m*
hiccup.

§horde, ord, *f* horde.

horaire, or-air, *m*
timetable (rail, etc).

horizon, or-e-zong, *m*
horizon.

horizontal, e,* or-e-zong-
tăhl, *a* horizontal.

horloge, or-losh, *f* clock.

horloger, or-losh-eh, *m*
watchmaker;
clockmaker.

horlogerie, or-losh-ree, *f*
watchmaking;
mouvement d'–, moov-
mahng d –, clockwork.

§hormis, or-me, *adv* but;
except.

horreur, or-rer, *f* horror;
frightful thing; dread;
awe; abhorrence.

horrible,* or-ree-bl, *a*
horrible; awful;
shocking.

horripilant, or-ree-pee-
lahng, *a* hair-raising;
(*fam*) exasperating.

§hors, or, *prep* out;
beyond; past; except;
–de combat, – der kong-
băh, disabled.

§hors-d'œuvre, or der-vr,
m hors d'œuvre; starter.

horticulteur, or-te-kEEl-
ter, *m* horticulturist.

hospice, oss-peess, *m*
asylum; hospital for old
and poor people;
hospice.

hospitali-er, ère,* oss-pe-
tăh-le-eh, *a* hospitable.

hostie, oss-tee, *f* victim;
host (holy bread).

hostile,* oss-teel, *a*
hostile; adverse.

hôte, oht, *m* host; guest.

hôtel, oh-tell, *m* hotel;
mansion; townhouse.

hôteli-er, ère, oh-ter-le-
eh, *mf* hotelier;
landlord.

hôtellerie, oh-tell-ree, *f*
inn; hostelry.

hôtesse, oh-tess, *f* hostess;
landlady; guest; **–de
l'air,** – der lair, flight
attendant; stewardess.

§houblon, oo-blong, *m*
hop.

§houille, oo'e-ye, *f* coal.

§houillère, oo'e-yair, *f*
coal-mine; colliery; *a*
coalbearing.

§houle, ool, *f* surge; swell
(of sea).

§houleu-x, se, oo-ler, *a*
swelling; rough.

§houppe, oop, *f* tuft;
powderpuff.

§hourra! oo-răh, *interj*
hurrah!.

§houspiller, oos-pee-yeh,
v to handle roughly; to
abuse.

§housse, ooss, *f* slipcover.

§houx, oo, *m* holly.

§hublot, E-bloh, *m*
porthole.

§huer, E-eh, *v* to hoot; to
boo.

huile, weel, *f* oil.

huis, wee, *m*: à **–clos,** ăh –
kloh, behind closed
doors; in camera (jud.).

huissier, weess-e-yeh, *m*

usher; bailiff.

§**huit,** weet, *a* eight;
eighth.

§**huitaine,** weet-ain, *f*
about eight; a week.

§**huitième,** weet-e-aym, *m*
& *a* eighth.

huître, wee-tr, *f* oyster.

humain, e,* E-mang, *a*
human; humane.

humains, E-mang, *mpl*
mankind.

humanité, E-măh-ne-teh, *f*
humanity; human
nature; *pl* humanities.

humble,* ung-bl, *a*
humble; lowly.

humecter, E-meck-teh, *v*
to moisten.

humer, E-meh, *v* to
inhale; to sip up.

humeur, E-mer, *f* humor;
temper; mood; fancy.

humide * E-meed, *a*
humid; damp; moist.

humiliant, e, E-me-le-
ahng, *a* humiliating.

humilier, E-me-le-eh, *v* to
humble.

humoriste, E-mor-isst, *m*
humorist.

§**huppé, e,** E-peh, *a*
crested; (*fam*) best; well-
off.

§**hurler,** EEr-leh, *v* to
howl; to yell.

hutte, EEt, *f* hut; shed.

hybride, e-breed, *a* hybrid.

hydravion, e-drăh-ve-ong,
m seaplane.

hydrogène, e-drosh-ain, *m*
hydrogen.

hyène, e-ain, *f* hyena.

hygiène, e-she-ain, *f*
hygiene.

hymne, eemn, *m* hymn;
anthem.

hypertension, e-pair-
tahng-se-ong, *f*
hypertension; high
blood pressure.

hypnotiser, ep-not-e-zeh,
v to hypnotize.

hypocrisie, e-pock-re-zee,
f hypocrisy.

hypocrite, e-pock-reet, *m*
hypocrite; *a**
hypocritical.

hypothécaire, e-pot-eh-
kair, *a* mortgage.

hypothèque, e-pot-eck, *f*
mortgage.

hypothèse, e-pot-ayz, *f*
hypothesis.

hystérique, ees-teh-reeck,
a hysterical.

ici, e-se, *adv* here; **par –,** păhr –, this way.

idéal, e-deh-ăhl, *m* ideal; *a** ideal.

idée, e-deh, *f* idea; notion; plan; outline; conceit; opinion.

identifier, e-dahnɡ-te-fe-eh, *v* to identify.

identique,* e-dahnɡ-teeck, *a* identical.

identité, e-dahnɡ-te-teh, *f* identity.

idiome, e-de-omm, *m* dialect; language.

idiot, e, e-de-o, *mf* idiot; *a* idiotic.

idiotie, e-de-oss-ee, *f* idiocy.

idiotisme, e-de-o-tissm, *m* idiom; idiocy.

idolâtre, e-doll-ah-tr, *m* idolater; *a* idolatrous.

idolâtrer, e-doll-ah-treh, *v* to idolize.

idole, e-dol, *f* idol.

if, eef, *m* yew.

ignare, een-yăhr, *a* ignoramus, ignorant.

ignoble, een-yob-l, *a* ignoble; base.

ignominie, een-yomm-e-nee, *f* ignominy.

ignominieu-x, se,* *a* een-yomm-een-e-er, ignominious.

ignorant, e, een-yor-ahnɡ, *mf* ignorant person; *a* ignorant.

ignoré, e, een-yor-eh, *a* unknown; hidden; secret.

ignorer, een-yor-eh, *v* to be ignorant of; not to know.

il, ill, *pron* he; it; there; *pl*

they; **– y a, – e** ăh, there is; there are.

île, eel, *f* island; isle.

illégal, e,* ill-leh-găhl, *a* illegal.

illégitime,* ill-leh-**she**-teem, *a* illegitimate; unlawful.

illettré, e, ill-lay-treh, *a* illiterate.

illicite,* ill-le-seet, *a* unlawful; illegal.

illimité, ill-le-me-teh, *a* unlimited.

illisible,* ill-le-zee-bl, *a* illegible.

illogique,* ill-losh-eeck, *a* illogical.

illumination, ill-lE-me-năh-se-onɡ, *f* illumination.

illuminé, e, ill-lE-me-neh, *mf* visionary; *a* illuminated; enlightened.

illusion, ill-lE-ze-onɡ, *f* illusion; delusion.

illusoire, ill-lE-zo'ăhr, *a* illusory; fallacious.

illustration, ill-lEs-trăh-se-onɡ, *f* illustration; celebrity.

illustre, ill-lEes-tr, *m* illustrious man; *a* illustrious.

illustré, ill-lEes-treh, *a* illustrated; *m* magazine (with pictures).

illustrer, ill-lEs-treh, *v* to illustrate.

îlot, ee-lo, *m* small island; plot; beat; block (of houses).

image, e-mähsh, *f* image; picture; likeness.

imagination, e-mäh-she-näh-se-ong, *f* imagination; invention.

imaginer, e-mäh-she-neh, *v* to imagine; to conceive; to contrive; **s'** –, to fancy.

imbécile, ang-beh-seell, *mf* idiot; fool; *a** imbecile; silly.

imberbe, ang-bairb, *a* beardless.

imbiber, ang-be-beh, *v* to soak; to imbibe.

imbroglio, ang-bro'e-lee-o, *m* confusion.

imbu, e, ang-bE, *a* imbued (**de**, with).

imbuvable, ang-bE-väh-bl, *a* undrinkable.

imiter, e-me-teh, *v* to imitate; to mimic.

immaculé, e, im-mäh-kE-leh, *a* immaculate.

immanquable,* ang-mahng-käh-bl, *a* infallible.

immatériel, le, im-mäh-teh-re-ell, *a* immaterial; intangible.

immatriculer, im-mäh-tre-kE-leh, *v* to register (car, etc); to enroll.

immédiat, e,* im-meh-de-äh, *a* immediate.

immensément, im-mahng-seh-mahng, *adv* immensely.

immensité, im-mahng-se-teh, *f* immensity.

immeuble, im-mer-bl, *m* real estate; fixture; building; apartment building.

immiscer (s'), sim-miss-eh, *v* to meddle (**dans,** with, in).

immobile, im-mob-eell, *a* motionless; unmovable.

immobili-er, ère, im-mob-e-le-eh, *a* of real estate; landed; **agence –ère,** äh-shahngs –, real estate office.

immobiliser, im-mob-e-le-zeh, *v* to realize.

immodéré, e, im-mod-eh-reh, *a* immoderate.

immodérément, im-mod-eh-reh-mahng, *adv* immoderately.

immodeste, im-mod-esst, *a* immodest.

immonde, im-mongd, *a* unclean; foul.

immoral, e,* im-mor-ähl, *a* immoral.

immortel, le,* im-mor-tell, *a* immortal.

immuable,* im-mE-äh-bl, *a* immutable.

immuniser, im-mE-ne-zeh, *v* to immunize.

immunité, im-mE-ne-teh, *f* immunity; exemption.

immutabilité, im-mE-täh-be-le-teh, *f* immutability.

impair, e, ang-pair, *a* odd; uneven.

impardonnable, ang-pähr-donn-äh-bl, *a* unforgivable.

imparfait, ang-pähr-fay, *m* imperfect tense; *a** imperfect.

impartial, e,* ang-pähr-se-ähl, *a* impartial.

impasse, ang-pahss, *f* dead end; "no through road"; dilemma; fix.

impassible,* ang-pähss-ee-bl, *a* impassive; unmoved.

impatiemment, ang-pähss-e-äh-mahng, *a* impatiently; eagerly.

impatient, e, ang-pähss-e-ahng, *a* impatient; eager; fidgety.

impatienter, ang-pähss-e-ahng-teh, *v* to make impatient; to provoke; **s'** –, to fret.

impayable, ang-pay-yäh-bl, *a* invaluable; (*fam*) very funny.

impénétrable,* ang-peh-neh-träh-bl, *a* inscrutable; impenetrable.

impératif, ang-peh-răh-teeff, *m* imperative mood.

impérati-f, ve,* ang-peh-răh-teeff, *a* imperative.

impératrice, ang-peh-răh-treess, *f* empress.

imperceptible,* ang-pair-sep-tee-bl, *a* imperceptible.

imperfection, ang-pair-feck-se-ong, *f* imperfection.

impérial, e,* ang-peh-re-ăhl, *a* imperial.

impériale, ang-peh-re-ăhl, *f* outside top (of a bus).

impérieu-x, se,* ang-peh-re-er, *a* imperious; urgent.

impérissable,* ang-peh-riss-ăh-bl, *a* imperishable.

imperméable, ang-pair-meh-ăh-bl, *m* raincoat; *a** impervious; waterproof.

impersonnel, le,* ang-pair-sonn-ell, *a* impersonal.

impertinemment, ang-pair-te-năh-mahng, *adv* impertinently.

impertinence, ang-pair-te-nahngss, *f* impertinence; insolence; rudeness.

impertinent, e, ang-pair-te-nahng, *mf* impertinent person; *a* impertinent.

imperturbable,* ang-pair-tEEr-băh-bl, *a* imperturbable.

impétueu-x, se,* ang-peh-tE-er, *a* impetuous.

impétuosité, ang-peh-tE-oz-e-teh, *f* impetuosity; vehemence.

impie, ang-pee, *mf* impious person; *a* impious; ungodly.

impiété, ang-pe-eh-teh, *f* impiety.

impitoyable,* ang-pe-to'ăh-yăh-bl, *a* pitiless.

implacable,* ang-plăh-kăh-bl, *a* implacable.

implanter, ang-plahng-teh, *v* to implant.

implicite,* ang-ple-seett, *a* implicit.

impliquer, ang-ple-keh, *v* to implicate; to involve; to imply.

implorer, ang-plor-eh, *v* to implore.

impoli,* e, ang-poll-e, *a* uncivil; rude; impolite.

impolitesse, ang-poll-e-tayss, *f* impoliteness; rudeness; incivility.

impopulaire, ang-pop-E-lair, *a* unpopular.

importance, ang-por-tahngss, *f* importance.

important, ang-por-tahng, *m* main point.

important, e, ang-por-tahng, *a* important.

importa-teur, trice, ang-por-tăh-ter, *mf* importer.

importer, ang-por-teh, *v* to import.

importer, ang-por-teh, *v* to matter (only used in 3rd person, infinitive and participles).

importun, e, ang-por-tung, *mf* intruder; *a* importunate.

importuner, ang-por-tE-neh, *v* to importune; to pester.

imposable, ang-pohz-ăh-bl, *a* taxable.

imposant, e, ang-pohz-ahng, *a* imposing.

imposer, ang-pohz-eh, *v* to impose; to tax.

imposition, ang-pohz-e-se-ong, *f* imposition; tax; assessment.

impossible, ang-poss-ee-bl, *m* impossibility; *a* impossible.

imposteur, ang-poss-ter, *m* impostor; *a* deceitful.

impôt, ang-poh, *m* tax; taxation; duty.

impotent, e, ang-pot-ahng, *mf* disabled; *a* infirm; impotent.

imprégner, ang-prehn-yeh, *v* to impregnate.

imprenable, ang-prer-năhl-bl, *a* impregnable.

impression, ang-press-e-ong, *f* impression; printing.

impressionner, ang-press-e-onn-eh, *v* to impress; to move (feelings).

imprévoyance, ang-preh-vo'ăh-yahngss, *f* improvidence.

imprévu, ang-preh-vE, *m* the unexpected.

imprévu, e, ang-preh-vE, *a* unforeseen; unexpected.

imprimé, ang-pre-meh, *m* printed paper; *pl* printed matter.

imprimer, ang-pre-meh, *v* to impress; to print; to stamp.

imprimerie, ang-preem-ree, *f* printing; printing-office.

imprimeur, ang-pre-mer, *m* printer.

improbable, ang-prob-ăh-bl, *a* unlikely.

improbe, ang-prob, *a* dishonest.

improducti-f, ve,* ang-prod-EEk-teeff, *a* unproductive.

impromptu, ang-prongp-tE, *m & adv* impromptu.

impropriété, ang-prop-re-e-teh, *f* impropriety (of language).

improvisa-teur, trice, ang-prov-e-zăh-ter, *mf & a* improviser.

improvisé, e, ang-prov-e-zeh, *pp & a* improvised; unprepared.

improviser, ang-prov-e-zeh, *v* to improvise.

improviste (à l'), ăh lang-prov-isst, *adv* unawares; suddenly.

imprudemment, ang-prE-dăh-mahng, *adv* imprudently.

imprudence, ang-prE-dahngss, *f* imprudence.

imprudent, e, ang-prE-dahng, *a* imprudent.

impudemment, ang-pE-dăh-mahng, *adv* impudently.

impudence, ang-pE-dahngss, *f* impudence.

impudent, e, ang-pE-dahng, *a* impudent.

impudique, ang-pE-deeck, *a* lewd; indecent.

impuissance, ang-pweess-ahngss, *f* impotence; powerlessness.

impuissant, e, ang-pweess-ahng, *a* impotent; ineffectual.

impulsi-f, ve,* ang-pEEl-seeff, *a* impulsive.

impulsion, ang-pEEl-se-ong, *f* impulse; impetus.

impunément, ang-pE-neh-mahng, *adv* with impunity.

impuni, e, ang-pE-ne, *a* unpunished.

impur, e, ang-pEEr, *a* impure; unclean.

impureté, ang-pEEr-teh, *f* impurity.

imputer, ang-pE-teh, *v* to impute; to ascribe; to charge.

inabordable, e-năh-bor-dăh-bl, *a* inaccessible.

inacceptable, e-năhck-sep-tăh-bl, *a* unacceptable.

inaccessible, e-năhck-sess-ee-bl, *a* unapproachable.

inaccoutumé, e, e-năh-koo-tE-meh, *a* unaccustomed; unusual.

inachevé, e, e-năhsh-veh, *a* unfinished.

inacti-f, ve,* e-năhck-teeff, *a* inactive.

inadéquat, e,* e-năh-deh-kwăh, *a* inadequate.

inadmissible, e-năhd-me-se-bl, *a* inadmissible.

inadvertance, e-năhd-vair-tahngss, *f* inadvertence; oversight.

inaltérable,* e-năhl-teh-răh-bl, *a* unalterable.

inamovible, e-năh-mov-ee-bl, *a* irremovable.

inanité, e-năh-ne-teh, *f* inanity; futility.

inaperçu, e, e-năh-pair-sE, *a* unseen; unnoticed.

inappliqué, e, e-năh-ple-keh, *a* inattentive.

inappréciable, e-năh-preh-se-ăh-bl, *a* invaluable.

inattaquable, e-năh-tăh-kăh-bl, *a* unassailable.

inattendu, e, e-năh-tahng-dE, *a* unexpected.

inauguration, e-noh-ghE-răh-se-ong, *f* opening; unveiling.

incandescent, e, ang-kahng-dayss-sahng, *a* incandescent.

incapable, ang-kăh-păh-bl, *a* incapable; unfit; incompetent.

incapacité, ang-kăh-păh-se-teh, *f* incapacity; incompetence.

incarcérer, ang-kăhr-seh-reh, *v* to imprison.

incarnat, e, ang-kăhr-năh, *a* flesh-colored; rosy.

incarné, e, ang-kăhr-neh, *a* incarnate.

incendie, ang-sahng-dèe, *m* fire; conflagration.

incendier, ang-sahng-de-eh, *v* to set on fire.

incertain, e, ang-sair-tang, *a* uncertain; undecided; wavering.

incertitude, ang-sair-te-tEEd, *f* uncertainty; instability.

incessamment, ang-sayss-săh-mahng, *adv* immediately.

incessant, e, ang-sayss-sahng, *a* incessant.

incidemment, ang-se-dăh-mahng, *adv* incidentally.

incident, ang-se-dahng, *m* incident; occurrence.

incident, e, ang-se-dahng, *a* incidental.

incinérer, ang-se-neh-reh, *v* to incinerate; to cremate.

incision, ang-se-ze-ong, *f* incision; lancing.

incitation, ang-se-tăh-se-ong, *f* incitement; instigation.

inciter, ang-se-teh, *v* to incite; to urge.

incivil, e, ang-se-veell, *a* uncivil; rude.

inclinaison, ang-kle-nay-zong, *f* tilting; incline.

inclination, ang-kle-năh-se-ong, *f* inclination; propensity; attachment.

incliner, ang-kle-neh, *v* to incline; to bend; s'–, to bow.

inclus, e, ang-klE, *a* enclosed; included; **ci-–, se –,** enclosed; herewith.

inclusi-f, ve,* ang-klE-zeeff, *a* inclusive.

incognito, ang-konn-yee-to, *m & adv* incognito.

incolore, ang-koll-or, *a* colorless.

incomber, ang-kong-beh, *v* to be incumbent (**à,** on).

incombustible, ang-kong-bEs-tee-bl, *a* incombustible; fireproof.

incommode, ang-kommod, *a* inconvenient; troublesome.

incommoder, ang-komm-odd-eh, *v* to inconvenience; to annoy; to disturb.

incommodité, ang-komm-odd-e-teh, *f* inconvenience; discomfort.

incomparable, * ang-kong-păh-răh-bl, *a* matchless.

incompatible, * ang-kong-păh-tee-bl, *a* incompatible; inconsistent.

incompétent, ang-kong-peh-tahng, *a* incompetent.

incompl-et, ète, * ang-kong-play, *a* incomplete.

incompréhensible, ang-kong-preh-ahng-see-bl,

incomprehensible.

incompris, e, ang-kong-pre, *pp* & *a* not understood; unappreciated.

inconcevable, ang-kongss-văh-bl, *a* inconceivable.

inconciliable, ang-kongse-le-ăh-bl, *a* irreconcilable.

inconduite, ang-kong-dweet, *f* misconduct.

incongru, e, ang-kong-grE, *a* incongruous; improper.

inconnu, e, ang-konn-E, *mf* unknown; stranger; *a* unknown.

inconsciemment, ang-kong-se-ăh-mahng, *adv* unconsciously.

inconscience, ang-kong-se-ahngss, *f* unconsciousness.

inconscient, e, ang-kong-se-ahng, *a* unconscious.

inconséquence, ang-kong-seh-kahngss, *f* inconsistency.

inconséquent, e, ang-kong-seh-kahng, *a* inconsistent.

inconstance, ang-kongss-tahngss, *f* inconstancy; fickleness.

inconstant, e, ang-kongss-tahng, *a* inconstant; unsteady; variable.

incontestable, * ang-kong-tess-tăh-bl, *a* unquestionable.

incontesté, e, ang-kong-tess-teh, *a* undisputed.

incontinent, e, ang-kong-te-nahng, *a* incontinent.

inconvenance, ang-kongv-nahngss, *f* impropriety.

inconvenant, e, ang-kongv-nahng, *a* improper; unbecoming.

inconvénient, ang-kong-veh-ne-ahng, *m* inconvenience; disadvantage.

incorporer, ang-kor-poh-reh, *v* incorporate.

incorrect, e, * ang-kor-reckt, *a* incorrect.

incrédule, ang-kreh-dEEl, *a* incredulous.

incroyable, * ang-kro'ăh-yăh-bl, *a* incredible; unbelievable.

incruster, ang-krEEs-teh, *v* to encrust (**de,** with); to inlay.

inculper, ang-kEEl-peh, *v* to charge; to accuse (**de,** with; of).

inculquer, ang-kEEl-keh, *v* to inculcate.

inculte, ang kEElt, *a* uncultivated; uneducated; rough.

incurable, ang-kE-răh-bl, *mf* & *a* incurable.

indécemment, ang-deh-săh-mahng, *adv* indecently.

indécent, e, ang-deh-sahng, *a* indecent.

indéchiffrable, ang-deh-she-frăh-bl, *a* undecipherable; incomprehensible.

indécis, e, ang-deh-se, *a* undecided; wavering.

indéfendable, ang-deh-fahng-dăh-bl, *a* indefensible.

indéfini, e, ang-deh-fe-ne, *a* indefinite.

indéfiniment, ang-deh-fe-ne-mahng, *adv* indefinitely.

indéfinissable, ang-deh-fe-niss-ăh-bl, *a* indefinable.

indélébile, ang-deh-leh-beell, *a* indelible.

indélicat, e, * ang-deh-le-kăh, *a* indelicate; unscrupulous.

indélicatesse, ang-deh-le-kăh-tayss, *f* indelicacy.

indemne, ang-daymn, *a* unhurt.

indemniser, ang-daym-ne-zeh, *v* to indemnify (**de,** for); to compensate.

indemnité, ang-daym-ne-teh, *f* indemnity; allowance.

indépendamment, ang-deh-pahng-dăh-mahng,

adv independently.

indépendant, e, ang-deh-pahng-dahng, *a* independent.

indescriptible, ang-dess-kreep-tee-bl, *a* indescribable.

indéterminé, e, ang-deh-tair-me-neh, *a* indeterminate; irresolute.

index, ang-dex, *m* index; forefinger.

indicateur, ang-de-käh-ter, *m* indicator; timetable.

indica-teur, trice, ang-de-käh-ter, *a* indicating; indicatory.

indicatif, ang-de-käh-teeff, *m* indicative mood.

indicati-f, ve, ang-de-käh-teeff, *a* indicative.

indice, ang-deess, *m* indication; sign; clue.

indicible, ang-deess-ee-bl, *a* inexpressible.

indifféremment, ang-de-feh-räh-mahng, *adv* indifferently; indiscriminately.

indifférent, e, ang-de-feh-rahng, *a* indifferent; immaterial.

indigène, ang-de-shain, *mf* & *a* native; indigenous.

indigent, ang-de-shahng, *m* pauper.

indigent, e, ang-de-shahng, *a* indigent; needy.

indigeste, ang-de-shaysst, *a* indigestible.

indigne,* ang-deen-yer, *a* unworthy; undeserving.

indigné, e, ang-deen-yeh, *a* indignant.

indigner, ang-deen-yeh, *v* to make indignant.

indignité, ang-deen-yee-teh, *f* unworthiness; indignity.

indiquer, ang-de-keh, *v* to indicate.

indirect, e,* ang-de-reckt, *a* indirect.

indiscipliné, ang-diss-e-plee-neh, *a* unruly.

indiscr-et, éte,* ang-diss-kray, *a* indiscreet.

indispensable,* ang-diss-pahng-säh-bl, *a* indispensable.

indisponible, ang-diss-ponn-ee-bl, *a* unavailable.

indisposer, ang-diss-poz-eh, *v* to upset; to antagonize.

indistinct, e,* ang-diss-tangkt, *a* indistinct.

individu, ang-de-ve-dE, *m* individual, person.

individuel, le,* ang-de-ve-dE-ell, *a* individual.

indocile, ang-doss-eell, *a* untractable; disobedient.

indolemment, ang-doll-äh-mahng, *adv* indolently.

indolent, e, ang-doll-ahng, *a* indolent; sluggish; lazy.

indolence, ang-doll-ahngss, *f* indolence; laziness.

indolore, ang-doll-or, *a* painless.

indomptable,* ang-dong-täh-bl, *a* indomitable; ungovernable.

indompté, e, ang-dong-teh, *a* untamed; unsubdued.

indubitable,* ang-dE-be-täh-bl, *a* indubitable.

induire, ang-dweer, *v* to induce; to lead; to infer.

indulgence, ang-dEEl-shahngss, *f* leniency.

indûment, ang-dEE-mahng, *adv* unduly.

industrie, ang-dEEs-tree, *f* industry; skill; trade.

industriel, ang-dEEs-tre-ell, *m* industrialist.

industriel, le,* ang-dEEs-tre-ell, *a* industrial.

industrieu-x, se,* ang-dEEs-tre-er, *a* industrious; skillful.

inébranlable,* e-neh-brahng-läh-bl, *a* immovable; resolute.

inédit, e, e-neh-dee, *a* unpublished; new.

ineffable,* e-neh-fãh-bl, *a* unspeakable.

ineffaçable, e-neh-fãh-sãh-bl, *a* indelible.

inefficace,* e-neh-fe-kãhss, *a* inefficient.

inégal, e,* e-neh-gãhl, *a* unequal; irregular; uneven.

inélégant, e, e-neh-leh-gahng, *a* inelegant.

inénarrable, e-neh-nãhr-rãh-bl, *a* indescribable.

inepte, * e-nehpt, *a* inept; silly.

ineptie, e-nehp-see, *f* ineptitude; absurdity.

inépuisable,* e-neh-pwee-zãh-bl, *a* inexhaustible.

inerte, e-nairt, *a* inert; lifeless; passive.

inertie, e-nair-see, *f* inertia.

inespéré, e, e-ness-peh-reh, *a* unhoped for.

inestimable, e-ness-te-mãh-bl, *a* invaluable.

inévitable,* e-neh-ve-tãh-bl, *a* unavoidable.

inexact, e,* e-negg-zãckt, *a* inaccurate; unpunctual.

inexcusable,* e-necks-kE-zãh-bl, *a* inexcusable.

inexécutable, e-negg-zeh-kE-tãh-bl, *a* impracticable.

inexercé, e, e-negg-zair-seh, *a* unskilled; untrained.

inexigible, e-negg-ze-shee-bl, *a* not demandable.

inexorable,* e-negg-zor-ãh-bl, *a* inexorable.

inexpérimenté, e, e-necks-peh-re-mahng-teh, *a* inexperienced; untried.

inexprimable,* e-necks-pre-mãh-bl, *a* inexpressible.

inextinguible, e-necks-tang-gwee-bl, *a* inextinguishable; uncontrollable.

infaillible,* ang-fah'e-ee-bl, *a* infallible.

infaisable, ang-fer-zãh-bl, *a* infeasible.

infamant, e, ang-fãh-mahng, *a* ignominious.

infame, ang-fahm, *mf* infamous person; *a* infamous; vile; filthy.

infamie, ang-fãh-mee, *f* infamy; infamous thing.

infanterie, ang-fahng-tree, *f* infantry.

infatigable, ang-fãh-te-gãh-bl, *a* indefatigable.

infatuer (s'), sang-fãh-tE-eh, *v* to become infatuated (**de**, with).

infécond, e, ang-feh-kong, *a* infertile; barren.

infect, e, ang-feckt, *a* stinking; foul.

infecter, ang-feck-teh, *v* to infect; to taint; to stink.

infection, ang-feck-se-ong, *f* infection.

inférer, ang-feh-reh, *v* to infer.

inférieur, e,* ang-feh-re-er, *a* inferior; lower.

infernal, e,* ang-fair-nãhl, *a* hellish.

infertile, ang-fair-teell, *a* unfruitful.

infester, ang-fess-teh, *v* to infest.

infidèle, ang-fe-dell, *mf* infidel; unbeliever.

infidèle, ang-fe-dell, *a* unfaithful; untrue; dishonest; unbelieving.

infiltrer (s'), sang-fill-treh, *v* to infiltrate.

infime, ang-feem, *a* lowest; (*fam*) tiny.

infini, e, ang-fe-ne, *a* infinite; endless; boundless.

infiniment, ang-fe-ne-mahng, *adv* infinitely; extremely.

infirme, ang-feerm, *a* infirm; disabled.

infirmerie, ang-feerm-re, *f* infirmary; sick room.

infirmi-er, ère, ang-feer-me-eh, *mf* nurse.

inflammable, ang-flăh-mǎh-bl, *a* inflammable.

inflammation, ang-flăh-mǎh-se-ong, *f* inflammation.

inflexible,* ang-fleck-see-bl, *a* inflexible.

infliger, ang-fle-sheh, *v* to inflict (**à,** on).

influent, e, ang-flE-ahng *a* influential.

influer, ang-flE-eh, *v* to exert an influence.

information, ang-for-mǎh-se-ong, *f* information; inquiry; *pl* news bulletin.

informe, ang-form, *a* shapeless.

informer, ang-for-meh, *v* to inform; to acquaint; **s' –,** to inquire.

infortune, ang-for-tEEn, *f* misfortune; adversity.

infortuné, e, ang-for-tE-neh, *mf* unfortunate person; *a* unfortunate.

infraction, ang-frähck-se-ong, *f* infraction; breach.

infranchissable, ang-frahng-shiss-ăh-bl, *a* impassable; insuperable.

infructueu-x, se,* ang-frEEk-tE- er, *a* unfruitful.

infus, e, ang-fE, *a* innate.

infuser, ang-fE-zeh, *v* to infuse; to steep.

infusion, ang-fEE-she-ong, *f* herb tea.

ingénier (s'), sang- sheh-ne-eh, *v* to strive.

ingénieur, ang- sheh-ne-er, *m* engineer.

ingénieu-x, se,* ang-sheh-ne-er, *a* ingenious.

ingénu, e, ang- sheh-nE, *mf & a* ingenuous person; ingenuous; candid.

ingénument, ang- sheh-nE-mahng, *adv* ingenuously.

ingérer (s'), sang- sheh-reh, *v* to meddle (**dans,** with).

ingrat, e, ang-grăh, *mf & a* ungrateful person; ungrateful; unprofitable; unpleasant.

ingrédient, ang-greh-de-ahng, *m* ingredient.

inguérissable, ang-greh-riss-ăh-bl, *a* incurable.

inhabile,* e-năh-beell, *a* unskillful.

inhabitable, e-năh-be-tăh-bl, *a* uninhabitable.

inhabité, e e-năh-be-teh, *a* uninhabited.

inhaler, e-năh-leh, *v* to inhale.

inhérent, e, e-neh-rahng, *a* inherent.

inhumain, e,* e-nE-mang, *a* inhuman; cruel.

inhumation, e-nE-măh-se-ong, *f* interment; burial.

inhumer, e-nE-meh, *v* to bury; to inter.

inimitié, e-ne-me-te-eh, *f* enmity; antipathy.

inique,* e-neeck, *a* iniquitous; unfair.

iniquité, e-ne-ke-teh, *f* iniquity; unfairness.

initial, e, e-ne-se-ăhl, *a* initial.

initiale, e-ne-se-ăhl, *f* initial.

initiative, e-ne-se-ă-teev, *f* initiative.

initier, e-ne-se-eh, *v* to initiate; to instruct; to admit.

injecter, ang- shayk-teh, *v* to inject.

injure, ang- shEer, *f* injury; wrong; insult.

injurieu-x, se,* ang- shE-re-**rr**, *a* injurious; offensive.

injurier, ang- shE-re-eh, *v* to abuse.

injuste,* ang- shEEst, *a* unjust; unfair; wrong.

inné, e, een-neh, *a* innate; inborn.

innocemment, e-noss-ăh-mahng, *adv* innocently.

innocent, e, e-noss-ahng, *mf* innocent person; simpleton; innocent; not guilty; harmless.

innombrable,* e-nong-brăh-bl, *a* innumerable.

inoccupé, e, e-nock-E-peh, *a* unoccupied.

inoculer, e-nock-E-leh, *v* to inoculate.

inoffensi-f, ve,* e-noff-ahng-seeff, *a* inoffensive.

inondation, e-nong-dăh-se-ong, *f* flood.

inonder, e-nong-deh, *v* to overflow; to flood.

inopiné, e, e-nop-E-neh, *a* unforeseen.

inopinément, e-nop-e-neh-mahng, *adv* unexpectedly.

inouï, e, e-noo-e, *a* unheard of; unprecedented.

inqui-et, ète, ang-ke-ay, *a* anxious; uneasy; worried.

inquiétant, e, ang-ke-eh-tahng, *a* alarming; worrying.

inquiéter, ang-ke-eh-teh, *v* to make uneasy; to alarm; to worry.

inquiétude, ang-ke-eh-tEEd, *f* anxiety; worry.

insalubre,* ang-săh-lEE-br, *a* unhealthy.

insatiable,* ang-săh-se-ăh-bl, *a* insatiable.

inscription, angss-krip-se-ong, *f* inscription; registration.

inscrire, angss-kreer, *v* to inscribe; to enter; to register.

insecte, ang-say-kt, *m* insect.

insensé, e, ang-sahng-seh, *mf & a* madman; madwoman; insane; senseless.

insensible,* ang-sahng-see-bl, *a* insensitive; unconscious; callous; imperceptible.

insérer, ang-seh-reh, *v* to insert; to put in.

insigne, ang-seen-yer, *a* notable.

insigne, ang-seen-yer, *m* badge; *pl* insignia.

insignifiant, e, ang-seen-yee-fe-ahng, *a* insignificant.

insinuant, e, ang-se-nE-ahng, *a* insinuating.

insinuer, ang-se-nE-eh, *v* to insinuate; to hint.

insipide, ang-se-peed, *a* insipid.

insistance, ang-siss-tahngss, *f* insistence.

insociable, ang-soss-e-ăh-bl, *a* unsociable.

insolation, ang-sol-ăh-se-ong, *f* sunstroke.

insolemment, ang-soll-ăh-mahng, *adv* insolently.

insolence, ang-soll-ahngss, *f* insolence.

insolent, e, ang-soll-ahng, *mf & a* insolent person;

insolent; impertinent.

insoluble, ang-soll-EE-bl, *a* insoluble.

insolvable, ang-soll-văh-bl, *a* insolvent.

insomnie, ang-somm-nee, *f* sleeplessness.

insondable, ang-song-dăh-bl, *a* unfathomable.

insouciance, ang-soo-se-ahngss, *f* insouciance.

insouciant, e, ang-soo-se-ahng, *a* insouciant.

insoucieu-x, se, ang-soo-se-er, *a* heedless.

insoutenable, ang-soot-năh-bl, *a* indefensible; unbearable.

inspecter, angss-peck-teh, *v* to inspect; to examine.

inspec-teur, trice, angss-peck-ter, *mf* inspector; examiner; surveyor.

inspiration, angss-pe-rah-se-ong, *f* inspiration.

inspirer, angss-pe-reh, *v* to inspire.

instable, angss-tăh-bl, *a* unstable.

installation, angss-tăh-lăh-se-ong, *f* installation; setting up; plant.

instamment, angss-tăh-mahng, *adv* earnestly; urgently.

instance, angss-tahngss, *f* entreaty; degree of

jurisdiction; suit.

instant, angss-tahng, *m*
instant; **à l' –,** ăh l –,
immediately; a moment
ago.

instinct, angss-tang, *m*
instinct.

instincti-f, ve,* angss-
tangk-teeff, *a*
instinctive.

instituer, angss-te-tE-eh, *v*
to institute; to establish;
to appoint.

institut, angss-te-tE, *m*
institute; institution;
school.

institu-teur, trice, angss-
te-tE-ter, *mf* elementary
schoolteacher; *f*
governess.

institution, angss-te-tE-se-
ong, *f* institution;
school.

instruction, angss-trEEk-
se-ong, *f* instruction;
judicial investigation.

instruire, angss-trweer, *v*
to instruct; to
investigate; to teach.

instruit, e, angss-trwee, *pp*
& *a* instructed; learned.

instrument, angss-trE-
mahng, *m* instrument;
tool.

instrumenter, angss-trE-
mahng-teh, *v* to draw
deeds, writs, etc.

instrumentiste, angss-trE-

mahng-teesst, *m*
instrumentalist.

insu (à l' – de), ăh lang-
sE-der, *prep* unknown to.

insuffisamment, ang-sE-fe-
zăh-mahng, *adv*
insufficiently.

insuffisant, e, ang-sE-fe-
zahng, *a* insufficient.

insulaire, ang-sE-lair, *mf*
& *a* islander; insular.

insulte, ang-sEElt, *f* insult;
abuse.

insulter, ang-sEEl-teh, *v* to
insult; to abuse.

insupportable,* ang-sE-
por-tăh-bl, *a*
unbearable; badly
behaved.

insurgé, e, ang-sEEr-sheh,
mf & *a* insurgent.

insurger (s'), sang-sEEr-
sheh, *v* to revolt; to
rebel.

insurmontable, ang-sEEr-
mong-tăh-bl, *a*
insurmountable.

insurrection, ang-sEEr-
rayk-se-ong, *f* uprising;
insurrection; revolt.

intact, e, ang-tăhckt, *a*
intact; whole;
undamaged.

intarissable,* ang-tăh-riss-
ăh-bl, *a* inexhaustible.

intègre,* ang-tay-gr, *a*
upright; just; honest.

intégrité, ang-tah-gze-tay,

f integrity; honesty.

intellectuel, le,* ang-tell-
leck-tE-ell, *a*
intellectual.

intelligemment, ang-tell-
le-**sh**ăh-mahng, *adv*
intelligently.

intelligence, ang-tell-le-
shahngss, *f* intelligence;
knowledge; skill;
harmony.

intelligent, e, ang-tell-le
shahng, *a* intelligent;
clever.

intempérie, ang-tahng-
peh-ree, *f* inclemency.

intempesti-f, ve,* ang-
tahng-pess-teeff, *a*
untimely.

intendant, ang-tahng-
dahng, *m* steward;
comptroller.

intense, ang-tahngss, *a*
intense.

intensi-f, ve, ang-tahng-
seeff, *a* intensive.

(s')intensifier, sang-tahng-
se-fe-eh, *v* escalate.

intenter, ang-tahng-teh, *v*
to institute
(proceedings); to sue.

intention, ang-tahng-se-
ong, *f* intention;
purpose.

intentionné, e, ang-tahng-
se-onn-eh, *a;* **bien** or
mal –, be-ang, măhl –,
well–, ill-disposed.

intercaler, ang-tair-kăh-leh, *v* to insert; to wedge in.

intercéder, ang-tair-seh-deh, *v* to intercede (**auprès de,** with).

intercepter, ang-tair-sep-teh, *v* to intercept.

interdire, ang-tair-deer, *v* to prohibit; to suspend; to forbid; (*fam*) to bewilder.

interdit, ang-tair-de, *m* interdict; ban.

interdit, e, ang-tair-de, *a* speechless.

intéressant, e, ang-teh-rayss-ahng, *a* interesting.

intéressé, e, ang-teh-rayss-eh, *pp* & *a* interested; selfish.

intéresser, ang-teh-rayss-eh, *v* to interest; to concern.

intérêt, ang-teh-ray, *m* interest; profit; share; concern.

intérieur, ang-teh-re-er, *m* inside; home.

intérieur, e,* ang-teh-re-er, *a* interior; inner.

intérimaire, ang-teh-re-mair, *a* temporary.

interjeter, ang-tair-sher-teh, *v* to lodge an appeal.

interlocu-teur, trice, ang-tair-lock-E-ter, *mf*

interlocutor.

interloquer, ang-tair-lock-eh, *v* to disconcert.

intermède, ang-tair-mayd, *m* interlude.

intermédiaire, ang-tair-meh-de-air, *m* & *a* medium; middleman; intermediate.

intermittence, ang-tair-mit-tahngss, *f* intermission.

internat, ang-tair-năh, *m* boarding school.

international, e, ang-tair-năh-se-on-ăhl, *a* international.

interne, ang-tairn, *mf* & *a* boarder; intern; internal.

interner, ang-tair-neh, *v* to intern.

interpeller, ang-tair-pel-leh, *v* to put a question to; to call upon.

interposer, ang-tair-poz-eh, *v* to interpose.

interprète, ang-tair-prayt, *m* interpreter.

interroga-teur, trice, ang-tair-rogh-ăh-ter, *mf* & *a* examiner; inquiring.

interrogation, ang-tair-rogh-ăh-se-ong, *f* interrogation; question.

interrogatoire, ang-tair-rogh-ăh-to'ăhr, *m* examination; cross-

examination.

interroger, ang-tair-rosh-eh, *v* to question; to examine.

interrompre, ang-tair-rong-pr, *v* to interrupt; to stop; **s'** –, to break off.

interrupteur, ang-tair-rEEp-ter, *m* switch.

intervalle, ang-tair-văhl, *m* interval.

intervenir, ang-tair-ver-neer, *v* to intervene; to interfere; to occur.

intervention, ang-tair-vahng-se-ong, *f* intervention.

intervertir, ang-tair-vair-teer, *v* to invert.

intestin, ang-tayss-tang, *m* intestine; bowel.

intimation, ang-te-măh-se-ong, *f* notification.

intime,* ang-teem, *mf* & *a* intimate friend; intimate; close; cozy.

intimer, ang-te-meh, *v* to notify.

intimider, ang-te-me-deh, *v* to intimidate.

intimité, ang-te-me-teh, *f* intimacy.

intitulé, e, ang-te-tE-leh, *pp* & *a* entitled.

intolérable,* ang-toll-eh-răh-bl, *a* insufferable.

intolérant, e, ang-toll-eh-rah*ng*, *a* intolerant.

intoxiquer, ang-tox-ick-eh, *v* to poison (food, etc).

intraduisible, ang-träh-dwe-zee-bl, *a* untranslatable.

intraitable, ang-tray-täh-bl, *a* intractable.

intransigeant, e, ang-trahng-ze-shahng, *a* intransigent.

intrépide,* ang-treh-peed, *a* undaunted; fearless.

intrigant, e, ang-tre-gahng, *mf* & *a* schemer; intriguing.

intriguer, ang-tre-gheh, *v* to perplex; to plot; to intrigue.

intrinsèque,* ang-trang-sayk, *a* intrinsic.

introduc-teur, trice, ang-trod-EEk-ter, *mf* introducer.

introduire, ang-trod-weer, *v* to introduce; s' –, to get into.

introuvable, ang-troo-văhl-bl, *a* not to be found.

intrus, e, ang-trE, *mf* intruder.

intuiti-f, ve,* ang-tE-e-teeff, *a* intuitive.

inusable, e-nE-zăh-bl, *a* everlasting.

inutile,* e-nE-teel, *a* useless; unnecessary.

inutilité, e-nE-te-le-teh, *f* uselessness; *pl* useless things.

invalide, ang-văh-leed, *a* & *mf* invalid; infirm; pensioner.

invalider, ang-văh-le-deh, *v* to invalidate.

invariable,* ang-văh-re-ăh-bl, *a* invariable.

invasion, ang-văh-se-ong, *f* invasion; irruption.

invectiver, ang-vayk-te-veh, *v* to inveigh.

invendable, ang-vahng-dăh-bl, *a* unsalable.

invendu, e, ang-vahng-dE, *a* unsold.

inventaire, ang-vahng-tair, *m* stocktaking; inventory.

inventer, ang-vahng-teh, *v* to invent.

inven-teur, trice, ang-vahng-ter, *mf* inventor; discoverer; *a* inventive.

inventi-f, ve, ang-vahng-teeff, *a* inventive.

inventorier, ang-vahng-tor-e-eh, *v* to make an inventory of.

inverse,* ang-vairss, *a* inverse; inverted.

investigation, ang-vayss-te-gah-se-ong, *f* investigation; inquiry.

investir, ang-vayss-teer, *v* to invest.

invétéré, e, ang-veh-teh-reh, *a* inveterate.

invisible,* ang-vee-zee-bl, *a* invisible; unseen.

invité, e, ang-ve-teh, *mf* guest.

inviter, ang-ve-teh, *v* to invite; to urge; to request.

involontaire,* ang-voll-ong-tair, *a* involuntary.

invoquer, ang-vock-eh, *v* to invoke.

invraisemblable,* ang-vrayss-ahng-blăh-bl, *a* unlikely; unbelievable.

invraisemblance, ang-vrayss-ahng-blahngss, *f* unlikelihood.

invulnérable,* ang-vEEl-neh-răh-bl, *a* invulnerable.

iode, e-od, *m* iodine.

irascible, e-răhss-ee-bl, *a* irritable.

irisé, e, e-re-zeh, *a* iridescent.

irlandais, e, eer-lahng-deh, *a* Irish; *mf* Irishman; Irishwoman; Irish.

ironie, e-ronn-ee, *f* irony.

ironique,* e-ronn-eeck, *a* ironical.

irréalisable, eer-reh-ăh-le-zăh-bl, *a* unrealizable.

irréductible, eer-reh-

dEEk-tee-bl, *a*
irreducible.

irréfléchi, e, eer-reh-fleh-
she, *a* thoughtless.

irréflexion, eer-reh-fleck-
se-*ong*, *f*
thoughtlessness.

irréguli-er, ère,* eer-reh-
ghE-le-eh, *a* irregular.

irrémissible,* eer-reh-
miss-ce-bl, *a*
unpardonable.

irrésolu, e,* eer-reh-zoll-
E, *a* irresolute.

irrespectueu-x, se,* eer-
ress-peck-tE- er, *a*
disrespectful.

irresponsable,* eer-ress-
pong-săh-bl, *a*
irresponsible

irrévocable,* eer-eh-
vock-ăh-bl, *a*
irrevocable.

irrigateur, eer-re-găh-ter,
m hose (garden).

irriguer, eer-re-gheh, *v* to
irrigate.

irriter, eer-re-teh, *v* to
irritate; to provoke.

isolé, e, e-zoll-eh, *a*
isolated; lonely;
detached.

isolement, e-zoll-mah*ng*,
m loneliness; seclusion.

issu, e, iss-E, *a* born;
sprung from.

issue, iss-E, *f* issue; outlet;
end.

isthme, issm, *m* isthmus.

itinéraire, e-te-neh-rair,
m itinerary; route;
guidebook.

ivoire, e-vo'ăhr, *m* ivory;
whiteness.

ivre, e-vr, *a* drunk;
intoxicated.

ivresse, e-vress, *f*
drunkenness; rapture.

ivrogne, e-vronn-yer, *m*
drunkard.

jabot, shăh-bo, *m* frill; crop (of a bird).

jacasser, shăh-kăhss-eh, *v* to chatter; to yak.

jacinthe, shăh-sangt, *f* hyacinth.

jadis, shăh-deess, *adv* formerly; of old.

jaillir, shah'e-eer, *v* to spout; to gush out; to spring forth.

jalon, shăh-long, *m* stake; pole; landmark.

jalouser, shăh-loo-zeh, *v* to envy.

jalousie, shăh-loo-zee, *f* jealousy; Venetian blind.

jalou-x, se, * shăh-loo, *a* jealous.

jamais, shăh-may, *adv* ever; never.

jambe, shahngb, *f* leg; shank.

jambon, shahng-bong, *m* ham.

jante, shahngt, *f* rim.

janvier, shahng-ve-eh, *m* January.

japonais, e, shah-po-neh, *a* Japanese; *mf* Japanese man, woman; Japanese.

japper, shăh-peh, *v* to yelp.

jaquette, shăh-kayt, *f* jacket.

jardin, shăhr-dang, *m* garden.

jardini-er, ère, shăhr-de-ne-eh, *mf* gardener.

jargon, shăhr-gong, *m* gibberish; jargon.

jarre, shăhr, *f* jar.

jarret, shăh-ray, *m* hamstring; hock; knuckle (veal).

jarretelle, shăhr-tell, *f* garter.

jaser, shah-zeh, *v* to chatter; to gossip.

jasmin, shăhss-mang, *m* jasmine.

jatte, shăht, *f* bowl.

jauge, shohsh, *f* gauge; tonnage.

jaunâtre, shoh-nah-tr, *a* yellowish.

jaune, shohn, *a* yellow.

jaunir, shoh-neer, *v* to make yellow; to turn yellow.

jaunisse, shoh-neess, *f* jaundice.

javelot, shăhv-lo, *m* javelin.

je (j' before a vowel), sher, *pron* I.

jésuite, sheh-zweet, *m* Jesuit.

Jésus, sheh-zE, *m* Jesus.

jet, shay, *m* throw; jet; ray.

jetée, sher-teh, *f* pier; jetty.

jeter, sher-teh, *v* to throw; to fling.

jeton, sher-tong, *m* chip;

token.

jeu, sher, *m* play; sport; gambling; set; acting; game.

jeudi, sher-de, *m* Thursday.

jeun (à), ăh-shung, *adv* fasting; on an empty stomach.

jeûne, shern, *m* fast; fasting.

jeune, shern, *a* young; junior; youthful.

jeûner, sher-neh, *v* to fast.

jeunesse, sher-ness, *f* youth; young people.

joaillerie, sho'ah-le-ree, *f* jewelry; jeweler's trade.

joie, sho'ăh, *f* joy; delight; gladness.

joignant, sho'ăhn-yahng, *pres part* & *a* adjoining; near to.

joindre, sho'ang-dr, *v* to join; to adjoin; to clasp; to get in touch.

joint, e, sho'ang, *a* joined; united; **ci-joint,** se-sho' ang, herewith; annexed.

joli, e, sholl-e, *a* pretty.

joliment, sholl-e-mahng, *adv* nicely; (*fam*) very; terribly.

jonc, shong, *m* rush; cane.

joncher, shong-sheh, *v* to strew; to scatter.

jonction, shongk-se-ong, *f* junction.

jongler, shong-gleh, *v* to juggle.

joue, shoo, *f* cheek.

jouer, shoo-eh, *v* to play; to gamble; to stake; to act; to deceive.

jouet, shoo-ay, *m* toy.

joueu-r, se, shoo-er, *mf* player; gambler.

joug, shoog, *m* yoke.

jouir, shoo-eer, *v* to enjoy; to possess; to use.

jouissance, shoo-iss-ahngss, *f* enjoyment; possession; use; joy.

joujou, shoo-shoo, *m* plaything; toy.

jour, shoohr, *m* day; daylight; gap.

journal, shoohr-năhl, *m* newspaper; journal; diary; record.

journali-er, ère, shoohr-năh-le-eh, *a* daily.

journée, shoohr-neh, *f* daytime; day's work.

journellement, shoohr-nell-mahng, *adv* daily.

jovial, e,* shov-e-ăhl, *a* jovial.

joyau, sho'ăh-yoh, *m* jewel.

joyeu-x, se,* sho'ăh-yer, *a* cheerful; merry; joyful.

jubilation, shE-be-lăh-se-ong, *f* rejoicing; jubilation.

jucher (se), ser **sh**E-sheh,

v to roost; to perch.

judiciaire,* shE-de-se-air, *a* judicial; legal.

judicieu-x, se,* shE-de-se-er, *a* judicious.

juge, shEEsh, *m* judge; magistrate.

jugement, shEEsh-mahng, *m* judgment; trial; sentence; opinion.

juger, shEE-sheh, *v* to judge; to try; to sentence; to believe.

jui-f, ve, shweef, *mf* & *a* Jew; Jewish.

juillet, shwe-yay, *m* July.

juin, shwang, *m* June.

juke-box, dshook-boks *m* juke box.

jumeau, jumelle, shE-moh, **sh**E-mell, *mf* & *a* twin.

jumelles, shE-mell, *fpl* binoculars.

jument, shE-mahng, *f* mare.

jupe, shEEp, *f* skirt.

jupon, shE-pong, *m* petticoat.

juré, shE-reh, *m* juror.

jurer, shE-reh, *v* to swear; to clash (colors, etc).

juridique,* shE-re-deeck, *a* judicial.

juron, shE-rong, *m* curse.

jury, shE-re, *m* jury.

jus, shE, *m* juice; gravy.

jusque, shEES-ker, *prep* to;

as far as; until; up to; down to; even.

juste, shEEst, *m* upright man; virtuous man; *a* just; correct; fair; tight.

juste, shEEst, *adv* just; right; exactly.

justement, shEEs-ter-mah*ng*, *adv* just so; exactly.

justesse, shEEs-tess, *f* accuracy; precision.

justice, shEEs-teess, *f* justice; fairness; law.

justifier, shEEs-te-fe-eh, *v* to justify; to prove.

jute, shEEt, *m* jute.

juteu-x, se, shEE-ter, *a* juicy.

juvénile, shE-veh-neel, *a* youthful.

juxtaposer, shEEx-tăh-po-zeh, *v* to place side by side.

kaolin, kăh-oll-*ang*, *m* clay (for china); kaolin.

képi, keh-pe, *m* military cap.

kermesse, kair-mess, *f* bazaar; charity fête.

kilo(gramme), ke-loh-grăhm; *m* kilo(gram).

kilomètre, ke-loh-met-tr, *m* kilometer.

kiosque, ke-osk, *m* kiosk; newsstand.

klaxon, klacks-*ong*, *m* horn.

klaxonner, klacks-on-eh, *v* to hoot.

krach, krăhck, *m* financial disaster.

kyste, kee-st, *m* cyst.

la, lăh, *f art* the; *pron* her;
it; *m* (music) A.

là, lăh, *adv* there; then.

labeur, lăh-ber, *m* labor;
toil; work.

laborieu-x, se,* lăh-bor-e-
er, *a* laborious.

labourer, lăh-boo-reh, *v* to
till; to plow.

laboureur, lăh-boo-rer, *m*
plowman.

lac, lăhck, *m* lake.

lacer, lăh-seh, *v* to lace.

lacet, lăh-say, *m* lace;
snare.

lâche, lahsh, *m* coward; *a**
loose; cowardly.

lâcher, lah-sheh, *v* to
slacken; to loosen; to
release.

lâcheté, lahsh-teh, *f*
cowardice; meanness.

laconique,* lăh-konn-
eeck, *a* laconic.

lacs, lah, *m* snares.

lacté, e, lăhck-teh, *a*
milky; **voie –e,** vo'ăh –,
Milky Way.

lacune, lăh-kEEn, *f* gap;
blank.

lagune, lăh-ghEEn, *f*
lagoon.

laid, e,* lay, *a* ugly; plain;
unbecoming.

laideron, layd-rong, *mf*
ugly creature.

laideur, lay-der, *f* ugliness.

lainage, lay-năhsh, *m*
woolen goods; woolly
garment.

laine, layn, *f* wool.

laisse, layss, *f* leash.

laisser, layss-eh, *v* to
leave; to bequeath; to
allow; to give up.

laissez-passer, layss-eh

păhss-eh, *m* pass.

lait, lay, *m* milk.

laitage, lay-tăhsh, *m* milk;
dairy produce.

laitance, lay-tahngss, *f* soft
roe.

laiterie, lay-tree, *f* dairy.

laiteu-x, se, lay-ter, *a*
milky.

laiti-er, ère, lay-te-eh, *m*
milkman; **produits –s,**
prod-wee –, dairy
produce.

laiton, lay-tong, *m* brass.

laitue, lay-tE, *f* lettuce.

lambeau, lahng-boh, *m*
rag; shred; scrap; bit.

lambris, lahng-bre, *m*
wainscot; paneling;
ceiling.

lame, lăhm, *f* plate; blade;
wave.

lamentable,* lăh-mahng-
tăh-bl, *a* woeful;
mournful; deplorable.

lamentation, lăh-mahng-
tăh-se-ong, *f* lament;
bewailing.

lampadaire, lahng-păh-
dair, *m* floor lamp.

lampe, lahngp, *f* lamp.

lampion, lahng-pe-ong, *m*
chinese lantern.

lance, lahngss, *f* lance;
spear.

lancer, lahng-seh, *v* to
throw; to fling; to issue;
to launch; to set

someone on his feet.

lancinant, e, lahng-se-nahng, *a* shooting (pain).

landau, aus, lahng-do, *m* baby carriage.

lande, lahngd, *f* barren land.

langage, lahng-gähsh, *m* language; speech; expression.

lange, lahngsh, *f* diaper; swaddling cloth.

langoureu-x, se,* lahng-ghoo-rer, *a* pining; melancholy.

langouste, lahng-ghoost, *f* crayfish.

langue, lahng-gh, *f* tongue; language; narrow strip (land).

languette, lahng-ghett, *f* small tongue (of wood, land, etc.); tab.

langueur, lahng-gher, *f* languor; weakness.

languir, lahng-gheer, *v* to languish; to pine away.

languissamment, lahng-ghiss-äh-mahng, *adv* languishingly.

lanière, läh-ne-air, *f* thong; lash; thin strap.

lanterne, lahng-tairn, *f* lantern; lamp.

lapider, läh-pe-deh, *v* to stone to death.

lapin, läh-pang, *m* rabbit.

laps, lähps, *m* lapse (of time).

laquais, läh-kay, *m* valet.

laque, lähck, *m* lacquer.

laquelle, läh-kell, *pron f* who; whom; which; that.

larcin, lähr-sang, *m* larceny.

lard, lähr, *m* bacon; lard.

larder, lähr-deh, *v* to lard.

lardon, lähr-dong, *m* piece of bacon; (*fig*) jibe.

large, lährsh, *m* breadth; width; open sea; *a* broad; generous.

largeur, lähr-sher, *f* breadth; width.

larme, lährm, *f* tear; drop.

larmoyer, lähr-mo'äh-yeh, *v* to weep; to whine.

larron, läh-rong, *m* thief.

larve, lährv, *f* larva; grub.

laryngite, läh-rang- sheet, *f* laryngitis.

la-s, sse, lah, *a* tired; weary.

lasci-f, ve,* lähss-eef, *a* lascivious; lewd.

lasser, lahss-eh, *v* to tire; to be weary; to fatigue.

latent, e, läh-tahng, *a* latent; concealed.

latte, läht, *f* lath.

lauréat, te, lor-eh-äh, *mf* laureate.

laurier, lor-e-eh, *m* laurel; bay.

lavabo, läh-väh-bo, *m* wash-bowl; lavatory; sink.

lavage, läh-vähsh, *m* washing; wash.

lavande, läh-vahngd, *f* lavender.

lavement, lähv-mahng, *m* enema.

laver, läh-veh, *v* to wash.

lave-vaisselle, lähv-vayss-ell, *m* dishwasher.

lavoir, läh-vo'ähr, *m* washing place.

layette, lay-yett, *f* baby clothes; layette.

le, ler, *m art* the; *m pron* him; it.

lécher, leh-sheh, *v* to lick.

leçon, ler-song, *f* lesson; lecture.

lec-teur, trice, leck-ter, *mf* reader; assistant.

lecture, leck-tEEr, *f* reading.

ledit, ler-de, *a* the aforementioned; *f* **ladite,** läh-deet.

légal, e,* leh-gähl, *a* legal; lawful.

légaliser, leh-gäh-le-zeh, *v* to legalize.

légataire, leh-gäh-tair, *mf* legatee.

légation, leh-gäh-se-ong, *f* legateship; legation.

légende, leh-shahngd, *f* legend; caption.

lég-er, ère,* leh-**sheh**, *a* light; faint; fickle.

légèreté, leh-**shair**-teh, *f* lightness; fickleness.

légion, leh-**she**-ong, *f* legion.

législation, leh-shees-lǎhse-ong, *f* legislation; set of laws.

légiste, leh-**sheesst**, *m* lawyer.

légitime,* leh-**she**-teem, *a* legitimate; lawful.

legs, leh, *m* legacy.

léguer, leh-**gheh**, *v* to bequeath.

légume, leh-**ghEEm**, *m* vegetable; greens.

lendemain, lahngd-mang, *m* next day; morrow.

lent, e,* lahng, *a* slow; sluggish.

lenteur, lahng-ter, *f* slowness; delay.

lentille, lahng-tee-ye, *f* lentil; lens; *pl* contacts.

léopard, leh-op-ǎhr, *m* leopard.

lèpre, laypr, *f* leprosy.

lépreu-x, se, leh-prer, *mf* & *a* leper; leprous.

lequel, ler-kell, *m pron* who; whom; which; that.

lesdits, lade-de, *a mpl* the aforementioned; *f* **lesdites,** lay-deet.

léser, leh-zeh, *v* to wrong;

to injure.

lésion, leh-ze-ong, *f* lesion; injury; wrong.

lesquels, lay-kell, *mpl* of **lequel**; *f* **lesquelles,** lay-kell who; whom; which; that.

lessive, layss-eev, *f* washing (of clothes); wash; laundry; detergent.

lest, lesst, *m* ballast.

leste,* lesst, *a* nimble.

lettre, lay-tr, *f* letter; note; *pl* literature; letters.

lettré, e, lay-treh, *a* learned; literary.

leur, ler, *pers pron* to them.

leur, leurs, ler, *poss a* their.

leurrer, ler-reh, *v* to lure; to decoy.

levain, ler-vang, *m* yeast.

levant, ler-vahng, *m* East; *a* rising.

levée, ler-veh, *f* raising; removal; levy; collection of mail.

lever, ler-veh, *v* to raise; to collect; **se–,** to stand up; to get up; *m* rising.

levier, ler-ve-eh, *m* lever; crowbar.

lèvre, lay-vr, *f* lip.

lévrier, leh-vre-eh, *m* greyhound.

levure, ler-vEEr, *f* yeast.

lézard, leh-zǎhr, *m* lizard.

lézarde, leh-zǎhrd, *f* crevice; crack.

liaison, lee-ay-zong, *f* joining; junction; affair.

liant, e, lee-ahng, *a* pliant; affable; sociable.

liasse, lee-ǎhss, *f* bundle; wad; file (of papers).

libellé, lee-bel-leh, *m* wording.

libellule, lee-bel-lEEl, *f* dragonfly.

libérer, lee-beh-reh, *v* to liberate; to discharge.

liberté, lee-bair-teh, *f* liberty; freedom; ease.

libraire, lee-brair, *m* bookseller.

librairie, lee-bray-ree, *f* bookstore.

libre,* lee-br, *a* free; bold; disengaged.

libre-échange, leebr-ehshahngsh, *m* free trade.

licence, lee-sahngss, *f* license; degree; licentiousness.

licencier, lee-sahng-se-eh, *v* to disband; to fire.

licencieu-x, se,* leesahng-se-er, *a* licentious.

licite,* lee-seett, *a* lawful; licit.

lie, lee, *f* dregs; (*fig*) scum.

liège, lee-aysh, *m* cork.

lien, lee-ang, *m* bond.

lier, lee-eh, *v* to bind; to

tie; to join; to thicken.

lierre, lee-air, *m* ivy.

lieu, lee-er, *m* place; spot.

lieutenant, lee-ert-nahng, *m* lieutenant.

lièvre, lee-ay-vr, *m* hare.

ligne, leen-yer, *f* line; row; rank.

ligoter, lee-got-eh, *v* to bind; to tie up.

ligue, leegh, *f* league.

lilas, lee-lăh, *m* lilac; *a* lilac-colored.

limace, lee-măhss, *f* slug.

limaçon, lee-măh-song, *m* snail.

limande, lee-mahngd, *f* lemon sole.

lime, leem, *f* file.

limer, lee-meh, *v* to file; to polish.

limier, lee-me-eh, *m* bloodhound; detective.

limite, lee-meet, *f* limit; boundary; landmark.

limitrophe, lee-me-trof, *a* bordering; adjacent.

limon, lee-mong, *m* slime; mud.

limonade, lee-monn-ăhd, *f* lemonade.

lin, lang, *m* flax; linen.

linceul, lang-serl, *m* shroud.

linge, langsh, *m* household linen; cloth; rag.

lingerie, langsh-ree, *f* lingerie; linen closet.

lingot, lang-go, *m* ingot.

linon, lee-nong, *m* lawn (fine linen).

linotte, lee-nott, *f* linnet; **tête de –,** tayt der –, scatterbrained person.

lion, ne, lee-ong, *mf* lion; lioness.

liqueur, lee-ker, *f* liqueur.

liquidation, lee-ke-dăh-se-ong, *f* liquidation; clearance.

liquide, lee-keed, *a* & *m* liquid.

lire, leer, *v* to read.

lis, leess, *m* lily.

lis-eur, euse, lee-zer, *mf* reader; *f* book cover.

lisible,* lee-zee-bl, *a* legible.

lisière, lee-ze-air, *f* selvage; border.

lisse, leess, *a* smooth; sleek; glossy.

liste, leest, *f* list; roll; schedule; catalog.

lit, lee, *m* bed; layer; channel.

litanie, lee-tăh-nee, *f* long story; *pl* litany.

literie, leet-ree, *f* bedding.

litière, lee-te-air, *f* litter (stable).

litige, lee-teesh, *m* litigation.

littéraire, lee-teh-rair, *a* literary.

littéral, e,* lee-teh-răhl, *a* literal.

littérateur, lee-teh-răh-ter, *m* man of letters.

littérature, lee-teh-răh-tEEr, *f* literature.

littoral, lee-tor-ăhl, *m* coast-line; *a* of the seacoast.

livide, lee-veed, *a* livid.

livraison, lee-vray-zong, *f* delivery.

livrée, lee-vreh, *f* livery; servants.

livrer, lee-vreh, *v* to deliver; to betray.

livret, lee-vray, *m* booklet; handbook; bank book.

livreur, lee-vrer, *m* delivery man.

local, lock-ăhl, *m* place; premises.

local, e,* lock-ăhl, *a* local.

locataire, lock-ăh-tair, *m* tenant; lodger.

location, lock-ăh-se-ong, *f* hiring; renting.

location de voitures, loh-kăh-se-ong-der-vo'ăh-tEEr *f* car rental.

locomo-teur, trice, lock-omm-ot-**er,** *a* locomotive.

locomotive, lock-omm-ot-eev, *f* locomotive; engine.

locution, lock-E-ong, *f* locution; expression.

loge, losh, *f* lodge; hut;

box.

logement, losh-mahng, *m* lodging; accommodation; quarters.

loger, losh-eh, *v* to lodge; to house; to dwell.

logique, losh-eeck, *f* logic; *a** logical.

logis, losh-e, *m* dwelling; house; home.

loi, lo'ăh, *f* law; act.

loin, lo'ang, *adv* far; distant.

lointain, e, lo'ang-tang, *a* remote; far off.

loisir, lo'ăh-zeer, *m* leisure; time.

long, ue,* long, *a* long.

longer, long- sheh, *v* to pass along; to walk along; to coast.

longtemps, long-tahng, *adv* long; a long while.

longueur, long-gher, *f* length.

longue-vue, long-gh-vE, *f* field-glass; telescope.

lopin, lop-ang, *m* patch of ground.

loque, lock, *f* rag; tatter.

loquet, lock-ay, *m* latch.

lorgner, lorn-yeh, *v* to ogle; to have an eye on.

lorgnette, lorn-yett, *f* opera-glasses; lorgnette.

lorgnon, lorn-yong, *m* lorgnette; pince-nez.

lors, lor, *adv* then; at the time; dès –, day –, ever since.

lorsque, lors-ker, *conj* when.

losange, loz-ahngsh, *m* lozenge; diamond.

lot, lo, *m* portion; share; prize.

loterie, lot-ree, *f* raffle; lottery.

lotir, lot-eer, *v* to allot; to portion.

louable,* loo-ăh-bl, *a* laudable; praiseworthy.

louage, loo-ăhsh, *m* hire; renting.

louange, loo-ahngsh, *f* praise.

louche, loosh, *f* soup-ladle; *a* squint-eyed; suspicious.

louer, loo-eh, *v* to rent; to hire; to praise.

loup, loo, *m* wolf.

loup-garou, loo-găh-roo, *m* werewolf.

loupe, loop, *f* magnifying glass; loupe.

lourd, e,* loor, *a* heavy; lumpish; clumsy.

lourdaud, loor-doh, *m* oaf; *a* clumsy; awkward.

lourdeur, loor-der, *f* heaviness; weight.

louve, loov, *f* female wolf.

loyal, e,* lo'ăh-yăhl, *a* honest; true; faithful.

loyauté, lo'ăh-yoh-teh, *f* honesty; fairness.

loyer, lo'ăh-yeh, *m* hire; rent.

lubie, lE-bee, *f* whim; fad.

lubrifiant, lE-bre-fe-ahng, *m* lubricant; *a* lubricating.

lubrifier, lE-bre-fe-eh, *v* to lubricate.

lucarne, lE-kăhrn, *f* skylight.

lucide,* lE-seedd, *a* lucid; clear.

lucrati-f, ve,* lE-krăh-teeff, *a* a lucrative.

lueur, lE- er, *f* glimmer; gleam.

lugubre,* lE-ghE-br, *a* lugubrious.

lui, lwe, *pers pron* he; him; to him; her; to her; it; to it.

luire, lweer, *v* to shine; to glitter.

luisant, e, lwe-zahng, *a* shining; glossy.

lumière, lE-me-air, *f* light; *pl* knowledge.

lumineu-x, se,* lE-me-ner, *a* luminous.

lunaire, lE-nair, *a* lunar.

lundi, lung-de, *m* Monday.

lune, lEEn, *f* moon; **–de miel,** – der me-ell, honeymoon.

lunette, lE-nayt, *f* telescope; *pl* glasses.

lustre, lEEs-tr, *m* luster; gloss; chandelier.

luth, lEEt, *m* lute.

lutin, lE-tang, *m* goblin; imp (of child).

lutiner, lE-te-neh, *v* to tease.

lutte, lEEt, *f* wrestling; struggle; contest; strife.

lutter, lE-teh, *v* to wrestle; to struggle.

luxe, lEEks, *m* luxury.

luxer, lEEk-seh, *v* to dislocate.

luxueu-x, se,* lEEk-sE- er, *a* luxurious.

luxure, lEEk-sEEr, *f* lust.

lycée, lee-seh, *m* secondary school; high school.

lyre, leer, *f* lyre.

lyrique, lee-reeck, *a* lyrical.

lyrisme, lee-reessm, *m* lyricism.

ma, măh, *poss af* my.

macabre, măh-kah-br, *a* macabre.

macédoine, măh-seh-do'ăhn, *f* mixed dish (of vegetables or fruit).

mâcher, mah-sheh, *v* to chew.

machinal, e,* măh-she-năhl, *a* mechanical.

machine, măh-sheen, *f* machine; engine; implement.

machiner, măh-she-neh, *v* to plot; to contrive.

mâchoire, mah-sho'ăhr, *f* jaw; jawbone.

mâchonner, mah-shonn-eh, *v* to munch.

maçon, măh-song, *m* mason; bricklayer; freemason.

madame, măh-dăhm, *f* madam; Mrs.

mademoiselle, măhd-mo'ăh-zell, *f* Miss; the young lady.

madone, măh-donn, *f* madonna.

madré, e, măh-dreh, *a* speckled; cunning.

magasin, măh-găh-zang, *m* shop; warehouse; stock store.

magasinage, măh-găh-ze-năhsh, *m* warehousing.

magazine, măh-găh-zeen, *m* magazine.

magie, măh-shee, *f* magic.

magique,* măh-sheeck, *a* magical.

magistral, e,* măh-shees-trăhl, *a* masterly; authoritative.

magistrat, măh-shees-trăh, *m* magistrate.

magistrature, măh-shees-trăh-tEEr, *f* prosecuting attorneys.

magnanime,* măhn-yăh-neem, *a* magnanimous.

magnétique, măhn-yeh-teeck, *a* magnetic.

magnétophone, măhn-yeh-toh-fonn, *m* tape recorder.

magnifique,* măhn-yee-feeck, *a* magnificent.

magot, mah-go, *m* baboon; grotesque figure; hoard

mai, may, *m* May; maypole.

maigre,* may-gr, *a* lean; thin; scanty; barren.

maigrir, may-greer, *v* to become thin; to lose weight.

maille, mah'e, *f* mesh; stitch; mail (chain).

maillot, mah'e-yo, *m* shirt; swimsuit (sports).

main, mang, *f* hand.

main-d'œuvre, mang-der-vr, *f* workmanship; labor.

main-forte, mang-fort, *f* assistance; help.

maint, e, mang, *a* many; several.

maintenant, mangt-nahng, *adv* now.

maintenir, mangt-neer, *v* to maintain; to keep up.

maintien, mang-te-ang, m
maintenance;
deportment;
countenance.

maire, mair, m mayor.

mairie, may-ree, f town
hall.

mais, may, conj but; **–oui,**
– we, "why, yes".

maïs, măh-eess, m maize.

maison, may-zong, f
house; home; firm.

maisonnette, may-zonn-
ett, f cottage; small
house.

maître, may-tr, m master;
owner; teacher.

maîtresse, may-tress, f
schoolmistress; mistress.

maîtrise, may-treez, f
mastery; self-control.

maîtriser, may-tre-zeh, v
to master; to keep under
control.

majesté, măh-shess-teh, f
majesty.

majestueu-x, se,* măh-
shess-tE-er, a majestic.

majeur, e, măh-sher, a
greater; major; **force –e,**
fors –, of necessity.

major, măh-shor, m
major.

majorité, măh-shor-e-teh,
f majority; coming of
age.

majuscule, măh-shEEs-
kEEl, f capital (letter).

mal, măhl, adv ill; badly;
amiss; on bad terms; m
evil; mischief;
misfortune; ache;
sickness.

malade, măh-lăhd, mf sick
person; patient; a ill;
sick.

maladie, măh-lăh-dee, f
illness.

maladi-f, ve,* măh-lăh-
deeff, a sickly.

maladresse, măh-lăh-
dress, f awkwardness;
blunder.

maladroit, e,* măh-lăh-
dro'ăh, a clumsy.

malaise, măh-layz, m
uneasiness; discomfort;
faintness; dizziness.

malaisé, e, măh-lay-zeh, a
difficult.

malappris, e, măhl-ăh-
pree, mf vulgar person; a
illbred.

malavisé, e, măhl-ăh-ve-
zeh, a ill-advised.

malaxer, măhl-acks-seh, v
to knead; to mix.

mâle, mahl, m male; a
male; manly; virile.

malchance, măhl-
shahngss, f bad luck.

maléfice, măh-leh-feess, m
witchcraft.

malencontreu-x, se,*
măh-lahng-kong-trer a
unlucky; unfortunate.

malentendu, măh-lahng-
tahng-dE, m
misunderstanding.

malfaisant, e, măhl-fer-
zahng, a mischievous;
noxious.

malfai-teur, trice, măhl-
fay-ter, mf criminal;
gangster; thief.

malgré, măhl-greh, prep in
spite of.

malhabile,* măhl-ăh-beel,
a unskillful.

malheur, măh-ler, m
unhappiness;
misfortune; bad luck.

malheureu-x, se,* măhl-
er-rer, mf & a unhappy;
wretched.

malhonnête,* măhl-onn-
ayt, a dishonest.

malice, măh-leess, f
malice; spite.

malicieu-x, se,* măh-le-
se-er, a spiteful;
mischievous.

malin, maligne,* măh-
lang, măh-leen-yer a
malignant; malicious;
mischievous; sly;
cunning.

malle, măhl, f trunk.

mallette, măh-lett, f small
suitcase.

malmener, măhl-mer-neh,
v to handle roughly; to
abuse.

malotru, e, măhl-ot-rE, mf

ill-bred person; boor.

malpropre,* măhl-propr, *a* slovenly; dirty.

malsain, e, măhl-sang, *a* unwholesome (things); unhealthy (persons).

malséant, e, măhl-seh-ahng, *a* unbecoming.

malsonnant, e, măhl-sonn-ahng, *a* ill-sounding; offensive.

maltraiter, măhl-tray-teh, *v* to maltreat.

malveillant, e, măhl-vay'e-ahng, *a* malevolent.

maman, măh-mahng, *f* mummy.

mamelle, măh-mell, *f* breast; udder.

mamelon, măh-mer-long, *m* nipple; teat.

mammifère, măh-me-fair, *m* mammal.

manche, mahngsh, *m* handle; *f* sleeve.

manchette, mahng-shett, *f* cuff.

manchon, mahng-shong, *m* muff.

manchot, e, mahng-sho, *a* & *mf* one-armed.

mandat, mahng-dăh, *m* mandate; money order; warrant.

mandataire, mahng-dăh-tair, *m* proxy; agent.

mander, mahng-deh, *v* to

send word; to send for.

manège, măh-naish, *m* riding school; roundabout; (*fam*) trick.

manette, măh-nett, *f* small handle.

mangeable, mahng-shăh-bl, *a* edible.

mangeaille, mahng-shăh'e, *f* feed; (*fam*) grub.

manger, mahng-sheh, *v* to eat; to squander; *m* food.

maniable, măh-ne-ăh-bl, *a* easy to handle.

maniaque, măh-ne-ăhck, *m* maniac; *a* eccentric.

manie, măh-nee, *f* mania; craze.

maniement, măh-ne-mahng, *m* handling; management.

manier, măh-ne-eh, *v* to handle; to manage; to govern.

manière, măh-ne-air, *f* manner; style; *pl* manners; airs.

maniéré, e, măh-ne-eh-reh, *a* affected.

manifestation, măh-ne-fes-tah-se-ong, *f* manifestation; political demonstration.

manifeste, măh-ne-fest, *m* manifesto; manifest; *a** manifest; evident.

manifester, măh-ne-fess-teh, *v* to manifest; to

demonstrate.

manipuler, măh-ne-pEleh, *v* to manipulate; to handle.

manivelle, măh-ne-vell, *f* handle; crank.

mannequin, măhn-kang, *m* dummy; fashion model; mannequin.

manœuvre, măh-ner-vr, *m* laborer; *f* move; drill.

manœuvrer, măh-ner-vreh, *v* to handle; to work; to maneuver.

manoir, măh-no'ăhr, *m* manor; mansion.

manque, mahngk, *m* lack; deficiency; failure.

manqué, é, mahng-keh, *a* missed; defective; failed.

manquement, mahngk-mahng, *m* omission; failure; oversight.

manquer, mahng-keh, *v* to fail; to want; to miss; to be very near to (doing something).

mansarde, mahng-săhrd, *f* attic.

manteau, mahng-toh, *m* mantle.

manuel, măh-nE-ell, *m* manual; textbook.

manuel, le,* măh-nE-ell, *a* manual.

manufacture, măh-nE-făhck-tEEr, *f* factory; manufacture.

manuscrit, măh-nEES-kree, *m* manuscript.

maquereau, măhck-roh, *m* mackerel.

maquette, măhck-ett, *f* model; dummy (book); mock-up

maquillage, măh-kee-yähsh, *m* makeup.

maquiller, măh-kee-yeh, *v* to make up (face); to disguise.

maraîch-er, ère, măh-ray-sheh, *a* & *m* truck farming; market-gardener.

marais, măh-ray, *m* marsh; swamp; bog.

marâtre, măh-rah-tr, *f* cruel stepmother.

marauder, măh-roh-deh, *v* to maraud; to plunder.

marbre, măhr-br, *m* marble; marble slab.

marchand, e, măhr-shahng, *mf* merchant; storekeeper; dealer; *a* salable; commercial.

marchandage, măhr-shahng-dăhsh, *m* bargaining.

marchandise, măhr-shahng-deez, *f* goods; wares.

marche, măhrsh, *f* stair; walking; march; progress; running (trains, etc).

marché, măhr-sheh, *m* market; bargain; purchase; contract; **bon –,** *bong –,* cheap; **meilleur –,** may-yer – cheaper.

marchepied, măhr-sherpe-eh, *m* footstool; step.

marcher, măhr-sheh, *v* to walk; to tread; to work; to move

mardi, măhr-de, *m* Tuesday.

mare, măhr, *f* pool; pond.

marécage, măh-reh-kähsh, *m* marsh; bog; swamp.

maréchal, măh-reh-shähl, *m* marshal; **–ferrant, –** feh-rahng, blacksmith.

marée, măh-reh, *f* tide; fish (fresh).

margarine, măhr-ghăh-reen, *f* margarine.

marge, măhrsh, *f* margin; border; time.

marguerite, măhr-gher-reet, *f* daisy; marguerite.

mari, măh-re, *m* husband.

mariage, măh-re-ăhsh, *m* marriage; wedding; union.

marié, e, măh-ree-eh, *mf* bridegroom; bride.

marier, măh-re-eh, *v* to marry; to unite; **se –,** to get married.

marin, măh-rang, *m* sailor; seaman.

marin, e, măh-rang, *a* marine; seagoing.

marinade, măh-re-năhd, *f* pickle; marinade.

marine, măh-reen, *f* navy; **bleu –,** bler –, navy blue.

marionnette, măh-re-onn-ett, *f* puppet; *pl* puppet show.

marmaille, măhr-mah'e, *f* crowd of kids.

marmite, măhr-meet, *f* pot (cooking).

marmot, măhr-mo, *m* brat; child.

marmotter, măhr-mot-eh, *v* to mutter.

maroquin, măh-rock-ang, *m* morocco leather.

marquant, e, măhr-kahng, *a* striking.

marque, măhrk, *f* mark; stamp; brand; token.

marquer, măhr-keh, *v* to mark.

marqueterie, măhr-kert-ree, *f* inlaid work.

marquis, e, măhr-ke, *mf* marquess; marchioness; marquee.

marraine, măh-rain, *f* godmother.

marrant, măh-rahng, *a* (*fam*) funny; amusing.

marron, măh-rong, *m* chestnut; *a* chestnut-colored; brown.

marronnier, măh-ronn-e-eh, *m* chestnut tree.

mars, măhrs, *m* March; Mars.

marseillaise, măhr-say'e-ayz, *f* Marseillaise.

marsouin, măhr-soo-ang *m* porpoise.

marteau, măhr-toh, *m* hammer; door knocker.

marteler, măhr-ter-leh, *v* to hammer.

martial, e,* măhr-se-ăhl, *a* martial.

martinet, măhr-te-nay, *m* swift; whip.

martre, măhr-tr, *f* martin (bird); sable.

martyre, măhr-teer, *m* martyrdom.

masculin, e, măhss-kE-lang, *a & m* masculine; male.

masque, măhsk, *m* mask; pretense.

masquer, măhss-keh, *v* to mask; to disguise; to hide.

massacrer, măhss-ăh-kreh, *v* to slaughter; to bungle.

masse, măhss, *f* mass; heap; bulk; lot; pool.

massif, măhss-eef, *m* thicket; clump of shrubs; chain of mountains.

massi-f, ve,* măhss-eef, *a*

massive; heavy; solid.

massue, măhss-E, *f* club.

mastic, măhss-teeck, *m* putty.

mastiquer, măhss-te-keh, *v* to cement; to masticate.

mat, măht, *m* mate (chess).

mat, e, măht, *a* mat; unpolished; dull; heavy.

mât, mah, *m* mast; pole.

matelas, măht-lăh, *m* mattress.

matelot, măht-lo, *m* sailor; seaman.

mater, măh-teh, *v* to checkmate; to mat; (*fam*) to curb; to subdue.

matériaux, măh-te-re-oh, *mpl* materials.

matériel, măh-teh-re-ell, *m* stock; plant.

matériel, le,* măh-teh-re-ell, *a* material.

maternel, le,* măh-tair-nell, *a* motherly; maternal; *f* nursery school.

maternité, măh-tair-ne-teh, *f* maternity; maternity ward.

mathématiques, măh-teh-măh-teeck, *fpl* mathematics.

matière, măh-te-air, *f* matter; material; subject; cause.

matin, măh-tang, *m* morning.

matinal, e, măh-te-năhl, *a* early.

matinée, măh-te-neh, *f* morning; matinee.

matois, e, măh-to 'ăh, *mf* sly person; *a* cunning.

matrice, măh-treess, *f* matrix; womb.

matricule, măh-tre-kEEl, *f* registration; roll.

maturité, măh-tE-re-teh, *f* maturity; ripeness.

maudire, moh-deer, *v* to curse.

maudit, e, moh-de, *a* cursed.

maugréer, moh-greh-eh, *v* to grumble.

maussade,* moh-săhd, *a* sulky.

mauvais, e, moh-vay, *a* evil; bad; ill; wrong.

mauve, mohv, *a & m* mauve.

me, mer, *pron* me; to me; at me.

mécanicien, meh-kăh-ne-se-ang, *m* mechanic; engineer.

mécanique, meh-kăh-neeck, *f* mechanics; machinery; *a** mechanical.

mécanisme, meh-kăh-nissm, *m* mechanism; machinery.

méchamment, meh-shǎh-mahng, *adv* wickedly; unkindly.

méchanceté, meh-shahngss-teh, *f* wickedness; unkindness.

méchant, e, meh-shahng, *mf* wicked person; naughty child; *a* wicked; ill-natured; naughty.

mèche, maysh, *f* wick; match; lock (of hair).

mécompte, meh-kongt, *m* miscalculation; disappointment.

méconnaissable, meh-konn-ess-ǎh-bl, *a* unrecognizable.

méconnu, e, meh-konn-E, *pp* & *a* unacknowledged; unappreciated.

mécontent, e, meh-kong-tahng, *a* discontented; unhappy.

mécréant, meh-kreh-ahng, *m* unbeliever.

médaille, meh-dah´e, *f* medal.

médaillon, meh-dah´e-yong, *m* medallion; locket.

médecin, mehd-sang, *m* physician; doctor.

médecine, mehd-seen, *f* medicine (art of).

médiat, e, meh-de-ǎh, *a* mediate.

média-teur, trice, meh-de-ǎh-ter, *mf* mediator.

médicament, meh-de-kǎh-mahng, *m* medicine.

médiocre,* meh-de-ockr, *a* mediocre.

médire, meh-deer, *v* to slander.

médisance, meh-de-zahngss, *f* slander.

méditer, meh-de-teh, *v* to meditate; to plan.

méduse, meh-DEEz, *f* jellyfish.

méfait, meh-fay, *m* misdeed.

méfiance, meh-fe-ahngss, *f* mistrust; caution.

méfiant, e, meh-fe-ahng, *a* mistrustful; suspicious.

méfier (se), ser meh-fe-eh, *v* to mistrust (**de**); to beware of.

mégarde (par), pǎhr meh-gǎhrd, *adv* inadvertently.

mégère, meh-shair, *f* shrew (of woman).

meilleur, e, may'e-er, *a* & *mf* better; best.

mélancolique,* meh-lahng-koll-eeck, *a* melancholy; gloomy.

mélange, meh-lahngsh, *m* mixture; blending; medley.

mélanger, meh-lahng-sheh, *v* to mix; to blend.

mêlée, may-leh, *f* fray;

scuffle; free-for-all.

mêler, may-leh, *v* to mix; to blend; to entangle.

mélodieu-x, se,* meh-lod-e-er, *a* melodious.

melon mer-long, *m* melon.

membrane, mahng-brǎhn, *f* membrane; film.

membre, mahng-br, *f* member; limb; penis.

même, maym, *a* same; even; very same; self.

mémoire, meh-mo'ǎhr, *m* memorandum; bill; *pl* memoirs; *f* memory; fame.

menaçant, e, mer-nǎh-sahng, *a* threatening.

menace, mer-nǎhss, *f* menace; threat.

menacer, mer-nǎhss-eh, *v* to threaten.

ménage, meh-nǎhsh, *m* housekeeping; household; housecleaning; married couple.

ménagement, meh-nǎhsh-mahng, *m* regard; caution; tact.

ménager, meh-nǎh-sheh, *v* to treat with care.

ménag-er, ère, meh-nǎh-sheh, *a* domestic; of the household.

ménagère, meh-nǎh-shair, *f* housewife.

mendiant, e, mahng-de-

191

ahng, *mf* & *a* beggar;
begging.

mendicité, mahng-de-se-
teh, *f* begging.

mendier, mahng-de-eh, *v*
to beg.

menées, mer-neh, *fpl*
intrigues.

mener, mer-neh, *v* to lead;
to head; to convey.

meneur, mer-ner, *m*
leader; ringleader.

méningite, meh-nang-
sheet, *f* meningitis.

menotte, mer-not, *f* little
hand; *pl* handcuffs.

mensonge, mahngss-
ongsh, *m* lie.

mensuel, le,* mahng-sE-
ell, *a* monthly.

mental, e,* mahng-tăhl, *a*
mental.

mentalité, mahng-tăh-le-
teh, *f* frame of mind;
mentality.

menteu-r, se, mahng-ter,
mf liar; *a* lying.

menthe, mahngt, *f* mint.

mentionner, mahng-se-
onn-eh, *v* to mention.

mentir, mahng-teer, *v* to
lie; to fib.

menton, mahng-tong, *m*
chin.

menu, mer-nE, *m* menu.

menu e, mer-nE, *a* thin;
slender; fine.

menuisier, mer-nwee-ze-

eh, *m* carpenter.

méprendre (se), ser meh-
prahng-dr, *v* to be
mistaken.

mépris, meh-pree, *m*
contempt; scorn.

méprisable, meh-pre-zăh-
bl, *a* contemptible;
despicable.

méprise, meh-preez, *f*
mistake.

mépriser, meh-pre-zeh, *v*
to despise; to scorn.

mer, mair, *f* sea; **mal de –,**
măhl der –, seasickness.

mercenaire, mair-ser-
nair, *m* & *a* mercenary.

mercerie, mair-ser-ree, *f*
notions store.

merci, mair-se, *m* thanks;
thank you; *f* mercy.

merci-er, ère, mair-se-eh,
mf notions dealer.

mercredi, mair-krer-de, *m*
Wednesday.

mère, mair, *f* mother; *a*
principal.

méridien, ne, meh-re-de-
ang, *a* meridian.

méridional, e, meh-re-de-
onn-ăhl, *a* & *mf*
southern; southerner.

mérite, meh-reet, *m* merit;
worth; talent.

mériter, meh-re-teh, *v* to
deserve; to be worth; to
require.

méritoire,* meh-re-to'ăhr,

a meritorious.

merlan, mair-lahng, *m*
whiting.

merle, mairl, *m* blackbird.

merveille, mair-vay'e, *f*
marvel; wonder; *adv phr*
à –, ăh –, excellently.

merveilleu-x, se,* mair-
vay'e-er, *a* wonderful.

mes, may, *poss a pl* my.

mésallier (se), ser meh-
zăh-le-eh, *v* to marry
beneath oneself.

mésange, meh-zahngsh, *f*
titmouse (bird).

mésaventure, meh-zăh-
vahng-tEEr, *f* mischance;
mishap.

mésestimer, meh-zess-te-
meh, *v* to undervalue.

mesquin, e,* mess-kang, *a*
mean; petty; stingy.

mesquinerie, mess-keen-
ree, *f* meanness;
pettiness.

message, mess-ăhsh, *m*
message; errand.

messag-er, ère, mess-ăh-
sheh, *mf* messenger.

messagerie, mess-ăhsh-
ree, *f* mail service;
shipping service.

messe, mayss, *f* mass.

mesure, mer-zEEr, *f*
measure; measurement;
proportion; step;
propriety; bar (music);
time.

mesuré, e, mer-zE-reh, *a* regular; guarded.

mesurer, mer-zE-reh, *v* to measure; to consider; to proportion.

mésuser, meh-zE-zeh, *v* to misuse.

métal, meh-tăhl, *m* metal.

métamorphose, meh-tăh-mor-fohz, *f* metamorphosis; transformation.

météore, meh-teh-or, *m* meteor.

météorologique, meh-teh-o-ro-lo-sheeck, *a* meteorological.

méthode, meh-tod, *f* method; way; system.

méthodique,* meh-tod-eeck, *a* methodical.

méticuleu-x, se,* meh-te-kE-ler, *a* meticulous; particular.

métier, meh-te-eh, *m* trade; profession; handicraft; loom.

métis, se, meh-tee, *mf* & *a* person of mixed race; of mixed race.

métrage, meh-trăhsh, *m* measuring; metric length; length of film.

mètre, met-tr, *m* meter; rule.

métrique, meh-treeck, *a* metric.

métropole, meh-trop-ol, *f* metropolis; mother country.

métropolitain, meh-trop-oll-e-tang, *a* metropolitan; **le métro,** lermeh-tro, *m* subway.

mets, may, *m* food; dish.

mettre, met-tr, *v* to put; to set; to wear.

meuble, mer-bl, *m* piece of furniture; *pl* furniture; *a* movable.

meubler, mer-bleh, *v* to furnish; to stock.

meule, merl, *f* grindstone; millstone.

meuni-er, ère, mer-ne-eh, *mf* miller.

meurtre, mer-tr, *m* murder.

meurtri-er, ère, mer-tre-eh, *mf* murderer; murderess; *a* deadly.

meurtrir, mer-treer, *v* to bruise.

meurtrissure, mer-triss-EEr, *f* bruise.

meute, mert, *f* pack; (*fam*) mob.

mi, me, *m* Mi (music); E.

mi, me, half; mid; semi-.

miasme, me-ăhssm, *m* miasma.

miauler, me-ohl-eh, *v* to mew.

microbe, me-krob, *m* microbe; (*fam*) germ.

microfilm, me-kroh-feelm, *m* microfilm.

microphone, me-krof-onn, *m* microphone.

microsillon, me-croh-se-yong, *m* long-playing record.

midi, me-de, *m* midday; noon; south (of France).

mie, me, *f* crumb (inside of a loaf).

miel, me-ell, *m* honey.

mielleu-x, se,* me-ell-er, *a* honeyed; bland; soft-spoken.

mien, ne, me-ang, *poss pron* mine.

miette, me-ett, *f* crumb; bit.

mieux, me-er, *adv* better; best; more; *m* best thing; *a* better.

mignon, ne, meen-yong, *a* cute.

migraine, me-grain, *f* migraine; headache.

mijaurée, me-shohr-eh, *f* affected woman.

mijoter, me-shot-eh, *v* to simmer.

milieu, me-le-er, *m* middle; circle; environment; social class.

militaire, me-le-tair, *m* soldier; *a* military.

mille, mill, *m* one thousand; *a* thousand.

milliard, mill-e-ăhr, *m*

one thousand millions.

millième, mill-e-aim, *m* & *a* thousandth.

million, mill-e-*ong*, *m* million.

millionième, mill-e-onn-e-emm, *m* & *a* millionth.

mime, meem, *m* mime.

minable, me-năh-bl, *a* shabby; pitiable.

minauder, me-nohd-eh, *v* to simper.

mince, mangss, *a* slender; slim; scanty.

mine, meen, *f* appearance; look; mine; lead (of pencil).

miner, me-neh, *v* to undermine; to wear away.

minerai, meen-ray, *m* ore.

minéral, e, me-neh-răhl, *a* mineral.

mineur, me-ner, *m* miner; *a* minor (music); minor.

mineur, e, me-ner, *a* minor; underage.

miniature, me-ne-ăh-tEEr, *f* miniature.

mini-er, ère, me-ne-eh, *a* mining.

minime, me-neem, *a* very small; trifling.

ministère, me-niss-tair, *m* ministry; services.

ministre, me-neestr, *m* minister; secretary of

state; clergyman.

minois, me-no'ăh, *m* (*fam*) pretty face.

minuit, me-nwe, *m* midnight.

minuscule, me-nEEs-kEEl, *f* small letter; *a* minute.

minute, me-nEEt, *f* minute; instant.

minutieu-x, se,* me-nEE-se-er, *a* particular; detailed.

miracle, me-răh-kl, *m* miracle; wonder.

miraculeu-x, se,* me-răh-kE-ler, *a* miraculous; wonderful.

mirage, me-răhsh, *m* mirage; delusion.

mirer, me-reh, *v* to aim at; **se–,** ser, to look at (oneself).

miroir, me-ro'ăhr, *m* mirror.

miroiter, me-ro'ăh-teh, *v* to flash; to glisten; **faire–, fehr–,** to promise.

mise, meez, *f* placing; dress; stake.

misérable, me-zeh-răh-bl, *mf* wretch.

misère, me-zair, *f* misery; poverty; trifle.

miséricorde, me-zeh-re-kord, *f* mercy.

mission, miss-e-*ong*, *f* mission.

missionnaire, miss-e-onn-air, *n* missionary.

mitaine, me-tain, *f* mitten.

mite, meet, *f* clothes moth; mite.

mi-temps, me-tah*ng*, *f* halftime; interval; part time.

mitiger, me-te-sheh, *v* to mitigate.

mitraille, me-trah'e, *f* grapeshot.

mitrailleuse, me-trah'e-erz, *f* machine gun.

mixte, meekst, *a* mixed; **école –,** eh-kol –, coed school.

mixtion, meeks-te-*ong*, *f* mixture; compounding; blending.

mobile, mob-eel, *m* moving body; motive; mobile; *a* movable; changing.

mobili-er, ère, mob-e-le-eh, *a* movable; personal.

mobiliser, mob-e-le-zeh, *v* to mobilize.

mobilité, mob-e-le-teh, *f* mobility; instability.

mode, mod, *m* mood; mode; method.

mode, mod, *f* fashion; way; *pl* millinery.

modèle, mod-ell, *m*

model; pattern.

modeler, mod-leh, *v* to model; to shape; to mold.

modération, mod-eh-räh-se-ong, *f* moderation.

modérer, mod-eh-reh, *v* to moderate.

moderne, mod-airn, *mf & a* modern style; modern.

modeste, * mod-est, *a* modest; unassuming.

modestie, mod-ess-tee, *f* modesty.

modifier, mod-e-fe-eh, *v* to modify.

modique, * mod-eeck, *a* moderate; small.

modiste, mod-eest, *f* milliner.

moelle, mwähl, *f* marrow (bone); pith.

moelleu-x, se, * mwähller, *a* marrowy; soft; mellow.

mœurs, mers, *fpl* manners; customs; morals.

moi, mwäh, *pers pron* I; me; to me; *m* self; ego.

moindre, * mwang-dr, *a* less; **le –,** ler **–,** the least.

moine, mwähn, *m* monk.

moineau, mwäh-noh, *m* sparrow.

moins, mwang, *adv* less; fewer; least; *prep* minus.

mois, mwäh, *m* month.

moisir, mwäh-zeer, *v* to go

moldy;(*fam*) to vegetate.

moisson, mwähss-ong, *f* harvest; crop.

moite, mwäht, *a* moist; damp; clammy.

moiteur, mwäh-ter, *f* moistness; dampness.

moitié, mwäh-te-eh, *f* half; *adv* half; partly.

mol, le, (* see **mou).**

molaire, moll-air, *f* molar tooth.

môle, mohl, *m* mole; pier.

molester, moll-ess-teh, *v* to molest; to annoy.

mollasse, moll-ähss, *a* flabby; spineless.

mollesse, moll-ess, *f* softness; indolence.

mollet, moll-ay, *m* calf (of leg).

molletonné, moll-tonn-eh, *a* lined with fleece; with raised nap.

mollir, moll-eer, *v* to soften; to slacken; to give way.

moment, mom-ahng, *m* moment; time; occasion.

momentané, * **e,** mom-ahng-täh-neh, *a* momentary.

momie, mom-ee, *f* mummy.

mon, mong, *poss a m* my; *f* **ma,** mäh, *pl* **mes,** may.

monarchie, monn-ähr-

shee, *f* monarchy.

monarque, monn-ährk, *m* monarch.

monastère, monn-ähss-tair, *m* monastery.

monceau, mong,soh, *m* heap.

mondain, e, * mong-dang, *a* worldly; mundane; fashionable.

monde, mongd, *m* world; mankind; people; society.

mondial, e, mong-de-ähl, *a* worldwide.

monétaire, monn-eh-tair, *a* monetary.

moniteur, monn-e-ter, *m* monitor; instructor; gazette.

monnaie, monn-ay, *f* money; coin; change; mint.

monocle, monn-ockl, *m* monocle.

monopole, monn-op-ol, *m* monopoly.

monotone, monn-ot-onn, *a* monotonous.

monseigneur, mong-sehn-yer, *m* Your Grace; Your Royal Highness.

monsieur, mer-se-er, *m* gentleman; Mr.; master; sir.

monstre, mongss-tr, *m* monster.

monstrueu-x, se, *

mongss-trE-**er**, *a*
monstrous; shocking.

mont, mong, *m* mount;
mountain.

montage, mong-tăhsh, *m*
raising; putting up.

montagnard, e, mong-
tăhn-yăhr, *mf*
mountaineer.

montagne, mong-tăhn-yer,
f mountain.

montant, mong-tahng, *m*
upright; rise; amount.

montant, e, mong-tahng, *a*
rising; uphill; high-
necked.

montée, mong-teh, *f* rise;
ascent; step.

monter, mong-teh, *v* to
ascend; to rise; to ride;
to set up; to mount
(jewel); se –, to amount.

monticule, mong-te-kEEl,
m hillock.

montre, mong-tr, *f* watch;
show; display window.

montrer, mong-treh, *v* to
show; to teach.

monture, mong-tEEr, *f*
mount; frame; setting.

monument, monn-E-
mahng, *m* monument.

moquer (se), ser mock-eh,
v to mock; to make fun
of.

moquerie, mock-ree, *f*
mockery; derision.

moquette, mock-ett, *f*
carpet.

moqueu-r, se, mock-**er**, *mf*
mocker; *a* mocking.

moral, e, * mor-ăhl, *m* state of
mind; morale; spirits.

moral, e, * mor-ăhl, *a*
moral; mental.

morale, mor-ăhl, *f* morals;
reprimand; moral (of
story).

morceau, mor-soh, *m*
piece; bit; morsel;
extract.

morceler, mor-ser-leh, *v*
to cut up into small
pieces; to parcel out.

mordant, e, mor-dahng, *a*
biting; sarcastic.

mordicus, mor-de-kEEss,
adv stubbornly;
doggedly.

mordre, mor-dr, *v* to bite;
to gnaw; to eat away.

morfondre (se), ser mor-
fong-dr, *v* to be chilled;
to be bored stiff waiting.

morgue, morgh, *f*
mortuary; arrogance.

moribond, e, mor-e-bong,
mf & a dying person;
dying.

morne, morn, *a* gloomy;
sad; dull.

morose, mor-ohz, *a*
morose.

morphine, mor-feen, *f*
morphine.

mors, mor, *m* bit; **prendre**

le –**aux dents,** prahng-dr
ler – oh dahng, to bolt.

morsure, mor-sEEr, *f* bite;
sting.

mort, mor, *f* death.

mort, e, mor, *mf* dead
person; *a* dead; stagnant;
spent.

mortalité, mor-tăh-le-teh,
f mortality; death rate.

mortel, le, * mor-tell, *a*
mortal; deadly; tedious.

mortier, mor-te-eh, *m*
mortar.

mortifier, mor-te-fe-eh, *v*
to mortify; to hang
(game).

morue, mor-EE, *f* codfish.

morveu-x, se, mor-ver, *mf*
dirty child; brat; *a*
snotty-nosed.

mot, moh, *m* word; saying;
hint.

moteur, mot-er, *m* motor;
engine.

mo-teur, trice, mot-er, *a*
motive; moving.

motif, mot-eeff, *m* motive;
reason.

motion, mo-se-ong, *f*
motion; proposal.

motiver, mot-e-veh, *v* to
state reason for; to
motivate.

motocyclette, mot-oss-e-
klett, *f* motorcycle.

motocycliste, mot-oss-e-
kleesst, *m* motorcyclist.

motte, mot, *f* clod; pat (of butter).

mou (**mol** before a word beginning with a vowel or **"h"** mute); *f* **molle**, moo, mol; *a* soft; indolent; muggy (weather).

mouchard, moo-shăhr, *m* (*fam*) sneak; informer.

mouche, moosh, *f* fly; beauty-spot; bull's eye.

moucher, moo-sheh, *v* to wipe the nose of; **se –**, to blow one's nose.

moucheron, moosh-rong, *m* gnat; snuff (candle).

mouchoir, moo-sho'ăhr, *m* handkerchief.

moudre, moodr, *v* to grind.

moue, moo, *f* pout.

mouette, moo-ett, *f* seagull.

mouillé, e, moo'e-yeh, *a* wet; soaked; anchored.

mouiller, moo'e-yeh, *v* to wet; to soak; to anchor.

moule, moo, *m* mold; cast; form; *f* mussel.

mouler, moo-leh, *v* to mold; to cast; to shape.

moulin, moo-lang, *m* mill; windmill; **– à paroles**, – ăh păh-rol, chatterbox.

moulu, e, moo-lE, *pp* & *a* ground.

mourant, e, moo-rahng, *mf* & *a* dying person; dying.

mourir, moo-reer, *v* to die; to die away; to go out (fire, light).

mousquetaire, mooss-ker-tair, *m* musketeer.

mousse, mooss, *m* ship's-boy; *f* moss; froth; lather.

mousseline, mooss-leen, *f* muslin; chiffon.

mousser, mooss-eh, *v* to foam; to lather; to sparkle; **faire –**, fair –, to froth.

mousseu-x, se, mooss-er, *a* frothy.

moustache, mooss-tăhsh, *f* moustache; whiskers (animals).

moustiquaire, mooss-te-kair, *m* mosquito net.

moustique, mooss-teeck, *m* mosquito.

moutarde, moo-tăhrd, *f* mustard.

mouton, moo-tong, *m* sheep; sheepskin.

mouvant, e, moo-vahng, *a* moving; shifting.

mouvement, moov-mahng, *m* movement; motion; disturbance.

mouvementé, e, moov-mahng-teh, *a* agitated; lively; eventful; fluctuating.

mouvoir, moo-vo'ăhr, *v* to move; to stir; to start.

moyen, mo'ăh-yang, *m* means; medium; power.

moyen, ne, mo'ăh-yang, *a* middle; mean; average.

moyennant, mo'ăh-yay-nahng *prep* on condition that; for a consideration.

moyenne, moăh-yain, *f* average; mean.

muer, mE-eh, *v* to molt; to break (voice).

muet, te, mE-ay, *mf* dumb person; *a* dumb; taciturn.

mufle, mEE-fl, *m* muzzle; (*fam*) face; bore.

mugir, mE-sheer, *v* to moo; to bellow; to roar.

mugissement, mE-shiss-mahng, *m* mooing; bellowing; roaring.

muguet, mE-ghay, *m* lily of the valley.

mule, mEEl, *f* female-mule; slipper.

mulet, mE-lay, *m* mule; mullet.

multiplier, mEEl-te-ple-eh, *v* to multiply.

multitude, mEEl-te-tEEd, *f* multitude.

municipalité, mE-ne-se-păh-le-teh, *f* municipality; town hall.

munificence, mE-ne-fe-sahngss, *f* munificence.

munir, mE-neer, *v* to provide; to supply; to arm (**de,** with).

munitions, mE-ne-se-*ong*, *fpl* ammunition; stores.

mur, mEEr, *m* wall; **au pied du –,** oh pe-eh dE –, in a corner.

mûr, e, * mEEr, *a* ripe; mature; mellow.

muraille, mE-rah'e, *f* wall; rampart.

mûre, mEEr, *f* mulberry; blackberry.

mûrir, mEE-reer, *v* to ripen; to mature.

murmure, mEEr-mEEr, *m* murmur; babbling; whisper.

murmurer, mEEr-me-reh, *v* to murmur; to grumble; to whisper.

muscade, mEEss-kăhd, *f* nutmeg.

muscat, mEEss-kăh, *m* muscatel.

muscle, mEEss-kl, *m* muscle.

musculeu-x, se, mEEss-kE-ler, *a* muscular.

museau, mE-zoh, *m* snout; muzzle; (*fam*) face.

musée, mE-zeh, *m* museum.

museler, mEEz-leh, *v* to muzzle.

muser, mE-zeh, *v* to loiter; to dawdle.

musicien, ne, mE-ze-se-*ang*, *mf* musician; *a* musical.

musique, mE-zeeck, *f* music; band.

mutation, mE-tăh-se-*ong*, *f* change; transfer.

mutiler, mE-te-leh, *v* to mutilate; to maim; to deface.

mutin, e, mE-tang, *mf* & *a* mutinous; unruly.

mutinerie, mE-teen-ree, *f* mutiny.

mutisme, mE-tissm, *m* muteness.

mutuel, le, * mE-tE-ell, *a* mutual.

myope, me-op, *a* myopic.

myosotis, me-oz-ot-iss, *m* forget-me-not.

myrte, meert, *m* myrtle.

mystère, miss-tair, *m* mystery.

mystérieu-x, se, * miss-teh-re-er, *a* mysterious.

mystifier, miss-te-fe-eh, *v* to mystify; to fool.

mystique, * miss-teeck, *mf* & *a* mystic; mystical.

myth, meth, *m* myth.

mythique, me-teek, *a* mythical.

nacelle, năh-sell, *f* small boat; basket (of balloon).

nacre, năh-kr, *f* mother-of-pearl.

nage, năhsh, *f* swimming.

nageoire, năh-sho'ăhr, *f* fin.

nager, năh-sheh, *v* to swim; to float.

nageu-r, se, năh-**sher**, *mf* swimmer.

naguère, năh-ghair, *adv* not long ago.

na-ïf, ïve,* năh-eeff, *a* gullible; naive.

nain, e, nang, *mf* dwarf; *a* dwarfish.

naissance, ness-ahngss, *f* birth; descent; rise.

naissant, e, ness-ahng, *a* newborn; rising; budding.

naître, nay-tr, *v* to be born; to spring; to dawn.

naïveté, năh-eev-teh, *f* naïveté; gullibility.

nantir, nahng-teer, *v* to provide; to secure.

nantissement, nahng-tiss-mahng, *m* security; pledge.

nappe, năhpp, *f* tablecloth; sheet (of water).

narcisse, năhr-seess, *m* narcissus; daffodil.

narcotique, năhr-ko-teeck, *m & a* narcotic.

narguer, năhr-gheh, *v* to flout; to scoff at.

narine, năh-reen, *f* nostril.

narration, năh-răh-se-ong, *f* narrative.

nasal, e,* năh-zăhl, *a* nasal.

nasiller, năh-zee-yeh, *v* to speak through the nose.

natal, e, năh-tăhl, *a* natal; native.

natalité, năh-tăh-le-teh, *f* birthrate.

natation, năh-tăh-se-ong, *f* swimming.

nati-f, ve, năh-teeff, *a* native.

nation, năh-se-ong, *f* nation.

national, e, năh-se-onn-ăhl, *a* national.

nationalité, năh-se-onn-ăh-le-teh, *f* nationality.

nationaux, năh-se-onn-oh, *mpl* nationals.

natte, năht, *f* mat; matting; plait.

naturaliser, năh-tE-răh-le-zeh, *v* to naturalize.

naturaliste, năh-tE-răh-leesst, *m* naturalist; taxidermist.

nature, năh-tEEr, *f* nature; kind; constitution; *a* plain (of cooking).

naturel, năh-tE-rell, *m* nature; character; native.

naturel, le,* năh-tE-rell, *a* natural; unaffected; illegitimate.

naufrage, noh-frăhsh, *m* shipwreck.

nauséabond, e, noh-zeh-ăh-bong, *a* nauseous.

nausée, noh-zeh, *f* nausea; disgust.

nautique, noh-teeck, *a* nautical; aquatic.

naval, e, nǎh-vǎhl, *a* naval.

navet, nǎh-vay, *m* turnip; (*fam*) bad film.

navette, nǎh-vett, *f* shuttle; **faire la –,** fair lǎh –, to go to and fro.

navigable, nǎh-ve-ghǎh-bl, *a* navigable; seaworthy.

naviguer, nǎh-ve-gheh, *v* to navigate; to sail.

navire, nǎh-veer, *m* ship; vessel.

navrant, e, nǎh-vrahng, *a* heartrending; distressing.

navrer, nǎh-vreh, *v* to break the heart of; to distress.

ne (n'), ner, *adv* not.

né, e, neh, *pp* & *a* born.

néanmoins, neh-ahng-mo'ang, *adv* nevertheless; for all that; however.

néant, neh-ahng, *m* naught; nothingness; worthlessness.

nébuleuse, neh-bE-lerz, *f* nebula.

nébuleu-x, se, neh-bE-ler, *a* nebulous; cloudy; obscure.

nécessaire, neh-sess-air, *m* the needful; necessaries; outfit; *a** necessary; needful.

nécessité, neh-sess-e-teh, *f* necessity; need; *pl* necessaries.

nécessiter, neh-sess-e-teh, *v* to necessitate; to compel.

nécessiteu-x, se, neh-sess-e-ter, *a* needy.

nef, neff, *f* nave.

néfaste, neh-fǎhsst, *a* ill-omened; unlucky; disastrous.

négati-f, ve,* neh-ghǎh-teeff, *a* negative; *m* negative (photo).

négligé, neh-gle-sheh, *m* negligee.

négligé, e, neh-gle-sheh, *pp* & *a* neglected; careless; slovenly.

négligeable, neh-gle-shǎh-bl, *a* negligible.

négligemment, neh-gle-shǎh-mahng, *adv* carelessly.

négligence, neh-gle-shahngss, *f* neglect; needlessness; oversight.

négligent, e, neh-gle-shahng, *a* negligent; careless.

négliger, neh-gle-sheh, *v* to neglect; to omit; to overlook; to disregard.

négoce, neh-goss, *m* trade; business; trafficking.

négociable, neh-goss-e-ǎh-bl, *a* negotiable.

négociant, neh-goss-e-ahng, *m* merchant.

négocier, neh-goss-e-eh, *v* to negotiate; to deal; to trade.

nègre, négresse, nay-gr, neh-gress, *mf* Negro; Negress.

négrillon, ne, neh-gree-yong, *mf* Negro boy, girl.

neige, naysh, *f* snow.

neiger, nay-sheh, *v* to snow.

neigeu-x, se, nay-sher, *a* snowy.

nénuphar, neh-nE-fǎhr, *m* water lily.

nerf, nair, *m* nerve; sinew; energy.

ne rien connaître à, ner-re-ang-konn-ay-trǎh *v* to be ignorant of something.

nerveu-x, se,* nair-ver, *a* nervous; vigorous; highly strung.

nervure, nair-vEEr, *f* nerve; cording; rib.

net, nett, *m* fair copy; *adv* plainly; entirely; at once; flatly.

net, te,* nett, *a* neat; clean; clear; net (price); sharp.

netteté, nett-teh, *f* cleanness; clearness; distinctness.

nettoiement, nay-to'ăh-mahng, *m* cleaning; clearing.

nettoyage, nay- to'ăh-yăhsh, *m* cleaning (at dry cleaners).

nettoyer, nay-to'ăh-yeh, *v* to clean; to wipe; to rid of; to clear.

neuf, nerf, *a* nine; ninth.

neu-f, ve, nerf, *a* new; fresh; raw; inexperienced.

neutre, ner-tr, *m & a* neuter; neutral.

neuvième, ner-ve-aym, *m & a* ninth.

neveu, ner-ver, *m* nephew.

névralgie, neh-vrăhl-shee, *f* neuralgia.

névrose, neh-vrohz, *f* neurosis.

névrosé, neh-vro-zeh, *a* neurotic.

nez, neh, *m* nose; face; scent; **–à –, – ăh –,** face to face.

ni, ne, *conj* neither; nor; either; or.

niable, ne-ăh-bl, *a* deniable.

niais, e,* ne-ay, *mf & a* silly person; simpleton; stupid.

niaiser, ne-ay-zeh, *v* to play the fool; to trifle.

niaiserie, ne-ayz-ree, *f* silliness; foolery.

niche, neesh, *f* nook; kennel; trick.

nichée, ne-sheh, *f* nestful; brood; lot.

nicher, ne-sheh, *v* to build a nest; to lodge; **se –,** to nestle.

nickelé, e, neek-leh, *pp & a* nickeled; nickel-plated.

nid, ne, *m* nest.

nièce, ne-ess, *f* niece.

nier, ne-eh, *v* to deny.

nigaud, e, ne-ghoh, *mf & a* simpleton; silly; foolish.

nimbe, nangb, *m* nimbus; halo.

nipper, ne-peh, *v* (*fam*) to rig out.

nitouche (sainte), sangt ne-toosh, *f* (*fam*) little hypocrite.

niveau, ne-voh, *m* level; standard.

niveler, neev-leh, *v* to level.

nivellement, ne-vell-mahng, *m* leveling.

noble, nobl, *mf & a* nobleman; noble; high.

noblesse, nob-less, *f* nobility.

noce, noss, *f* wedding; wedding party; *pl*
usually: **voyage de –s,** vo'ăh-yăhsh der –, honeymoon.

noci-f, ve, noss-eeff, *a* harmful.

nocturne, nock-tEErn, *m* (music) nocturne; *a* nocturnal; nightly.

Noël, no-ell, *m* Christmas.

nœud, ner, *m* knot; bow.

noir, no'ăr, *m* black; Negro.

noir, e, no'ăhr, *a* black; swarthy; dark; gloomy; wicked.

noirâtre, no'ăh-rah-tr, *a* blackish.

noiraud, e, no'ăh-roh, *mf & a* swarthy-looking person; swarthy.

noirceur, no'ăhr-ser, *f* blackness; atrocity.

noircir, no'ăhr-seer, *v* to blacken.

noisette, no'ăh-zett, *f* hazelnut; *a inv* nut-brown.

noix, no'ăh, *f* walnut; nut; kernel.

nom, nong, *m* name; fame; noun; **–de famille,** – der făh-mee-ye, last name.

nomade, nomm-ăhd, *mf & a* nomad; nomadic.

nombre, nong-br, *m* number; quantity.

nombreu-x, se, nong-brer,

a numerous; many.

nombril, nong-bre, *m* navel.

nomenclature, nomm-ahng-klāh-tEEr, *f* nomenclature.

nominal, e,* nomm-e-nǎhl, *a* nominal.

nominatif, nomm-e-nǎh-teeff, *m* nominative case.

nominati-f, ve, nomm-e-nǎh-teeff, *a* nominative; registered; personal.

nomination, nomm-e-nǎh-se-ong, *f* nomination; appointment.

nommément, nomm-eh-mahng, *adv* by name; particularly.

nommer, nomm-eh, *v* to call; to mention; to appoint; **se –,** to give one's name; to be called.

non, nong, *adv* no; not.

nonchalamment, nong-shǎh-lǎh-mahng, *adv* non-chalantly.

nonchalance, nong-shǎh-lahngss, *f* nonchalance.

nonne, nonn, *f* nun.

nonpareil, le, nong-pǎh-ray'e, *a* nonpareil; matchless.

non-sens, nong-sahngss, *m* absurd sentence.

nord, nor, *m* north; north wind; *a* north.

nord-est, nor-esst, *m* northeast.

nord-ouest, nor-wesst, *m* northwest.

normal, e,* nor-mǎhl, *a* normal; standard.

nos, noh, *poss a mfpl* our.

nostalgie, noss-tahl-shee, *f* nostalgia; homesickness.

notable,* not-ǎh-bl, *a* notable; considerable; eminent.

notaire, not-air, *m* notary.

notamment, not-ǎh-mahng, *adv* particularly.

note, not, *f* note; mark; bill; memorandum.

noter, not-eh, *v* to note; to notice; to bear in mind.

notice, not-eess, *f* notice; account; instructions.

notifier, not-e-fe-eh, *v* to notify.

notion, noss-e-ong, *f* notion; idea.

notoire,* not-o'ǎhr, *a* well-known; notorious.

notoriété, not-or-e-eh-teh, *f* notoriety.

notre, notr, *poss a m & f* our.

nôtre, noh-tr, *poss pron,* ours.

nouer, noo-eh, *v* to tie; to knot; to engage in.

noueu-x, se, noo-er, *a* knotty; knotted.

nougat, noo-gǎh, *m* nougat.

nourri, e, noo-re, *pp* & *a* fed; full; rich.

nourrice, noo-reess, *f* nurse; wet-nurse.

nourrir, noo-rEEr, *v* to feed; to nurse; to entertain (**de,** on; with).

nourrissant, e, noo-riss-ahng, *a* nourishing; nutritious.

nourrisson, noo-riss-ong, *m* newborn.

nourriture, noo-re-tEEr, *f* food; diet; sustenance.

nous, noo, *pers pron* we; us; to us; at us; ourselves; each other.

nouveau, noo-voh, *m* new thing; new person; *adv* newly.

nouveau (**nouvel** before a word beginning with a vowel or **h** mute), *f* **nouvelle,*** noo-voh, noo-vell, *a* new; novel; recent; fresh; additional; another.

nouveau-né, e, noo-voh-neh, *a* newborn.

nouveauté, noo-voh-teh, *f* newness; novelty; *pl* fancy articles.

nouvelle, noov-ell, *f* short story.

nova-teur, trice, nov-ăh-ter, *a* innovative.

novembre, nov-ahng-br, *m* November.

novice, nov-eess, *mf* novice; *a* inexperienced.

noyade, no'ăh-yăhd, *f* drowning.

noyau, no'ăh-yoh, *m* stone; kernel; nucleus; core.

noyer, no'ăh-yeh, *v* to drown; to swamp; to inundate; *m* walnut tree.

nu, nE, *m* bare part; nude; à –, ăh –, bare.

nu, e, nE, *a* bare; plain.

nuage, nE-ăhsh, *m* cloud; mist; gloom.

nuageu-x, se, nE-ăh-**sher,** *a* cloudy.

nuance, nE-ahngss, *f* shade; tint; very small difference.

nuancer, nE-ahngss-eh, *v* to shade; to vary.

nubile, nE-beel, *a* nubile; marriageable.

nucléaire, nEE-cleh-air, *a* nuclear.

nudité, nE-de-teh, *f* nakedness; *pl* naked figures.

nuée, nE-eh, *f* cloud; swarm; shower (of objects).

nuire (à), nweer ăh, *v* to hurt; to prejudice; to hinder.

nuisible,* nwee-zee-bl, *a* harmful; detrimental.

nuit, nwee, *f* night; darkness; –**blanche,** –blahngsh, sleepless night.

nul, le, nEEl, *a* no; not any; of no force; void; worth less; *pron* nobody; no one.

nullement, nEEl-mahng, *adv* by no means.

nullité, nEEl-le-teh, *f* nullity; incapacity; nonentity.

numérateur, nE-meh-răh-ter, *m* numerator.

numérique,* nE-meh-reeck, *a* numerical.

numéro, nE-meh-ro, *m* number; ticket; item (on program); issue (of magazines, etc).

numéroter, nE-meh-rot-eh, *v* to number.

nuptial, e, nEEp-se-ăhl, *a* nuptial.

nuque, nEEk, *f* nape of the neck.

nutriti-f, ve, nE-tre-teeff, *a* nourishing.

nylon, nee-long, *m* nylon.

nymphe, nangf, *f* nymph.

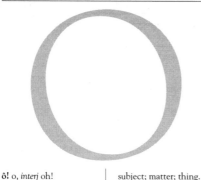

ô! o, *interj* oh!

obéir, ob-eh-eer, *v* to obey; to submit.

obéissance, ob-eh-iss-ahngss, *f* obedience; allegiance.

obéissant, e, ob-eh-iss-ahng, *a* obedient; dutiful.

obèse, ob-ayz, *a* obese; corpulent.

obésité, ob-eh-ze-teh, *f* obesity; corpulence.

objecter, ob-sheck-teh, *v* to object; to allege against.

objectif, ob-sheck-teeff, *m* lens; aim; target.

objecti-f, ive,* ob-sheck-teeff, *a* objective.

objection, ob-sheck-se-ong, *f* objection.

objet, ob-shay, *m* object; subject; matter; thing.

oblation, ob-lăh-se-ong, *f* offering.

obligataire, ob-le-găh-tair, *m* debenture holder.

obligation, ob-le-găh-se-ong, *f* obligation; duty; debenture; *v* to bond.

obligatoire,* ob-le-găh-to'ăhr, *a* obligatory; compulsory.

obligeamment, ob-le-shăh-mahng, *adv* obligingly.

obligeance, ob-le-shahngss, *f* obligingness; kindness.

obligeant, e, ob-le-shahng, *a* obliging; kind.

obliger, ob-le-sheh, *v* to oblige; to compel; to bind; to gratify.

oblique,* ob-leeck, *a* oblique; slanting; underhand.

obliquité, ob-le-kwe-teh, *f* obliquity; insincerity.

oblitérer, ob-le-teh-reh, *v* to obliterate; to cancel.

obscène, ob-sain, *a* obscene.

obscur, e, ob-skEEr, *a* dark; obscure; hidden; mysterious.

obscurcir, ob-skEEr-seer, *v* to obscure; to cloud; to darken.

obscurément, ob-skE-reh-mahng, *adv* obscurely.

obscurité, ob-skE-re-teh, *f* darkness; obscurity; mysteriousness.

obséder, ob-seh-deh, *v* to obsess.

obsèques, ob-sayk, *fpl* funeral.

obséquieu-x, se,* ob-seh-kee-er, *a* obsequious.

observa-teur, trice, ob-sair-văh-ter, *mf & a* observer; observant.

observation, ob-sair-văh-se-ong, *f* observation; observance; remark; reprimand.

observatoire, ob-sair-văh-to'ăhr, *m* observatory.

observer, ob-sair-veh, *v* to observe; to comply with.

obsession, ob-seh-se-ong, *f* obsession.

obstacle, obs-tăh-kl, *m* obstacle, hindrance.

obstination, obs-te-năh-se-ong, *f* obstinacy; stubbornness.

obstiné, e, obs-te-neh, *mf* & *a* obstinate person; obstinate; stubborn.

obstinément, obs-te-neh-mahng, *adv* obstinately.

obstiner (s'), obs-te-neh, *v* to be obstinate; to persist (à, in).

obstruer, obs-trE-eh, *v* to obstruct.

obtempérer (à), ob-tahng-peh-reh, *v* to obey (a summons, etc); to comply with.

obtenir, ob-ter-neer, *v* to obtain; to get; to procure.

obtus, e, ob-tE, *a* obtuse; dull.

obus, ob-EEz, or ob-E, *m* shell (artillery).

occasion, ock-ăh-ze-ong, *f* occasion; opportunity; bargain; **d'–,** secondhand.

occasionnel, le,* ock-ăh-ze-onn-ell, *a* occasional.

occasionner, ock-ăh-ze-onn-eh, *v* to occasion; to cause.

occident, ock-se-dahng, *m* West.

occidental, e, ock-se-dahng-tăhl, *a* western.

occulte, ock-EElt, *a* occult; secret.

occupant, e, ock-E-pang, *mf* & *a* occupier; occupying.

occupation, ock-E-păh-se-ong, *f* occupation; work; profession; capture (of a place).

occupé, e, ock-E-peh, *pp* & *a* occupied; engaged; busy; inhabited.

occuper, ock-E-peh, *v* to occupy; to employ; to inhabit.

occurrence, ock-E-rahngss, *f* occurrence.

océan, oss-eh-ahng, *m* ocean; sea.

océanique, oss-eh-ăh-neeck, *a* oceanic.

ocre, ockr, *f* ochre.

octobre, ock-tobr, *m* October.

octogénaire, ock-tosh-eh-nair, *mf* & *a* octogenarian.

octogone, ock-to-gonn, *m* octagon.

octroyer, ock-tro'ăh-yeh, *v* to grant.

oculaire,* ock-E-lair, *a* ocular.

oculiste, ock-E-lisst, *m* oculist.

odeur, od-er, *f* odor; smell; fragrance; repute.

odieu-x, se,* od-e-er, *a* odious; hateful; obnoxious.

odorant, e, od-or-ahng, *a* odorous; fragrant.

odorat, od-or-ăh, *m* sense of smell.

œil, er-ye, *m* eye; look; bud; *pl* **yeux,** yer.

œillade, er'e-yăhd, *f* glance; ogle; leer.

œillet, er'e-yay, *m* eyelet; pink; carnation.

œuf, erf, *m* egg; *pl* **œufs,** er.

œuvre, er-vr, *f* work; society; works.

offensant, e, off-ahng-sahng, *a* offensive.

offense, off-ahngss, *f* offense; trespass; contempt.

offensé, e, off-ahng-seh, *mf* & *a* offended party.

offenser, off-ahng-seh, *v* to offend; to injure; to shock.

offenseur, off-ahng-ser, *m* offender.

offensi-f, ve,* off-ahngss-eef, *a* offensive.

office, off-eess, *m* office; duty; worship; service; *f* pantry.

officiel, le,* off-eess-e-ell, *a* official.

officier, off-eess-e-eh, *v* to officiate; *m* officer.

officieu-x, se,* off-eess-e-er, *a* officious; semiofficial.

offrande, off-rahngd, *f* offering.

offre, ofr, *f* offer; tender; bidding.

offrir, off-reer, *v* to propose; to present; to bid.

offusquer, off-EEss-keh, *v* to obscure; to offend.

oh! o, *interj* oh!

oie, wăh, *f* goose.

oignon, onn-yong, *m* onion; bulb.

oindre, wang-dr, *v* to anoint.

oiseau, wăh-zoh, *m* bird.

oiseu-x, se,* wăh-zer, *a* idle; trifling; useless.

oisi-f, ve,* wăh-zeeff, *a* idle; unoccupied.

oisiveté, wăh-zeev-teh, *f* idleness.

oison, wăh-zong, *m* gosling; (*fig & fam*) simpleton.

olive, oll-eev, *f* olive; *a inv* olive-green.

olivier, oll-e-ve-eh, *m* olive tree.

olympique, oll-ang-peeck, *a* Olympic.

ombrage, ong-brăhsh, *m* shade; umbrage.

ombrageu-x, se,* ong-brăh-**sher**, *a* prickly; touchy.

ombre, ong-br, *f* shade; shadow; ghost.

ombrelle, ong-brell, *f* parasol.

ombreu-x, se, ong-brer, *a* shady.

omelette, omm-lett, *f* omelet.

omettre, omm-et-tr, *v* to omit; to leave out.

omission, omm-iss-e-ong, *f* omission.

omnibus, omm-ne-bEEss, *m* omnibus.

omoplate, omm-op-lăht, *f* shoulder blade.

on, ong *indefinite pron m sing* one; someone; anyone; people; we, you; they.

once, ongss, *f* ounce; grain; bit.

oncle, ong-kl, *m* uncle.

onction, ongk-se-ong, *f* unction.

onctueu-x, se,* ongk-tE-er, *a* unctuous; oily.

onde, ongd, *f* wave; surge; water; sea.

ondée, ong-deh, *f* shower.

ondoyant, e, ong-do'ăh-yahng, *a* undulating; flowing.

ondoyer, ong-do'ăh-yeh, *v* to undulate; to baptize privately.

onduler, ong-dE-leh, *v* to undulate; to wave (hair).

onéreu-x, se,* onn-eh-rer, *a* onerous.

ongle, ong-gl, *m* nail; claw.

onglée, ong-gleh, *f* numbness in the end of fingers (caused by cold).

onguent, ong-ghahng, *m* ointment; salve.

onze, ongz, *m & a* eleven.

onzième, ong-ze-aym, *m & a* eleventh.

opacité, op-ăh-se-teh, *f* opacity.

opaque, op-ăhck, *a* opaque.

opéra-teur, trice, op-eh-răh-ter, *mf* operator.

opération, op-eh-răh-se-ong, *f* operation; transaction.

opératoire, op-eh-răh-to'ăhr, *a* operative.

opérer, op-eh-reh, *v* to operate; to operate on; to work.

opiner, op-e-neh, *v* to give one's opinion.

opiniâtre, op-e-ne-ah-tr, *a* stubborn.

opiniâtrément, op-e-ne-ah-treh-mahng, *adv* stubbornly.

opiniâtrer (s'), sop-e-ne-ah-treh, *v* to be obstinate.

opinion, op-e-ne-ong, *f*

opinion.

opportun, e, op-or-tung, *a* opportune; timely; seasonable.

opportunité, op-or-tE-ne-teh, *f* opportuneness; seasonableness; opportunity.

opposant, e, op-o-zahng, *mf* opponent; *a* adverse.

opposé, op-oz-eh, *m* opposite; reverse.

opposé, e, op-oz-eh, *a* opposite; contrary; *pp* opposed.

opposer, op-oz-eh, *v* to oppose; **s'–,** to be opposed; to object (à, to).

opposition, op-oz-e-se-ong, *f* opposition; contrast.

oppresser, op-ress-eh, *v* to oppress.

oppression, op-ress-e-ong, *f* oppression.

opprimer, op-re-meh, *v* to oppress; to crush.

opprobre, op-robr, *m* disgrace; shame; opprobrium.

opter, op-teh, *v* to choose; to decide.

opticien, op-tiss-e-ang, *m* optician.

optimisme, op-te-mism, *m* optimism.

option, op-se-ong, *f* option.

optique, op-teeck, *f* optics; *a* optical; optic.

opulence, op-E-lahngss, *f* opulence; wealth.

opulent, e, op-E-lahng, *a* opulent; wealthy.

or, or, *conj* now; well.

or, or, *m* gold.

oracle, or-ăh-kl, *m* oracle.

orage, or-ăhsh, *m* storm; (*fig*) tumult.

orageu-x, se,* or-ăh-sher, *a* stormy.

oraison, or-ay-zong, *f* oration; orison.

oral, e,* or-ăhl, *a* oral; verbal; *m* oral examination.

orange, or-ahngsh, *f* orange; *a inv* orange-colored.

orangeade, or-ahng-shăhd, *f* orangeade.

oranger, or-ahng- sheh, *m* orange tree.

orateur, or-ăh-ter, *m* speaker; orator.

orbite, or-beet, *f* orbit; socket.

orchestre, or-kestr, *m* orchestra; band.

orchidée, or-ke-deh, *f* orchids.

ordinaire, or-de-nair, *m* the ordinary custom; *a** ordinary; common; vulgar.

ordinateur, or-de-năh-ter, *m* computer.

ordonnance, or-donn-ahngss, *f* prescription.

ordonna-teur, trice, or-donn-ăh-ter, *mf* organizer; manager; *a* directing.

ordonné, or-donn-eh, *a* orderly; tidy.

ordonner, or-donn-eh, *v* to order; to prescribe; to ordain.

ordre, or-dr, *m* order; discipline; warrant; decoration.

ordure, or-dEEr, *f* filth; filthy thing; *pl* rubbish.

orée, or-eh, *f* border; edge (of a wood, etc).

oreille, or-ay'e, *f* ear.

oreiller, or-ay'e-yeh, *m* pillow.

oreillons, or-ay'e-yong, *mpl* mumps.

orfèvre, or-fay-vr, *m* goldsmith; silversmith.

organe, or-ghăhn, *m* organ; voice; agent; spokesman.

organique,* or-ghăh-neeck, *a* organic.

organisa-teur, trice, or-ghăh-ne-zăh-ter, *mf & a* organizer.

organisation, or-ghăh-ne-zăh-se-ong, *f* organization.

organiser, or-ghäh-ne-zeh, *v* to organize; to get up.

organisme, or-ghäh-nism, *m* organism; structure.

organiste, or-ghäh-neesst, *m* organist.

orge, orsh, *f* barley.

orgelet, oar-je-lè, *m* sty (of eye).

orgie, or-shee, *f* revel; drinking bout; orgy.

orgue, orgh, *m* organ.

orgueil, or-gher'e, *m* pride; haughtiness.

orgueilleu-x, se,* or-gher'e-yer, *a* proud; haughty.

orient, or-e-ahng, *m* Orient; East.

oriental, e, or-e-ahng-tähl, *a* Eastern; oriental.

orienter, or-e-ahng-teh, *v* to point; to guide.

orifice, or-e-feess, *m* orifice; aperture.

originaire,* or-e-she-nair, *a* native; originating.

original, e, or-e-she-nähl, *mf* eccentric person; original; *a** original; novel; odd.

originalité, or-e-she-näh-le-teh, *f* originality; eccentricity.

origine, or-e-sheen, *f* origin; beginning; source; extraction.

orme, orm, *m* elm.

ornement, or-ner-mahng, *m* ornament.

orner, or-neh, *v* to adorn; to decorate; to deck.

ornière, or-ne-air, *f* rut; beaten track; groove.

orphelin, e, or-fer-lang, *mf* & *a* orphan.

orphelinat, or-fer-le-näh, *m* orphanage.

orteil, or-tay'e, *m* toe; **gros–**, grohz–, big toe.

orthographe, or-tog-rähf, *f* spelling.

ortie, or-tee, *f* nettle.

os, oss, *m* bone; *pl* **os**, oh.

osciller, oss-sil-leh, *v* to oscillate; (*fam*) to waver.

osé, e, o-zeh, *a* daring; bold; cheeky; *pp* attempted.

oseille, oz-ay'e, *f* sorrel.

oser, o-zeh, *v* to dare; to venture.

osier, o-ze-eh, *m* wicker; osier.

osselet, oss-lay, *m* small bone.

osseu-x, se, oss-er, *a* bony.

ostensible,* oss-tahng-see-bl, *a* ostensible.

otage, ot-ähsh, *m* hostage.

ôter, oht-eh, *v* to take away; to relieve; to pull off.

ou, oo, *conj* or; either; else.

où, oo, *adv* where;

whither; when; through which; at which; in which; to which.

ouate, oo-äht, *f* cotton-wool; wadding; padding.

oubli, oo-ble, *m* forgetfulness; oblivion.

oublier, oo-blee-yeh, *v* to forget; to neglect.

ouest, west, *m* West; *a inv* westerly; western.

oui, wee, *adv* yes.

ouï-dire, oo-e-deer, *m inv* hearsay.

ouïe, oo-ee, *f* hearing; *pl* gills.

ouïr, oo-eer, *v* to hear (not used very often).

ouragan, oo-räh-ghahng, *m* hurricane.

ourdir, oor-deer, *v* to warp; (*fig*) to plot.

ourlet, oor-lay, *m* hem.

ours, oors, *m* bear.

ourse, oors, *f* female bear.

outil, oo-te, *m* tool; implement.

outillage, oo-tee-yähsh, *m* tools; implements; plant.

outrage, oo-trähsh, *m* outrage; insult.

outrager, oo-träh-sheh, *v* to insult; to outrage.

outrageu-x, se,* oo-träh-sher, *a* outrageous.

outrance, oo-trahngss, *f* excess; **à –**, äh –, to the utmost.

outre, oo-tr, *f* goatskin bottle.

outre, oo-tr, *prep* beyond; besides; *adv* beyond.

outré, e, oo-treh, *pp* & *a* exaggerated; extravagant; indignant.

outremer, oo-trer-mair, *m* ultramarine; overseas.

outrepasser, oo-trer-pähss-eh, *v* to go beyond; to exceed.

outrer, oo-treh, *v* to overdo; to exasperate.

ouvert, e,* oo-vair, *pp* & *a* opened; open; bare; frank.

ouverture, oo-vair-tEEr, *f* opening; overture; inauguration; *pl* proposals.

ouvrable, oo-vrăh-bl, *a* workable; **jour –,shoo**r **–,** working day.

ouvrage, oo-vrähsh, *m* work; workmanship; piece of work.

ouvré, e, oo-vreh, *a* diapered; wrought; worked.

ouvre-boîtes, oo-vr-bo'äht, *m inv* can opener.

ouvri-er, ère, oo-vre-yeh, *mf* workman; work woman; laborer.

ouvrir, oo-vreer, *v* to open; to begin; to sharpen (appetite).

ovale, o-vähl, *a* & *m* oval.

ovation, o-văh-se-ong, *f* ovation.

ovipare, o-ve-păhr, *a* oviparous.

ovulation, o-VEE-lăh-se-ong, *f* ovulation.

oxyde, ox-eed, *m* oxide.

oxygène, ox-e-shenn, *m* oxygen.

ozone, oz-onn, *m* ozone.

pacifique,* păh-se-feeck, *a* peaceful; pacific.

pacte, păckt, *m* pact; compact; covenant.

pagaie, păh-gay, *f* paddle.

page, păhsh, *m* page (boy); *f* page (book).

paie, pay, *f* pay; wages.

paiement, pay-mahng, *m* payment.

païen, ne, păh-e-ang, *mf* & *a* pagan; heathen.

paillasse, pah'e-yăhss, *f* straw mattress.

paillasson, pah'e-yăhss-ong, *m* doormat.

paille, pah'e, *f* straw; chaff; flaw; mote; *a* straw-colored.

pain, pang, *m* bread; loaf; livelihood; **petit –,** per-te –, roll.

pain complet, pang (kong-play) *a* wholewheat bread.

pair, e, pair, *a* even; equal.

paire, pair, *f* pair; couple; brace.

pairie, pay-ree, *f* peerage.

paisible,* pay-zee-bl, *a* peaceful; quiet; still.

paître, pay-tr, *v* to graze; to feed on; to pasture.

paix, pay, *f* peace; quiet; rest.

palais, păh-lay, *m* palace; palate.

pâle, pahl, *a* pale; wan; white.

palefrenier, păhl-frer-ne-eh, *m* groom; stable boy.

pâleur, pah-ler, *f* paleness.

palier, păh-le-eh, *m* landing (of stairs); floor.

pâlir, pah-leer, *v* to turn pale; (*fig*) to wane.

palissade, păh-liss-ăhd, *f* paling; fence.

pallier, păhl-le-eh, *v* to palliate.

palme, păhlm, *f* palm; triumph.

palmier, păhl-me-eh, *m* palm tree.

pâlot, te, pah-loh, *a* palish; peaky.

palper, păhl-peh, *v* to feel; to finger.

palpiter, păhl-pe-teh, *v* to throb; to pant.

paludisme, păh-lEE-dism, *m* malaria.

pâmer (se), ser pah-meh, *v* to swoon; nearly to die (**de,** with).

pamplemousse, pang-pl-mooss, *m* grapefruit.

pan, pahng, *m* part of a wall; side; lappet; flap.

panache, păh-năhsh, *m* plume; tuft; (*fam*) flourish.

panaché, e, păh-năh-sheh, *a* variegated; mixed.

panaris, păh-năh-re, *m* whitlow.

pancarte, pahng-kăhrt, *f* placard; sign; notice.

pané, e, păh-neh, *a* covered with breadcrumbs.

panier, păh-ne-eh, *m* basket; hamper.

panique, păh-neeck, *f*

panic.

panne, păhn, *f* breakdown; failure; plush; lard.

panneau, păh-noh, *m* panel; board; trap; snare; sign.

panse, pahngss, *f* (*fam*) paunch; belly.

panser, pahngss-eh, *v* to dress (wound); to groom.

pantalon, pahng-tăh-long, *m* trousers; pants.

pantin, pahng-tang, *m* puppet.

pantoufle, pahng-too-fl, *f* slipper.

paon, ne, pahng, *mf* peacock; peahen.

papa, păh-păh, *m* daddy; dad.

papauté, păh-poh-teh, *f* papacy.

pape, păhp, *m* Pope.

paperasse, păhp-răhss, *f* old paper; wastepaper.

papier hygiénique, păh-pee-eh-e-she-eh-neeck *m* toilet paper.

papeterie, păhp-tree, *f* papermill; paper trade; stationery; stationer.

papetier, păhp-te-eh, *m* stationer.

papier, păh-pe-eh, *m* paper; –à lettres, – ăh let-tr, stationery.

papier d'emballage, păh-pe-eh-dahng-băh-lăhsh *m* wrapping paper.

papillon, păh-pee-yong, *m* butterfly; –de nuit, – der nwee, moth.

papillote, păh-pee-yot, *f* curlpaper.

paquebot, păhck-boh, *m* liner; steamer; ship.

pâquerette, pahck-rett, *f* daisy.

Pâques, pahk, *m* Easter.

paquet, păh-kay, *m* parcel; packet.

par, păhr, *prep* by; through; out of; per; about; for; with; in; into.

parachute, păh-răh-shEEt, *m* parachute.

parade, păh-răhd, *f* parade; display; show; parrying (fencing).

parader, păh-răh-deh, *v* to parade; to show off.

paradis, păh-răh-de, *m* Paradise; heaven; the gods (theater).

parafe, paraphe, păh-răhf, *m* flourish; initials.

parage, păh-răhsh, *m* extraction; birth; *pl* regions; latitudes.

paragraphe, păh-răh-grăf, *m* paragraph.

paraître, păh-ray-tr, *v* to appear; to look; to come out; to show; vient de –,

ve-ang der –, just out.

paralyser, păh-răh-le-zeh, *v* to paralyze.

paralysie, păh-răh-le-zee, *f* paralysis.

parapet, păh-răh-pay, *m* parapet.

parapluie, păh-răh-plwee, *m* umbrella.

parasite, păh-răh-zeet, *m* parasite; *a* parasitic.

paratonnerre, păh-răh-tonn-air, *m* lightning conductor.

paravent, păh-răh-vahng, *m* screen; folding screen.

parc, păhrk, *m* park; enclosure; playpen.

parcelle, păhr-sell, *f* small part; particle; plot.

parce que, păhr-ser ker, *conj* because.

parchemin, păhr-sher-mang, *m* parchment; *pl* diplomas.

parcimonieu-x, se, * păhr-se-monn-e-er, *a* parsimonious.

parcourir, păhr-koo-reer, *v* to travel over; to go through; to glance at.

parcours, păhr-koohr, *m* distance; line; journey; route.

pardessus, păhr-der-sE, *m* overcoat.

pardon, păhr-dong, *m* forgiveness; pardon.

pardonner, păhr-donn-eh, *v* to forgive; to excuse.

pare-brise, păhr-breez, *m* inv in pl windshield.

pare-chocs, păhr-shock, *m* inv in pl bumper.

pareil, le,* păh-ray'e, *a* like; similar; such; to match.

pareille, păh-ray'e, *f* the like; the same.

parent, e, păh-rahng, *mf* relative; kinsman; kinswoman; parents (father and mother); relatives; folks.

parenté, păh-rahng-teh, *f* relationship; consanguinity; kith and kin; family.

parer, păh-reh, *v* to adorn; to dress; to ward off; to provide for.

paresse, păh-ress, *f* idleness; sluggishness; indolence.

paresseu-x, se, păh-ress-er, *mf* idler; *a** idle; lazy; slothful.

parfaire, păhr-fair, *v* to perfect; to complete.

parfait, e,* păhr-fay, *a* perfect; faultless.

parfois, păhr-fo'ăh, *adv* sometimes; now and then.

parfum, păhr-fung, *m* perfume; scent.

parfumer, păhr-fE-meh, *v* to perfume; to scent.

pari, păh-ree, *m* bet; wager; stake.

parier, păh-re-eh, *v* to bet; to wager; to stake.

parité, păh-re-teh, *f* parity; equality.

parjure, păhr-shEEr, *m* perjury; perjurer.

parjurer (se), ser păhr-shE-reh, *v* to perjure oneself.

parlant, e, păhr-lahng, *a* speaking; talking.

parlement, păhr-ler-mahng, *m* Parliament.

parlementer, păhr-ler-mahng-teh, *v* to parley; to argue.

parler, păhr-leh, *v* to speak; *m* way of speaking.

parleu-r, se, păhr-ler, *mf* talker.

parmi, păhr-me, *prep* among; amongst; amid; amidst.

parodie, păh-rod-ee, *f* parody.

paroi, păh-ro'ăh, *f* wall; side; partition; coat.

paroisse, păh-ro'ăhss, *f* parish; parishioners.

paroissien, ne, păh-ro'ăhss-e-ang, *mf* parishioner.

parole, păh-rol, *f* word;

speech; saying right to speak; promise.

parquer, păhr-keh, *v* to pen up.

parquet, păhr-kay, *m* inlaid floor; flooring.

parrain, păh-rang, *m* godfather; sponsor.

parricide, păh-re-seed, *mf* parricide.

parsemer, păhr-ser-meh, *v* to strew (**de**, with).

part, păhr, *f* share; portion; participation.

partage, păhr-tăhsh, *m* sharing.

partance, păhr-tahngss, *f* departure; **en –**, ahng –, about to sail; bound (for).

partant, păhr-tahng, *adv* consequently.

partenaire, păhr-ter-nair, *mf* partner (at cards or dancing).

parterre, păhr-tair, *m* flower-bed; pit (theater).

parti, păhr-tee, *m* party; side; decision; profit.

partial, e,* păhr-se-ăhl, *a* partial; biased.

participation, păhr-te-se-păh-se-ong, *f* participation; share.

participe, păhr-te-seep, *m* participle.

participer, păhr-te-se-peh,

v to share (à, in).

particuli-er, ère, păhr-te-kE-le-eh *a* specific.

particularité, păhr-te-kE-lăh-re-teh, *f* peculiarity.

particule, păhr-te-kEEl, *f* particle.

particuli-er, ère, păhr-te-kE-le-eh, *mf* private person; individual; *a** particular; peculiar; odd.

partie, păhr-tee, *f* part; party; match; business; field; subject; (law) opponent.

partiel, le,* păhr-se-ell, *a* partial.

partir, păhr-teer, *v* to set out; to leave; to go off.

partition, păhr-te-se-ong, *f* partition; score (music).

partout, păhr-too, *adv* everywhere.

parure, păh-rEEr, *f* ornament; dress.

parvenir, păhr-ver-neer, *v* to reach; to succeed.

parvenu, e, păhr-ver-nE, *mf* upstart; self-made person.

parvis, păhr-ve, *m* parvis.

pas, pah, *m* step; gait; threshold; precedence.

pas, pah, *adv* not; not any; –**du tout,** – dE too, not at all.

passable,* păhss-ăh-bl, *a* passable; tolerable.

passag-er, ère, păhss-ăh-sheh, *mf* passenger; **a*** transitory.

passant, e, păhss-ahng, *mf* passer-by.

passe, păhss, *f* pass; spell; situation; channel.

passé, păhss-eh, *prep* after; *m* the past.

passé, e, păhss-eh, *pp* & *a* past; last; faded.

passer, păhss-eh, *v* to pass; to omit; to allow; to pass away; to fade; to cease; to spend (time).

passereau, păhss-roh, *m* sparrow.

passerelle, păhss-rell, *f* footbridge.

passible, păhss-ee-bl, *a* liable (**de,** to).

passif, păhss-eeff, *m* liabilities. **passi-f, ve*** păhss-eeff, *a* passive.

passion, păhss-e-ong, *f* passion.

passionnant, păhss-e-onn-ahng, *a* thrilling; fascinating.

passionné, e, păhss-e-onn-eh, *a* passionate; passionately fond (**de, pour,** of).

passionnément, păhss-e-onn-eh-mahng, *adv* passionately.

passoire, păhss-o'ăhr, *f* strainer; colander.

pastèque, păhss-teck, *f* watermelon.

pasteurisé, e, păhss-ter-e-zeh *a* pasteurized.

pastille, păhss-tee-ye, *f* pastille; lozenge.

patauger, păh-toh-sheh, *v* to dabble; to flounder; to make a mess of.

pâte, paht, *f* paste; dough; *pl* pasta.

pâté, pah-teh, *m* pie; pâté; blot of ink; block (of houses).

pâte d'amandes, păht-dăh-mahngd *f* marzipan .

patelin, păht-lang, *m* (*fam*) small village.

patente, păh-tahngt, *f* license; patent.

patère, păh-tair, *f* peg; curtain hook.

paternel, le,* păh-tair-nell, *a* fatherly; on the father's side.

pâteu-x, se,* pah-ter, *a* pasty; sticky; heavy (style, voice); dull.

patiemment, păh-se-ăh-mahng, *adv* patiently.

patience, păh-se-ahngss, *f* patience; puzzle.

patient, e, păh-se-ahng, *mf* patient; sufferer; *a* patient.

patienter, păh-se-ahng-teh, *v* to wait.

patinage (sur glace), păh-

te-**nähsh** (sEEr-glähss) *f*
ice skating.

patiner, päh-te-neh, *v* to
skate.

patinoire, päh-te-noähr *f*
ice rink.

patio, päh-te-oh *m* patio.

pâtisserie, päh-tiss-ree, *f*
pastry; bakery.

patois, päh-to'äh, *m*
dialect.

pâtre, pah-tr, *m* herdsman;
shepherd.

patrie, päh-tree, *f* native
country; fatherland;
home.

patrimoine, päh-tre-
mo'ähn, *m* patrimony.

patriote, päh-tre-ot, *m*
patriot; *a* patriotic.

patron, ne, päh-trong, *mf*
employer; patroness;
boss; skipper; pattern.

patronner, päh-tronn-eh,
v to patronize; to
stencil.

patrouille, päh-troo'ye, *f*
patrol.

patte, päht, *f* paw; foot;
leg; strap; flap.

pâturage, pah-tE-rähsh, *m*
pasture; grazing.

paume, pohm, *f* palm (of
the hands); tennis.

paupière, poh-pe-air, *f*
eyelid.

pause, pohz, *f* pause; stop;
rest.

pauvre, poh-vr, *m* poor
man; *a** poor; wretched.

pauvresse, poh-vress, *f*
beggar woman.

pauvreté, poh-vrer-teh, *f*
poverty; wretchedness.

pavaner (se), ser päh-väh-
neh, *v* to strut.

pavé, päh-veh, *m* paving
stone; pavement.

pavillon, päh-vee-yong, *m*
pavilion; flag.

pavoiser, päh-vo'äh-zeh, *v*
to deck with flags.

pavot, päh-voh, *m* poppy.

payant, e, pay-yahng, *mf*
payer; *a* paying; charged
for.

paye, see **paie.**

payement, see **paiement.**

payer, pay-yeh, *v* to pay;
to stand; to treat.

pays, pay-ee, *m* country;
home; place.

paysage, pay-ee-zähsh, *m*
landscape; scenery.

paysan, ne, pay-ee-zahng,
mf peasant; *a* rustic.

péage, peh-ähsh, *m* toll.

peau, poh, *f* skin; hide;
peel; life.

pêche, paysh, *f* fishing;
fishery; angling; peach.

péché, peh-sheh, *m* sin.

pécher, peh-sheh, *v* to sin;
to err.

pêcher, pay-sheh, *v* to
fish; to angle; *m* peach

tree.

pêcheu-r, se, pay-sher, *mf*
fisherman; fisherwoman.

péch-eur, eresse, peh-
sher, pehsh-ress, *mf*
sinner.

pécuniaire,* peh-kE-ne-
air, *a* pecuniary.

pédaler, peh-däh-leh, *v* to
pedal; to cycle.

pédant, e, peh-dahng, *mf*
pedant; *a* pedantic.

pédestre,* peh-dess-tr, *a*
pedestrian.

pédicure, peh-de-kEEr, *mf*
chiropodist; pedicure.

pedigree, peh-de-greh, *m*
pedigree.

peigne, payn-yer, *m* comb.

peigner, payn-yeh, *v* to
comb; **se –,** to comb
one's hair.

peignoir, payn-yo'ähr, *m*
dressing gown;
bathrobe.

peindre, pang-dr, *v* to
paint; to depict; to
represent.

peine, payn, *f* pain;
punishment; difficulty;
sorrow.

peiner, pay-neh, *v* to
grieve; to labor; to toil.

peintre, pang-tr, *m*
painter.

peinture, pang-tEEr, *f*
painting; picture;
description; paint.

péjorati-f, ve, peh-sho-răh-teef, *a* derogatory.

pêle-mêle, payl-mayl, *adv* pell-mell; *m* jumble.

peler, per-leh, *v* to peel; to pare.

pèlerin, payl-rang, *m* pilgrim.

pèlerinage, payl-re-năhsh, *m* pilgrimage.

pèlerine, payl-reen, *f* cape.

pelle, payl, *f* shovel; spade.

pelleterie, payl-tree, *f* fur trade; *pl* furs.

pellicule, payl-le-kEEl, *f* dandruff; film; roll (film).

pelote, plot, *f* pincushion; ball (of wool, etc).

pelouse, plooz, *f* lawn; grass plot.

peluche, plEEsh, *f* plush.

pelure, plEEr, *f* paring; peel; rind.

pénalité, peh-năh-le-teh, *f* penal system; penalty.

penaud, e, per-noh, *a* abashed; shamefaced.

penchant, pahng-shahng, *m* declivity; inclination; partiality.

pencher, pahng-sheh, *v* to incline; to lean.

pendaison, pahng-day-zong, *f* hanging.

pendant, pahng-dahng, *prep* during; *m* counterpart; earring.

(pendant) la nuit, (pahng-dahng) lăh-nwee *adv* overnight.

pendre, pahng-dr, *v* to hang; to hang up.

pendule, pahng-dEEl, *m* pendulum; *f* clock.

pêne, payn, *m* bolt (of a lock).

pénétrant, e, peh-neh-trahng, *a* penetrating; piercing; keen.

pénétrer, peh-neh-treh, *v* to penetrate; to enter.

pénible,* peh-nee-bl, *a* painful; laborious.

péniche, peh-neesh, *f* barge.

pénicilline, peh-ne-se-leen *f* penicillin.

pénitence, peh-ne-tahngss, *f* penance; penitence; repentance; disgrace.

pénitent, e, peh-ne-tahng, *mf* penitent; *a* penitent.

pénombre, peh-nong-br, *f* semidarkness; dim light.

pensant, e, pahng-sahng, *a* thinking.

pensée, pahng-seh, *f* thought; opinion; pansy.

penser, pahng-seh, *v* to think; to deem.

penseu-r, se, pahng-ser, *mf* thinker.

pensi-f, ve,* pahng-seeff, *a* pensive; thoughtful.

pension, pahng-se-ong, *f* pension; boardinghouse; boarding school.

pensionnaire, pahng-se-onn-air, *mf* boarder; pensioner.

pente, pahngt, *f* slope; gradient; bent.

pentecôte, pahngt-koht, *f* Pentecost.

pénurie, peh-nEE-ree, *f* scarcity; dearth; poverty.

pépier, peh-pe-eh, *v* to chirp.

pépin, peh-pang, *m* pip; kernel; hitch.

pépinière, peh-pe-ne-air, *f* nursery (tree).

percale, pair-kăhl, *f* cotton cambric.

perçant, e, pair-sahng, *a* piercing; sharp; shrill.

percé, e, pair-seh, *pp & a* pierced; in holes.

percepteur, pair-sep-ter, *m* tax collector.

percer, pair-seh, *v* to pierce; to bore.

percevoir, pair-ser-vo'ăhr, *v* to collect (taxes, etc); to perceive.

perche, pairsh, *f* pole; perch.

percher (se), pair-sheh, *v* to roost; to perch.

perdant, e, pair-dahng, *mf* loser; *a* losing.

perdre, pair-dr, *v* to lose;

to waste; to ruin; to corrupt.

perdrix, pair-dree, *f* partridge.

perdu, e, pair-dE, *pp & a* lost; ruined; done for; spoilt.

père, pair, *m* father.

perfectionnement, pair-feck-se-onn-mah*ng*, *m* improvement; perfecting.

perfectionner, pair-feck-se-onn-eh, *v* to improve; to perfect.

perfide, pair-feed, *mf* perfidious person; *a** perfidious.

perforer, pair-for-eh, *v* to bore; to punch.

péricliter, peh-re-kle-teh, *v* to be in jeopardy.

péril, peh-reel, *m* peril; danger.

périlleu-x, se,* peh-ree-yer, *a* perilous.

périmé, e, peh-re-meh, *a* out of date; lapsed.

période, peh-re-od, *f* period.

périodique, peh-re-od-eeck, *a* periodical; *m* periodical (publication).

péripétie, peh-re-peh-see, *f* ups and downs; *pl* vicissitudes.

périr, peh-reer, *v* to perish; to die; to be lost.

périssable, peh-riss-ăh-bl, *a* perishable.

perle, pair, *f* pearl; bead.

permanent, e, pair-măh-nah*ng*, *a* permanent; license; *f* permanent wave.

permanente, pair-măh-nah*ng*t *f* hair perm.

permettre, pair-met-tr, *v* to allow; to enable.

permis, pair-mee, *m* permit; licence; pass.

permis, e, pair-mee, *pp & a* allowed; allowable.

permis de conduire, pair-me-der-kong-dweer *m* drivers license.

permission, pair-miss-e-ong, *f* permission; leave.

pernicieu-x, se,* pair-ne-se-er, *a* pernicious; hurtful.

perpétuel, le,* pair-peh-tE-ell, *a* perpetual.

perpétuer, pair-peh-tE-eh, *v* to perpetuate.

perpétuité, pair-peh-twe-teh, *f* endlessness; à –, ăh –, for life.

perplexe, pair-plex, *a* perplexed.

perron, pay-rong, *m* flight of steps to house door.

perroquet, payr-ock-ay, *m* parrot.

perruche, pay-rEEsh, *f* parakeet.

perruque, pay-rEEk, *f* wig.

persécuter, pair-seh-kE-teh, *v* to persecute; to importune.

persévérance, pair-seh-veh-rah*ng*ss, *f* perseverance.

persévérer, pair-seh-veh-reh, *v* to persevere; to persist.

persienne, pair-se-ain, *f* shutter.

persil, pair-see, *m* parsley.

persistant, e, pair-siss-tah*ng*, *a* persistent.

persister, pair-siss-teh, *v* to persist (à, dans, in).

personnage, pair-sonn-ăhsh, *m* personage; somebody; character.

personnalité, pair-sonn-ăh-le-teh, *f* personality; person.

personne, pair-sonn, *pron* anybody; (with a negation) nobody; *f* person; individual.

(ne) personne, (ner) pair-sonn *pron* no one.

personnel, pair-sonn-ell, *m* staff.

personnel, le,* pair-sonn-ell, *a* personal.

personnifier, pair-sonn-e-fe-eh, *v* to personify; to impersonate.

perspective, pairs-peck-teev, *f* perspective;

prospect.

perspicace, pairs-pe-kähss, *a* perspicacious.

persuader, pair-sE-äh-deh, *v* to persuade; to convince; to prevail on.

persuasion, pair-sE-äh-ze-ong, *f* persuasion.

perte, pairt, *f* loss; waste; ruin; death.

pertinemment, pair-te-näh-mahng, *adv* pertinently.

perturba-teur, trice, pairt-tEEr-bäh-ter, *mf* disturber; *a* disturbing.

perturbation, pair-tEEr-bäh-se-ong, *f* disturbance.

perturber, pair-tEEr-beh, *v* to disrupt (disturb, break up).

pervers, e, pair-vair, *mf* evildoer; pervert; *a* perverse.

perversion, pair-vair-se-ong, *f* perversion.

pervertir, pair-vair, *v* to pervert; to corrupt.

pesamment, per-zäh-mahng, *adv* heavily.

pesant, e, per-zahng, *a* weighty; ponderous.

pesanteur, per-zahng-ter, *f* weight; gravity; dullness.

peser, per-zeh, *v* to weigh; to ponder; to be a burden.

peste, pesst, *f* plague; (*fam*) pest; bore.

pester, pess-teh, *v* to rave (contre, at).

pétillant, e, peh-tee-yahng, *a* sparkling; crackling.

pétiller, peh-tee-yeh, *v* to crackle; to sparkle.

petit, e, per-te, *mf* young child; young animal; *a* little; small.

petite-fille, per-teet-fee-ye, *f* granddaughter.

petit-fils, per-te-feess, *m* grandson.

pétition, peh-te-se-ong, *f* petition.

pétitionnaire, peh-te-se-onn-air, *mf* petitioner.

petits-enfants, per-te-zahng-fahng, *mpl* grandchildren.

pétri, e, peh-tre, *pp* & *a* kneaded.

pétrin, peh-trang, *m* kneading trough; (*fam*) **dans le –,** dahng ler –, in a mess.

pétrir, peh-treer, *v* to knead; to mold.

pétulant, e, peh-tE-lahng, *a* lively; full of spirits.

peu, per, *adv* little; not much; *m* little; few; bit.

peuplade, per-plähd, *f* tribe.

peuple, per-pl, *m* people;

nation; the masses.

peupler, per-pleh, *v* to populate (de, with); to throng.

peuplier, per-ple-eh, *m* poplar.

peur, per, *f* fear; fright; dread.

peureu-x, se,* per-rer, *a* timid; fearful.

peut-être, per-t'ay-tr, *adv* perhaps; maybe.

phare, fähr, *m* lighthouse; beacon; headlight.

pharmacie, fähr-mäh-see, *f* pharmacy; drugstore.

pharmacien, fähr-mäh-se-ang, *m* chemist.

phase, fahz, *f* phase; stage; turn.

phénomène, feh-nomm-ain, *m* phenomenon; (*fam*) freak.

philatéliste, fe-läh-teh-leesst, *m* stamp collector.

philosophe, fe-loz-off, *m* philosopher; *a* philosophical.

philosophie, fe-loz-off-ee, *f* philosophy.

philtre, feel-tr, *m* philter; love potion.

phonographe, fonn-og-rähf, *m* phonograph.

phoque, fock, *m* seal.

phosphore, foss-for, *m* phosphorous.

photocopie, fot-o-ko-pee, f photocopy.

photographe, fot-og-răhf, m photographer.

photographie, fot-og-răh-fee, f photograph; photography.

phrase, frahz, f sentence.

physicien, fe-ze-se-ang, m physicist.

physiologie, fe-ze-oll-osh-ee, f physiology.

physionomie, fe-ze-onn-omm-ee, f physiognomy; look; expression.

physique, fe-zeeck, m constitution; f physics; a* physical.

piaffer, pe-ăh-feh, v to paw the ground.

piailler, pe-ah'e-yeh, v to squall.

piano, pe-ăh-no, adv softly; m pianoforte.

pic, peek, m pickax; peak; woodpecker; à –, ăh –, perpendicularly.

picoter, pe-kot-eh, v to prick; to tease; to peck.

pie, pee, f magpie.

pièce, pe-ess, f piece; bit; play; room; document.

pied, pe-eh, m foot; footing; leg; stalk.

piédestal, pe-eh-dess-tăhl, m pedestal.

piège, pe-aysh, m snare; trap.

pierre, pe-ayr, f stone; flint; gem.

pierreries, pe-ay-rer-ree, fpl gems; precious stones.

pierreu-x, se, pe-ay-rer, a stony.

piété, pe-eh-teh, f piety.

piétiner, pe-eh-te-neh, v to trample; to mark time.

piéton, pe-eh-tong, m pedestrian.

piètre,* pe-ay-tr, a paltry; wretched; worthless.

pieu, pe-er, m stake.

pieuvre, pe-ervr f octopus.

pieu-x, se,* pe-er, a pious; godly.

pigeon, pe-shong, m pigeon; dove.

pigeonnier, pe-shonn-e-eh, m pigeon house; dovecote.

pigment, peeg-mahng, m pigment.

pignon, peen-yong, m gable.

pile, peel, f heap; pier; battery; reverse (of coin); (fam) thrashing.

piler, pe-leh, v to pound; to crush.

pilier, pe-le-eh, m pillar; post.

pillage, pee-yăhsh, m plundering; pillage.

piller, pee-yeh, v to plunder; to pillage; to ransack; to pilfer.

pilon, pe-long, m pestle; pounder; drumstick.

pilori, pe-lor-e, m pillory.

pilote, pe-lot, m pilot.

pilule, pe-lEEl, f pill.

pimbêche, pang-baish, f minx.

piment, pe-mahng, m pimento.

pimpant, e, pang-pahng, a spruce; smart.

pin, pang, m pine; pine tree.

pince, pangss, f pincers; pliers; crowbar; tongs.

pincé, e, pang-seh, a affected; stiff-necked.

pinceau, pang-soh, m brush.

pincée, pang-seh, f pinch (of salt, etc.).

pince-nez, pangss-neh, m pince-nez.

pincer, pang-seh, v to pluck (harp, guitar, etc.); to play; to catch in the act.

pince-sans-rire, pangss-sahng-reer, m person of dry humor.

pincettes, pang-sett, fpl tongs; tweezers.

ping-pong, pe-ng-pongg f table tennis.

pintade, pang-tăhd, f guinea fowl.

piocher, pe-osh-eh, *v* to dig; to work hard.

pion, pe-ong, *m* pawn.

pioncer, pe-ong-seh, *v* (*pop*) to snooze.

pionnier, pe-onn-e-eh, *m* pioneer.

pipe, peep, *f* tobacco pipe; pipe.

piquant, e, pe-kahng, *a* pricking; pungent; stinging; sharp.

pique, peek, *m* spade (cards).

pique-nique, peek-neek, *m* picnic.

piquer, pe-keh, *v* to prick; to sting; to bite; to goad; to spur; to rouse; to offend; to be pungent; –à la machine, – ăh lăh măh-sheen, to machine sew.

piquet, pe-kay, *m* stake; peg.

piqûre, pe-kEEr, *f* sting; bite; injection.

pirate, pe-răht, *m* pirate.

pire, peer, *a* worse; *m* le –, ler –, the worst.

pirouetter, pe-roo-ett-eh, *v* to whirl round.

pis, pee, *adv* worse; *m* udder.

pis-aller, pe-z'ăh-leh, *m* makeshift.

piscine, peess-seen, *f* swimming pool.

pissenlit, peess-ahng-lee, *m* dandelion.

piste, peesst, *f* track; trail; trace; scent; runway.

piste de ski, peest-der-ske *f* ski slope.

pistolet, peesst-toll-ay, *m* pistol.

piston, peess-tong, *m* piston; sucker; (*fam*) influence.

piteu-x, se,* pe-ter, *a* piteous; pitiable.

pitié, pe-te-eh, *f* pity; compassion.

pitoyable,* pe-to'ăh-yăh-bl, *a* pitiful; pitiable; wretched.

pittoresque,* pit-tor-esk, *a* picturesque; graphic.

pivot, pe-voh, *m* pivot; (*fig*) basis; support.

placard, plăh-kăhr, *m* cupboard; poster; bill.

place, plăhss, *f* place; spot; square; space; seat; situation; fortress.

placement, plăhss-mahng, *m* placing; sale; investment.

placer, plăhss-eh, *v* to place; to sell; to invest.

placide,* plăhss-eed, *a* placid.

plafond, plăh-fong, *m* ceiling.

plage, plăhsh, *f* beach; shore.

plagiaire, plăh-she-air, *m* plagiarist.

plaider, play-deh, *v* to plead; to argue; to intercede.

plaideu-r, se, play-der, *mf* litigant.

plaidoirie, play-do'ăh-ree, *f* pleading; address.

plaie, play, *f* wound; sore; plague.

plaignant, e, playn-yahng, *mf* plaintiff.

plaindre, plang-dr, *v* to pity; se –, to complain.

plaine, plain, *f* plain; flat open country.

plainte, plangt, *f* lamentation; complaint; charge.

plainti-f, ve,* plang-teeff, *a* plaintive; mournful.

plaire, plair, *v* to please; to be agreeable; to suit; s'il vous plaît, sill voo play, (if you) please.

plaisamment, play-zăh-mahng, *adv* pleasantly; humorously.

plaisant, e, play-zahng, *a* pleasing; funny; droll.

plaisanter, play-zahng-teh, *v* to jest; to test; to trifle (avec, with).

plaisanterie, play-zahng-tree, *f* joke; jest; fun; humor; mockery.

plaisir, play-zeer, *m*

pleasure; recreation.

plan, plahng, *m* plan; model; map; scheme.

plan, e, plahng, *a* level; even; flat.

planche, plahngsh, *f* plank; board; shelf; plate; garden bed.

planche de surf, plahngsh-der-sErf *f* surfboard.

plancher, plahng-sheh, floor.

planer, plăh-neh, *v* to soar; to hover; to smooth.

planeur, plăh-ner, *m* glider.

plante, plahngt, *f* plant; sole of the foot.

planté, e, plahng-teh, *pp* & *a* planted; situated; **bien –,** be-ang –, firmly set.

planter, plahng-teh, *v* to plant; to set; to fix.

planton, plahng-tong, *m* orderly.

plaque, plăhck, *f* plate; slab; badge; (license) plate.

plastique, plăhss-teeck, *m* plastic.

plastron, plăhss-trong, *m* breastplate; shirt front.

plat, e,* plăh, *a* flat; level; dull; straight (hair); *m* dish; course.

platane, plăh-tăhn, *m* plane tree.

plateau, plăh-toh, *m* tray; disk; plateau.

plâtrage, plah-trăhsh, *m* plastering; plasterwork.

plâtras, plah-trăh, *m* rubbish (plaster).

plâtre, plah-tr, *m* plaster; plastercast.

plâtrer, plah-treh, *v* to plaster; to patch up.

plausible,* ploh-zee-bl, *a* plausible.

plèbe, playb, *f* mob.

plein, e,* plang, *a* full; whole; broad; with young (animal).

plénière, pleh-ne-air, *af* plenary; full.

plénitude, pleh-ne-tEEd, *f* plenitude; fullness.

pleurer, pler-reh, *v* to weep; to cry; to mourn.

pleureu-r, se, pler-rer, *a* weeping; *mf* mourner.

pleurnicher, pler-ne-sheh, *v* to whimper; to snivel.

pleurs, pler, *mpl* tears; weeping; lament.

pleuvoir, pler-vo'ăhr, *v* to rain.

pli, ple, *m* fold; pleat; wrinkle; crease; bend; letter.

pliable, ple-ăh-bl, *a* flexible; docile.

pliant, ple-ahng, *m* folding

chair; *a* flexible; folding.

plier, plee-eh, *v* to fold; to bend; to give way.

plissé, e, pliss-eh, *pp* & *a* pleated; tucked.

plisser, pliss-eh, *v* to pleat; to crease; to corrugate.

plomb, plong, *m* lead; shot; sinker; plumb line; seal; fuse.

plombage, plong-băhsh, *m* leadwork; plumbing; sealing; filling (teeth).

plombier, plong-be-eh, *m* plumber.

plonger, plong- sheh, *v* to dive.

pluie, plwee, *f* rain.

plume, plEEm, *f* feather; nib; quill.

plupart (la), lăh plE-păhr, *f* most; the greatest part; most people.

pluriel, le, plE-re-ell, *m* & *a* plural.

plus, plE, *adv* more; **le –,** ler –, the most.

plusieurs, plE-ze-er, *pron* & *a* several.

plus-que-parfait, plEEs-ker-păhr-fay, *m* pluperfect.

plutôt, plE-toh, *adv* rather; sooner.

pluvieu-x, se, plE-ve-er, *a* rainy.

pneu, pner, *m* tire.

pneumatique, pner-măh-teeck, m express letter sent by a tube (in Paris).

poche, posh, f pocket; bag; pouch; net.

pocher, posh-eh, v to poach (egg); to bruise (eye).

pochette, posh-ett, f small pocket; kit.

poêle, po'ăhl, m stove; pall; f frying pan.

poème, po-emm, m poem.

poésie, po-eh-zee, f poetry; poems.

poète, po-ett, m poet.

poétique, po-eh-teeck, f poetics; a* poetical.

poids, po'ăh, m weight; burden.

poignant, e, po'ăhn-yahng, a poignant.

poignard, po'ăhn-yăhr, m dagger.

poigne, po'ăhn-yer, f grip; will; energy.

poignée, po'ăhn-yeh, f handful; handle.

poignet, po'ăhn-yay, m wrist; wristband; cuff.

poil, po'ăhl, m hair (animal); hair (on human body); bristle; (fam) mood; au –, super.

poilu, e, po'ăh-lE, a hairy; shaggy.

poinçon, po'ang-song, m bodkin; awl; punch; stamp; die.

poinçonner, po'ang-sonn-eh, v to punch (ticket, etc); to stamp.

poindre, po'ang-dr, v to dawn.

poing, po'ang, m fist; hand.

point, po'ang, adv no; not; none; never.

point, po'ang, m point; stop; stitch; dot; mark; full stop; degree.

pointe, po'angt, f point; tip; touch; dawn.

pointer, po'ang-teh, v to point; to prick; to aim; to soar.

pointillé, po'ang-tee-yeh, m stippling; dotted line.

pointilleu-x, se, po'ang-tee-yer, a captious; caviling.

pointu, e, po'ang-tE, a pointed; sharp.

pointure, po'ang-tEEr, f size (shoes, gloves, etc).

poire, po'ăhr, f pear; (slang) gullible person.

poireau, po'ăh-roh, m leek; wart.

poirier, po'ăh-re-eh, m pear tree.

pois, po'ăh, m pea; petits –, per-te –, green peas.

poison, po'ăh-zong, m poison.

poisseu-x, se, po'ăhss-er, a sticky.

poisson, po'ăhss-ong, m fish.

poissonnerie, po'ăhss-onn-ree, f fishmarket or shop.

poitrine, po'ăh-treen, f chest; breast; lungs; bosom; brisket.

poivre, po'ăh-vr, m pepper.

poivrier, po'ăh-vree-eh, f pepperpot.

poivron po'ăh-vrong, m green or red sweet pepper.

poix, po'ăh, f pitch; shoemaker's wax.

pôle, pohl, m pole.

polémique, poll-eh-meeck, f polemics; controversy; a polemical.

poli, e, poll-ee, a polished; polite; civil; refined.

police, poll-eess, f police; **agent de –,** ăh-shahng der –, policeman.

polichinelle, poll-e-she-nell, m buffoon.

polici-er, ère, poll-iss-e-eh, a of the police; m policeman.

poliment, poll-e-mahng, adv politely.

polir, poll-eer, v to polish; to brighten; to improve.

polisson, ne, poll-iss-ong, mf mischievous child;

scamp.

politesse, poll-e-tess, *f* politeness; civility; good breeding.

politique, poll-e-teeck, *f* policy; politics; *a** political; prudent; politic.

pollen, poll-ang *m* pollen.

polluer, poll-lE-eh, *v* to pollute.

pollution, poll-lE-se-ong *f* pollution.

poltron, ne, poll-trong, *mf* coward; *a* cowardly.

polythène, poll-e-tayn *m* polythene.

pommade, pomm-ăhd, *f* lip-salve; ointment.

pomme, pomm, *f* apple; **–de terre,** – der tair, potato.

pommé, e, pomm-eh, *a* rounded; (*fam*) downright.

pommelé, e, pomm-leh, *a* dappled; mottled.

pommette, pomm-ett, *f* cheekbone.

pommier, pomm-e-eh, *m* apple tree.

pompe, pongp, *f* pomp; pump.

pompe à essence, pongp-ăh-eh-sangss *f* gas pump.

pomper, pong-peh, *v* to pump up; to imbibe.

pompeu-x, se,* pong-per,

a pompous; stately.

pompier, pong-pe-eh, *m* fireman.

pomponner, pong-ponn-eh, *v* to adorn; **se –,** to smarten oneself.

ponce (pierre), pe-ayr pongss, *f* pumice stone.

ponctuation, pongk-tE-ah-se-ong, *f* punctuation.

ponctuel, le,* pongk-tE-ell, *a* punctual.

pondre, pongdr, *v* to lay eggs.

pont, pong, *m* bridge; deck.

pontage, pong-tăsh, *m med* bypass.

populace, pop-E-lăhss, *f* the masses.

populaire,* pop-E-lair, *a* popular.

population, pop-E-lăh-se-ong, *f* population.

populeu-x, se, pop-E-ler, *a* populous.

porc, por, *m* pig; swine; hog; pork.

porcelaine, por-ser-lain, *f* porcelain; chinaware.

porc-épic, por-keh-peeck, *m* porcupine.

porche, porsh, *m* porch.

pore, por, *m* pore.

poreu-x, se, por-er, *a* porous.

pornographie, por-nog-răhf-ee, *f* pornography.

port, por, *m* port; harbor; carriage; postage; deportment.

portable, por-tăh-bl, *a* wearable.

portail, por-tah'e, *m* portal.

portant, e, por-tahng, *a* bearing; **bien –,** be-ang –, in good health; **mal –,** măhl –, in bad health.

portati-f, ve, por-tăh-teeff, *a* a portable.

porte, port, *f* door; gate; doorway; threshold; pass.

porte-bagages, por-ter-băh-găhsh, *m* luggage rack.

porte-clefs, por-ter-kleh, *m inv* key ring.

portefeuille, por-ter-fer'e, *m* portfolio; wallet.

porte-monnaie, por-ter-monn-ay, *m* purse.

porte-parapluies, por-ter-păh-răh-plwee, *m* umbrella stand.

porte-plume, por-ter-plEEm, *m* penholder.

porter, por-teh, *v* to bear; to carry; to wear; to induce; to tell; **comment vous portez-vous?** komm-ahng voo por-teh voo? how are you?

porteu-r, se, por-ter, *mf* porter; carrier; holder.

porti-er, ère, por-te-eh,
mf doorkeeper.

portière, por-te-air, *f* door
(of car, train, etc).

portion, por-se-ong, *f*
portion; allowance.

portrait, por-tray, *m*
portrait; likeness.

pose, pohz, *f* putting; pose;
affectation.

posé, e, poh-zeh, *pp & a*
placed; sedate.

posément, poh-zeh-
mahng, *adv* sedately;
slowly.

poser, poh-zeh, *v* to place;
to pose.

poseu-r, se, poh-zer, *mf*
affected person.

positi-f, ve,* poh-ze-teeff,
a positive; matter-of-
fact.

position, poh-ze-se-ong, *f*
position; status; posture.

possédé, e, poss-eh-deh,
mf mad; *a* possessed.

posséder, poss-eh-deh, *v*
to possess; to enjoy.

possesseur, poss-ess-er, *m*
owner.

possession, poss-ess-e-ong,
f ownership; right;
possession.

possibilité, poss-e-be-le-
teh, *f* possibility.

possible, poss-ee-bl, *m*
utmost; *a* possible.

postal, e, poss-tăhl, *a*
postal.

poste, post, *m* post;
station; position; *f* post
office.

poste de télévision, post-
der-teh-leh-ve-se-ong *m*
television set.

poster, poss-teh, *v* to post;
to station.

postérieur, e,* poss-teh-
re-er, *a* subsequent;
later; hind.

postérité, poss-teh-re-teh,
f posterity; issue.

post-scriptum, post-skrip-
tom, *m* postscript.

postuler, poss-tE-leh, *v* to
apply for.

posture, poss-tEEr, *f*
posture; position.

pot, po, *m* pot; jug;
tankard; jar; crock;
carton (of yogurt).

potable, pot-ăh-bl, *a*
drinkable.

potage, pot-ăhsh, *m* soup;
pour tout –, poohr too
–, (*fam*) in all.

potager, e, pot-ăh-sheh, *m*
kitchen garden.

potasse, pot-ăhss, *f*
potash.

poteau, pot-oh, *m* post;
stake.

potelé, e, pot-leh, *a*
plump; fat.

potence, pot-ahngss, *f*
gallows; gibbet.

poterie, pot-ree, *f*
earthenware; pottery.

potier, pot-e-eh, *m* potter.

potin, pot-ang, *m* (*fam*)
gossip; clatter.

pou, poo, *m* louse.

pouce, pooss, *m* thumb;
big toe; inch.

poudre, poo-dr, *f* powder;
dust; gunpowder.

poudrier, poo-dre-eh, *m*
powder compact.

pouffer, poo-feh, *v* **–de
rire,** – der reer, to burst
out laughing.

poulailler, poo-lah'e-yeh,
m henhouse; (peanut
gallery) the gods.

poulain, poo-lang, *m* foal;
colt.

poule, pool, *f* hen.

poulet, poo-lay, *m*
chicken; (*fam*)
detective.

poulie, poo-lee, *f* pulley;
block.

pouls, poo, *m* pulse.

poumon, poo-mong, *m*
lung.

poupe, poop, *f* stern.

poupée, poo-peh, *f* doll;
puppet.

pour, poohr, *prep* for;
towards; to; in order to;
as to.

pourboire, poohr-bo'ăhr,
m gratuity; tip.

pourceau, poohr-soh, *m*

hog; pig; swine.

pourcentage, poohr-sahng-tähsh, *m* percentage.

pour étouffer une affaire, poo-reh-too-feh-E-näh-fair, *v* to cover-up.

pourparler, poohr-pährleh, *m* usually; *pl* parley; conference; negotiations.

pourpre, poohr-pr, *m & a* crimson; *f* purple dye.

pourquoi, poohr-kwäh, *adv & conj* why; wherefore; what ... for.

pourrir, poo-reer, *v* to rot.

pourriture, poo-re-tEEr, *f* decay; rot.

poursuite, poohr-sweet, *f* pursuit; *pl* proceedings.

poursuivre, poohr-swee-vr, *v* to pursue; to proceed against.

pourtant, poohr-tahng, *adv* yet; still; however.

pourtour, poohr-toohr, *m* circumference.

pour une personne, poohr-En-pair-sonn *f* single room.

pourvoi, poohr-vo'äh, *m* appeal.

pourvoir, poohr-vo'ähr, *v* to provide; to supply; to endow (**à,** for; **de,** with).

pourvu que, poohr-vE, ker, *conj* provided that.

pousser, pooss-eh, *v* to push; to thrust; to urge on; to utter; to grow.

poussette, pooss-ett, *f* stroller.

poussière, pooss-e-air, *f* dust; powder; spray.

poussin, pooss-ang, *m* chick.

poutre, pootr, *f* beam; rafter; girder.

pouvoir, poo-vo'ähr, *v* to be able; to be allowed.

pouvoir, poo-vo'ähr, *m* power; authority; power of attorney.

prairie, pray-ree, *f* meadow; prairie.

praline, präh-leen, *f* praline.

praticable, präh-te-käh-bl, *a* practicable; feasible.

praticien, ne, präh-te-se-ang, *mf* practitioner.

pratique, präh-teek, *f* practice; experience; *a** practical; useful.

pratiquer, präh-te-keh, *v* to practice; to use;† o make; to associate with.

pré, preh, *m* meadow.

préalable,* preh-äh-läh-bl, *a* previous; *adv phr* **au –,** first of all.

préavis, preh-ah-ve, *m* previous notice.

précaire,* preh-kair, *a* precarious.

précaution, preh-koh-se-ong, *f* precaution; caution.

précédemment, preh-seh-däh-mahng, *adv* previously.

précédent, e, preh-seh-dahng, *a* preceding; *m* precedent.

précéder, preh-seh-deh, *v* to precede.

précepteur, preh-sep-ter, *m* tutor.

prêcher, pray-sheh, *v* to preach; to lecture.

précieu-x, se,* preh-se-er, *a* precious; valuable; affected.

précipice, preh-se-peess, *m* precipice.

précipitamment, preh-se-pe-täh-mahng, *adv* hurriedly; headlong.

précipiter, preh-se-pe-teh, *v* to precipitate; to hurl headlong; to hasten.

précis, preh-se, *m* summary; précis.

précis, e, preh-se, *a* precise; exact; specific.

précisément, preh-se-zeh-mahng, *adv* precisely; just so.

préciser, preh-se-zeh, *v* to state precisely; to specify.

précité, e, preh-se-teh, *a* aforesaid.

précoce, preh-koss, *a* precocious; early.

préconiser, preh-konn-e-zeh, *v* to extol; to advocate.

prédicateur, preh-de-käh-ter, *m* preacher.

prédire, preh-deer, *v* to predict; to foretell.

préface, preh-fähss, *f* preface.

préférable,* preh-feh-räh-bl, *a* preferable; advisable.

préférer, preh-feh-reh, *v* to prefer; to like better.

préfet, preh-fay, *m* prefect; administrator (of French county).

préjudice, preh-shE-deess, *m* prejudice; wrong.

préjudiciable, preh-shE-de-se-äh-bl, *a* prejudicial.

préjugé, preh-shE-sheh, *m* prejudice; preconception.

prélasser (se) ser preh-lähss-eh, *v* to strut; to take one's ease.

prélever, prehl-veh, *v* to deduct beforehand; to levy.

préliminaire, preh-le-me-nair, *a* preliminary.

prélude, preh-lEEd, *m* prelude.

prématuré,* e, preh-mäh-tE-reh, *a* premature.

premier, prer-me-eh, *m* chief; leader; first.

premi-er, ère,* prer-me-eh, *a* first; former; early; next; leading.

prémunir, preh-mE-neer, *v* to forewarn; to caution.

prendre, prahngdr, *v* to take; to seize; to assume; to congeal; to set; to catch on.

prendre un bain de soleil, prahngdr-ung-bang-der-soll-a'ye *v* sunbathe.

preneu-r, se, prer-ner, *mf* taker; buyer.

prénom, preh-nong, *m* first name.

préoccuper, preh-ock-E-peh, *v* to preoccupy; to engross the mind; to disturb.

préparatif, preh-päh-räh-teeff, *m* preparation (used almost exclusively in the plural).

préparer, preh-päh-reh, *v* to prepare; to get ready.

prépondérance, preh-pong-deh-rahngss, *f* preponderance; sway.

préposé, preh-poh-zeh, *m* official in charge.

près, pray, *adv* & *prep* near; close by; **–de,** about to.

présage, preh-zähsh, *m* presage; omen.

présager, preh-zäh-sheh, *v* to forebode.

pré-salé, preh-säh-leh, *m* salt-meadow sheep.

presbyte, prez-beet, *mf* & *a* farsighted.

presbytère, prez-be-tair, *m* vicarage.

prescience, preh-se-ahngss, *f* prescience.

prescrire, press-kreer, *v* to order; to prescribe.

préséance, preh-seh-ahngss, *f* precedence.

présence, preh-zahngss, *f* presence.

présent, e, preh-zahng, *a* present.

présenter, preh-zahng-teh, *v* to present; to offer; to introduce.

présenta-teur, trice, preh-zahng-tah-tez, *mf* anchorman (new); anchorwoman (new).

préservati-f, ve, preh-zair-väh-teeff, *a* protective; *m* condom.

préserver, preh-zair-veh, *v* to preserve (**de,** from).

président, preh-ze-dahng, *m* president; chairman.

présider, preh-ze-deh, *v* to preside.

présomption, preh-zongp-se-ong, *f* presumption;

self-assurance.

présomptueu-x, se,* preh-zongp-tE- er, *a* presumptuous.

presque, press-ker, *adv* almost; nearly.

presqu'île, press-keel, *f* peninsula.

pressant, e, press-ahng, *a* pressing; urgent.

presse, press, *f* press; crowd; urgency; squeezer.

pressé, e, press-eh, *a* in a hurry; urgent.

pressentiment, press-ahng-te-mahng, *m* presentiment.

pressentir, press-ahng-teer, *v* to have a presentiment of.

presser, press-eh, *v* to press; to crowd; to urge.

pression, press-e-ong, *f* pressure.

prestance, press-tahngss, *f* fine presence.

preste,* presst, *a* quick; nimble.

prestidigitateur, press-te-de-she-tăh-ter, *m* conjuror.

prestige, press-teesh, *m* prestige.

prestigieu-x, se, press-te-she-er *a* glamorous (job).

présumer, preh-zE-meh, *v* to presume.

prêt, pray, *m* loan.

prêt, e, pray, *a* ready; prepared; willing.

prétendant, e, preh-tahng-dahng, *mf* claimant; pretender; suitor.

prétendre, preh-tahng-dr, *v* to claim; to intend; to maintain.

prétendu, e, preh-tahng-dE, *mf* intended (husband or wife); *a* so-called.

prête-nom, prayt-nong, *m* figurehead.

prétentieu-x, se,* preh-tahng-se-er, *a* pretentious; conceited.

prétention, preh-tahng-se-ong, *f* pretension; affectation.

prêter, pray-teh, *v* to lend; to ascribe; to give rise.

prêteu-r, se, pray-ter, *mf* lender.

prétexte, preh-text, *m* pretext; pretense.

prêtre, pray-tr, *m* priest.

preuve, prerv, *f* proof; evidence; token.

prévaloir, preh-văh-lo'ăhr, *v* to prevail.

prévenance, prehv-nahngss, *f* kind attention.

prévenant, prehv-nahng, *a* obliging; prepossessing.

prévenir, prehv-neer, *v* to advise; to inform.

prévention, prehv-vahng-se-ong, *f* imprisonment on suspicion; prevention.

prévenu, e, prehv-nE, *mf* accused; *a* prejudiced.

prévision, preh-ve-ze-ong, *f* forecast; anticipation.

prévoir, preh-vo'ăhr, *v* to foresee; to provide for or against.

prévoyance, preh-vo'ăh-yahngss, *f* foresight; forethought.

prier, pre-eh, *v* to pray; to entreat; to invite.

prière, pre-air, *f* prayer; entreaty; request.

primaire, pre-mair, *a* primary; elementary.

prime, preem, *f* premium; bonus; option.

primé, e, pre-meh, given a prize.

primer, pre-meh, *v* to surpass; to award a prize to.

primeur, pre-mer, *f* early fruit or vegetable; freshness.

primevère, preem-vair, *f* primrose.

primiti-f, ve,* pre-me-teeff, *a* primitive.

prince, sse, prangss, *mf* prince; princess.

princi-er, ère,* prang-se-eh, *a* princely.

principal, prang-se-pähl, *m* chief thing; main point; *a* principal; main.

principauté, prang-se-poh-te, *f* principality.

principe, prang-seep, *m* principle.

printani-er, ère, prang-tăh-ne-eh, *a* springlike.

printemps, prang-tahng, *m* spring; springtime.

priorité, pre-or-e-teh, *f* priority; right of way.

pris, e, pre, *pp* & *a* taken; occupied; busy.

prise, preez, *f* taking; hold; quarrel; catch.

priser, pre-zeh, *v* to value; to take snuff.

priseu-r, se, pre-zer, *mf* snuff-taker; appraiser.

prison, pre-zong, *f* prison.

prisonni-er, ère, pre-zonn-e-eh, *mf* & *a* prisoner.

privation, pre-văh-se-ong, *f* privation; loss.

privauté, pre-voh-teh, *f* familiarity.

privé, e, pre-veh, *a* private.

priver, pre-veh, *v* to deprive.

privilège, pre-ve-laysh, *m* privilege.

prix, pre, *m* price; value;

reward; prize; – de revient, de rer-ve-ang, *m* cost.

probabilité, prob-ăh-be-le-teh, *f* probability.

probable,* prob-ăh-bl, *a* probable; likely.

probant, e, prob-ahng, *a* conclusive; convincing.

probe, prob, *a* honest; upright.

probité, prob-e-teh, *f* honesty; uprightness.

problème, prob-laym, *m* problem.

procédé, pross-eh-deh, *m* process; behavior; method.

procéder, pross-eh-deh, *v* to proceed; to behave; to prosecute (**contre**, against).

procédure, pross-eh-dEEr, *f* proceedings; practice.

procès, pross-ay, *m* lawsuit; trial; litigation.

procès-verbal, pross-ay-vair-băhl, *m* report; minutes; record.

prochain, prosh-ang, *m* neighbor; fellow.

prochain, e, prosh-ang, *a* next; nearest.

prochainement, prosh-ain-mahng, *adv* shortly.

proche, prosh, *a* close; *mpl* relations; *adv* near.

proclamer, prock-lăh-

meh, *v* to proclaim.

procuration, prock-E-răh-se-ong, *f* proxy.

procurer, prock-E-reh, *v* to procure.

procureur, prock-E-rer, *m* state prosecutor/ general; attorney.

prodigalité, prod-e-găh-le-teh, *f* prodigality; extravagance.

prodige, prod-eesh, *m* prodigy; wonder.

prodigieu-x, se,* prod-e-she-er, *a* prodigious; wonderful.

prodigue, prod-eeg, *m* spendthrift; *a* prodigal.

prodiguer, prod-e-gheh, *v* to lavish; to squander.

produc-teur, trice, prod-EEk-ter, *mf* producer; *a* productive.

production, prod-EEk-se-ong, *f* production; product; output.

produire, prod-weer, *v* to produce; to yield; to show.

produit, prod-wee, *m* produce; product; proceeds.

produit pour la vaisselle, prod-wee-poohr-lăh-vayss-ell *m* dishwashing liquid.

profane, prof-ăhn, *mf* & *a* outsider; profane; lay.

profaner, prof-ăh-neh, *v* to profane.

proférer, prof-eh-reh, *v* to utter.

professer, prof-ess-eh, *v* to profess; to teach.

professeur, prof-ess-er, *m* professor; teacher.

profession, prof-ess-e-ong, *f* profession; business.

profil, prof-eel, *m* profile; section.

profit, prof-e, *m* profit; gain; utility.

profiter, prof-e-teh, *v* to profit (**de,** by); to take advantage (**de,** of).

profond, e, prof-ong, *a* deep; profound; sound.

profondément, prof-ong-deh-mahng, *adv* deeply.

profondeur, prof-ong-der, *f* depth; profoundness.

programme, prog-răhm, *m* program; bill; platform.

progrès, prog-ray, *m* progress; improvement.

prohiber, pro-e-beh, *v* to prohibit.

proie, prwăh, *f* prey.

projecteur, pro-sheck-ter, *m* projector; headlight.

projectile, pro-sheck-teel, *m* & *a* missile.

projection, prosh-eck-se-ong, *f* projection.

projet, prosh-ay, *m* project; scheme; rough draft.

projeter, prosh-teh, *v* to project; to plan.

prolétaire, proll-eh-tair, *m* & *a* proletarian.

prolonger, proll-ong-sheh, *v* to prolong; to protract; to lengthen.

promenade, promm-năhd, *f* walk; drive; ride; excursion.

promener, promm-neh, *v* to take about; to walk; **se –,** to take a walk.

promeneu-r, se, promm-ner, *mf* walker.

promesse, promm-ayss, *f* promise.

promettre, promm-ay-tr, *v* to promise; to look promising.

promontoire, promm-ong-to'ăhr, *m* promontory.

promouvoir, promm-oo-vo'ăhr, *v* to promote.

prompt, e,* prong, *a* prompt; sudden; hasty.

promptitude, prong-te-tEEd, *f* quickness.

promulguer, promm-EEl-gheh, *v* to promulgate.

pronom, pron-ong, *m* pronoun.

prononcé, e, pron-ong-seh, *pp* & *a* pronounced; decided.

prononcer, pron-ong-seh, *v* to pronounce; to utter.

propagande, prop-ăh-gahngd, *f* propaganda.

propager, prop-ăh-sheh, *v* to propagate; **se –,** to spread.

propension, prop-ahng-se-ong, *f* propensity.

prophétie, prof-eh-see, *f* prophecy.

propice, prop-eess, *a* propitious; favorable.

proportionnel, le,* prop-or-se-onn-ell, *a* proportional; commensurate.

propos, prop-oh, *m* purpose; talk.

proposer, prop-oh-zeh, *v* to propose; to move; **se –,** to intend; to mean.

proposition, prop-oh-ze-se-ong, *f* proposal; proposition; clause.

propre, propr, *m* own characteristic; *a* * own; proper; clean.

propreté, prop-rer-teh, *f* neatness; cleanliness.

propriétaire, prop-re-eh-tair, *mf* proprietor; landlord.

propriété, prop-re-eh-teh, *f* property; ownership; propriety.

propulsion, prop-EEl-se-ong, *f* propelling.

prorata, pro-răh-tăh, *m* proportion.

prorogation, pror-ogh-ăh-se-ong, f prorogation; adjournment.

proroger, pror-osh-eh, v to extend; to adjourn.

prosaïque, pro-zăh-eek, a prosaic.

prosateur, pro-zăh-ter, m prosewriter.

proscrire, pross-kreer, v to proscribe; to banish.

proscrit, e, pross-kre, mf exile; outlaw.

prose, prohz, f prose.

prospère, pross-pair, a prosperous.

prospérer, pross-peh-reh, v to prosper; to thrive.

prosterner (se), ser pross-tair-neh, v to prostrate oneself.

prostituée, pross-te-tE-eh, f prostitute.

protec-teur, trice, prot-eck-ter, mf & a protector; protective.

protectorat, prot-eck-tor-ăh, m protectorate.

protégé, e, prot-eh-**sheh**, mf protégé; dependent.

protéger, prot-eh-sheh, v to protect; to shield.

protestant, e, prot-ess-tahng, mf & a Protestant.

protester, prot-ess-teh, v to protest.

prouesse, proo-ess, f prowess; exploit.

prouver, proo-veh, v to prove; to show.

provenance, prov-nahngss, f origin; source.

provenir, prov-neer, v to proceed; to originate.

proverbe, prov-airb, m proverb.

proverbial, e,* prov-air-be-ăhl, a proverbial.

providence, prov-e-dahngss, f Providence.

province, prov-angss, f province; the country.

provincial, e, prov-ang-se-ăhl, mf & a provincial.

proviseur, prov-e-zer, m principal.

provision, prov-e-ze-ong, f provision; supply; retainer.

provisoire,* prov-e-zo'ăhr, a provisional.

provocant, e, prov-ock-ahng, a provoking; alluring.

provoca-teur, trice, prov-ock-ăh-ter, mf aggressor; agitator.

provoquer, prov-ock-eh, v to provoke; to challenge; to cause.

prudemment, prE-dăh-mahng, adv prudently.

prudence, prE-dahngss, f prudence.

pruderie, prEEd-ree, f prudishness.

prune, prEEn, f plum.

pruneau, prE-noh, m prune.

prunelle, prE-nell, f sloe; pupil (eye).

prunier, prE-ne-eh, m plum tree.

psaume, psohm, m psalm.

pseudonyme, pser-donn-eem, m pseudonym.

psychanalyste, pse-kăh-năh-leest mf psychoanalyst.

psychiatre, pse-ke-ah-tr, m psychiatrist.

psychologique, pse-koll-o-sheeck a psychological.

psychologue, pse-koll-og, m psychologist.

psychopathe, pse-ko-paht mf psychopath.

puant, e, pE-ahng, a stinking.

puanteur, pE-ahng-ter, f stench.

pubère, pE-bair, a pubescent.

public, pE-bleeck, m public.

publi-c, que,* pE-bleeck, a public; common.

publication, pE-bli-cah-se-ong, f publication; publishing.

publicité, pE-ble-se-teh, f publicity; advertisement.

publier, pE-ble-eh, *v* to publish.

puce, pEEss, *f* flea.

pucelle, pE-sell, *f* virgin.

pudeur, pE-der, *f* bashfulness; modesty; reserve.

pudique,* pE-deeck, *a* chaste; modest.

puer, pE-eh, *v* to stink; to smell strongly of.

puéril, e,* pE-eh-reel, *a* childish.

pugilat, pE- she-lăh, *m* boxing.

puis, pwee, *adv* then; afterwards; next; besides.

puiser, pwee-zeh, *v* to draw (water); to derive.

puisque, pweess-ker, *conj* since.

puissamment, pweess-ăh-mahng, *adv* powerfully; mightily.

puissance, pweess-ahngss, *f* power; force; influence.

puissant, e, pweess-ahng, *a* powerful; mighty; (*fam*) stout.

puits, pwee, *m* well; shaft; pit.

pull (-over), pEl (lo-vair) *m* pullover.

pulluler, pEEl-lE-leh, *v* to swarm.

pulsation, pEEl-săh-se-ong, *f* beating; throbbing.

pulvériser, pEEl-veh-re-zeh, *v* to pulverize.

punaise, pE-nayz, *f* bedbug; thumbtack.

punir, pE-neer, *v* to punish.

punition, pE-niss-e-ong, *f* punishment.

pupille, pE-peell, *mf* ward; *f* pupil (of eye).

pupitre, pE-pee-tr, *m* desk; music stand.

pur, e,* pEEr, *a* pure; genuine; clean; mere.

purée, pE-reh, *f* mash; purée; mashed potatoes.

pureté, pEEr-teh, *f* purity; chastity.

purgati-f, ve, pEEr-găh-teeff, *a* purgative.

purgatoire, pEEr-găh-to'ăhr, *m* purgatory.

purge, pEErsh, *f* purge; cleansing.

purger, pEEr-sheh, *v* to purge; to cleanse; to serve (jail).

purifier, pE-re-fe-eh, *v* to purify.

pus, pE, *m* pus; matter.

pusillanime, pE-zill-lăh-neemm, *a* fainthearted.

pustule, pEEs-tEEl, *f* pimple.

putréfier, pE-treh-fe-eh, *v* to putrefy; to rot.

puzzle, pEEzl *m* jigsaw.

pyramide, pe-răh-meedd, *f* pyramid.

quadragénaire, kwăh-dräh-sheh-nair, *mf & a* forty year old.

quadrillé, e, kăh-dree-yeh, *a* checkered.

quadruple, kwăh-drEE-pl, *m & a* quadruple.

quai, kay, *m* quay; wharf; platform.

qualification, kăh-le-fe-kăh-se-ong, *f* title.

qualifier, kăh-le-fe-eh, *v* to qualify; to call.

qualité, kăh-le-teh, *f* quality; property; rank; qualification.

quand, kahng, *adv* when (at what moment); *conj* when (at the time).

quant à, kahng t'ăh, *prep* as to; as for.

quantième, kahng-te-aym, *m* day of the month.

quantité, kahng-te-teh, *f* quantity.

quarantaine, kăh-rahng-tain, *f* about forty; quarantine.

quarante, kăh-rahngt, *m & a* forty.

quarantième, kăh-rahng-te-aym, *m & a* fortieth.

quart, kăhr, *m* quarter; (*nau*) watch; point (of compass).

quartier, kăhr-te-eh, *m* quarter; piece; neighborhood; district.

quartier des prostituées, kăhr-te-eh-deh-pross-te-tE-eh *m* red-light district.

quartiers défavorisés, kăhr-te-eh-deh-făh-vor-e-zeh *mpl* inner city.

quasi, kăh-ze, *adv* quasi; all but; almost.

quatorze, kăh-torz, *m & a* fourteen.

quatorzième, kăh-tor-ze-aym, *m & a* fourteenth.

quatre, kăh-tr, *m & a* four.

quatre-vingt-dix, kăh-trer-vang-deess, *m & a* ninety.

quatre-vingts, kăh-trer-vang, *a* eighty.

quatrième, kăh-tre-aym, *m & a* fourth.

quatuor, kwăh-tE-or, *m* quartet.

que, ker, *pron* whom; that; which; what.

que, ker, *adv* how; how much; how many; why.

que, ker, *conj* that; if; when; as; until; while; whether; lest; **ne...–,** ner...–, only.

quel, le, kell, *a* what; what a; which.

quelconque, kell-kongk, *a* whatever; any; (*fam*) commonplace.

quelque, kell-ker, *adv* some; about; *a* some;

any; a few.

quelquefois, kell-ker-fo'ăh, *adv* sometimes.

quelqu'un, e, kell-kung, *pron* somebody; one; *pl* **quelques-uns, unes,** kell-ker-z'ung, some; a few; any.

querelle, ker-rell, *f* quarrel; row.

question, kess-te-ong, *f* question; matter.

questionnaire, kess-te-onn-air, *m* set of questions; questionnaire.

quête, kayt, *f* quest; collection.

quêter, kay-teh, *v* to search; to make a collection.

queue, ker, *f* tail; train; cue; tailpiece.

qui, ke, *pron* who; whom; which; that; whoever; what.

quiconque, ke-kongk, *pron* whoever.

qui continue à évoluer, ke-kong-te-nE-ăh-eh-voll-E-eh *a* ongoing.

quille, kee-ye, *f* keel; skittle.

quincaillerie, kang-kah'e-ree, *f* hardware store.

quinquagénaire, kang-kwăh-**sh**eh-nair, *mf* & *a* to be fifty.

quinte, kangt, *f* coughing fit; fifth.

quintuple, kwang-tEE-pl, *m* & *a* fivefold.

quinzaine, kang-zain, *f* about fifteen; two weeks.

quinze, kangz, *m* & *a* fifteen; fifteenth.

quinzième, kang-ze-aym, *m* & *a* fifteenth.

quittance, ke-tahngss, *f* receipt; discharge.

quitte, keet, *a* clear; quit; –à, – ăh, at the risk of.

quitter, ke-teh, *v* to leave; to forsake; to depart.

qui-vive, ke-veev, *m* to be on the alert.

quoi, kwăh, *pron* what; which, that; (exclamation) what!

quoique, kwăh-ker, *conj* although.

quolibet, koll-e-bay, *m* gibe; jeer.

quota, kot-ăh, *m* quota.

quote-part, kot-păhr, *f* share.

quotidien, ne, kot-e-de-ang, *a* daily.

quotient, ko-sseahng, *m* quotient: I.Q.

R

rabâcher, răh-bah-sheh, *v* to repeat over and over again.

rabais, răh-bay, *m* abatement; rebate.

rabaisser, răh-bess-eh, *v* to lower; to humble.

rabattre, răh-băh-tr *v* to lower; to bring down; to deduct.

rabbin, răh-bang, *m* rabbi.

râblé, e, rah-bleh, *a* broad-backed; stocky.

raboter, răh-bot-eh, *v* to plane.

raboteu-x, se, răh-bot-er, *a* rugged; harsh; jagged.

rabougri, e, răh-boo-gre, *a* stunted.

raccommoder, răh-komm-od-eh, *v* to mend; to patch; to darn; to reconcile.

raccorder, răh-kor-deh, *v* to join; to unite.

raccourcir, răh-koohr-seer, *v* to shorten; to curtail.

raccrocher, răh-krosh-eh, *v* to hang up; **se –,** to clutch.

race, răhss, *f* race; stock; breed; family.

rachat, răh-shăh, *m* repurchase; atonement; redemption.

racheter, răh-shteh, *v* to buy back; to atone for.

rachitique, răh-she-teeck, *a* rickety.

racine, răh-seen, *f* root; origin.

racisme, răh-sism *m* racism.

raciste, răh-seest *a* & *mf* racist.

raclée, rah-kleh, *f* (*pop*) thrashing; licking.

racler, rah-kleh, *v* to scrape.

racoler, răh-koll-eh, *v* to recruit; to pick up.

racontar, răh-kong-tăhr, *m* gossip.

raconter, răh-kong-teh, *v* to relate; to tell.

rade, răhd, *f* harbor.

radeau, răh-doh, *m* raft.

radiateur, răh-de-ăh-ter, *m* radiator.

radieu-x, se,* răh-de-er, *a* radiant.

radio, răh-de-o, *f* radio.

radioactif, răh-de-o-ăhk-teef *a* radioactive.

radiodiffusion, răh-de-o-diff-E-ze-ong, *f* broadcasting.

radiographie, răh-de-o-grăh-fe, *f* X-ray photography; X-ray.

radis, răh-de, *m* radish.

radoter, răh-dot-eh, *v* to rave; to drivel.

radoucir, răh-doo-seer, *v* to soften; to calm.

rafale, răh-făhl, *f* squall.

raffermir, răh-fair-meer, *v* to strengthen; to make firm.

raffiné, e, răh-fe-neh, *a* refined; delicate.

raffinerie, răh-feen-ree, *f* sugar refinery.

raffoler, răh-foll-eh, *v* to dote (**de,** on); (*fam*) to be mad about.

rafler, rah-fleh, *v* to sweep off.

rafraîchir, răh-fray-sheer, *v* to cool; to brighten up.

rafraîchissement, răh-fray-shiss-mahng, *m* cooling; refreshing; *pl* refreshments.

rage, răhsh, *f* rabies; rage; violent pain.

rager, răh-sheh, *v* to fume; to be in a rage.

ragoût, răh-goo, *m* stew; relish.

ragoût (en cocotte), răh-goo, (ahng-kock-ot) *m* casserole (food).

raide, rayd, *adv* quickly; sharply; outright; *a* stiff; tight; steep; stubborn.

raideur, ray-der, *f* stiffness; tightness; sternness.

raidir, ray-deer, *v* to stiffen; to tighten.

raie, ray, *f* streak; stroke; parting (hair); skate (fish).

rail, rah'e, *m* rail (railroad).

railler, rah'e-yeh, *v* to scoff at; to mock.

raillerie, rah'e-ree, *f* mocking; banter; jeer.

rainure, ray-nEEr, *f* groove.

raisin, ray-zang, *m* grapes.

raison, ray-zong, *f* reason; cause; satisfaction; right; ratio.

raisonnable,* ray-zonn-ăh-bl, *a* reasonable; sensible.

raisonnement, ray-zonn-mahng, *m* reasoning; argument.

raisonner, ray-zonn-eh, *v* to reason.

rajeunir, răh-sher-neer, *v* to rejuvenate.

rajouter, răh-shoo-teh, *v* to add.

rajuster, răh-shEs-teh, *v* to readjust; to repair.

ralentir, răh-lahng-teer, *v* to slacken; to slow down.

râler, rah-leh, *v* to rattle (in one's throat); (*fam*) to fume.

rallier, răh-le-eh, *v* to rally; to rejoin.

rallonger, rah-long-sheh, *v* to lengthen; to let down.

ramage, răh-măhsh, *m* warbling; floral design.

ramas, răh-mah, *m* heap; set.

ramasser, răh-măhss-eh, *v* to gather; to pick up.

rame, răhm, *f* oar; ream

(paper); prop.

rameau, răh-moh, *m* bough; branch.

ramener, răhm-neh, *v* to bring back; to restore.

ramer, răh-meh, *v* to row; to stake (peas).

ramifier (se), ser răh-me-fe-eh, *v* to branch out.

ramollir, răh-moll-eer, *v* to soften; to weaken.

ramoner, răh-monn-eh, *v* to sweep (chimneys).

ramoneur, răh-monn-er, *m* chimneysweep.

rampant, e, rahng-pahng, *a* creeping; servile.

rampe, rahngp, *f* handrail; slope; footlights.

ramper, rahng-peh, *v* to crawl; to cringe.

rance, rahngss, *a* rancid.

rançon, rahng-song, *f* ransom.

rançonner, rahng-sonn-eh, *v* to ransom; (*fam*) to fleece.

rancune, rahng-kEEn, *f* rancor; grudge.

rang, rahng, *m* row; line; rank; range; rate.

rangée, rahng-sheh, *f* row; line; tier.

ranger, rahng-sheh, *v* to arrange; to tidy.

ranimer, răh-ne-meh, *v* to revive.

rapace, răh-păhss, *m* bird

of prey; *a* rapacious.

rapatrier, răh-păh-tre-eh, *v* to repatriate.

râpé, e, rah-peh, *pp* & *a* grated; threadbare.

râper, rah-peh, *v* to grate.

rapetisser, rahp-tiss-eh, *v* to shorten; to shrink.

rapide, răh-peed, *m* fast train; *a* * fast.

rapidité, răh-pe-de-teh, *f* swiftness; speed.

rappel, răh-pell, *m* recall; call to arms; repeal.

rappeler, răhp-leh, *v* to call again; to remind; **se** –, to remember.

rapport, răh-por, *m* report; tale; relation;. bearing.

rapporter, răh-por-teh, *v* to bring back; to report; to yield; to tell tales; **se** –à, to relate to.

rapporteur, răh-por-ter, *m* sneak; reporter; protractor.

rapprocher, răh-prosh-eh, *v* to bring near; to reconcile; to compare.

raquette, răh-kett, *f* racket.

raquette de tennis, răh-kett-der-teh-neess *f* tennis racket.

rare, * răhr, *a* rare; scarce; uncommon.

rareté, răhr-teh, *f* scarcity; rare object.

ras, e, rah, *a* shorn; flat; smooth.

rasade, răh-zăhd, *f* glassful.

raser, rah-zeh, *v* to shave; to graze; to skim; (*fam*) to bore.

rasoir, rah-zo'ăhr, *m* razor.

rassasier, răhss-ăh-ze-eh, *v* to satiate; to satisfy (hunger, etc).

rassemblement, răhss-ahng-bler-mahng, *m* gathering; crowd.

rassembler, răhss-ahng-bleh, *v* to reassemble; to gather; **se** –, to meet.

rasseoir, răhss-o'ăhr, *v* to reseat; to settle.

rasséréner, răhss-eh-reh-neh, *v* to clear up; to calm.

rassis, e, răhss-e, *a* stale; sedate.

rassurer, răhss-E-reh, *v* to reassure.

rat, răh, *m* rat.

ratatiné, e, răh-tăh-te-neh, *pp* & *a* shriveled up.

rate, răht, *f* spleen.

râteau, rah-toh, *m* rake.

râtelier, rah-ter-le-eh, *m* rack; (*fam*) denture.

rater, răh-teh, *v* to misfire; to fail.

ratifier, răh-te-fe-eh, *v* to ratify.

ration, răh-se-ong, *f* ration; share; allowance.

rationnel, le, * răh-se-onn-ell, *a* rational.

ratisser, răh-tiss-eh, *v* to scrape; to rake.

rattacher, răh-tăh-sheh, *v* to fasten; **se** –, to be connected (à, with).

rattraper, răh-trăh-peh, *v* to catch up; to recover; **se** –, to recoup oneself.

rature, răh-tEEr, *f* erasure.

rauque, rohk, *a* hoarse.

ravage, răh-văhsh, *m* ravage; devastation; havoc.

ravaler, răh-văh-leh, *v* to swallow again; to disparage.

ravi, răh-vee, *a* entranced; delighted.

ravin, răh-vang, *m* ravine.

ravir, răh-veer, *v* to rob; to carry off; to enrapture.

raviser (se), ser răh-ve-zeh, *v* to change one's mind.

ravissant, e, răh-viss-ahng, *a* ravishing; charming.

ravissement, răh-viss-mahng, *m* ravishment; rapture.

ravoir, răh-vo'ăhr, *v* to get back (only in *inf*).

rayer, ray-yeh, *v* to erase; to scratch; to strip.

rayon, ray-yong, *m* ray; bookshelf; radius; spoke; department.

rayonnement, ray-ongn-mahng *m* radiation.

rayonner, ray-yonn-eh, *v* to radiate.

rayure, ray-yEEr, *f* stripe.

réaction, reh-ăhck-se-ong, *f* reaction.

réagir, reh-ăh-**sheer**, *v* to react.

réaliser, reh-ăh-le-zeh, *v* to realize; to produce (film); to achieve.

réalité, reh-ăh-le-teh, *f* reality.

rébarbati-f, ve, reh-băhr-băh-teeff, *a* gruff; repulsive.

rebattu, e, rer-băh-tE, *a* trite; hackneyed.

rebelle, rer-bell, *mf* rebel; *a* rebellious.

rebondi, e, rer-bong-de, *a* plump; chubby.

rebondir, rer-bong-deer, *v* to rebound; to bounce.

rebord, rer-bor, *m* edge; brim.

rebours, rer-boohr, *m* wrong way; reverse.

rebrousse-poil (à), ăh rer-brooss-po'ăhl, *adv* the wrong way.

rebrousser, rer-brooss-eh, *v* to brush up; **–chemin,** – sher-mang, to retrace one's steps.

rebut, rer-bE, *m* rejection; scum; outcast.

rebuter, rer-bE-teh, *v* to repulse; to dishearten.

récalcitrant, e, reh-kăhl-se-trahng, *a* refractory.

recaler, rer-kăhl-eh, *v* to fail an exam.

recéler, rer-seh-leh, *v* to receive (stolen goods); to harbor.

récemment, reh-săh-mahng, *adv* recently.

recensement, rer-sahngss-mahng, *m* census.

récent, e, reh-sahng, *a* recent.

récépissé, reh-seh-piss-eh, *m* acknowledgment of receipt.

réception, reh-sep-se-ong, *f* reception; receipt; catching (sports).

recette, rer-sett, *f* receipt; returns; recipe.

receveu-r, se, rer-ser-ver, *mf* receiver; collector; conductor (bus, etc).

recevoir, rer-ser-vo'ăhr, *v* to receive; to admit.

rechange, rer-shahng-sh, *m* replacement; **de –,** spare.

réchaud, reh-shoh, *m* chafing dish; small stove.

réchauffer, reh-shoh-feh, *v* to reheat; to stir up.

recherche, rer-shairsh, *f* search; refinement; research.

recherché, e, rer-shair-sheh, *a* in great request; farfetched; choice.

rechercher, rer-shair-sheh, *v* to search; to seek.

rechute, rer-shEEt, *f* relapse.

récidive, reh-se-deev, *f* second offense.

récif, reh-seeff, *m* reef.

récipient, reh-se-pe-ahng, *m* container.

réciproque,* reh-se-prock, *a* reciprocal.

récit, reh-se, *m* account; narration.

réciter, reh-se-teh, *v* to recite; to relate.

réclamation, reh-klăh-măh-se-ong, *f* claim; complaint.

réclame, reh-klăhm, *f* advertisement.

réclamer, reh-klăh-meh, *v* to claim; to protest; to implore; to need.

reclus, e, rer-klE, *mf* recluse.

recoin, rer-ko'ang, *m* corner; nook.

récolte, reh-kollt, *f* harvest; crop.

recommandable, rer-komm-ahng-dăh-bl, *a* commendable; advisable.

recommandation, rer-komm-ahng-dăh-se-ong, *f* recommendation; advice.

recommander, rer-komm-ahng-deh, *v* to recommend; to advise; to register (letter).

recommencer, rer-komm-ahngss-eh, *v* to begin again; to do it again.

récompense, reh-kong-pahngss, *f* reward.

récompenser, reh-kong-pahngss-eh, *v* to reward.

réconcilier, reh-kong-se-le-eh, *v* to reconcile.

reconduire, rer-kong-dweer, *v* to lead back; to escort; to renew (document).

réconforter, reh-kong-for-teh, *v* to strengthen; to cheer up.

reconnaissance, rer-konn-ess-ahngss, *f* recognition; gratitude.

reconnaissant, e, rer-konn-ess-ahng, *a* grateful.

reconnaître, rer-konn-ay-tr, *v* to recognize; to acknowledge.

recourir, rer-koo-reer, *v* to have recourse.

recours, rer-koohr, *m* recourse; resource; appeal.

recouvrement, rer-koo-vrer-mahng, *m* recovery; collection (debts); covering.

recouvrer, rer-koo-vreh, *v* to regain; to collect.

recouvrir, rer-koo-vreer, *v* to recover; to cover.

récréation, reh-kreh-ăh-se-ong, *f* recreation; playtime.

recréer, rer-kreh-eh, *v* to create again.

récrier (se), ser reh-kre-eh, *v* to exclaim; to protest.

recrue, rer-krE, *f* recruit.

recruter, rer-krE-teh, *v* to recruit.

recteur, reck-ter, *m* rector.

rectifier, reck-te-fe-eh, *v* to rectify.

recto, reck-to, *m* right-hand page.

reçu, rer-sE, *m* receipt.

recueil, rer-ker'e, *m* collection.

recueillement, rer-ker'e-mahng, *m* meditation; composure; quietude.

recueillir, rer-ker'e-eer, *v* to gather; to collect; to

reap; **se –,** to collect one's thoughts.

recul, rer-kEEl, *m* retreat; retirement; room to move back.

reculé, e, rer-kE-leh, *a* distant; remote.

reculer, rer-kE-leh, *v* to move back; to defer.

reculons (à), ăh rer-kE-long, *adv* backwards.

récupérer, reh-kE-peh-reh, *v* to retrieve; to recover.

récurer, reh-kE-reh, *v* to scour; to clean.

récuser, reh-kE-seh, *v* to challenge; to object; **se –,** to decline.

rédac-teur, trice, reh-dăhck-ter, *mf* writer; editor.

rédaction, reh-dăhck-se-ong, *f* wording; editing; editorial staff; editorial office.

rédemption, reh-dahngp-se-ong, *f* redemption; redeeming.

redescendre, rer-deh-sahng-dr, *v* to come down again; to take down again.

redevable, rerd-văh-bl, *a* indebted.

redevance, rerd-vahngss, *f* rent; royalty; due.

rédiger, reh-de-sheh, *v* to draw up; to edit.

redire, rer-deer, *v* to say again; to find fault (à, with).

redite, rer-deet, *f* repetition.

redoubler, rer-doo-bleh, *v* to redouble; to increase; to repeat a year (in school).

redoutable, rer-doo-tăh-bl, *a* formidable.

redouter, rer-doo-teh, *v* to dread.

redresser, rer-dress-eh, *v* to straighten; to correct.

réduction, reh-dEEk-se-ong, *f* reduction; discount.

réduire, reh-dweer, *v* to reduce; to subdue; to compel.

réduit, reh-dwe, *m* nook; cubbyhole.

réel, le,* rer-ayl, *a* real.

réfectoire, reh-fehck-to'ăhr, *m* refectory.

référendum, reh-feh-rahng-dom *m* referendum.

référer, reh-feh-reh, *v* to refer.

réfléchir, reh-fleh-sheer, *v* to reflect; to ponder.

reflet, rer-flay, *m* reflection.

refléter, rer-fleh-teh, *v* to reflect.

réflexion, reh-fleck-se-ong, *f* reflection; (*fam*) remark.

refluer, rer-flE-eh, *v* to flow back.

reflux, rer-flE, *m* ebbing; ebb.

réforme, reh-form, *f* reform; reformation.

réformer, reh-for-meh, *v* to reform; to discharge.

refouler, rer-foo-leh, *v* to drive back; to repress (instinct, etc).

réfractaire, reh-frähck-tair, *a* refractory.

refrain, rer-frang, *m* refrain (song); chorus.

réfréner, rer-freh-neh, *v* to restrain.

réfrigérateur, reh-fre-sheh-răh-ter, *m* refrigerator.

refroidir, rer-fro'ăh-deer, *v* to cool; to chill.

refuge, rer-fEE sh, *m* refuge; shelter.

réfugié, e, reh-fE-she-eh, *mf* & *a* refugee.

réfugier (se) ser reh-fE-she-eh, *v* to take shelter.

refus, rer-fE, *m* refusal; denial.

refuser, rer-fE-zeh, *v* to refuse; to decline.

réfuter, reh-fE-teh, *v* to refute; to disprove.

régal, reh-găhl, *m* feast; relish; pleasure.

régaler, reh-găh-leh, *v* to entertain; **se –,** to enjoy oneself.

regard, rer-găhr, *m* look; glance.

regarder, rer-găhr-deh, *v* to look at; to concern.

régate, reh-găht, *f* boat race; regatta.

régénérer, reh-sheh-neh-reh, *v* to regenerate.

régie, reh-shee, *f* administration; excise.

régime, reh-sheem, *m* rule; diet.

région, reh-she-ong, *f* region.

régir, reh-sheer, *v* to govern; to rule.

régisseur, reh-shiss-er, *m* manager; steward.

registre, rer-shees-tr, *m* register; account.

règle, ray-gl, *f* ruler; rule; discipline; *pl* periods (menstrual).

réglé, e, reh-gleh, *pp* & *a* regular; steady.

règlement, ray-gler-mahng, *m* regulation; regulations; rules; settlement.

régler, reh-gleh, *v* to regulate; to rule; to adjust.

réglisse, reh-gleess, *f*

licorice.

règne, rayn-yer, *m* reign; prevalence.

régner, rehn-yeh, *v* to reign; to rule; to prevail.

regorger, rer-gor-sheh, *v* to overflow; to abound.

regret, rer-gray, *m* regret; sorrow.

regretter, rer-gray-teh, *v* to regret; to be sorry.

régularité, reh-ghE-läh-re-teh, *f* regularity.

régula-teur, trice, reh-ghE-läh-**ter,** *a* regulating; standard.

réguli-er, ère,* reh-ghE-le-eh, *a* regular.

réhabituer (se), ser reh-äh-be-tE-eh, *v* to become reaccustomed (**à,** to).

rehausser, rer-ohss-eh, *v* to raise; to enhance.

réimpression, reh-ang-press-e-ong, *f* reprint.

rein, rang, *m* kidney; *pl* loins; back.

reine, rayn, *f* queen; **–claude,** – klohd, greengage; plum.

réinstaller, reh-angs-täh-leh, *v* to reinstall; **se –,** to settle down again.

réintégrer, reh-ang-teh-greh, *v* to reinstate.

réitérer, reh-e-teh-reh, *v* to reiterate.

rejet, rer-**shay,** *m* rejection.

rejeter, rer **sh**-teh, *v* to throw back; to reject.

rejeton, rer **sh**-tong, *m* shoot; offspring.

rejoindre, rer-sho'**ang**-dr, *v* to rejoin; to join; to overtake; **se –,** to meet.

réjoui, e, reh-**sh**oo'e, *pp &* *a* delighted; jolly.

réjouir, reh-shoo-eer, *v* to rejoice; to delight; **se –,** to be delighted (**de,** at, with).

réjouissance, reh-shoo-iss-**ah**ngss, *f* rejoicing.

relâche, rer-lahsh, *f* respite; no performance (theater) ; port of call.

relâche, e, rer-lah-sheh, *a* slack; lax.

relâcher, rer-lah-sheh, *v* to loosen; to abate; to release.

relais, rer-lay, *m* relay; stage.

relater, rer-läh-teh, *v* to relate.

relati-f, ve,* rer-läh-teeff, *a* relative.

relation, rer-läh-se-ong, *f* relation; connection; *pl* intercourse; dealings.

relayer, rer-lay-yeh, *v* to relieve; to relay.

relevé, rerl-veh, *m* statement; abstract.

relevé, e, rerl-veh, *a* raised; high; noble; highly seasoned.

relever, rerl-veh, *v* to raise up again; to relieve; to notice; to dismiss.

relief, rer-le-eff, *m* relief; raised.

relier, rer-le-eh, *v* to bind again; to connect; (books) to bind.

relieur, rer-le-er, *m* bookbinder.

religieu-x, se, rer-le-she-er, *mf* monk; nun; a* religious.

religion, rer-le-she-ong, *f* religion.

reliquaire, rer-le-kair, *m* reliquary; shrine.

relire, rer-leer, *v* to read again.

reliure, rer-le-Er, *f* bookbinding; binding.

reluire, rer-lweer, *v* to shine; to glitter.

remanier, rer-mäh-ne-eh, *v* to handle again; to alter.

remarquable,* rer-mähr-käh-bl, *a* remarkable.

remarque, rer-mährk, *f* remark; observation.

remarquer, rer-mähr-keh, *v* to remark; to observe.

remblai, rahng-blay, *m* embankment.

rembourrer, rahng-boo-reh, v to stuff.

rembourser, rahng-boohr-seh, v to reimburse; to refund.

rembrunir, rahng-brE-neer, v to darken; to make sad.

remède, rer-mayd, m remedy.

remédier, rer-meh-de-eh, v to remedy (à).

remerciement, rer-mair-se-mahng, m thanks.

remercier, rer-mair-se-eh, v to thank (de, for).

remettre, rer-met-tr, v to put back again; to put off; to deliver; to restore; to hand; to recollect.

remise, rer-meez, f putting back; delivery; remittance; discount; putting off; shed.

rémission, reh-miss-e-ong, f forgiveness; remission.

remonte-pente, rer-mongt-pahngt m ski lift.

remonter, rer-mong-teh, v to go up again; to go back to; to wind up; to restock.

remontoir, rer-mong-to'ăhr, m winder (of watch).

remontrer, rer-mong-treh, v to show again; to remonstrate.

remords, rer-mor, m remorse.

remorque, rer-mork, f trailer.

remorquer, rer-mor-keh, v to tow.

rémouleur, reh-moo-ler, m grinder.

remous, rer-moo, m eddy; stir.

rempailler, rahng-pah-yeh, v to restuff with straw.

rempart, rahng-păhr, m rampart.

remplaçant, e, rahng-plăhss-ahng, mf substitute.

remplacer, rahng-plăhss-eh, v to replace; to succeed.

remplir, rahng-pleer, v to fill up; to fulfill.

remporter, rahng-por-teh, v to take back; to carry away; to win.

remue-ménage, rer-mE-meh-năhsh, m bustle; confusion.

remuer, rer-mE-eh, v to move; to stir; to wag.

rémunéra-teur, trice, reh-mE-neh-răh-ter, mf remunerator; a remunerative.

rémunérer, reh-mE-neh-reh, v to reward; to pay.

renaissance, rer-ness-ahngss, f rebirth; revival.

renaître, rer-nay-tr, v to

be born again; to revive.

renard, rer-năhr, m fox.

renchérir, rahng-sheh-reer, v to raise the price of; to become more expensive.

rencontre, rahng-kong-tr, f meeting; encounter.

rencontrer, rahng-kong-treh, v to meet; to come across; to hit upon.

rendement, rahngd-mahng, m yield; output.

rendez-vous, rahng-deh-voo, m appointment; meeting place.

rendre, rahng-dr, v to give back; to render; to yield; to surrender; to make; to express.

rêne, rayn, f usually pl rein.

renégat, rer-neh-găh, m renegade.

renfermé, rahng-fair-meh, m musty smell; withdrawn person.

renfermer, rahng-fair-meh, v to shut up; to contain.

renflement, rahng-fler-mahng, m swelling.

renfoncement, rahng-fongss-mahng, m hollow; recess.

renforcer, rahng-for-seh, v to strengthen; to reinforce.

renfort, rahng-for, *m*
reinforcement; help.

renfrogné, e, rahng-fronn-
yeh, *a* sullen; frowning.

rengaine, rahng-gain, *f*
(*fam*) old story.

rengorger (se), ser rahng-
gor-sheh, *v* to swagger.

reniement, rer-ne-mahng,
m denial; disowning.

renier, rer-ne-eh, *v* to
deny; to disown.

renifler, rer-ne-fleh, *v* to
sniff; to snivel.

renne, renn, *m* reindeer.

renom, rer-nong, *m*
renown.

renommé, e, rer-nomm-
eh, *a* renowned.

renommée, rer-nomm-eh,
f fame.

renoncer, rer-nongss-eh, *v*
to renounce; to give up.

renouer, rer-noo-eh, *v* to
tie again; to renew.

renouveler, rer-noov-leh,
v to renew; to revive.

renouvellement, rer-noo-
vell-mahng, *m* renewal;
renovation; increase.

renseignement, rahng-
sain-yer-mahng, *m*
information; inquiry.

renseigner, rahng-sain-
yeh, *v* to inform; se –, to
inquire.

rente, rahngt, *f* yearly
income; annuity; funds.

renti-er, ère, rahng-te-eh,
mf person of
independent means.

rentrée, rahng-treh, *f*
return; reopening;
payment.

rentrer, rahng-treh, *v* to
enter again; to return; to
gather in; to go home;
to be included in.

renversant, e, rahng-vair-
sahng, *a* stunning.

renverser, rahng-vair-seh,
v to upset; to reverse.

renvoi, rahng-vo'ăh, *m*
sending back; dismissal;
adjournment; reference.

renvoyer, rahng-vo'ăh-
yeh, *v* to send back; to
dismiss; to postpone; to
fire someone.

repaire, rer-pair, *m* den;
lair.

répandre, reh-pahng-dr, *v*
to spill; to spread; se –
to spread about.

répandu, reh-pahng-dE, *a*
widespread; widely
known.

reparaître, rer-păh-ray-tr,
v to reappear.

répara-teur, trice, reh-
păh-răh-ter, *a*
refreshing; restorative.

réparation, reh-păh-răh-
se-ong, *f* repair;
atonement.

réparer, reh-păh-reh, *v* to

repair; to atone for.

repartie, rer-păhr-tee, *f*
retort; repartee.

repartir, rer-păhr-teer, *v*
to set out again; to
retort.

répartir, reh-păhr-teer, *v*
to deal out; to
distribute.

repas, rer-pah, *m* meal;
repast.

repas froid, rer-păh-
fro'ăhd *m* packed lunch.

repasser, rer-pahss-eh, *v*
to pass again; to iron; to
grind; to think over.

repêcher, rer-pay-sheh, *v*
to fish up; (*fam*) to help
out.

repentir (se), ser rer-
pahng-teer, *v* to repent.

repentir, rer-pahng-teer,
m repentance.

répercuter, reh-pair-kE-
teh, *v* to reverberate.

repère, rer-pair, *m*
reference; **point de –**,
po'ang der –, landmark.

repérer, rer-peh-reh, *v* to
mark; to locate; se –, to
take one's bearings.

répertoire, reh-pair-
to'ăhr, *m* repertoire;
repertory.

répéter, reh-peh-teh, *v* to
repeat; to rehearse.

répétition, reh-peh-te-se-
ong, *f* repetition;

rehearsal.

répit, reh-pe, *m* respite.

repl-et, ète, rer-play, *a* fat; plump.

repli, rer-ple, *m* fold; winding; coil; retreat.

replier, rer-ple-eh, *v* to fold again; to coil.

réplique, reh-pleek, *f* rejoinder; cue; replica.

répliquer, reh-ple-keh, *v* to reply; to rejoin.

répondant, reh-pong-dahng, *m* surety; bail.

répondeur automatique or **téléphonique**, reh-pong-der-oh-toh-mäh-teeck, *m* answering machine.

répondre, rer-pong-dr, *v* to answer; to reply; to be security for.

réponse, reh-pongss, *f* answer; reply.

report, rer-por, *m* amount brought forward.

reportage, rer-por-tähsh, *m* coverage; report (newspaper); running commentary; scoop.

reporter, rer-por-teh, *v* to carry over; se –, to refer; *m* news reporter; journalist.

repos, rer-poh, *m* rest.

reposer, rer-poh-zeh, *v* to put back; to rest; se –, to rest; to rely.

repoussant, e, rer-pooss-ahng, *a* repulsive.

repousser, rer-pooss-eh, *v* to push back; to repel; to shoot out again.

reprendre, rer-prahng-dr, *v* to take back; to return; to resume.

représaille, rer-preh-zah'e, *fpl* reprisals; retaliation.

représentant, rer-preh-zahng-tahng, *m* representative.

représentation, rer-preh-zahng-täh-se-ong, *f* representation; performance.

représenter, rer-preh-zahng-teh, *v* to represent; to point out; to perform; to show well.

réprimande, reh-pre-mahngd, *f* rebuke.

réprimander, reh-pre-mahng-deh, *v* to rebuke

réprimer, reh-pre-meh, *v* to repress; to curb.

reprise, rer-preez, *f* resumption; repetition; darning.

repriser, rer-pree-zeh, *v* to mend; to darn.

reproche, rer-prosh, *m* reproach.

reprocher, rer-prosh-eh, *v* to reproach.

reproduire, rer-prod-weer,

v to reproduce; se –, to happen again.

réprouver, reh-proo-veh, *v* to reprobate; to disallow.

reptile, rehp-teel, *m* reptile.

repu, e, rer-pE, *a* satiated.

république, reh-pE-bleeck, *f* republic.

répudier, reh-pE-de-eh, *v* to repudiate.

répugnant, e, reh-pEEn-yahng, *a* repugnant.

répulsi-f, ve, reh-pEEl-siff, *a* repulsive.

réputation, reh-pE-täh-se-ong, *f* reputation; character.

réputer, reh-pE-teh, *v* to repute; to deem.

requérant, e, rer-keh-rahng, *m a* applicant; plaintiff.

requérir, rer-keh-reer, *v* to require; to demand.

requête, rer-kayt, *f* request; petition.

requin, rerkang, *m* shark.

requis, e, rerer-ke, *a* necessary; requisite.

réseau, reh-zoh, *m* net; network; system.

réserve, reh-zairv, *f* reservation; reserve; store.

réserver, reh-zair-veh, *v* to reserve.

réservoir, reh-zair-vo'ăhr, *m* reservoir; tank; pond.

résidence, reh-ze-dahngss, *f* residence; abode.

résider, reh-ze-deh, *v* to reside.

résidu, reh-ze-dE, *m* residue.

résignation, reh-zeen-yăh-se-ong, *f* resignation.

résigner, reh-zeen-yeh, *v* to resign.

résine, reh-zeen, *f* resin; rosin.

résistant, e, reh-zisstahng, *a* resistant; tough.

résister, reh-ziss-teh, *v* to resist.

résolu,* e, reh-zoll-E, *a* resolute.

résolution, reh-zoll-E-se-ong, *f* resolution.

résonner, reh-zonn-eh, *v* to resound.

résoudre, reh-zoo-dr, *v* to resolve; to dissolve.

respect, ress-pay, *m* respect; regard.

respectueu-x, se,* ress-payk-tE-er, *a* respectful.

respirer, ress-pe-reh, *v* to breathe; to inhale.

resplendir, ress-plahng-deer *v* to be resplendent.

resplendissant, e, ress-plahng-diss-ahng, *a* resplendent.

responsabilité, ress-pong-săh-be-le-teh, *f* responsibility.

responsable, ress-pongss-ăh-bl, *a* responsible; answerable.

ressaisir, rer-say-zeer, *v* to seize again; **se–,** to recover oneself.

ressembler, rer-sahng-bleh, *v* to resemble.

ressemeler, rer-serm-leh, *v* to resole.

ressentiment, rer-sahng-te-mahng, *m* resentment.

ressentir, rer-sahng-teer *v* to feel; to resent.

resserrer, rer-say-reh, *v* to tighten.

ressort, rer-sor, *m* spring; jurisdiction; department.

ressortir, rer-sor-teer, *v* to get out again; to stand out; to result from (**de**); to be in the jurisdiction of.

ressource, rer-soohrss, *f* resource.

ressusciter, reh-sE-se-teh, *v* to resuscitate.

restant, ress-tahng, *m* remainder.

restaurant, ress-toh-rahng, *m* restaurant.

restauration rapide, ress-toh-răh-se-ong-răh-peed, *f* fast food.

restaurer, ress-toh-reh, *v* to restore; to refresh.

reste, resst, *m* remainder; *pl* remnants; scraps; **du–,** dE–, besides.

rester, ress-teh, *v* to remain; to be left; to stay.

restituer, ress-te-tE-eh, *v* to refund; to restore.

restreindre, ress-trang-dr, *v* to restrict.

résultat, reh-zEEl-tăh, *m* result.

résulter, reh-zEEl-teh, *v* to result.

résumé, reh-zE-meh, *m* summary; resume.

résumer, reh-zE-meh, *v* to sum up; to summarize.

rétablir, reh-tăh-bleer, *v* to restore; to reestablish; **se–,** to recover.

rétablissement, reh-tăh-bliss-mahng, *m* restoration; recovery.

retard, rer-tăhr, *m* delay; enahng–, late.

retardataire, rer-tăhr-dăh-tair, *mf* & *a* straggler; in arrears.

retarder, rer-tăhr-deh, *v* to delay; to postpone; to be too slow.

retenir, rert-neer, *v* to detain; to withhold; to book.

retentir, rer-tahng-teer, *v*

to resound.

retentissant, e, rer-tahng-tiss-ahng, *a* resounding; noisy.

retentissement, rer-tahng-tiss-mahng, *m* resounding.

retenue, rert-nE, *f* modesty; reserve; stoppage; detention.

réti-f,ve, reh-teeff, *a* restive.

retiré, e, rer-te-reh, *pp* & *a* withdrawn; secluded; retired.

retirer, rer-te-reh, *v* to draw again; to withdraw; to retract.

retombée, rer-tong-beh, *f* fallout (radioactive).

retomber, rer-tong-beh, *v* to fall again; to fall back; to hang down.

rétorquer, reh-tor-keh, *v* to retort.

retoucher, rer-too-sheh, *v* to touch up.

retour, rer-toohr, *m* return; recurrence; reciprocity.

retourner, rertoohr-neh, *v* to turn; to return.

retracer, rer-trăhss-eh, *v* to retrace; to recall.

rétracter, reh-trăhck-teh, *v* to retract; to recant.

retrai-te, rer-trayt, *f* retreat; retirement;;

shelter.

retraiter, rer-tray-teh, *v* to pension off.

rétrécir, reh-treh-seer, *v* to narrow; to shrink.

rétribuer, reh-tre-bE-eh, *v* to remunerate.

rétribution, reh-tre-bE-se-ong, *f* reward; salary.

rétrograder, reh-trog-răh-deh, *v* to move back; to demote.

retrousser, rer-trooss-eh, *v* to tuck up; to turn up.

retrouver, rer-troo-veh, *v* to find again.

rétroviseur, reh-tro-ve-zer, *m* side-view mirror (auto).

réunion, reh-E-ne-ong, *f* reunion; meeting; gathering.

réunir, reh-E-neer, *v* to reunite; to gather; se –, to meet.

réussir, reh-EEss-eer, *v* to succeed; to thrive.

réussite, reh-EEss-eet, *f* success.

revanche, rer-vahngsh, *f* retaliation; revenge; return (games); en –, ahng –, in return.

rêve, rayv, *m* dream.

revêche, rer-vaysh, *a* peevish, cantankerous.

réveil, reh-vay'e, *m* awakening; alarm clock.

réveiller, reh-vay'e-yeh, *v* to awake; to rouse; to revive; se –, to wake up.

réveillon, reh-vay'e-yong, *m* midnight supper (New Year's and Christmas).

révéler, reh-veh-leh, *v* to reveal; to disclose.

revenant, rerv-nahng, *m* ghost.

revendeu-r, se, rer-vahng-der, *mf* retailer.

revendication, rer-vahng-de-käh-se-ong, *f* claim.

revendiquer, rer-vahng-de-keh, *v* to claim.

revendre, rer-vahng-dr, *v* to sell again.

revenir, rerv-neer, *v* to come back; to recur; to grow again; to amount; to please; to cost.

revenu, rerv-nE, *m* income; revenue.

rêver, ray-veh, *v* to dream; to muse.

reverbère, reh-vair-bair, *m* streetlight.

révérence, reh-veh-rahngss, *f* reverence; curtsy.

révérer, reh-veh-reh, *v* to revere.

rêverie, rayv-ree, *f* musing; dreaming.

revers, rer-vair, *m* back;

reverse; facing (coat).

revêtir, rer-vay-teer, *v* to clothe.

rêveu-r, se, ray-ver, *mf* dreamer; *a** dreaming; pensive.

revirement, rer-veer-mah*n*g, *m* sudden change; transfer.

reviser, réviser, rer-ve-zeh, reh-ve-zeh, *v* to revise.

revivre, rer-vee-vr, *v* to live again.

révocation, reh-vock-ăh-se-ong, *f* repeal; dismissal.

revoir, rer-vo'ăhr, *v* to see again; **au –,** oh –, goodbye.

révolte, reh-vollt, *f* revolt.

révolter, rer-voll-teh, *v* to rouse; to shock.

révolu, e, reh-voll-E, *a* in days gone by; past.

révolution, reh-voll-E-se-ong, *f* revolution.

revue, rer-vE, *f* review; survey; magazine.

rez-de-chaussée, reh-der-shohss-eh, *m* first floor.

rhabiller (se), ser răh-bee-yeh, *v* to get dressed again.

rhum, romm, *m* rum.

rhumatisme, rE-măh-tissm, *m* rheumatism.

rhume, rEEm, *m* cold.

riant, e, re-ahng, *a* smiling; pleasant.

ricaner, re-kăh-neh, *v* to sneer; to laugh unpleasantly.

riche, reesh, *a** rich; copious; fertile; *mf* wealthy person.

richesse, re-shess, *f* riches; wealth; fertility.

ricin, re-sang, *m* castor-oil plant.

ricochet, re-kosh-ay, *m* rebound.

ride, reed, *f* wrinkle; ripple.

rideau, re-doh, *m* curtain; screen.

rider, re-deh, *v* to wrinkle; to ripple.

ridicule, re-de-kEEl, *m* ridiculousness; *a** ridiculous.

ridiculiser, re-de-kE-le-zeh, *v* to ridicule.

rien, re-ang, *m* nothing; anything; trifle; **–que, –** ker, only; **cela ne fait –,** slăh n'fay –, that does not matter.

rieu-r, se, re-er, *n & a* laughter; laughing.

rigide,* re-sheed, *a* rigid; stern; strict.

rigole, re-gol, *f* trench; drain; gutter.

rigoler, re-goll-eh, *v* (*pop*) to laugh; to giggle.

rigolo,–ote, re-goll-o, *a* (*pop*) jolly; funny.

rigoureu-x, se,* re-goo-rer, *a* rigorous.

rigueur, re-gher, *f* rigor; **de –,** der –, indispensable.

rime, reem, *f* rhyme.

rincer, rang-seh, *v* to rinse.

ripaille, re-pah'e, *f* (*fam*) feasting.

riposte, re-post, *f* parry and thrust; repartee.

rire, reer, *v* to laugh; to scoff at; to joke; *m* laughter.

ris, re, *m* sweetbread.

risée, re-zeh, *f* laughingstock.

risible,* re-zee-bl, *a* laughable; ludicrous.

risqué, e, riss-keh, *a* hazardous; improper.

risquer, riss-keh, *v* to risk; to venture.

rivage, re-văhsh, *m* shore; bank.

rival, e, re-văhl, *a* rival.

rivaliser, re-văh-le-zeh, *v* to rival; to vie; to compete.

rive, reev, *f* bank; shore; border.

river, re-veh, *v* to rivet.

rivière, re-ve-air, *f* river; stream.

riz, re, *m* rice.

robe, rob, *f* robe; gown; dress; **–de chambre, –**

der shahng-br, bathrobe.

robinet, rob-e-nay, *m* faucet.

robuste, rob-EESt, *a* robust; sturdy; stalwart.

roc, rock, *m* rock.

rocailleu-x, se, rock-ah'e-er, *a* stony; rugged.

roche, rosh, *f* rock; boulder.

rocher, rosh-eh, *m* rock (mass of).

rock and roll, rock-eh-roll *m* rock and roll.

rôder, rohd-eh, *v* to prowl; to roam.

rogner, ronn-yeh, *v* to cut; to pare; to clip.

rognon, ronn-yong, *m* kidney (of edible animals).

roi, ro'ǎh, *m* king.

rôle, rohl, *m* roll; list; part; character.

roman, romm-ahng, *m* novel.

romance, romm-ahngss, *f* sentimental song.

romanci-er, ère, romm-ahngss-e-eh, *mf* novelist.

romanesque, romm-ǎhn-esk, *a* romantic.

romantique, romm-ahng-teeck *a* romantic.

romarin, romm-ǎh-rang, *m* rosemary.

rompre, rong-pr, *v* to break; to snap; to break

in.

ronce, rongss, *f* blackberry bush.

rond, e,* rong, *a* round; plump; full; (*fam*) drunk.

rond, rong, *m* round; circle.

ronde, rongd, *f* patrol; semibreve (music).

rondelle, rong-dell, *f* washer; slice.

rondeur, rong-der, *f* roundness; plumpness; frankness.

ronflant, e, rong-flahng, *a* snoring; bombastic.

ronfler, rong-fleh, *v* to snore; to roar.

ronger, rong-sheh, *v* to nibble; to corrode; to erode.

ronron, rong-rong, *m* purr.

rosaire, roz-air, *m* rosary.

rosbif, ross-beeff, *m* roast beef.

rose, rohz, *f* rose; *a* rose; rosy; pink; *m* pink (color).

roseau, roz-oh, *m* reed.

rosée, roh-zeh, *f* dew.

rosier, roh-ze-eh, *m* rosebush.

rosser, ross-eh, *v* (*fam*) to thrash.

rossignol, ross-een-yol, *m* nightingale; (*fam*) picklock; unsaleable

article.

rot, roh, *m* (*fam*) belch.

rôti, roh-te, *m* roast meat; joint.

rôtir, roh-teer, *v* to roast.

rotule, rot-EEl, *f* kneecap.

rouage, roo-ǎhsh, *m* wheel-work; machinery.

roucouler, roo-koo-leh, *v* to coo.

roue, roo, *f* wheel; **faire la –,** fair lǎh –, to strut; to turn cartwheels.

roué, e, roo-eh, *mf* rake; *a* sly; artful.

rouet, roo-ay, *m* spinning wheel.

rouge, roosh, *m* red color; red paint; *a* red.

rougeaud, e, roo-shoh, *a* (*fam*) red-faced.

rouge-gorge, roosh-gorsh, *m* robin.

rougeole, roo-shol, *f* measles.

rougeur, roo-sher, *f* redness.

rougir, roo-sheer, *v* to redden; to blush.

rouille, roo'e-ye, *f* rusty; blight.

rouillé, roo'e-yeh, *a* rust; rusted.

rouleau, roo-loh, *m* roll; roller.

roulement, rool-mahng, *m* rolling; rumbling; rotation.

rouler, roo-leh, *v* to roll; to wheel; to revolve.

roulette, roo-lett, *f* castor; roulette.

roulis, roo-le, *m* rolling.

roulotte, roo-lot, *f* caravan.

rouspéter, rooss-peh-teh, *v* (*pop*) to protest; to complain.

rousseur, rooss-er, *f* redness; **tache de** –, tähsh der –, freckle.

roussir, rooss-eer, *v* to redden; to singe; to scorch.

route, root, *f* road; route; course; journey.

routine, roo-teen, *f* routine; rote.

rou-x, sse, roo, *a* reddish; red-haired; russet.

royal, e,* ro'äh-yähl, *a* royal; regal.

royaume, ro'äh-yohm, *m* kingdom.

royauté, ro'äh-yoh-teh, *f* kingship; royalty.

ruade, rE-ähd, *f* kick (horse's).

ruban, rE-bahng, *m* ribbon.

rubéole, rE-beh-oll, *f* German measles.

rubis, rE-be, *m* ruby.

ruche, rEEsh, *f* beehive.

rude,* rEEd, *a* harsh; severe; uneven; rough.

rudesse, rE-dess, *f* harshness; roughness; severity.

rudoyer, rE-do'äh-yeh, *v* to treat roughly; to bully.

rue, rE, *f* street; road; thoroughfare.

ruelle, rE-ell, *f* lane; alley.

ruer, rE-eh, *v* to kick(horse's); **se** –, to rush.

rugby, rEg-be *m* rugby.

rugir, rE-sheer, *v* to roar.

rugissement, rE-shiss-mahng, *m* roaring; howling.

rugueu-x, se, rE-gher, *a* rough; rugged.

ruine, rween, *f* ruin; decay; downfall.

ruineu-x, se,* rwee-ner, *a* ruinous.

ruisseau, rweess-oh, *m* stream; brook; gutter.

ruisseler, rweess-leh, *v* to stream; to trickle down.

rumeur, rE-mer, *f* rumor; noise; report.

ruminant, e, rE-me-nahng, *m* & *a* ruminant; ruminating.

rupture, rEEp-tEEr, *f* rupture; breaking.

rural, e, rE-rähl, *a* rural.

ruse, rEEz, *f* cunning; artfulness; dodge.

rusé, e, rEE-zeh, *a* cunning; sly; wily; artful.

ruser, rEE-zeh, *v* to use cunning; to dodge.

rustaud, e, rEEss-toh, *a* boorish.

rustique, rEEss-teeck, *a* rural; rough.

rustre, rEEss-tr, *m* & *a* boor; boorish.

rut, rEEt, *m* rut.

rythme, reetm, *m* rhythm.

sa, săh, *poss af* his; her; its.

sabbat, săh-băh, *m* Sabbath.

sable, săh-bl, *m* sand; gravel.

sablonneu-x, se, săh-blonn-er, *a* sandy.

sabot, săh-bo, *m* wooden clog; hoof.

sabotage, săh-bot-ăhsh, *m* sabotage.

saboter, săh-bot-eh, *v* to bungle.

sabre, săh-br, *m* saber; broadsword.

sac, săhck, *m* sack; bag; knapsack.

sac à dos, săhk-ăh-doh *m* rucksack; backpack.

saccade, săh-kăhd, *f* jerk.

saccager, săh-kăh-sheh, *v* to ransack; to upset.

sac de couchage, săhk- der-koo-shăhsh *m* sleeping bag.

sacerdoce, săh-sair-doss, *m* priesthood.

sachet, săh-sheh *m* sachet; teabag.

sacoche, săh-kosh, *f* bag; saddlebag.

sacre, săh-kr, *m* consecration; coronation.

sacrement, săh-krer- mahng, *m* sacrament.

sacrer, săh-kreh, *v* to consecrate; to crown; to curse.

sacrifier, săh-kre-fe-eh, *v* to sacrifice.

sacrilège, săh-kre-laysh, *m* & *a* sacrilege; sacrilegious.

sacristain, săh-kriss-tang, *m* sexton.

sacristie, săh-kriss-tee, *f* vestry.

sagace,* săh-găhss, *a* sagacious; shrewd.

sage, săhsh, *a** wise; discreet; well-behaved.

sage-femme, săhsh-făhm, *f* midwife.

sagesse, săh-shess, *f* wisdom; prudence; good behavior.

saignant, e, sayn-yahng, *a* bleeding; underdone (meat); rare.

saigner, sayn-yeh, *v* to bleed.

saillie, sah'e-yee, *f* projection; spurt; (*fam*) outburst.

saillir, sah'e-yeer, *v* to jut out; to stand out.

sain, e,* sang, *a* sound; healthy; wholesome.

saindoux, sang-doo, *m* lard.

saint, e, sang, *mf* & *a** saint; holy; sacred.

sainteté, sang-ter-teh, *f* saintliness; holiness; sanctity.

saisie, say-zee, *f* seizure; distraint.

saisir, say-zeer, *v* to seize; to startle; to understand; to distrain.

saisissant, e, say-ziss-ahng, *a* startling; thrilling.

saisissement, say-ziss-

mahng, *m* shock; chill.

saison, say-zong, *f* season; time.

salade, săh-lăhd, *f* salad.

saladier, săh-lăh-de-eh, *m* salad bowl.

salaire, săh-lair, *m* wages; salary; (*fig*) reward.

salarié, e, săh-lăh-re-eh, *pp* & *a* paid.

sale,* săhl, *a* dirty; messy.

salé, e, săh-leh, *pp* & *a* salted; tasty; spicy (story).

saler, săh-leh, *v* to salt; (*fig*) to fleece.

saleté, săhl-teh, *f* dirtiness; nastiness; obscenity; dirty trick.

salière, săh-le-air, *f* saltbox.

salir, săh-leer, *v* to soil; to dirty; to taint.

salissant, săh-le-sahng, *a* soiling; messy; easily soiled.

salive, săh-leev, *f* saliva; spittle.

salle, săhl, *f* hall; large room; **–à manger,** – ăh mahng-**sheh,** dining room; **–d'attente,** – dăh-tahngt, waitingroom.

salon, săh-long, *m* living room; exhibition.

salopette, săh-lo-pet, *f* overalls; dungarees (jeans).

salubre, săhl-EE-br, *a* healthy; salubrious.

saluer, săh-lE-eh, *v* to salute; to bow; to greet.

salut, săh-lE, *m* salute; greeting; safety; salvation.

salutaire,* săh-lE-tair, *a* salutary; beneficial.

salutation, săh-lE-tăh-se-ong, *f* salutation; greetings.

samedi, săhm-de, *m* Saturday.

sanction, sahngk-se-ong, *f* sanction; penalty; approval.

sanctuaire, sahngk-tE-air, *m* sanctuary.

sandale, sahng-dăhl, *f* sandal.

sang, sahng, *m* blood; race; parentage.

sang-froid, sahng-fro'ăh, *m* coolness.

sanglant, e, sahng-glahng, *a* bloody; outrageous.

sangler, sahng-gleh, *v* to strap; to gird.

sanglier, sahng-gle-eh, *m* wild boar.

sangloter, sahng-glot-eh, *v* to sob.

sangsue, sahng-sE, fleech; (*fig*) extortioner.

sanguinaire, sahng-ghe-nair, *a* bloodthirsty.

sanitaire, săh-ne-tair, *a* sanitary.

sans, sahng, *prep* without; but for; ...less.

sans-façon, sahng-făh-song, *m* straightforwardness.

sans-gêne, sahng-**shayn,** *m* inconsiderateness.

sans plomb, sahng-plong *a* unleaded (gas, fuel).

santé, sahng-teh, *f* health.

saper, săh-peh, *v* to undermine.

sapeur, săh-per, **–pompier,** – pong-pe-eh, fireman.

sapin, săh-pang, *m* fir tree.

sarcasme, săhr-kăhssm, *m* sarcasm.

sarcler, săhr-kleh, *v* to weed.

sardine, săhr-deen, *f* sardine.

sarrau, săh-roh, *m* smock.

satané, e, săh-tăh-neh, *a* confounded.

satellite, săh-teh-leet, *m* satellite.

satiné, e, săh-te-neh, *a* satin-like; glazed; smooth.

satire, săh-teer, *f* satire.

satisfaction, săh-tiss-făhck-se-ong, *f* satisfaction.

satisfaire, săh-tiss-fair, *v* to satisfy; to meet.

satisfaisant, e, săh-tiss-fer-zahng, *a* satisfactory.

satisfait, e, săh-tiss-fay, *a* satisfied.

saturer, săh-tE-reh, *v* to saturate (**de,** with).

sauce, sohss, *f* sauce; gravy.

saucer, sohss-eh, *v* to sop; (*fam*) to drench; to reprimand.

saucière, sohss-e-air, *f* gravy-boat.

saucisse, sohss-eess, *f* sausage.

saucisson, sohss-iss-ong, *m* big, dry sausage.

sauf, sohff, *prep* save; except; but; subject to.

sau-f, ve, sohff, *a* safe; secure.

sauf-conduit, sohf-kong-dwee, *m* safe conduct.

sauge, sohsh, *f* sage.

saugrenu, e, soh-grer-nE, *a* absurd; preposterous.

saule, sohl, *m* willow; **–pleureur,** – pler-rer, weeping willow.

saumâtre, soh-mah-tr, *a* brackish; briny.

saumon, soh-mong, *m* salmon.

sauna. soh-năh *m* sauna.

saupoudrer, soh-poo-dreh, *v* to sprinkle (**de,** with).

saur, sor, *a* salted and smoked.

saut, soh, *m* leap; jump.

sauter, soh-teh, *v* to leap;

to jump; to blow up; to skip; to fry quickly.

sauterelle, soht-rell, *f* grasshopper.

sauteu-r, se, soh-ter, *mf* & *a* leaper; leaping.

sautiller, soh-tee-yeh, *v* to hop; to skip.

sauvage, soh-văhsh, *m* savage; *a** wild; untamed; shy; unsociable.

sauvagerie, soh-văhsh-ree, *f* savagery; unsociability.

sauvegarde, sohv-găhrd, *f* safeguard.

sauve-qui-peut, sohv-ke-per, *m* stampede.

sauver, soh-veh, *v* to save; to rescue; **se –,** to escape; to run away.

sauvetage, sohv-tăhsh, *m* lifesaving; rescue; salvage.

sauveur, soh-ver, *m* saver; deliverer.

savamment, săh-văh-mahng, *adv* skillfully; knowingly.

savant, e, săh-vahng, *m* scientist; scholar; *a* learned; skillful.

savate, săh-văht, *f* shoe.

saveur, săh-ver, *f* taste; savor; relish; flavor.

savoir, săh-vo'ăhr, *v* to know; to understand; to

be able to; *m* learning.

savoir-faire, săh-vo'ăhr-fair, *m* skill; ability.

savoir-vivre, săh-vo'ăhr-vee-vr, *m* good breeding.

savon, săh-vong, *m* soap.

savonner, săh-vonn-eh, *v* to soap; to lather.

savonnette, săh-vonn-ett, *f* bar of soap.

savourer, săh-voo-reh, *v* to relish.

scabreu-x, se, skăh-brer, *a* rugged; dangerous; ticklish.

scandaleu-x, se,* skahng-dăh-ler, *a* scandalous.

scarlatine, skăhr-lăh-teen, *f* scarlet fever.

sceau, soh, *m* seal.

scélérat, e, seh-leh-răh, *mf* & *a* scoundrel; villainous.

sceller, sell-eh, *v* to seal.

scénario, seh-năh-re-o, *m* scenario; screenplay.

scène, sayn, *f* scene; stage; row.

scepticisme, sehp-tiss-eessm, *m* skepticism.

sceptre, sayp-tr, *m* scepter.

schéma, sheh-măh, *m* diagram; schema.

scie, se, *f* saw.

sciemment, se-ăh-mahng, *adv* knowingly.

science, se-ahngss, *f* science; learning.

scientifique,* se-ahng-te-feeck, *a* scientific.

scier, se-eh, *v* to saw.

scierie, se-ree, *f* sawmill.

scintiller, sang-tee-yeh, *v* to twinkle (of star); to sparkle.

scission, siss-eong, *f* division; secession.

sciure, se-EEr, *f* sawdust.

scolaire, skoll-air, *a* scholastic; school.

scorbut, skor-bE, *m* scurvy.

scrupule, skrE-pEEl, *m* scruple; scrupulousness.

scrupuleu-x, se,* skrE-pE-ler, *a* scrupulous; precise.

scruter, skrE-teh, *v* to scrutinize.

scrutin, skrE-tang, *m* ballot; poll.

sculpter, skEEl-teh, *v* to sculpt; to carve.

se, ser, *pers pron* oneself; himself; herself; itself; themselves; each other; one another.

séance, seh-ahngss, *f* sitting; meeting; performance.

seau, soh, *m* bucket; pail.

sec, sayk, sèche,* saysh, *a* dry; harsh; barren.

sécher, seh-sheh, *v* to dry.

sécheresse, sehsh-ress, *f* dryness; drought;

barrenness.

second, ser-gong, *m* assistant; second floor.

second, e,* ser-gong, *a* second.

seconde, ser-gongd, *f* second (time).

seconder, ser-gong-deh, *v* to support; to further.

secouer, ser-koo-eh, *v* to shake; to shock; to stir up.

secourable, ser-koo-răh-bl, *a* helpful.

secourir, ser-koo-reer, *v* to help; to relieve.

secours, ser-koohr, *m* help; relief.

secousse, ser-kooss, *f* shake; jolt; blow; shock.

secret, ser-kray, *m* secret; secrecy.

secr-et, ète,* ser-kray, *a* secret; private.

secrétaire, ser-kreh-tair, *mf* secretary; writing desk.

secrétariat, ser-kreh-tăh-re-ăh, *m* secretaryship; secretariat.

sécréter, ser-kreh-teh, *v* to secrete.

sectaire, seck-tair, *mf & a* sectarian.

secte, seckt, *f* sect.

secteur, seckt-er, *m* sector; district area (served by electricity, etc).

section, seck-se-ong, *f* section; fare zone.

séculaire, seh-kE-lair, *a* age-old; time-honored.

séculi-er, ère, seh-kE-le-eh, *a* secular.

sécurité, seh-kE-re-teh, *f* security.

sédentaire, seh-dahng-tair, *a* sedentary.

séditieu-x, se,* seh-de-se-er, *a* seditious.

séduc-teur, trice, seh-dEEk-ter, *mf & a* seducer; fascinating; seductive.

séduire, seh-dweer, *v* to seduce; to delude; to captivate.

séduisànt, e, seh-dwee-zahng, *a* captivating; enticing; glamorous (person).

seigle, say-gl, *m* rye.

seigneur, sehn-yer, *m* lord.

sein, sang, *m* breast; bosom; (*fig*) womb; midst.

seize, sayz, *m & a* sixteen.

seizième, say-ze-aym, *m & a* sixteenth.

séjour, seh-shoohr, *m* stay; sojourn; living room.

séjourner, seh-shoohr-neh, *v* to stay; to dwell.

sel, sell, *m* salt; (*fam*) wit.

self-service, self-sair-veess *a* self-service.

selle, sell, *f* saddle; stool.

seller, sell-eh, *v* to saddle.

selon, ser-long, *prep* according to; **–que,** –ker, according as.

semailles, ser-mah'e, *fpl* sowing; sowing time.

semaine, ser-main, *f* week; week's wages.

semblable, sahng-blăh-bl, *m* fellow-man; *a** alike; similar.

semblant, sahng-blahng, *m* appearance; show; **faire –,** fair –, to pretend.

sembler, sahng-bleh, *v* to seem; to appear.

semelle, ser-mell, *f* sole (boots, shoes).

semence, ser-mahngss, *f* seed.

semer, ser-meh, *v* to sow; to scatter.

semestre, ser-mays-tr, *m* half-year.

semeu-r, se, ser-mer, *mf* sower.

semi, ser-me, *prefix* semi; half.

séminaire, seh-me-nair, *m* seminary.

semonce, ser-mongss, *f* lecture; reprimand; rebuke.

semoule, ser-mool, *f* semolina.

sénat, seh-năh, *m* senate.

senilité, seh-ne-le-teh, *f* senility.

sens, sahngss, *m* sense; senses; opinion; direction.

sensation, sahng-săh-se-ong, *f* sensation; excitement.

sensé, e, sahng-seh, *a* sensible; judicious.

sensibilité, sahng-se-be-le-teh, *f* sensibility; sensitivity.

sensible, sahng-see-bl, *a* sensitive; obvious; sore (of flesh, etc.).

sensiblement, sahng-se-bler-mahng, *adv* perceptibly; greatly.

sensuel, le,* sahng-sE-ell, *a* sensual.

sentence, sahng-tahngss, *f* sentence; maxim; judgment.

senteur, sahng-ter, *f* scent; fragrance.

senti, e, sahng-te, *a* felt; vividly expressed.

sentier, sahng-te-eh, *m* path.

sentiment, sahng-te-mahng, *m* sentiment; sense; feeling.

sentimental, e, sahng-te-mahng-tăhl *a* romantic.

sentinelle, sahng-te-nell, *f* sentry.

sentir, sahng-teer, *v* to feel; to smell; to taste of; to see; to foresee.

séparation, seh-păh-răh-se-ong, *f* separation.

séparer, seh-păh-reh, *v* to separate; to divide.

sept, sett, *m* & *a* seven.

septembre, sayp-tahng-br, *m* September.

septentrional, e, sayp-tahng-tre-onn-ăhl, *a* northern.

septième, say-te-aym, *m* & *a* seventh.

septuple, sayp-tE-pl, *m* & *a* septuple; sevenfold.

sépulture, seh-pEEl-tEEr, *f* tomb; burial.

séquestre, seh-kayss-tr, *m* sequestration; sequestrator.

serein, ser-rang, *m* evening dew.

sérénade, seh-reh-năhd, *f* serenade.

sérénité, seh-reh-ne-teh, *f* serenity.

sergent, sair-shahng, *m* sergeant.

série, seh-re, *f* series; set.

sérieu-x, se, * seh-re-er, *a* serious; earnest; grave.

serin, ser-rang, *m* canary; (*pop*) simpleton.

seringue, ser-rang-gh, *f* syringe.

serment, sair-mahng, *m*

oath.

sermon, sair-mong, *m*
sermon; lecture.

sermonner, sair-monn-eh,
v to lecture.

serpe, sairp, *f* billhook.

serpent, sair-pahng, *m*
serpent; snake.

serpenter, sair-pahng-teh,
v to meander.

serpette, sair-pett, *f*
pruning knife.

serpillière, sair-pe-yair, *f*
dishcloth.

serre, sair, *f* greenhouse;
pressing; talon.

serré, e, say-reh, *a* close;
compact; precise; tight.

serrer, say-reh, *v* to
squeeze; to tighten.

serrure, say-rEEr, *f* lock.

serrurier, say-rE-re-eh, *m*
locksmith.

servant, sair-vahng, *m*
gunner; *a* serving.

servante, sair-vahngt, *f*
servant.

serviable, sair-ve-ăh-bl, *a*
obliging.

service, sair-veess, *m*
service; attendance;
duty; set; divine service.

service des chambres,
sair-veess-deh-chang-br
m room service.

service de réanimation,
sair-veess-der-reh-ăh-
ne-măh-se-ong *m*

intensive care.

serviette, sair-ve-ett, *f*
napkin; towel; briefcase.

servile,* sair-veell, *a*
servile.

servir, sair-veer, *v* to
serve; to wait upon; **se
–de,** to use.

serviteur, sair-ve-ter, *m*
servant.

ses, say, *poss a pl* his; her;
its; one's.

session, sess-e-ong, *f*
session; sitting; term
(law).

seuil, ser'e, *m* threshold;
sill; doorstep; beginning.

seul, e,* serl, *a* only; sole;
alone; mere; single.

sève, sayv, *f* sap; (*fig*)
vigor.

sévère,* seh-vair, *a*
severe; stern; harsh.

sévir, seh-veer, *v* to
punish severely; to rage.

sevrer, ser-vreh, *v* to
wean.

sexagénaire, secks-ăh-
sheh-nair, *mf & a* sixty
year old.

sexe, secks, *m* sex.

sexiste, secks-eest *a* sexist.

sextuple, secks-tEE-pl, *m*
& a sixfold.

sexuel, le, secks-E-ell, *a*
sexual.

sexy, seck-se *a* sexy.

si, se, *adv* so; however;

yes; *conj* if; whether.

SIDA; sida; Sida, see-
dăh, *m* AIDS.

siècle, se-ay-kl, *m* century;
time; age.

siège, se-aysh, *m* seat; see;
siege.

siéger, se-eh-sheh, *v* to sit;
to hold sittings.

sien, ne (le, la), ler se-
ang, lăh se-enn, *poss
pron* his; hers; its.

sieste, se-esst, *f* siesta;
afternoon nap.

siffler, se-fleh, *v* to
whistle; to hiss.

sifflet, se-flay, *m* whistle;
hiss.

signal, seen-yăhl, *m*
signal.

signalé, e, seen-yăh-leh, *a*
signal.

signalement, seen-yăhl-
mahng, *m* description.

signaler, seen-yăh-leh, *v*
to signal; to point out.

signataire, seen-yăh-tair,
m signer.

signature, seen-yăh-tEEr, *f*
signature.

signe, seen-yer, *m* sign;
mark; token.

signer, seen-yeh, *v* to sign;
se –, to cross oneself.

signifier, seen-yee-fee-eh,
v to mean; to notify.

silence, se-lahngss, *m*
silence; stillness.

silencieu-x, se,* se-lahng-se-er, *a* silent; still.

sillon, see-yong, *m* furrow; trail; groove (record).

sillonner, see-yonn-eh, *v* to furrow; to plough.

simagrée, se-măh-greh, *f* grimace; *pl* fuss.

similaire, se-me-lair, *a* similar.

simple, sang-pl, *m* simpleton; *a** simple; single; plain; **(billet)** –, bee-yeh- sang pl, *a* one-way (ticket).

simplicité, sang-ple-se-teh, *f* simplicity.

simulacre, se-mE-lăh-kr, *m* image; sham.

simuler, se-mE-leh, *v* to simulate; to feign.

simultané, e, se-mEEl-tăh-neh, *a* simultaneous.

simultanément, se-mEEl-tăh-neh-mahng, *adv* simultaneously.

sincère,* sang-sair, *a* sincere; candid; true.

sincérité, sang-seh-re-teh, *f* sincerity; honesty.

singe, sangsh, *m* ape; monkey.

singer, sang-sheh, *v* to mimic.

singularité, sang-ghE-lăh-re-teh, *f* singularity.

singuli-er, ère,* sang-ghE-le-eh, *a* singular;

peculiar; odd.

sinistre, se-neess-tr, *m* disaster; *a** sinister; gloomy.

sinon, se-nong, *conj* if not; otherwise; else; except.

sinueu-x, se, se-nE-er, *a* winding.

sirène, se-rain, *f* mermaid; siren.

sirop, se-roh, *m* syrup.

sis, e, se, *a* situated.

site, seet, *m* site; landscape; scenery.

sitôt, se-toh, *adv* as soon; **–que,** – ker, as soon as.

situation, se-tE-ăh-se-ong, *f* situation; position.

situé, e, se-tE-eh, *a* situated.

six, seess (before a consonant, see), *m* & *a* six.

sixième, se-ze-aym, *m* & *a* sixth.

skateboard, sket-bor *m* skateboard.

ski, ske, *m* ski; skiing.

skier, ske-eh, *v* to ski.

ski nautique, ske-noh-teeck *m* waterskiing.

sobre,* sobr, *a* sober; temperate; sparing.

sobriété, sob-re-eh-teh, *f* sobriety.

sobriquet, sob-re-kay, *m* nickname.

soc, sock, *m* plowshare.

sociable, soss-e-ăh-bl, *a* sociable.

social, e,* soss-e-ăhl, *a* social.

socialisme, soss-e-ăh-leessm, *m* socialism.

sociétaire, soss-e-eh-tair, *mf* & *a* member; partner.

société, soss-e-eh-teh, *f* society; party; partnership; company.

sociologue, soss-e-o-log, *m* sociologist.

socle, soc-kl, *m* pedestal.

sœur, ser, *f* sister; nun.

sofa, soh-făh *m* sofa.

software, soft-wair *m* (*comput*) software.

soi, so'ăh, *pron* oneself; itself; self; himself; herself.

soi-disant, so'ăh-de-zahng, *a* would-be; so-called; *adv* supposedly.

soie, so'ăh, *f* silk; bristle.

soierie, so'ăh-ree, *f* silk; silk trade.

soif, so'ăhf, *f* thirst; **avoir** –, ăh-vo'ăhr –, to be thirsty.

soigné, e, so'ăhn-yeh, *a* done with care; well-groomed.

soigner, so'ăhn-yeh, *v* to take care of; to nurse.

soigneu-x, se,* so'ăhn-yer, *a* careful.

soin, so'ăng, *m* care; *pl*

attentions.

soir, so'ăhr, *m* evening;
night.

soirée, so'ăh-reh, *f*
evening (duration of);
evening party.

soit, so'ăh, *conj* either;
whether; or.

soit! so'ăh, *interj* so be it!
well and good!

soixantaine, so'ăhss-ahng-
tain, *f* about sixty.

soixante, so'ăhss-ahngt, *m*
& *a* sixty; **—dix,** – dess,
seventy.

soixantième, so'ăhss-ahng-
te-aym, *m* & *a* sixtieth.

sol, sol, *m* soil; ground;
the note G.

solaire, soll-air, *a* solar.

soldat, soll-dăh, *m* soldier.

solde, solld, *m* balance;
sale (of remnants); *f*
soldiers' pay.

solder, soll-deh, *v* to
settle; to sell off; to
disount

sole, sol, *f* sole (fish).

soleil, soll-ay'e, *m* sun;
sunshine.

solennel, le,* soll-ăh-nell,
a solemn.

solennité, soll-ăh-ne-teh,
f solemnity.

solidaire,* soll-e-dair, *a*
jointly liable;
interdependent.

solide,* soll-eed, *a* solid;

strong; firm; sound.

solitaire,* soll-e-tair, *a*
solitary; lonely.

solitude, soll-e-tEEd, *f*
solitude; loneliness.

solive, soll-eev, *f* joist;
rafter.

solliciter, soll-e-se-teh, *v*
to solicit; to urge; to
petition.

soluble, soll-E-bl, *a*
soluble; solvable.

solution, soll-E-se-ong, *f*
solution; break.

solvable, soll-văh-bl, *a*
solvent.

sombre, song-br, *a* dark;
gloomy; dismal; dull.

sombrer, song-breh, *v* to
sink; to founder.

sommaire, somm-air, *m* &
a* summary; abstract.

sommation, somm-ăh-se-
ong, *f* summons.

somme, somm, *m* nap; *f*
sum; **en –,** ahng –, on
the whole; in short.

sommeil, somm-ay'e, *m*
sleep.

sommeiller, somm-ay'e-
yeh, *v* to doze.

sommelier, somm-er-le-
eh, *m* sommelier.

sommer, somm-eh, *v* to
summon; to call upon.

sommet, somm-ay, *m*
summit; top; acme.

sommier, somm-e-eh, *m*

bedspring.

somnifère, somm-ne-fair,
m sleeping pill; soporific
(sleep-inducing).

somnolent, e, somm-noll-
ahng, *a* sleepy, drowsy.

somnoler, somm-no-leh, *v*
to drowse; to doze.

somptueu-x, se,* songpt-
tE-er, *a* sumptuous.

son, song, *poss a m* his;
her; its; one's.

son, song, *m* sound; bran.

sonate, sonn-ăht, *f* sonata.

sondage, song-dăhsh, *m*
poll; sounding; boring.

sonde, songd, *f* sounding
line; probe.

sonder, song-deh, *v* to
sound; to fathom; to
probe.

songe, songsh, *m* dream.

songer, song-sheh, *v* to
dream; to think; to
muse.

songerie, songsh-ree, *f*
dreaming.

songeu-r, se, song-sher,
mf a dreamer;
thoughtful.

sonnant, e, sonn-ahng, *a*
sounding; striking.

sonner, sonn-eh, *v* to
sound; to ring; to strike
(the hour).

sonnerie, sonn-ree, *f*
ringing; bells.

sonnette, sonn-ett, *f* small

bell; doorbell; buzzer.

sonore, sonn-or, *a* sonorous.

sorbet, sor-bay, *m* sherbert; sorbet.

sorcellerie, sor-sell-ree, *f* witchcraft; sorcery.

sorci-er, ère, sor-se-eh, *mf* & *a* sorcerer; wizard; witch.

sordide,* sor-deed, *a* sordid; disgusting; mean.

sornettes, sor-nett, *fpl* idle talk.

sort, sor, *m* fate; lot; spell.

sorte, sort, *f* sort; kind; manner.

sortie, sor-tee, *f* going out; way out; outburst.

sortir, sor-teer, *v* to go out; to emerge; to take out.

sosie, soz-ee, *m* doppelganger; double.

sot, te,* soh, sott, *a* silly; stupid; fool.

sottise, sot-eez, *f* silliness; foolishness; abuse (language); *pl* insults.

sou, soo, *m* old French coin; (*fam*) penny.

soubresaut, soo-brer-soh, *m* sudden start.

souche, soosh, *f* stump; stem; counterfoil; (*fig*) blockhead.

souci, sooss-e, *m* worry; concern; anxiety; marigold.

soucier (se), ser sooss-e-eh, *v* to care (**de,** about; for); to mind; to be concerned; to worry.

soucieu-x, se,* sooss-e-er, *a* anxious; careworn.

soucoupe, soo-koop, *f* saucer.

soudain, e,* soo-dang, *a* sudden; unexpected; *fig* overnight; **soudain,** *adv* suddenly.

soudaineté, soo-dain-teh, *f* suddenness.

soude, sood, *f* soda.

souder, soo-deh, *v* to solder; to weld.

soudure, soo-dEEr, *f* solder; soldering.

souffle, soo-fl, *m* breath; puff.

souffler, soo-fleh, *v* to blow; to breathe; to whisper; to prompt.

soufflet, soo-flay, *m* bellows; (*fam*) slap in the face; insult.

souffleter, soo-fler-teh, *v* to slap in the face; (*fig*) to insult.

souffrance, soo-frahngss, *f* suffering; pain; **en –,** ahng –, unsettled; in suspense.

souffrant, e, soo-frahng, *a* suffering; poorly.

souffrir, soo-freer, *v* to suffer; to allow; to be injured.

soufre, soo-fr, *m* sulfur.

souhait, soo-ay, *m* wish.

souhaiter, soo-ay-teh, *v* to wish; to desire.

souiller, soo'e-yeh, *v* to dirty; to soil.

soûl, soo, *m* (*fam*) fill.

soûl, e, soo, *a* drunk.

soulagement, soo-lăhsh-mahng, *m* relief; alleviation.

soulager, soo-lăh-sheh, *v* to relieve; to soothe.

soûler (se), ser soo-leh, *v* (*pop*) to get drunk.

soulèvement, soo-layv-mahng, *m* rising; upheaval; insurrection.

soulever, sool-veh, *v* to raise; to lift; to stir up; **se–,** to rise; to revolt.

soulier, soo-le-eh, *m* shoe.

souligner, soo-leen-yeh, *v* to underline; to emphasize.

soumettre, soo-met-tr, *v* to subdue; to submit; to lay before.

soumis, e, soo-me, *a* submissive.

soumission, soo-miss-e-ong, *f* submission; compliance.

soupape, soo-păhp, *f* valve.

soupçon, soop-song, *m*

suspicion; surmise; (*fig*) touch.

soupçonner, soop-sonn-eh, *v* to suspect.

soupe, soop, *f* soup.

souper, soo-peh, *v* to have supper.

soupeser, soo-per-zeh, *v* to weigh by hand.

soupière, soo-pe-air, *f* soup tureen.

soupir, soo-peer, *m* sigh.

soupirail, soo-pe-rah'e, *m* ventilator; basement window.

soupirer, soo-pe-reh, *v* to sigh.

souple,* soo-pl, *a* supple; flexible; compliant.

source, soohrss, *f* source; spring; authority.

sourcil, soohr-se, *m* eyebrow.

sourciller, soohr-see-yeh, *v* to frown.

sourd, e, soohr, *mf* & *a** deaf person; deaf; dull; secret; husky.

sourdine, soohr-deen, *f* damper; à la–, ăh lăh–, secretly.

souriant, e, soo-re-ahng, *a* smiling.

souricière, soo-riss-e-air, *f* mousetrap.

sourire, soo-reer, *v* to smile. *m* smile.

souris, soo-ree, *f* mouse.

sournois, e,* soohr-no'ăh, *a* sly; cunning; artful.

sous, soo, *prep* under; beneath; below.

souscripteur, sooss-krip-ter, *m* subscriber.

souscrire, sooss-kreer, *v* to subscribe; to sign.

sous-entendre, soo-z'ahng-tahng-dr, *v* to imply.

sous-entendu, soo-z'ahng-tahng-dE, *m* implication.

sous-marin, soo-măh-rang, *m* submarine. *a* underwater.

soussigné, e, sooss-een-yeh, *mf* & *a* the undersigned; undersigned.

sous-sol, sooss-ol, *m* basement.

sous-titre, soo-tee-tr, *m* subtitle.

soustraction, sooss-trăhck-se-ong, *f* subtraction.

soustraire, sooss-trair, *v* to subtract; to shelter; se –, to get away (à, from).

soutien-gorge, soo-te-ang-gorsh, *m* bra.

soutane, soo-tăhn, *f* cassock.

souteneur, soot-ner, *m* upholder.

soutenir, soot-neer, *v* to sustain; to support; to

assert; to stand.

soutenu, soot-nE, *pp* & *a* sustained; lofty.

souterrain, soo-tay-rang, *m* underground.

souterrain, e, soo-tay-rang, *a* underground; underhand.

soutien, soo-te-ang, *m* support; prop; supporter.

soutien-gorge, soo-te-ang-gorsh, *m* a bra(ssiere).

soutirer, soo-te-reh, *v* to draw off; (*fig*) to extract.

souvenir (se), ser soov-neer, *v* to remember (**de**).

souvenir, soov-neer, *m* remembrance; keepsake.

souvent, soo-vahng, *adv* often.

souverain, e, soov-rang, *mf* & *a** sovereign.

souveraineté, soov-rain-teh, *f* sovereignty; dominion.

soyeu-x, se, so'ah'e-er, *a* silky.

spacieu-x, se,* spăh-se-er, *a* roomy; spacious.

sparadrap, spăh-răh-drăp, *m* bandage.

spécial, e,* speh-se-ăhl, *a* special; particular.

spécialité, speh-se-ăhl-e-teh, *f* speciality; line of business; proprietary article.

spécifier, speh-se-fe-eh, *v* to specify.

spectacle, speck-täh-kl, *m* spectacle; show; play.

specta-teur, trice, speck-täh-ter, *mf* spectator; *pl* audience.

spectre, speck-tr, *m* specter; ghost.

spéculer, speh-kE-leh, *v* to speculate.

sperme, spairm, *m* sperm; semen.

sphère, sfair, *f* sphere; globe.

spirale, spe-rähl, *f* spiral; *a* spiral.

spirituel, le, * spe-re-tE-ell, *a* spiritual; witty.

spiritueu-x, se, spe-re-tE-er, *a* alcoholic.

splendeur, splahng-der, *f* splendor; magnificence.

splendide, * splahng-deed, *a* splendid; magnificent.

spongieu-x, se, spong-she-er, *a* spongy.

spontané, e, spong-täh-neh, *a* spontaneous.

spontanément, spong-täh-neh-mahng, *adv* spontaneously.

sport, spor, *m* sport; *a* casual (clothes).

sports d'hiver, spor-de-vair *mpl* winter sports.

squelette, sker-lett, *m* skeleton.

stable, stäh-bl, *a* stable; steady; durable.

stade, stähd *m* stadium.

stage, stähsh, *m* period of probation, course.

stagnant, e, stähgh-nahng, *a* stagnant; still.

stalle, stähl, *f* stall.

stance, stahngss, *f* stanza.

station, stäh-se-ong, *f* standing; subway stop; stand; station; taxi stand.

station de radio, stäh-se-ong-der-räh-de-oh *f* radio station.

stationner, stäh-se-onn-eh, *v* to stop; to park.

stationnement, stäh-se-onn-mahng, *m* parking.

station-service, stäh-se-ong-sair-veess *f* gas station.

statistique, stäh-tiss-teeck, *f* statistics. *a* statistical.

statue, stäh-tE, *f* statue.

statuer, stäh-tE-eh, *v* to decree; to rule.

stature, stäh-tEEr, *f* stature; height.

statut, stäh-tE, *m* statute; regulation; status.

sténodactylo(graphe), steh-no-dähck-te-log-rähf, *mf* shorthand typist.

sténographe, steh-nog-

rähf, *mf* stenographer.

sténographie, steh-nog-räh-fe, *f* shorthand.

stéréo, steh-reh-oh *f* stereo.

stéréophonique, steh-reh-o-fo-neeck, *a* stereophonic.

stérile, * steh-reel, *a* sterile; barren.

stérilité, steh-re-le-teh, *f* barrenness.

stigmate, stigg-mäht, *m* stigma; brand; stain.

stigmatiser, stigg-mäh-te-zeh, *v* to stigmatize; to denounce.

stimulant, e, ste-mE-lahng, *a* stimulating; *m* stimulant.

stimuler, ste-mE-leh, *v* to stimulate; to urge on.

stipuler, ste-pE-leh, *v* to stipulate.

stoïque, * sto-eeck, *a* stoical.

stomacal, e, stomm-äh-kähl, *a* stomach.

stoppage, stop-ähsh, *m* invisible mending.

store, stor, *m* blind.

strapontin, sträh-pong-tang, *m* jumpseat.

stratégie, sträh-teh-she *f* strategy.

strict, e, * strikt; *a* strict; severe; precise.

strident, e, stre-dahng, *a*

shrill.

trié, e, stre-eh, *a* striated; streaked; scored.

tructure, strEEk-tEEr, *f* structure; frame; build.

tudieu-x, se,* stE-de-er, *a* studious.

tupéfait, e, stE-peh-fay, *a* stupefied; amazed; flabbergasted.

tupéfier, stE-peh-fe-eh, *v* to stupefy; to amaze.

tupeur, stE-per, *f* stupor.

tupide,* stE-peed, *a* stupid.

tupidité, stE-pe-de-teh, *f* stupidity.

tyle, steel, *m* style.

tylo, stee-lo, *m* fountain pen; **–à bille, –** ăh bee-ye, ballpoint pen.

uaire, sE-air, *m* shroud.

uave,* sE-ăhv, *a* sweet; soft; suave.

ubdiviser, sEEb-de-ve-zeh, *v* to subdivide.

ubir, sE-beer, *v* to undergo; to suffer; to endure; to submit.

ubit, e,* sE-bee, *a* sudden.

ubjecti-f, ve,* sEEb-sheck-teeff, *a* subjective.

ubjonctif, sEEb-shongk-teeff, *a* subjunctive.

ubjuguer, sEEb-shE-gheh, *v* to subjugate.

ublime,* sEEb-leem, *a* sublime.

submerger, sEEb-mair-sheh, *v* to submerge, to swamp.

subordonner, sE-bor-donn-eh, *v* to subordinate.

subséquemment, sEEb-seh-kăh-mahng, *adv* subsequently.

subséquent, e, sEEb-seh-kahng, *a* subsequent.

subside, sEEb-seed, *m* subsidy.

subsister, sEEb-ziss-teh, *v* to subsist; to stand.

substance, sEEbs-tahngss, *f* substance.

substantiel, le,* sEEbs-tahngss-e-ell, *a* substantial.

substituer, sEEbs-te-tE-eh, *v* to substitute (à, for).

substitut, sEEbs-te-tE, *m* substitute; deputy.

subterfuge, sEEb-tair-fEEsh, *m* subterfuge.

subtil, e,* sEEb-teel, *a* subtle; sharp; acute; keen.

subtilité, sEEb-te-le-teh, *f* subtlety, acuteness.

subvenir, sEEb-ver-neer, *v* to provide (à, for); to help; to relieve.

subventionner, sEEb-vahng-se-onn-eh, *v* to subsidize.

subversi-f, ve,* sEEb-vair-seeff, *a* subversive.

suc, sEEk, *m* juice; essence; (*fig*) substance.

succéder, sEEk-seh-deh, *v* to succeed; to follow after.

succès, sEEk-say, *m* success.

successi-f, ve,* sEEk-sess-eeff, *a* successive.

succession, sEEk-sess-e-ong, *f* succession; inheritance.

succinct, e,* sEEk-sang, *a* succinct; concise.

succomber, sEE-kong-beh, *v* to succumb; to sink; to yield; to die.

succion, sEEk-se-ong, *f* suction.

succulent, e, sE-kE-lahng, *a* juicy, savory.

succursale, sE-kEEr-săhl, *f* branch (of store, etc).

sucer, sEEss-eh, *v* to suck; to suck in; to drain.

sucre, sEE-kr, *m* sugar.

sucre glace, sE-kr-glăhss *m* sugar.

sucrer, sE-kreh, *v* to sweeten; to sugar.

sucrerie, sE-krer-ree, *f* sugar refinery; *pl* sweets.

sucrier, sE-kre-eh, *m* sugar bowl.

sud, sEEd, *m* South; *a* south, southern.

suer, sE-eh, v to sweat;
(fig) to toil.

sueur, sE-er, f sweat,
perspiration; (fig) toil.

suffire, sE-feer, v to
suffice; to do; **cela
suffit,** ser-lăh sE-fe, that
will do.

suffisamment, sE-fe-zăh-
mahng, adv sufficiently.

suffisance, sE-fe-zahngss, f
sufficiency; conceit.

suffisant, e, sE-fe-zahng, a
sufficient; conceited.

suffocant, e, sE-fock-ahng,
a stifling.

suffoquer, sE-fock-eh, v to
suffocate; to stifle.

suffrage, sE-frăhsh, m
suffrage; approbation.

suggérer, sEEgh-sheh-reh,
v to suggest; to hint.

suicide, swee-seed, m
suicide.

suicider (se), ser swee-
see-deh, v to commit
suicide.

suie, swee, f soot.

suif, sweef, m tallow.

suinter, swang-teh, v to
ooze out; to leak.

suite, sweet, f suite;
consequence;
attendants; series;
sequence; sequel;
continuation; **tout de –,**
too der –, at once.

suivant, swee-vahng, prep
according to; **–que, –
ker,** according as.

suivant, e, swee-vahng, mf
attendant; a following,
next.

suivi, e, swee-ve, pp & a
followed; consistent;
sought after.

suivre, swee-vr, v to
follow; to result; to
study; **faire –,** fair –, to
forward.

sujet, sE-shay, m subject;
person; cause; topic.

sujet, te, sE-shay, a
subject; liable; inclined.

sujétion, sE-sheh-se-ong, f
subjection; constraint.

superbe,* sE-pairb, a
superb; majestic; proud.

supercherie, sE-pair-sher-
ree, f deceit; cheat;
fraud.

superficie, sE-pair-feess-
ee, f surface; area.

superficiel, le,* sE-pair-fe-
se-ell, a superficial;
shallow.

superflu, e, sE-pair-flE, a
superfluous.

supérieur, e,* sE-peh-re-
er, a upper; superior.

supermarché, soo-pair-
măhr-sheh m
supermarket.

superstitieu-x, se,* sE-
pair-ste-se-er, a
superstitious.

supplanter, sE-plahng-teh,
v to oust.

suppléant, e, sE-pleh-
ahng, mf & a substitute;
deputy.

suppléer, sE-pleh-eh, v to
make good; **–à,** to make
up for.

supplément, sE-pleh-
mahng, m supplement;
extra charge.

supplémentaire, sE-pleh-
mahng-tair, a
additional.

suppliant, e, sE-ple-ahng,
mf & a supplicant.

supplication, sE-ple-kăh-
se-ong, f entreaty.

supplice, sE-pleess, m
torture; (fig) torment.

supplier, sE-ple-eh, v to
entreat; to beseech.

supplique, sE-pleek, f
petition.

support, sE-por, m
support; stand.

supportable, sE-por-tăh-
bl, a bearable.

supporter, sE-por-teh, v to
support; to bear.

supposer, sE-poh-zeh, v to
suppose; (jur) to
substitute.

supposition, sE-poh-ze-se-
ong, f supposition; (jur)
substitution; forgery.

supprimer, sE-pre-meh, v
to suppress; to abolish.

supputer, sE-pE-teh, *v* to reckon; to calculate.

suprématie, sE-preh-mähss-ee, *f* supremacy.

suprême,* sE-praym, *a* supreme; crowning; last.

sur, sEEr, *prep* on; upon; over; above; by; out of; towards; concerning.

sur, e, sEEr, *a* sour.

sûr, e,* sEEr, *a* sure; safe; trustworthy.

surcroît, sEEr-kro'äh, *m* increase.

surdité, sEEr-de-teh, *f* deafness.

sûreté, sEEr-teh, *f* safety; security.

surexciter, sEEr-eck-se-teh, *v* to overexcite.

surf, sErf *m* surfing.

surface, sEEr-fähss, *f* surface; outside; area.

surfaire, sEEr-fair, *v* to overcharge; to overrate.

surfin, sEEr-fang, *a* superfine.

surgeler, sEEr-sher-leh, *v* to deep-freeze.

surgir, sEEr-sheer, *v* to arise; to appear suddenly.

surhumain, e, sEE -Er-E-mang, *a* superhuman.

surintendant, sEEr-ang-tahng-dahng, *m* superintendent.

surlendemain, sEEr-

lahngd-mang, *m* second day after.

surmener, sEEr-mer-neh, *v* to overwork.

surmonter, sEEr-mong-teh, *v* to overcome; to rise above (of fluids, etc.).

surnager, sEEr-näh-sheh, *v* to float; (*fig*) to survive.

surnaturel, le,* sEEr-näh-tE-rell, *a* supernatural.

surnom, sEEr-nong, *m* nickname.

surnuméraire, sEEr-nE-meh-rair, *m* & *a* supernumerary.

surpasser, sEEr-pähss-eh, *v* to exceed; to excel.

surplomber, sEEr-plong-beh, *v* to overhang.

surplus, sEEr-plE *m* surplus; **au –,** oh –, moreover.

surprenant, e, sEEr-prer-nahng, *a* surprising.

surprendre, sEEr-prahng-dr, *v* to surprise.

surprise, sEEr-preez, *f* surprise.

sursaut, sEEr-soh, *m* start; jump.

sursauter, sEEr-soh-teh, *v* to start; to give a jump; to be startled.

surseoir, sEEr-so'ähr, *v* to put off (à).

sursis, sEEr-see, *m* delay; suspension; reprieve.

surtaxe, sEEr-tähcks, *f* extra tax; surcharge.

surtout, sEEr-too, *adv* above all; particularly.

surveillance, sEEr-vay'e-ahngss, *f* superintendence; supervision.

surveiller, sEEr-vay'e-yeh, *v* to supervise; to keep an eye on.

survenir, sEEr-ver-neer, *v* to come unexpectedly.

survie, sEEr-vee, *f* survival.

survivance, sEEr-ve-vahngss, *f* relic.

survivre, sEEr-vee-vr, *v* to survive (à); to outlive.

sus, sEEss, *prep* on; **en –de,** ahng – der, over and above.

susceptibilité, sEEss-ep-te-be-le-teh, *f* touchiness.

susciter, sEEss-e-teh, *v* to raise up; to create.

susdit, e, sEEss-de, *a* aforesaid.

suspect, e, sEEss-paykt, *m* & *a* suspect.

suspecter, sEEss-payk-teh, *v* to suspect.

suspendre, sEEss-pahng-dr, *v* to suspend; to hang up.

suspens (en), ahng sEEss-pahng, *adv* in abeyance.

suture, sEE-tEEr, *f* suture;

point de –, po'*ang* der –,
stitch.

svelte, svaylt, *a* slender;
slim.

syllabe, seell-lǎhb, *f*
syllable.

sylvestre, sill-vays-tr, *a*
sylvan.

symbole, *sang*-bol, *m*
symbol.

symétrique,* se-meh-
treeck, *a* symmetrical.

sympathique,* *sang*-pǎh-
teeck, *a* sympathetic;
likable.

symptôme, *sang*p-tohm, *m*
symptom.

syncope, *sang*-kop, *f*
fainting fit; blackout.

syndicat, *sang*-de-kah, *m*
syndicate; –**d'initiative,**
– de-ne-se-ah-teev,
tourists' information
office.

syndicat d'initiative, *sang*-
de-kǎh-de-ne-se-ǎh-teev
m tourist office.

système, siss-taym, *m*
system.

ta, tăh, *poss a f sing*
familiar form of 'your.'

tabac, tăh-băh, *m* tobacco;
snuff.

tabatière, tăh-băh-te-air, *f*
snuffbox.

table, tăh-bl, *f* table;
board; index.

tableau, tăh-bloh, *m*
picture; painting;
blackboard; list

tablette, tăh-blett, *f* shelf;
lozenge; slab.

tablier, tăh-blee-eh, *m*
apron; workcoat.

tabouret, tăh-boo-ray, *m*
stool.

tache, tăhsh, *f* spot; stain;
blemish.

tâche, tahsh, *f* task; job.

tâcher, tah-sheh, *v* to
endeavor; to strive.

tacheté, e, tăhsh-teh, *a*
spotted; speckled.

tacite,* tăh-seet, *a*
implied; tacit.

taciturne, tăh-se-tEErn, *a*
taciturn; quiet.

tact, tăhckt, *m* touch; (*fig*)
tact; discretion.

taie, tay, *f* pillowcase.

taie d'oreiller, tay-dor-
ay'e-yeh *f* pillowcase.

taille, tah'e, *f* cut; waist;
height; pruning.

tailler, tah'e-yeh, *v* to cut;
to prune; to sharpen.

tailleur, tah'e-yer, *m*
tailor.

taillis, tah'e-ye, *m* copse;
thicket.

taire, tair, *v* to conceal; **se**
–, to be silent.

talc, tăhlk *m* talcum
powder.

talent, tăh-lahng, *m*
talent; (*fig*) ability.

talon, tăh-long, *m* heel;
voucher.

talonner, tăh-lonn-eh, *v*
to urge; to follow
closely.

talus, tăh-lE, *m* slope;
embankment.

tambour, tahng-boohr, *m*
drum; barrel.

tamis, tăh-mee, *m* sieve.

tampon, tahng-pong, *m*
plug; tampon; buffer.

tampon hygiénique,
tahng-pong-e-**she**-eh-
neeck *m* tampon.

tamponner, tahng-ponn-
eh, *v* to stop up; to
collide.

tancer, tahngss-eh, *v* to
scold.

tandis que, tahng-de ker,
conj while; whereas.

tangage, tahng-găhsh, *m*
pitching (of ship).

tanière, tăh-ne-air, *f* den;
lair.

tanner, tăh-neh, *v* to tan.

tant, tahng, *adv* so much;
as much; so many; as
many; **–mieux,** – me-er,
so much the better;
–pis, – pee, so much the
worse.

tante, tahngt, *f* aunt.

tantôt, tahng-toh, *adv*
presently; shortly; now
… now.

tapage, tăh-păhsh, *m*
uproar; row.

tape, tăhp, *f* slap; pat;
thump.

taper, tăh-peh, *v* to tap; to
pat; to strike.

tapir (se), ser tăh-peer, *v*
to squat; to crouch.

tapis, tăh-pe, *m* carpet;
rug; cover.

tapisserie, tăh-piss-ree, *f*
tapestry.

tapissier, tăh-piss-e-eh, *m*
upholsterer.

tapoter, tăhp-ot-eh, *v* to
tap; to strum.

taquiner, tăh-ke-neh, *v* to
tease.

tard, tăhr, *adv* late.

tarder, tăhr-deh, *v* to
delay; to be long.

tardi-f, ve,* tăhr-deeff, *a*
late; tardy; backward.

tare, tăhr, *f* (*fam*) blemish;
(*fam*) defect; tare.

taré, e, tăh-reh, *a*
damaged; spoiled.

tarif, tăh-reeff, *m* tariff;
price list; rate; scale of
prices.

tarir, tăh-reer, *v* to dry up.

tarte, tăhrt, *f* tart; pie.

tartine, tăhr-teen, *f* slice
of bread with butter and
jam.

tas, tah, *m* heap; pile; (*fig*)
lot.

tasse, tahss, *f* cup.

tasser, tahss-eh, *v* to heap
up; to press down; **se –,**
to settle.

tâter, tah-teh, *v* to feel; to
try; to taste.

tâtillon, ne, tah-tee-yong,
mf & *a* meddler;
meddlesome.

tâtonner, tah-tonn-eh, *v*
to grope; to feel one's
way.

tâtons (à), ăh tah-tong,
adv gropingly.

taudis, toh-dee, *m* hovel.

taupe, tohp, *f* mole.

taupinière, toh-pinn-e-
air, *f* molehill.

taureau, toh-roh, *m* bull.

taux, toh, *m* rate.

taverne, tăh-vairn, *f*
tavern.

taxer, tăhx-eh, *v* to tax; to
assess; to accuse.

te, ter, *pers pron mf sing*
(familiar form) you; to
you; yourself.

technique, teck-neeck, *a*
technical. *f* technique.

tee-shirt, tee-shert *m* T-
shirt.

teigne, tayn-yer, *f* moth;
ringworm.

teindre, tang-dr, *v* to dye;
to tint.

teint, tang, *m* complexion;
dye; color.

teinte, tangt, *f* tint; shade;
tinge.

teinture, tang-tEer, *f* dye;
dyeing; tincture.

tel, le, tell, *a* such; like;
–que, – ker, similar to;
such as.

télé, teh-leh *abbr f* TV.

télécopie teh-leh-ko-pee *f*
fax.

télégramme, teh-leh-
grăhm, *m* telegram.

télégraphier, teh-leh-
grăh-fe-eh, *v* to wire.

téléphone, teh-leh-fon, *m*
telephone.

téléphone de voiture, teh-
leh-fon-der-vo'ăh-tEEr,
m car phone.

téléphone public, teh-leh-
fonn-pE-bleeck *f*
payphone.

téléphonique, teh-leh-
fonn-eeck, *a* telephonic;
cabine –, kăh-been –,
phone booth.

télescope, teh-less-kop, *m*
telescope.

télévision, teh-leh-ve-ze-
ong, *f* television.

télévision par câble, teh-
leh-ve-se-ong-păhr-kah-
bl, *f* cable television.

tellement, tell-mahng, *adv*
so; so much; **–que,** –
ker, so that.

téméraire,* teh-meh-rair,
a rash; foolhardy.

témoignage, teh-mo'ăhn-
yăhsh, *m* testimony;

evidence.

témoigner, teh-mo'ăhn-yeh, *v* to show; to testify.

témoin, teh-mo-ang, *m* witness.

tempe, tahngp, *f* temple.

tempérament, tahng-peh-răh-mahng, *m* temperament; constitution.

tempérant, e, tahng-peh-rahng, *a* temperate.

température, tahng-peh-răh-tEEr, *f* temperature.

tempérer, tahng-peh-reh, *v* to moderate; to allay.

tempête, tahng-payt, *f* tempest; storm.

tempêter, tahng-pay-teh, *v* to storm; to fume.

temple, tahng-pl, *m* temple.

temporaire,* tahng-por-air, *a* temporary.

temporel, le,* tahng-por-ell, *a* temporal.

temps, tahng, *m* time; while; period; season; weather; tense; beat.

tenace, ter-năhss, *a* tenacious.

tenailles, ter-nah'e, *fpl* pincers.

tendance, tahng-dahngss, *f* tendency; leaning.

tendon, tahng-dong, *m* sinew.

tendre, tahng-dr, *v* to

stretch; to strain; to hold out; to tend.

tendre,* tahng-dr, *a* tender; affectionate; new.

tendresse, tahng-dress, *f* tenderness.

tendu, e, tahng-dE, *a* tight; stretched; tense.

ténèbres, teh-nay-br, *fpl* darkness; gloom.

teneur, ter-ner, *f* tenor; purport.

tenir, ter-neer, *v* to hold; to keep; to last; to deem; to depend on; –à, – ăh, to value; to care about.

tension, tahng-se-ong, *f* tension.

tension artérielle, tahng-se-ong-ăhr-teh-re-ell, *f* blood pressure.

tentant, e, tahng-tahng, *a* tempting.

tentation, tahng-tăh-se-ong, *f* temptation.

tentative, tahng-tăh-teev, *f* attempt; endeavor.

tente, tahngt, *f* tent.

tenter, tahng-teh, *v* to attempt; to tempt.

tenture, tahng-tEEr, *f* hangings; wallpaper.

ténu, e, teh-nE, *a* slender; thin.

tenue, ter-nEE, *f* holding; behavior; attitude; dress.

térébenthine, teh-reh-

bahng-teen, *f* turpentine.

terme, tairm, *m* term; limit; *pl* condition.

terminaison, tair-me-nay-zong, *f* ending.

terminal, tair-me-năhl *m* terminal (computer, oil).

terminale, tair-me-năhl *a* terminal.

terminer, tair-me-neh, *v* to finish; to conclude.

terminus, tair-me-nEs *m* terminal (*rail*).

terne, tairn, *a* dull; colorless.

ternir, tair-neer, *v* to tarnish; to dim.

terrain, tay-rang, *m* ground; soil; piece of land.

terrasse, tay-răhss, *f* terrace.

terrasser, tay-răhss-eh, *v* to bank up; to throw on the ground.

terre, tair, *f* earth; ground; land; estate; the world.

terrestre, tay-ress-tr, *a* terrestrial.

terreur, tay-rer, *f* terror; dread; awe.

terrible,* tay-ree-bl, *a* terrible; dreadful; frightful.

terrifier, tay-re-fe-eh, *v* to terrify.

terrine, tay-reen, *f*
earthen dish; pâté.

territoire, tay-re-to'ăhr, *m*
territory.

terroriste, teh-ro-rest *mf*
terrorist.

tertre, tair-tr, *m* hillock.

tes, tay, *poss a mf pl*
(familiar form) your.

test, tayst *m* quiz.

testament, tess-tăh-
mahng, *m* testament;
will.

têtard, teh-tahr, *m*
tadpole.

tête, tayt, *f* head; top;
wits; (*fig*) presence of
mind.

téter, teh-teh, *v* to suck
(at the breast).

tétine, teh-teen, *f* teat.

têtu, e, tay-tE, *a* stubborn;
headstrong.

texte, text, *m* text;
subject.

textile, tex-teell, *m*
textile; material; *a*
textile.

textuel, le, * tex-tE-ell, *a*
textual.

thé, teh, *m* tea; tea party.

théâtral, e, teh-ah-trăhl, *a*
theatrical.

théâtre, teh-ah-tr, *m*
theater; stage; plays;
coup de –, koo der–,
unexpected event.

théière, teh-yair, *f* teapot.

thème, taym, *m* topic;
theme; exercise (in
school).

théorie, teh-or-ee, *f*
theory; procession.

théorique, * teh-or-eeck, *a*
theoretical.

thérapie, teh-rah-pee, *f*
therapy.

thermomètre, tair-
momm-ay-tr, *m*
thermometer.

thèse, tayz, *f* thesis;
argument.

thon, tong, *m* tuna fish.

thorax, to-racks, *m*
thorax; chest.

thrombose coronarienne,
trong-bohz-kor-oh-năh-
re-en, *f* coronary.

thym, tang, *m* thyme.

tibia, te-be-ăh, *m*
shinbone.

tic, teek, *m* tic; habit.

ticket, te-kay, *m* ticket
(bus, etc).

tiède, * te-aid, *a* lukewarm;
tepid; indifferent.

tiédir, te-eh-deer, *v* to
grow lukewarm.

tien, ne, te-ang, *poss pron
mf* (familiar form) yours.

tier-s, ce, te-air, *mf* third
person; *a* third.

tige, teesh, *f* stem; stalk;
trunk; rod; shaft.

tigre, tigresse, tee-gr, tee-
gress, *mf* tiger; tigress.

tilleul, tee-yerl, *m* lime
tree; lime blossom.

timbale, tang-băhl, *f*
kettledrum; metal cup.

timbre, tang-br, *m* bell;
(*fig*) tone; stamp.

timbré, e, tang-breh, *a*
stamped; sonorous;
(*fam*) mad.

timide, * te-meed, *a* timid;
shy; bashful.

timoré, e, te-mor-eh, *a*
timorous.

tintamarre, tang-tăh-
măhr, *m* uproar;
hubbub; clatter.

tinter, tang-teh, *v* to ring;
to tinkle; to toll.

tir, teer, *m* shooting;
firing; rifle range.

tirage, te-răhsh, *m*
drawing; draft; printing;
circulation
(newspapers).

tiraillement, te-rah'e-
mahng, *m* pulling; pain.

tire-bouchon, teer-boo-
shong, *m* corkscrew.

tiré, e, te-reh, *a* drawn
(face); worn out.

tirelire, teer-leer, *f*
piggybank.

tirer, te-reh, *v* to draw; to
pull; to drag; to verge
on; to shoot.

tiret, te-reh, *m* hyphen;
dash.

tiroir, te-ro'ăhr, *m* drawer;

slide.

tisane, te-zähn, *f* infusion.

tison, te-zong, *m* fire brand.

tisonnier, te-zonn-e-eh, *m* poker.

tisser, teess-eh, *v* to weave.

tissu, teess-E, *m* material; fabric.

titre, tee-tr, *m* title; right; certificate.

tituber, tee-tE-beh, *v* to stagger; to lurch.

titulaire, tee-tE-lair, *mf* holder; titular.

tocsin, tock-sang, *m* alarm bell.

tohu-bohu, toh-E-boh-E, *m* confusion; chaos.

toi, to'äh, *pers pron mf sing* (familiar form) you (subject or object).

toile, to'ähl, *f* cloth; linen; canvas; picture.

toilette, to'äh-lett, *f* wash; dress; toilet; dressing table.

toiser, to'äh-zeh, *v* to measure; (*fig*) to eye (someone).

toison, to'äh-zong, *f* fleece; (*fam*) mop of hair.

toit, to'äh, *m* roof; (*fam*) home.

tôle, tohl, *f* sheet.

tolérable, toll-eh-răh-bl, *a* tolerable.

tolérance, toll-eh-rahngss, *f* toleration.

tolérer, toll-eh-reh, *v* to tolerate.

tomate, tomm-äht, *f* tomato.

tombant, e, tong-bahng, *a* falling.

tombe, tongb, *f* tomb; grave.

tombeau, tong-boh, *m* tomb; grave; tombstone.

tomber, tong-beh, *v* to fall; to abate; –sur, to come across.

tome, tohm, *m* tome; volume.

ton, tong, *poss a m sing* (familiar form) your; *m* tone; style; shade.

tondeuse, tong-derz, *f* lawnmower; shears.

tondre, tong-dr, *v* to shear; to mow; to clip.

tonne, tonn, *f* ton.

tonneau, tonn-oh, *m* cask; barrel.

tonner, tonn-eh, *v* to thunder.

tonnerre, tonn-air, *m* thunder.

toque, took, *f* cap.

toqué, e, tock-eh, *a* (*fam*) crazy.

torche, torsh, *f* torch.

torchon, tor-shong, *m* dishcloth; duster.

tordre, tor-dr, *v* to wring; to twist; se –, to writhe.

torpeur, tor-per, *f* torpor; numbness.

torpille, tor-pee-ye, *f* torpedo.

torpilleur, tor-pee-yer, *m* torpedo boat.

torréfier, tor-reh-fe-eh, *v* to roast.

torrent, tor-rahng, *m* torrent.

torrentiel, le, tor-rahng-se-ell, *a* torrential.

torse, torss, *m* torso; trunk; chest.

tort, tor, *m* wrong; harm; injury; **avoir –,** äh-vo'ähr –, to be wrong.

tortiller, tor-tee-yeh, *v* to twist; to shuffle; se –, to wriggle.

tortue, tor-tE, *f* tortoise; turtle.

tortueu-x, se,* tor-tE- er, *a* winding; crooked.

torture, tor-tEer, *f* torture.

tôt, toh, *adv* soon; early.

total, tot-ăhl, *m* total.

total, e,* tot-ăhl, *a* total; whole.

touchant, too-shahng, *prep* concerning; regarding.

touchant, e, too-shahng, *a* touching; affecting.

touche, toosh, *f* touch; stroke; key.

toucher, too-sheh, v to touch; to cash; to hit; to affect; to be contiguous to.

toucher, too-sheh, m touch; feeling.

touffe, toof, f tuft; bunch; clump.

touffu, e, too-fE, a tufted; bushy; thick.

toujours, too-shoohr, adv always; ever; nevertheless.

toupet, too-pay, m tuft; (fam) impudence; cheek.

toupie, too-pee, f top (spinning).

tour, toohr, m turn; revolution; circumference; trick; trip; lathe.

tour, toohr, f tower.

tourbe, toohrb, f peat; turf; mob.

tourbillon, toohr-bee-yong, m whirlwind.

tourelle, too-rell, f turret.

touriste, too-risst, mf tourist; tripper.

tourment, toohr-mahng, m torment; anguish.

tourmente, toohr-mahngt, f tempest; (fig) turmoil.

tourmenté, e, toohr-mahng-teh, a stormy; worried.

tourmenter, toohr-

mahng-teh, v to torment.

tournant, toohr-nahng, m turning; bend; corner.

tournée, toohr-neh, f round; walk.

tourner, toohr-neh, v to turn; to change.

tourneur, toohr-ner, m turner.

tournevis, toohr-ner-veess, m screwdriver.

tournoi, toohr-no'ăh, m tournament.

tournoyer, toohr-no'ăh-yeh, v to whirl round.

tournure, toohr-nEEr, f figure; appearance; turn; course.

tourte, toohrt, f tart; fruitpie.

tourterelle, toohr-ter-rell, f turtledove.

toussaint (la), lăh-tooss-ang, f All Saints' Day.

tousser, tooss-eh, v to cough.

tout, too, adv wholly; quite. m all; the whole; chief point.

tout, e, too, a all; whole.

tout, too, pron all; everything.

tout-à-l'égout, toot-ăh-leh-ghoo, m main sewer.

toutefois, toot-fo'ăh, adv yet; however.

toute-puissance, toot-

pweess-ahngss, f omnipotence.

tout(e) petit(e) enfant, too-per-te-ahng-fahng mf toddler.

tout-puissant, too-pweess-sahng, m Almighty; a all-powerful.

toux, too, f cough; coughing.

toxique, tox-eeck, m poison. a poisonous; toxic.

trac, trăhck, m (fam) fright; stage fright.

tracas, trăh-kah, m bother; anxiety; worries.

tracasser, trăh-kăhss-eh, v to worry; to plague.

trace, trăhss, f trace; track; footstep.

tracé, trăhss-eh, m outline; planning; line.

tracer, trăhss-eh, v to trace; to draw out; to lay down.

tracteur, trăhk-ter m tractor.

traduc-teur, trice, mf translator.

traduction, trăh-dEEk-se-ong, f translation; translating.

traduire, trăh-dweer, v to translate.

trafic, trăh-feek, m traffic; trade.

trafiquer, trăh-fe-keh, v to

trade; to traffic.

tragique,* trăh-**sheeck**, a
tragic(al).

trahir, trăh-**eer**, v to
betray; to deceive.

trahison, trăh-e-**zong**, f
treachery; betrayal;
treason.

train, trang, m train; pace;
rate; speed; way; style.

traînard, tray-**năhr**, m
straggler; slowpoke.

traîneau, tray-**noh**, m sled.

traînée, tray-**neh**, f train;
trail.

traîner, tray-**neh**, v to
drag; to drawl; to lag
behind; to lie about.

traire, trayr, v to milk.

trait, tray, m dart; arrow;
stroke; dash (of the pen,
etc.); touch; draft (of
liquor); act; feature.

traitable, tray-**tăh**-bl, a
tractable.

traite, trayt, f journey;
draft; trading (on the
African coast).

traité, tray-**teh**, m treatise;
treaty.

traitement, trayt-**mahng**,
m treatment; salary.

traiter, tray-**teh**, v to treat;
to handle; to negotiate.

traître, sse, tray-tr, mf & a
traitor; traitress;
treacherous.

traîtreusement, tray-**trerz**-

mahng, adv
treacherously.

traîtrise, tray-**treez**, f
treachery; betrayal.

trajet, trăh-**shay**, m
journey; passage;
distance.

trame, trăhm, f woof;
weft; web; plot;
framework.

tramer, trăh-**meh**, v to
weave; to plot.

tranchant, trahng-**shahng**,
m edge.

tranchant, e, trahng-
shahng, a sharp; cutting;
peremptory.

tranche, trahngsh, f slice.

tranchée, trahng-**sheh**, f
trench; pl gripes.

trancher, trahng-**sheh**, v
to cut off; to decide; to
solve; to contrast (sur,
with).

tranquilisant, trahng-ke-
le-**zahng** m tranquilizer.

tranquille,* trahng-**keel**, a
quiet; peaceful; easy.

tranquilliser, trahng-ke-
le-**zeh**, v to calm.

tranquillité, trahng-ke-le-
teh, f calm; stillness.

transatlantique, trahngss-
ăht-lahng-teeck, m
transatlantic liner. a
transatlantic.

transborder, trahngss-bor-
deh, v to transship.

transcrire, trahngss-**kreer**,
v to transcribe.

transe, trahngss, f fright;
apprehension; trance.

transférer, trahngss-feh-
reh, v to transfer.

transfert, trahngss-**fair**, m
transfer.

transformer, trahngss-for-
meh, v to transform; to
change into.

transfusion, trahngss-fe-
ze-ong, f transfusion.

transi, e, trahng-**ze**, pp & a
chilled; benumbed.

transiger, trahng-ze-**sheh**,
v to compromise.

transitoire,* trahng-ze-
to'**ăhr**, a transitory.

transmettre, trahngss-met-
tr, v to transmit; to
broadcast.

transparence, trahngss-
păh-**rahngss**, f
transparency.

transparent, trahngss-păh-
rahng, a transparent.

transpiration, trahngss-pe-
răh-**se-ong**, f
perspiration.

transpirer, trahngss-pe-
reh, v to perspire; to
transpire; to sweat.

transport, trahngss-**por**, m
carriage; conveyance;
rapture.

transporter, trahngss-por-
teh, v to convey; to

enrapture.

transvaser, trahngss-vah-zeh, *v* to decant.

trappe, trăhp, *f* trapdoor; trap; pitfall.

trapu, e, trăh-pE, *a* thickset; dumpy.

traquenard, trăhck-năhr, *m* (*fig*) snare; trap.

traquer, trăh-keh, *v* to hunt out; to surround.

travail, trăh-vah'e, *m* work; labor; toil.

travailler, trăh-vah'e-yeh, *v* to work; too work on; to ferment (of wines).

travers, trăh-vair, *m* breadth; defect; oddity; à –, ăh –, across.

traversée, trăh-vair-seh, *f* passage; crossing.

traverser, trăh-vair-seh, *v* to cross; to travel over; to thwart.

traversin, trăh-vair-sang, *m* bolster.

travestir, trăh-vess-teer, *v* to disguise; to travesty.

trébucher, treh-bE-sheh, *v* to stumble.

trèfle, tray-fl, *m* clover; clubs (cards).

treillage, tray'e-yăhsh, *m* latticework.

treille, tray'e, *f* climbing vine.

treize, trayz, *m* & *a* thirteen.

treizième, tray-ze-aym, *m* & *a* thirteenth.

tréma, treh-mah, *m* diaeresis.

tremblement, trahng-bler-mahng, *m* shake; tremor; –de terre, – der tair, earthquake.

trembler, trahng-bleh, *v* to tremble; to quake; to shake; to quaver; to fear.

trémousser (se), ser treh-mooss-eh, *v* to bestir oneself.

tremper, trahng-peh, *v* to dip; to soak; to temper (steel).

trentaine, trahng-tenn, *f* about thirty.

trente, trahngt, *m* & *a* thirty.

trentième, trahng-te-aym, *m* & *a* thirtieth.

trépasser, treh-pahss-eh, *v* to die.

trépied, treh-pe-eh, *m* tripod.

trépigner, treh-peen-yeh, *v* to stamp.

très, tray, *adv* very; very much; most.

trésor, treh-zor, *m* treasure; treasury.

trésori-er, ère, treh-zor-e-eh, *mf* treasurer.

tressaillir, tress-sah'e-yeer, *v* to start; to thrill; to shudder.

tresse, trayss, *f* plait.

tréteau, treh-toh, *m* trestle; *pl* stage.

treuil, trer-e, *m* windlass.

trêve, trayv, *f* truce; –de, – der, no more.

tri, triage, tre, tre-ăhsh, *m* sorting; picking.

tribu, tre-bE, *f* tribe.

tribunal, tre-bE-năhl, *m* tribunal; bench; courthouse.

tribune, tre-bEen, *f* tribune; (*fig*) platform; (*fig*) grandstand.

tribut, tre-bE, *m* tribute.

tricher, tre-sheh, *v* to cheat.

tricot, tre-ko, *m* knitting; sweater.

tricoter, tre-ko-teh, *v* to knit.

tricycle, tre-see-kl, *m* tricycle.

trier, tre-eh, *v* to sort; to pick; to choose.

trimbaler, trang-băh-leh, *v* (*fam*) to carry about; to trail (children) about.

trimestre, tre-mess-tr, *m* quarter; term.

tringle, trang-gl, *f* rod; curtain rod.

trinquer, trang-keh, *v* to touch glasses; (*fam*) to drink together.

triompher, tre-ong-feh, *v* to triumph.

tripe, treep, f tripe; (fam) pl guts.

triple,* tre-pl, a treble; triple.

tripoter, tre-pot-eh, v to mess about.

triste,* trisst, a sad; gloomy; dreary.

tristesse, triss-tess, f sadness; gloom; melancholy.

triturer, tre-tE-reh, v to grind; to masticate.

troc, trock, m barter; exchange in kind.

trognon, tronn-yong, m core (of a pear); stump (of a cabbage).

trois, tro'ăh, m & a three.

troisième, tro'ăh-ze-aym, m & a third.

trombe, trongb, f waterspout.

trombone, trong-bonn, f trombone; paper clip.

trompe, trongp, f horn; trunk (of elephants, etc.); proboscis.

tromper, trong-peh, v to deceive; to cheat; **se –,** to make a mistake.

trompette, trong-pett, f trumpet.

trompeu-r, se, trong-per, mf & a* deceiver; betrayer; deceitful.

tronc, trong, m trunk; collection box.

tronçon, trong-song, m stump.

trône, trohn, m throne.

tronquer, trong-keh, v to mutilate; to cut off.

trop, tro, adv too; too much; too many.

troquer, trock-eh, v to barter; to exchange.

trotter, trot-eh, v to trot; to run.

trottinette, trot-e-nett, f child's scooter.

trottoir, trot-o'ăhr, m pavement.

trou, troo, m hole; gap; mouth.

trouble, troo-bl, m disturbance; perplexity; a muddy; dull; confused.

troubler, troo-bleh, v to disturb; to make muddy; to put about.

trouer, troo-eh, v to hole; to pierce.

troupe, troop, f troupe; gang; set; crew; pl troops.

troupeau, troo-poh, m flock; herd.

troupier, troo-pe-eh, m soldier; trooper.

trousse, trooss, f truss; bundle; case; kit.

trousseau, trooss-oh, m bunch of (keys); trousseau.

trouvaille, troo-vah'e, f discovery.

trouver, troo-veh, v to find; to think; to consider.

truc, trEEk, m (fam) trick; thing.

truffe, trEEf, f truffle.

truie, trwee, f sow.

truite, trweet, f trout.

truquer, trE-keh, v to fake.

tu, tE, pers pron sing (familiar form) you.

tuba, tEEb-ăh m snorkel.

tube, tEEb, m tube; pipe.

tuer, tE-eh, v to kill; to slaughter.

tuerie, tE-ree, f slaughter.

tue-tête (à), ăh tE-tayt, adv at the top of one's voice.

tuile, tweel, f tile.

tumeur, tE-mer, f tumor; growth.

tumulte, tE-mEElt, m tumult; turmoil.

turbot, tEEr-bo, m turbot.

turbulence, tEEr-bE-lahngss m turbulence.

turbulent, tEEr-bE-lahng, a turbulent; boisterous.

tutelle, tE-tell, f tutelage; protection; guardianship.

tu-teur, trice, tE-ter, mf guardian.

tutoyer, tE-to'ăh-yeh, v to address as **tu**; to be on familiar terms with.

tuyau, twee-yoh, *m* pipe; tube; funnel; (*fam*) tip.

type, teep, *m* type; symbol; (*pop*) man; guy.

typhon, te-*fong*, *m* typhoon.

typique, te-peeck, *a* typical.

tyran, te-rah*ng*, *m* tyrant.

tyrannie, te-răhn-nee, *f* tyranny.

tzigane, tse-găhn, *mf* & *a* gypsy.

ulcère, EEl-sair, *m* ulcer.

ulcéré, EEl-seh-reh, *pp* & *a* ulcerated; (*fig*) embittered.

ultérieur, e,* EEl-teh-re-er, *a* subsequent; ulterior.

un, e, ung, *a* & *n* one; unit; first.

un, e, ung, *indef art* & *pron* an; one; any.

unanime,* E-năh-neem, *a* unanimous.

uni, e, E-ne, *a* united; smooth; even; level; plain.

unième, E-ne-aym, *a* first (used only in compounds: **vingt et unième,** twenty-first, etc).

unifier, E-ne-fe-eh, *v* to unify.

uniforme, E-ne-form, *a* & *m* uniform.

uniformément, E-ne-for-meh-mahng, *adv* uniformly.

union, E-ne-ong, *f* union; marriage; harmony.

unique,* E-neeck, *a* only; sole; unique; matchless.

unir, E-neer, *v* to unite; to smooth.

unisson, E-niss-ong, *m* unison.

unité, E-ne-teh, *f* unity; unit.

univers, E-ne-vair, *m* universe.

universel, le,* E-ne-vair-sell, *a* universal.

universitaire, E-ne-vair-se-tair, *mf* & *a* member of the university; belonging to the university.

université, E-ne-vair-se-teh, *f* university.

urbain, e, EEr-bang, *a* urban.

urbanité, EEr-băh-ne-teh, *f* urbanity.

urgence, EEr-**shahng**ss, *f* urgency; emergency.

urgent, e, EEr-**shah**ng, *a* urgent.

urine, E-reen, *f* urine.

uriner, E-reen-eh, *v* to urinate.

urinoir, E-re-no'ăhr, *m* urinal.

urne, EE rn, *f* urn.

usage, E-zăhsh, *m* use; custom; habit; wear.

usagé, e, E-zăh-sheh, *a* that has been used.

usé, e, E-zeh, *pp* & *a* worn-out; stale; hackneyed.

user, E-zeh, *v* to wear; to spend; **–de,** to make use of

usine, E-zeen, *f* factory; plant.

usité, e, E-ze-teh, *a* in use; customary.

ustensile, EEss-**tah**ng-seel, *m* utensil.

usuel, le,* E-zE-ell, *a* usual.

usure, E-zEEr, *f* wear; usury.

usurpa-teur, trice, E-zEEr-

273

păh-**ter**, *mf* & *a* usurper;
usurping.

usurper, E-zEEr-peh, *v* to
usurp.

ut, EEt, *m* C (of music).

utérus, E-teh-rEss, *m*
uterus; womb.

utile, E-teel, *m* & *a**
utility; useful;
serviceable.

utiliser, E-te-le-zeh, *v* to
utilize; to make use of.

utilité, E-te-le-teh, *f*
utility; usefulness.

utopique, E-top-eeck, *a*
utopian.

vacance, văh-kahngss, *f*
vacancy; *pl* vacation;
holiday.

vacant, e, văh-kahng, *a*
vacant; unoccupied.

vacarme, văh-kăhrm, *m*
hubbub; uproar; din.

vaccination, văhck-seen-
ăh-se-ong, *f* vaccination.

vacciner, văhck-seen-eh,
v to vaccinate.

vache, văhsh, *f* cow;
cowhide.

vaciller, văh-sill-leh or
văh-see-yeh, *v* to waver;
to wobble.

va-et-vient, văh-eh-ve-
ang, *m* coming and
going.

vagabond, e, văh-găh-
bong, *a & mf* vagabond;
vagrant.

vague, văhg, *m* vagueness;

empty space; *a** vague;
indistinct; vacant; waste
(land).

vague, văhg, *f* wave;
billow; generation.

vague de chaleur, văhg-
der-shăh-**ler** *f* heat
wave.

vaillamment, vah'e-yăh-
mahng, *adv* valiantly.

vaillance, vah'e-yahngss, *f*
valor; bravery.

vaillant, e, vah'e-yahng, *a*
valiant; brave; gallant.

vain, e,* vang, *a* vain;
fruitless; vainglorious.

vaincre, vang-kr, *v* to
vanquish; to conquer; to
defeat.

vaincu, vang-kE, *m & a*
conquered; vanquished.

vainqueur, vang-ker, *m*
victor; prizewinner; *a*

victorious.

vaisseau, vayss-oh, *m*
vessel; ship; structure.

vaisselle, vayss-ell, *f*
dishes; washing up.

val, văhl, *m* vale; valley;
dale.

valable,* văh-lăh-bl, *a*
valid.

valet, văh-lay, *m* footman;
knave (cards).

valeur, văh-ler, *f* value;
worth; courage; *pl*
securities.

valeureu-x, se,* văh-ler-
rer, *a* valiant; brave.

valide,* văh-leed, *a* valid.

validité, văh-le-de-teh, *f*
validity.

valise, văh-leez, *f* suitcase.

vallée, văh-leh, *f* valley;
vale; dale.

vallon, văh-long, *m* dale;
small valley.

valoir, văh-lo'ăhr, *v* to be
worth; to yield.

valse, văhls, *f* waltz.

valve, văhlv, *f* valve.

vanille, văh-nee-ye, *f*
vanilla.

vanité, văh-ne-teh, *f*
vanity.

vaniteu-x, se,* văh-ne-
ter, *a* vain; vainglorious.

vanne, văhn, *f* sluice;
watergate.

vanner, văh-neh, *v* to
winnow.

vannerie, văhn-ner-ree, *f* basketwork.

vantard, e, vahng-tăhr, *mf* & *a* boaster; boastful; boasting.

vanter, vahng-teh, *v* to praise; to extol; **se –,** to boast.

vapeur, văh-per, *m* steamer; *f* vapor; steam.

vaporeu-x, se,* văh-por-er, *a* vaporous; hazy.

vaporiser, văh-por-e-zeh, *v* to vaporize; to spray.

vaquer, văh-keh, *v* to be vacant; **-à, – ăh,** to attend to.

vareuse, văh-rerz, *f* pea jacket.

variable,* văh-re-ăh-bl, *a* variable; changeable.

variation, văh-re-ăh-se-ong, *f* variation.

varice, văh-reess, *f* varicose vein.

varicelle, văh-re-sell, *f* chicken pox.

varier, văh-re-eh, *v* to vary; to differ.

variété, văh-re-eh-teh, *f* variety.

variole, văh-re-ol, *f* smallpox.

vase, vahz, *m* vase; urn; vessel; *f* mud; slime.

vaseu-x, se, vah-zer, *a* muddy; miry.

vaste,* văhsst, *a* vast; spacious; wide; great.

va-tout, văh-too, *m* last stake.

vaurien, ne, voh-re-ang, *mf* worthless person.

vautour, voh-toohr, *m* vulture.

vautrer (se), ser voh-treh, *v* to wallow; to sprawl.

veau, voh, *m* calf; calf's leather; veal.

vedette, ver-dett, *f* motorboat; star (film).

végétal, e, veh-sheh-tăhl, *a* vegetable.

véhément, e,* veh-eh-mahng, *a* vehement.

véhicule, veh-e-kEEl, *m* vehicle.

veille, vay'e, *f* wakefulness; watch; eve.

veillée, vay'e-yeh, *f* sitting up; vigil.

veiller, vay'e-yeh, *v* to sit up; to watch; to be awake; **–(á)** to see to.

veilleuse, vay'e-yerz, *f* night-light; pilot light.

veine, vayn, *f* vein; (*fam*) luck.

velléité, veh-leh-e-teh, *f* slight desire.

vélo, veh-lo, *m* (*fam*) bicycle.

vélodrome, veh-lod-rohm, *m* cycling track.

vélo tout terrain, (veh-lo) too-tay-rang *m* mountain bike.

velours, ver-loohr, *m* velvet.

velouté, e, ver-loo-teh, *a* velvety; soft; rich (soup, etc).

velu, e, ver-lE, *a* hairy; shaggy.

venaison, ver-nay-zong, *f* venison.

venant, e, ver-nahng, *a* coming; thriving; **á tout –,** ăh-too–, to all and sundry.

vendable, vahng-dăh-bl, *a* marketable.

vendange, vahng-dahng sh, *f* vintage; grape harvest.

vendeu-r, se, vahng-der, *mf* seller; salesman (-woman).

vendre, vahng-dr, *v* to sell; to betray.

vendredi, vahng-drer-de, *m* Friday.

vénéneu-x, se, veh-neh-ner, *a* poisonous.

vénérer, veh-neh-reh, *v* to venerate.

vénérien, ne, veh-neh-re-ang, *a* venereal.

vengeance, vahng-shahngss, *f* revenge.

venger, vahng- sheh, *v* to avenge; to revenge.

veng-eur, eresse, vahng-sher, *mf* & *a* avenger.

véniel, le, veh-ne-ell, *a* venial.

venimeu-x, se, ver-ne-mer, *a* venomous.

venin, ver-nang, *m* venom; (*fig*) spite; (*fig*) rancor.

venir, ver-neer, *v* to come; to arrive; to happen; to grow; **—de,**—der, to have just...

vent, vahng, *m* wind; scent; (*fig*) emptiness.

venter, vahngt, *f* sale.

vente, vahng-teh, *v* to be windy.

ventilateur, vahng-te-lăh-ter, *m* ventilator; fan.

ventouse, vahng-tooz, *f* suction cup.

ventre, vahng-tr, *m* abdomen; belly; stomach.

ventru, e, vahng-trE, *a* corpulent; big-bellied.

venu, e, ver-nE, *mf* comer.

venue, ver-nE, *f* coming; arrival; growth.

vêpres, vay-pr, *fpl* vespers.

ver, vair, *m* worm; maggot.

verbal, e,* vair-băhl, *a* verbal.

verbe, vairb, *m* verb.

verbeu-x, se, vair-ber, *a* verbose.

verbiage, vair-be-ăhsh, *m* verbiage; mere talk.

verdâtre, vair-dah-tr, *a* greenish.

verdeur, vair-der, *f* greenness; tartness.

verdir, vair-deer, *v* to grow green; to make green.

verdoyant, e, vair-do'aăh-yahng, *a* verdant.

verdure, vair-dEEr, *f* greenness; verdure; foliage.

véreu-x, se, veh-rer, *a* worm-eaten; (*fam*) suspicious; dishonest.

verge, vairsh, *m f* penis; *pl* birch rod.

verger, vair-sheh, *m* orchard.

verglas, vair-glah, *m* black ice.

vergogne (sans), sahng vair-gonn-yer, *f* shameless.

véridique,* veh-re-deeck, *a* veracious; truthful.

vérifier, veh-re-fe-eh, *v* to verify; to check.

véritable,* veh-re-tăh-bl, *a* true; genuine; downright.

vérité, veh-re-teh, *f* truth.

vermeil, vair-may'e, *m* vermeil.

vermeil, le, vair-may'e, *a* ruby; rosy; vermilion.

vermine, vair-meen, *f* vermin.

vermisseau, vair-miss-oh, *m* small worm.

vermoulu, e, vair-moo-lE, *a* worm-eaten.

vernir, vair-neer, *v* to varnish.

vernis, vair-ne, *m* varnish; japan (japonaiserie); French polish.

vérole (petite), per-teet veh-rol, *f* smallpox.

verre, vair, *m* glass.

verrerie, vay-rer-ree, *f* glassworks.

verrou, vay-roo, *m* bolt.

verrouiller, vay-roo'e-yeh, *v* to bolt.

verrue, vay-rE, *f* wart.

vers, vair, *prep* towards; about.

vers, vair, *m* verse; line.

versant, vair-sahng, *m* slope; bank.

verse (à), ăh vairss, *adv* in torrents (rain).

versé, e, vair-seh, *a* well-versed; well up (**dans, en,** in).

versement, vair-ser-mahng, *m* payment; partial installment.

verser, vair-seh, *v* to pour; to shed; to lodge; to pay in; to overturn.

verset, vair-say, *m* verse (Bible, etc.).

verso, vair-so, *m* back; reverse (of paper, etc.).

vert, e, vair, *a* green; unripe; sharp; *m* color green.

vertement, vair-ter-mah*ng*, *adv* sharply; severely.

vertical, e,* vair-te-kăhl, *a* vertical.

vertige, vair-teesh, *m* giddiness; vertigo.

vertigineu-x, se, vair-te-she-ner, *a* giddy; dizzy.

vertu, vair-tE, *f* virtue; chastity; power; property.

vertueu-x, se,* vair-tE-er, *a* virtuous.

verve, vairv, *f* animation; zest; spirits.

vessie, vayss-ee, *f* bladder.

veste, vaysst, *f* jacket.

vestiaire, vayss-te-air, *m* cloakroom; locker room; changing room (sport).

vestibule, vayss-te-bEEl, *m* vestibule.

vestige, vayss-teesh, *m* vestige; remains; track.

veston, vayss-tong, *m* jacket.

vêtement, vaytt-mah*ng*, *m* garment; *pl* clothes.

vétérinaire, veh-teh-re-nair, *m & a* veterinarian; veterinary.

vêtir, vay-teer, *v* to clothe; to dress; to array.

veu-f, ve, verf, *mf & a* widower; widow; widowed.

veule, verl, *a* weak; soft.

veuvage, ver-văhsh, *m* widowhood.

vexatoire, veck-săh-to'ăhr, *a* vexatious.

vexer, veck-seh, *v* to vex; to annoy.

viable, ve-ăh-bl, *a* viable.

viag-er, ère, ve-ăh-sheh, *a* for life.

viande, ve-ahngd, *f* meat; flesh.

vibrant, e, ve-brahng, *a* vibrating.

vibrer, ve-breh, *v* to vibrate.

vicaire, ve-kair, *m* curate.

vice, veess, *m* vice; defect; blemish; flaw.

vice versa, vess-vair-săh *adv* vice versa.

vicié, e, veess-e-eh, *a* vitiated; corrupt.

vicier, veess-e-eh, *v* to vitiate; to corrupt.

vicieu-x, se,* veess-e-er, *a* vicious; faulty; depraved.

vicomte, ve-kongt, *m* viscount.

vicomtesse, ve-kong-tess, *f* viscountess.

victime, vick-teem, *f* victim.

victoire, vick-to'ăhr, *f* victory.

victorieu-x, se,* vick-tor-e-er, *a* victorious.

victuaille, vick-tE-ah'e, *f* victuals; *pl* provisions.

vidange, ve-dahng sh, *f* clearing out; draining.

vide, veed, *m* empty space; vacuum; *a* empty.

vidéo, ve-deh-oh *f* video (film).

vidéocassette, vee-deh-oh-kăh-sett *f* video cassette.

vider, vee-deh, *v* to empty; to drain; to settle.

vie, vee, *f* life; living; existence.

vieillard, ve-ay'e-ăhr, *m* old man.

vieille, ve-ay'e, *f* old woman.

vieillerie, ve-ay'e-ree, *f* old things.

vieillesse, ve-ay'e-ess, *f* old age.

vieillir, ve-ay'e-eer, *v* to grow old; to age.

vierge, ve-airsh, *f* virgin.

vieux, ve-er, *m* old man; *pl* old folk.

vieux (before a vowel or **h** mute: **vieil**), *f* **vieille,** ve-er, ve-ay'e, *a* old.

vi-f, ve,* veef, *a* alive; sharp; quick-tempered; bright (of colors); strong; running.

vif-argent, veef-ăhr-**shah**ng, *m* quicksilver (mercury).

vigie, ve-**shee**, *f* lookout.

vigilamment, ve-she-lăh-mahng, *adv* vigilantly.

vigilance, ve-she-lahngss, *f* vigilance.

vigilant, e, ve-she-lăhng, *a* vigilant.

vigne, veen-yer, *f* vine; vineyard.

vigneron, veen-yer-rong, *m* winegrower.

vignoble, veen-yo-bl, *m* vineyard.

vigoureu-x, se,* ve-goo-rer, *a* vigorous; sturdy; energetic.

vigueur, ve-gher, *f* vigor; strength.

vil, e,* veel, *a* vile; base; mean; despicable.

vilain, e,* ve-lang, *a* ugly; nasty; naughty (child).

vilenie, ve-ler-nee, *f* meanness; dirty trick; *pl* abuse.

village, ve-lăhsh, *m* village.

villageois, e, ve-lăh-sho'ăh, *mf* & *a* villager; rustic.

ville, veel, *f* town; city.

vin, vang, *m* wine.

vinaigre, ve-nay-gr, *m* vinegar.

vinaigrette, ve-nay-grett, *f* oil and vinegar dressing; vinagrette.

vindicati-f, ve, vang-de-kăh-teeff, *a* revengeful.

vingt, vang, *m* & *a* twenty; twentieth.

vingtaine, vang-tain, *f* about twenty.

vingtième, vang-te-aym, *m* & *a* twentieth.

viol, ve-ol, *m* rape.

violation, ve-oll-ăh-se-ong, *f* violation; infringement.

violemment, ve-oll-ăh-mahng, *adv* violently.

violence, ve-oll-ahngss, *f* violence.

violent, e, ve-oll-ahng, *a* violent.

violer, ve-oll-eh, *v* to violate; to infringe; to rape.

violet, te, ve-oll-ay, *a* violet-colored; *m* color violet.

violette, ve-oll-ett, *f* violet.

violon, ve-oll-ong, *m* violin; violinist; (*pop*) prison.

vipère, ve-pair, *f* viper; adder.

virage, ve-răhsh, *m* turning; bend; toning (photography); changing (of color).

virement, veer-mahng, *m* transfer (finance).

virer, ve-reh, *v* to turn; to take a bend; (*naut*) to tack.

virgule, veer-ghEEl, *f* comma.

viril, e,* ve-reel, *a* manly; virile.

virilité, ve-re-le-teh, *m* manhood; virility; vigor.

virtuel, le,* veer-tE-ell, *a* virtual.

virulence, ve-rE-lahngss, *f* virulence.

virus, ve-rEEss, *m* virus.

vis, veess, *f* screw.

visa, ve-zăh, *m* signature; visa.

visage, ve-zăhsh, *m* face; visage; look.

vis-à-vis, ve-zăh-ve, *adv* in relation to.

viscère, veess-sair, *m* viscus; entrails.

visée, ve-zeh, *f* aim; design; end.

viser, ve-zeh, *v* to aim at; to aspire to; to endorse.

visible,* ve-zee-bl, *a* visible.

visière, ve-ze-air, *f* visor (of a helmet); peak (of caps, etc.).

vision, ve-ze-ong, *f* vision; sight; phantom.

visionnaire, ve-ze-onn-air, *a* visionary.

visite, ve-zeet, *f* visit;

search; medical examination.

visiter, ve-ze-teh, *v* to visit; to inspect; to search.

visqueu-x, se, veess-ker, *a* viscous; sticky.

visser, veess-eh, *v* to screw on.

visuel, le,* ve-zE-ell, *a* visual.

vital, e, ve-tăhl, *a* vital.

vitalité, ve-tăh-le-teh, *f* vitality.

vitamine, ve-tăh-meen *f* vitamin.

vite, veet, *adv* quickly; fast; *a* quick; swift.

vitesse, ve-tess, *f* quickness; speed.

vitesse maximale permise, ve-tess-măhks-e-măhl *f* speed limit.

viticulture, ve-te-kEEl-tEEr, *f* wine-growing.

vitrail, ve-trah'e, *m* stained glass window.

vitre, vee-tr, *f* pane; windowpane.

vitrier, ve-tre-eh, *m* glazier.

vitrine, ve-treen, *f* store window; display cabinet.

vivace, ve-văhss, *a* long-lived; deep-rooted.

vivacité, ve-văhss-e-teh, *f* vivacity; hastiness (of temper).

vivant, ve-vahng, *m* living person; lifetime.

vivant, e, ve-vahng, *a* living; alive; lively.

vivier, ve-ve-eh, *m* fish pond; breeding ground.

vivre, vee-vr, *v* to live; to board.

vivres, vee-vr, *mpl* food; provisions.

vocable, vock-ăh-bl, *m* word; term.

vocabulaire, vock-ăh-bE-lair, *m* vocabulary; word list.

vocal, e, vock-ăhl, *a* vocal.

vocatif, vock-ăh-teeff, *m* vocative case.

vocation, vock-ăh-se-ong, *f* vocation; calling.

vociférer, voss-e-feh-reh, *v* to bawl; to cry out.

vœu, ver, *m* vow; wish.

vogue, vogh, *f* vogue; fashion.

voguer, vogh-eh, *v* to sail.

voici, vo'ăh-se, *adv* here is; here are.

voie, vo'ăh, *f* way; road; track; (*fig*) gauge; means.

voilà, vo'ăh-lăh, *adv* there is; there are.

voile, vo'ăhl, *m* veil; voile; *f* sail.

voiler, vo'ăh-leh, *v* to veil; to cloak; to conceal.

voilier, vo'ăh-le-eh, *m* sail-maker; sailboat.

voir, vo'ăhr, *v* to see; to behold; to inspect; to visit; to meet.

voire, vo'ăhr, *adv* indeed; nay; even.

voisin, e, vo'ăh-zang, *mf* neighbor; *a* adjoining.

voisinage, vo'ăh-ze-năhsh, *m* neighborhood.

voiture, vo'ăh-tEEr, *f* automobile; cart; carriage.

voix, vo'ăh, *f* voice; tone; vote.

vol, vol, *m* flight; theft.

volage, voll-ăhsh, *a* fickle.

volaille, voll-ah'e, *f* poultry.

volant, voll-ahng, *m* shuttlecock; steering wheel.

vol à l'étalalge, voll-ăh-leh-tăh-lăhsh *m* shoplifting.

volant, e, voll-ahng, *a* flying; loose.

volcan, voll-kahng, *m* volcano.

volée, voll-eh, *f* flight (of birds); flock; volley (of guns); shower (of blows); peal (of bells).

voler, voll-eh, *v* to fly; to soar; to steal; **il ne l'a pas volé,** ill ner lăh păh voll-eh, it serves him right.

volet, voll-ay, *m* shutter.

voleu-r, se, voll-er, *mf* thief; robber.

voliére, voll-e-air, *f* aviary.

vol libre, voll-lee-br *m* hang-gliding.

volontaire, voll-ong-tair, *m* volunteer; *a** voluntary; headstrong.

volonté, voll-ong-teh, *f* will; *pl* whims; caprices.

volontiers, voll-ong-te-eh, *adv* willingly.

voltage, voll-tăhsh, *m* voltage.

volte-face, voll-ter-făhss, *f* turning round; about-face.

voltiger, voll-te-sheh, *v* to flutter; to perform on rope, trapeze, etc.

voltigeur, voll-te-sher, *m* performer on rope, trapeze, etc.

volubilité, voll-E-be-le-teh, *f* volubility.

volume, voll-EEm, *m* volume; bulk; mass; size.

volumineu-x, se, voll-E-me-ner, *a* voluminous.

volupté, voll-EEp-teh, *f* voluptuousness; luxury.

vomir, vomm-eer, *v* to vomit; to throw up.

vomissement, vomm-iss-mahng, *m* vomiting.

vomitif, vomm-e-teeff, *m* emetic.

vorace,* vor-ăhss, *a* voracious; ravenous.

voracité, vor-ăhss-e-teh, *f* voracity; ravenousness.

vote, vot, *m* vote; suffrage; poll; division.

voter, vot-eh, *v* to vote.

votre, votr, *poss a* your; *pl* **vos,** voh.

vôtre (le, la, les) ler, lăh, leh voh-tr, *poss pron* yours.

vouer, voo-eh, *v* to devote; to vow; to dedicate.

vouloir, voo-lo'ăhr, *v* to be willing; to want; to require; to order; to consent.

vouloir, voo-lo'ăhr, *m* will.

voulu, e, voo-lE, *pp* & *a* wanted; required; intentional.

vous, voo, *pers pron* you.

voûte, voot, *f* vault.

vouvoyer, voo-vo'ăh-yeh, *v* to address as **vous**.

voyage, vo'ăh-yăhsh, *m* travel; journey; trip.

voyager, vo'ăh-yăh-sheh, *v* to travel; to journey.

voyageu-r, se, vo'ăh-yăh-sher, *mf* & *a* traveler; passenger; traveling.

voyant, e, vo'ăh-yahng, *mf* fortune-teller; *a* showy; gaudy.

voyelle, vo'ăh-yell, *f* vowel.

voyou, vo'ăh-yoo, *m* hooligan; ruffian.

vrac (en) ahng vrăhck, *adv* in bulk.

vrai, vray, *m* truth.

vrai, e, vray, *a* true; genuine; regular; errant.

vraiment, vray-mahng, *adv* truly; indeed.

vraisemblable,* vray-sahng-blăh-bl, *a* likely.

vraisemblance, vray-sahng-blahngss, *f* likelihood.

vrille, vree-ye, *f* gimlet.

vu, vE, *prep* seeing; considering; *m* sight; examination.

vu, e, vE, *pp* & *a* seen; examined.

vue, vE, *f* sight; view; prospect; design; purpose.

vulgaire, vEEl-ghair, *m* the common people; *a** vulgar; coarse.

wagon, văh-go*ng m*
carriage; car; – **lit,** – lee,
Pullman car.

xérès, keh-rayss, *m* sherry.

y, e, *pron* to it; at it; by it;
for it; to them; at them,
etc.

y, e, *adv* there; within; –
compris, – kong-pree,
including.

yaourt, yah-oort, *m*
yogurt.

yacht, e-ăhck, *m* yacht.

yeux, e-er, *mpl* eyes.

youyou, yoo-yoo, *m*
dinghy.

zèbre, zay-br, *m* zebra.
zébré, e, zeh-breh, *a* striped.
zéla-teur, trice, zeh-läh-ter, *mf* zealot.
zèle, zayl, *m* zeal; ardor; earnestness.
zénith, zeh-neet, *m* zenith.
zéphir, zeh-feer, *m* zephyr; gentle breeze.
zeppelin, zehp-lang, *m* zeppelin.
zéro, zeh-ro, *m* zero; (*fig*) cipher; (*fig*) nobody.
zeste, zaysst, *m* zest; peel; zeal.
zézaiement, zeh-zay-mah*ng*, *m* lisping; limp.
zézayer, zeh-zay-yeh, *v* to lisp.
zibeline, zeeb-leen, *f* sable.
zigzaguer, zeeg-zäh-gheh, *v* to stagger; to zigzag.

zinc, zangk, *m* zinc.
zingueur, zang-gher, *m* zinc worker.
zizanie, zze-zah-nee, *f* ill-feeling.
zodiaque, zod-e-ähck, *m* zodiac.
zona, zoh-näh, *m* shingles.
zone, zohn, *f* zone.
zoo, zoh, *m* (*fam*) zoo.
zoologie, zo-oll-osh-ee, *f* zoology.
zoophyte, zo-off-eet, *m* zoophyte.
zut! zEEt, *interj* (*fam*) nuts!

ENGLISH · FRENCH
ANGLAIS · FRANÇAIS

Pour l'explication de la
prononciation figurée,
lire avec soin la page 5.

a, é, *art* un, une.

abandon, a-bănn´-d'n, *v* abandonner; **–ed**, *a* abandonné; (morally) dissolu.

abase, a-béce´, *v* abaisser; humilier.

abash, a-băche´, *v* déconcerter.

abate, a-béte´, *v* diminuer.

abbey, ăb´ei, *n* abbay *f*.

abbot, ăb´-otte, *n* abbé *m*.

abbreviate, ab-bri´-vi-éte, *v* abréger.

abdicate, ăb´-di-quéte, *v* abdiquer.

abdomen, ăb-dau´-menn, *n* abdomen *m*.

abduction, ăb-doc´-ch'n, *n* enlèvement *m*.

abeyance, a-bé´-annce, *n* suspension *f*.

abide, a-bäïde´, *v* demeurer; **–by**, s'en tenir à.

ability, a-bil´-i-ti, *n* habileté *f*; capacité *f*.

ablaze, a-bléze´, *a* en flammes; enflammé.

able, é´-b'l, *a* capable; habile; **to be –**, pouvoir.

abnormal*, ăb-nôr´-m'l, *a* anormal.

aboard, a-bôrde´, *adv* à bord.

abode, a-bôde´, *n* demeure *f*.

abolish, a-bol´-iche, *v* abolir.

abominable, a-bomm´-inn-a-b'l, *a* abominable.

aboriginal, ab-ŏr-idj´-inn-'l, *a* aborigène.

abortion, a-bôr´-ch'n, *n* avortement *m*.

abound, a-bâ´´ounnde, *v* abonder.

about, a-bâoute´, *adv* environ; à peu près; autour. *prep* auprès de; autour de; au sujet de.

above, a-bove´, *adv* en haut; au-dessus; ci-dessus. *prep* au-dessus de; plus de; sur.

abrasion, a-bré´-j'n, *n* écorchure *f*.

abreast, a-breste´, *adv* de front.

abroad, a-brôde´, *adv* à l'étranger.

abrupt*, a-bropte´, *a* brusque; (steep) escarpé.

abscess, ăb´-sesse, *n* abcès *m*.

abscond, ăb-skonnde´, *v* s'enfuir; se cacher.

absence, ăb´-sennce, *n* absence *f*.

absent, ăb´-sennte, *a* absent. *v* (– oneself) s'absenter; **–ee**, *n* absent *m* absente *f*; **–minded**, *a* distrait.

absolute*, ăb´-sŏ-lioute, *a* absolu.

absolve, ăb-zolve´, *v* absoudre.

absorb, ăb-sorb´, *v* absorber.

abstain, ab-sténe´, *v* s'abstenir de.

abstainer, ab-sténe´-'r, *n* abstinent *m*.

abstemious*, ab-sti´-mi-*euce*, *a* sobre.

abstinence, ăb´-sti-nennce, *n* abstinence *f*.

abstract, ăb-străcte´, *v* abstraire; résumer.

abstract, ăb´-străcte, *n* résumé *m*. *a* abstrait.

absurd*, ăb-seurde´, *a* absurde.

abundant, *a*-bonne´d'nt, *a* abondant.

abuse, *a*-biouze´, *v* abuser de; injurier.

abuse, *a*-biouce´, *n* abus *m*; injures *fpl*.

abusive*, *a*-biou´-cive, *a* injurieux; abusif.

abyss, *a*-bisse´, *n* abîme *m*.

academy, *a*-kăd´-é-mi, *n* académie *f*.

accede, ăx-îde´, *v* accéder; monter (sur).

accelerate, ăx-el´-é-réte, *v* accélérer.

accent, ăx-ennte´, *v* accentuer.

accent, ăx´-ennte, *n* accent *m*.

accentuate, ăx-ennte´-iou-éte, *v* accentuer.

accept, ăx-epte´, *v* accepter; –ance, *n* acceptation *f*.

access, ăx´-esse, *n* accès *m*.

accession, ăx-ech'n, *n* avènement *m*.

accessory, ăx´-ess-ŏ-ri, *n* complice *m*; accessoire *m*.

accident, ăx´-i-dennte, *n* accident *m*.

accidental*, ăx-i-denn´-t'l, *a* accidentel; accessoire.

acclaim, ac-cléme´, *v* acclamer.

accommodate, ac-comm´-mŏ-déte, *v* accommoder; loger; fournir.

accommodation, ac-comm-mŏ-dé´-ch'n, *n* logement *m*; arrangement *m*; aménagement *m*.

accompaniment, ac-comm´-pa-ni-m'nt, *n* accompagnement *m*.

accompanist, ac-comm´-pa-nisste, *n* accompagnateur *m*; accompagnatrice *f*.

accompany, ac-comm´-pa-ni, *v* accompagner.

accomplice, ac-comm´-plisse, *n* complice *m*.

accomplish, ac-comm´-pliche, *v* accomplir.

accomplishment, ac-comm´-pliche-m'nt, *n* accomplissement *m*; –s, talents *mpl*.

accord, ac-côrde´, *v* accorder. *n* accord *m*; of one's own –, de plein

gré; in –ance with, d'accord avec; –ing to, *prep* selon, d'après; –ingly, *adv* en conséquence.

accordion, ac-côr´-di'n, *n* accordéon *m*.

accost, ac-coste´, *v* accoster; aborder.

account, *a*-câ°ounnte´, *n* (bill) compte *m*; on –, (payment) en acompte; –able, *a* responsable; –ant, *n* comptable *m*.

accrue, ac-croue´, *v* provenir (de); s'accumuler.

accumulate, ac-kiou´-miou-léte, *v* (s')accumuler.

accuracy, ă´-kiou-ra-ci, *n* exactitude *f*; précision *f*.

accurate*, ă´-kiou-réte, *a* exact; correct; juste.

accursed, *a*-keur´-st, *a* maudit.

accusation, ac-kiou-zé´-ch'n, *n* accusation *f*.

accuse, *a*-kiouze´, *v* accuser.

accustom, *a*-coss´-t'm, *v* accoutumer; habituer.

ace, éce, *n* (cards) as *m*.

ache, éque, *n* douleur *f*; mal *m*. *v* faire mal.

achieve, *a*-tchîve´, *v* accomplir; –ment, *n* accomplissement *m*;

exploit *m*.

acid, ă´-side, *n* & *a* acide *m*.

acidity, *a*-side´-i-ti, *n* acidité *f*; (*med*) aigreurs *fpl*.

acknowledge, ăc-nol´-èdje, *v* reconnaître; accuser réception de.

acorn, é´-côrne, *n* gland *m*.

acoustics, *a*-couss´-tiks, *npl* acoustique *f*.

acquaint, *a*-couénnte´, *v* informer; –ance, *n* connaissance *f*.

acquiesce, ă-coui-esse´, *v* acquiescer (à).

acquire, *a*-couâïre´, *v* acquérir; apprendre.

acquisition, *a*-coui-zi´-ch'n, *n* acquisition *f*.

acquit, *a*-couitte´, *v* acquitter.

acquittal, *a*-coui´-t'l, *n* acquittement *m*.

acre, é´-*keur*, *n* acre *m*.

acrid, ăc´-ridde, *a* âcre.

across, *a*-crosse´, *adv* à travers; de l'autre côté. *prep* au travers de.

act, ăcte, *n* action *f*; (deed) acte *m*; (of a play) acte *m*; (law) loi *f*. *v* agir; (in theater) jouer; –or, *n* acteur *m*; –ress, actrice *f*.

action, ăk´-ch'n, *n* action

f; procès *m*; combat *m*.

active*, ăc´-tive, *a* actif; alerte; agile.

actual*, ăc´-tiou-al, *a* réel; actuel.

actuate, ăc´-tiou-éte, *v* mettre en action; animer; faire agir.

acumen, *a*-kiou´-mène, *n* perspicacité *f*.

acute, *a*-kioute´, *a* aigu.

acuteness, *a*-kioute´-nesse, *n* acuité *f*; finesse *f*.

adamant, ăd´-*a*-mannte, *a* inflexible.

adapt, *a*-dăpt´, *v* adapter; –oneself, s'adapter.

adaptation, *a*-dăpp-té´-ch'n, *n* adaptation *f*.

add, ădde, *v* additionner; –to, ajouter à; –ition, *n* addition *f*; –itional, *a* supplémentaire.

adder, ăd´-*eur*, *n* (snake) vipère *f*.

addict, ăd´-icte´, *n* personne adonnée (à) *f*; –ed, *a* adonné (à).

address, ad-dresse´, *n* adresse *f*; (speech) discours *m*; *v* (letters, etc.) adresser; (a meeting) prendre la parole; –ee, *n* destinataire *m* & *f*.

adequate, ăd´-i-couéte, *a* proportionnel; suffisant.

adhere, ăd-hîre´, *v* adhérer; s'en tenir à; –nt, *a* & *n*, adhérent *m*; partisan *m*.

adhesive, ăd-hî´-cive, *n* colle *f*. *a* adhésif.

adjacent, ad-jé´-sennte, *a* adjacent (à); avoisinant.

adjourn, ad-jeurne´, *v* ajourner; remettre. *n* remise *f*.

adjournment, ad-jeurne´-m'nt, *n* ajournement *m*.

adjunct, ăd´-jonn-kt, *n* accessoire *m*. *a* adjoint.

adjust, ad-joste´, *v* ajuster; régler.

adjustment, ad-joste´-m'nt, *n* ajustement *m*.

adjutant, ăd´-djou-t'nt, *n* adjudant-major *m*.

administer, ad-minn´-isse-teur, *v* administrer.

admirable, ăd´-mi-ra-b'l, *a* admirable.

admiral, ăd´-mi-ral, *n* amiral *m*; –ty, amirauté *f*.

admire, ad-mâïre´, *v* admirer.

admission, ad-mi´-ch'n, *n* admission *f*; entrée *f*.

admit, ad-mitte´, *v* admettre; laisser entrer.

admittance, ad-mit´-t'nce, *n* entrée *f*; aveu *m*.

admonish, ad-monn´-iche, *v* exhorter.

adopt, a-dopte´, v adopter.

adore, a-daure´, v adorer.

adorn, a-dôrne´, v parer; **–ment,** n parure f.

adrift, a-drifte´, adv (naut) à la dérive.

adroit*, a-drô'îte´, a adroit; habile.

adult, a-dolte´, n adulte m & f. a adulte.

adulterate, a-dol´-té-réte, v falsifier; corrompre.

adultery, a-dol´-té-ri, n adultère m.

advance, ăd-vânnce´, v avancer; (price) hausser; faire avancer. n (progress) progrès m; (money) avance f; (prices) hausse f; **in –,** d'avance; **–ment,** n avancement m; progrès m.

advantage, ăd-vănn´-tèdje, n avantage m.

advantageous*, ăd-vann-té´-djeusse, a avantageux.

advent, ăd´-vennte, n venue f; (eccl) Avent m.

adventure, ad-venn´-tioure, n aventure f.

adventurer, ad-venn´-tiou-r'r, n aventurier m.

adventurous, ad-venn´-tiou-reuce, a aventureux.

adversary, ăd´-veur-sa-ri,

n adversaire m & f.

adverse*, ăd´-veursse, a défavorable; adverse; opposé.

advertise, ăd´-veur-tâïze, v annoncer; faire de la réclame.

advertisement, ad-veur´-tize-m'nt, n annonce f; réclame f.

advertising, ăd-veur-tăï´-zinng, n publicité f.

advice, ad-văïsse´, n conseil m.

advisable, ad-vâï´-za-b'l, a prudent; préférable.

advise, ad-vâïze´, v conseiller; aviser.

adviser, ad-vâï´-z'r, n conseiller m.

advocate, ad´-vŏ-kéte, n avocat m. v soutenir.

aerial, é-i´-ri-al, n antenne f. a aérien.

afar, a-fare´, adv loin; de loin; au loin.

affable, ăf´-fa-b'l, a affable.

affair, a-faire´, n affaire f; (love) aventure f; liaison f.

affect, a-fecte´, v affecter; émouvoir; prétendre; **–ed,** a (manners, style) maniéré; (moved) affecté, ému; **–ing,** touchant; **–ion,** n affection f; tendresse f.

affectionate*, a-féque´-chŏ-néte, a affectueux.

affidavit, ă-fi-dé´-vitte, n déposition sous serment f.

affiliate, a-fil´-i-éte, v affilier.

affinity, a-fine´-i-ti, n affinité f.

affirm, a-feurme´, v affirmer; **–ative*,** a affirmatif.

affirmation, ă-feur-mê´-ch'n, n affirmation f.

affix, a-fixe´, v apposer; attacher.

afflict, a-flicte´, v affliger; **–ion,** n affliction f.

affluence, ă-flou-ennce, n affluence f; opulence f.

afford, a-faurde´, v avoir les moyens de.

affray, a-fré´, n échauffourée f; rixe f.

affront, a-fronnte´, n affront m. v affronter; insulter.

aflame, a-fléme´, adv & a enflammé; en flammes.

afloat, a-flôte´, adv à flot.

afraid, a-fréde´, **to be –,** v avoir peur; être effrayé.

afresh, a-fréche´, adv de nouveau.

aft, ăfte, adv (naut) à l'arrière.

after, âf´-t'r, adv après; suivant. prep après;

–noon, n après-midi m & f; **–wards,** adv ensuite.

again, a-guénne´, adv encore; de nouveau.

against, a-gué´-n'ste, prep contre.

age, é´-dje, n âge m; (period) siècle m. **to be of –,** v être majeur; **–d,** a âgé; vieux.

agency, é´-djenn-ci, n agence f; entremise f; bureau m.

agenda, ă-djenn´-d'r, n ordre du jour m.

agent, é´-dj'nt, n agent m; représentant m.

aggravate, ăg´-gra-véte, v aggraver; empirer; (fam) agacer.

aggregate, ăg´-gri-guette, v rassembler. n total m.

aggression, a-grè´-ch'n, n agression f; attaque f.

aggressive*, a-gresse´-ive, a agressif.

aggrieve, a-grîve´, v chagriner.

aghast, a-gâsste´, a consterné; bouche bée.

agile, ă-djâïl, a agile.

agitate, ă-dji-téte, v agiter.

agitation, a-dji-té´-ch'n, n agitation f.

ago, a-gau´, adv passé; **long –,** il y a longtemps.

agonize, ăg´-o-nâïze, v

agoniser; torturer.

agony, ăg´-o-ni, n agonie f; (mental) angoisse f.

agree, a-grî´, v s'accorder; être d'accord; consentir; **–able,** a agréable; **–ment,** n accord m; contrat m.

agricultural, ăg-gri-kol´-tiou-r'l, a agricole.

agriculture, ăg´-gri-kol-tioure, n agriculture f.

aground, a-grâ´ounnde, adv (naut) échoué.

ahead, a-hêdde´, adv en avant; devant.

aid, éde, n aide f; secours m; v aider.

aids, éds, n sida m.

ail, éle, v avoir mal; **–ing,** a souffrant.

ailment, éle´-m'nt, n maladie f; mal m.

aim, éme, v viser. n but m; visée f; **–less,** a sans but.

air, aire, v aérer; n air m; **––conditioned,** a climatisé; **––hostess,** hôtesse de l'air f; **––plane,** avion m; **––port,** aéroport m; **––tight,** a hermétique.

aisle, âïle, n nef f; allée f.

ajar, a-djârre´, a entrouvert.

akin, a-quinne´, a apparenté; de même nature.

alabaster, ăl´-a-băss-t'r, n albâtre m.

alarm, a-lârme´, n alarme f; **–clock,** réveil m.

alarming*, a-lârme´-ing, a alarmant.

album, ăl´-bomme, n album m.

alcohol, ăl-koh-holl, n alcool m.

alert, a-leurte´, a éveillé; **on the –,** sur ses gardes; **–ness,** n vigilance f; vivacité f.

alias, é-li-ăsse, adv autrement dit. n nom supposé m.

alibi, ăl´-i-bâï, n alibi m.

alien, é´-lienne, n étranger m. a étranger.

alight, a-lâîte´, v descendre se; se poser sur; (aero) atterrir. a allumé; en flammes.

alike, a-lâïke´, adv également. a semblable.

alive, a-lâïve´, a vivant; éveillé.

all, oale, adv entièrement. a tout; **–right,** adv très bien; **not at –,** pas du tout.

allay, a-lé´, v adoucir; calmer.

allege, a-lèdje´, v alléguer; **–d,** a présumé.

allegiance, a-li´-dji-annce, n allégeance f.

allergic, *a*-leur´-djique, *a* allergique.

alleviate, *a*-li´-vi-éte, *v* adoucir; soulager.

alley, ǎl´-lie, n ruelle f; allée f; **blind –,** impasse f.

alliance, *a*-lâï´-annce, n alliance f.

allied, ǎl´-lâïde, *a* allié.

allot, *a*-lotte´, *v* assigner; **–ment,** n part f.

allow, *a*-lâ´ou´, *v* allouer; permettre; admettre

allowance, *a*-lâ´ou´-annce, n concession f; (monetary) allocation f; (rebate) remisé f; argent de poche.

alloy, *a*-lôïe´, n alliage m. *v* allier.

allude, *a*-lioude´, *v* faire allusion (à).

allure, *a*-lioure´, *v* attirer; séduire.

alluring, *a*-liou´-rinng, *a* alléchant.

allusion, *a*-liou´-j'n, n allusion f.

ally, *a*-lâï´, n allié m. *v* allier.

Almighty, oal-mâï´-ti, n Tout-Puissant m.

almond, â´-mônnde, n amande f.

almost, oale´-mauste, *adv* presque.

aloft, *a*-lofte´, *adv* en l'air.

alone, *a*-laune´, *a* seul; solitaire.

along, *a*-lonng´, *prep* le long de.

aloof, *a*-loufe´, *adv* & *a* distant; réservé.

aloud, *a*-lâ´oude´, *adv* à haute voix; tout haut.

already, oal-redd´-i, *adv* déjà.

also, oal´-sau, *adv* aussi; également.

altar, oal´-t'r, n autel m.

alter, oal´-t'r, *v* changer; modifier.

alteration, oal-teur-é´-ch'n, n modification f.

alternate*, oal-teur´-néte, *a* alternatif.

alternating, oal-teur-né´-tinng, *a* alternant.

alternative, oal-teur´-né-tive, n alternative f.

although, oal-dzau´, *conj* quoique; bien que.

altitude, ǎl´-ti-tioude, n altitude f; élévation f.

altogether, oal-tou-gué´-dzeur, *adv* tout à fait.

aluminium, *a*-lioue-mine´-i-omme, n aluminium m.

always, oal´-ouèze, *adv* toujours.

amass, *a*-mâsse´, *v* amasser.

amateur, ǎmm´-*a*-tioure, n amateur m.

amaze, *a*-méze´, *v* étonner; stupéfier; ébahir.

amazement, *a*-méze´-m'nt, n stupéfaction f.

ambassador, am-bǎss´-*a*-deur, n ambassadeur m.

amber, ǎmm´-b'r, n ambre m.

ambiguous*, ǎmm-bi-ghiou-eusse, *a* ambigu.

ambition, amm-bi-ch'n, n ambition f.

ambitious*, amm-bi-cheusse, *a* ambitieux.

ambulance, ǎmm´-biou-l'nse, n ambulance f.

ambush, ǎmm´-bouche, n embuscade f.

ameliorate, *a*-mill´-ior-éte, *v* améliorer.

amenable, *a*-mî´-na-b'l, *a* disposé à; justiciable de.

amend, *a*-mennde´, *v* modifier; corriger; réformer; **–ment,** n modification m; **make –s,** *v* dédommager (de).

amenity, *a*-mî-nit-ti, n agrément m; commodité f.

amethyst, ǎmm´-î-tsist, n améthyste f.

amiable, é´-mi-a-b'l, *a* aimable.

amicable, ǎmm´-i-ca-b'l, *a* amical.

amid, amidst, *a*-midde´, *a*-midste´, *prep* au milieu

de; –**ships**, *adv* par le travers.

amiss, *a*-mice´, *a* de travers. *adv* mal; **take –**, prendre en mauvaise part.

ammonia, *a*-mau´-ni-*a*, *n* ammoniaque *f*.

ammunition, ămm-ioue-ni´-ch'n, *n* munitions *fpl*.

amnesty, ămm´-nesse-ti, *n* amnistie *f*.

among(st), *a*-monng´(ste), *prep* parmi.

amorous*, ămm´-*o*-reuce, *a* amoureux.

amount, *a*-mâ´´ounnte, *n* montant *m*; quantité *f*; *v* s'élever à.

ample, ămm´-p'l, *a* ample; abondant.

amplify, ămm´-pli-fâï, *v* amplifier.

amputate, amm´-pioue-téte, *v* amputer.

amuse, *a*-miouze´, *v* amuser.

amusement, *a*-miouze´-m'nt, *n* amusement *m*.

an, ănne, *art* un; une.

analogous, *a*-năl´-*o*-gueusse, *a* analogue.

analysis, *a*-nă´-li-sice, *n* analyse *f*.

analyze, ănn´-*a*-lâïze, *v* analyser.

anarchy, ănn´-ar-ki, *n* anarchie *f*.

ancestor, ănn´-cèsse-*teur*, *n* ancêtre *m* & *f*.

anchor, ain´-n'g-keur, *n* ancre *f*. *v* ancrer.

anchorage, ain´-n'g-keur-édje, *n* mouillage *m*; ancrage *m*

anchovy, ann-tchô´-vi, *n* anchois *m*.

ancient*, énn´-tchi-ennte, *a* ancien; âgé.

and, ănnde, *conj* et.

anesthetize, *a*-nîce-*tz*-eur-tăïze, *v* anesthésier.

angel, énne´-dj'l, *n* ange *m*.

anger, ain´-n'gheur, *n* colère *f*. *v* mettre en colère.

angina, ănn-djăï´-na, *n* angine *f*; – **pectoris**; anginede poitrine.

angle, ain´-n'gl, *n* angle *m*. *v* (fish) pêcher à la ligne; **–r**, *n* pêcheur à la ligne *m*.

angling, ain´-n'glinng, *n* pêche à la ligne *f*.

angry, ain´-n'gri, *a* en colère; (vexed) irrité.

anguish, ain´-n'gouiche, *n* angoisse *f*.

animal, ă´-ni-mal, *n* & *a* animal *m*.

animate, ănn´-i-méte, *v* animer; **–d**, *a* animé.

animosity, *a*-ni-mo´-zi-ti,

n animosité *f*.

aniseed, ănn´-i-sîde, *n* anis *m*.

ankle, ain´-n'kl, *n* cheville *f*.

annals, ănn´-*a*lz, *npl* annales *fpl*.

annex, *a*-nex´, *v* annexer; *n* annexe *f*.

annihilate, *a*-năï´-hi-léte, *v* anéantir; annihiler.

anniversary, *a*-ni-veur´-seu-ri, *n* anniversaire de mariage *m*.

annotate, ănn´-nau-téte, *v* annoter.

announce, *a*-nâ´´ounnce, *v* annoncer.

annoy, *a*-noa'ï´, *v* ennuyer.

annoyance, *a*-noa'ï´-n'se, *n* désagrément *m*.

annual, ă´-niou-*eul*, *n* annuaire *m*. *a** annuel.

annuity, *a*-niou´-i-ti, *n* rente annuelle *f*.

annul, *a*-nol´, *v* annuler; **–ment**, *n* annulation *f*.

anoint, *a*-nô´innte´, *v* oindre.

anomalous, *a*-nom´-*a*-leuce, *a* abnormal.

anonymous*, *a*-no´-ni-meuce, *a* anonyme.

another, *a*-nodzr´, *a* un(e) autre.

answer, ănn´-s'r, *v* répondre; résoudre. *n* réponse *f*.

ant, ännte, *n* fourmi *f.*

antagonist, änn-tăgue´-au-nist, *n* antagoniste *m.*

antecedent, ănn-ti-ci´-dennte, *n* & *a* antécédent *m.*

antedate, ănn-ti-déte, *v* antidater; avancer.

antelope, ănn-ti-laupe, *n* antilope *f.*

anterior, ănn-ti´-ri-*eur*, *a* antérieur.

anteroom, ănn´-ti-roume, *n* antichambre *f.*

anthem, ănn´-tzème, *n* hymne national *m.*

anticipate, ănn-ti´-ci-péte, *v* anticiper; s'attendre à.

anticipation, ănn-tice-i-pé´-ch'n, *n* anticipation *f*; attente *f.*

antics, ănn´-tikss, *npl* gambades *fpl*; singeries *fpl.*

antidote, ănn´-ti-daute, *n* antidote *m.*

antifreeze, ănn´ti-frîze, *n* anti-gel *m inv.*

antipathy, ănn-ti´-pa-tsi, *n* antipathie *f.*

antipodes, ănn-ti´-pŏ-dize, *npl* antipodes *mpl.*

antiquarian, ănn-ti-coué´-ri-anne, *n* antiquaire *m.*

antiquated, ănn´-ti-coué-tedde, *a* vieilli; suranné.

antique, ănn-tique´, *n* antiquité *f. a* ancien.

antiseptic, ănn-ti-sepp´-tique, *n* & *a* antiseptique *m.*

antler, ănn´-t'leur, *n* (stag, etc) bois *mpl.*

anvil, ănn´-vil, *n* enclume *f.*

anxiety, aingue-zâï´-é-ti, *n* inquiétude *f*; anxiété.

anxious, aink´-chieuce, *a* inquiet; désireux.

any, ènn´-i, *a* quelque; l'un ou l'autre; **–body,** *pron* quelqu'un; **–how,** *adv* de toute façon; n'importe comment; **–one,** *pron* n'importe lequel; **–where,** n'importe où.

apart, a-pârte´, *adv* à part; en dehors.

apartment, a-pârte´-m'nt, *n* appartement *m.*

apathy, ă´-pa-tsi, *n* apathie *f.*

ape, épe, *n* singe sans queue *m.*

aperture, ă´-peur-tioure, *n* ouverture *f*; orifice *m.*

apologize, a-pol´-ŏ-djâïze, *v* faire des excuses.

apology, a-pol´-ŏ-dji, *n* excuses *fpl.*

apostle, a-po´-s'l, *n* apôtre *m.*

appall, a-poal´, *v* épouvanter; **–ling,** *a* épouvantable.

apparatus, ăp-pa-ré´-teuce, *n* appareil *m.*

apparent*, a-pă´-rennte, *a* évident; apparent.

apparition, ăp-pa-ri-ch'n, *n* apparition *f.*

appeal, a-pîle, *v* faire appel; attirer. *n* appel *m.*

appear, a-pîre´, *v* paraître; sembler; (law) comparaître.

appearance, a-pî´-r'ns, *n* apparence *f.*

appease, a-pîze´, *v* apaiser; **–ment,** *n* apaisement *m.*

append, a-pennde´, *v* apposer; annexer; attacher.

appendix, ăp-penne´-dikse, *n* appendice *m*; annexe *f.*

appetite, ăp´-pi-tâïte, *n* appétit *m.*

appetizing, ăp´-pi-tâï-zing, *a* appétissant.

applaud, a-ploade´, *v* applaudir.

applause, a-ploaze´, *n* applaudissement *m.*

apple, ăpp´-'l, *n* pomme *f*; **–tree,** pommier *m.*

appliance, a-plâï´-annce, *n* appareil *m*, instrument *m*; electro ménager *m.*

applicant, ă´-pli-k'nt, *n* candidat *m.*

application, ăp-pli-ké´-ch'n, *n* demande *f*;

application.

apply, *a*-plâï´, *v* appliquer; solliciter; **–to,** s'adresser à; **–for a job,** poser sa candidature.

appoint, *a*-pô´ïnnte´, *v* nommer; **–ment,** *n* rendez vous *m*; nomination *f*; situation *f*.

apportion, *a*-pôr´-ch'n, *v* répartir.

appraise, *a*-préze´, *v* évaluer; **–r,** *n* commissaire priseur *m*; **appraisal,** évaluation *f*.

appreciable, *a*p-pri´-chi-*a*-b'l, *a* appréciable.

appreciate, *a*-pri´-chi-éte, *v* apprécier.

appreciation, *a*p-pri-chi-é´-ch'n, *n* appréciation *f*.

apprehend, *a*p-pri-hennde´, *v* saisir; craindre.

apprehension, *a*p-pri-henn´-ch'n, *n* crainte *f*; arrestation *f*.

apprehensive*, *a*p-pri-henn´-cive, *a* craintif.

apprentice, *a*-prenn´-tice, *v* mettre en apprentissage. *n* apprenti *m*; **–ship,** apprentissage *m*.

approach, *a*-prautche´, *v* (s')approcher (de).

appropriate*, *a*-prau´-pri-

éte, *a* convenable.

approval, *a*-prou´-v'l, *n* approbation *f*.

approve, *a*-prouve´, *v* approuver.

approximate*, *a*-prox´-i-méte, *a* approximatif.

apricot, é´-pri-cotte, *n* abricot *m*.

April, é´prile, *n* avril *m*.

apron, é´-preune, *n* tablier *m*.

apt, âpte, *a* apte; propre à; enclin à.

aptitude, *a*p´-ti-tioude, *n* aptitude *f*; disposition *f*.

aqueduct, *a*´-coui-dokte, *n* aqueduc *m*.

aqueous, *a*´-coui-*euce*, *a* aqueux.

aquiline, *a*´-coui-linne, *a* aquilin.

arable, *a*r´-*a*-b'l, *a* labourable.

arbitrary, *a*r´-bi-tra-ri, *a* arbitraire.

arbitrate, *a*r´-bi-tréte, *v* arbitrer; juger.

arbitration, *a*r´-bi-tré-ch'n, *n* arbitrage *m*.

arbitrator, *a*r´-bi-tré-*teur*, *n* arbitre *m*.

arbor, *a*r-*beur*, *n* tonnelle *f*.

arc, *a*rc, *n* arc *m*; **–-lamp,** lampe à arc *f*.

arcade, *a*r-kéde´, *n* arcade *f*, galerie *f*.

arch, *a*rtche, *n* arche *f*; **–way,** vôute *f*.

arch, *a*rtche, *a* archi–; **–bishop,** *a*r archevêque *m*; **–deacon,** archidiacre *m*; **–duke,** archiduc *m*.

archer, *a*rtch´-*eur*, *n* archer *m*; **–y,** tir à l'arc *m*.

architect, *a*r´-ki-tecte, *n* architecte *m*.

archives, *a*r´-kâïvz, *n*pl archives *f*pl.

arctic, *a*rc´-tik, *a* arctique.

ardent, *a*r´-d'nt, *a* ardent; véhément.

ardor, *a*r´-*deur*, *n* ardeur *f*; zèle *m*.

arduous*, *a*r´-diou-*euce*, *a* ardu; difficile.

area, aï´-ri-*a*, *n* surface *f*; zone *f*; région *f*.

arena, *a*-ri´-na, *n* arène *f*.

argue, *a*r´-ghiou, *v* raisonner; discuter; se disputer.

argument, *a*r´-ghiou-m'nt, *n* argument *m*; discussion *f*.

arise, *a*-râïze´, *v* s'élever; provenir de.

aristocracy, *a*-rice-to´-cra-ci, *n* aristocratie *f*.

aristocratic, *a*-rice´-to-cra´-tik, *a* aristocratique.

arithmetic, *a*-rits´-mé-tique, *n* arithmétique *f*.

ark, *a*rque, *n* arche *f*;

Noah's –,arche de Noé f.

arm, ărme, n bras m; **– chair,** fauteuil m; **–ful,** brassée f; **–let,** brassard m; **–pit,** aisselle f.

arm, ărme, v armer; **–ament,** n armement m; **–or,** armure f; blindage m; **–ored,** a blindé; **–ory,** n armurerie f; **–s,** (mil) armes fpl; (heraldry) armoiries fpl; **–y,** armée f.

aromatic, a-rau-mă´-tik, a aromatique n; aromate m.

around, a-ră´ounnde´, prep autour de. adv à l'entour.

arouse, a-râ´ouze´, v exciter; (awake) éveiller.

arrange, a-réne´-dje, v arranger; disposer.

array, a-ré´, v ranger; revêtir. n ordre m.

arrears, a-rirze´, npl arrérages mpl; **to be in –** être en retard; âvoir de l'arriéré.

arrest, a-reste´, v arrêter. n arrestation f.

arrival, a-râi´-v'l, n arrivée f; (com) arrivage m.

arrive, a-râïve´, v arriver.

arrogant, ăr´-ro-gannte, a arrogant.

arrow, ăr´-rau, n flèche f.

arsenal, âr´-s'n-'l, n arsenal m.

arson, âr´-s'n, n incendie par malveillance m.

art, ărte, n art m; habileté f.

artery, âr´-teur-i, n artère f.

artful, ârte´-foull, a (sly) rusé.

artichoke, âr´-ti-tchauke, n artichaut m; **Jerusalem–,**n topinambour m.

article, âr´-ti-k'l, n article m; clause f.

articulate, ăr-ti´-kiou-léte, v articuler. a articulé.

artifice, âr´-ti-fisse, n artifice m; ruse f.

artificial*, âr-ti-fi´-ch'l, a artificiel.

artillery, âr-til´-eur-i, n artillerie f.

artisan, âr´-ti-zănne, n artisan m.

artist, âr´-tisste, n artiste m & f.

artless*, ârte´-lesse, a simple; naïf.

as, ăze, conj comme; car; aussi; que; à mesure que; puisque; **–for, –to,** quant à; **–soon –,**aussitôt que; **–well,** aussi.

asbestos, ass-bess´-teuce, n amiante m.

ascend, a-cennde´, v

monter.

ascendancy, a-cenn´-denn-ci, n ascendant m.

ascent, a-cennte´, n ascension f; montée f.

ascertain, a-seur-téne´, v s'assurer de; constater.

ascribe, ass-crâïbe´, v attribuer; imputer.

ash, ăche, n cendre f; (tree) frêne m; **–tray,** cendrier m.

ashamed, a-chémmde´, a honteux.

ashore, a-chaure´, adv à terre; (naut) échoué.

aside, a-sâïde, adv de côté; à l'écart; à part.

ask, ăske, v demander; inviter.

askew, ass-kiou´, adv de travers.

asleep, a-slîpe´, a endormi; **fall –,**v s'endormir.

asp, ăspe, n (snake) aspic m.

asparagus, ass-păr´-a-gheuce, n asperge f.

aspect, ăss´-pecte, n aspect.

aspen, ăss´-p'n, n tremble m.

asphyxia, ăss-fik´-si-a, n asphyxie f.

aspirate, ăss´-pi-réte, v aspirer. a aspiré.

aspire, ass-pâïre´, v

aspirer (à).

assail, a-céle´, v assaillir;
–**ant,** n assaillant m.

assassinate, a-sǎss´-i-néte,
v assassiner.

assault, a-soalte´, v
attaquer. n attaque f.

assay, a-cé´, v (metals)
essayer. n essai m.

assemble, a-cemm´-b'l, v
assembler; se réunir.

assembly, a-cemm´-bli, n
assemblée f; montage m.

assent, a-cennte´, n
assentiment m. v
consentir à.

assert, a-seurte´, v
affirmer; revendiquer;
–**ion,** n assertion f;
revendication f.

assess, a-cesse´, v taxer;
évaluer.

assessment, a-cesse´-m'nt,
n évaluation f.

asset, ǎs´-sèt, n avoir m.

assets, ǎs-sètse, npl actif
m.

assiduous, a-ci´-diou-
euce, a appliqué; assidu.

assign, a-sâïne´, v assigner
à; (law) transférer; –**ee,**
n cessionnaire m;
–**ment,** transfert m.

assist, a-ciste´, v aider;
secourir.

assistant, a-ciss´-t'nt, n
aide m; commis m. a
auxiliaire.

associate, a-sau´-chi-éte, v
associer. n associé m.

assort, a-sôrte´, v assortir.

assortment, a-sôrte´-m'nt,
n assortiment m.

assuage, a-souédje, v
calmer; adoucir.

assume, a-sioume´, v
supposer; prendre sur
soi.

assuming, a-siou´-minng,
a prétentieux; arrogant.

assumption, a-sommp´-
ch'n, n présomption f.

assurance, a-chou´-r'ns, n
assurance f.

assure, a-choure´, v
assurer.

asterisk, ǎss´-teu-risque, n
astérisque f.

astern, a-steurne´, adv
(naut) à l'arrière.

asthma, ǎss´-ma, n asthme
m.

astir, a-steur´, a en
mouvement; (up)
debout.

astonish, ass-tonn´-iche, v
étonner.

astound, ass-tâ'ounnde´, v
stupéfier; ébahir.

astray, ass-tré´, a égaré.

astride, ass-trâïde´, adv à
califourchon.

astronaut, ǎss´-tro-nôt, n
astronaute m.

astute*, ass-tioute´, a fin;
avisé.

asylum, a-sâï´-leume, n
asile m.

at, ǎtte, prep à; chez.

athlete, ǎ´-tslite, n athlète
m.

atmosphere, atte´-moss-
fire, n atmosphère f;
(fam) ambiance f.

atom, ǎ´-tôme, n atome m.

atomizer, ǎ´-to-mâï-z'r, n
vaporisateur m;
atomiseur m.

atone, a-taune´, v expier;
–**ment,** n expiation f.

atrocious*, a-trau´-
cheuce, a atroce.

atrophy, ât´-rau-fi, n
atrophie f. v atrophier.

attach, a-tâtche´, v
attacher; joindre; (law)
saisir.

attachment, a-tǎtch´-
m'nt, n attachement m.

attack, a-tǎque´, v
attaquer. n attaque f.

attain, a-téne´, v
atteindre; –**ment,** n
talent m.

attempt, a-temmpte´, v
tenter; essayer. n
tentative f; essai m;
(crime) attentat m.

attend, a-ntende´, v
assister à; –**to,** s'occuper
de.

attendance, a-tenn´d'ns, n
service m; auditoire m;
présence f.

attendant, *a*-tenn´-d'nt, *n* ouvreuse *f*.

attention, *a*-tenn´-ch'n, *n* attention *f*.

attest, *a*-teste´, *v* attester.

attic, ăt´-tique, *n* grenier *m*; mansarde *f*.

attire, *a*-tăïre´, *v* vêtir; parer. *n* vêtements *mpl*.

attitude, ăt´-ti-tioude, *n* attitude *f*; pose *f*.

attorney, *a*-teur´-ni, *n* avoué *m*; **power of –,** procuration *f*.

attract, *a*-trăcte´, *v* attirer; **–ion,** *n* attraction *f*; (personal) attrait *m*; **–ive,** *a* attirant; séduisant.

attribute, *a*-tri´-bioute, *v* attribuer. *n* attribut *m*.

auburn, ô´-beurne, *a* auburn.

auction, ôque´-ch'n, *n* vente aux enchères *f*.

auctioneer, ôque´-ch'n-îre, *n* commissaire-priseur *m*.

audacious*, ô-dé´-cheuce, *a* audacieux.

audacity, ô-dăss´-i-ti, *n* audace *f*.

audible, ô´-di-b'l, *a* distinct; intelligible.

audience, ô´-di-ennce, *n* (assembly) auditoire *m*; spectateurs *mpl*.

audit, ô´-ditte, *v* apurer; vérifier; **–or,** *cn* censeur *m*; vérificateur *m*.

augment, ôgue-mennte´, *v* augmenter.

augur, ô´-*gueur,* *v* augurer. *n* augure *m*.

August, ô´-gueusste, *n* août *m*.

august, ô-gueusste´, *a* auguste.

aunt, ânnte, *n* tante *f*.

auspicious*, ôss-pi´-cheuce, *a* propice.

austere, ô-stîre´, *a* austère.

authentic, ô-tsenn´-tique, *a* authentique.

author, ô´-*tseur,* *n* auteur *m*.

authoritative, ô-tsor´-i-ta-tive, *a* autoritaire.

authority, ô-tsor´-i-ti, *n* autorité *f*.

authorize, ô-tsŏr-âï´ze, *v* autoriser.

automatic, ô-tŏ-mătt´-ique, *a* automatique.

autumn, ô´-*teumme,* *n* automne *m*.

auxiliary, ôg-zil´-i-a-ri, *a* auxiliaire.

avail, *a*-véle´, *n* avantage *m*; utilité *f*. *v* servir à; **–oneself of,** profiter de.

available, *a*-véle´-*a*-b'l, *a* valable; disponible.

avalanche, ă´-*va*-lanche, *n* avalanche *f*.

avarice, ă´-*va*-risse, *n* avarice *f*.

avaricious*, a-va-ri´-cheuce, *a* avare.

avenge, *a*-venndje´, *v* venger.

avenue, ă´-vi-ni'ou, *n* avenue *f*.

average, ă´-*veu*-rédje, *n* moyenne *f*. *a* moyen.

aversion, *a*-veur´-ch'n, *n* aversion *f*; répugnance *f*.

avert, *a*-veurte´, *v* détourner; écarter.

aviary, é´-vi-a-ri, *n* volière *f*.

aviation, é-vi-é´-ch'n, *n* aviation *f*.

avidity, *a*-vid´-i-ti, *n* avidité *f*.

avoid, *a*-vô´ïde´, *v* éviter.

await, *a*-ouéte´, *v* attendre.

awake, *a*-ouéque´, *v* s'éveiller; réveiller.

awakening, *a*-ouéque´-ninng, *n* réveil *m*.

award, *a*-ouôrde´, *v* adjuger; accorder; (prize) décerner. *n* récompense *f* ; prix *m*.

aware, *a*-ouère´, **to be –,** *v* savoir; être au courant.

away, *a*-oué´, *adv* absent; loin; **far –,** au loin.

awe, oa, *n* crainte *f*; admiration *f*; **to be held in awe by someone,** en imposer à quelqu'un; **to**

stand in awe of someone, avoir une crainte respectueuse de quelqu'un.

awful, oa´-foull, *a* terrible; imposant.

awhile, *a*-ou'âïle´, *adv* pour un instant.

awkward, oa´-koueurde, *a* gêné; (clumsy) gauche; **–ness,** *n* gaucherie *f*.

awning, oann´-inng, *n* banne *f*.

awry, *a*-râï´, *adv* de travers.

ax, ăx, *n* hache *f*.

axis, ăk´-siss, *n* axe *m*.

axle, ăk´-s'l, *n* essieu *m*.

azure, ă´-jioure, *n* azur *m*.

B

babble, băb´-b'l, n babil m. v babiller.

baby, bé´-bi, n bébé m.

bachelor, bătch´-eul-eur, n célibataire m; bachelier m.

back, băque, n dos m; arrière m. v (support) soutenir; (car) aller en arrière; (return) de retour; **–bone,** n épine dorsale f; **–ground,** fond m; **–ward,** adv en arrière. a (mentally) arriéré.

bacon, bé´-k'n, n lard m.

bad, bădde, a mauvais; méchant; **–ly,** adv mal; gravement.

badge, bàdje, n insigne m.

badger, băd´-jeur, n blaireau m. v harceler.

baffle, băf´-f'l, v déjouer; confondre, déconcerter.

bag, băgue, n sac m. v mettre en sac.

baggage, băgg´-idje, n bagage m.

bail, béle, v cautionner. n caution f; **out on –,** sous caution.

bailiff, bé´-liff, n huissier m.

bait, béte, n appât m. v amorcer; (molest) tourmenter.

bake, béque, v cuire au four; **–r,** n boulanger m; **–ry,** boulangerie f.

balaclava, n băla´-kla-vas, n passe-montagne m.

balance, băl´-n'ce, v équilibrer; balancer. n équilibre m; (com.) solde m; **–sheet,**

bilan m.

balcony, băl´-kau-ni, n balcon m.

bald, boalde, a chauve; **–ness,** n calvitie f.

bale, béle, n balle f; ballot m. v emballer; (naut) écoper.

balk, boak, v frustrer; contrarier.

ball, boale, n balle f; (hard) boule f; (foot) ballon m; (dance) bal m.

ballast, băl´-aste, n lest m. v (weight) lester.

ballet, băl´-lay, n ballet m.

balloon, bal-loune´, n ballon m.

ballot, băl´-lŏtte, v voter. n scrutin m.

ballpoint, boale poa´´innte, n stylo à bille m.

balm, bâ´me, n baume m.

bamboo, bămm-bou´, n bambou m.

ban, bănne, n ban m; interdiction f. v interdir.

banana, ba-na´-na, n banane f.

band, bănnde, n bande f; (brass) fanfare f; (string) orchestre m; (ribbon) bandeau m; (gang) bande f. v se liguer; **–age,** n bandage m; **–leader,** chef de musique m.

bandy, bănn´-di, a bancal.

bang, bain-nng, *v* claquer (door); frapper; cogner. *n* détonation *f*; claquement *m*.

banish, bănn´-iche, *v* bannir.

banister, bănn´-iss-t'r, *n* rampe *f*.

bank, bain´-nk, *n* banque *f*; (river) rive *f*; (mound) talus *m*. *v* (money) déposer dans une banque; **–er,** *n* banquier *m*; **–ing- account,** compte en banque *m*; **– note,** billet de banque *m*; **–rupt,** *a* insolvable; en banque route; **–ruptcy,** *n* faillite *f*.

banner, bann´-eur, *n* bannière *f*; étendard *m*.

banquet, bănn´-couette, *n* banquet *m*; festin *m*.

banter, bănn´-teur, *n* raillerie *f*. *v* railler.

baptism, băp´-tizme, *n* baptême *m*.

bar, bâre, *n* bar *m*, (metal) barre *f*; (law) barreau *m*. *v* barrer; defendre.

barb, bârbe, *n* barbe *f*; **–ed,** *a* barbelé.

barbarian, bâre-bé´-ri-ann, *n* & *a* barbare *mf*.

barbarity, bâre-băr´-i-ti, *n* barbarie *f*.

barber, bâre-*beur*, *n* barbier *m*; coiffeur *m*.

bare, bère, *v* mettre à nu. *a* nu; **–faced,** effronté; **–footed,** nu-pieds; **–ly,** *adv* à peine; **–ness,** *n* nudité *f*; dénuement *m*.

bargain, bâre´-guinne, *v* marchander. *n* occasion *f*; bonne affaire *f*.

barge, bârdje, *n* chaland *m*; péniche *f*.

bark, bârque, *v* aboyer. *n* aboiement *m*; (tree) écorce *f*.

barley, bâre´-li, *n* orge *f*.

barn, bâre-'n, *n* grange *f*.

barometer, ba-ro´-mi-teur, *n* baromètre *m*.

baron, bă´-reune, *n* baron *m*; **–ess,** baronne *f*.

barracks, băr´-axe, *npl* caserne *f*.

barrel, băr´-el, *n* tonneau *m*; (gun) canon de fusil *m*.

barren, băr´-enne, *a* stérile; (land) aride.

barrier, băr´-i-eur, *n* barrière *f*.

barrow, băr´-au, *n* brouette *f*.

barter, bâre´-teur, *v* échanger. *n* échange *m*.

base, béce, *v* baser. *n* base *f*. *a* vil; **–less,** sans fondement; **–ment,** *n* sous-sol *m*; **–ness,** bassesse *f*.

bash, băch, *v* cogner; *n*

coup *m*.

bashful*, bâche´-foull, *a* timide.

bashfulness, bâche´-foull-nesse, *n* timidité *f*.

basin, bé-s'n, *n* (bowl) bol *m*; (wash) lavabo *m*.

basis, bé´-cisse, *n* base *f*; fondement *m*.

bask, bâsque, *v* se chauffer au soleil.

basket, bâsse´-kett, *n* panier *m*; corbeille *f*.

bass, béce, *n* basse *f*; (fish) bar *m*.

bassoon, băss´oun, *n* basson *m*.

baste, béste, *v* (cooking) arroser de graisse; (sewing) bâtir; faufiler.

bat, bătte, *n* bat *m*; (animal) chauve-souris *f*.

batch, bătche, *n* fournée *f*; (articles, etc.) tas *m*.

bath, bâts, *n* bain *m*; (tub) baignoire *f*; **–room,** salle de bain *f*.

bathe, bé-dze, *v* se baigner; **–r,** *n* baigneur *m*; baigneuse *f*; **bathing suit,** *n* maillot de bain *m*.

batter, bătt´-eur, *n* pâte à friture *f*. *v* démolir.

battery, băt´-trî, *n* pile *f*; batterie *f*.

battle, bătt´-'l, *n* bataille *f*;

–ship, cuirassé *m.*

bawl, boal, *v* brailler.

bay, bé, *n* (*geog*) baie *f. a*
(color) bai. *v* aboyer (à);
at –, aux abois; **–tree,** *n*
laurier *m.*

bayonet, bé´-onn-ette, *n*
baïonnette *f.*

be, bî, *v* être.

beach, bîtche, *n* plage *f;*
rivage *m;* grève *f.*

beacon, bi´-k'n, *n* phare
m; (*naut*) balise *f.*

bead, bîde, *n* perle *f;*
(drop) goutte *f.*

beak, bîke, *n* bec *m.*

beam, bîme, *n* rayon *m;*
(wood) poutre *f.*

bean, bîne, *n* haricot *m;*
(broad) fève *f.*

bear, bère, *n* ours *m. v*
donner naissance à;
porter; endurer; **–able,** *a*
supportable.

beard, birde, *n* barbe *f;*
–ed, *a* barbu; **–less,** *a*
imberbe.

beast, bîste, *n* bête *f;* **wild
–,** fauve *m.*

beat, bîte, *v* battre. *n* coup
m; (pulse, etc)
battement *m;* secteur *m.*

beautiful*, bioue´-ti-foull,
a beau; magnifique.

beautify, bioue´-ti-fâï, *v*
embellir.

beauty, bioue´-ti, *n* beauté
f; **–spot,** grain de beauté

m.

beaver, bî´-veur, *n* castor
m.

becalm, bi-câme´, *v*
calmer; (*naut*) abriter du
vent.

because, bi-coaze´e, *conj*
parce que; **–of,** à cause
de.

beckon, bekk´n, *v* faire
signe.

become, bi-komme´, *v*
devenir.

becoming, bi-komm´-
inng, *a* convenable;
(conduct) bienséant;
(dress) qui va bien;
seyant.

bed, bedde, *n* lit *m;*
flower- –, plate-bande *f;*
–ding, literie *f;* **–pan,**
bassin de lit *m;* **–ridden,**
a alité; **–room,** *n*
chambre à coucher *f.*

bedeck, bi-dèque´, *v* parer;
orner.

bee, bî, *n* abeille *f;* **–hive,**
ruche *f.*

beech, bîtche, *n* hêtre *m.*

beef, bîfe, *n* boeuf *m;* **–
steak,** bifteck *m.*

beer, bîre, *n* bière *f.*

beet, bîte´, *n* betterave *f.*

beetle, bî´-t'l, *n* coléoptère
m; **black –,** cafard *m.*

befitting, bi-fitt´-inng, *a*
convenable à.

before, bi-foare´, *adv &*

prep (time) avant;
(place) devant; **–hand,**
adv d'avance; à l'avance.

befriend, bi-frennde´, *v*
traiter en ami; aider.

beg, bègue, *v* (alms)
mendier; (request, etc)
prier; **–gar,** *n* mendiant
m; **–ging,** mendicité *f.*

begin, bi-guinne´, *v*
commencer; **–ner,** *n*
débutant *m;* **–ning,**
commencement *m.*

begrudge, bi-grodge´, *v*
donner à contre-cœur.

beguile, bi-gâïle´, *v*
tromper; séduire.

behalf, bi-hâfe´, **on –of,**
en faveur de; au nom de;
de la part de.

behave, bi-héve´, *v* se
conduire; se comporter.

behavior, bi-hé´-vieur, *n*
conduite *f;* tenue *f.*

behead, bi-hédde´, *v*
décapiter.

behind, bi-hâïnnde´, *adv*
en arrière. *prep* derrière;
en retard de; *n* derrière
m.

behold, bi-haulde´, *v* voir.
interj regardez!

being, bî´-inng, *n*
existence *f;* (human)
être *m.*

belch, beltche, *v* (pop)
roter. (pop) rot *m.*

belfry, bel´-fri, *n* beffroi *m;*

clocher *m*.

belie, bi-lâî´, *v* démentir.

belief, bi-lîfe´, *n* croyance *f*; foi *f*.

believable, bi-lîve´-*a*-b'l, *a* croyable.

believe, bi-lîve´, *v* croire; –r, *n* croyant *m*.

bell, belle, *n* cloche *f*; sonnette *f*; grelot *m*.

belligerent, bel-lidj´-*eur*-'nt, *a* & *n* belligérant *m*.

bellow, bél´-lô, *v* beugler; mugir.

bellows, bél´-lôze, *npl* soufflet *m*.

belly, bél´-li, *n* ventre *m*.

belong, bi-lonng´, *v* appartenir.

belongings, bi-lonng´-inngze, *npl* affaires *fpl*.

beloved, bi-lo´-vèdde, *n* & *a* bien-aimé *m*.

below, bi-lau´, *adv* & *prep* au-dessous; en bas.

belt, bellte, *n* ceinture *f*; (*mech*) courroie *f*.

bemoan, bi-maune´, *v* gémir sur; se lamenter.

bench, benntche, *n* banc *m*; tribunal *m*; établi *m*.

bend, bennde, *v* courber; plier. *n* courbure *f*; (road, etc) coude *m*; tournant *m*; virage *m*.

beneath, bi-nîts´, *adv* & *prep* sous; au-dessous.

benediction, benn-i-dic´-

ch'n, *n* bénédiction *f*.

benefactor, benn-i-fâque´-teur, *n* bienfaiteur *m*.

beneficial*, benn-i-fi´-cheul, *a* salutaire; avantageux.

beneficiary, benn-i-fi´-chi-*eur*-i, *n* bénéficiaire *mf*.

benefit, benn´-i-fite, *v* profiter. *n* bénéfice *m*.

benevolence, bi-nèv´-ŏ-lennce, *n* bienveillance *f*.

benevolent, bi-nèv´-ŏ-lennte, *a* bienveillant; charitable.

benign, bi-nâîne´, *a* bénin; doux.

bent, bennte, *pp* courbé; résolu. *n* (*fig*) penchant *m*.

bequeath, bi-kouîds´, *v* léguer.

bequest, bi-koueste´, *n* legs *m*.

bereave, bi-rîve´, *v* priver de; –ment, *n* perte *f*.

berry, bê´-ri, *n* baie *f*.

berth, beurts, *n* couchette *f*.

beseech, bi-cîtche´, *v* supplier; implorer.

beside, bi-sâîde´, *prep* à côté de; hors de.

besides, bi-sâïdze´, *adv* en outre; d'ailleurs. *prep* en plus; excepté.

besiege, bi-cîdje, *v* assiéger.

besotted, bi-sotte´-èdde, *a* abruti.

best, besste, *adv* le mieux. *a* & *n* le meilleur.

bestial, bess´-ti'l, *a* bestial.

bestir, bi-steur´, *v* –oneself, se remuer.

bestow, bi-stau´, *v* accorder; conférer; –al, *n* don *m*.

bet, bette, *v* parier. *n* pari *m*.

betoken, bi-tau´-k'n, *v* indiquer; dénoter.

betray, bi-tré´, *v* trahir; –al, *n* trahison *f*.

betroth, bi-traudz´, *v* fiancer.

betrothal, bi-traudz´-'l, *n* fiançailles *fpl*.

better, bett´r, *v* améliorer. *adv* mieux. *a* meilleur.

betterment, bett´-eur-m'nt, *n* amélioration *f*.

between, bi-touîne´, *prep* entre.

bevel, bév´'l, *v* tailler en biseau; **beveled**, *a* de biais; en biseau.

beverage, bèv´-*eur*-idj, *n* boisson *f*; breuvage *m*.

bewail, bi-ouéle´, *v* déplorer.

beware, bi-ouère´, *v* se méfier de; prendre garde à.

bewilder, bi-ouile´-deur, v
ahurir; déconcerter.

bewilderment, bi-ouile´-
deur-m'nt, n
ahurissement m.

bewitch, bi-ouitche´, v
ensorceler; enchanter.

beyond, bi-ionnde´, adv
au delà; là-bas. prep au
delà de.

bias, baï´-asse, n biais m;
préjugé m; **biased,** a
partial.

Bible, baï´-b'l, n bible f.

bicker, bik´eur, v se
quereller; se chamailler.

bicycle, baï´-ci-k'l, n
bicyclette f.

bid, bide, v commander;
prier; (auction) faire
une offre; n offre f;
enchère f; **–ding,**
commandement m;
enchère f.

bide, baïde, v attendre;
endurer.

bier, bîre, n corbillard m,
bière f.

big, bigue, a gros; grand;
vaste.

bigot, bigg-eute, n bigot m;
–ed, a bigot.

bilberry, bil´-bê-ri, n
airêlle f.

bile, baîle, n bile f.

bilingual, baï-linn´-guou'l,
a bilingue.

bilious, bi´-li-euce, a
bilieux.

bill, bil, n note f; compte
m, facture f; (restaurant)
addition f; (bird) bec m;
(poster) affiche f; **–of
exchange,** lettre de
change f; **–of fare,** menu
m; **–of lading**
connaissement m.

billet, bil´-ette, v loger. n
(mil) logement m.

billiards, bil´-lieurdze, npl
billard m.

bin, bine, n huche f;
(wine) porte-bouteilles
m; poubelle f.

bind, baînnde, v lier;
obliger; (books) relier;
–ing n reliure f. a
obligatoire; **–up,** v
bander.

binocular(s), bi-nok´-
ioue-leur(ze), n jumelle
f.

biography, baï-o´-grã-fi, n
biographie f.

birch, beurtche, n (tree)
bouleau m; (punitive)
verges fpl.

bird, beurde, n oiseau m.

birth, beurts, n naissance
f; **–day,** anniversaire m;
—mark, tache de
naissance f; **–place,** lieu
natal m; **–rate,** natalité
f.

biscuit, biss´-kitte, n
biscuit m.

bishop, bich´-eup, n
évêque m.

bit, bitte, n morceau m;
(horse) mors m.

bite, baîte, v mordre,
morsure f; piqûre f.

biting, baît´-inng, a
mordant.

bitter*, bitt´-eur, a amer;
–ness, n amertume f.

black, blăque, v (shoes)
cirer; noircir. a noir. n
noir m; **–berry,** n mûre f;
–bird, merle m;
–currant, cassis m; **–en,**
v noircir; **–mail,**
chantage m. v faire
chanter; **–mailer,** n
maître chanteur m;
–smith, forgeron m.

bladder, blăd´-eur, n vessie
f.

blade, bléde, n lame f;
(grass) brin m; (oar) plat
m.

blame, bléme, v blâmer. n
blâme m; faute f.

blameless*, bléme´-lesse,
a irréprochable.

blanch, blânntche, v
blanchir; pâlir.

bland, blănnde, a doux;
–ishment, n flatterie f.

blank, blain-n'k, n blanc
m. a blanc; (mind) vide.

blanket, blaing´-kette, n
couverture f.

blare, blére, v retentir.

blaspheme, blass-fîme´, v blasphémer.

blasphemy, blass´-fé-mi, n blasphème m.

blast, blâsste, v (explode) faire sauter; (blight) flétrir. n (trumpet) son m; coup m.

blatant, blé´-t'nt, a bruyant.

blaze, bléze, v flamber. n flamme f; éclat m.

bleach, blîtche, v blanchir; décolorer.

bleak, blîque, a froid; exposé aux vents; morne.

bleat, blîte, v bêler. n bêlement m.

bleed, blîde, v saigner; –ing, n saignement m.

blemish, blèm´-iche, n tache f. v tacher.

blend, blennde, v mélanger. n mélange m.

bless, bless, v bénir; –ed, a béni.

blessing, bless´-inng, n bénédiction f.

blight, blâïte, n nielle f; rouille f; (fam) influence néfaste.

blind, blâïnnde, n (window) store m; (venetian) jalousie f. n & a (sight) aveugle m & f. v aveugler. –fold, bander les yeux; –ness,

n aveuglement m; cécité f.

blink, blinng-k, v clignoter; n battement (m) de paupière; –er, n œillère f.

bliss, blisse, n félicité m; béatitude f.

blissful, bliss´-foull, a bienheureux.

blister, bliss´-t'r, n ampoule f; cloque f.

blithe*, blâïdz, a gai; joyeux.

blizzard, bliz´-eurde, n tempête de neige f.

bloated, blau´-tedde, a boursouflé; bouffi. **bloater,** n hareng fumé m.

block, bloque, v bloquer. n bloc m; billot m; obstacle m; (of houses) pâté de maisons m; –ade blocus m; –head, n imbécile m & f.

blood, blodde, n sang m; –hound, limier m; –shot, a injecté de sang; –thirsty, sanguinaire; –y, sanglant.

blossom, bloss-eume, v fleurir. n fleur f m.

blot, blotte, v tacher; (dry) sécher. n tache f; (ink) pâté m; –ting **paper,** papier buvard m.

blotch, blotche, n tache f.

blouse, blâ´-ouze, n blouse f; (woman's shirt) chemisier m.

blow, blau, n coup m. v souffler; (trumpet) sonner; (nose) se moucher.

blubber, blob´-eur, n (whale) graisse de baleine f.

bludgeon, blod´-jeune, n matraque f.

blue, blou, a & n bleu; –bell, n jacinthe des bois f; clochette f.

bluff, bloffe, n bluff m. v bluffer.

bluish, bloue´-iche, a bleuâtre.

blunder, blonne´-deur, n maladresse f. v commettre une maladresse.

blunt, blonnt, v émousser. a* brusque; émoussé.

blur, bleure, v brouiller. n tache f.

blush, bloche, v rougir. m rougeur f.

bluster, bloce´-teur, v faire du vacarme. n fanfaronnade f; –er, n fanfaron m; –ing, a tapageur; (wind) violent.

boar, baure, n (wild) sanglier m.

board, baurde, n planche

f; (directors) conseil d'administration m; (food) pension f. v garnir de planches;

bulletin–, n tableau d'annonces m; **–er,** pensionnaire m & f; **–ing house,** pension f; **–ing school,** pensionnat m; pension f.

boast, bauste, v se vanter.

boaster, baus´-t'r, n vantard m.

boat, baute, n bateau m; (row) bateau à rames m; **motor–,** canot à moteur m; **steam–,** vapeur m; **–hook,** gaffe f.

bob, bobbe, v ballotter; osciller; s'agiter.

bobbin, bob´-ine, n bobine f.

bodice, bod´-ice, n corsage m.

bodkin, bode´-kinne, n passe-lacet m; poinçon m.

body, bod´-i, n corps m; (vehicle) carrosserie f.

bog, bogue, n marécage m; **–gy,** a marécageux.

bogeyman, bau´-gui-mănne, n croquemitaine m.

boil, boa´ïle, v faire bouillir; bouillir. n (med) furoncle m.

boiler, boa´ïl´-eur, n

chaudière f.

boisterous*, bo´ïce´-teur-euce, a bruyant; turbulent.

bold*, bôlde, a hardi; audacieux; effronté.

boldness, bôlde´-nesse, n hardiesse f; effronterie f.

bolster, bôle´-steur, n traversin m. v (fig) soutenir.

bolt, bôlte, v verrouiller; décamper. n verrou m.

bomb, bomme, n bombe f; **–ard,** v bombarder.

bond, bonnde, n (tie) lien m; (word) engagement m; bon m.

bondage, bonnd´-idj, n esclavage m; servitude f.

bone, baune, n os m; (fish) arête f.

bonfire, bonn´-fâïre, n feu de joie m.

bonnet, bonn´-ette, n chapeau m; bonnet.

bonus, bau´-neuce, n prime f.

bony, bau´-ni, a osseux.

boob, boub, n (pop) gaffe f. v faire une gaffe.

book, bouk, n livre m. v inscrire; réserver; **–binder,** n relieur m; **–case,** bibliothèque f; **–ing office,** guichet m; **–keeper,** comptable m; **–seller,** libraire m;

–shop, librairie f.

boom, boume, n (com) boom m; (noise)grondement m; (spar) bout-dehors m. v gronder; (com) faire hausser; être à la hausse.

boon, boune, n bienfait m.

boor, boure, n rustre m; **–ish,** a grossier.

boot, boute, n botte f; **–maker,** bottier m.

booth, boudz, n cabine f.

booty, boue´-ti, n butin m.

border, bôre´-d'r, n frontière f; bord m; bordure f; **–ing,** a (adjacent) contigu à; touchant.

bore, bôre, v percer; (ground) forer; (weary) ennuyer. n calibre m; (person) raseur m; raseuse f; barbe f.

born, bôrne, pp né.

borrow, bor´-au, v emprunter.

bosom, bou´-zeume, n sein m.

boss, bosse, n (fam) patron m. v diriger.

botanist, bott´-a-niste, n botaniste mf.

botany, bott´-a-ni, n botanique f.

both, bôts, a les deux; ensemble.

bother, bô´-dz'r, v

tracasser. n ennui m.

bottle, bott´-'l, v mettre
en bouteilles. n bouteille
f.

bottom, bott´-eume, n
fond m; bas m; derrière
n:.

bottomless, bott´-eume-
lesse, a sans fond.

boudoir, bou´-do'ar, n
boudoir m.

bough, bâ'ou, n rameau m;
branche f.

bounce, bâ'ounnce, v
rebondir.

bound, bâ'ounn´-de, v
borner; (jump) bondir. n
(jump) bond m; **–ary,**
borne f limites fpl; **–for,**
à destination de.

bountiful*, bâ'ounn´-ti-
foull, a généreux.

bounty, bâ'ounn´-ti, n
libéralité f; prime f.

bouquet, bou-kay, n
bouquet m.

bout, bâ'oute, n accès m.

bow, bâ'ou, v saluer;
s'incliner. n salut m;
révérence f; (ship) avant
m.

bow, bau, n (archery) arc
m; (tie: knot) nœud m;
(violin) archet m.

bowels, bâ'ou´-elze, n
boyaux mpl; intestins
mpl.

bowl, baule, n bol m;

(ball) boule f. v jouer
aux boules; (cricket)
lancer la balle.

box, boxe, v boxer. n boîte
f; (theater) loge f; (on
the ears) gifle f; **–ing,**
boxe f.

boy, boa´i, n garçon m;
–cott, v boycotter. n
boycottage m; **–hood,**
enfance f.

brace, bréce, v lier;
fortifier. n (mech)
vilebrequin m; (two)
couple m; **–s,** bretelles
fpl; appareil dentaire m.

bracelet, bréce´-lette, n
bracelet m.

bracing, bréce´-inng, a
fortifiant; tonique.

bracken, brǎk´-'n, n
fougère f.

bracket, brǎk´-ette, n
console f; parenthèse f.

brackish, brǎk´-iche, a
saumâtre.

brag, brǎgue, v se vanter;
–gart, n vantard m.

braid, bréde, v tresser. n
tresse f; (dress) galon m.

brain, bréne, n
(substance) cervelle f;
(mind) cerveau m;
brainy. a (fam)
intelligent.

braise, bréze, v braiser.

brake, bréque, n frein m. v
freiner.

bramble, brǎmm´-b'l, n
ronce f.

bran, brǎnne, n son m.

branch, brǎnntche, n
branche f; (com)
succursale f.

brand, brǎnnde, n marque
f; (fire) brandon m. v
marquer; stigmatiser;
–ish, brandir.

brandy, brǎnn´-di, n eau
de vie f.

brass, brǎce, n laiton m,
cuivre jaune m.

brasserie (fam **bra**), brǎ´-
ssiaire (brǎ), n
soutiengorge f.

bravado, bra-vâ´-dô, n
bravade f.

brave*, bréve, a brave;
courageux. v braver; **–ry,**
n bravoure f.

brawl, broale, v se
chamailler.

brawn, broanne, n
fromage de tête m;
muscles mpl; **–y,** a
musclé.

bray, bré, v braire.

brazen, bré´-z'n, a de
laiton; (insolent)
effronté.

Brazil nut, bra-zile´-notte,
n noix du Brésil f.

breach, brîtche, n fracture
f; violation f; rupture f.

bread, brède, n pain m;
(pop) argent.

breadth, brèdts, n largeur f.

break, bréque, v casser; (amity, etc) rompre; (law) violer; (smash) briser. n brisure f; (pause) pause f; (school) récréation; **–age,** casse f; **–down,** rupture f; écroulement m; dépression f; (mech) panne f; **–er,** (naut) grosse vague f; **–water,** brise-lames m.

breakfast, brèque´-fâste, n petit-déjeuner m.

bream, brîmme, n brème f.

breast, breste, n sein m; poitrine f.

breath, brè-ts, n haleine f; souffle m; **–less,** a essouflé.

breathe, brî-dz, v respirer.

breech, brîtche, n (firearms) culasse f.

breed, brîde, v élever; procréer; se reproduire; n race f; espèce f; **–er,** éleveur m; **–ing,** élevage m; éducation f.

breeze, brîze, n brise f.

brevity, brèv´-i-ti, n brièveté f.

brew, broue, v brasser; faire infuser; **–er,** n brasseur m.

brewery, broue´-eur-i, n brasserie f.

briar, brâî´-eur, n (bramble) ronce f; églantier m.

bribe, brâîbe, v corrompre; (fam) graisser la pâte. n paiement illicite m.

bribery, brâî´-beur-i, n corruption f.

brick, brique, n brique f; **–layer,** macon m.

bridal, brâî´-d'l, a nuptial.

bride, brâîde, n mariée f; **–groom,** marié m; **–smaid,** demoiselle d'honneur f.

bridge, bridje, n pont m; (naut) passerelle f; bridge m.

bridle, brâî´-d'l, n bride f. v brider.

brief, brîfe, n dossier m. a* bref; **–case,** n serviette f; **–ing,** instruction f; directives f.

brigade, bri-guéde´, n brigade f.

bright*, brâîte, a luisant; lumineux; intelligent; **–en,** v faire briller; (enliven) égayer; (weather) s'éclaircir; **–ness,** n éclat m; vivacité f.

brilliancy, bril´-iann-ci, n éclat m; lustre m.

brilliant, bril´-iannte, a brillant; éclatant.

brim, brime, n bord m; **–over,** v déborder.

brimstone, brime´-staune, n soufre m.

brine, brâîne, n saumure f.

bring, brinng, v apporter; conduire; **–forward,** (com) reporter; **–in,** (com) rapporter; **–up,** élever.

brink, brinng-k, n bord m.

brisk, brisque, a vif; animé; **–ness,** n vivacité f.

brisket, briss´-quette, n poitrine de bœuf f.

bristle, briss´-'l, n poil raide m; soie f. v se hérisser.

bristly, briss´-li, a poilu; hérissé.

brittle, britt´-'l, a fragile; cassant.

broad, broad, a large; (accent) prononcé.

broadcast, broade´-câste, v radiodiffuser.

broadcasting, broade´-câste-inng, n émission f.

brocade, brô-quéde´, n brocart m.

broccoli, broque´-o-li, n brocoli m.

brogue, braugue, n patois m; chaussure f.

broil, broa´île, v griller.

broker, brau´-keur, n courtier m; stock–,agent de change m; **–age,**

courtage *m*.

bronchitis, bronng-kâî´-tice, *n* bronchite *f*.

bronze, bronnze, *n* bronze *m*. *v* bronzer.

brooch, brautche, *n* broche *f*.

brood, broude, *v* couver; (*fam*) remâcher; ruminer (une idée). *n* couvée *f*.

brook, brouque, *n* ruisseau *m*.

broom, broume, *n* balai *m*; (plant) genêt *m*.

broth, brots, *n* bouillon *m*.

brother, brodz´-eur, *n* frère *m* –**hood**, fraternité *f*; (*eccl*) confrérie *f*; –**in-law**, beau-frère *m*; –**ly**, *a* fraternel.

brow, brâ´ou, *n* front *m*; sourcil *m*; –**beat**, *v* intimider.

brown, brâ´oune, *v* brunir. *a* brun; marron; –**ish**, brunâtre.

browse, brâ´ouze, *v* brouter; regarder sans acheter.

bruise, brouze, *n* contusion *f*; bleu *m*. *v* meurtrir.

brunette, brou-nette´, *n* brunette *f*.

brunt, bronnte, *n* choc *m*; violence *f*.

brush, broche, *n* brosse *f*. *v* brosser; (sweep)

balayer.

brushwood, broche´-ou´oude, *n* broussailles *fpl*.

brusque, breuske, *a* brusque.

brussels sprouts, bross´-lze-spr´outse, *npl* choux de Bruxelles *mpl*.

brutal*, broue´-t'l, *a* brutal; –**ity**, *n* brutalité *f*.

brutalize, broue´-t'l-âïze, *v* abrutir; brutaliser.

brute, broute, *n* brute *f*.

bubble, bo´-b'l, *n* bulle *f*. *v* bouillonner; (wine) pétiller.

buck, boque, *a* mâle. *n* (deer) daim *m*.

bucket, bok´-ette, *n* seau *m*; baquet *m*.

buckle, bo´-k'l, *n* boucle *f*. *v* boucler; attacher.

bud, bodde, *n* bourgeon *m*; (flower) bouton *m*. *v* bourgeonner; fleurir.

budge, bodje, *v* bouger.

budget, bodj´-ette, *n* budget *m*.

buff, boffe, *a* couleur chamois. *v* polir.

buffalo, boff´-a-lau, *n* buffle *m*.

buffer, boff´-eur, *n* tampon (de choc) *m*.

buffet, boff´-ette, *n* (bar) buffet *m*. *v* battre.

buffoon, beuf-foune´, *n*

bouffon *m*.

bug, bogue, *n* punaise *f*; insecte *m*; –**bear**, (*fam*) bête noire *f*.

bugle, bioue´-g'l, *n* (*mil*) clairon *m*.

build, bilde, *v* bâtir. *n* forme *f*; –**er**, constructeur *m*; –**ing**, bâtiment *m*.

bulb, bolbe, *n* bulbe *m*; (lamp) ampoule électrique *f*.

bulge, bol-dj, *v* bomber; gonfler.

bulk, bolke, *n* volume *m*; **in** –, en gros.

bulky, boll´-ki, *a* volumineux; encombrant.

bull, boull, *n* taureau *m*; (stock exchange) haussier *m*; –**dog**, bouledogue *m*; –**finch**, bouvreuil *m*; –**'s eye**, (target) mouche *f*.

bullet, boull´-ette, *n* balle *f*.

bulletin, boull´-i-tinne, *n* bulletin *m*.

bullion, boull´-ieune, *n* or en barres *m*.

bully, boull´-i, *v* malmener. *n* tyran *m*; brute *f*.

bulrush, boull´-roche, *n* jonc *m*.

bulwark, boull´-

ou'eurque. n rempart m;
(naut) pavois m.

bumblebee, bomm´-b'l-bî,
n bourdon m.

bump, bommpe, n coup m;
secousse f; (swelling)
bosse f. v heurter;
cogner.

bumper, bomm´-peur, n
(glass) rasade f (of car)
pare-chocs m.

bumptious, bommpe´-
cheuce, a arrogant.

bunch, bonntche, v
grouper; se tasser. n
(vegetables) botte f;
(flowers) bouquet m;
(grapes) grappe de raisin
f; (keys) trousseau de
clefs m; groupe m.

bundle, bonn´-d'l, n
paquet m; ballot m; (of
wood) fagot m.

bung, bonng, n bondon m;
–hole, bonde f.

bungalow, bonng´-ga-lau,
n bungalow m.

bungle, bonng´-g'l, v
gâcher; **–r,** n gâcheur m.

bunion, bonn´-ieune, n
oignon aux pieds m.

bunker, bonng´-keur, n
(coal) soute à charbon f.

bunting, bonn´-tinng, n
étamine f; (flags)
drapeaux mpl.

buoy, bôa'ï, n bouée f;
–ancy, légèreté f; (fam)

entrain m; **–ant,** a
flottable; (fam) plein
d'entrain.

burden, beur´-d'n, v
charger; accabler. n
fardeau m; charge f;
–some, a lourd.

bureau, biou´-rau, n
(furniture) bureau m;
secrétaire m; (office)
bureau m; office m.

bureaucracy, biou-rau-
cra-si, n bureaucratie f.

burglar, beur´-gleur, n
cambrioleur m.

burglary, beur´-gleur-i, n
cambriolage m.

burial, bè´-ri-al, n
enterrement m.

burial ground, bè´-ri-al-
grâ´ounnde, n cimetière
m.

burlesque, beur-lesque´, n
& a burlesque m.

burly, beur´-li, a
corpulent.

burn, beurne, v brûler;
(arson) incendier. n
brûlure f; **–er,** (gas;
lamp) bec m.

burr, beurre, n (botanical)
carde f.

burrow, beurr´-au, v
terrer. n terrier m.

bursar, beurr´-sar, n
(school) économe m.

burst, beurste, v éclater;
(crack) crever; sauter.

bury, bèr-i, v enterrer.

bus, boss, n autobus m.

bush, bouche, n buisson
m; fourré m; **–y,** a touffu.

business, biz´-nesse, n
affaires fpl; occupation f.

bust, bosste, n buste m;
poitrine f.

bustle, boss´'l, v se remuer.
n mouvement m; remue-
ménage m.

bustling, boss´-linng, a
affairé.

busy, biz´-i, a occupé;
affairé.

but, botte, conj mais. adv
seulement.

butcher, boutt´-cheur, n
boucher m. v massacrer.

butler, bott-leur, n maître
d'hôtel m.

butt, bott, n bout m; (gun)
crosse f; (cask) tonneau
m. v buter.

butter, bott-eur, v beurrer.
n beurre m; **–cup,**
bouton d'or m; **–dish,**
beurrier m; **–fly,**
papillon m.

buttock, bott´-ŏque, n
fesse f; culotte de bœuf m.

button, bott´-'n, n bouton
m. v boutonner; **–hole,**
n boutonnière f.

buxom, box´-eume, a
(woman) bien en chair;
grassouillette.

buy, bâî, v acheter; **–er,** n

acheteur *m*; acheteuse *f*.
buzz, bozze, *v* bourdonner.
buzzard, bozz´-*eu*rde, *n*
buse *f*.
by, bâï, *prep* par; près de;
–**gone,** *a* passé; —
stander, *n* spectateur *m*;
—**word,** dicton *m*.
bylaw, bâï´-loa, *n*
réglement *m*; arrêté *m*.
bypass, bâï´-pâsse, *v*
contourner, éviter.

cab, căbbe, n taxi m.

cabbage, căb´-ădj, n chou m.

cabin, căb´-inn, n cabine f; (hut) cabane f.

cabinet, căb´-inn-ett, n cabinet m; meuble m; vitrine f; classeur m; –maker, ébéniste m.

cable, ké´-b'l, n câble m. v câbler.

cablegram, ké´-b'l-grămme, n câblogramme m.

cackle, căk´-'l, v caqueter. n caquet m.

cage, kédje, n cage f. v mettre en cage.

cajole, ca-djaule´, v cajoler.

cake, kéque, n gâteau m. v se coaguler.

calabash, căl´-a-băche, n calebasse f.

calamitous, ca-lămm´-i-teuce, a désastreux.

calamity, ca-lămm´-i-ti, n calamité f.

calculate, căl´-kiou-léte, v calculer.

calculator, căl´-kiou-lă-teur, n calculette m.

calendar, căl´-ènn-deur, n calendrier m.

calf, câfe, n veau m; (leg) mollet m.

calico, căl´-i-kô, n calicot m.

call, coal, v appeler; (name) nommer; (visit) visiter; passer chez. n appel m; visite f.

callous, căl´-euce, a (unfeeling) insensible; endurci.

calm, câme, v calmer. n & a* calme m.

calorie, călor´-ri, n calorie f.

cambric, kéme´-brique, n batiste f.

camel, cămm´-'l, n chameau m.

cameo, cămm´-î-ô, n camée f.

camera, cămm´-eur-a, n appareil photographique m; **in –,** à huis clos; **cameraman,** n cameraman m.

camomile, cămm´-ô-mâîle, n camomille f.

camp, cămmpe, v camper. n camp m; –**cot,** lit de camp m; **to go camping,** faire du camping.

campaign, cămm-péne´, n campagne f.

camphor, cămm´-feur, n camphre m.

can, cănne, n bidon m; (of food) boîte f. v (preserve) conserver en boîte.

can, cănne, v pouvoir; savoir.

canal, cănn-ăl´, n canal m.

canary, că-né´-ri, n canari m, serin m.

cancel, cănn-s'l, v annuler.

cancer, cănn´-ceur, n cancer m.

candid*, cănn´-dide, a candide; franc.

candidate, cănn´-di-déte, n candidat m.

candle, cănn´-d'l, n bougie f; chandelle f; **–stick,** bougeoir m; chandelier m.

candor, cănn´-deur, n candeur f; franchise f.

candy, cănn´-di, n bonbons mpl. v cristalliser.

cane, quéne, n canne f.

canine, că-nåïnne´, a canin. n (tooth) canine f.

canister, cănn´-iss-teur, n boîte en fer blanc f.

canker, caing´-k'r, n chancre m.

canned, cănn´-d, a en boîte; en conserve.

cannibal, cănn´-i-b'l, n & a cannibale m & f.

cannon, cănn´-eune, n canon m.

canoe, ca-noue´, n périssoire f; (native) pirogue f; canoe m.

canon, cănn´-eune, n (title) chanoine m; (law) canon m.

can opener, cănn´-ôp-neur, n ouvre-boîte(s) m.

canopy, cănn´-ŏ-pi, n baldaquin m.

cant, cănnte, n hypocrisie f.

cantankerous, cănn-taing´-keur-euce, a revêche.

canteen, cănn-tîne, n cantine f.

canter, cănn´-teur, v aller au petit galop.

canvas, cănn´-vasse, n toile f; (sail) voile f.

canvass, cănn´-vasse, v solliciter.

cap, căppe, n casquette f; (of bottle) capsule f; (pen) capuchon m.

capable, qué´-pa-b'l, a capable; competent.

capacity, ca-păsse´-i-ti, n capacité f.

cape, quépe, n (geog) cap m; (cover) cape f.

caper, ca´-peur, n cambriole; gambade f; (cooking) câpre f.

capital, căp´-i-t'l, n (city) capitale f; (money) capital m; (letter) majuscule f.

capitulate, ca-pitte´-ioue-léte, v capituler.

capricious*, ca-prich´-euce, a capricieux.

capsize, căp-sâïze´, v chavirer.

capstan, căp´-stănne, n cabestan m.

capsule, căp´-sioulle, n capsule f.

captain, căp´-t'n, n

capitaine m; (sport) chef d'équipe m.

caption, căp´-ch'n, n légende f.

captive, căp´-tive, n & a captif m; captive f.

captivity, căp-tive´-i-ti, n captivité f.

capture, căp´-tioure, v capturer. n prise f.

car, câre, n automobile f; voiture f; (aero) nacelle f.

caramel, căr´-a-m'l, n caramel m.

carat, căr´-atte, n carat m.

caravan, căr´-a-vănne, n caravane f; roulotte f.

caraway, căr´-a-oué, n (seed) carvi m.

carbide, căr´-bâïde, n carbure m.

carbolic, căr-bol´-ique, a phénique; **–acid,** n phénol m.

carbon, căr´-b'n, n carbone m; **––copy,** n double m; **–paper,** n papier carbone m.

carbuncle, căr´-bonng-k'l, n (med) anthrax m.

carburetor, căr-bi´-oue-rett´-'r, n carburateur m.

carcass, căr´-casse, n carcasse f.

card, cârde, v carder. n carte f; **–board,** carton m.

cardinal, căr´-di-n'l, *n* cardinal *m*. *a* cardinal.

care, quére, *n* soin *m*; attention *f*; inquiétude *f*. *v* se soucier de; **take –!***interj* attention!; **take –of,** *v* faire attention à; **–for,** aimer; **–ful*****,** *a* soigneux; prudent; **–less,** négligent; sans soin; **–lessness,** *n* négligence *f*; **c/o,** chez; aux bons soins de; **–taker,** *n* gardien *m*; concierge *m* & *f*.

career, *ca*-rîre´, *n* carrière *f*.

caress, *ca*-resse´, *v* caresser. *n* caresse *f*.

cargo, căr´-gau, *n* cargaison *f*.

caricature, căr´-i-*ca*-tioure´, *n* caricature *f*.

carmine, câr´-mine, *n* carmin *m*.

carnage, câr´-nidj, *n* carnage *m*.

carnal***,** câr´-n'l, *a* charnel.

carnation, câr-né´-ch'n, *n* œillet *m*.

carnival, câr´-ni-v'l, *n* carnaval *m*.

carol, căr´-ŏl, *n* cantique de Noël *m*.

carp, cârpe, *n* (fish) carpe *f*. *v* chicaner sur.

carpenter, căr´-penn-*teur*, *n* charpentier *m*.

carpet, câr´-pette, *n* tapis *m*; moquette *f*.

carriage, căr´-idj, *n* voiture *f*; (freight) port *m*; (deportment) maintien *m*; (rail) wagon *m*.

carrier, căr´-i-*eur*, *n* entrepreneur de transports *m*; (on car, cycle, etc) porte-bagages *m*; **–pigeon,** pigeon voyageur *m*.

carrion, căr´-ri-*eu*ne, *n* charogne *f*.

carrot, câr´-ŏtte, *n* carotte *f*.

carry, căr´-i, *v* porter; transporter.

cart, cârte, *v* transporter; (*fam*) trimbaler. *n* charette *f*; **–age,** camionnage *m*.

cartoon, câr-toune´, *n* caricature *f*; dessin animé *m*.

cartridge, câr´-tridj, *n* cartouche *f*.

carve, cârve, *v* (wood) sculpter; (meat) découper.

carving, câr´-vinng, *n* sculpture *f*; découpage *m*.

cascade, căsse-quéde´, *n* cascade *f*.

case, quéce, *n* (box) caisse *f*; (cigarette etc) étui *m*; (jewel) écrin *m*; cas *m*; affaire *f*; **in –,** au cas où.

casement, quéce´-m'nt, *n* croisée *f*; fenêtre *f*.

cash, căche, *n* argent *m*; argent liquide *m*. *v* encaisser; **––book,** *n* livre de caisse *m*.

cashier, căche-îre´, *n* caissier *m*; caissière *f*.

cashmere, căche´-mîre, *n* cachemire *m*.

cask, câsque, *n* tonneau *m*, baril *m*; fût *m*.

casket, câsse´-quette, *n* cassette *f*; écrin *m*; cercueil *m*.

cassock, căss´-ŏque, *n* soutane *f*.

cast, câste, *n* (throw) coup *m*; (theater) distribution des rôles *f*; (metal) moule *m*. *v* (throw) jeter; lancer; (metal) couler; **–iron,** *n* fonte *m*.

castanet, căsse´-*ta*-nette, *n* castagnette *f*.

caste, câste, *n* caste *f*.

castigate, căsse´-ti-guéte, *v* châtier.

castle, câ´-s'l, *n* château *m*.

castor, câsse´-*tŏr*, *n* (wheel) roulette *f*.

castor oil, câsse´-*tŏr*-oa'ile, *n* huile de ricin *f*.

casual, căj´-iou-*eul*, *a*

fortuit; indifférent; détaché.

casualty, căj´iou-*eul*-ti, n accidenté m; (mil) perte f.

cat, cătte, n chat m.

catalog, căt´-*a*-logue, n catalogue m.

catarrh, ca-târre´, n catarrhe m.

catastrophe, ca-tăce´-trŏ-fi, n catastrophe f.

catch, cătche, n prise f. v attraper; **–ing,** a contagieux; **–up,** v rattraper.

category, căt´-i-gŏr-i, n catégorie f.

cater, qué´-teur, v approvisionner; **–er,** n traiteur m.

caterpillar, căt´-*eur*-pil-*eur,* n chenille f.

cathedral, ca-tsi´-dralle, n cathédrale f.

catholic, că´-tsŏ-lique, n & a catholique m & f.

cattle, căt´-t'l, n bétail m.

cauldron, côl-t'-dronne, n chaudron m; chaudière f.

cauliflower, col´-i-flâ'ou-*eur,* n chou-fleur m.

caulk, côke, v calfater.

cause, côze, n cause f. v causer; occasionner.

caustic, côce´-tique, n & a caustique m.

cauterize, cô´-teur-âïze, v cautériser.

caution, cô´-ch'n, n prudence f; (warning) avis m. v avertir.

cautious, cô´-cheuce, a prudent.

cavalier, căv-a-lîre´, n cavalier m.

cavalry, căv´-al-ri, n cavalerie f.

cave, quéve, n caverne f; (animals') antre m.

cavil, căv´-il, v chicaner.

cavity, căv´-i-ti, n cavité f; carie f.

cease, sîce, v cesser; **–less,** a incessant.

cedar, sî-deur, n cèdre m.

cede, sîde, v céder.

ceiling, sîl´-inng, n plafond m.

celebrate, sell´-i-bréte, v célébrer; **–d,** a célèbre.

celery, sell´-*eur*-i, n céleri m.

celestial, si-lesse´-ti-'l, a céleste.

celibacy, sell´-i-ba-ci, n célibat m.

cell, selle, n cellule f.

cellar, sell´-*eur,* n cave f.

celluloid, sell´-ioue-lo-ide, n celluloïde m.

cement, sé-mennté´, n ciment m. v cimenter.

cemetery, sém´-i-teur-i, n cimetière m.

cenotaph, senn´-ô-tă?e, n cénotaphe m.

censor, senn´-seur, n censeur m; **–ship,** censure f.

censure, senn´-chioure, v censurer. n censure f.

census, senn´-ceusse, n recensement m.

cent, sennte, n sou m; centime m; **per –,** pour cent; **–enary,** a centenaire; **–ury,** n siècle m.

center, senn´-t'r, n centre m. v placer au centre.

central, senn´-tr'l, a central; **–heating,** chauffage central m; **–ize,** v centraliser.

cereal, sî-rî-'l, n céréale f.

ceremonious, sair-i-mau´-ni-*euce,* a cérémonieux.

ceremony, sair´-i-mau-ni, n cérémonie f.

certain*, seur´-t'n, a certain.

certificate, seur-tif´-i-quéte, n certificat m; acte m.

certify, seur´-ti-fâï, v certifier; (law) attester.

cessation, saiss-sé´-ch'n, n cessation f; suspension f.

cesspool, saiss´-poule, n fosse d'aisances f.

chafe, tchéfe, v irriter;

écorcher.

chaff, tchâffe, *v* taquiner. *n* (husk) menue paille *f*.

chaffinch, tchăf´-finntche, *n* pinson *m*.

chain, tchéne, *n* chaîne *f*; **–up,** *v* enchaîner.

chair, tchaire, *n* chaise *f*; **–man,** président *m*.

chalice, tchăl´-isse, *n* calice *m*.

chalk, tchôque, *n* craie *f*; **–y,** *a* crayeux.

challenge, tchăl´-inndje, *v* défier. *n* défi *m*.

chamber, tchéme´-b'r, *n* chambre *f*; **–lain,** chambellan *m*; **—maid,** femme de chambre *f*; **— pot,** pot de chambre *m*.

chamois, chăme´-oï, *n* chamois *m*.

champion, tchăme´-pi-*eune*, *n* champion *m*. *v* soutenir.

chance, tchânnce, *n* hasard *m*; (opportunity) occasion *f*. *a* fortuit. *v* risquer.

chancel, tchânn´-s'l, *n* sanctuaire *m*.

chancellor, tchânn´-seul-*eur*, *n* chancelier *m*.

chancery, tchânn´-ceu-ri, *n* chancellerie *f*.

chandelier, chănn-di-lîre´, *n* lustre *m*.

change, tchéne-dje, *v* changer. *n* changement *m*; (cash) monnaie *f*; **–able,** *a* variable; **–less,** immuable.

channel, tchănn´-'l, *v* creuser. *n* canal *m*; voie *f*; (TV) chaîne *f*; **the English –,** La Manche *f*.

chant, tchânnte, *v* chanter. *n* chant *m*; plain-chant *m*.

chaos, qué´-oce, *n* chaos *m*.

chap, tchăpe, (hands, lips, etc.) *v* gercer. *n* gerçure *f*; (person) type *m*.

chapel, tchăp´-'l, *n* chapelle *f*.

chaperon, chăpe´-*eur*-aune, *v* chaperonner. *n* chaperon *m*.

chaplain, tchăp´-l'n, *n* aumônier *m*; chapelain *m*.

chapter, tchăp´-teur, *n* chapitre *m*.

char, tchâre, *v* carboniser; (clean) faire le ménage; **–woman,** *n* femme de ménage *f*.

character, kăr´-ac-teur, *n* caractère *m*; genre *m*; personnage *m*.

charcoal, tchâr´-caule, *n* charbon de bois *m*; (art) fusain *m*.

charge, tchârdje, *n* attaque *f*; accusation *f*; (load) chargement *m*; (price) prix *m*. *v* attaquer; accuser; charger; (price) demander; **to take –,** se charger de.

chariot, tchăr´-i-otte, *n* char *m*.

charitable, tchăr´-i-ta-b'l, *a* charitable.

charity, tchăr´-i-ti, *n* charité *f*.

charm, tchârme, *v* charmer. *n* charme *m*.

charming, tchărm´-inng, *a* charmant.

chart, tchârte, *n* carte *f*; carte marine *f*; graphique *m*; tableau *m*.

charter, tchâr´-teur, *n* charte *f*. *v* (hire) affréter.

chary, tché´-ri, *a* circonspect; économe.

chase, tchéce, *v* chasser. *n* chasse *f*.

chasm, căz´m, *n* abîme *m*.

chaste*, tchéste, *a* chaste; **–n,** *v* châtier; purifier.

chastise, tchàss-tâïze´, *v* châtier.

chat, tchătte, *v* bavarder. *n* causerie *f*; **–ter,** caquet *m*. *v* jaser; (teeth) claquer; **–terbox,** *n* moulin à paroles *m*.

chattel, tchătt´-'l, *n* mobilier *m*; effets *mpl*.

chauffeur, chau´-feur, n chauffeur m.

cheap*, tchîpe, a & adv bon marché; **–en,** v baisser les prix; discréditer (réputation); **–er,** a meilleur marché; **–ness,** n bon marché m; médiocrité f.

cheat, tchîte, v tricher. n tricheur m; tricheuse f.

cheating, tchîte´-inng, n tricherie f.

check, tchéque, n chèque m; (restraint; chess) échec m; (verification) contrôle m; (pattern) à carreaux mpl. v (stop) arrêter; (repress) réprimer; (verify) vérifier; in échec et mat m. v mater; **– book,** carnet de chèques m.

checkered, tchèque´curde, a varié; mouvementé.

cheek, tchîque, n joue f; (fam) toupet m.

cheer, tchîre, n gaieté f; (applause) acclamation f. v acclamer; (brighten) égayer; **to –** (someone) **up,** remonter le moral (de quelqu'un); **–ful,** a joyeux; gai; **–less,** triste; sombre.

cheese, tchîze, n fromage m.

chemical, quèm´-i-k'l, a chimique.

chemist, quèm´-isste, n pharmacien,-ne m & f; chimiste m; (shop) pharmacie f; **–ry,** chimie f.

cherish, tchèr´-iche, v chérir.

cherry, tchèr´-i, n cerise f; **–tree,** cerisier m.

cherub, tchèr´-eub, n chérubin m.

chess, tchèss, n échecs mpl.

chest, tchèste, n coffre m; boîte f; (box) caisse f; (human) poitrine f; **–of drawers,** commode f.

chestnut, tchèste´-notte, n marron m; châtaigne f; (tree) châtaignier m. a châtain; **horse –,**n marron d'Inde m; (tree) marronnier m.

chew, tchiou, v mâcher.

chicken, tchik´-enne, n poulet m; **–pox,** varicelle f.

chide, tchâide, v réprimander.

chief, tchîfe, n chef m; (fam) patron m. a* principal.

chilblain, tchil´-bléne, n engelure f.

child, tchâilde, n enfant m & f; **–hood,** enfance f;

–ish, a enfantin.

chill, tchill, n coup de froid m. v refroidir; réfrigérer.

chilly, tchil´-i, a un peu froid; frais.

chime, tchâïme, v carillonner. n carillon m.

chimney, tchime´-ni, n cheminée f.

chimneysweep, tchime´-ni-soûpe, n ramoneur m.

chin, tchine, n menton m.

china, tchâï´-na, n porcelaine f.

chintz, tchine'tse, n perse f.

chip, tchipe, v tailler par éclats; ébrécher. n fragment m; éclat m; pomme frite f.

chiropodist, câï-rop´-o-diste, n pédicure m.

chirp, tcheurpe, v gazouiller.

chisel, tchiz´-'l, n ciseau m. v ciseler.

chivalrous, chiv´-al-reusse, a courtois; chevaleresque.

chives, tchâïvze, npl ciboulette f.

chloride, clau´-râïde, n chlorure m.

chlorine, clau´-rine, n chlore m.

chloroform, clau´-roforme, n chloroforme m.

chocolate, tchok´-ŏ-léte, n chocolat m.

choice, tchoa´ïce, n choix m. a choisi; surfin.

choir, couaï´r, n chœur m.

choke, tchauque, v étouffer; (block up) boucher; (car) n starter m.

cholera, col´-eur-a, n choléra m.

choose, tchouze, v choisir; **choosy,** a (fam) difficile.

chop, tchoppe, n côtelette f. v hacher; –**off,** couper; –**per,** n hachoir m.

choral, co´-r'l, a choral.

chord, côrde, n (mus) accord m.

chorister, cor´-iss-teur, n choriste m.

chorus, cô´-eusse, n chœur m; refrain m.

Christ, craïsste, n le Christ.

christen, criss´-'n, v baptiser; –**ing,** n baptême m.

Christian, criss´-ti-'n, n & a chrétien m; chrétienne f.

Christianity, criss-ti-ann´-i-ti, n christianisme m.

Christmas, criss´-meusse, n Noël m; –**tree,** arbre de Noël m.

chronic, cronn´-ique, a chronique.

chronicle, cronn´-i-k'l, n chronique f.

chrysanthemum, cri-sanne´-tsi-meumme, n chrysanthème m.

chuck, tcho´-k, v jeter; lancer; flanquer.

chuckle, tcho´-k'l, v rire tout bas; glousser. n gloussement m.

church, tcheurtche, n église f; –**yard,** cimetière m.

churlish, cheur´-liche, a revêche; maussade.

churn, tcheurne, v baratter. n baratte f.

cider, sâï-d'r, n cidre m.

cigar, si-gâre´, n cigare m.

cigarette, sig-a-rette´, n cigarette f; –**butt,** (fam) mégot m.

cinder, sinn´-d'r, n cendre f.

cinema, si´-ni-ma, n cinéma m.

cinnamon, sin´-na-meune, n cannelle f.

cipher, sâï´-f'r, v chiffrer. n chiffre m; zéro m.

circle, seur´-k'l, v entourer; tourner autour de. n cercle m.

circuit, seur-kitte, n circuit m; tournée f.

circuitous, seur-kiou´-i-teusse, a détourné.

circular, seur´-kiou-l'r, n & a circulaire f.

circulate, seur´-kiou-léte, v circuler; faire circuler.

circulation, seur-kiou-lé´-ch'n, n circulation f; (newspaper, etc) tirage m.

circumference, seur-komm´-feur´-'nce, n circonférence f.

circumflex, seur´-keume-flèxe, a circonflexe.

circumscribe, seur´-keume-scrâïbe, v circonscrire.

circumspect, seur´-keume-specte, a circonspect.

circumstance, seur´-keume-stännce, n circonstance f.

circumstantial, seur-keume-stänn´-ch'l, a circonstanciel; –**evidence,** n preuve indirecte f.

circus, seur´-keusse, n cirque m; (place) rondpoint m.

cistern, siss-teurne, n citerne f; (lavatory) réservoir de chasse d'eau m.

cite, sâïte, v citer.

citizen, sit´-i-z'n, n citoyen m; –**ship,** nationalité f.

city, sit´-i, n cité f; grande

ville.

civil, siv´-il, *a* civil; **–ian,** *n* civil *m*; **–isation,** civilization *f*; **–ity,** politesse *f*; civilité *f*.

claim, cléme, *n* réclamation *f*; (inheritance) droit *m*; prétention *f*; demande de remboursement *f*. *v* réclamer; prétendre; **–ant,** *n* prétendant *m*.

clammy, clă´-mi, *a* (hands) moite; (weather) humide.

clamor, clămm´-eur, *v* vociférer. *n* clameur *f*.

clamp, clămmpe, *n* crampon *m*. *v* cramponner.

clan, clănne, *n* clan *m*; tribu *f*; (*fam*) clique *f*.

clandestine, clănne-desse´-tinne, *a* clandestin.

clang, clainng, *n* bruit métallique *m*; résonnement *m*. *v* retentir.

clap, clăppe, *v* applaudir. *n* (thunder) coup *m*.

clapping, clăpp´-inng, *n* applaudissement *m*.

claret, clăr´-ette, *n* vin rouge de Bordeaux *m*.

clarify, clăr´-i-făï, *v* clarifier; éclaircir.

clarinet, clăr´-i-nette, *n*

clarinette *f*.

clash, clăche, *n* choc *m*; conflit *m*; *v* (se) heurter; (of colors) jurer.

clasp, clâsspe, *v* étreindre. *n* étreinte *f*; (catch) fermoir *m*.

class, clâss, *n* classe *f*; (school) classe *f*; cours *m*. *v* classer.

classify, clâss´-i-făï, *v* classifier.

clatter, clătt´-eur, *n* fracas *m*. *v* retentir.

clause, cloaze, *n* clause *f*; (gram) proposition *f*.

claw, cloa, *v* griffer. *n* griffe *f*; (bird of prey) serre *f*; (crab, etc) pince *f*.

clay, clé, *n* argile *f*; **–ey,** *a* argileux.

clean, clîne, *v* nettoyer. *a* propre. *adv* absolument; **–ing,** *n* nettoyage *m*; **–liness,** propreté *f*.

cleanse, clènnz, *v* purifier.

clear, clîre, *a* clair; net. *v* éclaircir; évacuer; dégager; (table) desservir; **–ness,** *n* clarté *f*.

clearance, clîr´-annce, *n* dégagement *m*; (customs) dédouanement *m*; (sale) liquidation *f*.

cleave, clîve, *v* fendre;

(cling) s'attacher à.

cleft, clefte, *n* fente *f*.

clemency, clémm´-enn-ci, *n* clémence *f*.

clench, clentche, *v* serrer.

clergy, cleur´-dji, *n* clergé *m*; **–man,** pasteur *m*; prêtre *m*.

clerical, clé´-ri-k'l, *a* clérical; de bureau; **–error,** *n* erreur de plume *f*; faute decopiste *f*.

clerk, clărque, *n* employé *m*; (law) clerc *m*.

clever*, clèv´-eur, *a* habile; intelligent; **–ness,** *n* habileté *f*.

click, clique, *n* déclic *m*.

client, clâï´-ennte, *n* client, **-ente** *m* & *f*; **-ele,** clientèle *f*.

cliff, cliffe, *n* falaise *f*.

climate, clâï´-méte, *n* climat *m*.

climax, clâï´-măxe, *n* comble *m*; point culminant *m*; apogée *f*.

climb, clâïmme, *v* monter; grimper; (mountain, etc) gravir.

clinch, *v* conclure.

cling, clinng, *v* se cramponner; adhérer.

clinic, clinn´-ik, *n* clinique *f*; **–al,** *a* clinique.

clink, clinnque, *v* tinter;

(glasses) trinquer.

clip, clippe, v (cut) tondre; couper; agrafer; rogner.

cloak, clauque, n manteau m; cape f. v (fig) voiler; **—room,** vestiaire m; (station) consigne f.

clock, cloque, n horloge f; pendule f; **—maker,** horloger m; **—work,** mouvement d'horlogerie m.

clod, clodde, n motte de terre f.

clog, clogue, n entrave f; (shoe) sabot m. v obstruer.

cloister, cloa'iss´-t'r, n cloître m.

close, clauze, n fin f. v fermer; terminer. a (weather) lourd; proche. adv (near) près de.

closet, cloz´-ette, n cabinet m; placard m.

closure, clau´-jeure, n fermeture f; résolution f.

clot, clotte, v cailler. n caillot m.

cloth, clots, n drap m; tissu m; **table— ,** nappe f.

clothe, claudz, v habiller; vêtir.

clothes, claudz-z, npl vêtements mpl; **—brush,** brosse à habits f.

clothing, claudz´-inng, n

vêtements mpl.

cloud, clâ'oude, n nuage m. v obscurcir; **—y,** a nuageux.

clout, clâ'oute, n claque f; gifle f; influence f.

clove, clauve, n clou de girofle m.

clover, clauv´-'r, n trèfle m; **to be in —,** être comme coq en pâte.

clown, clâ'oune, n clown m.

club, clobbe, n club m; (cards) trèfle m; (stick) massue f; **golf —,** club m; **—foot,** pied bot m.

cluck, cloque, v glousser. n gloussement m.

clue, cloue, n indice m.

clump, clommpe, n (trees) bosquet m; (flowers) massif m; touffe f.

clumsiness, clomme´-zi-nesse, n maladresse f.

clumsy, clomme´-zi, a maladroit; gauche.

cluster, closs´-teur, n groupe m; (fruit) grappe f; (trees) bosquet m. v se grouper.

clutch, clotche, n griffe f; (motor) embrayage m. v saisir.

coach, cautche, n (motor) car m; (rail) wagon m; (tutor) répétiteur m. v donner des leçons

particulières; (sport) entraîner.

coagulate, cau-âgue´-ioue-léte, v coaguler.

coal, caule, n houille f, charbon de terre m; **—mine,** mine f.

coalition, cau-à-li´-ch'n, n coalition f.

coarse*, course, a grossier; gros; **—ness,** n grossièreté f; rudesse f.

coast, causste, n côte f; littoral m. v côtoyer.

coast guard, causste´-gârde, n garde-côte m.

coat, caute, n manteau m; pardessus m; (animal) manteau m, pelage; (paint) couche f.

coax, cauxe, v enjôler; encourager.

cob, cobbe, n (horse) cob m; (swan) cygne mâle m; (nut) noisette f; (corn) épi de mais m.

cobbler, cob´-bleur, n cordonnier m.

cobweb, cob´-ouèbbe, n toile d'araignée f.

cochineal, cotch´-i-nîl, n cochenille f.

cock, coque, n (bird) coq m; (gun) chien m; (turn valve) robinet m; **—ade,** cocarde f; **—erel,** cochet m; **—roach,** blatte f; cafard m.

cockle, coque´-'l, n coque f.

cocoa, cau´-cau, n cacao m.

coconut, cau´-cau-notte, n noix de coco f.

cocoon, co-coune´, n cocon m.

cod, codde, n morue f; — **liver oil,** huile de foie de morue f.

coddle, cod´-d'l, v choyer; dorloter.

code, caude, n code m.

codicil, codd´-i-sile, n codicille m.

coeducation, cau-èd-iou-ké´-ch'n, n coéducation f; enseignement mixte m.

coerce, cau-eurce´, v contraindre.

coffee, cof´-i, n café m; — **pot,** cafetière f.

coffer, cof´-eur, n coffre m; caisse f.

coffin, cof´-inne, n cercueil m.

cog, cogue, n dent de roue f; —**wheel,** roue dentée f.

coherent*, cau-hî´-r'nt, a cohérent.

cohesion, cau-hî´-j'n, n cohésion f.

coil, coa´ile, n rouleau m; (electric) bobine f. v enrouler; (reptile) s'enrouler.

coin, coa´inne, n pièce de monnaie f.

coincide, cau-inn-çâîde´, v coïncider.

coincidence, cau-inn´-si-d'ns, n coïncidence f.

coke, cauque, n coke m.

cold, caulde, n froid m; (med) rhume m. a* froid.

colic, col´-ique, n colique f.

collaborate, cŏl-la´-bo-réte, v collaborer.

collaborator, col-la´-bo-ra-t'r, collaborateur m.

collapse, cŏl-lăpse´, v s'affaisser. n effondrement m.

collar, col´-eur, n col m; (dog) collier m; —**bone,** clavicule f.

collate, col-léte´, v collationner; assembler.

colleague, col´-ligue, n collègue m.

collect, cŏl-lècte´, v rassembler; (stamps, etc) collectionner; (money) encaisser; (charity) quêter; –**ion,** n collection f; (charity) quête f; (postal) levée f; –**ive*,** a collectif; –**or,** n collectionneur m; (tax) percepteur m.

college, col´-idj, n collège

m; école f.

collide, cŏl-lâïde´, v se heurter; se tamponner.

collier, col´-i-eur, n mineur m; –**y,** houillère f.

collision, cŏl-li´-j'n, n collision f; rencontre f; (railroad) tamponnement m; (ships) abordage m.

colloquial*, cŏl-lau´-coui-al, a familier.

collusion, cŏl-lioue´-j'n, n collusion f.

colon, cau´-l'n, n deux points mpl; (anat) côlon m.

colonel, queur´-n'l, n colonel m.

colonist, col´-ŏnn-iste, n colon m.

colonnade, col-ŏnn-éde´, n colonnade f.

colony, col´-ŏ-ni, n colonie f.

color, col´-eur, n couleur f. v colorier.

coloring, col´-eur-inng, n coloris m; teint m.

colossal, cau-loss´-'l, a colossal.

colt, caulte, n poulain m.

column, col´-eume, n colonne f.

coma, cau´-mǎ, n (med) coma m.

comb, caume, n peigne m;

(bird) crête f. v peigner.

combat, comm´-batte, n combat m. v combattre; **–ant,** n combattant m; **–ive,** a batailleur.

combination, comm-bi-né´-ch'n, n combinaison f.

combine, cŏmm-bâîne´, v combiner.

combustion, cŏmm´-bosse´-tch'n, n combustion f.

come, comme, v venir; arriver; **–down,** descendre; **–in,** entrer; **–off,** se détacher; **–out,** sortir; **–up,** monter.

comedian, cŏ-mi´-di-anne, n comédien m.

comedy, comm´-i-di, n comédie f.

comet, comm´-ette, n comète f.

comfort, comm´-feurte, n confort m; consolation f; (relief) soulagement m. v consoler.

comfortable, comm´-feurta-b'l, a confortable.

comic, comm´-ique, a comique.

coming, comm´-inng, a proche; futur. n venue f.

comma, comm´-ma, n virgule f.

command, cŏmm-ânnde´, v commander; dominer.

n ordre m; (knowledge) facilité f; **–er,** commandant m; **–ment(s),** commandement(s) m (pl).

commence, cŏmm-ennce´, v commencer; **–ment,** n commencement m.

commend, cŏmm-ennde´, v recommander; (praise) louer; **–ation,** n éloge m; louange f.

comment, comm´-ennte, n commentaire m; observation f. v commenter; **commentary,** n commentaire m.

commerce, comm´-eurce, n commerce m.

commercial, cŏmm-eur´-ch'l, a commercial.

commiserate, cŏmm-iz´-eur-éte, v plaindre.

commission, cŏmm-ich´-'n, v charger de. n commission f; (mil) brevet m.

commit, cŏmm-itte´, v commettre; envoyer en prison; (bind) engager.

commitment, cŏmm-it´-ment, n engagement m; responsabilité f.

committee, cŏmm-it´-ti, n comité m.

commodious, cŏmm-aud´-i-euce, a spacieux.

commodity, cŏmm-od´-i-ti, n produit m; marchandise f.

common, comm´-'n, a commun; ordinaire; **–place,** banal.

commotion, cŏmm-au´-ch'n, n commotion f.

commune, cŏmm-ioune´, n commune f. v converser.

communicate, cŏmm-ioue´-ni-quéte, v communiquer.

communication, cŏmm-ioue´-ni-qué´-ch'n, n communication f.

communion, cŏmm-ioue´-nieune, n communion f.

communism, comm´-ioue-niz'm, n communisme m.

communist, cŏmm´-ioue-nisste, a & n communiste mf.

community, cŏmm-ioue´-ni-ti, n communauté f.

commute, cŏmm-moute´, v (é)changer; commuer.

compact, comm´-păcte, n pacte m; (powder) poudrier m. a compact.

companion, cŏmm-pănn´-ieune, n compagnon m; **–ship,** n camaraderie f.

company, comm´-pa-ni, n compagnie f.

comparative*, cŏmm-păr´-*a*-tive, *a* comparatif.

compare, cŏmm-père´, *v* comparer.

comparison, cŏmm-păr´-i-s'n, *n* comparaison *f*.

compartment, cŏmm-parte´-m'nt, *n* compartiment *m*; case *f*.

compass, comm´-passe, *n* (magnetic) boussole *f*; (a pair of) **-es**, *pl* compas *m*.

compassionate, cŏmm-păch´-eune-éte, *a* compatissant.

compel, cŏmm-pel´, *v* contraindre; forcer.

compensate, comm´-penn-séte, *v* compenser.

compensation, cŏmm-penn-sé´-ch'n, *n* compensation *f*.

compete, cŏmm-pîte´, *v* concourir.

competence, comm´-pi-t'nce, *n* compétence *f*.

competent*, *a* capable; compétent.

competition, cŏmm-pi-ti´-ch'n, *n* (com) concurrence *f*; (games, sport) concours *m*.

competitor, cŏmm-pett´-i-*teur*, *n* (com) concurrent *m*; (sport, etc) compétiteur *m*.

compile, cŏmm-pâïle´, *v* compiler; composer.

complacent, cŏmm-plé´-cennte, *a* content de soirmême.

complain, cŏmm-pléne´, *v* se plaindre.

complaint, cŏmm-plénnte´, *n* plainte *f*; maladie *f*.

complement, comm´-plî-m'nt, *n* effectif *m*; complément.

complete, cŏmm-plîte´, *v* achever. *a** complet.

completion, cŏmm-plî-ch'n, *n* achèvement *m*.

complex, comm´-plexe, *a* compliqué; complexe. *n* complexe *m*.

complexion, cŏmm-plèque´-ch'n, *n* (face) teint *m*.

compliance, cŏmm-plâï´-'nt, *n* conformité *f*.

compliant, cŏmm-plâï´-'nt, *a* complaisant; soumis.

complicate, comm´-pli-quéte, *v* compliquer.

compliment, comm´-pli-m'nt, *n* compliment *m*. *v* faire des compliments; **-s**, *npl* compliments *mpl*.

comply, cŏmm-plâï´, *v* **-with**, se conformer à.

component, cŏmm-pau´-n'nt, *n* composant *m*.

compose, cŏmm-pauze´, *v* composer; calmer.

composer, cŏmm-pau´-zeur, *n* compositeur *m*.

composition, cŏmm-pau-si´-ch'n, *n* composition *f*.

compositor, cŏmm-po´-zi-t'r, *n* compositeur *m*.

composure, cŏmm-pau´-jeure, *n* calme *m*; sang-froid *m*.

compound, comm´-pâ'ounnde, *v* composer. *n* espace clos *m*. *a* composé; **-interest**, intérêt composé *m*.

comprehend, cŏmm-pri-hennde´, *v* comprendre.

comprehension, cŏmm-pri-henn´-ch'n, *n* compréhension *f*.

compress, cŏmm-presse´, *v* comprimer. *n* compresse *f*.

comprise, cŏmm-prâïze´, *v* contenir; comprendre.

compromise, comm´-prŏ-mâïze, *n* compromis *m*. *v* compromettre.

compulsion, cŏmm-pol´-ch'n, *n* contrainte *f*.

compulsory, cŏmm-pol´-sŏr-i, *a* obligatoire.

compunction, cŏmm-ponnk´-ch'n, *n* remords *m*.

computation, cŏmm-piou-

te-ch'n, *n* calcul *m*;
computation *f*.

compute, cŏmm-pioute´, *v*
estimer; calculer.

computer, cŏmm-piou´-t'r,
n ordinateur *m*.

comrade, comm´-réde, *n*
camarade *m* & *f*;
compagnon *m*.

concave, conn´-quéve, *a*
concave.

conceal, cŏnn-cîle´, *v*
cacher.

concede, cŏnn-cîde´, *v*
concéder.

conceit, cŏnn-cîte´, *n*
vanité *f*; prétention *f*;
–ed, *a* prétentieux.

conceive, cŏnn-cîve´, *v*
concevoir; (s') imaginer.

concentrate, conn´-seune-
tréte, *v* concentrer.

conception, cŏnn-seppe´-
ch'n, *n* conception *f*.

concern, cŏnn-seurne´, *n*
affaire *f*; (disquiet) souci
m. *v* concerner; **to be**
–ed, s'inquiéter.

concert, conn´-seurte, *n*
concert *m*.

concession, cŏnn-sèch´-
eune, *n* concession *f*.

conciliate, cŏnn-cil´-i-éte,
v concilier.

concise, cŏnn-sâîce´, *a*
concis.

conclude, cŏnn-cloude´, *v*
conclure.

conclusion, cŏnn-cloue´-
j'n, *n* conclusion *f*.

conclusive, cŏnn-cloue´-
cive, *a* concluant.

concoct, cŏnn-cocte´, *v*
élaborer; préparer;
combiner.

concord, conn´-côrde, *n*
concorde *f*; accord *m*.

concrete, conn´-crîte, *n*
béton *m*. *a* concret.

concur, cŏnn-queur´, *v*
concourir; être d'accord.

concussion, cŏnn-coch´-
'n, *n* choc *m*; (*med*)
commotion *f*.

condemn, cŏnn-demme´,
v condamner.

condense, cŏnn-dennce´,
v condenser.

condescend, cŏnn-di-
cennde´, *v*
condescendre.

condescension, cŏnn-di-
cenn´-ch'n, *n*
condescendance *f*.

condition, cŏnn-di´-ch'n,
n condition *f*.

conditional*, cŏnn-dich´-
eun-'l, *a* conditionnel.

condole, cŏnn-daule´, *v*
exprimer ses
condoléances.

condolence, cŏnn-daul´-
'ns, *n* condoléance *f*.

condone, cŏnn-daune´, *v*
pardonner; fermer les
yeux sur.

conducive, cŏnn-dioue´-
cive, *a* contribuant à.

conduct, cŏnn-docte´, *v*
conduire; (*mus*) diriger.
n conduite *f*.

conductor, cŏnn-doct´-'r,
n conducteur *m*; chef
d'orchestre *m*.

cone, caune, *n* cône *m*;
(ice cream) cornet *m*.

confectioner, cŏnn-
féque´-cheunn-*eur*, *n*
confiseur *m*; (shop)
confiserie *f*; **–y,** bonbons
mpl; confiserie *f*.

confederate, cŏnn-féd´-
eur-éte, *n* & *a* confédéré
m; complice *m*.

confederation, cŏnn-féd´-
eur-é-'ch'n, *n*
confédération *f*.

confer, cŏnn-feur´, *v*
conférer; accorder.

conference, cŏnn´-feur-
ennce, *n* conférence *f*;
congrès *m*.

confess, cŏnn-fesse´, *v*
avouer; (*eccl*) confesser.

confession, cŏnn-fé´-ch'n,
n aveu *m*; (*eccl*)
confession *f*.

confide, cŏnn-fâïde´, *v*
confier; se confier à.

confidence, cŏnn´-fi-d'ns,
n confidence *f*; (faith)
confiance *f*.

confident, cŏnn´-fi-
dennte, *a* confiant;

assuré.

confidential*, cŏnn-fi-denn´-ch'l, *a* confidentiel.

confine, cŏnn-fâïne´, *v* limiter; enfermer; **–ment**, *n* emprisonnement *m*; (birth) accouchement *m*.

confirm, cŏnn-feurme´, *v* confirmer.

confirmation, cŏnn-feur-mé´-ch'n, *n* confirmation *f*.

confiscate, cŏnn´-fisse-quéte, *v* confisquer.

conflagration, cŏnn-fla-gré´-ch'n, *n* incendie *m*; conflagration *f*.

conflict, cŏnn´-flicte, *n* conflit *m*; (combat) lutte *f*. *v* être en conflit.

conflicting, cŏnn-flique´-tinng, *a* contradictoire.

conform, cŏnn-foarme´, *v* se conformer.

confound, cŏnn-fâ´ounnde´, *v* confondre.

confront, cŏnn-fronnte´, *v* confronter; affronter.

confuse, cŏnn-fiouze´, *v* déconcerter; embrouiller.

confusion, cŏnn-fiouē´-j'n, *n* confusion *f*.

congeal, cŏnn-djîle´, *v* congeler; se congeler.

congenial, cŏnn-djî´-ni-al, *a* sympathique.

congenital, cŏnn-djenn´-i-t'l, *a* (med) congénital.

congest, cŏnn-djeste´, *v* entasser; congestionner; **–ion**, *n* (traffic) embouteillage *m*; (med) congestion *f*.

congratulate, cŏnn-grăt´-iou-léte, *v* féliciter.

congratulation, cŏnn-grăt-iou-lé´-ch'n, *n* félicitation *f*.

congregate, conng´-gri-guéte, *v* se rassembler.

congregation, cŏnn-gri-guē´-ch'n, *n* assemblée *f*; congrégation *f*.

congress, conng´-gresse, *n* congrès *m*.

conjecture, cŏnn-djéque-tioure, *n* conjecture *f*. *v* conjecturer.

conjugal, cŏnn´-djoue-g'l, *a* conjugal.

conjunction, cŏnn-djonngk´-ch'n, *n* conjonction *f*.

conjurer, conn´-djeur-*eur*, *n* prestidigitateur *m*.

connect, cŏnn-necte´, *v* unir; relier à.

connection, cŏnn-nec´-ch'n, *n* rapport *m*; lien *m*; (train, etc) correspondance *f*.

connoisseur, cŏnn-oss-

eur´, *n* connaisseur *m*.

conquer, conng´-qu*eur*, *v* conquérir; vaincre.

conqueror, conng´-queur-*eur*, *n* conquérant *m*.

conquest, conng´-coueste, *n* conquête *f*.

conscience, conn´-chennce, *n* conscience *f*.

conscientious*, cŏnn-chienn´-cheuce, *a* consciencieux.

conscious, conn´-cheuce, *a* conscient; **–ness**, *n* conscience *f*; (med) connaissance *f*.

conscript, conn´-scripte, *n* conscrit *m*.

consecrate, conn´-ci-créte, *v* consacrer; bénir.

consecutive*, cŏnn-sèk´-iou-tive, *a* consécutif.

consent, cŏnn-cennte´, *v* consentir. *n* consentement *m*.

consequence, conn´-ci-couènnce, *n* conséquence *f*.

consequently, conn´-ci-couènn-tli, *adv* par conséquent.

conservative, cŏnn-seur´-va-tive, *n & a* conservateur, -trice *m & f*.

conservatory, cŏnn-seur´-va-*teur*-i, *n* serre *f*; conservatoire *f*.

conserve, cŏnn-seurve´, v
conserver.

consider, cŏnn-cid´-eur, v
considérer; **–able,** a
considérable; **–ate,**
attentionné; **–ation,** n
considération f; **–ing,**
prep vu; étant donné.

consign, cŏnn-sâïne´, v
livrer; consigner; confier
à; **–ee,** n destinataire m;
–ment, envoi m; **–or,**
expéditeur m.

consist, cŏnn-cisste´, v
consister; **–ency,** n
consistance f; **–ent,** a
compatible; conforme;
logique; stable.

consolation, cŏnn-saule-
é´-ch'n, n consolation f.

console, cŏnn-saule´, v
consoler.

consonant, conn´-so-
nennte, n consonne f.

conspicuous, cŏnn-spik´-
iou-euce, a apparent; en
évidence; **to make
oneself –,** se faire
remarquer.

conspiracy, cŏnn-spir´-a-
ci, n complot m.

conspirator, cŏnn-spir´-é-
teur, n conspirateur m.

conspire, cŏnn-spâïre´, v
conspirer.

constable, conn´-sta-b'l, n
agent de police m.

constabulary, cŏnn-stăb´-

iou-la-ri, n gendarmerie
f; police f.

constancy, conn´-stann-
ci, n constance f.

constant, conn´-stannte, a
constant; continuel.

constipation, cŏnn-sti-
pé´-ch'n, n constipation
f.

constituency, cŏnn-sti´-
tiou-enn-ci, n
circonscription
électorale f; électeurs
mpl.

constituent, cŏnn-sti´-
tiou-'nt, n électeur m.

constitute, cŏnn´-sti-
tioute, v constituer.

constitution, cŏnn-sti-
tiou´-ch'n, n
constitution f.

constrain, cŏnn-stréne´, v
contraindre.

constraint, cŏnn-
strénnte´, n contrainte f.

constriction, cŏnn-stric´-
ch'n, n rétrécissement
m; resserrement m.

construct, cŏnn-strocte´, v
construire.

construction, cŏnn-stroc´-
ch'n, n construction f.

construe, cŏnn-stroue, v
construire; interpréter.

consul, conn´-seul, n
consul m; **–ate,** consulat
m.

consult, cŏnn-solte´, v

consulter; –ation, n
consultation f.

consume, cŏnn-sioume´, v
consumer; (food)
consommer.

consumer, cŏnn-sioue´-
meur, n consommateur
m.

consummate, conn´-
somm-éte, v
consommer; a âchevé.

consummation, cŏnn-
somm-mé´-ch'n, n
consommation f;
accomplissement m.

consumption, cŏnn-
sommp´-ch'n, n (use)
consommation f; (med)
comsomption
pulmonaire f.

consumptive, cŏnn-
sommp´-tive, a & n
tuberculeux.

contact, conn´-tăcte, n
contact m; **–lens,** verre
de contact m.

contagious, cŏnn-té-
djeuce, a contagieux.

contain, cŏnn-téne´, v
contenir; retenir.

contaminate, cŏnn-
tămm´-i-néte, v
contaminer.

contemplate, cŏnn´-
temm-pléte, v
contempler; projeter.

contemporary, cŏnn-
temm´-pŏ-ra-ri, n & a

contemporain, -aine.

contempt, cŏnn-temmp´-
't, n mépris m; – of
court, refus de
comparaître.

contemptible, cŏnn-
temmp´-ti-b'l, a
méprisable.

contend, cŏnn-tennde´, v
contester; (maintain)
soutenir.

content, cŏnn-tennte´, v
contenter. a satisfait;
–ment, n contentement
m.

content, cŏnn´-tennte, n
contenu m.

contention, cŏnn-tenn´-
ch'n, n prétention f.

contentious, cŏnn-tenn´-
cheuce, a discutable.

contents, cŏnn´-tenn-ts,
npl contenu m.

contest, cŏnn-tesste´, v
contester. n concours m;
match m.

contiguous, cŏnn-tigue´-
iou-euce, a contigu.

continent, cŏnn´-ti-
nennte, n continent m.

contingency, cŏnn-tinn´-
djenn-ci, n éventualité f.

contingent, cŏnn-tinn´-
djennte, a éventuel;
contingent.

continual*, cŏnn-tinn´-
iou'l, a continuel.

continuation, cŏnn-tinn´-

iou-é´-ch'n, n
continuation f.

continue, cŏnn-tinn´-
ioue, v continuer.

continuous*, cŏnn-tinn´-
iou-euce, a continu.

contortion, cŏnn-toar´-
ch'n, n contorsion f.

contraband, cŏnn´-tra-
bănnde, n contrebande
f.

contract, cŏnn´-trăcte, n
contrat m. v contracter;
–ion, n contraction f;
–or, fournisseur m;
(builder) entrepreneur
m.

contradict, cŏnn-tra-
dicte´, v contredire;
–ion, n contradiction f.

contrary, cŏnn´-tra-ri, n
& a contraire m.

contrast, cŏnn´-traste, n
contraste m.

contrast, cŏnn-traste´, v
contraster.

contravene, cŏnn-tra-
vîne´, v enfreindre.

contravention, cŏnn-tra-
venn´-ch'n, n
contravention f.

contribute, cŏnn-trib´-
ioute, v contribuer.

contribution, cŏnn-trib-
iou´-ch'n, n
contribution f; (literary)
article m.

contrite, cŏnn´-trăïte, a

contrit.

contrivance, cŏnn-trăï´-
v'nce, n invention f;
dispositif m; (fam)
manigance f.

contrive, cŏnn-trăïve´, v
inventer; trouver
moyen; (fam) machiner.

control, cŏnn-traule´, v
contrôler; (feelings) (se)
maîtriser. n contrôle m;
(feelings) maîtrise f;
(authority) direction f;
–ler, contrôleur m.

controversial, cŏnn-trŏ-
veur´-ch'l, a polémique.

controversy, cŏnn´-trŏ-
veur-ci, n controverse f.

convalescence, cŏnn-va-
less-ennce,
convalescence f.

convalescent, cŏnn-va-
less´-'nt, a & n
convalescent.

convenience, cŏnn-vî´-
ennce, n convenance f;
commodité f.

convenient, cŏnn-vî´-ni-
ennte, a commode.

convent, cŏnn´-vennte, n
couvent m.

convention, cŏnn-venn´-
ch'n, n convention f.

converge, cŏnn-veurdje´,
v converger.

conversant, cŏnn-veur´-
s'nt, a au courant de.

conversation, cŏnn-veurcé´-ch'n, n conversation f.

converse, cŏnn-veurse´, v s'entretenir.

conversion, cŏnn-veur´-ch'n, n conversion f.

convert, cŏnn-veurte´, v convertir. n converti m.

convex, conn´-vexe, a convexe.

convey, cŏnn-vé´, v transporter; transmettre; présenter; **–ance,** n transport m; (law) transfert m.

convict, cŏnn-victe´, v condamner; **–ion,** n condamnation f; (belief) conviction f.

convict, conn´-victe, n forçat m; bagnard m.

convince, cŏnn-vinnce´, v convaincre.

convivial, cŏnn-viv´-ial, a jovial; sociable; digne de bons convives.

convoy, cŏnn-voa'i´, v convoyer; escorter. n convoi m.

convulse, cŏnn-vol´, v convulser.

convulsion, cŏnn-vol´-ch'n, n convulsion f.

coo, cou, v roucouler.

cook, couk, v faire cuire; faire la cuisine; cuire. n cuisinier, -ère m & f.

cookery, couk´-eur-i, n

cuisine f.

cool, coule, v refroidir. a frais; froid; **–ness,** n fraîcheur f; (nerve) sang-froid m.

coop, coupe, n cage à poulets f.

cooperate, cau-op´-eur-éte, v coopérer.

cope, caupe, v **–with,** se débrouiller de.

copious*, cau-pi-euce, a copieux.

copper, cop´-eur, n cuivre m. a de cuivre.

coppice, copse, cop´-ice, copce, n taillis m.

copy, cop´-i, v copier. n copie f; (of book) exemplaire m; (newspaper, etc) numéro m; **–right,** droits d'auteur m.

coquetry, coque´-éte-ri, n coquetterie f.

coral, cor´-al, n corail m.

cord, côrde, v corder. n corde f.

cordial, côr´-di-al, a cordial.

corduroy, coar´-diou-roa'ï, n velours côtelé m.

core, caure, n cœur m; trognon m.

cork, corque, v boucher. n liège m; (stopper) bouchon m; **–screw,** tire-bouchon m.

corn, côrne, n blé m; (foot, etc) cor m.

corner, côr´-n'r, n coin m; (road bend) tournant m; virage m, accaparer; acculer.

cornflower, côrne´-flâ'ou-eur, n bluet m.

cornice, cor´-nice, n corniche f.

coronation, cor-ŏ-né´-ch'n, n couronnement m.

coroner, cor´-o-neur, n magistrat enquêteur m.

coronet, cor´-o-nette, n couronne f.

corporal, coar´-pŏ-r'l, n caporal m; (artillery and cavalry) brigadier m. a corporel.

corporation, coar´-pŏ-ré´-ch'n, n corporation f.

corps, core, n corps m.

corpse, coarpse, n cadavre m.

corpulence, cor´-piou-lenn-ce, n corpulence f.

corpulent, cor´-piou-l'nt, a corpulent.

corpuscle, cor´-peuss-'l, n corpuscule m.

correct*, cŏr-recte´, a correct. v corriger; **–ive,** a correctif; **–ness,** n exactitude f.

correspond, cŏr-i-sponnde´, v

correspondre; **–ence,** n correspondance f.

corridor, cŏr´-i-doar, n corridor m; couloir m.

corroborate, cŏr-rôb´-ŏ-réte, v corroborer.

corroboration, cŏr-rôb´-ŏ-ré´-ch'n, n corroboration f.

corrode, cŏr-raude´, v corroder.

corrosive, cŏr-rau´-sive, n & a corrosif m.

corrugated, cor´-rou-gué-tedde, **–paper,** n papier ondulé m; **–iron,** tôle ondulée f.

corrupt, cŏr-ropte´, v corrompre. a corrompu.

corruption, cŏr-rope´-ch'n, n corruption f.

corset, cor´-cette, n corset m.

cortege, cŏr-téje´, n cortège m.

cost, coste, n prix m; (expense) frais mpl. v coûter; **–ly,** a coûteux; **–s,** npl (law) dépens mpl.

costume, cosse´-tioume, n costume m.

cot, cotte, n lit d'enfant m.

cottage, cot´-idj, n (thatched) chaumière f; cottage m.

cotton, cot´-t'n, n coton m; **–wool,** ouate f;

(med) coton hydrophile m.

couch, câ´-outche, n canapé m; divan m.

cough, coaf, v tousser. n toux f.

council, câ´-ounn´-cil, n conseil m; **–lor,** conseiller m.

counsel, câ´-ounn´-s'l, n avocat conseil m. v conseiller; **–or,** conseiller m; (law) conseil m.

count, câ´-ounnte, v compter. n compte m; **–inghouse,** la comptabilité f; **–less,** a innombrable.

count, câ´-ounnte, n (title) comte m; **–ess,** comtesse f.

countenance, câ´-ounn´-teu-nannce, v approuver. n contenance f.

counter, câ´-ounn´-teur, n comptoir m; (games) jeton m. adv contre; **–act,** v contrarier; neutraliser; (frustrate) déjouer; **–balance,** contrebalancer; **–feit,** v contrefaire. a faux. n faux m; **–foil,** talon m; **–mand,** v contremander. n contre-ordre m; **–pane,** couvre-lit m;

–part, contre-partie f; **–sign,** v contresigner. n mot d'ordre m.

country, connⁿ-tri, n (state) pays m; (rural) campagne f.

county, câ´-ounn´-ti, n comté m.

couple, cop´-p'l, v accoupler. n couple m.

courage, cor´-idj, n courage m.

courageous*, keur-é´-djeuce, a courageux.

course, corse, n (river, tuition) cours m; (direction) route f; (race) champ de courses m; (meals) plat m; **of –,** adv naturellement.

court, côrte, n (royal) cour f; (law) tribunal m; (tennis) court m. v faire la cour à; **–ier,** n courtisan m; **– martial,** conseil de guerre m; **–ship,** cour f; **–yard,** cour f.

courteous*, keur´-ti-euce, a courtois.

courtesy, keur´-ti-ci, n courtoisie f.

cousin, co´-z'n, n cousin m; cousine f.

cove, cauve, n (geog) anse f; petite baie f.

covenant, cov´-nannte, n pacte m; contrat m. v

stipuler.

cover, cov´-*eur*, *n* couverture *f*; (lid) couvercle *m*; (shelter) abri *m*. *v* couvrir.

covet, cov´-*ette*, *v* convoiter.

cow, câ'ou, *n* vache *f*. *v* intimider: **–slip,** *n* coucou *m*.

coward, câ'ou´-*eurde*, *n* lâche *m* & *f*; **–ice,** lâcheté *f*.

cower, câ'ou´-*eur*, *v* se tapir.

cowl, câ'oule, *n* (hood, chimney) capuchon *m*.

coy, côa'ï, *a* réservé; timide.

cozy, cauz´-i, *a* confortable; à l'aise.

crab, crăbbe, *n* crabe *m*; **–apple,** pomme sauvage *f*.

crack, crăque, *n* (small) craquelure *f*; fente *f*; (glass) fêlure *f*; (noise) craquement *m*; (whip) claquement *m*. *v* craqueler; fendre; fêler; craquer; claquer; (nuts) casser; **–er,** *n* (firework) pétard *m*; (nut) cassenoisette *m*; **–le,** *v* craquer; (fire) pétiller.

cradle, cré´-d'l, *n* (crib) berceau *m*.

craft, crâfte, *n* (trade) métier *m*; (*naut*)

embarcation *f*; (cunning) ruse *f*; **–sman,** artisan *m*; **–y,** *a* rusé.

crag, crăgue, *n* rocher à pic *m*.

cram, crămme, *v* bourrer.

cramp, crămmpe, *n* crampe *f*.

cranberry, crănne´-bê-ri, *n* airelle *f*.

crane, créne, *n* grue *f*.

crank, crain-ngk, *n* (*mech*) manivelle *f*.

crash, crăche, *v* (break) briser; (*aero*) s'écraser; (car) se tamponner. *n* (car, train) accident *m*; (noise) fracas *m*.

crate, créte, *n* caisse *f*, cageot *m*.

crater, cré-*teur*, *n* cratère *m*.

crave, créve *v* implorer; désirer ardemment.

craving, créve´-inng, *n* désir ardent *m*.

crawl, croal, *v* ramper.

crayfish, cré´-fiche, *n* écrevisse *f*; (sea) langouste *f*.

crayon, cré´-onn, *n* pastel *m*.

craze, créze, *n* (mode) manie *f*; engouement *m*.

crazy, cré´-zi, *a* toqué; fou.

creak, crîque, *v* grincer. *n* craquement *m*.

cream, crîme, *n* crème *f*;

–y, *a* crémeux.

crease, crîce, *n* (press) pli *m*; (crush) faux pli *m*. *v* se froisser.

create, cri-éte´, *v* créer; produire.

creature, crî´-tioure, *n* créature *f*.

credentials, cri-denn´-ch'lz, *npl* lettres de créance *fpl*; papiers d'identité *mpl*.

credible, crèd´-i-b'l, *a* croyable.

credit, crèd´-itte, *n* crédit *m*. *v* créditer; **–able,** *a* estimable; honorable; **–or,** *n* créancier *m*.

credulous, crèd´-iou-*leuce*, *a* crédule.

creed, crîde, *n* croyance *f*.

creek, crîque, *n* crique *f*.

creep, crîpe, *v* se traîner; (silently) se glisser; (plants, animals, etc) ramper.

creeper, crî´-*peur*, *n* plante grimpante *f*.

cremate, cri-méte´, *v* incinérer.

cremation, cri-mé´-ch'n, *n* crémation *f*.

creole, crî´-ôle, *n* & *a* créole *m* & *f*.

crescent, cress´-'nt, *n* croissant *m*.

cress, cresse, *n* cresson *m*.

crest, cresste, *n* (heraldry)

armes *fpl*; (seal, etc) écusson; *m* (hill, bird's) crête *f*; **–fallen,** *a* penaud; abattu.

crevice, crév´-ice, *n* crevasse *f*.

crew, croue, *n* (*naut*) équipage *m*.

crick, crique, *n* crampe *f*; (neck) torticolis *m*.

cricket, cri´-quette, *n* grillon *m*; (game) cricket *m*.

crime, crâîme, *n* crime *m*.

criminal, crimm´-i-n'l, *n* & *a* criminel *m* & *f*.

crimson, crimm´-z'n, *n* & *a* cramoisi *m*.

cringe, crinn´-dje, *v* faire des courbettes; se blottir.

crinkle, crinn´-k'l, *v* froisser. *n* froissement *m*.

cripple, crip´-p'l, *n* estropié *m*. *v* estropier.

crisis, crâî´-cisse, *n* crise *f*.

crisp, crispe, *a* (food) croustillant.

criterion, crâî-ti´-ri-*eu*ne, *n* critère *m*.

critic, cri´-tique, *n* critique *m*; **–al*,** *a* critique.

criticism, crit´-i-ci-z'm, *n* critique *f*.

criticize, crit´-i-sâïze, *v* critiquer.

croak, crauque, *v* (bird) croasser; (frog) coasser.

n croassement *m*; coassement *m*.

crochet, cro´-ché, *n* crochet *m*. *v* faire du crochet.

crockery, crok´-*eu*-ri, *n* vaisselle *f*.

crocodile, crok´-o-dâïle, *n* crocodile *m*.

crocus, cro´-qu*euce*, *n* crocus *m*.

crook, crouk, *n* (*pers*) escroc *m*.

crooked, crouk´-edde, *a* tordu; de travers; malhonnête.

crop, crope, *n* récolte *f*; (haircut) coupe *f*. *v* tondre.

cross, crosse, *n* croix *f*. *a* fâché; entravers. *v* (intersect) croiser; **––examine,** interroger; **–ing,** *n* traversée *f*; **–out,** *v* rayer; **–over,** traverser; **––road,** *n* carrefour *m*.

crotchet, crotch´-ette, *n* (music) noire *f*.

crouch, crâ´outche, *v* se tapir; s'accroupir.

crow, crau, *n* corbeau *m*. *v* (cock) chanter.

crowbar, crau´-bâre, *n* pince *f*.

crowd, crâ´oude, *n* foule *f*. *v* encombrer; (s') entasser.

crown, crâ´ounne, *n*

couronne *f*; (top) sommet *m*. *v* couronner.

crucible, croue´-ci-b'l, *n* creuset *m*.

crucifix, croue´-ci-fixe, *n* crucifix *m*.

crucify, croue´-ci-fâï, *v* crucifier.

crude*, croude, *a* (raw) cru; (vulgar) grossier.

cruel*, croue´-*eul*, *a* cruel; **–ty,** *a* cruauté *f*.

cruise, crouze, *v* faire une croisière. *n* croisière *f*.

cruiser, croue´-zeur, *n* croiseur *m*.

crumb, cromme, *n* mie *f*; (particle) miette *f*.

crumble, cromm´-b'l, *v* tomber en poussière; émietter.

crumple, cromm´-p'l, *v* chiffonner.

crunch, cronntche, *v* croquer.

crush, croche, *v* écraser; (pound) broyer. *n* cohue *f*.

crust, crosste, *n* croûte *f*; **–y,** *a* croustillant.

crutch, crotche, *n* béquille *f*.

cry, crâï, *v* crier; (weep) pleurer. *n* cri *m*.

cryptic, cripe´-tic *a* occulte.

crystal, criss´-t'l, *n* cristal *m*.

cub, cobbe, n (bear) ourson m; (lion) lionceau m.

cube, kioube, n cube m.

cuckoo, cou´-coue, n coucou m.

cucumber, kiou´-commb'r, n concombre m.

cud, code, n (to chew the –) ruminer.

cuddle, cod´-d'l, v caresser.

cudgel, codd´-j'l, n gourdin m.

cue, kioue, n (billiard) queue f; (acting) réplique f; avis m.

cuff, coffe, n manchette f.

culinary, kiou´-li-na-ri, a culinaire.

culminate, col´-mi-néte, v culminer.

culpability, col-pa-bile´-i-ti, n culpabilité f.

culpable, col´-pa-b'l, a coupable.

culprit, col´-pritte, n coupable m & f.

cultivate, col´-ti-véte, v cultiver.

culture, col´-tioure, n culture f.

cumbersome, comm´-beur-somme, a encombrant.

cunning*, conn´-inng, n ruse f. a rusé

cup, coppe, n tasse f; (trophy) coupe f.

cupboard, cob´-eurde, n placard m; armoire f.

cupola, kiou´-po-la, n coupole f.

cur, keur, n cabot m; (fig) vil individu m.

curate, kiou´-réte, n vicaire m.

curb, keurbe, n frein m; rebord de trottoir m. v (fig) réprimer.

curd, keurde, n lait caillé m.

curdle, keur´-d'l, v se figer; (milk) se cailler.

cure, kioure, n traitement m; (remedy) remède m. v guérir; (meat, fish, etc) saler; fumer.

curiosity, kiou-ri-o´-si-ti, n curiosité f.

curious*, kiou´-ri-euce, a curieux.

curl, keurle, v (hair) friser. n boucle f.

currant, cor´-annte, n (dried) groseille f.

currency, cor´-enn-ci, n monnaie f; **foreign –,** n devises fpl.

current, cor´-ennte, n courant m. a courant.

curse, keurce, n malédiction f. v maudire.

cursory, keur´-so-ri, a rapide; superficiel.

curt, keurte, a bref;

brusque.

curtail, keur-télé, v abréger; **–ment,** n raccourcissement m.

curtain, keur-t'n, n rideau m.

curtsy, keurtt´-ci, n révérence f.

curve, keurve, n courbe f. v courber.

cushion, cou´-ch'n, n coussin m.

custard, cosse´-teurde, n flan m; crème cuite f.

custody, cosse´-tô-di, n garde f; détention f.

custom, cosse´-teume, n coutume f; douane fpl; **–ary,** a d'usage; **–er,** n client m; **–house,** douane f; **–s-duty,** droits de douane mpl.

cut, cotte, n coupure f; (joint, etc) tranche f; coupe f. v couper; (suit diamonds, etc) trailer; **–lery,** argenterie f; **–let,** côtelette f; **–ter,** n (tailor) coupeur m.

cuticle, kiou´-ti-k'l, n cuticule f.

cuttlefish, cott´-'l-fiche, n seiche f.

cyclamen, sique´-lä-menn, n cyclamen m.

cycle, saï´-k'l, n cycle m; (vehicle) bicyclette f. v faire de la bicyclette.

cylinder, sill´-inn-d*eu*r, *n*
  cylindre *m*.
cynical, sinn´-i-k'l, *a*
  cynique.
cypress, săï´-presse, *n*
  cyprès *m*.

dabble, dăbb-'l, *v*
s'occuper; barboter;
(shares) boursicoter.

daffodil, dăff´-o-dile, *n*
narcisse sauvage *m*;
jonquille *f*.

dagger, dăgg´-'r, *n*
poignard *m*.

dahlia, dél´-i-ă, *n* dahlia
m.

daily, dé´-li, *a* quotidien.

dainty, dénne´-ti, *a*
délicat.

dairy, dé´-ri, *n* laiterie *f*;
(shop) crèmerie *f*.

daisy, dé´-zi, *n* (field)
pâquerette *f*.

dale, déle, *n* vallon *m*.

dam, dăme, *n* digue *f*;
barrage *m*. *v* endiguer.

damage, dămm´-idj, *n*
dommage *m*; dégât *m*;
avarie *f*. *v* endommager;

abîmer.

damask, dămm´-asque, *n*
damas *m*.

damn, dămme, *v* damner.
interj zut!

damnation, dămm-né´-
ch'n, *n* damnation *f*.

damp, dămmpe, *v*
mouiller. *a* humide.

dampness, dămmpe´-
nesse, *n* humidité *f*;
moiteur *f*.

damson, dămm´-s'n, *n*
prune de Damas *f*.

dance, dânnce, *v* danser. *n*
danse *f*.

dancer, dânne´-ceur, *n*
danseur *m*; danseuse *f*.

dandelion, dănn´-di-lâï-
onn, *n* pissenlit *m*.

dandruff, dănnde´-rof, *n*
pellicules *fpl*.

danger, déne´-djeur, *n*

danger *m*; **–ous*,** *a*
dangereux; **–ously,** *adv*
dangereusement.

dangle, dănn´-g'l, *v*
pendiller; se balancer.

dare, daire, *v* oser;
(challenge) défier.

daring, daire´-inng, *n*
audace *f*. *a** audacieux.

dark, dârque, *a* sombre;
(skin) brun; **–ness,** *n*
obscurité *f*.

darling, dâre´-linng, *n* & *a*
chéri, -ie *m* & *f*.

darn, dârne, *v* repriser. *n*
reprise *f*.

dart, dârte, *n* dard *m*;
(game) fléchette *f*;
(sewing) pince *f*.

dash, dâche, *n* (short line)
trait *m*. *v* lancer; (rush)
s'élancer.

data, dé´-ta, *npl* données
fpl; information *f*.

data processing, dé´-ta-
prau´-cess-inng, *n*
informatique *f*.

date, déte, *n* date *f*; (fruit)
datte *f*. *v* dater; **–d,** *a*
démodé; qui date.

daughter, doa´-t'r, *n* fille *f*;
—in-law, belle-fille *f*.

daunt, doannt, *v*
décourager; intimider.

dauntless, doannte´-lesse,
a intrépide.

dawdle, doa´-d'l, *v* flâner;
traîner.

dawn, doanne, n aurore f.
v faire jour.

day, dé, n jour m; journée
f; **–break,** point du jour
m; aube f.

dazzle, dǎz´-z'l, v éblouir.

deacon, dî´-k'n, n diacre
m.

dead, dède, a mort; **–en,** v
amortir; **–ly,** a mortel.

deaf, deffe, a sourd; **–en,** v
assourdir.

deafness, deff´-nesse, n
surdité f.

deal, dîle, n quantité f;
(business) affaire f; v
(trade) faire des affaires;
(attend to) s'occuper de;
(cards) donner.

dealer, dîl´-eur, n
négociant m.

dean, dîne, n doyen m.

dear*, dîre, a cher.

dearth, deurts, n manque
m; pénurie f.

death, dèts, n mort f.

debar, di-bâre´, v exclure;
priver de.

debase, di-béce´, v avilir;
dégrader.

debate, di-béte´, v
discuter. n débat m.

debauch, di-boatch´- v
débaucher.

debauchery, di-boatch´-
eur-i, n débauche f.

debenture, di-benn´-
tioure, n obligation f.

debility, di-bile´-i-ti, n
débilité f.

debit, dèb´-itte, n débit m.
v débiter.

debt, dette, n dette f; **–or,**
débiteur m.

decadence, dè´-ca-dennce,
n décadence f.

decant, di-cânnte´, v
décanter; **–er,** n carafe f.

decapitate, di-cǎpe´-i-téte,
v décapiter.

decay, di-qué´, n (decline)
décadence f; (rot)
délabrement m. v
détériorer; pourrir;
(teeth) carier.

decease, di-cîce´, n décès
m; **–d,** a décédé.

deceit, di-cîte´, n
tromperie f; **–ful*,** a
trompeur.

deceive, di-cîve´, v
décevoir; tromper.

December, di-semm´-b'r,
n décembre m.

decency, dî´-cenn-ci, n
(moral) décence f.

decent, dî´-cennte, a
décent; (nice)
convenable.

deception, di-cepp´-ch'n,
n tromperie f.

deceptive, di-cepp´-tive, a
trompeur.

decide, di-sâide´, v
décider; **–d,** * a décidé.

decimal, dé´-ci-m'l, a
décimal.

decipher, di-sâi´-f'r, v
déchiffrer.

decision, di-ci´-j'n, n
décision f.

decisive,* di-sâi´-cive, a
décisif.

deck, dèque, n pont m. v
orner.

declaim, di-cléme´, v
déclamer.

declaration, di-cla-ré´-
ch'n, n déclaration f.

declare, di-clére´, v
déclarer; se déclarer.

declension, di-clenn´-
ch'n, n déclinaison f.

decline, di-clâine´, n
baisse f; (slope) pente f;
(decadence) déclin m. v
refuser; (grammar)
décliner.

decompose, di-cǒmm-
pauze´, v décomposer.

decompress, di-comm-
presse´, v décomprimer.

decorate, dè´-cǒ-réte, v
décorer.

decorous, dè-cô´-reuce, a
décent; convenable.

decoy, di-coa'ï´, n piège m;
(bird) appeau m; (bait)
appât m. v leurrer.

decrease, di-crîce´, v
décroître; (knitting)
diminuer. n diminution
f.

decree, di-crî´, n décret m.

v décréter.

decry, di-crâî´, *v* décrier.

dedicate, dè´-di-quéte, *v* dédier.

deduce, di-diouce´, *v* déduire.

deduct, di-docte´, *v* déduire.

deduction, di-doc´-ch'n, *n* déduction *f*; (*com*) remise *f*.

deed, dîde, *n* action *f*; (heroic) exploit *m*; (law) acte *m*; titre *m*.

deem, dîme, *v* juger; estimer.

deep, dîpe, *a* profond; –en, *v* approfondir.

deep freeze, dîpe´-frîze, *n* congélateur *m*.

deer, dire, *n* daim *m*; (red) cerf *m*.

deface, di-féce´, *v* dégrader; mutiler.

defamation, dé-fa-mé´-ch'n, *n* diffamation *f*.

defame, di-féme´, *v* diffamer.

default, di-foalte´, *n* défaut de payement *m*; (law) contumace *f*. *v* faire défaut.

defeat, di-fîte´, *n* défaite *f*. *v* vaincre; déjouer.

defect, di-fecte´, *n* défaut *m*; –ive, *a* défectueux.

defend, di-fennde´, *v* défendre; –ant, *n*

défendeur *m*; –er, défenseur *m*.

defense, di-fennce´, *n* défense *f*.

defenseless, di-fennce´-lesse, *a* sans défense.

defensive, di-fenn´-cive, *n* défensive *f*. *a* défensif.

defer, di-feur´, *v* différer; ajourner; **to – someone's judgement**, en déférer à quelqu'un.

deference, dèf´-eur-ennce, *n* déférence *f*.

defiance, di-faî´-'nce, *n* défi *m*.

deficiency, di-fich´-enn-ci, *n* manque *m*.

deficient, di-fich´-'nt, *a* défectueux; insuffisant.

deficit, dèf´-i-cite, *n* déficit *m*.

defile, di-faîle´, *v* souiller.

define, di-faîne´, *v* définir.

definite, dèf´-i-nitte, *a* déterminé; défini.

definition, dèf-i-ni´-ch'n, *n* définition *f*.

deflect, di-flecte´, *v* dévier.

deform, di-foarme´, *v* déformer; –ed, *a* difforme.

defraud, di-froade´, *v* frauder.

defray, di-fré´, *v* défrayer.

deft*, defte, *a* adroit; (clever) habile; (quick) leste.

defunct, di-fonnkt´, *a* défunt.

defy, di-faî´, *v* défier; provoquer.

degenerate, di-djènn´-eur-éte, *v* dégénérer. *n* & *a* dégénéré *m*.

degrade, di-gréde´, *v* dégrader.

degree, di-grî´, *n* degré *m*; (university) licence *f*.

dehydrate, dí´-hâî-dréte, *v* déshydrater.

deign, déne, *v* daigner.

deject, di-djèque't´, *v* décourager; déprimer.

dejection, di-djèque´-ch'n, *n* abattement *m*.

delay, di-lé´, *n* retard *m*; délai *m*. *v* tarder; différer.

delegate, dèl´-i-guéte, *v* délégué *m*.

delete, di-lîte´, *v* effacer; rayer; supprimer.

deletion, de-lîch'n, *n* effacement *m*; rature *f*.

deliberate, di-lib´-eur-éte, *v* délibérer. *a** délibéré.

delicacy, dèl´-i-ca-ci, *n* délicatesse *f*.

delicate*, dèl´-i-quéte, *a* délicat.

delicious*, di-lich´-euce, *a* délicieux.

delight, di-lâîte, *v* enchanter. *n* délices *fpl*; joie *f*.

delightful*, di-lâïte´-foull, *a* délicieux.

delineate, di-linn´-i-éte, *v* tracer.

delinquent, di-linng´-couente, *n* délinquant, - e *m* & *f*.

delirious*, di-lir´-i-euce, *a* en délire.

delirium, di-lir´-i-eume, *n* délire *m*.

deliver, di-liv´-eur, *v* (letters) distribuer; (goods) livrer; (set free, rid) délivrer; **–y,** *n* délivrance *f*; (letters) distribution *f*; (goods) livraison *f*.

delude, di-lioude´, *v* tromper.

delusion, di-liou´-j'n, *n* illusion *f*.

demand, di-mânnde´, *v* exiger. *n* demande *f*.

demeanor, di-mî´-neur, *n* conduite *f*; tenue *f*.

demented, di-menn´-tedde, *n* & *a* dément *m*.

democratic, dè-mo-crâ´-tique, *a* démocratique.

demolish, di-mol´-iche, *v* démolir.

demon, dî´-mŏnne, *n* démon *m*.

demonstrate, dè-´-monn-stréte, *v* démontrer; donner une démonstration.

demonstrative, di-monn´-stra-tive, *a* démonstratif; expansif.

demoralize, di-mô-rǎ-lâïze, *v* démoraliser.

demur, di-meure´, *v* hésiter.

demure, di-mioure´, *a* modeste.

den, dènne, *n* tanière *f*; repaire *m*; cabinet de travail *m*.

denial, di-nâï´-'l, *n* dénégation *f*.

denomination, di-nŏmm-i-né´-ch'n, *n* dénomination *f*.

denote, di-naute´, *v* dénoter.

denounce, di-nâ'ounnce´, *v* dénoncer.

dense, dènnce, *a* dense; épais; (person) stupide.

dent, dènnte, *n* marque *f*; creux *m*. *v* cabosser; bosseler.

dentist, dènn´-tiste, *n* dentiste *m*.

denude, di-nioude´, *v* dénuder.

deny, di-nâï´, *v* nier.

deodorant, di-ô´-deur-'nt, *n* déodorant *m*.

deodorize, di-ô´-deur-âïze, *v* désodoriser.

depart, di-pârte´, *v* partir; **–ment,** *n* branche *f*; service *m*; (shop) rayon *m*; **–ure,** départ *m*.

depend (upon), di-pennde´, *v* (contingent) dépendre; (trust) compter sur; **–ent,** *a* dépendant; à charge.

depict, di-picte´, *v* dépeindre.

depletion, di-plî´-ch'n, *n* épuisement *m*.

deplore, di-plaure´, *v* déplorer.

deport, di-paurte´, *v* déporter.

deportment, di-paurte´-m'nt, *n* maintien *m*.

depose, di-pauze´, *v* déposer.

deposit, di-pauz´-itte, *n* (bank, sediment) dépôt *m*; (on account) acompte *m*; arrhes *fpl*. *v* déposer; **–or,** *n* déposant *m*.

depot, depp´-au, *n* dépôt *m*.

deprave, di-préve´, *v* dépraver.

deprecate, dè´-pri-quéte, *v* désapprouver.

depreciate, di-prî´-chi-éte, *v* déprécier.

depress, di-press´, *v* déprimer; décourager; **–ion,** *n* (trade) crise *f*; (spirits) abattement *m*; dépression *f*; (hollow) affaissement *m*.

deprive, di-prâïve´, *v* priver.

depth, depts, *n* profondeur *f.*

deputation, dè-piou-té´-ch'n, *n* députation *f.*

deputy, dèp´-iou-ti, *n* représentant *m*; remplaçant *m.*

derailment, di-réle´-m'nt, *n* déraillement *m.*

derange, di-rénndje´, *v* déranger.

derangement, di-rénndje´-m'nt, *n* dérangement *m.*

derelict, dèr´-i-licte, *a* abandonné. *n* (ship) épave *f.*

deride, di-râïde´, *v* railler.

derision, di-rî´-jeune, *n* dérision *f.*

derisive*, di-râï´-cive, *a* dérisoire.

derive, di-râïve´, *v* dériver; provenir.

descend, di-cennde´, *v* descendre; **–ant,** *n* descendant, -ante *m* & *f.*

descent, di-cennte´, *n* descente *f*; origine *f.*

describe, diss-crâïbe´, *v* décrire.

description, diss-crippe´-ch'n, *n* description *f.*

desecrate, dess´-si-créte, *v* profaner.

desert, dèz´-eurte, *n* désert *m.*

desert, diz-eurte´, *v* abandonner; (*mil*) déserter; **–er,** *n* déserteur *m*; **–ion,** désertion *f*; abandon *m.*

deserve, di-zeurve´, *v* mériter.

design, di-zâïne, *n* (sketch) dessin *m*; (intention) dessein *m*; (pattern) modèle *m*; motif *m*. *v* dessiner; (plan) projeter; créer; **–ing,** *a* intrigant.

desirable, di-zâï´-ra-b'l, *a* désirable; souhaitable.

desire, di-zâïre´, *v* désirer. *n* désir *m.*

desirous, di-zâï´-reuce, *a* désireux.

desist, di-zisst´, *v* cesser; se désister.

desk, dessque, *n* bureau *m*; (school) pupitre *m.*

desolate, dess´-ŏ-léte, *a* désolé; désert.

despair, diss-pair´, *n* désespoir *m*. *v* désespérer.

desperate*, dess´-peur-éte, *a* désespéré; forcené.

despicable, dess´-pi-ca-b'l, *a* méprisable.

despise, diss-pâïze´, *v* mépriser.

despite, diss-pâïte´, *prep* en dépit de; malgré.

despoil, diss-poa´ïle´, *v* dépouiller.

despondent, diss-ponn´-d'nt, *a* découragé; déprimé.

despot, dess´-pŏtte, *n* despote *m.*

dessert, di-zeurte´, *n* dessert *m.*

destination, dèss-ti-né´-ch'n, *n* destination *f.*

destiny, dess´-ti-ni, *n* sort *m*; destin *m.*

destitute, dess´-ti-tioute, *a* indigent; dénué.

destitution, dess-ti-tiou´-ch'n, *n* dénuement *m.*

destroy, diss-troa´ï´, *v* détruire.

destruction, diss-trok´-ch'n, *n* destruction *f.*

destructive, diss-trok´-tive, *a* destructif.

desultory, dé´-seul-to-ri, *a* irrégulier; décousu.

detach, di-tâtche´, *v* détacher; **–able,** *a* détachable.

detail, di-téle´, *v* détailler. *n* détail *m.*

detain, di-téne´, *v* détenir; retenir.

detect, di-tecte´, *v* découvrir; surprendre.

detective, di-tèque´-tive, *n* détective *m*; **–novel,** roman policier *m.*

detention, di-tenn´-ch'n,

n détention *f*; (*sch*) retenue *f*.

deter, di-teur´, *v* dissuader; détourner; **–rent,** *n* préventif; (nuclear, etc) arme de dissuasion *f*.

deteriorate, di-tî´-ri-o-réte, *v* détériorer.

determine, di-teur´-minne, *v* déterminer; décider.

detest, di-tesste´, *v* détester.

dethrone, di-tsrône´, *v* détrôner.

detonation, di-to-né´-ch'n, *n* explosion *f*.

detour, di-tour´, *n* détour *m*.

detract, di-trăcte´, *v* enlever (à); dénigrer.

detrimental*, dèt-ri-menn´-t'l, *a* préjudiciable.

deuce, diouce, *n* (tennis) égalité *f*; (cards, etc) deux *m*.

devaluate, di-val´-iou-éte, *v* dévaluer, **–tion,** *n* dévaluation *f*.

devastate, dè´-vass-téte, *v* dévaster.

develop, di-vèl´-ŏpe, *v* développer.

development, di-vèl´-ope-m'nt, *n* développement *m*; fait *m*.

deviate, dî´-vi-éte, *v* dévier.

device, di-vâïce´, *n* moyen *m*; dispositif *m*; appareil *m*; truc *m*.

devil, dév´-'l, *n* diable *m*; **–ry,** diablerie *f*.

devise, di-vâïze´, *v* inventer; tramer; (law) léguer.

devoid, di-voa´ïde´, *a* dénué; dépourvu.

devote, di-vaute´, *v* dévouer; **–oneself to,** se consacrer à.

devour, di-vâ´oure´, *v* dévorer.

devout*, di-vâ´oute´, *a* dévot; pieux.

dew, dioue, *n* rosée *f*.

dexterous*, deks´-teur-euce, *a* adroit; habile.

diabetes, dâï-a-bî´-tize, *n* diabète *m*.

diabolical*, dâï-a-bol-i-k'l, *a* diabolique.

diagnose, dâï-ăgue-nauze´, *v* diagnostiquer.

diagonal, dâï-ăgue´-o-n'l, *a* diagonal.

diagram, dâï´-a-grâmme, *n* diagramme *m*; schéma *m*.

dial, dâï´-al, *n* cadran *m*. *v* composer un numéro de téléphone.

dialect, dâï-a-lecte, *n* dialecte *m*.

dialogue, dâï-a-logue, *n*

dialogue *m*.

diameter, dâï-ămm´-i-teur, *n* diamètre *m*.

diamond, dâï´-a-meunnde, *n* diamant *m*; (cards) carreau *m*.

diarrhea, dâï-a-rî´-a, *n* diarrhée *f*.

diary, dâï´-a-ri, *n* journal *m*; (pocket) agenda *m*.

dice, dâïce, *npl* dés *mpl*.

dictaphone, dic´-ta-faune, *n* machine à dicter *f*.

dictate, dic-téte´, *v* dicter; faire la loi; **dictator,** dictateur *m*.

dictionary, dic´-chŏnn-a-ri, *n* dictionnaire *m*.

die, dâï, *v* mourir.

diet, dâï´-ette, *v* (to go on a –) faire un régime. *n* régime *m*.

differ, dif´-eur, *v* différer; **–ence,** *n* différence *f*; **–ent,** *a* différent.

difficult, diff´-i-keulte, *a* difficile; **–y,** *n* difficulté *f*.

diffident, diff´-i-d'nt, *a* défiant de soi-même.

diffuse, dif-fiouze´, *v* répandre. *a* diffus.

dig, digue, *v* (garden) bêcher; (excavate) creuser; (archeol) faire des fouilles.

digest, di-djeste´, *v* digérer; **–ion,** *n*

digestion *f.*

dignified dig´-ni-fàïde, *a* digne.

dignitary, dig´-ni-ta-ri, *n* dignitaire *m.*

dignity, dig´-ni-ti, *n* dignité *f.*

digression, di-grèch´-eunne, *n* digression *f.*

dike, dâïke, *n* digue *f.*

dilapidated, di-lăpp´-i-détedde, *a* délabré.

dilapidation, di-lăpp´-i-dé-ch'n, *n* délabrement *m.*

dilate, di-léte´, *v* dilater; se dilater.

dilatory, dil´-a-tŏ-ri, *a* tardif; dilatoire.

dilemma, di-lemm´-ma, *n* dilemme *m.*

diligence, dil´-i-djennce, *n* diligence *f.*

diligent*, dil´-i-djennte, *a* appliqué.

dilute, di-lioute´, *v* diluer; (wine) couper.

dim, dime, *v* obscurcir. *a* trouble; faible.

dimension, di-menn´-ch'n, *n* dimension *f.*

diminish, di-minn´-iche, *v* diminuer.

dimple, dime´-p'l, *n* fossette *f.*

din, dinn, *n* vacarme *m.* *v* assourdir.

dine, dâïne, *v* dîner.

dingy, dinn´-dji, *a* sombre; sale; défraîchi.

dining, dâï´-ninng, **–car,** *n* wagon-restaurant *m;* **–room,** salle à manger *f.*

dinner, dinn´-eur, *n* dîner *m.*

dip, dippe, *v* plonger; tremper; baisser subitement; (slope) incliner.

diphtheria, diff-tsî´-ri-a, *n* diphtérie *f.*

diplomacy, di-plau´-ma-ci, *n* diplomatie *f.*

diplomat, dippe´-lau-mătte, *n* diplomate *m.*

dire, dâïre, *a* cruel; terrible; affreux.

direct, di-recte´, *v* diriger; indiquer. *a* direct; **–ion,** *n* direction *f;* **–ly,** *adv* tout de suite; directement; **–or,** *n* directeur *m;* administrateur *m;* **–ory,** annuaire *m.*

dirt, deurte, *n* saleté *f;* ordure *f.*

dirty, deur´-ti, *a* sale. *v* salir.

disability, diss-a-bile´-i-ti, *n* incapacité *f.*

disable, diss-é´-b'l, *v* mutiler; rendre infirme; (*mech*) mettre hors de service.

disadvantage, diss-ăd-

vânne´-tidj, *n* désavantage *m.*

disagree, diss-a-grî´, *v* être en désaccord.

disagreeable, diss-a-grî´-a-b'l, *a* désagréable.

disallow, diss-a-la'ou´, *v* refuser; désapprouver; désavouer.

disappear, diss-a-pîre, *v* disparaître.

disappearance, diss-ap-pîr´-'nce, *n* disparition *f.*

disappoint, diss-a-poa'innte´, *v* décevoir; **–ment,** *n* déception *f.*

disapprove, diss-a-prouve´, *v* désapprouver.

disarm, diss-ârme´, *v* désarmer; **–ament,** *n* désarmement *m.*

disaster, diz-âsse´-teur, *n* désastre *m;* accident *m.*

disastrous*, diz-âsse´-treuce, *a* désastreux.

discard, diss-cârde´, *v* rejeter.

discern, diz-zeurne´, *v* discerner.

discharge, diss-tchârdje´, *n* (dismissal) congé *m;* (gun) décharge *f;* (*med*) suppuration *f;* perte *f. v* congédier; décharger; (fulfill) remplir; (acquit) acquitter; (release) libérer.

disciple, diss-sâï´-p'l, *n*

disciple *m*.
discipline, diss´-si-plinne, *n* discipline *f*.
disclaim, diss-cléme´, *v* renier; répudier.
disclose, diss-clauze´, *v* révéler.
disclosure, diss-clau´-jioure, *n* révélation *f*.
discolor, diss-col´-*eur*, *v* décolorer.
discomfort, diss-comm´-feurte, *n* incommodité *f*; manque de confort *m*; (uneasy) malaise *m*.
disconnect, diss-cŏnn-necte´, *v* disjoindre; couper.
discontent, diss-cŏnn-tennte´, *n* mécontentement *m*; **–ed,** *a* mécontent.
discontinue, diss-cŏnn-tinn´-ioue, *v* cesser.
discord, diss´-coarde, *n* discorde *f*.
discount, diss´-câ´ounnte, *n* (com) remise *f*; (fin) escompte *m*.
discourage, diss-cor´-idj, *v* décourager.
discourse, diss-course´, *v* discourir. *n* discours *m*.
discourteous, diss-keur´-ti-*euce*, *a* discourtois.
discover, diss-cov´-*eur*, *v* découvrir.
discovery, diss-cov´-*eur*-i,

n découverte *f*.
discreet*, diss-crîte´, *a* discret.
discrepancy, diss-crèp´-ann-ci, *n* différence *f*.
discriminate, diss-crimm´-i-néte, *v* discerner; destinguer.
discuss, diss-cosse´, *v* discuter.
discussion, diss-coch´-'n, *n* discussion *f*.
disdain, diss-déne´, *v* dédaigner. *n* dédain *m*.
disdainful*, diss-déne´-foull, *a* dédaigneux.
disease, di-zîze´, *n* maladie *f*; **–d,** *a* malade.
disembark, diss-emm-bârke´, *v* débarquer; **–ation** *n* débarquement *m*.
disengaged, diss-enn-guédje´, *a* libre.
disentangle, diss-enn-tain´-g'l, *v* démêler.
disfigure, diss-figue´-*eur*, *v* défigurer.
disgrace, diss-gréce´, *n* disgrâce *f*; (shame) honte *f*. *v* déshonorer; **–ful,** *a* honteux.
disguise, diss-gâîze´, *v* déguiser. *n* déguisement *m*.
disgust, diss-gosste´, *v* dégoûter. *n* dégoût *m*; **–ing,** *a* dégoûtant.

dish, diche, *n* plat *m*; (food) mets *m*; **––cloth,** torchon *m*; **–up,** *v* servir.
dishearten, diss-hâre´-t'n, *v* décourager.
disheveled, di-chè´-vellde, *a* échevelé.
dishonest, diss-onn´-este, *a* malhonnête.
dishonor, diss-onn´-*eur*, *v* déshonorer. *n* déshonneur *m*.
dishwashing liquid, diche-ou'oache-inng-lik-ouide, *n* produit pour la vaisselle *m*.
disillusion, diss-il-lioue´-j'n, *v* désillusionner.
disinclination, diss-inn-cli-né´-ch'n, *n* aversion *f*.
disinfect, diss-inn-fecte´, *v* désinfecter; **–ant** *n* désinfectant *m*.
disinherit, diss-inn-hèr´-itte, *v* déshériter.
disintegrate, diss-inn´-teur-gréte, *v* désintégrer.
disintegration, diss-inn-teur-gré´-ch'n, *n* désintégration *m*.
disjointed, diss-djoa´inn´-tedde, *a* désarticulé.
disk, disque, *n* disque *m*.
dislike, diss-lâîque´, *v* ne pas aimer. *n* aversion *f*.
dislocate, diss´-lo-kéte, *v* disloquer.

disloyal, diss-lo´-ial, *a* déloyal.

dismal*, diz´-m'l, *a* triste; lugubre; sombre.

dismay, diss-mé´, *v* consterner. *n* consternation *f.*

dismiss, diss-mice´, *v* congédier; (mentally) écarter.

dismount, diss-mâ´ounnte´, *v* descendre de.

disobedient, diss-o-bî´-di-ennte, *a* désobéissant.

disobey, diss-o-bé´, *v* désobéir.

disorder, diss-oar´-deur, *n* désordre *m.*

disorganization, diss-oar-ga-nâï-zé´-ch'n, *n* désorganisation *f.*

disorganize, diss-oar´-ga-nâïze, *v* désorganiser.

disown, diz-aune´, *v* renier.

disparage, diss-pår´-idj, *v* dénigrer.

dispatch, diss-pătché, *v* expédier; *n* dépêche *f*; envoi *m.*

dispel, diss-pelle´, *v* chasser; dissiper.

dispensary, diss-penn´-sa-ri, *n* dispensaire *m.*

disperse, diss-peurce´, *v* disperser.

display, diss-plé´, *v* exposer. *n* (com) étalage *m.*

displease, diss-plîze´, *v* déplaire.

displeasure, diss-plè´-jeure, *n* mécontentement *m.*

disposal, diss-pau-z'l, *n* disposition *f.*

dispose, diss-pauze´, *v* disposer; se débarrasser.

disprove, diss-prouve´, *v* réfuter.

disputable, diss-pioue´-ta-b'l, *a* contestable.

dispute, diss-piout´e, *v* se disputer; contester. *n* dispute *f*; contestation *f.*

disqualify, diss-couoll´-i-fâî, *v* disqualifier.

disquiet, diss-couâî´-ètte, *v* inquiéter. *n* inquiétude *f.*

disregard, diss-ri-gârde´, *v* négliger; ne pas observer; faire peu de cas de. *n* mépris *m*; indifférence *f.*

disrepute, diss-ri-pioute´, *n* discrédit *m*; mauvaise réputation *f.*

disrespect, diss-ri-specte´, *n* manque de respect *m*; irrévérence *f*; –ful, *a* irrespectueux.

dissatisfy, diss-săt´-is-fâï, *v* mécontenter.

dissect, diss-secte´, *v* disséquer.

dissemble, diss-semm´-b'l, *v* dissimuler.

dissent, diss-sennte´, *v* différer d'opinion.

dissimilar, diss-simm´-i-l'r, *a* dissemblable.

dissipate, diss´-si-péte, *v* dissiper.

dissociate, diss-sau´-chi-éte, *v* dissocier; se désintéresser.

dissolute, diss´-sŏ-lioute, *a* dissolu.

dissolve, diss-solv´, *v* dissoudre.

dissuade, diss-souéde´, *v* dissuader.

distance, diss´-tannce, *n* distance *f.*

distant, diss´-tannte, *a* éloigné; distant.

distasteful, diss-téste´-foull, *a* répugnant.

distemper, diss-temm´-peur, *n* (paint) détrempe *f*; (veterinary) maladie des chiens *f.*

distend, diss-tennde´, *v* dilater; gonfler.

distill, diss-till´, *v* distiller.

distinct*, diss-tinng´-kt, *a* distinct; clair.

distinction, diss-tinng´-kch'n, *n* distinction *f.*

distinguish, diss-tinng´-gouiche, *v* distinguer.

distort, diss-toarte´, *v*

distract, diss-trăkt´, v
distraire; détourner;
affoler; **–ion,** n
distraction f.

distrain, diss-tréne´, v
saisir.

distress, diss-tresse´, n
détresse f.; (poverty)
misère f. v affliger; **–ing,**
a affligeant; pénible.

distribute, diss-trib´-ioute,
v distribuer.

distributor, diss-trib´-iou-
t´r, n concessionnaire m;
(in car, etc) distributeur
m.

district, diss´-tricte, n
région f; arrondissement
m.

distrust, diss-trosste´, v se
mefier de. n méfiance f.

disturb, diss-teurbe´, v
déranger; **–ance,** n
dérangement m; (mob)
désordre m.

disuse, diss-iouce´, n
désuétude f.

ditch, ditche, n fossé m.

dive, dâïve, v plonger.

diver, dâï´-veur, n
plongeur m; (salvage,
etc) scaphandrier m.

diverge, di-veurdje´, v
diverger.

diverse, dâî-veurse´, a
divers; varié.

diversion, di-veur´-ch´n, n
diversion f;
divertissement m.

divert, di-veurte´, v
détourner; distraire.

divest, di-veste´, v
dépouiller de; (clothes)
dévêtir.

divide, di-vâîde´, v diviser;
partager.

divine, di-vâîne´, v
deviner. a* divin.

division, di-vi´-j´n, n
division f.

divorce, di-vaurce´, v
divorcer. n divorce m.

divulge, di-voldje´, v
divulguer.

dizzy, diz´-i, a étourdi;
vertigineux.

do, doue, v faire;
accomplir; suffire; jouer
le rôle de.

docile, do´-sâïle, a docile.

dock, doc, n bassin m;
(court) banc des accusés
m; **dry –,** cale sèche f.

doctor, doc´-t´r, n docteur
m.

doctrine, doc´-trine, n
doctrine f.

document, doc´-iou-m´nt,
n document m.

documentary, doc´-iou-
menn´-ta-ri, n
documentaire m.

dodge, dodje, v esquiver;
éviter. n truc m.

dog, dogue, n chien m;
–ged*, a tenace.

dole, daule, v distribuer. n
allocation de chômage f.

doleful*, daule´-foull, a
plaintif; triste.

doll, dolle, n poupée f.

domain, dau-méne´, n
domaine m.

dome, daume, n dôme m.

domestic, do-mess´-tique,
n & a domestique m & f.

domesticated, do-mess´-ti-
qué-tedde, a bonne
ménagère.

domicile, domm´-i-sâïle, n
domicile m.

dominate, domm´-i-néte,
v dominer.

domineer, domm-i-nîre´, v
régenter.

donation, dau-né-ch´n, n
donation f.

donkey, donng´-qui, n âne
m; baudet m.

donor, dau´-neur, n
donateur m.

doom, doume, n (fate)
sort m. v condamner.

doomsday, doumze´-dé, n
jugement dernier m.

door, daur, n porte f;
(vehicle) portière f; **––
keeper,** concierge m & f;
––mat, paillasson m; **––
step,** pas de la porte m.

dormitory, dor´-mi-to-ri, n
dortoir m.

dose, dauce, n dose f. v doser.

dot, dotte, n point m. v mettre un point sur; (art) pointiller.

dote, daute, v raffoler (de).

double, dob´-'l, v doubler. n & a double m.

doubt, dâ´oute, v douter. n doute m; **–ful,** a douteux; indécis; **–less,** adv sans doute.

douche, douche, n douche f. v doucher.

dough, dau, n pâte f.

dove, douve, n colombe f; **–cote,** colombier m.

dowager, dâ´ou´-édj´eur, n douairière f.

down, dâ´ounn, adv & prep en bas. n (feathers) duvet m; **–cast,** a abattu; **–fall,** n chute f; ruine f; **–pour,** pluie torrentielle f; **–stairs,** adv en bas; **–wards,** vers le bas.

dowry, dâ´ou´-ri, n dot f.

doze, dauze, v somnoler. n somme m.

dozen, doz´-'n, n douzaine f.

drab, drâbbe, a terne.

draft, drâfte, n (money) traite f; (sketch) esquisse f; (writing) brouillon m; project m; v rédiger; n courant d'air

m; (drinking) coup m; **–board,** damier m.

draftsman, drâfts´-mănne, n dessinateur m.

drag, drăgue, v traîner; (water) draguer.

dragon, drăgue´eune, n dragon m; **–fly,** lɪbellule f.

drain, dréne, v faire égoutter; faire écouler; (land) drainer. n égout m; **–age,** système d'égouts m; **–pipe,** gouttière f.

drake, dréke, n canard m.

drama, drâm´-a, n drame m.

dramatic, dra-ma´-tique, a dramatique.

draper, dré´-peur, n marchand de nouveautés m.

drastic, drass´-tique, a énergique; drastique; draconien.

draw, droa, n (lottery) tirage m; (game) partie nulle f. v (pull) tirer; (pull out) arracher; (attract) attirer; (sketch) dessiner; (bill) tirer; (money) retirer; **–back,** n inconvénient m; **–er,** n (furniture) tiroir m; **–ing,** (sketch) dessin m.

drawl, droal, v parler

d'une voix traînante; n débit (m) traînant.

dread, drèdde, v redouter. n terreur f; **–ful*,** a terrible.

dream, drîme, n rêve m. v rêver.

dreary, drî´-ri, a triste; morne; monotone.

dredge, drèdje, v draguer; **–r,** n dragueur m.

dregs, drègze, npl lie f; sédiment m.

drench, drenntche, v tremper.

dress, dresse, n robe f; toilette f; costume m. v habiller; vêtir; (wounds) panser; **–ing,** n (med) pansement m; (culinary) assaisonnement m; **–ing gown,** robe de chambre f; peignoir m; **–ing room,** cabinet de toilette m.

dressmaker, dresse´-mék´-eur, n couturière f.

dribble, drib´-'l, v baver; (of water) dégoutter.

drift, drifte, n (naut) dérive f; (snow, etc) monceau m; (tendency) but m. v dériver; **–wood,** bois flottant m.

drill, drile, n (mil) exercice m; (tool) foret m. v exercer; forer; percer.

drink, drinnque, n boisson f. v boire.

drip, drippe, v dégoutter. n goutte f.

dripping, dripp´-inng, n (fat) graisse de rôti f.

drive, drâïve, v conduire. n (approach) allée f; (outing) promenade en . . (auto, etc) f; (of car) conduite f.

driver, drâï´-veur, n conducteur m; chauffeur m.

drizzle, driz´-z'l, v pleuvasser. n bruine f.

droll, draule, a drôle.

drone, draune, n faux-bourdon m. v bourdonner.

droop, droupe, v languir; (plants) tomber.

drop, droppe, n chute f; (liquid) goutte f; (prices) baisse f. v tomber; (let fall) laisser tomber.

drought, drâ´oute, n sécheresse f.

drown, drâ´ounne, v noyer; se noyer.

drowsy, drâ´au´-zi, a somnolent.

drudge, drodje, v trimer; **–ry,** n corvée f.

drug, drogue, v droguer. n drogue f.

drum, dromme, n tambour

m; **–mer,** tambour m.

drunk, dronnque, a ivre; soûl; **–ard,** ivrogne m; **–enness,** ivresse f; ivrognerie f.

dry, drâï, v sécher. a* sec; **–-cleaning,** nettoyage à sec m.

dryness, drâï´-ness, n sécheresse f.

dubious*, dioue´-bi-euce, a douteux.

duchess, dotch´-esse, n duchesse f.

duck, doque, n canard m; cane f. v plonger; se baisser.

due, dioue, n dû m; (toll, rights, etc) droits mpl. a (owing) dû; (bill) échu.

duel, dioue´-'l, n duel m.

duet, diou-ette´, n duo m.

duke, diouque, n duc m.

dull, dolle, a (weather) gris; (tedious) ennuyeux; (mind) lent; (metal) terne.

duly, dioue´-li, adv dûment; en temps voulu.

dumb, domme, a muet; (fam) bête; **–found,** v confondre.

dummy, domm´-i, n mannequin m; (sham) simulacre m; (cards) le mort m.

dump, dommpe, v déposer.

n dépôt m.

dung, donng, n (horse) crottin m; (cow) bouse de vache f; (manure) fumier m.

dungeon, donn´-djeune, n cachot m.

dupe, dioupe, v duper. n dupe f.

duplicate, dioue´-pli-quéte, n duplicata m; a double. v faire le double; tirer (des copies).

durable, dioue´-ra-b'l, a durable.

duration, dioue-ré´-ch'n, n durée f.

during, dioue´-rinng, prep pendant.

dusk, dossque, n crépuscule m.

dusky, doss´-ki, a sombre; (color) noirâtre.

dust, dosste, n poussière f. v épousseter; **–er,** n chiffon m.

dutiful*, dioue´-ti-foull, a obéissant; dévoué.

duty, dioue´-ti, n devoir m; (customs) droits mpl; (task) fonction f.

dwarf, douoarfe, n & a nain m & f. v rapetisser.

dwell, douelle, v demeurer; habiter; **–er,** n habitant m; **–ing,** n demeure f.

dwindle, douinn´-d'l, v

diminuer; s'amoindrir.

dye, dâï, *n* teinture *f. v*
teindre.

dynamite, dâïn´-*a*-mâïte,
n dynamite *f.*

dynamo, dâï´-n*a*-mau, *n*
dynamo *f.*

dysentery, diss´-'n-tri, *n*
dysenterie *f.*

E

each, îtche, *pron* chacun, -une. *a* chaque; **–other,** *pron* l'un l'autre; l'une l'autre; les uns; les autres.

eager, î´-gueur, *a* avide; ardent.

eagerness, î´-gueur-nesse, *n* avidité *f*; empressement *m*.

eagle, î´-g'l, *n* aigle *m* & *f*.

ear, îre, *n* oreille *f*; (corn) épi *m*; – **-ring,** boucle d'oreille *f*; **-wig,** perce-oreille *m*.

earl, eurle, *n* comte *m*.

early, eur´-li, *adv* de bonne heure, tôt. *a* matinal; tôt.

earn, eurne, *v* gagner; mériter; **-ings,** *npl* salaire *m*.

earnest*, eur´-nesste, *a* sérieux; sincère; empressé.

earth, eurts, *n* terre *f*; monde *m*. *v* (electricity) mettre à la terre; **–enware,** *n* faïence *f*; **–ly,** *a* terrestre; **–quake,** *n* tremblement de terre *m*.

ease, îze, *n* aise *f*; repos *m*; (facility) facilité *f*. *v* soulager.

easel, î´-z'l, *n* chevalet *m*.

easily, î´-zi-li, *adv* facilement.

east, îsste, *n* est *m*; **–erly,** *a* d'est; **–ern,** oriental.

Easter, îss´-teur, *n* Pâques *m*.

easy, î´-zi, *a* facile; **–chair,** *n* fauteuil *m*.

eat, île, *v* manger; (worm; acid) ronger; **–able,** *a* mangeable; **–ables,** *npl* comestibles *mpl*.

eavesdropper, îvz´-dropp-eur, *n* oreille indiscrète *f* (aux portes).

ebb, èbe, *v* refluer. *n* reflux *m*.

ebony, èb´-ŏ-ni, *n* èbène *f*.

eccentric, èque-senn-´-trique, *a* excentrique.

echo, èk´-au, *n* écho *m*. *v* répéter.

eclipse, i-klipse´, *n* éclipse *f*. *v* éclipser.

economize, i-konn´-ŏ-mäize, *v* économiser.

economy, i-konn´-ŏ-mi, *n* économie *f*.

ecstasy, ex´-ta-zi, *n* extase *f*.

eddy, éd´-i, *n* tourbillon *m*; remous *m*.

edge, èdje, *n* bord *m*; (blade) tranchant *m*. *v* border.

edible, éd´-i-b'l, *n* & *a* comestible *m*.

edify, èd´-i-fäï, *v* édifier.

edit, èd´-itte, *v* éditer; **–ion,** *n* édition *f*; **–or,** rédacteur *m*; **–orial,** *a* éditorial.

educate, èd´-iou-quéte, *v* instruire; éduquer.

education, èd-iou-ké´-ch'n, *n* éducation *f*; enseignement *m*; études *fpl*.

eel, île, n anguille f.

efface, ef-féce´, v effacer.

effect, ef-fecte´, v effectuer. n effet m; **–ive*,** a efficace; effectif; **–ual*,** efficace.

effeminate, ef-femm´-i-néte, a efféminé.

effervescent, ef-feur-vess´-'nt, a effervescent.

efficiency, ef-fich´-enn-ci, n efficacité f; capacité f.

efficient, ef-fich´-ennt, a (person) capable; compétent.

effort, ef´-feurte, n effort m.

effrontery, ef-fron´-teur-i, n effronterie f.

effusive, ef-fioue´-cive, a expansif.

egg, ègg, n œuf m; **–-cup,** coquetier m.

egotism, ègg´-au-tizme, n égoïsme m.

eiderdown, aî´-deur-dâ'ounne, n édredon m.

eight, éte, n & a huit m; **–een,** dix-huit m; **–eenth,** dix-huitième m; **–h,** huitième m; **–ieth,** quatre vingtième m; **–y,** quatre-vingts m.

either, aî´-dzeur, pron l'un ou l'autre, conj ou; soit.

eject, i-djecte´, v expulser.

elaborate, i-lâb´-ŏ-réte, a soigné; raffiné; élaboré. v élaborer.

elapse, i-lâpse´, v s'écouler.

elastic, i-lâss´-tique, n & a élastique m.

elate, i-léte´, v exalter; transporter; **–d,** a exalté; transporté.

elbow, el´-bau, n coude m. v coudoyer.

elder, el´-deur, n & a aîné m & f; (tree) sureau m.

elderly, el´-deur-li, a d'un certain âge.

eldest, el´-deste, n & a aîné m & f.

elect, i-lecte´, v élire; nommer. n & a élu m.

election, i-léque-ch'n, n élection f.

electric(al)*, i-léque´-trique('l), a électrique.

electrician, i-léquetri´-ch'n, n électricien m.

electricity, i-léque-tri´-ci-ti, n électricité f.

electrify, i-lèque´-tri-fâî, v électriser; électrifier.

electron, i-lèque´-tronne, n électron m; **–ics,** électronique f.

electroplate, i-lèqu´-tro-pléte, n plaqué m. v plaquer.

elegance, el´-i-gannce, n élégance f.

elegant*, el´-i-gannte, a élégant.

element, el´-i-m'nt, n élément m.

elementary, i-li-menn´-ta-ri, a élémentaire.

elephant, el´-i-fannte, n éléphant m.

elevate, el´-i-véte, v élever; exalter.

elevator, el´-évé-teur, n ascenseur m.

eleven, i-lèv´-'n, n & a onze m; **–th,** onzième m.

elicit, i-liss´-ite, v faire jaillir; mettre au jour; provoquer.

eligible, el´-i-dji-b'l, a éligible; n un bon parti.

eliminate, i-lime´-i-néte, v éliminer.

elite, é-lîte´, n élite f.

elk, elk, n élan m.

elm, elme, n orme m.

elongate, î´-longue-éte, v prolonger; allonger.

elope, i-laupe´, v se laisser; enlever.

elopement, i-laupe´-m'nt, n fugue amoureuse f; fuite f.

eloquent, el´-ŏ-couennte, a éloquent.

else, elce, a autre. adv autrement; **–where,** ailleurs.

elucidate, i-lioue´-ci-déte, v éclaircir; élucider.

elude, i-lioude´, v éviter; éluder.

elusive, i-lioue´-sive, *a* évasif.

emaciate, i-mé´-chi-éte, *v* amaigrir.

emanate, emm´-*a*-néte, *v* émaner.

emancipate, i-männ´-ci-péte, *v* émanciper.

embalm, emm-bǎme´, *v* embaumer.

embankment, emm-bainque´-m'nt, *n* terrassement *m*; (railroad) remblai *m*; (river) quai *m*.

embark, emm-bǎrke´, *v* embarquer.

embarrass, emm-bǎr´-*ass*, *v* gêner.

embarrassment, emm-bǎr´-*ass*-m'nt, *n* gêne *f* & *m*.

embassy, emm´-bǎss-i, *n* ambassade *f*.

embellish, emm-bell´-iche, *v* embellir.

ember, emm´-beur, *n* braise *f*.

embezzle, emm-bez´-z'l, *v* détourner.

embitter, emm-bitt´-eur, *v* (fig) aigrir.

embody, emm-bod´-i, *v* incorporer; personnifier.

embrace, emm-bréce´, *n* étreinte *f*. *v* étreindre.

embroider, emm-broa'i´-d'r, *v* broder.

embroidery, emm-broa'i´-deur-i, *n* broderie *f*.

embroil, emm-broa'il´, *v* embrouiller.

emerald, emm´-*eur*-alde, *n* émeraude *f*.

emerge, i-meurdje´, *v* surgir; émerger; **–ncy,** *n* circonstance imprévue *f*; cas d'urgence *m*.

emetic, i-mett´-ique, *n* émétique *m*.

emigrant, emm´-i-grannte, *n* émigrant, -e *m* & *f*.

emigrate, emm´-i-gréte, *v* émigrer.

eminence, emm´-i-nennce, *n* éminence *f*.

eminent, emm´-i-nennte, *a* éminent; célèbre.

emissary, emm´-is-*sa*-ri, *n* émissaire *m*.

emit, i-mitte´, *v* émettre; dégager; exhaler.

emotion, i-mau-´ch'n, *n* émotion *f*; **–al,** *a* émotif; ému.

emperor, emm´-*peu-reu* *n* empereur *m*.

emphasis, emm´-*fa*-cice, *n* insistance *f*.

emphasize, emm´-*fa*-sǎïze, *v* appuyer sur; mettre en valeur.

emphatic, emm-fǎte´-ique, *a* emphatique.

empire, emm´-pǎire, *n* empire *m*.

employ, emm-ploa'i´, *v* employer; **–er,** *n* patron *m*; employeur *m*; **–ment,** emploi *m*.

empower, emm-pâ'ou´-eur, *v* autoriser; mettre à même de.

empress, emm´-presse, *n* impératrice *f*.

empty, emm´-pti, *a* vide. *v* vider.

emulate, emm´-iou-léte, *v* rivaliser avec.

enable, enn-é´-b'l, *v* permettre de.

enact, enn-âcte´, *v* décréter.

enamel, enn-ǎmm´-'l, *n* émail *m*. *v* émailler.

enamored, enn-ǎmm´-eurde, *a* épris de.

encamp, enn-cǎmmpe´, *v* camper.

enchant, enn-tchǎnnte´, *v* enchanter; **–ment,** *n* enchantement *m*.

encircle, enn-seur´-k'l, *v* entourer.

enclose, enn-clauze´, *v* (field) clôturer; (in) enfermer; joindre.

enclosure, enn-clau´-jeure, *n* enclos *m*; (com) pièce jointe *f*.

encore, an-coare´, *v* bisser. *interj* bis!

encounter, enn-câ'ounn´-

teur, *v* rencontrer. *n* recontre *f*.

encourage, enn-cor´-idj, *v* encourager; **–ment**, *n* encouragement *m*.

encroach, enn-craoutche´, *v* empiéter; (time, etc) abuser de;**–ment**, *n* empiètement *m*; usurpation *f*.

encumber, enn-comm´-beur, *v* encombrer.

encumbrance, enn-comm´-brannce, *n* embarras *m*; (property) charges *fpl*.

encyclopedia, en-sâï´-clau-pî´-di-a, *n* encyclopédie *f*.

end, ènnde, *n* fin *f*; bout *m*. *v* finir.

endanger, enn-dénn´-djeur, *v* mettre en danger.

endear, enn-dîre´, *v* rendre cher.

endeavor, enn-dèv´-eur, *v* s'efforcer. *n* effort *m*.

endive, enn´-dive, *n* endive *f*.

endless, ènnde´-lesse, *a* sans fin.

endorse, enn-doarse´, *v* endosser; approuver; **–ment**, *n* endossement *m*; sanction *f*; approbation *f*.

endow, enn-dâ'ou´, *v*

doter; **–with,** douer de.

endurance, enn-dioue´-rannce, *n* résistance *f*.

endure, enn-dioure´, *v* endurer; supporter.

enema, enn´-i-ma, *n* lavement *m*.

enemy, enn´-i-mi, *n* ennemi *m*.

energetic, enn-eur-djett´-ique, *a* énergique.

energy, enn´-eur-dji, *n* énergie *f*; force *f*.

enervate, enn-eur-véte, *v* affaiblir; énerver.

enforce, enn-faurce´, *v* faire observer; imposer.

engage, enn-guédje´, *v* engager; embaucher; **–d,** *a* fiancé; (reserved) retenu, occupé; **–ment**, *n* fiançailles *fpl*; (mil) combat *m*; (obligation) engagement *m*; (appointment) rendez-vous *m*.

engaging, enn-guédj´-inng, *a* engageant, attirant.

engender, enn-djenn´-d'r, *v* engendrer.

engine, enn´-djinne, *n* machine *f*; (rail) locomotive *f*; (car) moteur *m*; **–er,** mécanicien *m*; (profession) ingénieur *m*; **–ering**, génie *m*.

English, inng´-gliche, *n & a* anglais, *m & f*; (language) *n* anglais *m*.

engrave, enn-gréve´, *v* graver; **–r,** *n* graveur *m*; **–ing**, *n* gravure *f*.

engross, enn-grausse´, *v* absorber.

engulf, enn-golf´, *v* engouffrer.

enhance, enn-hânnce´, *v* rehausser; mettre en valeur.

enjoy, enn-djoa'ï´, *v* jouir de; **–ment**, *n* jouissance *f*; plaisir *m*; **–oneself,** *v* s'amuser.

enlarge, enn-lârdje´, *v* agrandir; dilater.

enlargement, enn-lârdje´-m'nt, *n* agrandissement *m*.

enlighten, enn-lâï´-t'n, *v* éclairer; illuminer.

enlist, enn-lisste´, *v* enrôler; s'engager.

enliven, enn-jâï´-v'n, *v* animer; égayer.

enmity, enn´-mi-ti, *n* inimitié *f*; hostilité *f*.

enormous, i-nôr´-meuce, *a* énorme.

enough, i-noff´, *adv & a* assez.

enrage, enn-rédje´, *v* exaspérer, faire enrager.

enrapture, enn-râp´-tioure, *v* ravir,

transporter.

enrich, enn-ritche´, v
enrichir.

enrol, enn-raule´, v
enrôler; s'inscrire.

ensign, enn´-sâine, n
(flag) enseigne f; (naval
flag) pavillon m; (rank)
enseigne f.

enslave, enn-sléve´, v
asservir; captiver.

ensnare, enn-snére´, v
prendre au piège.

ensue, enn-sioue´, v
s'ensuivre.

ensure, enn-choure´,
s'assurer de; rendre sûr.

entail, enn-téle´, v
entraîner; (law)
substituer.

entangle, enn-tănn´-g'l, v
emmêler.

enter, enn´-teur, v entrer;
–**up,** inscrire.

enterprise, enn´-teur-
prâïze, n entreprise f;
(boldness) esprit
d'entreprise m.

entertain, enn-teur-téne´,
v divertir; (guests)
recevoir; (consider)
admettre; –**ment,** n
divertissement m.

enthrall, enn´-tsroale v
captiver, séduire.

enthusiasm, enn-tsioue´-
zi-ăzme, n enthousiasme
m.

entice, enn-tâïce´, v
tenter; séduire.

entire*, enn-tâïre´, a
entier, complet.

entitle, enn-tâï´-t'l, v
intituler; donner droit à.

entomb, enn-toum´, v
ensevelir.

entrance, enn´-trannce, n
entrée f.

entrance, enn-trânnse´, v
hypnotiser; transporter;
ravir.

entreat, enn-trîte´, v
supplier; implorer.

entrench, enn-trenche´, v
se retrancher.

entrust, enn-trosste´, v
confier à.

entry, enn´-tri, n entrée f;
(record) écriture f.

entwine, enn-tou´äïne´, v
enrouler; enlacer.

enumerate, i-niou´-mé-
réte, v énumérer.

envelop, enn-vel´-ŏpe, v
envelopper.

envelope, enn´-vel-ôpe, n
enveloppe f.

envious*, enn´-vî-euce, a
envieux.

environs, enn-vâï´-
ronnze, npl environs
mpl.

envoy, enn´-voa'ï, n
envoyé m.

envy, enn´-vi, n envie f. v
envier.

epic, èp´-i-k, a épique.

epicure, èp´-i-kioure, n
gourmet m.

epidemic, èp-i-demm´-
ique, n épidémie f.

episode, èp´-i-saude, n
épisode m.

epistle, è-piss´-'l, n épître
f.

epoch, i´-poque, n époque
f.

equal, î´-coual, n & a*
égal, -e m & f. v égaler;
–**ity,** n égalité f; –**ize,** v
égaliser.

equator, i-coué´teur, n
équateur m.

equilibrium, i-coui-lib´-ri-
eume, n équilibre m.

equip, i-coupe´, v
équiper; munir.

equitable, èk´-oui-ta-b'l, a
équitable.

equity, èk´-oui-ti, n équité
f; justice f.

equivalent, i-coui´-va-
lennte, n & a équivalent
m.

era, i´-ra, n ère f.

eradicate, é-răd´-i-quéte, v
extirper; déraciner;
exterminer.

erase, i-réze´, v (rub out)
effacer; (cross out) rayer.

eraser, i-ré´-zeur, n gomme
f; (metal) grattoir m.

erect, i-recte´, v ériger;
bâtir. a droit; debout.

ermine, eur´-mine, *n*
hermine *f*.

erosion, i-rau´-j'n, *n*
érosion; usure *f*.

err, eure, *v* errer;
(mistake) se tromper.

errand, èrr´-annde, *n*
commission *f*.

erratic, err-rât´-tique, *a*
changeant, irrégulier.

erroneous*, err-rau´-ni-
euce, a erroné.

error, èrr´-*eur, n* erreur *f*;
faute.

eruption, i-rope´-ch'n, *n*
éruption *f*.

escape, ess-képe´, *n* fuite *f*.
évasion *f*. *v* échapper.

escort, ess-kôrte´, *n*
escorte *f*; cavalier *m*. *v*
escorter.

especially, ess-péch´-al-li,
adv surtout.

essay, ès´-sé, *n* essai *m*;
composition *f*.

essential*, ess-senn´-ch'l,
a essentiel.

establish, ess-tăb´-liche, *v*
établir.

establishment, ess-tăb´-
liche-m'nt, *n*
établissement *m*.

estate, ess-téte´, *n*
propriété *f*; biens *mpl*;
(status) rang *m*;
(possessions) succession
f.

esteem, ess-tîme´, *v*

estimer. *n* estime *f*.

estimate, ess´-ti-méte, *n*
évaluation *f*; (cost)
devis *m*. *v* évaluer;
estimer.

estrange, ess-tréne´-dje, *v*
aliéner.

etch, ètch, *v* graver.

etching, ètch´-inng, *n*
gravure à l'eau-forte *f*.

eternal*, i-teur´-n'l, *a*
éternel.

eternity, i-teur´-ni-ti, *n*
éternité *f*.

ether, î´-*tseur, n* éther *m*.

ethical, é´-tsi-k'l, *a* moral.

ethics, é´-tsiks, *npl* morale
f.

evacuate, i-văk´-iou-éte, *v*
évacuer.

evade, i-véde´, *v* éviter;
éluder.

evaporate, i-văp´-ŏ-réte, *v*
s'évaporer.

evasive*, i-vé´-cive, *a*
évasif.

eve, îve, *n* veille *f*.

even, î´-v'n, *adv* même. *a*
égal; pair; quitte;
(smooth) uni.

evening, ive´-ninng, *n* soir
m; soirée *f*; **–dress,**
tenue de soirée *f*; robe
du soir *f*.

evensong, i´-venn-sonng,
n service du soir *m*.

event, i-vennte´, *n*
évènement *m*; cas *m*;

–ful, *a* accidenté;
mémorable; **–ually,** *adv*
finalement.

ever, èv´-'r, *adv* toujours;
(at any time) jamais.

everlasting*, èv´-eur-lâst-
inng, *a* éternel.

every, év´-ri, *a* chaque;
tous les; **–body,** *n* tout le
monde; **–thing,** tout *m*;
–where, *adv* partout.

evict, i-victe´, *v* expulser;
–ion, *n* expulsion *f*.

evidence, èv´-i-dennce, *n*
évidence *f*; preuve *f*;
déposition *f*; **give –,***v*
déposer.

evident, èv´-i-dennte, *a*
évident.

evil, î´-v'l, *n* mal *m*. *a*
mauvais; méchant;
malin.

evince, i-vinnce´, *v*
manifester; faire preuve
de.

evoke, i-vauque´, *v*
évoquer.

evolution, î´-vau-lioue-
ch'n, *n* évolution *f*;
développement *m*.

evolve, i-volve´, *v*
émettre; évoluer.

ewe, ioue, *n* brebis *f*.

exact, egg-zăct´, *a** exact.
v exiger; **–ing,** *a*
exigeant; **–itude,** *n*
exactitude *f*.

exaggerate, egg-zădj´-iréte, *v* exagérer.

exaggeration, egg-zădj-i-ré´-ch'n, *n* exagération *f*.

exalt, egg-zoalt´, *v* exalter.

examination, egg-zămm-inn-é´-ch'n, *n* examen *m*; inspection *f*; (legal) interrogatoire *m*.

examine, egg-zămm´-inne, *v* examiner.

example, egg-zămm´-p'l, *n* exemple *m*.

exasperate, egg-zăss´-peur-éte, *v* exaspérer.

excavate, ex´-ca-véte *v* faire des fouilles.

exceed, ex-cîde´, *v* excéder; dépasser.

exceedingly, ex-cîd´-inng-li, *adv* excessivement.

excel, ex-celle´, *v* exceller; –lent, *a* excellent.

except, ek-cepte´, *v* excepter. *prep* sauf; excepté; –ion, *n* exception *f*; take –ion, *v* s'offenser; –ional *a* exceptionnel.

excerpt, ek-seurpte´, *n* extrait *m*.

excess, ek-cesse´, *n* excès *m*; (surplus) excédent *m*.

excessive, ek-cess´-ive, *a* excessif.

exchange, ex-tchéne´-dje, *n* échange *m*; (money) change *m*; (telephone) central *m*. *v* échanger.

excise, ek-sâïze´, *v* retrancher; supprimer; exciser.

excitable, ek-sâï´-ta-b'l, *a* excitable; nerveux.

excite, ek-sâïte´, *v* exciter; agiter.

excitement, ek-sâïte´-m'nt, *n* émotion *f*; agitation *f*.

exciting, ek-sâï´-tinng, *a* passionnant.

exclaim, ex-cléme´, *v* s'écrier.

exclamation, ex-clă-mé´-ch'n, *n* exclamation.

exclude, ex-cloude´, *v* exclure.

exclusive*, ex-cloue´-cive, *a* exclusif.

excruciating, ex-croue´-chi-éte-inng, *a* atroce.

excursion, ex-kor´-ch'n, *n* excursion *f*.

excuse, ex-kiouze´, *v* excuser. *n* excuse *f*.

execute, ex´-ci-kioute, *v* exécuter; accomplir.

executioner, ex-ci-kiou´-chŏnn-*eur*, *n* bourreau *m*.

executor, ex-cè´-kioue-*teur*, *n* exécuteur *m*.

exempt, eg-zemmpte, *v* dispenser. *a* dispensé.

exemption, egg-zemmpte´-ch'n, *n* dispense *f*.

exercise, ex´-*eur*-sâïze, *n*

exercice *m*. *v* exercer.

exert, egg-zeurte´, *v* s'efforcer; –ion, *n* effort *m*.

exhaust, eg-zôste´, *v* épuiser. *n* (mech) échappement *m*.

exhaustion, egg-zôst´n, *n* epuisement *m*.

exhibit, egg-zib´-itte, *v* exposer; montrer. *n* article exposé *m*.

exhibition, egg-zi-bi´-ch'n, *n* exposition *f*.

exhilarate, egg-zil´-ă-réte, *v* réjouir.

exhilarating, egg-zil´-*a*-réte-inng, *a* vivifiant.

exigency, ek´-si-djenn-ci, *n* exigence *f*.

exile, ek-sâïle, *v* exiler. *n* exil *m*; (person) exilé *m*.

exist, egg-zisste´, *v* exister; –ence, *n* existence *f*.

exit, ek´-citte, *n* sortie *f*.

exonerate, egg-zonn´-eur-éte, *v* exonérer; disculper; innocenter.

exorbitant, ek-sôre´-bi-t'nt, *a* exorbitant.

expand, ex-pănnde´, *v* dilater; –ing, *a* extensible.

expansion, ex-pănn-ch'n, *n* expansion *f*.

expect, ex-pecte´, *v* attendre; s'attendre à; –ation, *n* attente *f*.

expedient, ex-pî´-di-ennte, n expédient m. a convenable.

expedite, ex´-pi-dâîte, v accélérer; expédier.

expel, ex-pelle´, v expulser, renvoyer.

expend, ex-pennde´, v dépenser.

expenditure, ex-penn´-ditioure, n dépense f.

expense, ex-pennse´, n dépense f, frais mpl.

expensive*, ex-penn´-cive, a coûteux, cher.

experience, ex-pi´-ri-ennce, n expérience f. v éprouver, faire l'expérience de.

experiment, ex-pair´-i-mennte, n expérience f. v expérimenter.

expert, ex-peurte´, n & a expert m.

expire, ex-pâîre´, v expirer.

explain, ex-pléne´, v expliquer.

explanation, ex-pla-né´-ch'n, n explication f.

explicit, ex-pli´-site, a explicite, clair.

explode, ex-plaude´, v faire explosion.

exploit, ex-ploa'ite´, n exploit m v exploiter.

explore, ex-plaure´, v explorer.

explorer, ex-plaur´-eur, n explorateur m.

explosion, ex-plau-j'n, n explosion f.

export, ex-paurte´, v exporter; n exportation f; **–er,** n exportateur m.

expose, ex-pauze´, v exposer; (fraud) démasquer; (plot) dévoiler.

expostulate, ex-poss´-tiouléte, v faire des remontrances.

exposure, ex-pau´-jeure, n exposition f; scandale m.

expound, ex-pâ'ounnde´, v exposer; expliquer.

express, ex-presse´, n express m; rapide m. a exprès. v exprimer; **–ion,** n expression f.

expulsion, ex-pol´-ch'n, n expulsion f.

exquisite*, ex´-coui-zite, a exquis.

extend, ex-tennde´, v étendre; s'étendre.

extensive, ex-tenn´-cive, a étendu; vaste.

extent, ex-tennte´, n étendue f; point m; degré m.

extenuating, ex-tenn´-iou-é´-tinng, a atténuant.

exterior, ex-ti´-ri-eur, n & a extérieur m.

exterminate, ex-teur´-minéte, v exterminer.

exterminator, ex-teur´-mi-na-teur, n exterminateur m.

external*, ex-teur´-n'l, a externe; extérieur.

extinct, ex-tinng´-kt, a éteint; (race, etc) disparu.

extinguish, ex-tinng´-gouiche, v éteindre.

extortion, ex-tôr´-ch'n, n extorsion f.

extort, ex-tôrte´, v extorquer.

extra, ex´-tra, a en plus. n supplément m; **–ordinary,** a extraordinaire.

extract, ex-trăcte´, v extraire. n extrait m.

extravagant, ex-tră´-vagannte, a dépensier.

extreme, ex-trîme´, n extrême m. a* extrême.

extremity, ex-trè´-mi-ti, n extrémité f.

extricate, ex´-tri-kéte, v dégager de.

eye, âî, n œil m; trou m; **–ball,** globe m (de l'œil); **–brow,** sourcil m; **–lash,** cil m; **–let,** œillet m; **–lid,** paupière f; **–sight,** vue f; **–witness,** témoin oculaire m.

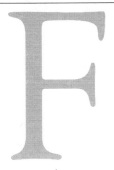

fable, fé´-b'l, *n* fable *f*.

fabric, făb´-rik, *n* étoffe *f*; tissu *m*; structure *f*; **–ation,** fabrication *f*; invention *f*.

fabulous*, făb´-iou-leuce, *a* fabuleux.

façade, fă-sade´, *n* façade *f*.

face, féce, *n* figure *f*; visage *m*; face *f*; (clock) cadran *m*; apparence *f*. *v* faire face à; **–cream,** *n* crème pour le visage *f*.

facilitate, fa-cil´-i-téte, *v* faciliter.

facsimile, făk-simm´-i-li, *n* fac-similé *m*.

fact, făct, *n* fait *m*.

factor, făk´-tŏr, *n* facteur *m*; élément *m*.

factory, făk´-teur-i, *n* fabrique *f*; usine *f*.

faculty, făk´-eul-ti, *n* faculté *f*; aptitude *f*.

fade, féde, *v* se faner; (color) passer.

fail, féle, *v* manquer; faillir; (exam, etc) échouer; **without –,** sans faute; **–ing,** *n* défaut *m*. *prep* à défaut de; faute de; **–ure,** échec *m*; (insolvency) faillite *f*; (of person) raté, -ée *m* & *f*.

faint, fé-nnte, *v* s'évanouir; *n* évanouissement *m*. *a** léger; faible.

fair, fère, *a* juste; équitable; assez bon; considérable; beau; (hair) blond. *n* foire *f*; **–ness,** équité *f*; beauté *f*; honnêteté *f*.

fairy, fé´-ri, *n* fée *f*.

faith, féts, *n* foi *f*; confiance *f*; **–ful*,** *a* fidèle.

fake, féke, *n* objet (*m*) truqué; imposteur *m*; feinte *f* (sport); *a* falsifié; truqué. *v* faire semblant.

fall, foal, *n* chute *f*; descente *f*; (prices) baisse *f*. *v* tomber; baisser.

fallacy, făl´-la-ci, *n* fausseté *f*; illusion *f*.

false*, foalse, *a* faux; artificiel.

falsehood, foalse´-houde, *n* mensonge *m*.

falsification, foal´-si-fi-qué-ch'n, *n* falsification *m*.

falsify, foal´-si-făï, *v* falsifier.

falter, foal´-teur, *v* hésiter; (speech) balbutier.

fame, féme, *n* renommée *f*; **–d,** *a* célèbre; renommé.

familiar*, fa-mil´-i-eur, *a* familier, intime.

family, fămm´-i-li, *n* famille *f*.

famine, fămm´-inn, *n* famine *f*.

famish, fămm´-iche, *v* affamer.

famous, féme´-euce, *a* fameux, célèbre.

fan, fănne, *n* éventail *m*;

ventilateur *m.* *v* éventer.

fanatic, fă-năt´-ique, n &
 a fanatique *m* & *f.*

fanaticism, fă-năt´-i-
 cizme, *n* fanatisme *m.*

fancy, fănn´-ci, n
 imagination *f;* (liking)
 goût *m;* (desire) envie *f.*
 v imaginer; avoir envie
 de.

fang, fainng, n (dog) croc
 m; (snake) crochet *m.*

fantastic, fănn-tăss´-tique,
 a fantastique.

fantasy, fănn´-ta-zi, n
 fantaisie *f.*

far, făre, *adv* loin. *a*
 lointain; éloigné.

farce, fărce, n farce *f.*

fare, fère, n prix du
 parcours *m;* (food)
 nourriture *f;* voyageur *m.*

farewell, fère-ouel´, n
 adieu *m.*

farm, fărme, n ferme *f;*
 –er, fermier *m.*

farther, făre´dzeur, *adv*
 plus loin. *a* plus éloigné.

fascinate, făss´-ci-néte, *v*
 fasciner.

fascinating, făss´-ci-né-
 tinng, *a* séduisant;
 enchanteur.

fashion, făche´-eune, n
 mode *f.* *v* façonner; **to
 be in –,**être à la mode;
 –able, *a* à la mode.

fast, făste, *a* rapide; ferme;

(color) bon teint. n
 jeûne *m.* *v* jeûner.

fasten, făs´-s'n, *v* attacher;
 fixer; (close) fermer.

fastidious*, făss-tid´-i-
 euce, *a* difficile;
 exigeant.

fat, fătte, n graisse *f;*
 (meat) gras *m. a*
 (person) gros; (animal)
 gras; **–ten,** *v* engraisser;
 –ty, *a* graisseux, gras.

fatal*, fé-t'l, *a* fatal;
 mortel.

fate, féte, n destin *m;* sort
 m; **–d,** *a* destiné.

father, fă´-dzeur, n père *m;*
 –in-law, beau-père *m;*
 –ly, *a* paternel.

fatigue, fa-tîgue´, *v*
 fatiguer. n fatigue *f.*

fault, foalte, n faute *f;*
 (defect) défaut *m;*
 –less*, *a* impeccable;
 faire plaisir; **–y,**
 défectueux.

favor, fé´-veur, n faveur *f;*
 grâce *f;* (com) honorée *f.*
 v favoriser; **to do**
 (someone) **a –,** rendre
 service; **–able,** *a*
 favorable; propice; **–ite,**
 n & *a* favori, -te *m* & *f.*

fawn, foanne, n faon *m.*

fear, fîre, *v* craindre. n
 crainte *f;* peur *f;* **–ful,** *a*
 effroyable; craintif;
 –less, intrépide.

feasible, fî´-zi-b'l, *a*
 praticable; faisable.

feast, fîsste, n fête *f;* festin
 m. *v* régaler; se régaler.

feat, fîte, n exploit *m;*
 (skill) tour de force *m.*

feather, fè´-dzeur, n plume
 f. *v* emplumer.

feature, fît´-ieure, n trait
 m; particularité *f.*

February, fè´-brou-èr-i, n
 février *m.*

federation, fé´-deur-é-
 ch'n, *n* fédération *f.*

fee, fî, n honoraires *mpl;*
 prix *m.*

feeble, fî´-b'l, *a* faible;
 débile.

feed, fîde, *v* nourrir;
 (cattle) paître.

feel, fîle, *v* sentir; tâter. n
 toucher *m;* **–er,** *n*
 (insects) antenne *f;*
 –ing, toucher *m;*
 sensation *f;* sentiment
 m.

feign, féne, *v* feindre,
 simuler.

fell, fèle, *v* abattre;
 assommer.

fellow, fèl´-au, n membre
 m; collègue *m;* (pop)
 garçon *m;* homme *m;*
 –ship, camaraderie *f.*

felony, fèl´-au-ni, n crime
 m.

felt, fèlte, n feutre *m.*

female, fî´-méle, n & *a*

femelle f; a & n **féminin**
m.

feminine, fème´-i-ninn, a
& n **féminin** m.

fence, fènnce, n **clôture** f.
v **entourer**;
(swordsmanship) **faire
de l'escrime.**

fencing, fènn-cinng, n
escrime f.

fender, fenn´-deur, n
garde-feu m; (auto) **aile**
f.

ferment, feur-mennté´, v
fermenter. n **ferment** m.

fern, feurne, n **fougère** f.

ferocious*, fi-rau´-cheuce,
a **féroce.**

ferret, fèr´-ette, n **furet** m.
v **fureter.**

ferry, fèr´-i, n **bac** m. v
passer en bac.

fertile, feur´-tâïle, a
fertile.

fertilize, feur-ti-lâïze, v
fertiliser.

fervent, feur´-vennte, a
fervent; ardent.

fester, fess´-teur, v
s'envenimer.

festival, fess´-ti-v'l, n **fête**
f; **festival** m. a **de fête.**

festive, fess´-tive, a
joyeux; de fête.

festoon, fess-touné´, n
feston m. v **festonner.**

fetch, fètche, v **aller
chercher.**

fetter, fèt´-teur, v
enchaîner; –s, npl **fers**
mpl.

fetus, fî´-teuce, n **embryon**
m; **foetus** m.

feud, fioude, n **inimitié** f;
–al, a **féodal.**

fever, fî´-veur, n **fièvre** f;
–ish, a **fiévreux.**

few, fioue, a **peu de; a –,**
quelques.

fiber, fâï´-beur, n **fibre** f.

fickle, fik´-'l, a **volage;
inconstant.**

fiction, fique´-ch'n, n
fiction f; **roman** m.

fictitious*, fique-tich´-
euce, a **fictif; faux.**

fidelity, fi-dél´-i-ti, n
fidélité f.

fidget, fid´-jette, v **remuer;
–y,** a **remuant; agité.**

field, filde, n **champ** m;
pré m; (games) **terrain**
m.

fiend, fînnde, n **démon** m;
–ish, a **diabolique.**

fierce*, fîrce, a **féroce;
farouche; furieux.**

fiery, fâï´-eu-ri, a **ardent;
fougueux.**

fifteen, fiff´-tîne, n & a
quinze m; **–th,** n & a
quinzième m & f.

fifth, fifts, n & a
cinquième m & f.

fiftieth, fiff´-ti-its, n & a
cinquantième m & f.

fifty, fiff´-ti, n & a
cinquante m.

fig, figue, n **figue** f; **–tree,**
figuier m.

fight, fâïte, v **se battre;
combattre.** n **combat** m.

figure, figue´-ioure, n
figure f; **forme** f; **ligne** f;
(number) **chiffre** m;
tournure.

file, fâïle, n (tool) **lime** f;
(office) **classeur** m;
dossier m; (mil) **file** f. v
limer; classer.

filigree, fil´-i-grî, n
filigrane f.

fill, file, v **remplir.** n
suffisance f.

filly, fil´-i, n **pouliche** f.

film, filme, n **voile** m;
(snapshots, etc)
pellicule f; (cinema)
film m. v **filmer.**

filter, fil´-teur, v **filtrer.** n
filtre m.

filth, filts, n **saleté** f; **–y,** a
sale.

fin, fine, n **nageoire** f.

final*, fâï´-n'l, a **final;
décisif.**

finance, fi-nännce´, n
finance f. v
commanditer.

financial*, fi-nänn´-ch'l, a
financier.

finch, finntche, n **pinson**
m.

find, fâïnnde, v **trouver.**

fine, faïïnne, *v* mettre à l'amende. *n* amende *f*. *a* fin; délicat; beau; subtil; excellent.

finery, fâï´-*neur*-i, *n* parure *f*.

finger, finng´-*gueur*, *n* doigt *m*. *v* toucher.

finish, finn´-iche, *v* finir; terminer. *n* fin *f*.

fir, feur, *n* sapin *m*.

fire, fâïre, *n* feu *m*; (conflagration) incendie *m*. *v* incendier; (gun, etc) tirer; **–alarm,** *n* avertisseur d'incendie *m*; **–department,** corps de pompiers *m*; **–engine,** pompe à incendie *f*; **–escape,** échelle de sauvetage *f*; **–man,** pompier *m*; **–place,** foyer *m*; cheminée *f*; **–proof,** *a* ininflammable; **–works,** *npl* feu d'artifice *m*.

firm, feurme, *n* maison (de commerce) *f*. *a** solide; ferme.

first, feurste, *n* & *a** premier; d'abord.

fish, fiche, *n* poisson *m*. *v* pêcher; **–bone,** *n* arête *f*; **–erman,** pêcheur *m*; **–hook,** hameçon *m*.

fishing, fich´-inng, *n* pêche *f*; **–rod,** canne à pêche *f*.

fissure, fich´-ioure, *n* fissure *f*; fente *f*.

fist, fiste, *n* poing *m*.

fistula, fiss´-tioue-la, *n* fistule *f*.

fit, fite, *v* ajuster; (clothes) aller; correspondre; poser; adapter. *n* (*med*) attaque *f*. *a* convenable; propre à; en forme.

fittings, fitt´-inngs, *npl* garnitures *fpl*; accessoires *mpl*.

five, fâïve, *n* & *a* cinq *m*.

fix, fixe, *v* fixer; arranger; préparer. *n* position *f*; combine *f*.

fixture, fixe´-tioure, *n* objet fixé à demeure *m*.

fizzy, fiz´-i, *a* gazeux.

flabby, flâb´-i, *a* flasque; mollasse.

flag, flague, *n* drapeau *m*; (*naut*) pavillon *m*; **–ship,** vaisseau amiral *m*; **–staff,** hampe de drapeau *f*.

flagon, flâg´-ŏnn, *n* flacon *m*.

flagrant, flé´-grannte, *a* flagrant.

flake, fléke, *n* (metal) lame *f*; (snow, etc) flocon *m*.

flaky, flé´-ki, *a* (pastry) feuilleté.

flame, fléme, *n* flamme *f*. *v* flamber.

flange, flânndje, *n* rebord *m*; (wheel) boudin *m*.

flank, flain´-ngk, *v* flanquer; border. *n* flanc *m*.

flannel, flânn´-'l, *n* flanelle *f*.

flap, flâppe, *n* battant *m*; (pocket) patte *f*; (wings) coup d'aile *m*. *v* battre.

flare, flère, *n* vive clarté *f*; flamme *f*. *v* flamboyer; (trousers, etc) évaser.

flash, flâche, *n* éclat *m*; (lightning) éclair *m*; (guns, etc) feu *m*.

flask, flâsske, *n* flacon *m*.

flat, flâtte, *n* appartement *m*; (*mus*) bémol *m*. *a* plat.

flatten, flâtt´-'n, *v* aplatir.

flatter, flâtt´-*eur*, *v* flatter; **–ing*,** *a* flatteur; **–y,** *n* flatterie *f*.

flavor, flé´-*veur*, *n* saveur *f*; goût *m*; (wine) bouquet *m*. *v* assaisonner.

flaw, floa, *n* défaut *m*.

flax, flâxe, *n* lin *m*.

flea, flî, *n* puce *f*.

flee, flî, *v* fuir; s'enfuir.

fleece, flîce, *n* toison *f*. *v* tondre; (rob) écorcher.

fleet, flîte, *n* flotte *f*. *a** rapide; léger.

flesh, flèche, *n* chair *f*.

flexible, flè´-xi-b'l, *a* flexible; souple.

flicker, flik´-*eur*, *v* vaciller;

clignoter. n battement m.

flight, flâïte, n (fleeing) fuite f; (birds, planes) vol m; (stairs) escalier m.

flight attendant, flâïte a-tten´d'nt, n hotesse de l'air f.

flimsy, flimm´-zi, a léger; fragile; (paper) papier pelure m.

flinch, flinntche, v broncher; fléchir.

fling, flinng, v lancer.

flint, flinnte, n silex m; (lighter) pierre f (à briquet).

flippant*, flipp´-annte, a léger; (pers) désinvolte.

flirt, fleurte, v flirter. n flirt m & f.

float, flaute, n (angler's) flotteur m. v flotter; (on back) faire la planche; (a company) lancer.

flock, floque, n troupeau m; (birds) vol m. v s'attrouper.

flog, flogue, v fouetter.

flood, flodde, v inonder. n inondation f; (tide) marée f.

floor, flaure, n plancher m; (story) étage m.

florid, flor´-ide, a fleuri; flamboyant.

florist, flor´-isste, n

fleuriste m & f.

floss, flosse, n bourre de soie f; fil dentaire m.

flounce, flâ'ounnce, n (dress) volant m. v se démener.

flour, flâ'oueur, n farine f.

flourish, flor´-iche, n brandissement m; (mus) fanfare f. v prospérer; (brandish) brandir.

flout, flâ'oute, v se moquer de.

flow, flau, n écoulement m; (river) cours m. v couler.

flower, flâ'ou´-eur, n fleur f. v fleurir.

fluctuate, floc´-tiou-éte, v fluctuer.

flue, floue, n tuyau de cheminée m.

fluency, floue´-enn-ci, n facilité f.

fluent, floue´-ennte, a facile; coulant.

fluff, floff, n duvet m; peluches fpl; –y, a peluches; duveteux.

fluid, floue´-idd, n & a fluide m.

fluke, flouque, n (chance) coup de hasard m.

flurry, flor´-i, n émoi m. v agiter; troubler.

flush, floche, v (redden) rougir; (rinse) laver à grande eau. n rougeur f.

a (level) au niveau de.

fluster, floce´-teur, v déconcerter. n agitation f.

flute, floute, n flûte f; –d, a cannelé.

flutter, flott´-eur, v palpiter; battre des ailes.

fly, flâï, n mouche f; (trouser) n braguette f. v voler; (flag) flotter.

foal, faule, n poulain m. v pouliner.

foam, faume, n écume f. v écumer.

focus, fau´-keuce, v mettre au point; régler. n foyer m.

fodder, fod´'r, n fourrage m.

foe, fau, n ennemi m.

fog, fogue, n brouillard m;–**gy**, a brumeux; — **horn**, n sirène f; trompede brume.

foil, foa´ile, n (fencing) fleuret m; (metal) feuille f. v déjouer.

foist, foa´iste, v imposer; introduire; fourrer.

fold, faulde, n (clothes, etc) pli m; (sheep) bercail m. v plier; (arms) croiser.

foliage, fau´-li-édje, n feuillage m.

folk, fauke, n gens mpl & fpl.

follow, foll´-au, v suivre;
(fig) s'ensuivre.

follower, foll´-au'r, n
partisan m; disciple m.

folly, foll´-i, m folie f;
(stupidity) sottise f.

foment, fo-mennte´, v
fomenter.

fond, fonnde, a
affectueux; **to be –of,**
aimer.

fondle, fonn´-d'l, v
choyer; caresser.

font, fonnte, n fonts
baptismaux mpl.

food, foude, n nourriture f;
(a food) aliment m.

fool, foull, n imbécile m &
f. v duper; **–hardy,** a
téméraire; **–ish,** sot;
imprudent.

foot, foutt, n pied m;
–ball, football m; **–path,**
sentier m; (pavement)
trottoir m; (print) trace
de pas f; **–step,** pas m.

for, fôr, prep pour;
pendant. conj car.

forage, for´-idj, n fourrage
m. v fourrager.

forbear, fôr-bére´, v
supporter; s'abstenir.

forbearance, fôr-bèr´-
annce, n indulgence f.

forbid, fôr-bide´, v
défendre; **–ding,** a
repoussant.

force, fôrce, v forcer. n

force f; **–ful,** a
vigoureux.

forceps, for´-seppse, n
pince f; forceps m.

forcible, fôr´-ci-b'l, a
énergique; par force.

ford, fôrde, v passer à gué.
n gué m.

fore, fore, n avant m. a
antérieur; **–arm,** n
avant-bras m; **–bode,** v
présager; **–boding,** n
présage m; **–cast,**
prévision f. v prévoir;
–close, v (law) forclore;
–fathers, n aïeux mpl;
–finger, index m;
–going, a précédent;
–gone, préconçu;
–ground, n premier plan
m; **–head,** front m;
–man, contremaître m;
–most, a le plus avancé;
principal; **–runner,** n
précurseur m; **–see,** v
prévoir; **–sight,** n
prévoyance f; **–stall,** v
devancer; **–taste,** n
avant-goût m; **–tell,** v
prédire; **–thought,** n
préméditation f; **–warn,**
v avertir.

foreign, for´-ine, a
étranger; **–er,** n étranger,
-éren m & f.

forest, for´-este, n forêt f.

forfeit, for´-fite, n gage m;
(law) dédit m. v perdre;

renoncer.

forge, fordje, v forger;
(falsify) contrefaire. n
forge f; **–ry,** contrefaçon
f; faux m.

forget, fôr-guette´, v
oublier; **–ful,** a oublieux;
négligent; **–fulness,** n
oubli m; **––me-not,**
(flower) myosotis m.

forgive, fôr-guive´, v
pardonner.

forgiveness, fôr-guive´-
nesse, n pardon m.

forgo, fore-gau´, v
renoncer à; s'abstenir
de.

fork, forque, n fourchette
f; (tool) fourche f;
(road) bifurcation f. v
bifurquer.

forlorn, fôr-lôrne´, a
abandonné; désespéré.

form, fôrme, n forme f; (a
form to fill up) formule
f; (seat) banc m; (class)
classe f. v former; **–al**, a
de forme; formel;
officiel; **–ality,** n
formalité f; **–ation,**
formation f; **–er,** a
précédent; ancien;
–erly, adv autrefois.

forsake, fôr-céque´, v
délaisser; abandonner.

fort, fôrte, n fort m;
–ification, fortification
f; **–ify,** v fortifier; **–ress,**

n forteresse *f*.

forth, fôrts, *adv* en avant;
désormais; **–coming,** *a*
prochain; **–with,** *adv*
sur-le-champ.

fortieth, fôr´-ti-its, *n* & *a*
quarantième *m* & *f*.

fortitude, fôr´-ti-tioude, *n*
courage *m*.

fortnight, forte´-nâîte, *n*
quinzaine *f*; quinze jours.

fortunate*, fôr´-tiou-néte,
a heureux; fortuné.

fortune, fôr´-tioune, *n*
fortune *f*; (fate) sort *m*.

forty, fôr´-ti, *n* & *a*
quarante *m*.

forward, fôr´-ouarde, *v*
expédier; faire suivre.
adv en avant. *a* avancé;
effronté; **–ness,**
effronterie *f*.

fossil, foss´-il, *n* & *a*
fossile *m*

foster, fosse´-t'r, *v* élever;
encourager; **–parents,**
npl parents nourriciers
mpl.

foul, fâ´-oule, *v* souiller. *a**
sale; impur; obscène;
(unfair) déloyal.

foul play, fâ´-oule-plé, *n*
quelque chose de louche
m.

found, fâ´-ounnde, *v*
fonder; (metal) fondre;
–ation, *n* fondation *f*;
(*fig*) fondement *m*; **–er,**

v sombrer. *n* fondateur
m; **–ling,** enfant trouvé
m; **–ry,** fonderie *f*.

fountain, fâ´ounn´-tinne,
n fontaine *f*; **–pen,** stylo
m.

four, fôr, *n* & *a* quatre *m*;
–fold, *a* quadruple;
–teen, *n* & *a* quatorze
m; **–teenth,** *n* & *a*
quartozième *m*; **–th,**
quatrième *m* & *f*.

fowl, fâ´oule, *n* volaille *f*.

fox, foxe, *n* renard *m*;
–terrier, fox-terrier *m*.

fraction, frăck´-ch'n, *n*
fraction *f*.

fracture, frăck´-tioure, *v*
fracturer. *n* fracture *f*.

fragile, frăd´-jile, *a* fragile.

fragment, frăgue´-m'nt, *n*
fragment *m*.

fragrance, fré´-grannce, *n*
perfum *m*.

fragrant, fré´-grannt, *a*
parfumé.

frail, fréle, *a* frêle; **–ty,** *n*
fragilité *f*.

frame, fréme, *n* forme *f*;
cadre *m*; (car) chassis *m*.
v former; (picture, etc)
encadrer; **–s,** (glasses) *n*
monture *f*.

franchise, frănn´-tchâîze,
n franchise *f*.

frank*, frain-ngk, *a* franc;
–ness, *n* franchise *f*.

frantic, frănn´-tique, *a*

frénétique; furieux.

fraud, froade, *n* fraude *f*;
imposteur *m*; **–ulent*,** *a*
frauduleux.

fray, fré, *n* (scuffle)
bagarre *f*. *v* (material)
s'effiler.

freak, frîque, *n*
phénomène *m*; monstre
m; **–ish,** *a* bizarre.

freckle, frèk´-'l, *n* tache de
rousseur *f*.

free, frî, *v* libérer; délivrer.
a libre; gratuit; **–dom,** *n*
liberté *f*; **–trade,** libre-
échange *m*.

freeze, frîze, *v* geler;
glacer; congeler.

freezing, frîz´-inng, *n*
congélation *f*. *a* glacial.

freight, fréte, *n* fret *m*;
cargaison *f*. *v* affréter.

frenzy, frenn´-zi, *n*
frénésie *f*.

frequency, fri´-couenn-ci,
n fréquence *f*.

frequent, fri´-couennte, *a*
fréquent. *v* fréquenter.

fresh*, frèche, *a* frais;
–ness, *n* fraîcheur *f*.

fret, frette, *v* se
tourmenter; **–ful,** *a*
irritable; **—saw,** *n* scie à
découper; **–work,**
découpage *m*.

friar, frâî´-'r, *n* moine *m*;
–y, monastère *m*.

friction, frique´-ch'n, *n*

friction f; frottement m.

Friday, frâï´-dé, n
vendredi m; **Good –,**
vendredi saint m.

friend, frennde, n ami m;
–liness, bienveillance f;
a amical; **–ship,** n amitié
f.

fright, frâïte, n frayeur f;
peur f; **–en,** v effrayer;
–ful, a effroyable;
épouvantable.

frigid, fridj´-ide, a glacial;
frigide.

frill, frile, n volant m,
ruche f.

fringe, frinndje, n frange f;
bord m. v border.

frisk, frisk, v gambader;
fouiller.

frisky, frisk´-i, a frétillant;
animé.

fritter, fritt´-'r, n beignet
m. v morceler; **–away,**
dissiper; gaspiller.

frivolous*, friv´-ŏ-leuce, a
frivole.

frock, froque, n (dress)
robe f.

frog, frogue, n grenouille f.

frolic, frol´-ique, v
folâtrer. n espièglerie f.

from, fromme, prep de;
depuis; de la part de;
d'après.

front, fronnte, n devant
m; (mil) front m; a de
face; **–age,** n façade f.

frontier, fronnt´-i-eur, n &
a frontière f.

frost, froste, v glacer. n
gelée f; (hoar) givre m;
—bitten, a gelé; **–y,**
glacé.

froth, frôts, n écume f;
mousse f. v écumer;
mousser.

frown, frâ'oune, v froncer
les sourcils. n
froncement de sourcils
m.

frugal*, froue´-g'l, a
frugal.

fruit, froute, n fruit m;
–ful, a fructueux; **–less,**
stérile.

frustrate, fross-tréte´, v
frustrer.

fry, frâï, v frire; faire frire.

fuchsia, fioue´-chi-a, n
fuchsia m.

fuel, fioue´-eul, n
combustible m.

fugitive, fioue´-dji-tive, n
& a fugitif, –ive m & f.

fugue, fiougue, n fugue f.

fulcrum, feul´-creum, n
point d'appui m.

fulfill, foull-fill´, v
accomplir; réaliser;
satisfaire; **–ment,** n
accomplissement m;
réalisation f.

full, foull, a plein;
complet.

fullness, foull´-nesse, n

plénitude f; abondance
f.

fulsome, foull´-seumme, a
vil; écœurant.

fume, fioume, n vapeur f.
v (rage) rager.

fun, fonne, n amusement
m; (joke) plaisanterie f;
–ny, a drôle; amusant.

function, fonnk´-ch'n, n
fonction f. v
fonctionner.

fund, fonnde, n fonds mpl;
caisse f.

fundamental*, fonn-da-
menn´-t'l, a
fondamental f.

funeral, fioue´-neur-'l, n
enterrement m;
funérailles fpl.

funnel, fonn´-'l, n
entonnoir m; (smoke)
cheminée f.

fur, feure, n fourrure f;
(boiler) tartre m. v
incruster; **–rier,** n
fourreur m.

furious*, fioue´-ri-euce, a
furieux.

furnace, feur´-nisse, n four
m; fourneau m; (ship,
etc) foyer m.

furnish, feur´-niche, v
meubler; fournir.

furniture, feur´-ni-tioure,
n meubles mpl.

furrow, for´-au, v
sillonner. n sillon m.

further, feur´dzeur, *adv* en
plus; plus loin. *a*
supplémentaire. *v*
avancer; seconder.

furtive*, feur´-tive, *a*
furtif.

fury, fioue´-ri, *n* furie *f*.

fuse, fiouze, *n* (time) fusée
f; (electric) plomb *m*;
fusible *m*; *v* fuser; sauter.

fuss, foce, *n* embarras *m*;
cérémonies *fpl*; (*fam*)
des histoires *fpl*.

futile, fioue´-tâïle, *a* futile;
frivole.

future, fioue´-tioure, *n*
avenir *m*. *a* futur.

gable, gué´-b'l, n pignon m.

gaff, găffe, n gaffe f.

gag, găgue, v bâillonner. n bâillon m; (fam) blague f.

gaiety, gué´-i-ti, n gaieté f.

gaily, gué´-li, adv gaiement.

gain, guéne, n gain m. v gagner; atteindre.

gait, guéte, n démarche f; (horse) allure f.

gaiter, gué´-t'r, n guêtre f.

galaxy, găl´-ak-ci, n galaxie f.

gale, guéle, n tempête f; coup de vent m.

gall, goal, n bile f. v irriter; —**stone,** n calcul biliaire m; —**bladder,** n vésicule biliaire f.

gallant, găl´-'nt, a brave; galant.

gallantry, găl´-ann-tri, n bravoure f; galanterie f.

gallery, găl´-eur-i, n galerie f.

gallop, găl´-pe, v galoper. n galop m.

gallows, găl´-auze, n potence f; gibet m.

galvanism, găl´-vann-izme, n galvanisme m.

galvanize, găl´-vann-âïze, v galvaniser.

gamble, gămm´-b'l, v jouer de l'argent; miser; —**r,** n joueur m.

game, guéme, n jeu m; partie f; (birds, etc) gibier m; —**keeper,** garde-chasse m.

gander, gănn´-d'r, n jars m.

gang, gain´-ng, n équipe f; bande f; —**way,** passage m; (ship) passerelle f.

gap, găppe, n brèche f; ouverture f; trou m; écart m.

gape, guépe, v regarder bouche bée; s'ouvrir.

garage, ga-râdge´, n garage m.

garb, gârbe, n costume m; habit m.

garbage, gâr´-bidj, n ordures fpl.

garden, găr´-d'n, n jardin m; (kitchen) (jardin) potager m; —**er,** jardinier m; —**ing,** jardinage m.

gargle, găr´-g'l, v se gargariser. n gargarisme m.

garland, gâr´-lannde, n guirlande f. v orner de guirlandes.

garlic, gâr´-lique, n ail m.

garment, gâr´-m'nt, n vêtement m.

garnish, gâr´-niche, v garnir. n garniture f.

garret, găr´-ette, n mansarde f.

garrison, găr´-i-s'n, n garnison f.

garrulous, găr´-ou-leuce, a bavard.

garter, gâr´-t'r, n jarretière f.

gas, găce, n gaz m; —**eous,** a gazeux; —**works,** usine à gaz f.

gash, gâche, v balafrer. n balafre f; coupure f.

gasp, gâsspe, v haleter. n soupir convulsif m.

gastric, gâss´-trique, a gastrique.

gate, guéte, n porte f; (iron) grille f; (wooden) barrière f.

gather, gǎdz´-eur, v rassembler; (pluck) cueillir; (conclude) comprendre; **–ing,** n réunion f; (med) abcès m.

gaudy, goa´-di, a voyant; criard.

gauge, guédje, n indicateur m. n (tool) calibre m; (railroad) entre-rail m; (size) mesure f. v mesurer; estimer.

gaunt, goannte, a maigre; décharné.

gauze, goaze, n gaze f; (wire) toile métallique f.

gawky, goa´-ki, a dégingandé; gauche.

gay, gué, a gai; joyeux; dissolu; homosexuel.

gaze, guéze, v regarder fixement. n regard fixe m.

gazelle, ga-zelle´, n gazelle f.

gazette, ga-zette´, n gazette f.

gear, guîeur, n équipment; (car) boîte de vitesse f.

gelatin, djell´-a-tinn, n gélatine f.

gelding, guêl´-dinng, n cheval hongre m.

gem, djème, n pierre précieuse f.

gender, djenn´-d'r, n genre m.

general, djenn´-eu-ral, n général m. a* général.

generalize, djenn´-eu-ra-lâîze, v généraliser.

generate, djenn´-eur-éte, v produire; engendrer.

generation, djenn-eur-é´-ch'n, n génération f.

generosity, djenn-eur-o´-si-ti, n générosité f.

generous*, djenn´-eur-euce, a généreux.

genial, dji´-ni-al, a doux; cordial.

genitive, djenn´-i-tive, n & a génitif m.

genius, dji´-ni-euce, n génie m.

genteel, djenn-tîle´, a comme il faut.

gentle, djenn´-t'l, a doux; **–man,** n homme bien élevé m; monsieur m; **–ness,** n douceur f.

gently, djenn´-tli, adv doucement.

genuine*, djenn´-iou-ine, a authentique; sincère.

–ness, n authenticité f; sincérité f.

geography, dji-og´-rǎ-fi, n géographie f.

geology, dji-ol´-o-dji, n géologie f.

geometry, dji-omm´-e-tri, n géométrie f.

geranium, dji-ré´-ni-omm, n géranium m.

germ, djeurme, n germe m; microbe m.

germinate, djeur´-mi-néte, v germer.

gesticulate, djesse-tik´-ioue-léte, v gesticuler.

gesture, djesse´-tioure, n geste m.

get, guette, v obtenir; (earn) gagner; (fetch) aller chercher; (attain) arriver; **–back,** recouvrer; **–down,** descendre; **–off,** descendre; **–on,** progresser; monter; s'entendre; **–out,** sortir; **–up,** se lever.

geyser, gui´-zeur, n geyser m; chauffe-bain m.

ghastly, gâce´-tli, a blême; (awful) épouvantable.

gherkin, gueur´-quine, n cornichon m.

ghost, gôsste, n revenant m; fantôme m.

giant, djâî´-nte, n géant m; **–ess,** géante f.

gibberish, guib´-*eur*-iche, n baragouin m.

gibbet, djib´-ette, n gibet m; potence f.

gibe, djâïbe, v se moquer de. n raillerie f.

giblets, djib´-*le*tce, npl abatis mpl.

giddiness, guid´-i-ness, n vertige m.

giddy, guid´-i, a étourdi; vertigineux; qui donne le vertige.

gift, guifte, n don m; cadeau m; talent m.

gifted, guif´-tédde, a doué.

gigantic, djâï-gănne´-tique, a gigantesque.

giggle, guig´-l, v rire nerveusement.

gild, guilde, v dorer.

gilding, gilt, guild´-inng, guilte, n dorure f.

gills, guilze, npl branchies fpl.

gimlet, guime´-lette, n vrille f.

gin, djine, n gin m.

ginger, djinn´-djeur, n gingembre m.

giraffe, dji-raffe´, n girafe f.

girder, gueur´-d'r, n poutre f; traverse f.

girdle, gueur´-d'l, n gaine f. v ceindre.

girl, gueurle, n fille f; jeune fille f; **–hood,** jeunesse f.

girth, gueurts, n contour m; (horse) sangle f.

gist, djisste, n substance f; essentiel m.

give, guive, v donner; remettre; **–in,** céder; **–up,** renoncer à.

gizzard, guiz´-*eur*de, n gésier m.

glacier, glé´-ci-*eur,* n glacier m.

glad, glădde, a heureux; content; **–den,** v réjouir; **–ness,** n joie f; plaisir m.

glade, gléde, n clairière f; percée f.

glance, glânnce, n coup d'œil m. v jeter un coup d'oeil; **–off,** dévier; ricocher.

gland, glănnde, n glande f.

glare, glère, n clarté f; (stare) regard fixe m. v éblouir; regarder fixement.

glaring, glèr´-inng, a éblouissant; voyant; (of fact, etc) manifeste.

glass, glâce, n verre m; miroir m; (pane) vitre f; **–es,** (spectacles) n lunettes fpl; **–ware,** verrerie f; **–y,** a vitreux.

glaze, gléze, v vitrer; (cake, etc) glacer; (pottery) émailler. n (luster) lustre m; émail m.

glazier, glé´-jeur, n vitrier m.

gleam, glîme, n lueur f; (ray) rayon m. v luire; briller.

glean, glîne, v glaner; **–er,** n glaneur, -euse m & f.

glee, glî, n joie f.

glen, glène, n vallon m.

glib, glibbe, a (of the tongue) bien déliée.

glide, glâïde, v glisser; planer; **–r,** n (aircraft) planeur m.

glimmer, glimm´-'r, v luire faiblement. n lueur f.

glimpse, glimmpse, n coup d'œil m; aperçu m.

glint, glinnte, n trait de lumière m. v luire.

glisten, gliss´-'n, v étinceler; reluire.

glitter, glitt´'r, v briller; étinceler. n éclat m.

gloat, glaute, v se réjouir de; couver des yeux.

globe, glaube, n globe m; sphère f.

globular, globb´-iou-l'r, a sphérique.

gloom, gloume, n obscurité f; (dismal) tristesse f.

gloomy, gloumm´-i, a obscur; (dismal) triste.

glorify, glau-ri-fâï, v glorifier.

glorious*, glau´-ri-*euce*, *a* glorieux; superbe.

glory, glau´-ri, n gloire *f*. *v* –**in**, se glorifier de.

gloss, glsse, n lustre m; –**y**, *a* luisant, brillant.

glove, glove, n gant m.

glow, glau, n éclat m; rougeur *f*. *v* luire; rougir.

glue, gloue, n colle *f*. *v* coller.

glum, gleumme, *a* morose.

glut, glotte, *v* (market) inonder; (of food) (se) gorger. n excès m.

glutton, glott´-n, n glouton, -onne m & *f*.

gnarled, nârlde, *a* noueux.

gnash, nâche, *v* grincer; –**ing**, n grincement m.

gnat, nâtte, n cousin m; moucheron m.

gnaw, noa, *v* ronger.

go, gau, *v* aller; partir; (mech) marcher; –**away**, s'en aller; partir; –**back**, retourner; –**down**, descendre; –**out**, sortir; –**up**, monter; –**without**, se passer de.

goad, gaude, n aiguillon m. *v* aiguillonner; inciter.

goal, gaule, n but m.

goat, gaute, n chèvre *f*; **male** –, bouc m.

gobble, gob´-l, *v* avaler avidement; dévorer.

goblin, gob´-linne, n lutin

m; farfadet m.

god, godde, m, Dieu m; dieu m; –**child**, filleul, -e m & *f*; –**dess**, déesse *f*; –**father**, parrain m; –**liness**, n piété *f*; –**ly**, *a* pieux; –**mother**, n marraine *f*.

goggles, gog´-g'lze, npl grosses lunettes fpl.

goiter, go'i´-teur, n goître m.

gold, gaulde, n or m; –**en**, *a* d'or; –**finch**, n chardonneret m; –**fish**, poisson rouge m; –**leaf**, or en feuille m; –**smith**, orfèvre m.

golf, golf, n golf m; – **course**, terrain de golf m.

gong, gon-ng, n gong m.

good, goudd, n bien m; avantage m. *a* bon; sage; –**bye!** *interj* adieu! au revoir! –**morning**, –**afternoon**, –**day**, bonjour; –**night**, bonsoir.

good-natured, goudd-nét´-tiour'd, *a* d'un bon naturel.

goodness, goudd´-nesse, n bonté *f*.

goods, goudd´-ze, npl marchandises fpl; effets mpl.

goodwill, goudd-ouil´, n

bienveillance *f*.

goose, goûce, n oie *f*.

gooseberry, goûce´-beur-i, n groseille à maquereau *f*.

gore, gôre, n (blood) sang m. *v* encorner.

gorge, gôrdje, n gorge *f*. *v* se gorger de.

gorgeous*, gôr´-djeuce, *a* somptueux; splendide.

gorilla, go-ril´-la, n gorille m.

gorse, gôrse, n ajonc m.

gosling, goz´-linng, n oison m.

gospel, goss´-p'l, n évangile m.

gossip, goss´-ippe, *v* bavarder; papoter. n potin m; cancans mpl; (person) commère *f*.

gouge, gâ´oudje, n gouge *f*. *v* gouger; arracher.

gout, gâ´oute, n goutte *f*.

govern, gov´-eurne, *v* gouverner; –**ess**, n gouvernante *f*; –**ment**, gouvernement m; –**or**, gouverneur m; (mech) régulateur m.

gown, gâ´oune, n robe *f*.

grab, grâbe, *v* empoigner; saisir. n (mech) benne preneuse *f*.

grace, gréce, n grâce *f*; –**ful***, *a* gracieux.

gracious*, gré´-cheuce, *a*

gracieux.

grade, gréde, n grade m; degré m; rang m. v classer; graduer.

gradient, gré´-di-ennte, n pente f; rampe f.

gradual*, grăd´-iou-eul, a progressif.

graduate, grăd´-iou-éte, n diplômé, -e m & f. v graduer; obtenir des diplômes.

graft, grâfte, n greffe f; (fig) corruption f. v greffer.

grain, gréne, n grain m. v (paint) veiner.

grammar, grămm´-'r, n grammaire f.

granary, grănn´-a-ri, n grenier m.

grand*, grănnde, a grandiose; magnifique; –**daughter**, n petite-fille f; –**father**, grand-père m; –**mother**, grand-mère f; –**son**, petit-fils m.

grant, grănnte, v accorder. n subvention f; bourse f.

grape, grépe, n raisin m.

grapefruit, grépe´-froute, n pamplemousse m.

grapple, grăp´-p'l, n (hook) grappin m. v lutter.

grasp, grâsspe, v empoigner; (understand) comprendre. n étreinte f; –**ing**, a avide.

grass, grâsse, n herbe f; (lawn) gazon m; –**hopper**, sauterelle f; –**y**, a herbeux.

grate, gréte, n (fire) grille f. v grincer; (cookery, etc) râper.

grateful, gréte´-foull, a reconnaissant.

gratification, gră-ti-fi-qué´-ch'n, n satisfaction f.

gratify, gră´-ti-fâï, v satisfaire; –**ing**, a agréable.

grating, gré´-tinng, n grillage m. a grinçant.

gratis, gré´-tisse, adv gratis.

gratitude, gră-ti-tioude, n reconnaissance f.

gratuitous*, gra-tiou´-i-teuce, a gratuit.

gratuity, gra-tiou´-i-ti, n pourboire m.

grave, gréve, n tombe f. a* grave; –**stone**, pierre tombale f; –**yard**, cimetière m.

gravel, grăv´-'l, n gravier m.

gravitate, grăv´-i-téte, v graviter.

gravity, grăv´-i-ti, n gravité f.

gravy, gré´-vi, n jus m; sauce f.

gray, gré, a gris; (complexion) blême.

graze, gréze, n écorchure f. v effleurer; érafler; (feed) paître.

grease, grîce, n graisse f. v graisser.

greasy, grî´-zi, a graisseux.

great*, gréte, a grand; –**ness**, n grandeur f.

greed, grîde, n gourmandise f; avidité f; –**ily**, adv goulûment; –**y**, a gourmand; avide.

green, grîne, n & a vert m; –**gage**, n Reine-claude f; –**house**, serre f; –**ish**, a verdâtre.

greet, grîte, v saluer; –**ing**, n salutation f.

grenade, gre-néde´, n grenade f.

greyhound, gré´-hâ´ounnde, n lévrier m.

grief, grîfe, n chagrin m; douleur f.

grievance, grî´-v'nce, n grief m; doléance f.

grieve, grîve, v s'affliger; chagriner.

grievous, grî´-veuce, a grave; accablant.

grill, grile, v griller. n gril m.

grim*, grime, a sinistre; menaçant.

grimace, gri-méce´, n

grimace *f*.

grime, grâïme, *n* saleté *f*; (dirt) crasse *f*.

grin, grinne, *v* grimacer; sourire à belles dents. *n* large sourire *m*.

grind, grâïnnde, *v* moudre; (sharpen) aiguiser.

grinder, grâïnn´-*deur*, *n* rémouleur *m*; broyeur *m*; (coffee, etc) moulin *m*.

grip, grippe, *n* (action) étreinte *f*; (handle) poignée *f*; prise *f*. *v* empoigner; saisir.

gripe, grâïpe, *v* (bowels) donner à la colique.

grisly, grize´-li, *a* affreux; horrible.

grit, gritte, *n* gravier *m*; sable *m*; –ty, *a* graveleux.

groan, graune, *v* gémir. *n* gémissement *m*.

grocer, grau´-*ceur*, *n* épicier *m*; –y, épicerie *f*.

grog, grgue, *n* grog *m*.

groin, grô'ine, *n* aine *f*; (arch) arête *f*.

groom, groume, *n* palefrenier *m*.

groove, grouve, *v* rainer; creuser. *n* rainure *f*.

grope, graupe, *v* tâtonner.

gross, grauce, *n* (12 dozen) grosse *f*; *a* (coarse) grossier; (obvious) flagrant;

–**weight**, *n* poids brut *m*.

ground, grâ´ounnde, *v* (naut) échouer. *n* terrain *m*; terre *f*; (reason) motif *m*; base *f*; –**floor**, rez-de- chaussée *m*; –**less**, *a* sans fondement; –**work**, *n* base *f*.

group, groupe, *n* groupe *m*. *v* grouper.

grouse, grâ´ouce, *n* coq de bruyère *m*. *v* grogner; se plaindre.

grove, grauve, *n* bocage *m*; bosquet *m*.

grovel, grov´-´-l, *v* (fig) ramper.

grow, grau, *v* pousser; croître; grandir; cultiver; –**er**, *n* cultivateur *m*; –**n up**, adulte *m* & *f*; –**th**, croissance *f*.

growl, grâ´oule, *n* grognement *m*. *v* grogner.

grub, grobbe, *n* larve *f*; asticot *m*; maugeaille.

grudge, grodje, *n* rancune *f*. *v* donner à regret; envier à.

gruel, groue´-´l, *n* gruau *m*.

gruesome, groue´-somme, *a* affreux; macabre.

gruff*, groffe, *a* brusque; rude.

grumble, gromm´-b'l, *v* grommeler; se plaindre; –**r**, *n* grognon *m*.

grunt, gronnte, *v* grogner. *n* grognement *m*.

guarantee, ga-rann-tî´, *v* garantir. *n* garantie *f*.

guard, gârde, *n* garde *f*. *v* garder; –**ed**, *a* circonspect.

guardian, găr´-di-anne, *n* gardien *m*; (trustee) tuteur *m*.

guess, guesse, *v* deviner.

guest, guesse, *n* invité -ée *m* & *f*; (hotel) client -e *m* & *f*.

guidance, gâï´-d'nce, *n* direction *f*; conduite *f*; orientation *f*.

guide, gâïde, *v* guider. *n* guide *m*.

guild, guilde, *n* corps de métier *m*; corporation *f*.

guile, gâïle, *n* astuce *f*; artifice *m*; –**less**, *a* ingénu.

guilt, guilte, *n* culpabilité *f*; –**y**, *a* coupable.

guinea, gui´-ni, *n* guinée *f*; –**fowl**, pintade *f*; –**pig**, cochon d'Inde *m*.

guise, guâïze, *n* façon *f*; apparence *f*.

guitar, gui-târe´, *n* guitare *f*.

gulf, golfe, *n* (geog) golfe *m*; (abyss) gouffre *m*.

gull, golle, *n* mouette *f*. *v* duper.

gullet, goll´-ette, *n*

gosier *m.*

gulp, golpe, *v* avaler. *n* gorgée *f.*

gum, gomme, *n* gomme *f;* (teeth) gencive *f.*

gun, gonne, *n* fusil *m;* (artillery) canon *m;* **–ner,** canonnier *m;* **–powder,** poudre à canon *f;* **–smith,** armurier *m.*

gurgle, gueur´-g'l, *v* gargouiller. *n* gargouillement *m.*

gush, goche, *v* jaillir. *n* jaillissement *m.*

gust, gosste, *n* coup de vent *m;* rafale *f.*

gut, gotte, *n* boyau *m. v* vider.

gutter, gott´-'r, *n* gouttière *f;* (street) ruisseau *m.*

guy, gaille, *n* type *m;* individu *m.*

gymnasium, djimm-né´-zi-mme, *n* gymnase *m.*

gymnastics, djimm-năss´-tikse, *npl* gymnastique *f.*

gypsy, djip´-ci, *n* bohémien *m;* tzigane *m.*

haberdashery, hăb´-*eur*-dăch-'ri, n mercerie f.

habit, hăb´-itte, n habitude f; coutume f.

habitable, hăb´-i-*ta*-b'l, a habitable.

habitual*, ha-bit´-iou-*eul*, a habituel.

hack, hăque, v écharper; hacher; couper.

hackneyed, hăque´-nidde, a rebattu; banal.

haddock, hăd´-oque, n aiglefin fumé m; haddock m.

hag, hăgue, n mégère f; **–gard**, a hagard.

haggle, hăgg´-'l, v marchander.

hail, héle, n grêle f. v grêler; (greet) saluer.

hair, hère, n poil m; (of head only) cheveu m; (horse) crin m; **–brush**, brosse à cheveux f; **–dresser**, coiffeur, -euse m & f; **–pin**, épingle à cheveux f; **–y**, a poilu; chevelu.

hake, héke, n merluche f.

half, hâfe, n moitié f; demi, -e m & f. a demi. adv à moitié.

halibut, hăl´-i-botte, n flétan m.

hall, hoal, n vestibule m; entrée f; salle f; **–mark**, poinçon de contrôle m.

hallow, hal´-lau, v sanctifier.

hallucination, hal-liou-ci-né´-ch'n, n hallucination f.

halo, hé´-lau, n auréole m; (astronomy) halo m.

halt, hoalte, n arrêt m. v arrêter. interj halte!

halter, hoal-t'r, n licou m.

halve, hâve, v partager en deux.

ham, hămme, n jambon m.

hamlet, hămm´-lette, n hameau m.

hammer, hămm´-'r, n marteau m. v marteler.

hammock, hămm´-oque, n hamac m.

hamper, hămm´-p'r, n panier m; bourriche f. v gêner.

hand, hănnde, n main f; (clock) aiguille f. v passer; donner; **–bag**, n sac à main m; **–book**, manuel m; **–cuffs**, menottes fpl; **–ful**, poignée f; **–kerchief**, mouchoir m; **–le**, manche f; (door) bouton m. v manier; **–made**, a fait à la main; **–rail**, n rampe f; **–y**, a utile; commode; à portée.

handsome*, hănn´-somme, a beau; généreux.

hang, hain-ng, v pendre;

–**up,** v accrocher.

hangar, hain´-gueur, n hangar m.

hanger, hain´-gueur, n cintre m.

hanker, hain´-nkeur, v désirer ardemment.

happen, hăp´-p'n, v arriver; se passer.

happily, hăpp´-i-li, adv heureusement.

happiness, hăpp´-i-nesse, n bonheur m.

happy, hăpp´-i, a heureux.

harangue, hă-raingue, n harangue f. v haranguer.

harass, hăr´-ăce, v harceler.

harassment, hăz´-acemennt, n harcèlement m; tracasseries f.

harbor, hăr´-b'r, n port m. v héberger.

hard, hârde, a dur; difficile; –**en,** v durcir; (refl) s'endurcir; –**ly,** adv à peine; durement; –**ness,** n dureté f; –**ship,** peine f; privation f; –**ware,** quincaillerie f; –**y,** a robuste.

hare, hârde, n lièvre m; – **lip,** bec de lièvre m.

harm, hârm, n mal m; tort m. v faire du mal; –**ful,** a nuisible; –**less,** inoffensif.

harmonious*, hâr-mô´-nieuce, a harmonieux.

harmonize, hăr´-mönnâïze, v harmoniser.

harness, hăr´-nesse, n équipment m; (horse) harnais m. v harnacher; (to a cart) atteler; (forces) utiliser.

harp, hârpe, n harpe f. v rabâcher.

harpoon, hâr-poune´, n harpon m.

harrow, hăr´-au, n herse f. v (fig) tourmenter.

harsh, hârche, a (sound) discordant; (severe) dur; (color) criard.

harvest, hăr´-veste, n moisson f; récolte f. v moissonner; récolter.

hash, hăche, n hachis m; (fig) gâchis m. v hacher.

hassock, hăs´-soque, n coussin m.

haste, héste, n hâte f; –**n,** v hâter; se hâter.

hastily, héce´-ti-li, adv à la hâte.

hat, hătte, n chapeau m.

hatch, hătche, n trappe f; (naut) écoutille f. v (eggs) couver; (plot) tramer.

hatchet, hătch´-ette, n hachette f.

hate, héte, n haine f. v haïr; –**ful*,** a odieux.

hatred, hé´-tredde, n haine f.

haughtiness, hoa´-tinesse, n hauteur f; arrogance f.

haughty, hoa´-ti, a hautain; altier.

haul, hoale, n tirage m; (catch) coup de filet m. v tirer; (boat) haler; (drag) traîner.

haunch, hoanntche, n hanche f; arrière-train m.

haunt, hoannte, v hanter; (fig) fréquenter. n rendez-vous m; (animals) repaire m.

have, hâve, v avoir; posséder.

haversack, hăve´-eursăque, n havresac m.

havoc, hăv´-ôque, n dégât m; ravage m.

hawk, hoaque, n épervier m. v colporter.

hawker, hoak´-'r, n colporteur m.

hawthorn, hoa´-tsôrne, n aubépine f.

hay, hé, n foin m; –**fever,** rhume des foins m; –**loft,** grange f; –**making,** fenaison f.

hazard, hăz´-arde, n hasard m. v hasarder.

hazardous, hăz´-ar-deuce, a hasardeux.

haze, héze, n brume f.

hazel, hé´-z'l, n noisetier m; **—nut,** noisette f.

hazy, hé´-zi, a brumeux

he, hî, pron il; lui.

head, hedde, n tête f; chef m; principal m; directeur m; **—ache,** mal de tête m; **—ing,** en tête m; titre m; **—land,** promontoire m; **—light,** phare m; **—long,** adv tête baissée; aveuglément; **—master,** n directeur m; **— quarters,** quartier général m; **—strong,** a entêté; opiniâtre; **—way,** progrès m.

heady, hedd´-i, a capiteux.

heal, hîle, v guérir; cicatriser; **—ing,** n guérison f. a curatif.

health, hêlts, n santé f.

healthy, hêlts´-i, a sain; (climate) salubre.

heap, hîpe, n tas m. v entasser; amonceler.

hear, hîre, v entendre; **—ing,** n (sense) ouïe f; (judicial) audience f; **—say,** ouï-dire m.

hearse, heurce, n corbillard m.

heart, hârte, n cœur m; courage m; **—attack,** n crise cardiaque f; **— broken,** a brisé de douleur; **—burn,** n

aigreurs d'estomac fpl; **—ily,** adv cordialement; **—less,** a sans cœur.

hearth, hârts, n foyer m.

heat, hîte, n chaleur f. v chauffer; **—er,** n réchaud m; radiateur m; **—ing,** chauffage m.

heath, hîts, n lande f; bruyère f.

heathen, hî´-dz'n, n & a païen, -enne m & f.

heather, hèdz´-eur, n bruyère f.

heave, hîve, v hisser; (sigh) pousser un soupir.

heaven, hèv´-'n, n ciel m; **—ly,** a céleste.

heaviness, hèv´-i-nesse, n poids m; pesanteur f; lourdeur f.

heavy, hèv´-i, a lourd; pesant.

hectic, hèk´-tik, a agité; mouvementé.

hedge, hêdje, n haie f; **—hog,** hérisson m.

heed, hîde, v tenir compte de. n attention f; **—ful*,** a attentif; **—less,** inattentif; étourdi.

heel, hîle, n talon m.

heifer, hèf´-'r, n génisse f.

height, hâïte, n hauteur f; (person) taille f.

heighten, hâï´-t'n, v rehausser; augmenter.

heinous*, hé´-neuce, a

atroce; abominable.

§heir, aire, n héritier m; **—ess,** héritière f.

helicopter, he´-li-cop-t'r, n hélicoptère.

hell, hêle, n enfer m; **—ish,** a infernal.

helm, hêlme, n barre f; (wheel) gouvernail m.

helmet, hêle´-mette, n casque m.

helmsman, hêlmze´-männe, n timonier m.

help, helpe, n aide f; (in distress) secours m. interj au secours! v aider; secourir; **—er,** n aide m; **—ful,** a utile; serviable; **—less,** impuissant.

hem, hemme, n ourlet m. v faire un ourlet; **—in,** cerner.

hemisphere, hemm´-i-sfire, n hémisphère m.

hemlock, hemm´-loque, n cigüe f.

hemorrhage, hém´ridje, n hémorragie f.

hemp, hemmpe, n chanvre m.

hen, henne, n poule f.

hence, hennce, adv d'ici; **—forth,** désormais.

her, heur, pron elle, la. poss a son; sa; ses.

herb, heurbe, n herbe f; **—alist,** herboriste m.

herd, heurde, n troupe f;

troupeau *m*. *v*
s'attrouper; **–sman,** *n*
pâtre *m*.

here, *hîre, adv* ici; **–about,**
près d'ici; **–after,** ci-
après; dorénavant; **–by,**
par ceci; **–in,** là-dedans;
ci-inclus; **–of,** de ceci;
–upon, là-dessus; **–with,**
avec ceci; ci-joint.

hereditary, he-redd´-i-ta-
ri, *a* héréditaire.

heresy, hèr´-i-ci, *n* hérésie
f.

heretic, hèr´-i-tique, *n*
hérétique *m & f*.

hermit, heur´-mitte, *n*
ermite *m*; **–age,** ermitage
m.

hernia, hêr´-ni-a, *n* hernie
f.

hero, hi´rau, *n* héros *m*.

heroic, hi-rau´-ique, *a*
héroïque.

heroine, hêr´-o-inn, *n*
héroïne *f*.

heroism, hêr´-o-izme, *n*
héroïsme *m*.

herring, hair´-inng, *n*
hareng *m*.

hers, heurze, *poss pron* le
sien, la sienne; les siens,
les siennes.

herself, heur-self´, *pron*
elle-même.

hesitate, hêz´-i-téte, *v*
hésiter.

hesitation, hêz-i-té´-ch'n,

n hésitation *f*.

hew, hioue, *v* couper;
(stone) tailler.

hiccup, hik´-eupe, *n*
hoquet *m*. *v* avoir le
hoquet.

hide, hâïde, *v* cacher. *n*
peau *f*; cuir *m*.

hideous*, hid´-i-euce, *a*
hideux.

hiding, hâï´-dinng *n* (*fig*)
raclée *f*.

hiding place, hâï´-dinng-
pléce, *n* cachette *f*.

high, hâï, *a* haut; élevé;
(game) faisandé; **–est,** le
plus élevé; le plus haut;
–fidelity, haute fidélité;
–way, grand-route *f*.

hilarity, hil-ăr´-i-ti, *n*
hilarité *f*.

hill, hile, *n* colline *f*;
(road) côte *f*.

hilly, hil´-i, *a* accidenté; à
pentes; montagneux.

hilt, hilte, *n* garde *f*;
(handle) poignée *f*.

him, himme, *pron* le, lui;
–self, lui-même.

hind, hâïnnde, *n* biche *f*. *a*
de derrière.

hinder, hinn´-d'r, *v*
empêcher; gêner.

hindmost, hâïnnd´-
mauste, *a* dernier.

hindrance, hinn´-
drannce, *n*
empêchement *m*;

obstacle *m*.

hinge, hinndje, *n*
charnière *f*; (door) gond
m.

hint, hinnte, *n*
insinuation *f*. *v* insinuer.

hip, hippe, *n* hanche *f*.

hire, hâïre, *v* louer. *n*
location *f*.

his, hize, *poss pron* le sien,
la sienne; les siens, les
siennes. *poss a* son, sa,
ses.

hiss, hice, *v* siffler. *n*
sifflement *m*.

historian, hice-to´-ri-
anne, *n* historien *m*.

historical, hice-to´-ri-k'l,
a historique.

history, hice´-tŏr-i, *n*
histoire *f*.

hit, hitte, *v* frapper;
(target, etc) toucher. *n*
coup *m*.

hitch, hitch, *n* (obstacle)
anicroche *f*; (*naut*)
amarre *f*. *v* (pull up)
remonter; (hook on)
attacher; **–hike,** *v* faire
de l'auto-stop.

hither, hidz´-'r, *adv* ici; par
ici; **–to,** *adv* jusqu'ici.

hive, hâïve, *n* ruche *f*.

hoard, haurde, *v* amasser;
(food, etc) accaparer; *n*
amas *m*.

hoarding, haurd´-inng, *n*
palissade *f*;

accumulation f.

hoarse, haurse, a rauque; enroué.

hoax, hauxe, n mystification f; tour m. v mystifier; jouer un tour.

hobble, hobb´-l, v clopiner; boitiller.

hobby, hobb´-i, n passe-temps favori m.

hock, hoque, n vin du Rhin m; (leg) jarret m.

hoe, hau, n binette f; houe f. v biner.

hog, hogue, n cochon m; porc m.

hogshead, hogz´-hédde, n tonneau m.

hoist, hoa'isste, v hisser.

hold, haulde, v tenir; contenir. n prise f; (ship) cale f; **–back,** v retenir; **–er,** n possesseur m, détenteur m; (shares, etc) actionnaire m & f; **–ing,** possession f; (com) participation f; **–on,** v tenir ferme; **–over,** ajourner.

hole, haule, n trou m.

holiday, holl´-i-dé, n jour de fête m; (leave) congé m.

holidays, holl´-i-dêze, npl vacances fpl.

holiness, hau´-li-nesse, n sainteté f.

hollow, holl´-au, n cavité

f. a creux. v creuser.

holly, holl´-i, n houx m.

holy, hau´-li, a saint, sacré; **–water,** n eau bénite f; **–week,** semaine sainte f.

homage, home´-idj, n hommage m.

home, hôme, n maison f; (circle) foyer m; chez soi m; (homeland) patrie f; **at –,** chez soi; **–less,** a sans abri; **–ly,** intime; (to be) **–sick,** (avoir) le mal du pays; **–work,** n devoirs mpl.

§**honest*,** onn´-este, a honnête; **–y,** n honnêteté f.

honey, honn´-i, n miel m; **–moon,** lune de miel f; **–suckle,** chèvrefeuille m.

§**honor,** onn´-eur, n honneur m. v honorer.

§**honorable,** onn´-eur-a-b'l, a honorable.

§**honorary,** onn´-eur-a-ri, a honoraire.

hood, houdd, n capuchon m; (vehicle) capote f.

hoodwink, houdd´-ouinnque, v tromper.

hoof, houff, n sabot m.

hook, houk, n crochet m; (large) croc m; (naut) gaffe f; (fish) hameçon m. v accrocher; **–and-**

eye, n agrafe f.

hoop, houpp, n cercle m; (toy) cerceau m.

hoot, houte, n (owl) hululement m; (derision) huée f; (motor) coup de klaxon m. v hululer; huer; (motor) klaxonner; **–er,** n klaxon m.

hop, hoppe, v sautiller. n saut m; (plant) houblon m.

hope, hôpe, v espérer. n espoir m; **–ful,** a encourageant; plein d'espoir; **–less,** sans espoir; inutile.

horizon, ho-râï´-zonne, n horizon m.

horizontal, hor-i-zonn´-t'l, a horizontal.

horn, hoarne, n corne f; (motor) klaxon m; (hunt) cor de chasse m.

hornet, hoar´-nette, n frelon m.

horrible, hor´-i-b'l, a horrible.

horrid*, hor´-ride, a horrible; affreux.

horrify, hor´-ri-fâï, v épouvanter; horrifier.

horror, hor´-rör, n horreur f.

horse, horce, n cheval m; **–back (on),** adv à cheval; **–hair,** n crin m; **––power,** puissance (f) en chevaux; —**radish,** n raifort m; —**shoe,** fer à cheval.

hose, hauze, n tuyau d'arrosage m.

hospitable, hoss´-pi-ta-b'l, a hospitalier.

hospital, hoss´-pi-t'l, n hôpital m.

host, hauste, n (friend) hôte m; (army) armée f; (sacrament) hostie f; foule f; —**ess,** hôtesse f.

hostage, hoss´-tidj, n otage m.

hostel, hoss´-tell, n pension f; **youth** —,n auberge de la jeunesse f.

hostile, hoss´-tâïle a hostile.

hot, hotte, a chaud; (food, sauces, etc) épicé; fort.

hotel, hô-tel´, n hôtel m.

hothouse, hott´-hâ-ouce, n serre f.

hound, hâ´ounnde, n chien de chasse m. v chasser; traquer.

§**hour,** âour, n heure f; —**ly,** adv d'heure en heure.

house, hâ´ouce, v loger. n maison f; —**hold,** maison f; —**keeper,** femme de charge f; —**work,** ménage m.

hovel, hov´-'l, n taudis m; bouge m.

hover, hov´-'r, v voltiger;

planer; hésiter.

hovercraft, hov´-'r-crâfte, n aéroglisseur m.

how, hâ´ou, adv comment; —**ever,** cependant; —**much, many?** combien?

howl, hâ´oule, v hurler. n hurlement m.

hub, hobbe, n moyeu m.

huddle, hod´-d'l, v se presser les uns contre les autres.

hue, hi´oue, n couleur f; (shade) nuance f.

hug, hogue, v étreindre. n étreinte f.

huge, hioudje, a immense; énorme; vaste.

hulk, holke, n (naut) ponton m.

hull, holle, n (naut) coque f.

hum, homme, v (insect) bourdonner; (engine) vrombir; (voice) fredonner. n bourdonnement m.

human*, hi´oue´-manne, a & n humain m.

humane, hi´oue-méne´, a humain; compatissant.

humanity, hi´oue-mă´-ni-ti, n humanité f.

humble, homm´-b'l, a humble. v humilier.

humidity, hi´oue-mid´-i-ti, n humidité f.

humiliate, hi´oue-mil´-i-éte, v humilier.

humiliation, hi´oue-mil-i-ét´-ch'n, n humiliation f.

humor, hi´oue´-meur, v complaire à. n (temper) humeur f; (wit) esprit m; humour m.

humorous*, hi´oue´-meur-euce, a comique.

hunch, honntche, n bosse f; —**back,** bossu m.

hundred, honn´-dredde, n & a cent m; —**th,** a & n centième m & f.

hunger, honng´-gueur, v avoir faim; désirer; n faim f.

hungry, honng´-gri, a affamé; **to be** —,v avoir faim.

hunt, honnte, v chasser. n chasse f.

hurdle, heur´-d'l, n claie f; (sport) obstacle m.

hurl, heurle, v lancer; précipiter.

hurricane, hor´-i-cane, n ouragan m.

hurry, hor´-i, v se dépêcher. n hâte f.

hurt, heurte, v faire mal; (feeling) blesser.

hurtful, heurte´foull, a nuisible; blessant.

husband, hoze´-bǎnnde, n mari m. v ménager.

hush! hoche, interj chut!

–up, v étouffer; n silence m.

husk, hossque, n (seeds) cosse f.

husky, hoss´-ki, a (voice) rauque; enroué.

hustle, hoss´-'l, v se presser; bousculer.

hut, hotte, n hutte f baraque f.

hutch, hotche, n cabane à lapins f; clapier m.

hyacinth, hâï´-a-sinnts, n jacinthe f.

hydrant, hâï´-drannte, n bouche d'incendie f.

hydraulic, hâï-drau´-lique, a hydraulique.

hydro, hâï´-drau, **–gen,** n hydrogène m; **–phobia,** hydrophobie f; **–plane,** hydravion m.

hygiene, hâï´-djeen, n hygiène f.

hygienic, hâï-djeenn´-ique, a hygiénique.

hymn, himme, n hymne f.

hyphen, hâï´-fenne, n trait d'union m.

hypocrisy, hip-o´-cri-si, n hypocrisie f.

hypocrite, hip´-ŏ-crite, n hypocrite m & f.

hypodermic, hâï-po-deur´-mique, a hypodermique.

hypothetical, hâï-po-tsè´-ti-k'l, a hypothétique;

supposé.

hysterical*, hice-tèr´-i-k'l, a hystérique.

I, âï, *pron* je; moi.

ice, âïce, *n* glace *f*. *v* glacer; frapper; **–berg,** *n* iceberg *m*; **–cream,** *n* glace *f*.

icicle, âï´-ci-k'l, *n* glaçon *m*.

icy, âï´-ci, *a* glacial; glacé.

idea, âï-dî´-*a*, *n* idée *f*.

ideal, âï-dî´-*eul*, *n* & *a* idéal *m* **–ize,** *v* idéaliser.

identical*, âï-denn´-ti-k'l, *a* identique.

identify, âï-denn´-ti-fâï, *v* identifier.

identity, âï-denn´-ti-ti, *n* identité *f*.

idiom, i´-di-ômme, *n* idiome *m*.

idiot, i´-di-*eute*, *n* idiot, -e *m* & *f*; **–ic,** *a* idiot.

idle, âï´-d'l, *v* flâner. *a* oisif, paresseux; **–ness,** *n* oisiveté *f*; **–r,** flâneur *m*.

idol, âï´-dôl, *n* idole *f*; **–ize,** *v* adorer.

if, if, *conj* si; **even –,** même si.

ignite, igue-nâïte´, *v* allumer; enflammer.

ignition, igue-ni´-ch'n, *n* (spark) allumage *m*; (car, etc) contact *m*.

ignoble, igue-nau´-b'l, *a* ignoble.

ignominious*, igue-nŏ-minn´-i-*euce*, *a* ignominieux.

ignominy, igue´-no-mi-ni, *n* ignominie *f*.

ignorance, igue´-nŏ-r'nce, *n* ignorance *f*.

ignorant, *a* ignorant.

ignore, igue-nore´, *v* ne pas tenir compte de; faire semblant de ne pas

voir.

ill, il, *a* malade; **–ness,** *n* maladie *f*.

illegal*, il-lî´-gal, *a* illégal.

illegible, il-lèdj´-i-b'l, *a* illisible.

illegitimate*, il-li-djitt´-i-méte, *a* illégitime.

illiterate, il-li´-*teur*-éte, *n* & *a* illettré, -e *m* & *f*.

illogical*, il-lodj´-i-k'l, *a* illogique.

illuminate, il-lioue´-mi-néte, *v* éclairer; illuminer.

illumination, il-lioue-mi-né´-ch'n, *n* illumination *f*; éclairage *m*.

illusion, il-lioue´-j'n, *n* illusion *f*.

illusory, il-lioue´-so-ri, *a* illusoire.

illustrate, il´-leuce-tréte, *v* illustrer; élucider.

illustration, il-leuce-tré´-ch'n, *n* illustration *f*.

illustrious, il-loss´-tri-*euce*, *a* illustre; célèbre.

image, imm´-idj, *n* image *f*; portrait *m*.

imagination, i-mădj-i-né´-ch'n, *n* imagination *f*.

imagine, i-mădj´-inne, *v* imaginer; s'imaginer.

imbecile, imm´-bi-sîle, *n* & *a* imbécile *m* & *f*.

imbue, imm-bioue´, *v* imprégner; pénétrer.

imitate, imm´-i-téte, *v* imiter.

immaculate*, imm-mǎque´-iou-léte, *a* immaculé; impeccable.

immaterial, imm-ma-tî-ri-*eul*, *a* sans importance; indifférent.

immature, imm-ma-tioure´, *a* pas mûr.

immeasurable, imm-mèj´-iou-ra-b'l, *a* incommensurable; infini.

immediate*, imm-mî´-di-éte, *a* immédiat.

immense, imm-mennce´, *a* immense.

immensity, imm-menn´-ci-ti, *n* immensité *f*.

immerge, imm-meurdje´, *v* immerger; plonger.

immigrant, imm´-mi-grannt, *n* & *a* immigrant, -e *m* & *f*.

immigrate, imm´-mi-gréte, *v* immigrer.

imminent, imm´-mi-nennte, *a* imminent.

immoderate*, imm-mod´-eur-éte, *a* immodéré.

immodest*, imm-mod´-este, *a* immodeste.

immoral*, imm-mor-´-'l,.*a* immoral.

immortal*, imm-mor-´-t'l, *a* immortel.

immortalize, imm-mor´-tal-âïze, *v* immortaliser.

immovable, imm-mouv´-a-b'l, *a* inébranlable.

immune, imm-mioune´, *a* immunisé.

immunity, imm-mioue´,ni-ti, *n* immunité *f*.

immunization, imm´-mioue-nâï-zé-ch'n, *n* immunisation *f*.

imp, immpe, *n* lutin *m*; (*fig*) petit diable *m*.

impact, imm´-pǎcte, *n* choc *m*; impact *m*.

impair, imm-paire´, *v* détériorer; abîmer.

impale, imm-péle´ *v* empaler.

impart, imm-pârte´, *v* communiquer.

impartial*, imm-pâr´-ch'l, *a* impartial.

impassable, imm-pǎss´-a-b'l, *a* impraticable.

impassive*, imm-pǎss´-ive, *a* impassible.

impatience, imm-pé´-ch'nce, *n* impatience *f*.

impatient, imm-pé´-ch'nt, *a* impatient.

impede, imm-pîde´, *v* empêcher; gêner.

impediment, imm-pèd´-i-'m'nt, *n* empêchement *m*.

impel, imm-pelle´, *v* forcer; pousser.

impending, imm-penn´-dinng, *a* imminent.

imperative, imm-pair´-a-tive, *n* & *a* impératif *m*.

imperfect*, imm-peur´-fecte, *n* & *a* imparfait *m*.

imperfection, imm-peur-fèque´-ch'n, *n* imperfection *f*.

imperial, imm-pî´-ri-*eul*, *a* impérial.

imperil, imm-pair´-il, *v* mettre en danger.

imperishable, imm-pair´-i-cha-b'l, *a* impérissable.

impersonal, imm-peur´-sŏ-n'l, *a* impersonnel.

impersonate, imm-peur´-sŏ-néte, *v* personnifier.

impertinence, imm-peur´-ti-n'nce, *n* impertinence *f*.

impertinent*, imm-peur´-ti-nennte, *a* impertinent.

impervious*, imm-peur´-vi-*euce*, *a* impénétrable.

impetuous*, imm-pett´-iou-*euce*, *a* impétueux.

impetus, imm-´pi-*teuce*, *n* impulsion *f*; élan *m*.

implant, imm-plânnte´, *v* implanter; inculquer.

implement, imm-´pli-m'nt, *n* instrument *m*; outil *m*.

implicate, imm´-pli-quéte, *v* impliquer.

implication, imm-pli-qué´-ch´n, *n* implication *f*; sous-entendu *m*.

implicit*, imm-pliss´-itte, *a* implicite.

implore, imm-plore´, *v* implorer.

imply, imm-plâï´, *v* impliquer; insinuer.

impolite*, imm-po-lâïte´, *a* impoli.

import, imm´-porte, *v* importer. *n* importation *f*; **–er,** importateur *m*.

importance, imm-por´-tannce, *n* importance *f*.

important, imm-por´-t'nt, *a* important.

impose, imm-pauze´, *v* imposer; **–upon,** abuser de.

imposing, imm-pauze´-inng, *a* imposant.

imposition, imm-po-zi´-ch'n, *n* abus *m*; (tax) impôt *m*.

impossibility, imm-poss´-i-bi-li-ti, *n* impossibilité *f*.

impossible, imm-poss´-i-b'l, *a* impossible.

impostor, imm-poss´-t'r, *n* imposteur *m*.

impotent, imm´-po-tennte, *a* impuissant.

impound, imm-pâ'ounnde´, *v* (animals) mettre en fourrière;

(law) déposer au greffe; saisir (des marchandises).

impoverish, imm-pov´-eur-iche, *v* appauvrir.

impracticable, imm-prăc´-ti-ca-b'l, *a* impraticable.

impregnable, imm-pregg´-na-b'l, *a* imprenable.

impregnate, imm-pregg´-néte, *v* imprégner; (fertilize) féconder.

impress, imm-presse´, *v* imprimer; (feelings) faire une impression; (make clear) faire bien comprendre; **–ion,** *n* impression *f*; **(stamp)** empreinte *f*; **–ive,** *a* frappant; émouvant.

imprint, imm-prinnte´, *n* marque *f*; empreinte *f*. *v* empreindre; (mind) imprimer.

imprison, imm-prize´-onn, *v* emprisonner; **–ment,** *n* emprisonnement *m*.

improbable, imm-prob´-a-b'l, *a* improbable.

improper, imm-prop´-'r, *a* inconvenant.

improve, imm-prouve´, *v* améliorer; se perfectionner; **–ment,** *n* amélioration *f*.

improvident, imm-prove´-i-dennte, *a* imprévoyant.

improvisations, imm´-pro-vâïz, *v* improviser.

improvise, imm´-prove-i-zé-ch´n, *n* improvisation *f*.

imprudent*, imm-proue´-dennte, *a* imprudent.

impudence, imm´-pioue-dennce, *n* insolence *f*.

impudent*, imm´-pioue-dennte, *a* insolent.

impulse, imm´-polse, *n* impulsion *f*; élan *m*.

impure*, imm-pioure´, *a* impur.

impurity, imm-pioue´-ri-ti, *n* impureté *f*.

impute, imm-pioute´, *v* imputer.

in, inne, *prep* dans; en; à; *adv* dedans.

inability, inn-a-bil´-i-ti, *n* impuissance *f*.

inaccessible, inn-ăc-sess´-i-b'l, *a* inaccessible.

inaccuracy, inn-ăc´-quiou-ra-ci, *n* inexactitude *f*.

inaccurate*, inn-ăc´-quiou-réte, *a* inexact.

inadequate, inn-ăd´-i-couéte, *a* insuffisant.

inadvertent*, inn-ăd´-veur´-tennte, *a* inattentif.

inane, inn-éne´, *a* inepte.

inanimate, inn-ănn´-i-méte, *a* inanimé.

inapt, inn-ăpte´, *a* inapte;
–itude, *n* inaptitude *f*.

inasmuch as, inn-*a*ze-
motche´ ăze, *conj* vu
que.

inaudible, inn-oa-di-b'l, *a*
inaudible.

inaugurate, inn-oa-
guioue-réte, *v* inaugurer.

inborn, inn´-boarne, *a*
inné.

incalculable, inn-cal´-
kiou-*la*-b'l, *a*
incalculable.

incapable, inn-qué´-*pa*-b'l,
a incapable.

incapacitate, inn-ca-păss´-
i-ti'ete, *v* rendre
incapable.

incapacity, inn-ca-păss´-i-
ti, *n* incapacité *f*.

incarnation, inn-câr-né´-
ch'n, *n* incarnation *f*.

incautious*, inn-cô´-
cheuce, *a* imprudent.

incense, inn-cennse´, *n*
encens *m*. *v* provoquer.

incentive, inn-cenn´-tive,
n motif *m*; stimulant *m*.

incessant, inn-cess´-
annte, *a* incessant.

inch, inntche, *n* pouce
anglais *m*.

incident, inn´-ci-dennt, *n*
incident *m*; –al, *a*
fortuit.

incision, inn-ci´-j'n, *n*
incision *f*.

incite, inn-sâïte´, *v*
inciter.

inclination, inn-cli-né´-
ch'n, *n* inclination *f*;
(disposition) penchant
m.

incline, inn´-clâïne, *n*
(slope) pente *f*. *v*
incliner.

include, inn-cloude´, *v*
comprendre; renfermer.

inclusive*, inn-cooue´-
cive, *a* inclusif; compris.

incoherent, inn-co-hî´-
rennte, *a* incohérent.

income, inn´-comme, *n*
revenu *m*; rentes *fpl*;
–tax, impôt sur le
revenu *m*.

incoming, inn´-comm-
inng, *a* entrant;
nouveau.

incomparable, inn-
comm´-pa-*ra*-b'l, *a*
incomparable.

incompatible, inn-comm-
patt´-i-b'l, *a*
incompatible.

incompetent, inn-comm´-
pi-tennte, *a*
incompétent.

incomplete*, inn-comm-
plîte´, *a* incomplet.

incomprehensible, inn-
comm-pré-henn´-si-b'l,
a incompréhensible.

inconceivable, inn-cŏnn-
cî´-*va*-b'l, *a*
inconcevable.

inconclusive, inn-cŏnn-
cloue´-cive, *a*
inconcluant.

incongruous*, inn-
conng´-grou-*eu*ce, *a*
incongru.

inconsiderable, inn-cŏnn-
si-*deur-a*-b'l, *a*
insignifiant.

inconsiderate, inn-cŏnn-
si-*deur*-éte, *a* sans
égards.

inconsistent*, inn-cŏnn-
ciss´-tennte, *a* illogique.

inconsolable, inn-cŏnn-
sol´-*a*-b'l, *a*
inconsolable.

inconstant, inn-conn´-
stannte, *a* inconstant.

inconvenience, inn-cŏnn-
vî´-ni-ennce, *v*
déranger; gêner. *n*
dérangement *m*;
inconvénient *m*.

inconvenient, inn-cŏnn-
v´-ni-ennte, *a*
incommode.

incorporate, inn-kor´-po-
réte, *v* incorporer.

incorrect*, inn-cŏr-recte´,
a inexact; (behavior)
incorrect.

incorrigible, inn-cor´-i-
dji-b'l, *a* incorrigible.

increase, inn-crîce´, *v*
augmenter; accroître. *n*
augmentation *f*;

accroissement *m*.

incredible, inn-crèd´-i-b'l, *a* incroyable.

incredulous, inn-crèd´-iou-leuce, *a* incrédule.

incriminate, inn-crimm´-inn-éte, *v* incriminer.

incubate, inn´-kioue-béte, *v* couver; incuber.

incubation, inn´-kioue-bé-ch'n, *n* incubation *f*.

incubator, inn´-kioue-bé-teur, *n* couveuse *f*.

inculcate, inn´-kol-quéte, *v* inculquer.

incur, inn-queur´, *v* encourir; (expenses) faire.

incurable, inn-kiou´-ra-b'l, *a* incurable.

indebted, inn-dett´-èdde, *a* endetté; redevable.

indecent, inn-dî´-cennte, *a* indécent.

indecision, inn-di-si´-j'n, *n* indécision *f*.

indecisive, inn-di-sâï´-cive, *a* indécis.

indeed, inn-dîde´, *adv* en effet; vraiment.

indefatigable, inn-di-fätt´-i-gǎ-b'l, *a* infatigable.

indefensible, inn-di-fenn´-si-b'l, *a* indéfendable.

indefinite*, inn-dèf´-i-nitte, *a* indéfini.

indelible, inn-dèl´-i-b'l, *a*

indélébile; ineffaçable.

indemnify, inn-demm´-ni-fâï, *v* indemniser.

indemnity, inn-demm´-ni-ti, *n* indemnité *f*.

independence, inn-di-penn´-dennce, *n* indépendance *f*.

independent*, inn-di-penn´-dennte, *a* indépendant.

indescribable, inn-di-scrâï´-ba-b'l, *a* indescriptible.

indestructible, inn-di-strok´-ti-b'l, *a* indestructible.

index, inn´-dexe, *n* table des matières *f*; index *m*.

index finger, inn´-dexe-finng´-gueur, *n* index *m*.

indicate, inn´-di-quéte, *v* indiquer.

indication, inn-di-qué´-ch'n, *n* indication *f*.

indicator, inn´-di-qué-teur, *n* indicateur *m*.

indict, inn-dâïte´, *v* poursuivre.

indifference, inn-dif´-eur-ennce, *n* indifférence *f*.

indifferent*, inn-dif´-eur-ennte, *a* indifférent.

indigestible, inn-di-djess´-ti-b'l, *a* indigeste.

indigestion, inn-di-djess´-ti-'n, *n* indigestion *f*.

indignant, inn-dig´-

nannte, *a* indigné.

indignity, inn-dig´-ni-ti, *n* indignité *f*.

indigo, inn´-di-go, *n* indigo *m*.

indirect*, inn-di-recte´, *a* indirect.

indiscreet*, inn-disscrîte´, *a* indiscret.

indiscriminate, inn-disscrimm´-i-néte, *a* sans discernement; –ly, *adv* indistinctement.

indispensable, inn-disspenn´-sa-b'l, *a* indispensable.

indisposed, inn-disspauz'd´, *a* indisposé.

indisputable, inn-disspiou´-ta-b'l, *a* incontestable.

indistinct*, inn-disstinng´kt´, *a* indistinct.

indistinguishable, inn-diss-tinng´-gouich-a-b'l, *a* imperceptible; indistinct.

individual*, inn-di-vid´-iou-al, *a* individuel. *n* individu *m*.

indolent, inn´-dǒ-lennte, *a* indolent.

indoor, inn-daur´, *a* d'intérieur.

indoors, inn-daurze´, *adv* à l'intérieur; à la maison.

induce, inn-diouce´, *v* provoquer; causer;

induire.

inducement, inn-diouce´-m'nt. n stimulant m; motif m.

indulge, inn-doldje´, v gâter; se livrer à; s'abandonner à.

indulgent*, inn-dol´-djennte, a indulgent.

industrial*, inn-doss´-tri-al, a industriel.

industrious*, inn-doss´-tri-euce, a laborieux.

industry, inn´-doss-tri, n industrie f.

inebriated, inn-i´-bri-é-tedde, a ivre.

ineffective*, inn-èf-fèque´-tive, a inefficace.

inefficient*, inn-èf-fich´-ennte, a inefficace; incapable.

inept, inn-epte´, a inepte; absurde.

inequality, inn-i-couol´-i-ti, n inégalité f.

inert, inn-eurte´, a inerte.

inestimable, inn-ess´-ti-ma-b'l, a inestimable.

inevitable, inn-èv´-i-ta-b'l, a inévitable.

inexcusable, inn-èks-kiou'é-za-b'l, a inexcusable.

inexhaustible, inn-èks-hauss´-ti-b'l, a inépuisable.

inexpedient, inn-èks-pî´-di-ennte, a inopportun.

inexpensive, inn-èks-penn´-cive, a bon marché.

inexperienced, inn-èks-pî´-ri-enncd, a inexpérimenté; sans expérience.

inexplicable, inn-èks-pli-ka-b'l, a inexplicable.

inexpressible, inn-èks-press´-si-b'l, a inexprimable.

infallible, inn-fàll´-i-b'l, a infaillible.

infamous, inn´-fa-meuce, a infâme.

infancy, inn´-fann-ci, n première; enfance f; (law) minorité f.

infant, inn´-fannte, n enfant m; enbasâge; (law) mineur, -e m & f.

infantry, inn´-fann-tri, n infanterie f.

infatuation, inn-fàtt-iou-é´-ch'n, n engouement.

infect, inn-fèkte´, v infecter; **–ious*,** a contagieux.

infer, inn-feur´, v inférer; déduire.

inference, inn´-feur-'nce, n déduction f.

inferior, inn-fi´-ri-eur, n & a inférieur m.

infernal*, inn-feur-n'l, a infernal.

infest, inn-feste´, v infester.

infidel, inn´-fi-d'l, n & a infidèle m & f.

infiltrate, inn´-file-tréte, v infiltrer; imprégner.

infinite*, inn´-fi-nite, a infini.

infirm, inn-feurme´, a infirme; maladif.

infirmary, inn-feurm´-a-ri, n infirmerie f.

inflame, inn-fléme´, v enflammer.

inflammable, inn-flàmm´-a-b'l, a inflammable.

inflammation, inn-fla-mé´-ch'n, n inflammation f.

inflate, inn-fléte, v gonfler; (prices) hausser.

inflation, inn-flé´-ch'n, n inflation f.

inflexible, inn-flèk´-si-b'l, a inflexible.

inflict, inn-flickte´, v infliger.

influence, inn´-flou-ennce, n influence f. v influencer.

influential, inn-flou-enn´-ch'l, a influent; **to be –,** avoir de l'influence.

influenza, inn-flou-enn´-za, n grippe f.

inform, inn-foarme´, v informer; **–al,** a sans cérémonie; **–ation,** n renseignements *mpl.*

infrequent, inn-frî´-
couennte, *a* infréquent,
rare.

infringe, inn-frinndje´, *v*
empiéter; transgresser.

infringement, inn-
frinndje´-m'nt, *n*
infraction *f.*

infuriate, inn-fiou-ri-éte,
v rendre furieux.

infuse, inn-fiouze´, *v*
verser; (tea, etc) infuser.

ingenious*, inn-djî´-ni-
euce, a ingénieux.

ingenuity, inn-dji-niou´-i-
ti, *n* ingénuité *f.*

ingot, inng´-gŏtte, *n*
lingot *m.*

ingrained, inn-grénnde´, *a*
enraciné; invétéré.

ingratiate, inn-gré´-chi-
éte, *v* –oneself with, se
faire bien voir de
quelqu'un.

ingratitude, inn-grätt´-i-
tioude, *n* ingratitude *f.*

ingredient, inn-grî´-di-
ennte, *n* ingrédient *m.*

inhabit, inn-hăb´-itte, *v*
habiter; –able, *a*
habitable; –ant, *n*
habitant m.

inhale, inn-héle´, *v*
aspirer; (smoke) avaler.

inherent*, inn-hî´-r'nt, *a*
inhérent.

inherit, inn-hér´-itte, *v*

hériter; –ance, *n*
succession *f;* héritage *m.*

inhibit, inn-hi-bitte, *v*
empêcher; inhiber;
–ion, *n* inhibition *f.*

inhospitable, inn-hoss´-
pit-a-b'l, *a* inhospitalier.

inhuman*, inn-hioue´-
m'n, *a* inhumain.

iniquitous, inn-ik´-oui-
teuce, a inique.

initial, inn-i´-ch'l, *n*
initiale *f. a** initial;
premier.

initiate, inn-i´-chi-éte, *v*
initier; commencer.

inject, inn-djecte´, *v*
injecter; –ion, *n*
injection *f;* piqûre *f.*

injudicious*, inn-djiou-
dich´-euce, *a* peu
judicieux.

injunction, inn-djonnk´-
ch'n, *n* injonction *f.*

injure, inn-djioure, *v*
blesser; abîmer; nuire à.

injurious*, inn-djioue´-ri-
euce, a nuisible.

injury, inn´-djeur-i, *n*
blessure *f;* tort m.

injustice, inn-djoss´-tice,
n injustice *f.*

ink, inng´-k, *n* encre *f;*
–stand, *n* encrier m.

inlaid, inn-léde´, *a*
incrusté; (wood)
marqueté.

inland, inn´-lănnde, *n & a*

intérieur m.

inlet, inn´-lette, *n* entrée
f; (geog) bras de mer *m.*

inmate, inn´-méte, *n*
pensionnaire *m & f;*
interné *m.*

inmost, inn´-mauste, *a* le
plus profond.

inn, inn, *n* auberge *f;*
–keeper, aubergiste *m.*

inner, inn´-'r, *a* intérieur;
secret.

innocent, inn´-o-cennte,
a innocent.

innocuous*, inn-o´-kiou-
euce, a inoffensif.

innovation, inn-no-vé´-
ch'n, *n* innovation *f.*

innumerable, inn-nioue´-
meur-a-b'l, *a*
innombrable.

inoculate, inn-o´-kiou-
léte, *v* inoculer.

inoffensive, inn-o-fenn´-
cive, *a* inoffensif.

inopportune, inn-opp´-or-
tioune, *a* inopportun.

inquest, inn´-coueste, *n*
enquête *f.*

inquire, inn-couâire, *v*
demander; s'informer.

inquiry, inn-couâ´i´-ri, *n*
demande *f;* enquête *f.*

Inquisition, inn-couiz-i´-
ch'n, *n* Inquisition *f.*

inquisitive*, inn-couiz´-i-
tive, *a* curieux.

insane, inn-séne´, *a* fou;

dément.

insanity, inn-sann´-i-ti, n folie f; démence f.

insatiable, inn-sé´-chi-a-b'l, a insatiable.

inscription, inn-scripe´-ch'n, n inscription f.

insect, inn´-secte, n insecte m.

insecure, inn-ci-kioure´, a peu sûr; insécurisé; incertain; peu solide.

insensible, inn-senn´-si-b'l, a insensible; (unconscious) sans connaissance.

inseparable, inn-sép´-a-ra-b'l, a inséparable.

insert, inn-seurte´, v insérer; introduire; –ion, n insertion f; (advertisement) annonce f.

inside, inn-sâïde´, n intérieur m. a intérieur. adv en dedans.

insidious*, inn-si´-di-euce, a insidieux.

insignificant, inn-sigg-nif´-i-k'nt, a insignifiant.

insincere*, inn-sinn-cire´, a faux.

insinuate, inn-sinn´-iou-éte, v insinuer.

insipid*, inn-sipp´-idde, a insipide; fade.

insist, inn-sisste´, v exiger;

insister.

insolence, inn´-sŏ-lennce, n insolence f.

insolent, inn´-sŏ-lennte, a insolent.

insolvent, inn-soll´-vennte, a insolvable.

inspect, inn-specte´, v inspecter; –ion n inspection f; –or, inspecteur m.

inspiration, inn-spi-ré´-ch'n, n inspiration f.

inspire, inn-spâïre, v inspirer; –d, a inspiré.

install, inn-stoale´, v installer; (mech) monter; –ation, n installation f; montage m.

installment, inn-stoale´-m'nt, n versement partiel m; (of story etc.) épisode m; **to pay by –s,** v payer à tempérament.

instance, inn´-stannce, n exemple m; cas m.

instant, inn´-stannte, n instant m. a (date) courant; –aneous*, instantané; –ly, adv à l'instant.

instead of, inn-stedde´ ove, adv au lieu de.

instep, inn´-steppe, n cou-de-pied m.

instigate, inn´-sti-guéte, v inciter.

instill, inn-stille´, v

instiller.

instinct, inn´-stinng-kt, n instinct m.

institute, inn´-sti-tioute, n institut m. v instituer.

institution, inn-sti-tiou´-ch'n, n institution f; établissement m.

instruct, inn-strocte´, v instruire; charger de.

instruction, inn-stroc´-ch'n, n instruction f.

instrument, inn-strou-m'nt, n instrument m.

insubordinate, inn-seub-oar´-din-néte, a insubordonné.

insufferable, inn-sof´-feur-a-b'l, a insupportable.

insufficient, inn-sof-fi´-chennte, a insuffisant.

insulation, inn-siou-lé´-ch'n, n isolation f; (heat, pipes, etc) calorifugeage m.

insult, inn-sollté, v insulter. n insulte f.

insurance, inn-chou´-r'nce, n assurance f.

insure, inn-choure´, v assurer.

insurrection, inn-seur-rèque´-ch'n, n insurrection f.

integrate, inn´-teur-grète, v rendre entier; intégrer.

intellect, inn´-teur-lecte, n intelligence f; intellect

m; **–ual,** *a* intellectuel.

intelligence, inn-tel´-li-dj'nce, *n* intelligence *f*.

intelligent*, inn-tel´-li-dj'nt, *a* intelligent.

intemperate*, inn-temm´-peur-éte, *a* immodéré.

intend, inn-tennde´, *v* se proposer; avoir l'intention de.

intense*, inn-tennce´, *a* intense; vif.

intent, inn-tennte´, *n* dessein *m*. *a* appliqué; **–ion,** *n* intention *f*; **–ionally,** *adv* exprès.

inter, inn-teur´, *v* enterrer; **–ment,** *n* enterrement *m*.

inter, inn´-teur, **–cept,** *v* intercepter; **–change,** échanger; **–course,** *n* commerce *m*; relations *fpl*; rapports *mpl*; **–fere,** *v* se mêler de; **–ference,** *f*; (radio) bruit parasite *m*; **–lude,** intermède *m*; **–mediate,** *a* intermédiaire; **–mingle,** *v* s'entremêler; **–mittent,** *a* intermittent; **–mix,** *v* entremêler; **–national,** *a* international; **–rupt,** *v* interrompre; **–val,** intervalle *m*; (theater) entracte *m*; **–vene,** *v* intervenir; **–vention,** *n*

intervention *f*; **–view,** entrevue *f*; (for news) interview *f*. *v* interviewer.

interest, inn´-teur-reste, intérêt *m*. *v* intéresser; **–ing,** *a* intéressant.

interior, inn-tî´-ri-eur, *n* & *a* intérieur *m*.

intern, inn-teurne´, *v* interner.

internal*, inn-teur-n'l, *a* interne.

interpret, inn-teur´-prette, *v* interpréter.

internet, inn-teur´-naite, *n* internet *m*.

interpreter, inn-teur´-prett-'r, *n* interprète *m*.

interrogate, inn-terr´-ŏ-guéte, *v* interroger.

intestate, inn-tess´-téte, *a* intestat.

intestine, inn-tess´-tinne, *n* intestin *m*.

intimacy, inn´-ti-ma-ci. *n* intimité *f*.

intimate, inn´-ti-méte, *v* signaler; donner à entendre. *a** intime.

intimation, inn-ti-mé´-ch'n, *n* indice *m*; avis *m*.

intimidate, inn-ti´-mi-déte, *v* intimider.

into, inn´-tou, *prep* dans; en.

intolerable, inn-tol´-eur-a-b'l, *a* intolérable.

intoxicate, inn-toks´-i-quéte, *v* enivrer; griser.

intrepid*, inn-trepp´-ide, *a* intrépide.

intricate*, inn´-tri-quéte, *a* compliqué; embrouillé.

intrigue, inn-trîgue´, *n* intrigue *f*. *v* intriguer.

intriguing, inn-trî´-guinng, *a* intrigant.

intrinsic, inn-trinn´-sique, *a* intrinsèque.

introduce, inn-trŏ-diouce´, *v* introduire; présenter.

introductory, inn-trŏ-doc´-tŏ-ri, *a* préliminaire.

intrude, inn-troude´, *v* s'imposer; déranger; être de trop.

intuition, inn-tiou-i´-ch'n, *n* intuition *f*.

inundate, inn´-ŏnn-déte, *v* inonder.

inundation, inn-ŏnn-dé´-ch'n, *n* inondation *f*.

inure, inn-ioure´, *v* endurcir; accoutumer.

invade, inn-véde´, *v* envahir; **–r,** *n* envahisseur *m*.

invalid, inn´-va-lide, *n* malade *m* & *f*; infirme *m* & *f*.

invalid, inn-văl´-ide, *a* nul; non valable.

invaluable, inn-văl´-iou-a-b'l, *a* inestimable.

invariable, inn-vé´-ri-a-b'l, *a* invariable.

invasion, inn-vé´-j'n, *n* invasion *f*.

inveigle, inn-vî´-g'l, *v* séduire, attirer dans.

invent, inn-vennte´, *v* inventer; **–ion,** *n* invention *f*; **–or,** inventeur *m*.

inventory, inn´-venn-to-ri, *n* inventaire *m*.

invert, inn-veurte´, *v* intervertir; renverser.

invest, inn-vesst´, *v* investir; (money) placer; **–ment,** *n* placement *m*; **–or,** épargnant *m*.

investigate, inn-vess´-ti-guéte, *v* rechercher; faire une enquête.

inveterate, inn-vett´-eur-éte, *a* invétéré.

invigorate, inn-vig´-ŏr-éte, *v* fortifier.

invincible, inn-vinn´-ci-b'l, *a* invincible.

invisible, inn-viz´-i-b'l, *a* invisible.

invitation, inn-vi-té´-ch'n, *n* invitation *f*.

invite, inn-vâîte´, *v* inviter.

invoice, inn´-voa'ice, *n* facture *f*.

invoke, inn-vauke´, *v* invoquer.

involuntary, inn-vol´-onn-ta-ri, *a* involontaire.

involve, inn-volve´, *v* impliquer; entraîner; **–d,** *a* compliqué.

inward*, inn´-oueurde, *a* intérieur.

iodine, âî´-o-dine, *n* iode *m*.

ire, âîre, *n* courroux *m*; ire *f*; colère *f*.

iris, âï´-rice, *n* iris *m*.

irksome, eurk´-somme, *a* ennuyeux; pénible.

iron, âî´-eurne, *n* fer *m*; (flat) fer à repasser *m*. *a* de fer. *v* repasser.

ironic, âî-ronn´-ik, *a* ironique.

irony, âï´-rŏnn-i, *n* ironie *f*.

irreconcilable, ir-rèk-ŏnn-sâï´-la-b'l, *a* irréconciliable; incompatible.

irregular*, ir-regg´-iou-l'r, *a* irrégulier.

irrelevant, ir-rèl´-i-v'nt, *a* hors de propos.

irreproachable, ir-ri-prautch´-a-b'l, *a* irréprochable.

irresistible, ir-ri-ziss´-ti-b'l, *a* irrésistible.

irrespective, ir-ress-pèk´-tive, *adv* sans tenir compte de.

irresponsible, ir-ress-ponn´-ci-b'l, *a* irresponsable.

irretrievable, ir-ri-trî´-va-b'l, *a* irréparable.

irrigate, ir´-ri-guéte, *v* irriguer; arroser.

irritable, ir´-ri-ta-b'l, *a* irritable; irascible.

irritate, ir´-ri-téte, *v* irriter; agacer.

island, âî´-lannde, *n* île *f*; **–er,** *n* insulaire *m & f*.

isle, âîlle, *n* île *f*; (islet) îlot *m*.

isolate, âî´-sŏ-léte, *v* isoler.

isolation, âï-sŏ-lé´-ch'n, *n* isolement *m*.

issue, i´-chiou, *n* progéniture *f*; (edition) numéro *m*; (result) issue *f*; résultat *m*. *v* émettre; publier; émaner; donner; délivrer.

isthmus, iss´-meuce, *n* isthme *m*.

it, itt, *pron* il, elle; le; la; lui; il; cela.

italic, i-tal´-ique, *n & a* (type) italique *m*.

itch, itch, *v* démanger. *n* démangeaison *f*.

item, âï´-temme, *n* article *m*; chose *f*; (news) article *m*.

its, itse, *poss pron* le sien,

la sienne; les siens, les siennes. *poss a* son; sa; ses.

itself, itt-self´, *pron* lui-même, elle-même.

ivory, âï´-*veur*-i, *n* ivoire *m.*

ivy, âï´-vi, *n* lierre *m.*

jeopardize, djèp´-*eur*-dâïze, *v* compromettre.

jeopardy, djèp´-*eur*-di, *n* danger *m*; péril *m*.

jerk, djeurque, *v* donner une secousse. *n* secousse *f*.

jersey, djeur´-zi, *n* jersey *m*; tricot *m*.

jest, djesste, *n* plaisanterie *f*. *v* plaisanter.

jester, djess´-t´r, *n* farceur *m*; (court) bouffon *m*.

jet, djett, *n* (mineral) jais *m*; (liquid) jet *m*; (aircraft) avion à réaction *m*.

jettison, djett´-i-sonn, *v* jeter à la mer.

jetty, djett´-i, *n* jetée *f*.

Jew, djioue, *n* Juif *m*; –ish, *a* juif, -ve.

jewel, djioue´-l, *n* bijou *m*; joyau *m*; –er, bijoutier *m*; –ry, bijouterie *f*.

jig, djigue, *n* gigue *f*.

jilt, djillte, *v* délaisser; plaquer.

jingle, djinng´-g'l, *v* tinter. *n* tintement *m*.

job, djobbe, *n* situation *f*; emploi *m*; (task) besogne *f*; travail *m*; job *m*.

jockey, djok´-i, *n* jockey *m*.

jocular, djok´-iou-l'r, *a*

jabber, jăb´-'r, *v* jacasser. *n* baragouinage *m*.

jack, djăque, *n* (*mech*) cric *m*.

jackal, djăk´-oale, *n* chacal *m*.

jacket, djăk´-ette, *n* veston *m*; veste *f*; jaquette *f*.

jade, djéde, *n* (stone) jade *m*.

jaded, djé´-dédde, *a* éreinté.

jag, djágue, *n* brèche *f*. *v* ébrécher –ged, *a* entaillé; dentelé.

jail, djéle, *n* prison *f*; –er, geôlier *m*.

jam, djămme, *n* (conserve) confiture *f*; (traffic) embouteillage *m*. *v* (lock) coincer; (crowd) presser.

January, djănn´-iou-èr-i, *n* janvier *m*.

jar, djârre, *n* pot *m*; bocal *m*; (shock) secousse *f*. *v* agacer.

jaundice, djoann´-dice, *n* jaunisse *f*.

jaw, djoa, *n* mâchoire *f*.

jay, djé, *n* geai *m*.

jealous*, djèl´-*euce*, *a* jaloux; –y, *n* jalousie *f*.

jeer, djire, *v* railler. *n* raillerie *f*.

jelly, djèl´-i, *n* gelée *f*; –fish, méduse *f*.

jovial.

join, djoa´ine, *v* joindre; unir; (club) devenir membre; **–in,** prendre part à.

joiner, djoa´inn´-r, *n* menuisier *m*.

joint, djoa´innte, *n* joint *m*; (anatomy) articulation *f*; (meat) quartier *m*; (roast) rôti *m*. *a* uni, collectif.

jointly, djoa´innt´-li, *adv* conjointement.

joke, djauke, *n* plaisanterie *f*; blague *f*. *v* plaisanter.

joker, djauk´-´r, *n* farceur *m*.

jolly, djoll´-i, *a* gai.

jolt, djault, *n* cahot *m*; chôc. *v* cahoter; secouer.

jostle, djoss´-´l, *v* bousculer.

journal, djeur´-n'l, *n* journal *m*; **–ism,** journalisme *m*; **–ist,** journaliste *m* & *f*.

journey, djeur´-ni, *n* voyage *m*. *v* voyager.

jovial*, djau´-vi-al, *a* jovial; joyeux.

joy, djoa´i, *n* joie *f*; **–ful*,** *a* joyeux.

jubilant, djoue´-bi-l'nt, *a* réjoui.

judge, djodje, *n* juge *m*; connaisseur *m*. *v* juger.

judgment, djodje´-m'nt, *n* jugement *m*. **–day,** jour du jugement.

judicial*, djoue-di´-ch'l, *a* judiciaire.

judicious*, djoue-di´-cheuce, *a* judicieux.

jug, djogue, *n* cruche *f*; pot *m*; (large) broc *m*.

juggle, djogg´-g'l, *v* jongler.

juggler, djogg´-l'r, *n* jongleur *m*.

juice, djouce, *n* jus *m*; (botanical) suc *m*.

juicy, djoue´-ci, *a* juteux; succulent.

July, djou-lâï´, *n* juillet *m*.

jumble, djomm´-b'l, *n* fouillis *m*. *v* emmêler.

jump, djommpe, *v* sauter. *n* saut *m*.

junction, djonngk´-ch'n, *n* jonction *f*; (railroad) embranchement *m*; (road) carrefour *m*.

juncture, djonngk´-tioure, *n* conjoncture *f*.

June, djoune, *n* juin *m*.

jungle, djonng´-g'l, *n* jungle *f*.

junior, djoue´-ni-*eur*, *n* & *a* cadet *m*. *a* jeune.

juniper, djoue´-ni-p'r, *n* genièvre *m*.

jurisdiction, djoue-rice-dik´-ch'n, *n* juridiction *f*.

juror, djoue´-*reur*, *n* juré *m*.

jury, djoue´-ri, *n* jury *m*.

just, djosste, *a* & *adv* juste; **–ice,** *n* justice *f*; **–ification,** justification *f*; **–ify,** *v* justifier; **–ly,** *adv* justement.

jut, djotte, *v* faire saillie.

juvenile, djoue´-vi-nâïle, *a* d'enfants; jeune.

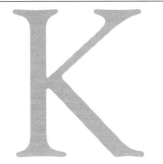

kangaroo, kănng´-*ga*-roo, n kangourou m.

keel, kîle, n quille f.

keen*, kînne, a ardent; (blade) affilé.

keenness, kîn´-nesse, n acuité f; empressement m.

keep, kîpe, n entretien m. v garder; maintenir; tenir; rester; **–back,** retenir; **–off,** éviter; se tenir éloigné de; **–up,** maintenir; **–er,** n gardien m; **–sake,** souvenir m.

keg, quègue, n caque f; barillet m.

kennel, quènn´-´l, n chenil m.

kernel, queur´-n'l, n noyau m; amande f.

kettle, quètt´-´l, n bouilloire f; **–drum,** timbale f.

key, kî, n clef f; (music) clef f; (piano) touche f; **–board,** clavier m; **–hole,** trou de serrure m.

kick, kique, v donner un coup de pied; ruer. n coup de pied m; (horse) ruade f.

kid, kidde, n chevreau m. fam gosse m & f.

kidnap, kidd´-năppe, v enlever; kidnapper.

kidney, kidd´-ni, n rein m; (cookery) rognon m.

kill, kille, v tuer.

kiln, kilne, n four m.

kin, kinne, n parenté f. a allié; **–dred,** de même nature.

kind, kâïnnde, n espèce f; genre m; sorte f. a* bon; aimable; **–ness,** n bonté f.

kindergarten, kinn´-d'r-gar-t'n, n jardin d'enfants m; école maternelle f.

kindle, kinn´-d'l, v allumer; (fig) enflammer.

king, kinng, n roi m; **–dom,** royaume m.

kipper, kipp´-*eur*, n hareng fumé m.

kiss, kisse, n baiser m. v embrasser.

kit, kitte, n équipement m; trousse f.

kitchen, kitt´-chine, n cuisine f.

kite, kâïte, n cerf-volant m; (bird) milan m.

kitten, kit´-t'n, n chaton m.

knack, năque, n don m; talent m; truc m.

knapsack, năpp´-săque, n havresac m.

knave, néve, n coquin m; (cards) valet m.

knead, nîde, v pétrir.

knee, nî, n genou m; **–cap,** rotule f.

kneel, nîle, v s'agenouiller; se mettre à genoux.

knell, nêle, n glas m.

knife, nâïfe, n couteau m; **pen–,** canif m.

knight, nâïte, *n* chevalier
m; (chess) cavalier *m*.

knit, nitte, *v* tricoter;
–**ting,** *n* tricot *m*.

knob, nobbe, *n* bouton *m*;
poignée.

knock, noque, *n* coup *m. v*
frapper; –**against,**
heurter; –**down,**
renverser; –**er,** *n* (door)

knot, not, *n* nœud *m. v*
nouer.

knotty, nott´-i, *a* noueux;
(*fig*) embrouillé.

know, nau, *v* savoir;
connaître.

knowledge, noll´-idj, *n*
connaissance *f*; savoir *m*.

knuckle, nok´-'l, *n*
articulation *f*; jointure *f*.

label, lé´-b'l, n étiquette f. v mettre une étiquette.

labor, lé´-beur, v travailler; peiner. n travail m; labeur m; **–er,** travailleur m; a noeuvre.

laboratory, lăb´-o-ra-to-ri, n laboratoire m.

laborious*, la-bau´-ri-euce, a laborieux; pénible.

lace, léce, n dentelle f; (shoe, etc) lacet m. v lacer.

lacerate, lăss´-eur-éte, v lacérer.

lack, lăque, v manquer de. n manque m.

lacquer, lăk´-'r, n laque f. v laquer.

lad, lădde, n garcon m; jeune homme m.

ladder, lădd´-'r, n échelle f.

ladle, lé´-d'l, n louche f. v servir.

lady, lé´-di, n dame f; **–bug,** coccinelle f; (fam) bête à bon Dieu f.

lag, lăgue, v traîner; rester en arrière.

lagoon, la-goune´, n lagune f.

lair, lère, n repaire m.

lake, léque, n lac m.

lamb, lămme, n agneau m; **leg of –,** gigot m.

lame, léme, a boiteux. v estropier.

lament, la-mennte´, v se lamenter. n plainte f.

lamp, lămmpe, n lampe f; (street lamp) réverbère m; (electric bulb) ampoule électrique f.

lance, lânnce, n lance f;

(med) bistouri m. v (med) ouvrir au bistouri.

land, lânnde, n terre f; (home) pays m. v débarquer; (aircraft) atterrir; **–ing,** débarquement m; (quay) débarcadère m; (stairs) palier m; **–lady,** patronne f; maîtresse; propriétaire f; **–lord,** propriétaire m; **–mark,** point de repère m; **–scape,** paysage m; **–slide,** éboulement deterre m.

lane, léne, n (country) chemin m; (town) ruelle f; (traffic) file f.

language, lănng´-gouidje, n langage m; langue f.

languid, lănng´-gouide, a languissant.

languish, lănng´-gouiche, v languir.

lanky, lain´-nki, a grand et maigre.

lantern, lănn´-teurne, n lanterne f.

lap, lăppe, n genoux mpl; (sport) tour m. v (drink) laper.

lapel, lă-pèl´, n revers d'habit m.

lapse, lăpse, v s'écouler; retomber. n cours m; erreur f.

larceny, lăr´-ci-ni, n

larcin *m*.

lard, lârde, *n* saindoux *m*;
  –er, garde-manger *m*.

large*, lârdje, *a* grand;
  gros; fort; considérable.

lark, lârque, *n* alouette *f*.

lash, lăche, *n* (whip) fouet
  m; (stroke) coup de
  fouet *m*; (eye) cil *m*. *v*
  fouetter; (bind)
  attacher.

lassitude, lăss´-i-tioude, *n*
  lassitude *f*.

last, lăsste, *v* durer. *a*
  dernier; **–ing,** durable.

latch, lătche, *n* loquet *m*.
  v fermer au loquet.

late, léte, *adv* tard. *a* en
  retard; tard; récent;
  tardif; (deceased) feu; **to
  be –,** *v* être en retard.

lately, léte´-li, *adv*
  dernièrement.

latent, lé´-tennte, *a* caché;
  latent.

lathe, lédz, *n* tour *m*.

lather, lădz´-´r, *n* mousse
  de savon *f*. *v* savonner.

latitude, lăt´-i-tioude, *n*
  latitude *f*.

latter*, lătt´-´r, *a* dernier
  (des deux).

lattice, lătt´-ice, *n* treillis
  m.

laudable, loa´-da-b'l, *a*
  louable.

laugh, lâfe, *v* rire. *n* rire *m*;
  –able, *a* risible; **–ter,**

rires *mpl*; hilarité *f*.

launch, loanntche, *n*
  (boat) chaloupe *f*. *v*
  lancer; **–ing,** *n*
  lancement *m*; mis à
  l'eau.

launderette, loann´-deur-
  rète, *n* laverie *f*.

laundress, loann´-dresse,
  n blanchisseuse *f*.

laundry, loann´-dri, *n*
  blanchisserie *f*.

laundry powder, loann´-
  dri-pâ'ou-d'r, *n* lessive *f*.

laurel, lau´-r'l, *n* laurier *m*.

lavatory, lăv´-a-tŏ-ri, *n*
  lavabo *m*; toilette *f*.

lavender, lăv´-enn-d'r, *n*
  lavande *f*.

lavish, lăv´-iche, *a**
  prodigue; somptueux. *v*
  prodiguer.

law, loa, *n* loi *f*;
  (jurisprudence) droit *m*;
  –ful*, *a* légal; licite;
  légitime; **–suit,** *n* procès
  m; **–yer,** avocat *m*;
  (solicitor) avoué *m*.

lawn, loanne, *n* pelouse *f*.

lax, lăxe, *a* lâche; relâché;
  mou.

laxative, lăx´-a-tive, *n* & *a*
  laxatif *m*.

lay, lé, *v* coucher; placer;
  mettre; (hen) pondre.

layer, lé´-*eur*, *n* couche *f*.

layman, lé´-mănne, *n*
  laïque *m*.

laziness, lé´-zi-nesse, *n*
  paresse *f*.

lazy, lé´-zi, *a* paresseux.

lead, lèdde, *n* plomb *m*;
  (pencil) mine *f*; (*naut*)
  sonde *f*. *v* plomber.

lead, lîde, *v* conduire;
  guider. *n* (dog) laisse *f*;
  –ing, *a* premier;
  principal.

leader, lîde´-'r, *n* guide *m*;
  conducteur *m*; chef *m*;
  –ship, direction *f*;
  conduite *f*.

leaf, lîfe, *n* feuille *f*;
  (table) rallonge *f*.

leaflet, lîfe´-lett, *n*
  prospectus *m*.

league, lîgue, *n* ligue *f*;
  (measurement) lieue *f*.

leak, lîque, *v* fuir; (boats,
  etc) faire eau. *n* fuite *f*.

lean, lîne, *n* & *a* maigre *m*;
  –against, –on, *v*
  s'appuyer; **–out,** se
  pencher.

leap, lîpe, *v* sauter; bondir.
  n saut *m*.

leap year, lîpe´-i-ïre, *n*
  année bissextile *f*.

learn, leurne, *v* apprendre;
  –ed, *a* savant; **–er,** *n*
  étudiant *m*; apprenti *m*;
  –ing, (study) étude *f*;
  (knowledge) savoir *m*;
  érudition *f*.

lease, lîce, *v* louer. *n* bail
  m.

leash, lîche, n laisse f. v
tenir en laisse.

least, lîste, adv le moins. a
le moindre.

leather, lèdz´-´r, n cuir m;
(patent) cuir verni m.

leave, lîve, n permission f.
v partir; s'en aller;
quitter; abandonner;
laisser; (bequeath)
léguer; –out, omettre;
exclure.

lecture, lèque´tioure, n
conférence f;
réprimande f. v faire une
conférence;
réprimander.

lecturer, lèque´-tiour-'r, n
conférencier m.

ledge, lèdje, n rebord m.

leech, lîtche, n sangsue f.

leek, lîque, n poireau m.

leer, lîre, v lorgner.

left, lefte, a & n gauche f;
–handed, gaucher.

leg, lègue, n jambe f;
(animal) patte f;
(mutton, lamb) gigot m;
(fowl) cuisse f;
(furniture) pied m.

legacy, lègg´-a-ci, n legs m;
héritage.

legal,* lî´-g'l, a légal;
licite; –ize, v légaliser.

legation, li-gé´-ch'n, n
légation f.

legend, lèdj´-ennde, n
légende f.

legible, lèdj´-i-b'l, a
lisible.

legion, lî´-dj'n, n légion f.

legislate, lèdj´-iss-léte, v
légiférer.

legislation, lèdj-iss-lé´-
ch'n, n législation f.

legitimacy, lidj-itt´-i-ma-
ci, n légitimité f.

legitimate*, lidj-itt´-i-
méte, a légitime.

leisure, lè´-jeure, n loisir
m; convenance f.

leisurely, lè´-jeur-li, adv à
loisir.

lemon, lèmm´-'n, n citron
m; –ade, limonade f.

lend, lennde, v prêter.

length, lenng´-ts, n
longueur f; (time) durée
f; –en, v allonger;
prolonger; –ways, adv
en longueur; –y, a long,
prolongé.

leniency, lî´-ni-enn-ci, n
indulgence f.

lenient, lî´-ni-ennte, a
indulgent.

lens, lennze, n lentille f;
verre m.

Lent, lennte, n carême m.

lentil, lenn´-t'l, n lentille
f.

leopard, lèp´-eurde, n
léopard m.

leper, lèp´-'r, n lépreux, -
euse m & f.

leprosy, lèp´-rŏ-si, n
lèpre f.

less, lesse, adv moins. n &
a moindre m.

lessee, less-î´, n locataire
m.

lessen, less´-'n, v
diminuer; (pain) alléger.

lesson, less´-'n, n leçon f.

let, lette, v laisser;
permettre; (lease) louer.

letter, lett´-r, n lettre f.

lettuce, lett´-ice, n laitue
f.

level, lèv´-l, n niveau m. a
de niveau; uni. v
niveler; (plane) aplanir.

lever, lî´-v'r, n levier m.

levity, lèv´-i-ti, n légèreté
f.

levy, lèv´-i, v (taxes)
imposer. n impôt m;
(troops) levée f.

lewd*, lioude, a
impudique.

lewdness, lioude´-nesse, n
impudicité f.

liabilities, lâï-a-bil´-i-tèze,
npl (com) passif m.

liability, lâï-a-bil´-i-ti, n
responsabilité f.

liable, lâï´-a-b'l, a
responsable; –to, exposé
à; responsable de.

liar, lâï´-eur, n menteur, -
euse m & f.

libel, lâï´-b'l, n
diffamation f. v diffamer.

libelous, lâï´-bel-euce, a

diffamatoire.

liberal, lib´-eur'l, *n* & *a**
libéral *m.*

liberate, lib´-*eur*-éte, *v*
délivrer; libérer.

liberty, lib´-*eur*-ti, *n*
liberté *f.*

librarian, lâï´-brè´-ri-
anne, *n* bibliothécaire
m.

library, lâï´-bré-ri, *n*
bibliothèque *f.*

license, lâï´-cennce, *n*
permis *m*; autorisation *f.*
v autoriser.

licentious, lâï-cenn´-
cheuce, *a* licencieux;
libertin.

lichen, lâï-k'n *n* lichen
m.

lick, lique, *v* lécher; **–up,**
laper.

licorice, lik´-*eur*-ice, *n*
réglisse *f.*

lid, lidde, *n* couvercle *m*;
(eye) paupière *f.*

lie, lâï, *n* (untruth)
mensonge *m. v* mentir;
(in a place, situation) se
trouver; **–down,**
(repose) se coucher.

lieutenant, lêf-tenn´-
annte, *n* lieutenant *m.*

life, lâïfe, *n* vie *f*;
(vivacity) vivacité *f*; **—
belt,** ceinture de
sauvetage *f*; **—boat,**
canot de sauvetage *m*;

–insurance, assurance
sur la vie *f*; **–less,** *a*
inanimé; sans vie; **–like,**
naturel; **–long,** de toute
la vie; **—size,** grandeur
nature; **–time,** *n* cours
de la vie *m.*

lift, lifte, *n* ascenseur *m. v*
lever; soulever.

light, lâïte, *n* lumière *f*;
clarté *f. a** léger; clair *v.*
allumer; éclairer; **–en,**
alléger; **–er,** *n* briquet *m*;
(boat) allège *f*; **–house,**
phare *m*; **–ing,** éclairage
m; **–ness,** légèreté *f.*

lightning, lâïte´-ninng, *n*
(flash) éclair *m*; (strike)
foudre *f*; **– conductor,**
paratonnerre *m.*

like, lâïque, *v* aimer. *a*
pareil; égal; **–lihood,** *n*
probabilité *f*; **–ly,** *a*
probable; **–ness,** *n*
ressemblance *f*; **–wise,**
adv de même.

liking, lâïque´-inng, *n*
goût *m*; penchant *m.*

lilac, lâï´-laque, *n* lilas *m.*

lily, lil´-i, *n* lis *m*; **—of the
valley,** muguet *m.*

limb, limm, *n* (anatomy)
membre *m.*

lime, lâïme, *n* chaux *f*;
(birdlime) glu *f*; (fruit)
limette *f*; citron vert;
(tree) tilleul *m.*

limit, limm´-itte, *n* limite

f. v limiter.

limp, limmpe, *v* boiter. *a*
(soft) mou, flasque.

limpet, limm´-pette, *n*
patelle *f.*

line, lâïne, *n* ligne *f*; file *f*;
queue *f*; (business)
partie *f*; (rope) corde *f. v*
(garment) doubler.

lineage, linn´-i-idj, *n*
lignée *f.*

linen, linn´-enne, *n* toile
f; (laundry) linge *m.*

liner, lâï´-neur, *n* paquebot
m.

linger, linn´-gueur, *v*
tarder; languir.

linguist, linn´-gouiste, *n*
linguiste *m* & *f.*

lining, lâïnn´-inng, *n*
doublure *f.*

link, linnque, *v*
enchaîner; unir. *n*
chaînon *m*; (cuff links)
boutons de manchettes
mpl.

linnet, linn´-ette, *n* linot
m.

linseed, linn´-cîde, *n*
graine de lin *f.*

lion, lâï´-*eu*ne, *n* lion *m*;
–ess, lionne *f.*

lip, lippe, *n* lèvre *f*; **—
stick,** rouge à lèvres *m.*

liquefy, lik´-oui-fâï, *v*
liquéfier.

liqueur, li-kioure´, *n*
liqueur *f.*

liquid, lik´-ouide, n & a
liquide m.

liquidate, lik´-oui-déte, v
liquider; (debts)
acquitter.

liquidation, lik-oui-dé´-
ch´n, n liquidation f.

liquor, lik´-eur, n alcool m.

lisp, lisspe, v zézayer. n
zézaiement m.

list, lisste, n liste f; (naut)
bande f. v (naut) donner
de la bande.

listen, liss´-n, v écouter.

listener, liss´-neur, n
auditeur -euse m & f.

literal*, litt´-eur-al, a
littéral.

literary, litt´-eur-a-ri, a
littéraire.

literature, litt´-eur-a-
tioure, n littérature f.

lithograph, lits´-o-gräfe, n
lithographie f. v
lithographier.

litigate, litt´i-guéte, v
plaider.

litigation, litt-i-gué´-ch´n,
n litige m.

litter, litt´-´r, n (stretcher,
stable) litière f;
(untidiness) fouillis m;
(young) portée f. v
(scatter) éparpiller;
joncher.

little, lit´-t´l, a (quantity,
time) peu de; (size)
petit. adv peu.

live, live, v vivre; habiter;
(dwell) demeurer.

live, lâïve, a vivant; vif;
–ly, animé.

liver, liv´-eur, n foie m.

livid, liv´-ide, a livide.

living, liv´-inng, n vie f;
(eccl) bénéfice m. a
vivant; –room, n salle
de séjour m.

lizard, liz´-eurde, n lézard
m.

load, laude, v charger. n
charge f.

loaf, laufe, n pain m.

loafer, lau´-feur, n (idler)
fainéant m; mocassin m.

loam, laume, n terre glaise
f; –y, a glaiseux.

loan, laune, n prêt m;
emprunt m.

loathe, laudz´, v détester;
abhorrer.

loathing, laudz´-inng, n
aversion f; dégoût m.

loathsome, laudze´-seume,
a répugnant; odieux.

lobby, lob´-i, n
antichambre f; couloir
m.

lobe, laube, n lobe m.

lobster, lob´-st´r, n homard
m.

local*, lau´-k´l, a local; du
pays; régional; –ity, n
localité f.

locate, lau´-kéte´, v situer;
déterminer la position.

location, lau-ké´-ch´n, n
emplacement m.

lock, loque, n serrure f;
(hair) mèche f; bouche
f;(canal, etc) écluse f. v
fermer à clef; –et, n
médaillon m; –in (or
up), v enfermer; –jaw, n
tétanos m; –out, v laisser
dehors; –smith, n
serrurier m.

locomotive, lau´-ko-mau-
tive, n locomotive f.

locust, lau´-keusste, n
criquet m; locuste f.

lodge, lodje, n loge f. v
loger.

lodger, lodj´-´r, n locataire
m & f.

lodging, lodj´-inng, n
logement m.

loft, lofte, n grenier m; –y,
a haut; (fig) hautain.

log, logue, n bûche f; –
book, (ship) journal de
bord m.

logic, lodj´-ique, n logique
f; –al*, a logique.

loin, lô´ine, n (mutton)
filet m (veal) longe f.

loiter, loa´i-t´r, v flâner;
–behind, traîner.

loll, lolle, v se prélasser;
(tongue) pendre la
langue.

lollipop, loll´-i-poppe, n
sucette f.

loneliness, laune´-li-nesse,

n solitude *f*.
lone(ly), laune´(-li), *a*
solitaire; isolé.
long, lonng, *a* long. *adv*
longtemps; **–for,** *v*
désirer ardemment;
–ing, *n* désir ardent *m*.
longitude, lonn´-dji-
tioude, *n* longitude *f*.
look, louk, *n* regard *m*. *v*
regarder; (seem) avoir
l'air; **–after,** (take care
of) s'occuper de;
–at, regarder; **–for,** *v*
chercher; **–out,** *v*
regarder par. *n* (*naut*)
vigie *f*. *interj* gare!
loom, loume, *n* métier *m*.
v paraître au loin.
loop, loupe, *n* boucle *f*.
–hole, (fort, etc)
meurtrière *f*. ;
échappatoire; **–the loop,**
v boucler la boucle.
loose, louce, *a* lâche;
(tooth) branlante;
(morals) relâché; **–n,** *v*
relâcher; desserrer.
loot, loute, *n* butin *m*. *v*
piller.
lop, loppe, *v* (prune)
élaguer; **–off,** couper.
loquacious, lo-coué´-
cheuce, *a* loquace.
Lord, lôrde, *n* (Deity) le
Seigneur *m*; Dieu *m*.
Lord's Prayer, lôrdze prè´-
eur, *n* Pater *m*.

lose, louze, *v* perdre;
(clock) retarder; **–r,** *n*
perdant *m*.
loss, losse, *n* perte *f*.
lot, lotte, *n* (auction) lot
m; (fate) sort *m*; (many)
beaucoup.
lotion, lau´-ch'n, *n* lotion
f.
lottery, lott´-*eur*-i, *n*
loterie *f*.
loud*, lâ'oude, *a* fort;
haut; (colors) voyant; **––
speaker,** *n* (radio) haut-
parleur *m*.
lounge, lâ-ounndje, *n*
grand vestibule *m*; salon
m. *v* flâner.
louse, lâ'ouce, *n* pou *m*.
lout, lâ'oute, *n* rustre *m*;
(clumsy) lourdaud *m*.
love, love, *v* aimer. *n*
amour *m*; affection *f*;
–liness, beauté *f*; **–ly,** *a*
charmant; **–r,** *n*
amoureux *m*; (illicit)
amant *m*.
low, lau, *v* mugir. *a* bas;
vulgaire; **–er,** *v* baisser;
humilier; **–land,** *n* pays
plat *m*; terrain bay.
loyal*, lo´-ial, *a* loyal;
fidèle; **–ty,** *n* loyauté *f*.
lozenge, loz´-enndje, *n*
losange *f*; pastille *f*.
lubricate, lioue´-bri-quéte,
v lubrifier; graisser.
lucid*, lioue´-cide, *a*

lucide.
luck, loque, *n* chance *f*;
fortune *f* **–y,** *a* fortuné;
veinard.
ludicrous*, lioue´-di-
cr*euce*, *a* risible;
ridicule.
luggage, logg´-idj, *n*
bagages *mpl*.
lukewarm, liouke´-
ouârme, *a* tiède.
lull, lolle, *v* endormir;
(child) bercer. *n* calme
m.
lullaby, loll´-*a*-bâï, *n*
berceuse *f*.
lumbago, lomm-bé´-go, *n*
lumbago *m*.
lumber, lomm´-b'r, *n*
(timber) bois de
charpente *m*. (old
things) vieilleries *fpl*.
luminous*, loue´-minn-
euce, *a* lumineux.
lump, lommpe, *n* morceau
m; (med) grosseur *f*; **–y,** *a*
grumeleux.
lunacy, loue´-na-ci, *n*
aliénation mentale *f*;
folie *f*.
lunar, loue´-n'r, *a* lunaire.
lunatic, loue´na-tique, *n*
fou *m*; folle *f*.
lunch, lonntche, *n*
déjeuner *m*. *v* déjeuner.
lung, lonng, *n* poumon *m*.
lurch, leurtche, *n* secousse
f; (ship) coup de roulis

m; **to leave in the –,**
laisser dans l'embarras.
lure, lioure, *n* leurre *m*. *v*
leurrer; attirer.
lurid, lioue´-ride, *a* (color)
blafard.
lurk, leurque, *v* (hide) se
cacher.
luscious, loch´-euce, *a*
succulent.
lust, losste, *n* luxure *f*;
(greed) convoitise *f*. *v*
convoiter; **–ful,** *a*
sensuel.
luster, loss´-teur, *n* lustre
m.
lute, lioute, *n* luth *m*.
luxurious*, lok-siou´-ri-
euce, *a* luxueux.
luxury, lok´-seur-i, *n* luxe
m; somptuosité *f*.
lymph, limmfe, *n* lymphe
f.
lynch, lintche, *v* lyncher.

macaroon, măc-*a*-
rounne´, n macaron m.
mace, méce, n (staff)
masse f; massue f;
(spice) macis; gaz
incapacitant m.
machine, m*a*-chîne´, n
machine f; **–ry,**
mécanisme m; **–gun,**
mitrailleuse f; **sewing,–,**
machine à coudre f.
machinist, m*a*-chînn´-
iste, n mécanicien m.
mackerel, măc´-r'l, n
maquereau m.
mad, mădde, a fou; (dog)
enragé; **–man,** n aliéné
m; **–ness,** folie f.
madam, măd´-*a*me, n
madame f.
magazine, mă-g*a*-zine´, n
(periodical) magazine m;
(gun) magasin m;

(powder) poudrière f.
maggot, măgg´-*eu*te, n ver
m; larve f; asticot m.
magic, mădj´-ique, n
magie f. a magique.
magistrate, mădj´-iss-
tréte, n magistrat m.
magnanimity, măg´-nă-
nimm´-i-ti, n
magnanimité f.
magnanimous*, măg-
nănn´-i-m*eu*ce, a
magnanime.
magnet, măg´-néte, n
aimant m; **–ic,** a
magnétique. **–ism,** n
magnétisme m; **–ize,** v
magnétiser; aimanter.
magneto, măg-nî´-tau, n
magnéto f.
magnificent*, măg-nif´-i-
cennte, a magnifique.
magnify, măg´-ni-fâï, v

grossir; **–ing glass,** n
loupe f.
magnitude, măg´-ni-
tioude, n grandeur f;
importance f.
magpie, măg´-pâï, n pie f.
mahogany, m*a*-hog´-*a*-ni,
n acajou m.
maid, méde, n (young girl)
jeune fille f; (servant)
bonne f; **–en,** vierge f;
old –, vieille fille f.
mail, méle, n (post)
courrier m; (armor)
cotte de mailles f. v
expédier par la poste; **–**
bag, n sac de poste m; **–**
boat, paquebot poste m.
maim, méme, v mutiler.
main, méne, a* principal;
essentiel. n (pipe, cable)
conduit principal m;
–land, terre ferme f.
maintain, méne-téne´, v
maintenir; soutenir.
maintenance, méne´-t*eu*-
n*a*nnce, n maintien m;
soutien m.
maize, méze, n maiis m.
majestic, m*a*-djess´-tique,
a majestueux.
majesty, mădj´-ess-ti, n
majesté f.
major, mé´-djeur, n (mil)
commandant m. a
majeur; **–ity,** n majorité
f.
make, méque, v faire;

fabriquer. n façon f;
marque f; **—believe,** v
faire semblant; **—r,** n
fabricant m; **—shift,**
expédient m; **—up,** (face)
maquillage m. v
maquiller.

malady, măl´-a-di, n
maladie f.

malaria, ma-lé´-ri-a, n
paludisme m.

male, méle, n & a mâle m.

malediction, ma-lè-
dique´-ch'n, n
malédiction f.

malevolent*, ma-lè-v´-ŏl-
ennte, a malveillant.

malice, măl´-ice, n malice
f; malveillance f.

malicious*, ma-li´-cheuce,
a méchant; malveillant.

malign, ma-lâïne´, v
diffamer; calomnier.

malignant, ma-ligue´-
nannte, a malfaisant;
(med) malin.

malinger, ma-linng´-gueur,
v faire le malade.

malingerer, ma-linng´-
gueur-eur, n simulateur
m.

mallet, măl´-ette, n
maillet m.

mallow, măl´-au, n mauve
f.

malt, moalte, n malt m.

maltreat, măl-trîte´, v
maltraiter.

mammal, mămm´-'l, n
mammifère m.

man, mănne, v armer. n
homme m; **—hood,**
virilité f; **—kind,** genre
humain m; **—ly,** a viril;
—slaughter, homicide m.

manacle, mănn´-a-k'l, v
mettre les menottes.

manage, mănn´-idj, v
(business) diriger;
(accomplish, control)
parvenir à; arriver à;
—ment, n administration
f; gestion f; direction f;
—r, directeur m; gérant
m.

mandate, mănn´-déte, n
ordre m; (law) mandat
m.

mandolin, mănn´-dau-
linne, n mandoline f.

mane, méne, n (of a horse,
lion) crinière f.

maneuver, ma-noue´-v'r, v
manœuvrer. n
manœuvre f.

mangle, main´-ng'l, v
mutiler. n (laundry)
essoreuse f. v essorer.

mania, mé´-ni-a, n manie
f; folie f.

maniac, mé´-ni-ăque, n
fou furieux m.

manicure, mănn´-i-
kioure, v faire les ongles.

manifest, mănn´-i-feste,
a* manifeste. v

manifester.

manifold, mănn´-i-faulde,
a multiple; divers.

manipulate, ma-nipp´-
iou-léte, v manipuler.

manner, mănn´-'r, n
manière f; façon f.

manners, mănn´-eurze, npl
manières fpl.

manor, mănn´-ŏr, n
manoir m.

mansion, mănn´-ch'n, n
(country) château m.

mantelpiece, mănn´-t'l-
pîce, n cheminée f.

manual*, mănn´-iou-'l, n
& a manuel m.

manufacture, mănn-iou-
făc´-tioure, v fabriquer. n
fabrication f; **—r,**
fabricant m.

manure, ma-nioure´, v
fumer. n fumier m;
engrais m.

manuscript, mănn´-iou-
scripte, n manuscrit m.

many, menn´-i, a
beaucoup.

map, măppe, n carte f;
(town) plan m.

maple, mé´-p'l, n érable m.

mar, mâre, v gâter;
défigurer.

marble, mâr´-b'l, n marbre
m; (toy) bille f.

march, mârtche, v
marcher. n marche f.

March, mârtche, v

mars *m*.

marchioness, mâr´-cheunn-esse, *n* marquise *f*.

mare, mère, *n* jument *f*.

margarine, mâr´-ga-rinne, *m* margarine *f*.

margin, mâr´-djinne, *n* marge *f*.

marginal*, mâr´-djinn-'l, *a* marginal.

marigold, mar´-i-gaulde, *n* souci *m*.

marine, ma-rîne´, *a* marin. *n* fusilier marin *m*.

mariner, mar´-i-neur, *n* marin *m*.

maritime, mar´-i-tâïmme, *a* maritime.

mark, mârque, *v* marquer. *n* marque *f*; **book--,** signet *m*; **trade--,** marque de fabrique *f*.

market, mâr´-kette, *n* marché *m*.

marmalade, mâr´-meu-léde, *n* confiture d'oranges *f*.

marmot, mâr´-motte, *n* marmotte *f*.

maroon, ma-rouné, *a* (couleur) bordeaux. *v* abandonner.

marquee, mâr-ki´, *n* (tent) marquise *f*.

marquess, mâr´-couesse, *n* marquis *m*.

marriage, mâr´-idj, *n* mariage *m*.

married, măr´-idde, *a* marié; **--couple,** *n* ménage *m*; couple *m*.

marrow, măr´-au, *n* moelle *f*; (vegetable) courge *f*.

marry, măr´-i, *v* marier; se marier; épouser.

marsh, mârche, *n* marais *m*.

marshal, mâr´-ch'l, *n* maréchal *m*.

mart, mârte, *n* marché *m*; (auction) salle de ventes *f*.

marten, mâr´-tenne, *n* martre *f*.

martial*, mâr´-ch'l, *a* martial; **court--,** *n* conseil de guerre *m*; **--law,** état de siège *m*.

martyr, mâr´-teur, *n* martyr *m*. *v* martyriser.

martyrdom, mâr´-teur-deume, *n* martyre *m*.

marvel, mâr´-v'l, *n* merveille *f*. *v* s'émerveiller.

marvelous*, mâr´-veul-euce, *a* merveilleux.

masculine, măss´-kiou-line, *n* & *a* masculin *m*.

mash, măche, *n* purée *f*; mélange *m*. *v* écraser.

mask, mâssque, *n* masque *m*. *v* masquer.

mason, mé´-s'n, *n* maçon *m*; **--ry,** *n* maçonnerie *f*.

masquerade, măss-keur-éde´, *v* se déguiser. *n* mascarade *f*.

mass, măsse, *n* masse *f*; (*eccl*) messe *f*. *v* masser.

massacre, măss´-a-k'r, *n* massacre *m*. *v* massacrer.

massage, mass-âge´, *n* massage *m*. *v* masser.

massive*, măss´-ive, *a* massif.

mast, mâste, *n* mât *m*.

master, mâss´-t'r, *v* maîtriser; surmonter. *n* maître *m*; patron *m*; professeur *m*; **--ful*,** impérieux; expert; **--ly,** *a* magistral; **--piece,** chef-d'œuvre *m*.

masticate, măss´-ti-quéte, *v* mastiquer.

mastiff, măss´-tif, *n* mâtin *m*.

mat, mătte, *n* natte *f*; (door) paillasson *m*.

match, mătche, *n* allumette *f*; (contest) match *m*. *v* assortir; **--less,** *a* incomparable.

mate, méte, *n* camarade *m* & *f* époux *m*; épouse *f*; second maître *m*. *v* accoupler.

material, ma-ti´-ri-al, *n* matière *f*; (building, etc) matériaux *mpl*; (cloth) tissu *m*.

materialize, ma-ti´-ri-al-âîze, v matérialiser.

maternal*, ma-teur´-n'l, a maternel.

maternity, ma-teur´-ni-ti, n maternité f.

mathematics, mă-tsi-măt´-ikse, n mathématiques fpl.

matrimony, măt´-ri-mŏn-i, n mariage m.

matrix, mé´-trikse, n matrice f.

matron, mé´-tr'n, n infirmière en chef f.

matter, măt´-'r, n matière f; (pus) pus m; (business, subject) affaire f. v avoir de l'importance.

matting, mătt´-innng, n natte f; (straw) paillasson m.

mattress, măt´-tress, n matelas m.

mature, ma-tioure´, v mûrir; (bill) échoir. a mûr.

maturity, ma-tiou´-ri-ti, n maturité f; échéance f.

maul, moale, v déchirer à coups de griffes.

mauve, mauve, n & a mauve m.

maxim, măx´-simm, n maxime f.

maximum, măx´-si-momm, n & a maximum m.

may, mé, v pouvoir.

May, mé, n mai m; — **flower,** aubépine f.

mayor, mè´-eur, n maire m.

maze, méze, n labyrinthe m.

me, mie, pron moi; me.

meadow, mèd´-au, n pré m; prairie f.

meager*, mî´-gueur, a maigre.

meal, mîle, n farine f; (repast) repas m.

mean, mîne, a avare; (action) bas. v avoir l'intention de; vouloir dire; –**ing,** n signification f; –**ingless,** a dénué de sens.

means, minn´ze, npl moyens mpl.

meanwhile, mine´-houâîle, adv en attendant.

measles, mîz´-'lz, n rougeole f.

measure, mèj´-eur, n mesure f; (tape) mètre (en ruban) m. v mesurer; –**ments,** n les mesures fpl.

meat, mîte, n viande f.

mechanic, mi-cănn´-ique, n ouvrier mécanicien m; –**al,** a mécanique; –**s,** n mécanique f.

mechanism, mè´-cănn-

izme, n mécanisme m.

medal, mèd´-'l, n médaille f.

meddle, mèd´-'l, v se mêler de.

mediate, mî-di-éte, v intervenir (en faveur de).

medical*, mèd´-i-k'l, a médical.

medicine, mèd´-cine, n médecine f.

medieval, mèd-i-î´-v'l, a du moyen âge.

mediocre, mî´-di-ô-keur, a médiocre.

meditate, mèd´-i-téte, v méditer.

medium, mî´-di-ŏmme, n moyen m; (person) entremise f; (spiritualist) médium m.

meek*, mîque, a doux; humble.

meet, mîte, v rencontrer; (obligations) remplir.

meeting, mî´-tinng, n rencontre f; réunion f.

melancholy, mèl´-annn-cŏl-i, n mélancolie f.

mellow, mèl´-au, a doux; moelleux.

melodious*, mèl-au´-di-euce, a mélodieux.

melody, mèl´-o-di, n mélodie f.

melon, mèl´-eune, n melon m.

melt, melte, *v* to fondre.

member, memm´-b'r, *n* membre *m*; **–ship,** sociétariat *m*; les membres d'une société; cotisation *f*.

memento, mi-menn´-to, *n* mémento *m*.

memoir, memm´-ouâre, *n* mémoire *m*.

memorable, memm´-ŏ-ra-b'l, *a* mémorable.

memorandum, memm-ŏ-rănn´-d'm, *n* note *f*; mémorandum *m*.

memorial, mi-mau´-ri-al, *n* monument commémoratif *m*.

memory, memm´-ŏ-ri, *n* mémoire *f*.

menace, menn´-ace, *v* menacer. *n* menace *f*.

menagerie, mi-nădj´-eur-i, *n* ménagerie *f*.

mend, mennde, *v* réparer; (sew) raccommoder.

menial, mî´-ni-al, *a* servile. *n* domestique *m* & *f*; *a* inférieur; subalterne.

mental*, menn´-t'l, *a* mental.

mention, menn´-ch'n, *v* mentionner. *n* mention *f*.

menu, menn´-iou, *n* menu *m*; carte *f*.

mercantile, meur´-kann-tâile, *a* mercantile.

merchandise, meur´-tchann-dâïze, *n* marchandise *f*.

merchant, meur´-tch'nt, *n* négociant *m*; marchand *m*. *a* commercial; (fleet) marchand.

merciful*, meur´-ci-foull, *a* clément; miséricordieux.

mercury, meur´-kiou-ri, *n* mercure *m*.

mercy, meur´-ci, *n* grâce *f*; indulgence *f*.

mere, mîre, *a** pur; simple; seul. *n* lac *m*.

merge, meurdje, *v* fondre; absorber; **–r,** *n* fusion *f*.

meridian, mi-ri´-di-ann, *n* méridien *m*. *a* méridien.

merit, mair´-itte, *n* mérite *m*. *v* mériter.

meritorious*, mair-i-tau´-ri-euce, *a* méritoire.

mermaid, meur´-méde, *n* sirène *f*.

merriment, mair´-i-m'nt, *n* gaieté *f*; joie *f*.

merry, mair´-i, *a* joyeux.

mesh, maiche, *n* maille *f*.

mesmerize, mez´-meur-âïze, *v* hypnotiser.

mess, messe, *n* mess *m*; (dirt) saleté *f*; (spoil) gâchis *m*. *v* salir.

message, mess´-sédje, *n* message *m*.

messenger, mess´-enn-dj´r, *n* coursier, -ère *m* & *f*; (restaurant, hôtel, etc) chasseur *m*.

metal, mett´-'l, *n* métal *m*; **–lic,** *a* métallique.

meteor, mî´-ti-ŏre, *n* météore *m*.

meter, mî´-teur, *n* compteur *m*.

method, maits´-ŏde, *n* méthode *f*.

metropolis, mi-trop´-ŏ-lice, *n* métropole *f*.

mica, mâî´-ka, *n* mica *m*.

microscope, mâî´-cross-kaupe, *n* microscope *m*.

middle, midd´-'l, *n* centre *m*; milieu *m*. *a* moyen; **–aged,** *a* d'un certain âge; **–class (es),** *n* (people) classe moyenne *f*; **–man,** intermédiaire *m*.

midge, midje, *n* cousin *m*; moucheron *m*.

midget, midj´-ette, *n* nain, -e *m* & *f*.

midnight, midd´-nâïte, *n* minuit *m*.

midshipman, midd´-chipp-mănne, *n* aspirant de marine *m*.

midwife, midd´-ouâïfe, *n* sage-femme *f*.

mien, mîne, *n* mine *f*; air *m*.

might, maîte, *n* force *f*; puissance *f*.

mighty, maï´-ti, *a* puissant; fort.

migrate, maî´-gréte, *v* émigrer.

mild*, maîlde, *a* doux; léger; tempéré.

mildew, mil´-dioue, *n* moisissure *f*.

mile, maîle, *n* mille *m*; **–stone,** borne *f*.

military, mil´-i-ta-ri, *n* & *a* militaire *f*.

milk, milque, *n* lait *m. v* traire; **–y,** *a* laiteux; **–y way,** *n* voie lactée *f*.

mill, mill, *n* moulin *m*; **–er,** meunier *m*.

milliner, mill´-i-n'r, *n* modiste *f*; **–y,** modes *fpl*.

million, mill´ieune, *n* million *m*.

millionaire, mill´ionn-air, *n* millionnaire *m*.

mimic, mimm´-ique, *v* mimer. *n* mime *m*.

mince, minnce, *v* hacher; (words) mâcher.

mind, maînnde, *n* esprit *m*; opinion *f. v* faire attention à; (nurse) soigner; **–ful,** *a* attentif.

mine, maîne, *poss pron* le mien, la mienne; les miens, les miennes; à moi.

mine, maîne, *n* mine *f. v*

miner; **–r,** *n* mineur *m*.

mineral, minn´-eur-al, *n* & *a* minéral *m*.

mingle, minng´-g'l, *v* mélanger; se mêler.

miniature, minn´-i-a-tioure, *n* miniature *f*.

minimize, minn´-i-maîze, *v* réduire; diminuer.

minister, minn´-iss-t'r, *n* pasteur *m*.

ministry, minn´-iss-tri, *n* ministère *m*.

mink, minque, *n* vison *m*.

minor, maî´-neur, *n* mineur, -e *m* & *f. a* mineur.

minority, minn-or´-i-ti, *n* minorité *f*.

minstrel, minn´-str'l, *n* ménestrel *m*.

mint, minnte, *n* la Monnaie *f*; (plant) menthe *f. v* frapper de la monnaie.

minuet, minn´-iou-ette, *n* menuet *m*.

minus, maî´-neuce, *a* & *adv* moins. *prep* sans.

minute, minn´-itte, *n* minute *f*.

minute, maîn-ioute´, *a* menu; (exact) minutieux.

miracle, mir´-a-k'l, *n* miracle *m*.

miraculous*, mi-răk´-iou-leuce, *a* miraculeux.

mirage, mi-râge´, *n* mirage *m*.

mire, maîre, *n* fange *f*; boue *f*; bourbe *f*.

mirror, mir´-eur, *n* miroir *m. v* refléter.

mirth, meurts, *n* gaieté *f*; hilarité *f*.

mis, miss, **–adventure,** *n* mésaventure *f*; **–apprehension,** malentendu *m*; **–appropriate,** *v* détourner; **–behave,** se conduire mal; **–carriage,** *n* (*med*) fausse couche *f*; **–carry,** *v* échouer; (*med*) faire une fausse couche; **–conduct,** *n* mauvaise conduite *f*; **–construction,** mésinterprétation *f*; **–count,** *v* mal compter; **–demeanor,** (law) délit *m*; **–direct,** *v* mal diriger; calamité *f*; **–giving,** crainte *f*; **–govern,** *v* mal gouverner; **–guide,** égarer; (fig) mal conseiller; **–hap,** *n* contretemps *m*; accident *m*; **–inform,** *v* mal renseigner; **–judge,** mal juger; **–lay,** égarer; **–lead,** tromper; **–manage,** mal gérer; **–place,** mal placer;

-print, n faute d'impression f;

-pronounce, v mal prononcer; **-represent,** fausser; **-statement,** n rapport inexact m; **-take,** v se tromper. n erreur f; **-taken,** a erroné; **-trust,** v se méfier de. n méfiance f; **-understand,** v mal comprendre; **-understanding,** n malentendu m; **-use,** v abuser de.

miscellaneous, miss-s'l-lé´-ni-euce, a varié; divers.

mischief, miss´-tchife, n mal m; dommage m; (of child) bêtise f.

mischievous*, miss´-tchiveuce, a malicieux.

miser, mâï´-z'r, n avare m & f; **-ly,** a mesquin.

miserable, miz´-eur-a b'l, a misérable; triste.

misery, miz´-eur-i, n misère f; tourment m.

Miss, mice, n mademoiselle f.

miss, mice, v manquer; (someone's absence) regretter; **-ing,** a absent; perdu; manquant.

missile, miss´-âïl, n projectile m.

mission, mich´-eune, n mission f.

missionary, mich´-eune-ri, n (eccl) missionaire m & f.

mist, miste, n brume f; **-y,** a brumeux.

Mister, (Mr) miss´teur, n monsieur m.

mistletoe, miss´-s'l-tau, n gui m.

mistress, miss´-tresse, n madame f; (school) maîtresse f; (kept) maîtresse f.

miter, mâï´-teur, n mitre f.

mitigate, mit´-i-guéte, v adoucir; mitiger.

mix, mixe, v mêler, mélanger; (salad) tourner; **-ed,** a mixte; **-ture,** n mélange m.

moan, maune, v gémir; grogner; n gémissement m.

moat, maute, n fossé m.

mob, mobbe, n foule f; bande f. clique f. bande (f) de gangsters. v houspiller; (enthusiasm) presser par la foule.

mobile, mô´-bâïle, a & n mobile m.

mobilize, môb´-il-âïze, v mobiliser.

mock, moque, v se moquer. a simulé; faux; **-ery,** n moquerie f; **-ingly,** adv en se moquant.

mode, maude, n manière f; (fashion) mode f.

model, modd´-'l n modèle m; (fashion) mannequin m. v modeler.

moderate, modd´-eur-éte, v modérer. a* modéré; passable.

moderation, modd-eur-é´-ch'n, n modération f.

modern, modd´eurne, a moderne.

modest*, modd´este, a modeste.

modify, modd´-i-fâï, v modifier.

Mohammedan, mô-hamm´-é-danne, n & a mahométan, -e m & f.

moist, moa´isste, a moite, humide; **-en,** v humecter; **-ure,** n humidité f.

mold, maulde, v mouler. n moule m; (mildew) moisissure f; (earth) terreau m; **-er,** mouleur m; **-ing,** moulure f; **-y,** a moisi.

mole, maule, n taupe f; (mark) grain de beauté m; (jetty) môle m; **-hill,** taupinière f.

molest, mo-leste´, v molester.

mollify, moll´-i-fâï, v adoucir.

molten, maule´-t'n, *a*
fondu; en fusion.

moment, mau´-m'nt, *n*
moment *m*; **–ous,** *a*
important; mémorable.

momentum, mau-menn´-
tomme, *n* (impetus)
impulsion *f*.

monarch, monn´-eurque,
n monarque *m*.

monarchy, monn´-eur-ki,
n monarchie *f*.

monastery, monn´-ass-tri,
n monastère *m*.

Monday, monn´-dé, *n*
lundi *m*.

monetary, monn´-eu-ta-ri,
a monétaire.

money, monn´-i, *n* argent
m; (coin) monnaie *f*; **–-
lender,** prêteur d'argent
m; **–-order,** mandat-
poste *m*.

mongrel, monng´-gr'l, *n* &
a bâtard, -e *m* & *f*.

monk, monng´-k, *n* moine
m.

monkey, monng´-ki, *n*
singe *m*.

monocle, monn´-o-k'l, *n*
monocle *m*.

monogram, monn´-ô-
grämme, *n*
monogramme *m*.

monopolize, mǒnn-op´-ǒ-
lǎïze, *v* monopoliser.

monopoly, mǒnn-op´-ǒ-li,
n monopole *m*.

monotonous*, mǒnn-ot´-
nǒ-neuce, *a* monotone.

monster, monn´-st'r, *n*
monstre *m*.

monstrous*, monn´-
streuce, *a* monstrueux.

month, monnts, *n* mois *m*;
–ly, *a* mensuel.

monument, monn´-iou-
m'nt, *n* monument *m*.

mood, moude, *n* humeur *f*;
(grammar) mode *m*.

moody, moud´-i, *a*
d'humeur changeante.

moon, moune, *n* lune *f*;
–light, clair de lune *m*.

Moor, mou'r, *n* Maure *m*;
–ish, *a* mauresque.

mop, moppe, *n* balai à
laver *m*. *v* éponger.

mope, maupe, *v* s'attrister;
s'ennuyer.

moral, mor´al, *n* morale *f*.
a* moral; **–ity,** *n*
moralité *f*; **–s,** mœurs
fpl; moralité *f*.

morale, mo-râl´, *n* moral
m.

morass, mo-răce´, *n*
marécage *m*; marais *m*.

moratorium, môr-a-tô´-ri-
omme, *n* moratorium *m*.

morbid*, môr´-bidde, *a*
morbide.

more, môre, *a* & *adv* plus;
plus de; davantage;
encore.

moreover, môr-au´-v'r, *adv*

en outre; de plus.

morning, môr´-ninng, *n*
matin *m*; (period)
matinée *f*; **good
–,**bonjour.

morocco, mo-rok´-au, *n*
(leather) maroquin *m*.

morose*, mǒ-rauce´, *a*
morose.

morphine, moar´-fi-a, *n*
morphine *f*.

morsel, môr´s'l, *n* morceau
m.

mortal, môr´-t'l, *n* & *a**
mortel, -elle *m* & *f*; **–ity,**
mortalité *f*.

mortar, môr´-t'r, *n* mortier
m.

mortgage, môr´-guédje, *n*
hypothèque *f*. *v*
hypothéquer; **–e,** *n*
créancier hypothécaire
m; **–r,** débiteur
hypothécaire *m*.

mortification, môr´-ti-fi-
qué´-ch'n, *n*
mortification *f*.

mortify, môr´-ti-fäï, *v*
mortifier.

mortuary, môr´-tiou-a-ri,
n morgue *f*.

mosaic, mǒ-zé´-ique, *n* &
a mosaïque *f*.

mosque, mosske, *n*
mosquée *f*.

mosquito, moss-kî´-tau, *n*
moustique *m*.

moss, moss, *n* mousse *f*.

most, mauste, *adv*
extrêmement, le plus. *n*
la plupart *f*; **–ly,** *adv*
principalement.

moth, motz, *n* papillon de
nuit *m*; (clothes) mite *f*.

mother, modz´-*eur*, *n* mère
f; **–hood,** maternité *f*; **—
in-law,** belle-mère *f*; **—
of-pearl,** nacre *f*; **–ly,** *a*
maternel.

motion, mau´-ch'n, *n*
mouvement *m*.

motionless, mau´-ch'n-
lesse, *a* immobile.

motive, mau´-tive, *n* motif
m. *a* moteur.

motor, mau´-t'r, *n* moteur
m; **—car,** automobile *f*;
—cycle, motocyclette *f*;
–ing, automobilisme *m*;
–ist, automobiliste *m* &
f.

mottled, mot´-t'ld, *a*
bigarré.

motto, mot´-tau, *n* devise
f.

mound, mâ´ounnde, *n*
monticule *m*.

mount, mâ´ounnte, *n*
mont *m*; (horse, jewels)
monture *f*; (picture)
cadre *m*. *v* monter.

mountain, mâ´ounn´-
tinne, *n* montagne *f*;
–eer, montagnard, -e *m*
& *f*; **–ous,** *a*
montagneux.

mourn, môrne, *v* se
lamenter; pleurer; **–ful*,**
a triste; lugubre; **–ing,** *n*
deuil *m*.

mouse, mâ´ouce, *n* souris
f; **—trap,** souricière *f*.

moustache, mousse-
tache´, *n* moustache *f*.

mouth, mâouth, *n* bouche
f; gueule *f*; (river)
embouchure *f*; **–ful,**
bouchée *f*; **–piece,**
embouchure *f*; (*fig*)
porte-parole *m*.

movable, moue´-va-b'l, *a*
mobile.

move, mouve, *v* mouvoir;
(house) déménager;
(fidget) se remuer; (stir)
bouger. *n* mouvement *m*;
(*fig*) coup *m*.

mow, mau, *v* faucher;
(lawn) tondre.

mower, mau´-*eur*, *n*
tondeuse *f*.

much, motche, *adv*
beaucoup; **how** –?
combien?

mud, modde, *n* boue *f*;
–dy, *a* boueux.

muddle, modd´-'l, *n*
confusion *f*; fouillis *m*. *v*
embrouiller.

muff, moffe, *n* manchon
m; **–le,** *v* (sound)
étouffer; (cover)
emmitoufler; **–ler,** *n*
écharpe *f*.

mug, mogue, *n* gobelet *m*;
pot *m*.

Muhammadan, mô-
hamm´-é-danne, *n* & *a*
Mahometan,
-e *m* & *f*.

mulberry, moll´-bèr-î, *n*
mûre *f*; **–tree,** mûrier *m*.

mule, mioule, *n* mulet *m*;
mule *f*.

mullet, mol´-ette, *n* mulet
m; **red** –,rouget *m*.

multiplication, mole´-ti-
pli-qué´-ch'n, *n*
multiplication *f*.

multiply, moll´-ti-plâï, *v*
multiplier.

multitude, moll´-ti-tioude,
n multitude *f*.

mummy, momm´-i, *n*
momie *f*.

mumps, mommpse, *npl*
oreillons *mpl*.

munch, monntche, *v*
mâcher; (crunch)
croquer.

municipal, miou-niss´-i-
p'l *a* municipal.

munition, miou-ni´-ch'n,
n munition *f*.

murder, meur´-d'r, *v*
assassiner. *n* assassinat
m; **–er,** assassin *m*; **–ous,**
a meurtrier.

murky, meur´-ki, *a* obscur;
ténébreux.

murmur, meur´-m'r,
v murmurer. *n*

murmure m.

muscle, moss´-'l, n muscle m.

muse, miouze, v musarder; méditer. n muse f.

museum, mioue-zî-omme, n musée m.

mushroom, moche´-roumme, n champignon m.

music, mi'oue´-zique, n musique f; **–al,** a musical.

musician, mi'oue-zi´-ch'n, n musicien, -enne m & f.

musk, mossque, n musc m.

muslin, moze´-linne, n mousseline f.

mussel, moss´-'l, n moule f.

must, moste, v devoir; falloir.

mustard, moss´-t'rd, n moutarde f.

muster, moss´-t'r, v rassembler; (mil) faire l'appel.

musty, moss´-ti, a moisi.

mute, mioute, n & a muet, -ette m & f.

mutilate, mioue´-ti-léte, v mutiler.

mutineer, mioue-ti-nîre´, n mutin m; révolté m.

mutinous, mioue´-ti-neuce, a en révolte.

mutiny, mioue´-ti-ni, n

mutinerie f. v se mutiner m.

mutt, meutt, n corniaud (chien) m.

mutter, mott´-'r, v marmotter.

mutual*, mioue´-tiou-al, a mutuel.

muzzle, mozz´-'l, n (for dogs, etc) muselière f; (snout) museau m; (gun) bouche f. v museler.

my, mâï, poss a mon; ma; mes; **–self,** pron moi-même.

myrtle, meur´-t'l, n myrte f.

mysterious*, miss-tî´-ri-euce, a mystérieux.

mystery, miss´-teur-i, n mystère m.

mystify, miss´-ti-fâï, v mystifier.

myth, mits, n mythe m; **–ology,** mythologie f.

nag, năgue, *v* gronder; harceler. *n* canasson *m.*

nail, néle, *n* (metal) clou *m;* (human) ongle *m. v* clouer; **–brush,** *n* brosse à ongles *f;* **–file,** lime à ongles *f.*

naive*, nâ-ive', *a* naïf.

naked, né'-kedde, *a* nu; (trees, etc) dépouillé.

name, néme, *v* appeler; (specify) nommer. *n* nom *m;* **Christian –,** prénom *m;* **last –,** nom de famille *m;* **–less,** *a* anonyme; **–ly,** *adv* à savoir; **–sake,** *n* homonyme *m.*

nap, năppe, *n* (sleep) somme *m;* (cloth) poil *m.*

nape, népe, *n* nuque *f.*

naphtha, năph'-tsa, *n* naphte *m.*

napkin, năpp'-kinne, *n* serviette *f.*

narcissus, năr-siss'-euce, *n* narcisse *m.*

narcotic, năr-cott'-ique, *n & a* narcotique *m.*

narrative, năr'-ra-tive, *n* narration *f.*

narrow, năr'-au, *v* rétrécir. *a** étroit; **–minded,** étroit d'esprit; **–ness,** *n* étroitesse *f.*

nasal*, né'-z'l, *a* nasal.

nasturtium, nass-teur'-ch'm, *n* capucine *f.*

nasty, nâsse'-ti, *a* méchant; (*fig*) mauvais; (dirty) sale.

nation, né'-ch'n, *n* nation *f;* pays *m.*

national, năch'-eunn-'l, *a* national.

nationality, năch-eunn-al'-i-ti, *n* nationalité *f.*

native, né'-tive, *n & a* natif, -ive *m & f,* indigène *m & f. a* natal (**my native country,** mon pays natal).

natural*, năt'-tiou-r'l, *a* naturel.

naturalization, năt'-tiou-ral-âï-zé'-ch'n, *n* naturalisation *f.*

nature, nét'-tioure, *n* nature *f.*

naught, noate, *n* rien *m;* zéro *m.*

naughty, noa'-ti, *a* vilain; pas sage.

nauseous, nô'-si-euce, *a* nauséabond; écœurant.

nautical, nô'-ti-k'l, *a* nautique.

naval, né'-v'l, *a* naval; maritime; **–officer,** officier de marine *m.*

navel, né'-v'l, *n* nombril *m.*

navigate, nă'-vi-guéte, *v* naviguer.

navigation, nă-vi-gué'-ch'n, *n* navigation *f.*

navigator, năv'-i-gué-*teur,* *n* navigateur *m.*

navy, né'-vi, *n* marine *f;* **–blue,** *a* bleu marine.

near, nîeuz, *a* proche. *prep* près de. *adv* près. *v* s'approcher de; **–ly,** *adv*

presque; **–ness,** n
proximité f; **––sighted,** n
& a myope m & f.

neat, nîte, a (spruce)
soigné; (dainty) délicat;
(tidy) rangé; (not
diluted) pur.

neatness, nîte´-ness, n
netteté f; (clean)
propreté f.

necessarily, nèss´-ess-a-ri-
li, adv nécessairement.

necessary, nèss´-ess-a-ri, a
nécessaire.

necessitate, ni-sess´-i-téte,
v nécessiter.

necessity, ni-sess´-i-ti, n
nécessité f.

neck, nèque, n cou m;
(bottle) goulot m; **–lace,**
collier m; **––tie,** cravate
f.

need, nîde, v avoir besoin
de. n besoin m; **–ful*,** a
nécessaire; **–less*,**
inutile; **–y,** nécessiteux.

needle, nî´-d'l, n aiguille f.

negation, ni-gué´-ch'n, n
négation f.

negative, negg´-a-tive, n
négative f. a* négatif.

neglect, nig-lecte´, v
négliger. n négligence f.

negligence, negg´-li-
djennce, n négligence f.

negligent, negg´-li-dj'nt, a
négligent.

negotiate, ni-gau-chi-éte,

v négocier.

negotiation, ni-gau´-chi-
é-´ch'n, n négociation f.

neigh, né, v hennir. n
hennissement m.

neighbor, nè´-b'r, n voisin
m; **–hood,** voisinage m;
–ly, a bon voisin.

neither, nâï´-dz'r, pron & a
ni l'un ni l'autre. adv
non plus;–... **nor,** conj
ni...ni.

nephew, név´-iou, n
neveu m.

nerve, neurve, n nerf m;
(fam) (pluck, etc) sang
froid m; (fig) (cheek)
audace f.

nervous*, neur´-veuce, a
nerveux; timide;
excitable.

nest, nesste, n nid m. v
nicher.

nestle, ness´-'l, v se
nicher; se blottir.

net, nett, n filet m. a
(weight, etc) net.

nettle, nett´-'l, n ortie f.

network, nett´-oueurque,
n réseau m.

neuralgia, nioue-rall´-dji-
a, n névralgie f.

neuter, nioue´-teur, n & a
neutre m.

neutral, nioue´-tr'l, a
neutre.

never, nèv´-'r, adv
(ne)...jamais; **–more,**

plus jamais; **–theless,**
adv néanmoins.

new, nioue, a neuf;
nouveau; frais; **–year,** n
nouvel an m; **–Year's
Day,** jour de l'an m.

news, niouze, npl
nouvelles fpl; (radio, TV)
informations fpl; **–agent,**
marchand de journaux
m; **–paper,** journal m.

next, nexte, a prochain
(of future time); suivant
(of past time); (beside) à
côté, voisin. adv ensuite.

nib, nibbe, n plume f.

nibble, nib´-b'l, v
grignoter; (rats, etc)
ronger.

nice*, nâïce, a agréable;
sympathique; (fam)
aimable; (subtle)
scrupuleux.

nickel, nique´-'l, n nickel
m; 5 "cents".

nickname, nique´-néme, n
surnom m.

nicotine, nique´-ô-tinne,
n nicotine f.

niece, nîce, n nièce f.

night, nâïte, n nuit f; **––
gown,** chemise de nuit f;
–fall, tombée de la nuit
f; **–ingale,** rossignol m;
–ly, adv tous les soirs;
–mare, n cauchemar m.

nimble, nimm´-b'l, a leste;
agile; vif.

nine, nâîne, *n* & *a* neuf *m*; *m* & *a* **–teen,** dix-neuf *m*; *m* & *a* **–teenth,** dix-neuvième *m* & *f*; **–tieth,** *m* & *a* quatrevingt-dixième *m* & *f*; **–ty,** *m* & *a* quatre-vingt-dix *m*.

ninth, nâînnts, *n* & *a* neuvième *m* & *f*.

nip, nippe, *v* pincer; filer; **–off,** couper (le bout de).

nipple, nip´-p'l, *n* mamelon *m*; tétine *f*.

nitrate, nâï´-tréte, *n* nitrate *m*.

nitrogen, nâï´-trô-dj'n, *n* azote *m*; nitrogène *m*.

no, nau, *adv* non; pas; ne … pas. *a* aucun.

nobility, no-bil´-i-ti, *n* noblesse *f*.

noble, nau´-b'l, *n* noble *m*. *a* noble; généreux.

nobody, nau´-bŏdd-i, *n* personne sans importance *f*. *pron* personne.

nod, nodde, *v* faire un signe de tête. *n* signe de tête *m*.

noise, noa´ize, *n* bruit *m*; **–less*,** *a* silencieux.

noisily, noa´iz´-i-li, *adv* bruyamment.

noisy, noa´´-i-zi, *a* bruyant; tapageur.

nominal*, nomm´-i-n'l, *a*

nominal.

nominate, nomm´-i-néte, *v* nommer; proposer.

nominee, nomm-i-nî´, *n* personne désignée *f*.

non, nonne, **– commissioned officer,** *n* sous- officier *m*; **–plussed,** *a* confus; dérouté; **–sense,** *n* absurdité *f*; **–stop,** *a* continu; (train, etc) direct.

nook, nouk, *n* coin *m*.

noon, noune, *n* midi *m*.

noose, nouce, *n* nœud coulant *m*.

normal*, nôr´-m'l, *a* normal.

north, nôrts, *n* nord *m*; **–erly,** *adv* au nord. *a* du nord.

nose, nauze, *n* nez *m*.

nostril, noss´-tr'l, *n* narine *f*; naseau (of a horse, etc.) *m*.

not, notte, *adv* ne … pas; ne … point; pas.

notable, nauté´-a-b'l, *a* notable; insigne.

notary, nauté´-a-ri, *n* notaire *m*.

notch, notche, *v* entailler. *n* entaille *f*; coche *f*.

note, naute, *v* noter; remarquer. *n* note *f*; (currency) billet de banque *m*; **–book,**

carnet *m*; **–d,** *a* fameux; célèbre; **–paper,** *n* papier à lettres *m*; **–worthy,** *a* digne de remarque.

nothing, no´-tsinng, *n* rien *m*; **for –,** *adv* en vain.

notice, nau´-tice, *v* remarquer; faire attention; observer. *n* avis *m*; affiche *f*; (to quit, to give notice) donner congé *m*; **–able,** *a* perceptible.

notify, nau´-ti-fâï, *v* notifier; signaler.

notion, nau´-ch'n, *n* notion *f*; idée *f*.

notoriety, nau-tŏ-râï´-è-ti, *n* notoriété *f*.

notorious, nau-tau´-ri-euce, *a* notoire; insigne.

notwithstanding, nott-ouidz-stännd´-inng, *prep* & *conj* néanmoins; malgré.

noun, na´oune, *n* nom *m*; substantif *m*.

nourish, nor´-iche, *v* nourrir; **–ing,** *a* nourrissant; **–ment,** *n* nourriture *f*.

novel, nov´´-'l, *n* roman *m*. *a* nouveau; **–ist,** *n* romancier *m*; **–ty,** nouveauté *f*; innovation *f*.

November, no-vemm´-b'r,

n novembre *m*.

novice, nov´-ice, *n* novice *m* & *f*.

now, nâ'ou, *adv* maintenant; **–adays,** de nos jours; **–and then,** de temps en temps.

nowhere, nau´-houère, *adv* nulle part.

noxious, noque´-cheuce, *a* nuisible; pernicieux.

nozzle, noz´-z'l, *n* bout *m*; lance (de tuyau) *f*.

nuclear, nioue´-kl-îr, *a* nucléaire.

nucleus, nioue´-kli-euce, *n* noyau *m*.

nude, nioude, *n* & *a* nu *m*.

nudge, nodje, *v* & *n* coup de coude *m*.

nugget, nogg´-itte, *n* pépite *f*.

nuisance, nioue´-s'nce, *n* (annoyance) plaie *f*; (bother) ennui *m*.

null, nolle, *a* nul; **–ify,** *v* annule.

numb, nomme, *a* engourdi. *v* engourdir; **–ness,** *n* engourdissement *m*.

number, nomm´-b'r, *n* nombre *m*; (of a series) numéro *m*. *v* numéroter; **–less,** *a* innombrable.

numerous, nioue´-meur-euce, *a* nombreux.

nun, nonne, *n* nonne *f*; religieuse *f*.

nuptial, nopp´-ch'l, *a* nuptial; **–s,** *npl* noces *fpl*.

nurse, neurce, *n* infirmière *f*; (male) infirmier *m*. *v* soigner; (suckle) nourrir; **–ry school,** *n* maternelle *f*; (plants, etc) pépinière *f*; **–ry rhyme,** conte de nourrice *m*.

nurture, noitshoi, *v* élever; s'occuper de; nourire. *n* nouriture *f*.

nut, notte, *n* noix *f*; (hazel) noisette *f*; (pea) cacahuète *f*; (*mech*) écrou *m*; **–cracker,** casse-noisettes *m*; **–meg,** muscade *f*; **–shell,** coquille de noix *f*.

nutriment, nioue´-tri-m'nt, *n* nourriture *f*.

nutritious, nioue-tri´-cheuce, *a* nutritif.

nuzzle, nozeul, *v* fouiner; fourrer son nez.

nylon, nâî´-lonn, *n* nylon *m*.

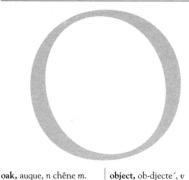

oak, auque, n chêne m.

oar, ore, n rame f; aviron m; **–sman,** rameur de pointe m.

oasis, au-é´-cisse, n oasis f.

oat, aute, n avoine f; **–meal,** farine d'avoine m.

oath, auts, n serment m; (profane) juron m.

obdurate*, ob´-diou-rête, a endurci; obstiné.

obedience, o-bî´-di-ennce, n obéissance f.

obedient, o-bî´-di-ennte, a obéissant.

obese, au-bîce´, a obèse.

obesity, au-bîs´-i-ti, n obésité f.

obey, o-bé´, v obéir.

obituary, o-bit´-iou-a-ri, n nécrologie f. a nécrologique.

object, ob-djecte´, v protester; s'opposer à.

object, ob´-djecte, n objet m; (aim) but m; (grammar) complément m; **–ion,** objection f; **–ionable,** a répréhensible; **–ive,** n & a objectif m.

obligation, o-bli-gé´-ch'n, n obligation f.

obligatory, ob´-lî-ga-to-ri, a obligatoire.

oblige, o-blâïdje´, v obliger; (favor) rendre service.

obliging*, o-blâïdj´-inng, a obligeant.

obliterate, ob-litt´-eur-éte, v effacer.

oblivion, ob-liv´-i-eune, n oubli m.

oblivious, ob-liv´-i-euce, a

oublieux.

oblong, ob´-lonng, a oblong. n rectangle m.

obnoxious*, ob-noque´-cheuce, a odieux; insupportble; repoussant.

obscene*, ob-cîne´, a obscène.

obscure, ob-skioure´, v obscurcir. a* obscur.

observant, ob-zeur´-v'nt, n & a observateur m.

observation, ob-zeur-vé´-ch'n, n observation f.

observatory, ob-zeur´-va-tŏ-ri, n observatoire m.

observe, ob-zeurve´, v observer; remarquer.

obsolete, ob´-sôlîte, a suranné; hors d'usage.

obstacle, ob´-stă-k'l, n obstacle m.

obstinacy, ob´-sti-na-ci, n obstination f; opiniâtreté f.

obstinate, ob´-sti-néte, a entêté; obstiné.

obstruct, ob-strocte´, v encombrer; (hinder) empêcher; **–ion,** n encombrement m.

obtain, ob-téne´, v obtenir; se procurer.

obtrude, ob-troude´, v s'imposer.

obtrusive*, ob-trouce´-cive, a importun.

obvious*, ob´-vi-*euce*, *a*
évident; clair.

occasion, o-qué´-j´n, *n*
occasion *f*; **–al**, *a*
occasionnel; **–ally**, *adv*
de temps en temps.

occult, ok´-kolte, *a*
occulte; secret.

occupation, ok-kiou-pé´-
ch´n *n* occupation *f*.

occupier, ok´-kiou-pâï-*eur*,
n occupant *m*; (tenant)
locataire *m* & *f*.

occupy, ok´-kiou-pâï, *v* de
occuper; s'occuper (to
be occupied in).

occur, ok-keure´, *v* (to the
mind) venir à l'esprit;
(happen) arriver;
(opportunity) se
présenter.

occurrence, ok-keur´-
ennse, *n* événement *m*.

ocean, au´-ch´n, *n* océan
m.

ocher, ô´-keur, *n* ocre *f*.

octagon, ok´-ta-gonne, *n*
octogone *m*.

octagonal, ok-ta´-gonn-al,
a octogonal.

octave, ok´-téve, *n* octave
f.

October, ok-tau´-b'r, *n*
octobre *m*.

octopus, ok´-tau-p*euce*, *n*
pieuvre *f*; poulpe *m*.

oculist, ok´-iou-liste, *n*
oculiste *m*.

odd, odde, *a* (number)
impair; (single)
dépareillé; (strange)
étrange; **–ly**, *adv*
singulièrement; **–s**, *npl*
(betting) chances *fpl*; **–s
and ends**, bricoles *fpl*.

odious*, au´-di-*euce*, *a*
odieux; détestable.

odium, au´-di-*eume*, *n*
odieux *m*; (hatred)
haine *f*.

odor, o´-d'r, *n* odeur *f*;
(sweet) parfum *m*.

of, ove, *prep* de; (among)
parmi.

off, of, *adv* loin; à
distance. *prep* de.

offal, of-f'l, *n* abats *mpl*;
(refuse) rebut *m*.

offend, of-fennde´, *v*
offenser.

offense, of-fennce´, *n*
offense *f*; (law) délit *m*.

offensive, of-fenn´-cive,
a* offensif. *n* offensive *f*.

offer, of´-f'r, *v* offrir. *n*
offre *f*; **–ing**, offrande *f*.

office, of´-ice, *n* bureau *m*;
fonctions publiques *fpl*.

officer, of´-iss-'r, *n* (*mil*)
officier *m*.

official, of-ich´-'l, *n*
fonctionnaire *m*. *a**
officiel.

officious*, of-ich´-*euce*, *a*
officieux.

offspring, of´-sprinng, *n*

descendant *m*.

oft, often, ofte, of´-'n, *adv*
souvent; fréquemment.

ogle, au´-g'l, *v* lorgner.

oil, oa'ile, *n* huile *f*. *v*
lubrifier; **–cloth**, *n* toile
cirée *f*.

ointment, ô'innte´-m'nt, *n*
pommade *f*.

old, aulde, *a* vieux; âgé;
antique; ancien.

old-fashioned, aulde-
fâch´-*eun*'d, *a* démodé.

olive, ol´-ive, *n* olive *f*; –
oil, huile d'olive *f*.

omelette, omm´-lette, *n*
omelette *f*.

omen, au´-menne, *n*
augure *m*; présage *m*.

ominous*, o´-mi-*neuce*, *a*
de mauvais augure.

omission, o-mîch´-'n, *n*
omission *f*, oubli *m*.

omit, o-mitte´, *v* omettre.

omnipotent, omm-nip´-o-
tennte, *a* tout-puissant.

on, onne, *prep* en; à; sur.
adv (upon) dessus;
(onward) en avant;
(date) le; **–foot**, à pied.

once, ou'onnce, *adv* une
fois; (formerly)
autrefois; **all at –**,tout
d'un coup; **at –**,tout de
suite; **–more**, encore
une fois.

one, ou'onne, *n* & *a* un
m; une *f*; *pron*

(impersonal) on.

onerous*, onn´-eur-euce, a onéreux.

oneself, ou´onne´-selfe, pron soi-même.

onion, onn´-ieune, n oignon m.

only, aune´-li, adv seulement. a unique; seul.

onslaught, onn´-sloate, n assaut m.

onward, onn´-oueurde, adv en avant.

onyx, onn´-ix, n onyx m.

ooze, ouze, v suinter; dégouliner. n vase f; fange f.

opal, au´-pal, n opale f.

opaque, ŏ-péque´, a opaque.

open, ôp´-'n, v ouvrir. a* ouvert; –air, en plein air; –er, n (tool) ouvre... m; –ing, ouverture f; occasion f.

opera, op´-eur-a, n opéra m.

operate, op´-eur-éte, v faire marcher; (med) opérer.

operation, op-eur-é´-ch'n, n opération f.

operator, op´-eur-é-teur, n opérator m.

opinion, ŏ-pinn´-ieune, n opinion f.

opponent, ŏ-pau´-nennte,

n adversaire m.

opportune, op´-ŏr-tioune, a opportun; à propos.

opportunity, ŏ-por-tioue´-ni-ti, n occasion f.

oppose, ŏp-auze´, v opposer; s'opposer.

opposite, op´-ŏ-zitte, adv en face de. a opposé. n opposé m.

opposition, ŏp-pô-zi´-ch'n, n opposition f; (com) concurrence f.

oppress, ŏp-presse´, v opprimer; –ion, n oppression f; –ive, a tyrannique; (atmosphere) accablant.

optician, ŏp-tich´-'n, n opticien m.

option, op´-ch'n, n option f; –al, a facultatif.

opulent, op´-iou-lennte, a opulent.

or, aur, conj ou; –else, ou bien.

oral*, au´-r'l, a oral.

orange, or´-inndje, n orange f.

orator, or´-a-t'r, n orateur m.

oratory, or´-a-tŏ-ri, n éloquence f.

orb, oarbe, n (sphere) globe m; orbe m; sphère f.

orbit, oar´-bitte, n orbite f.

orchard, oar´-tcheurde, n verger m.

orchestra, oar´kess-tra, n orchestre m.

orchid, or´-kidde, n orchidée f.

ordain, oar-déne´, v ordonner.

ordeal, oar´-dîle, n épreuve f.

order, oar´-deur, n ordre m; (goods) commande f. v commander; –ly, a ordonné; (quiet) calme. n planton m.

ordinary, oar´-di-na-ri, a ordinaire.

ordnance, oard´-nannce, n artillerie f.

ore, aure, n minerai m.

organ, oar´-guenne, n orgue m; (med) organe m.

organic, oar-gănn´-ique, a organique.

organization, oar´-ga-nâîzé´-ch'n, n organisation f.

organize, oar´-ga-nâîze, v organiser.

orgy, oar´-dji, n orgie f.

orient, au´-ri-ennte, n orient m; –al, a oriental.

origin, or´-i-djinne, n origine f; –al*, a original.

originate, ŏr-idj´-i-néte, v provenir de.

ornament, oar´-na-mennte, n ornement m.

ornamental, oar´-na-menn´-t'l, a ornemental.

orphan, oar´-f'n, n orphelin, -e m & f; **–age,** orphelinat m.

orthodox, or´-tsŏ-dŏxe, n & a orthodoxe m & f.

orthography, oar-tsog´-ra-fi, n orthographe f.

oscillate, os´-sil-léte, v osciller.

ostentatious*, oss-tennté´-cheuce, a fastueux.

ostrich, oss´-tritche, n autruche f.

other, o´-dz'r, a autre; **the –one,** pron l'autre.

otherwise, o´-dz'r-ou'ãîze, adv autrement.

otter, ot´-t'r, n loutre f.

ought, oate, v devoir; falloir.

our, â'our, poss a notres; nos pl.

ours, â'ourze, poss pron le nôtre ms; la nôtre fs; les nôtres mfpl.

ourselves, â'our-celves´, pron nous-mêmes.

out, â'oute, adv hors, dehors; (extinguished) éteint; (issued) paru; **–bid,** v surenchérir; **–break,** n insurrection f; épidémie f; **–burst,** n explosion f; **–cast,**

proscrit m; **–cry,** clameur f; **–do,** v surpasser; **–fit,** n équipement m; **–fitter,** confectionneur m; (ships) armateur m; **–grow,** v devenir trop grand pour; **–last,** survivre à; dépasser...; **–law,** n proscrit m. v proscrire; **–lay,** n dépenses fpl; **–let,** débouché m; issue f; **–line,** v esquisser; **–live,** survivre à; **–look,** n perspective f; aspect m; **–lying,** a éloigné; **–number,** v surpasser en nombre; **–post,** n avant-poste m; **–put,** rendement m; **–rage,** outrage m; **–rageous,** a outrageux; exorbitant; **–right,** adv entièrement; **–run,** v dépasser en vitesse; **–side,** adv en dehors. n extérieur m; dehors m; **–size,** grande taille f; **–skirts,** confins mpl; **–standing,** a saillant; (debts) impayé; **–ward,** adv à l'extérieur. a extérieur; **–ward bound,** (naut) à destination de l'étranger; **–wit,** v surpasser en finesse.

oval, au´-v'l, n & a ovale m.

ovary, au´-va-ri, n ovaire m.

oven, o´-v'n, n four m.

over, au´-v'r, adv par-dessus. prep sur; au-dessus de; **–alls,** n salopette f; **–bearing,** a arrogant; **–board,** adv par-dessus bord; **–cast,** n couvert; **–charge,** n surcharge f; **–coat,** (woman) manteau m; (man) pardessus m; **–come,** v vaincre; triompher de; **–do,** surmener; exagérer; **–dose,** n dose trop forte f; **–draw,** v excéder son crédit; **–due,** a en retard; (debt) arriéré; **–flow,** v déborder; **–grow,** trop grandir; (botanical) recouvrir; **–hang,** surplomber; **–haul,** (mech) examiner; mettre en état; **–hear,** surprendre une conversation; **–joyed,** pp transporté de joie; **–land,** adv par voie de terre; **–lap,** v chevaucher; **–load,** surcharger; **–look,** avoir vue sur; (forget) oublier; (pardon) laisser passer; **–power,** (vanquish) maîtriser; (heat, fumes,

etc) accabler; **–rate,**
surestimer; **–rule,** (set
aside) rejeter; **–run,**
envahir; infester; **–seas,**
a d'outremer; **–see,** *v*
surveiller; **–seer,** *n*
surveillant *m*; **–sight,**
inadvertance *f*; **–sleep,** *v*
dormir trop longtemps;
–take, rattraper; (car,
etc) doubler; **–throw,**
renverser; **–time,** *n*
(work) travail
supplémentaire *m*;
–turn, *v* renverser; se
renverser; **–weight,** *n*
excédent de poids *m*;
–whelm, *v* accabler;
écraser; **–work,** *v*
surmener. *n* surmenage
m.

owe, au, *v* devoir.

owing, au´-inng, dû; **–to,**
prep à cause de.

owl, â'oule, *n* hibou *m*.

own, aune, *v* posséder;
(admit) avouer. *a* propre
(à soi).

owner, aune´-'r, *n*
propriétaire *m*.

ox, oxe, *n* boeuf *m*.

oxygen, ok´-si-dj'n, *n*
oxygène *m*.

oyster, oa'iss´-t'r, *n* huître
f; **–bed,** parc à huîtres
m.

ozone, ozone, *n* ozone *f*.

pace, péce, n pas m; (speed) allure f. v mesurer.

pacify, păss´-i-fâï, v pacifier; calmer.

pack, păque, v emballer; empaqueter; (a case) faire les valises. n paquet m; (load) charge f; (cards) jeu m; (gang) bande f; (animals) troupeau m; (hounds) meute f; **–age,** colis m; **–et,** paquet m; **–ing,** emballage m; (mech) garniture f.

pact, păcte, n pacte m.

pad, pădde, v (stuff) rembourrer. n (stamp pad) tampon m; (writing) bloc-notes m.

padding, pădd´-inng, n rembourrage m.

paddle, păd´-d'l, v pagayer; (feet, hands) patauger. n pagaie f; **–steamer,** vapeur à roues m; **–wheel,** roue à aubes f.

paddock, pădd´-ŏque, n (meadow) enclos m.

padlock, păd´-lŏque, n cadenas m. v cadenasser.

pagan, pé´-ganne, n & a païen m.

page, pédje, n page f; **–boy,** chasseur m.

pageant, pă´-djannte, n cortège m; spectacle; pompeux m.

pail, péle, n seau m.

pain, péne, v faire mal. n douleur f; **–ful,** a* douloureux; **–less,** sans douleur.

paint, péne-te, v peindre. n peinture f; (art)

couleur f; **–brush,** pinceau m; **–er,** peintre m; **–ing,** (picture) tableau m.

pair, père, n paire f; couple (of married people, etc.) m.

pajamas, pi-djâ´-maze, npl pyjamas m.

palace, păl´-ace, n palais m.

palatable, păl´-a-ta-b'l, a agréable au goût.

palate, păl´-ate, n palais m.

pale, péle, a pâle. v pâlir; **–ness,** n pâleur f.

palette, păl´-ette, n palette f.

paling, péle´-inng, n palissade f.

palm, pâme, n (tree) palmier m; (hand) paume f; **–ist,** chiromancien m; **–istry,** chiromancie f; **–Sunday,** dimanche des Rameaux m.

palpitation, păl-pi-té´-ch'n, n palpitation f.

pamper, pămm´-p'r, v choyer.

pamphlet, pămm´-flitte, n brochure f.

pan, pănne, n (frying) poêle f; **–cake,** crêpe f.

pane, péne, n vitre f; carreau m.

panel, pănn´-'l, n panneau m; (persons) liste f.

pang, pain-ng, n angoisse f.

panic, pănn´-ique, n panique f.

pansy, pănn´-zi, n pensée f.

pant, pănnte, v haleter.

panther, pănn´-tseur, n panthère f.

pantomime, pănn´-taumâïme, n (Christmas) féerie f; pantomime f.

pantry, pănn´-tri, n (food) garde-manger m.

pants, pănntse, npl pantalon m.

papal, pé´-pal, a papal.

paper, pé´-p'r, v tapisser. n papier m; **news-,** journal m; **wall- –,** papier peint m.

par, pâre, n pair m; egalité f.

parable, păr´-a-b'l, n parabole f.

parachute, pă´-ra-choute, n parachute m.

parade, pa-réde´, v parader. n parade f.

paradise, pă´-ra-dâïce, n paradis m.

paraffin, pă´-ra-finne, n paraffine f; **–lamp,** (colloq) lampe à pétrole f.

paragraph, pă´-ra-grăfe, n

paragraphe m.

parallel, pă-ral-lelle, a parallèle; (fig) (similar) semblable.

paralysis, pa-ral´-i-sisse, n paralysie f.

paralyze, pă´-ra-lâïze, v paralyser.

parasite, pă´-ra-sâïte, n parasite m.

parcel, pâr-s'l, n paquet m; colis m.

parched, pârtch´-'t, a desséché; aride.

parchment, pârtch´-m'nt, n parchemin m.

pardon, pâr-d'n, v pardonner; excuser. n pardon m; (law, official) grâce f.

parents, pè´-renntse, npl parents mpl.

parish, păr´-iche, n (civil) commune f; (eccl) paroisse f.

park, pârque, n parc m; **–ing,** (motors) stationnement m; **–ing meter,** n parcomètre m.

parley, pâr-li, v parlementer. n pourparlers mpl.

parliament, pâr-li-mennte, n parlement m.

parlor, pâr´-l'r, n petit salon m.

parochial, pa-rau-ki-al, a communal; paroissial.

parrot, păr´-ŏtte, n perroquet m.

parry, păr´-i, v parer. n (fenc.) parade f.

parsimonious*, pâr-ci-mau´-ni-euce, a parcimonieux.

parsley, pârce´-li, n persil m.

parsnip, pârce´-nippe, n (bot.) panais m.

parson, pâr´-s'n, n (Protestant) pasteur m; (catholic) prêtre m.

parsonage, pâr´-sŏnn-idj, n presbytère m.

part, pârte, v séparer; (hair) faire la raie; n (share) (actor's) rôle m; (district) partie f.

partake, pâr-téque´, v participer à.

partial*, pâr´-ch'l, a partial; **–ity,** n (fig) prédilection f.

participate, pâr-tiss´-i-péte, v participer à or de.

participle, pâr´-ti-ci-p'l, n (grammar) participe m.

particle, pâr´-ti-c'l, n particule f.

particular, par-tik´-iou-l'r, a spécial; exigeant; (exact) minutieux; **–s,** npl détails mpl.

parting, pârt´-inng, n séparation f; (hair) raie f.

partition, pâr-ti´-ch'n, n
(wall) cloison f.

partner, pârte´n'r, n
(business) associé m;
(games) partenaire m &
f; (dance) danseur m.

partnership, pârte´-n'r-
chippe, n association f.

partridge, pârte´-ridje, n
perdrix f.

party, pâr´-ti, n (political)
parti m; féte f; (evening)
soirée f.

pass, pâsse, v passer;
(overtake) dépasser;
(meet) rencontrer;
(exam) réussir;
(mountain) passe f; —
book, livre de compte
m; **–port,** passeport m.

passage, pâss´-idj, n
passage m; (house)
corridor m; (sea)
traversée f.

passenger, pâss´-inn-dj'r, a
& n voyageur, -euse m
& f; (naut) passager, -
ère m & f.

passer-by, pâsse´-r-bâï, n
passant, -e m & f.

passion, pâch´-ŏnne, n
passion f; (anger) colère
f.

passionate*, pâch´-ŏnn-
éte, a passionné.

past, pâsst, n & a passé m.
prep au-delà de.

paste, péste, n pâte f;
(adhesive) colle f. v
coller (for pastry).

pastime, pâsse´-tâïme, n
passe-temps m.

pastries, péss´-trize, npl
pâtisserie f; gâteaux mpl.

pastry, péss´-tri, pâte f.

pasture, pâsse´-tioure, n
pâturage m.

pat, pâtte, v caresser de la
main. n caresse f.

patch, pâtche, v rapiécer.
n pièce f.

patent, pé´-tennte, v
breveter. n brevet
d'invention m. a
breveté; – **leather,** n cuir
verni m.

paternal*, pa-teur´-n'l, a
paternel.

path, pâts, n sentier m;
(garden) allée f.

pathetic, pâ-tsé´-tique, a
pathétique.

patience, pé´-ch'nce, n
patience f.

patient, pé´-ch'nt, n
malade m & f. a*
patient.

patriot, pé´-tri-ŏtte, n
patriote m & f; –**ic,** a
(person) patriote;
(thing) patriotique.

patrol, pa-traule´, n
patrouille f. v faire une
ronde.

patronize, pâ´-trŏnn-âïse,
v favoriser; (fig) faire

l'important.

pattern, pâtt´-eurne, n
modèle m; (sample)
échantillon m; (paper,
etc) patron m.

paunch, poanche, n panse
f, ventre m.

pauper, poa´-p'r, n pauvre
m & f.

pause, poaze, v faire une
pause; s'arrêter. n pause
f.

pave, péve, v paver;
–**ment,** n trottoir m.

pavilion, pă-vil´-ieunne, n
pavilion m.

paw, poa, n patte f. v (as a
horse) piaffer.

pawn, poanne, n (fig) gage
m; (chess) pion m; v
mettre en gage;
–**broker's shop,** n mont-
de-piété m.

pay, pé, v payer. n
(military) solde f;
(workman's) salaire m;
–**able,** a payable; –**er,** n
payeur m; –**ment,**
paiement m.

pea, pî, n pois m; –**nut,**
cacahuète f.

peace, pîce, n paix f;
–**ful*,** a paisible.

peach, pîtche, n pêche f; –
tree, pêcher m.

peacock, pî´-coque, n
paon m.

peak, pique, n (mountain)

pic m; (fig) sommet m.

peal, pîle, n (bells) carillon m; (thunder) coup de tonnerre m.

pear, père, n poire f; — **tree,** poirier m.

pearl, peurle, n perle f.

peasant, pèz´-'nt, n paysan, -anne m & f; **-ry,** les paysans mpl.

peat, pîte, n tourbe f.

pebble, pèb´-b'l, n (on sea shore) galet m.

peck, pèque, v picoter. n (of a bird) coup de bec m.

peculiar*, pi-kiou´-li-eur, a singulier.

peculiarity, pi-kiou-li-ǎr´-i-ti, n singularité f.

pedal, pède-'l, n pédale f. v pédaler.

pedantic, pé-dǎnn´-tique, a (person) pédant; (thing) pédantesque.

peddler, pèd´-l'r, n colporteur m.

pedestal, pèd´-ess-t'l, n piédestal m.

pedestrian, pi-dess´-tri-anne, n piéton m.

pedigree, pèd´-i-grî, n généalogie f; (dog) pedigree m.

peel, pîle, n pelure f. v peler; éplucher.

peep, pîpe, v jeter un coup d'œil. n coup d'œil m.

peer, pîre, n pair m; **-age,** pairie f.

peevish*, pî´-viche, a grincheux; maussade.

peg, pègue, n cheville f; (for hats, etc) patère f; **clothes- –,**pince à linge f.

pellet, pel´-lite, n boulette f; (shot) grain de plomb m.

pelt, pelte, n peau f. v assaillir à coups de ...

pen, pène, n stylo m; (cattle, etc) parc m; **-holder,** porte-plume m; **-knife,** canif m; **--nib,** plume f.

penal, pî´-n'l, a pénal; **-servitude,** n travaux forcés mpl.

penalty, penn´-al-ti, n peine f; (fine) amende f.

penance, penn´-'nce, n pénitence f.

pencil, penn´-s'l, n crayon m.

pendant, penn´-dennte, n (jewel) pendentif m.

pending, penn´-dinng, prep en suspens.

pendulum, penn´-diou-leume, n pendule m.

penetrate, penn´-i-tréte, v pénétrer.

penguin, penn´-gouinne, n pingouin m.

penicillin, penn´-i-sil-inne, n pénicilline f.

peninsula, penn-inn´-siou-la, n péninsule f.

penis, pî´-nisse, n pénis m.

penitent, penn´-i-tennte, n & a pénitent, -e m & f.

penniless, penn´-i-less, a sans le sou.

pension, penn´-ch'n pension f. v mettre à la retraite; **-er,** n retraité, -e m & f; (of mil. or naval homes) invalide m.

pensive*, penn´-cive, a pensif.

penurious, pi-niou´-ri-euce, a indigent.

people, pî-p'l, n gens m & fpl; (community) peuple m.

pepper, pèp´-'r, n poivre m; **-mint,** menthe poivrée f.

per, peure, prep par; **-cent,** pour cent; **-centage,** n pourcentage m.

perceive, peur-cîve´, v apercevoir; (to recognize) s'apercevoir de.

perception, peur-sèpp´-ch'n, n perception f.

perch, peurtche, n (for fowls, etc.) perchoir m; (fish) perche f.

peremptory, pair´-emmp-tŏ-ri, *a* péremptoire.

perfect, peur´-fècte, *a** parfait. *v* perfectionner.

perfection, peur-fèque´-ch'n, *n* perfection *f*.

perfidious*, peur-fid´-i-*euce*, *a* perfide.

perforate, peur´-fo-réte, *v* perforer.

perform, peur-foarme´, *v* exécuter; (stage) représenter; **–ance,** *n* exécution *f*; représentation *f*.

perfume, peur´-fioume, *n* parfum *m*. *v* parfumer.

perhaps, peur-hăpse´, *adv* peut-être.

peril, pèr´-ile, *n* péril *m*; **–ous,** *a* périlleux.

period, pi´-ri-ode, *n* période *f*; **menstrual –s,** règles *fpl*; **–ical,** *a* périodique.

periscope, pèr´-iss-kôpe, *n* périscope *m*.

perish, pèr´-iche, *v* périr; (spoil) avarier.

perishable, pèr´-iche-*a*-b'l, *a* périssable.

perjury, peur´-djiou-ri, *n* parjure *m*.

perm, peurme, *n* permanente *f*.

permanent*, peur´-ma-nennte, *a* permanent.

permeate, peur´-mi-éte, *v* pénétrer.

permission, peur-mich´n, *n* permission *f*.

permit, peur´-mitte, *n* permis *m*. *v* permettre.

pernicious*, peur-nich´-*euce*, *a* pernicieux.

perpendicular, peur-penn-di´-kiou-lar, *n & a* perpendiculaire *f*.

perpetrate, peur´-pi-tréte, *v* commettre.

perpetual*, peur-pett´-iou-*al*, *a* perpétuel.

perplex, peur-plexe´, *v* embarrasser.

persecute, peur´-si-kioute, *v* persécuter.

persecution, peur-si-kiou-ch'n, *n* persécution *f*.

perseverance, peur-si-vir´-'nce, *n* persévérance *f*.

persevere, peur-si-vire´, *v* persévérer.

persist, peur-sisste´, *v* persister.

person, peur´-s'n, *n* personne *f*; **–al,** *a** personnel; **–ality,** *n* personnalité *f*.

personify, peur-sonn´-i-făï, *v* personnifier.

personnel, peur´-sŏ-nèl, *n* personnel *m*.

perspective, peur-spèque´-tive, *n* perspective *f*.

perspicacity, peur-spi-kă´-ci-ti, *n* perspicacité *f*.

perspiration, peur-spi-ré´-ch'n, *n* transpiration *f*.

perspire, peur-spâïre´, *v* transpirer; suer.

persuade, peur-souéde´, *v* persuader.

persuasion, peur-soué´-j'n, *n* persuasion *f*.

pert, peurte, *a* éveillé; impertinent.

pertinent, peur´-ti-nennte, *a* à propos.

perturb, peur-teurbe´, *v* troubler; agiter.

perusal, peur-ouze´-'l, *n* examen *m*; lecture *f*.

peruse, peur-ouze´, *v* lire attentivement.

perverse, peur-veurce´, *a* pervers; dépravé.

pervert, peur-veurte´, *v* pervertir; dénaturer.

pest, peste, *n* peste *f*.

pester, pess´-t'r, *v* tourmenter; importuner.

pet, pette, *n* favori *m*; (child) chéri *m*. *v* choyer; (spoil) gâter.

petal, pett´-'l, *n* pétale *m*.

petition, pi-ti´-ch'n, *n* (law) requête *f*. *v* (law) présenter une requête; **–er,** *n* pétitionnaire *m & f*.

petrify, pett´-ri-făï, *v* pétrifier.

petroleum, pè-trau´-li-*eume*, *n* pétrole *m*.

petticoat, pett´-i-caute, n
jupon m.

petty, pett´-i, a mesquin;
—cash, n argent pour
menus frais m.

petulance, pett´-ioul-'nce,
n pétulance f.

pew, pioue, n banc d'église
m.

pewter, pioue´-t'r, n étain
m.

phantom, fănn´-teume, n
fantôme m; spectre m.

phase, féze, n phase f.

pheasant, fèz´-nt, n faisan
m.

phenomenon, fi-nomm´-i-
nŏnne, n phénomène m.

philosopher, fi-loss´-ŏf-'r,
n philosophe m.

phlegm, flemme, n flegme
m.

phosphate, fosse´-féte, n
phosphate m.

phosphorus, fosse´-fo-
reuce, n phosphore m.

photograph, fau´-to-gràfe,
n photographie f.

photographer, fau-tog´-
ràf-'r, n photographe m.

phrase, fréze, n phrase f;
locution f.

physical, fiz´-zi-k'l, a
physique.

physician, fi-zi´-ch'n, n
médecin m.

physics, fiz´-zix, npl la
physique f.

piano, pi-ă´-nau, n piano
m; **grand —,** piano à
queue m.

pick, pique, n pic m; **(—
axe)** pioche f. v choisir;
(gather) cueillir;
(bones) ronger; **—up,**
ramasser; **—pocket,** n
pickpocket m.

pickle, pik-'l, v conserver
au vinaigre.

pickles, pik-'lze, npl
conserves au vinaigre
fpl; cornichon m.

picnic, pik´-nique, n
pique-nique m.

picture, pik´-tioure, n
tableau m; illustration f;
portrait m; film m.

pie, păï, n (meat) pâté m;
(fruit-open) tourte f.

piece, pîce, n pièce f;
(fragment, portion)
morceau m; **—meal,** adv
par morceaux; **—work,** n
travail à pièce m.

pier, pire, n jetée f.

pierce, pirce, v percer.

piercing, pire´-cinng, a
perçant.

piety, păï´-i-ti, n piété f.

pig, pigue, n cochon m;
porc m; **—iron,** fonte en
gueuse f; **—sty,** porcherie
f.

pigeon, pid´-jinne, n
pigeon m.

pigeonhole, pid´-jinne-

haule, n (papers) case f.

pike, păïque, n (weapon)
pique f; (fish) brochet
m.

pilchard, pill´-chârde, n
pilchard m; sardine f.

pile, pâïle, n (building)
pieu m; (heap) tas m;
(carpet, etc) poil m. v
empiler.

piles, pâïlze, npl (med)
hémorroïdes fpl.

pilfer, pill´-f'r, v chiper.

pilgrim, pill´-grimme, n
pèlerin, -e m & f.

pilgrimage, pill´-grimm-
idj, n pèlerinage m.

pill, pile, n pilule f.

pillage, pill´-idj, n pillage
m. v piller.

pillar, pill´-'r, n pilier m.

pillow, pill´-au, n oreiller
m; **—case,** taie d'oreiller
f.

pilot, pâï´-leutte, n pilote
m. v piloter.

pimple, pimm´-p'l, n
bouton m; pustule f.

pin, pinne, n épingle f;
(safety) épingle de
sûreté f. v épingler.

pinafore, pinn´-a-faure, n
tablier m.

pincers, pinn´-ceurze, npl
pince fpl; tenailles fpl.

pinch, pinntche, v pincer;
(press) gêner. n (salt,
etc) pincée f.

pine, pâîne, n pin m; — **apple,** ananas m.

pinion, pinn´-ieune, n (tech) pignon m. v lier les bras.

pink, pinng-k, a rose. n œillet m.

pinnacle, pinn´-a-k'l, n pinacle m.

pint, pâînnte, n pinte f.

pioneer, pâî-o-nîr´, n pionnier m; (mil) sapeur m.

pious*, pâî´-euce, a pieux.

pip, pippe, n pépin m.

pipe, pâïpe, n tuyau m; conduit m; (tobacco) pipe f.

pirate, pâî´-réte, n pirate m.

pistol, piss´-t'l, n pistolet m.

piston, piss´-t'n, n piston m.

pit, pitte, n fosse f; (mine) mine f; (theater) parterre m.

pitch, pitche, n poix f; (mus) ton m. v (naut) tanguer; (throw) lancer.

pitcher, pitch´-'r, n (jug) cruche f.

pitchfork, pitche´-foarque, n fourche f.

pitfall, pit´-foale, n piège m.

pith, pits, n moelle f.

pitiful*, pitt´-i-foull, a pitoyable.

pitiless*, pitt´-i-lesse, a impitoyable.

pity, pitt´-i, n pitié f. v avoir pitié de; plaindre; **what a —!**interj quel dommage!

pivot, piv´-eute, n pivot m.

placard, plă´-kârde, n affiche f. v placarder.

place, pléce, n place f; (locality) lieu m; endroit m. v mettre.

placid*, plăss´-ide, a placide; calme.

plagiarism, plé´-dji-a-rizme, n plagiat m.

plague, plégue, n peste f. v tourmenter.

plain, pléne, n plaine f. a simple; clair; évident; (looks, etc) ordinaire.

plaint, pléne-te, n plainte f; lamentation f; —**iff,** plaignant, -e m & f; —**ive*,** a plaintif.

plait, plăte, n natte f. v (hair) tresser; (fold) plisser.

plan, plănne, n plan m; projet m. v projeter.

plane, pléne, v raboter. n rabot m; —**tree,** platane m.

planet, plănn´-ette, n planète f.

plank, plain-nk, n

planche f.

plant, plânnte, v planter. n plante f; (mech) outillage m; —**ation,** plantation f.

plaster, plâsse´-t'r, v plâtrer. n plâtre m; (med) emplâtre m.

plastic, plăsse´-tique, n plastique m.

plate, pléte, v argenter; (to cover with gold) dorer; nickeler. n assiette f; (silver) argenterie f; (photo) plaque f.

plateglass, pléte´-glâce, n glace f.

platform, plătt´-fôrme, n estrade f; (station) quai m.

platinum, plătt´-i-nomme, n platine m.

play, plé v jouer. n jeu m; (theater) pièce f; —**er,** musicien, -ienne m & f; acteur m; actrice f; joueur, -euse m & f; —**ful*,** a enjoué; —**ground,** n terrain de jeux m; (school) cour f; —**ing cards,** cartes à jouer fpl.

plea, plî, n procès m; (law) prétexte m; défense f.

plead, plîde, v alléguer; (law) plaider.

pleasant*, plè´-z'nt, a plaisant; agréable.

please, plîze, *v* plaire;
contenter. *interj* s'il vous
plaît!

pleasing, plî´-zinng, *a*
agréable; aimable.

pleasure, plè´-jeure, *n*
plaisir *m*.

pleat, plîte, *n* pli *m*; **–ed**, *a*
plissé.

pledge, plèdje, *n* gage *m*;
(surety) garantie *f*. *v*
(pawn) mettre en gage.

plenty, plenn´-ti, *n*
abondance *f*.

pleurisy, plioue´-ri-si, *n*
pleurésie *f*.

pliable, plâï´-a-b'l, *a*
flexible.

pliers, plâï´-eurze, *npl*
pinces *fpl*.

plight, plâïte, *n* état *m*;
situation *f*.

plod, plodde, *v* (work)
bûcher; **–along,** (walk)
marcher péniblement.

plodder, plodde´-'r, *n*
bûcheur, -euse *m & f*.

plot, plotte, *v* tramer. *n*
complot *m*; (land)
parcelle *f*; (story, etc)
sujet *m*; **–ter,**
conspirateur *m*.

plover, plov´-'r, *n* (*ornit*)
pluvier *m*.

plow, plâ´ou, *n* charrue *f*. *v*
labourer.

plowman, plâ´ou´-manne,
n laboureur *m*.

pluck, ploque, *v* (poultry)
cueillir; (flowers, fruit,
etc.) plumer. *n* courage
m.

plug, plogue, *v* boucher. *n*
bouchon *m*; tampon *m*;
spark –,bougie
d'allumage *f*; **wall
–,**prise de courant.

plum, plomme, *n* prune *f*;
–tree, prunier *m*.

plumage, ploue´-midj, *n*
plumage *m*.

plumb, plomme, *v* (*naut.*)
sonder. *n* plomb *m*; **–ing,**
plombage *m*.

plumber, plomm´-eur, *n*
plombier *m*.

plump, plommpe, *a* gras;
(person) potelé.

plunder, plonn´-d'r, *v*
piller *n* pillage *m*.

plunderer, plonn´-deur-
eur, *n* pillard *m*.

plunge, plonndje, *v*
plonger. *n* plongeon *m*.

plural, ploue´-r'l, *n & a*
pluriel *m*.

plus, plosse, *prep* plus.

plush, ploche, *n* peluche *f*.

ply, plâï, *v* (trade) exercer;
(3-ply wool) laine à
trois fils *f*; **–between,** *v*
faire le service entre. . . .

pneumatic, niou-mätt´-
ique, *a* pneumatique.

pneumonia, niou-mau´-
ni-*a*, *n* pneumonie *f*.

poach, pautche, *v*
braconner; (eggs)
pocher.

poacher, pautch´-'r, *n*
braconnier *m*.

pocket, pok´-ette, *v*
empocher. *n* poche *f*.

pod, pode, *n* cosse *f*;
(garlic) gousse *f*.

poem, pau´-emme, *n*
poème *m*.

poet, pau´-ette, *n* poète *m*;
–ry, poésie *f*.

point, poa˝innte, *v*
indiquer; (finger)
montrer; (sharpen)
tailler. *n* (tip) pointe *f*;
(punctuation, position)
point *m*; **–ed,** *a* pointu;
(*fig*) direct; **–er,** *n* (rod)
baguette *f*; (dog) chien
d'arrêt *m*.

poise, poa´ize, *n* équilibre
m; (person) maintien *m*.

poison, poa'i´-z'n, *n*
poison *m*. *v*
empoisonner; **–ous,** *a*
(of plants) vénéneux;
(animal) venimeux.

poke, pauke, *v* (to push)
pousser; (fire) attiser.

poker, pau´-keur, *n*
tisonnier *m*; (cards)
poker *m*.

pole, paule, *n* perche *f*;
(arctic) pôle *m*.

police, pŏ-lîce´, *n* police *f*;
–man, agent *m*;

–station, commissariat de police *m.*

policy, pol´-i-ci, *n* politique *f*; (insurance) police *f.*

polish, pol´-iche, *n* (gloss) luisant *m*; (shoes) cirage *m*; (furniture, etc) cire *f. v* polir (shoes); cirer.

polite*, pŏ-lâïte´, *a* poli.
–ness, *n* politesse *f.*

political, pŏ-lite´-i-k'l, *a* politique.

politician, pŏl-i-tiche´-ann, *n* homme politique *m.*

politics, pol´-i-tikse, *n* politique *f.*

poll, paule, *n* élection *f*; scrutin *m. v* voter.

pollute, pŏl-lioute´, *v* polluer.

pollution, pol-liou-ch'n, *n* pollution *f.*

pomade, pau-méde´, *n* pommade *f.*

pomegranate, pomm´-grănn-éte, *n* grenade *f.*

pomp, pommpe, *n* pompe *f*; **–ous*,** *a* pompeux.

pond, ponnde, *n* étang *m.*

ponder, ponn´-d'r, *v* réfléchir; méditer.

ponderous*, ponn´-deur-euce, *a* lourd; pesant.

pony, pau´-ni, *n* poney *m.*

poodle, poue´-d'l, *n* caniche *m.*

pool, poule, *n* (water) mare *f*; (swimming) piscine *f*; (cards) cagnotte *f*; poule *f. v* mettre en commun.

poop, poue´pe, *n* poupe *f.*

poor, pou´eur, *a* pauvre. *n* les pauvres *mpl.*

pop, poppe, *v* sauter. *n* (of a cork) bruit d'un bouchon qui saute *m.*

Pope, paupe, *n* pape *m.*

poplar, pop´-l'r, *n* peuplier *m.*

poplin, pop´-linne, *n* popeline *f.*

poppy, pop´-i, *n* (field poppy) coquelicot *m.*

populace, pop´-iou-léce, *n* peuple *m*; foule *f.*

popular*, pop´-iou-l'r, *a* populaire.

populate, pop´-iou-léte, *v* peupler.

population, pop-iou-lé´-ch'n, *n* population *f.*

populous, pop´-iou-leuce, *a* populeux.

porcelain, por´-ce-linne, *n* porcelaine *f.*

porch, paurtche, *n* porche *m*; (Phil.) le Portique *m.*

porcupine, poar´-kiou-pâïne, *n* porc-épic *m.*

pore, paure, *n* pore *m*; **–over,** *v* étudier assidûment.

pork, paurque, *n* porc *m*;

–butcher, charcutier *m.*

porous, pau´-reuce, *a* poreux.

porpoise, poar´-peuce, *n* marsouin *m.*

porridge, por´-idj, *n* bouillie de gruau d'avoine *f.*

port, poar´te, *n* (wine) porto *m*; (harbor) port *m*; (naut) bâbord *m*; **– hole,** hublot *m.*

portable, paur´-ta-b'l, *a* portatif.

portend, poar-tennde´, *v* présager.

porter, paur´-t'r, *n* (luggage) porteur *m*; (door) portier *m*; **–age,** factage *m.*

portfolio, paurt-fau´-li-au, *n* serviette *f.*

portion, paur´-ch'n, *n* portion *f*; (share) part *f.*

portly, paurt´-li, *a* corpulent; d'un port majestueux.

portmanteau, paurt-mănn´-tau, *n* valise *f.*

portrait, paur´-tréte, *n* portrait *m.*

portray, paur-tré´, *v* peindre; (describe) décrire.

pose, pause, *n* pose *f. v* poser; **–as,** se faire passer pour.

position, po-zi´-ch'n, *n*

position f; situation f.

positive*, poz´-i-tive, a
positif; certain.

possess, pô-zesse´, v
posséder; **–ion**, n
possession f.

possessor, pô-zess´-eur, n
possesseur m.

possibility, poss-i-bil´-i-ti,
n possibilité f.

possible, poss´-i-b'l, a
possible.

possibly, poss´-i-bli, adv
peut-être.

post, pauste, n (Phil) poste
f; courrier m; (wood,
etc) poteau m; (job)
emploi m; place f; v
mettre à la poste; **–age**,
n port m; **–card**, carte
postale f; **–date**, v
postdater; **–er**, n affiche
f **–paid**, a franco; **–man**,
n facteur m; **–master**,
receveur des postes m; **–
mortem**, autopsie f; **–
office**, bureau de poste
m; **–pone**, v remettre;
–script, n postscriptum
m.

posterior, poss-ti-ri-eur, n
& a postérieur m.

posterity, poss-tèr´-i-ti, n
postérité f.

posture, poss´-tioure, n
posture f.

pot, potte, n pot m;
(cooking) marmite f.

potash, pot´-ăche, n
potasse f.

potato, po-té´-tau, n
pomme de terre f.

potent, pau´-tennte, a
puissant; (fig) efficace.

potion, pau´-ch'n, n
potion f.

pottery, pot´-eur-i, n
poterie f.

pouch, pâ'outche, n poche
f; (tobacco) blague f.

poulterer, paule´-teur-eur,
n marchand de volailles
m.

poultice, paule´-tice, n
cataplasme m.

poultry, paule´-tri, n
volaille f.

pounce, pâ'ounce, v (on,
upon) fondre sur.

pound, pâ'ounde, n livre
sterling f; (weight) livre
f; (animals) fourrière f. v
(pulverize) broyer.

pour, paure, v verser;
(rain) pleuvoir à verse.

pour out, paure â'oute, v
verser; (serve) servir.

pout, pâ'oute, v faire la
moue.

poverty, pov´-eur-ti, n
pauvreté f.

powder, pâ'ou´-d'r, n
poudre f. v pulvériser;
(face) poudrer.

power, pâ'ou-eur, n
pouvoir m; (mech) force

f; (state) puissance f;
–ful*, a puissant; **–less**,
impuissant.

pox, poxe, **small– –**,n
variole f; **chicken–
–**,varicelle f.

practicable, prăque´-ti-ca-
b'l, a praticable.

practical*, prăque´-ti-c'l, a
pratique.

practice, prăque´-tice, n
pratique f; (custom)
coutume f;
(professional) clientèle
f; (exercise) exercise m;
(mus) s'exerce;
(profession) exercer.

practitioner, prăque-
tiche´-onn-eur, n
praticien m.

praise, préze, v louer. n
louange f; éloge m.

praiseworthy, préze´-
oueur-dzi, a louable.

pram, prămme, n landau
m.

prance, prănnce, v se
cabrer; (fig) se pavaner.

prank, prain-nk, n
escapade f; farce f.

prawn, proanne, n
bouquet m.

pray, pré, v prier.

prayer, préeur, n prière f; **–
book**, livre de prières m;
Lord's Prayer, pater m.

preach, prîtche, v prêcher;
–er, n prédicateur m.

precarious*, pri-ké'-ri-euce, *a* précaire.

precaution, pri-koa'-ch'n *n* précaution *f.*

precede, prî-cîde', *v* précéder.

precedence, prè'-sid-ennce, *n* préséance *f.*

precedent, prè'-sid-ennte, *n* (example) précédent *m.*

precept, prî'-cèpte, *n* précepte *m.*

precinct, prî'-cinng-kt, *n* enceinte *f.*

precious*, prè'-cheuce, *a* précieux.

precipice, prèce'-i-pice, *n* précipice *m.*

precise*, pri-sâïce', *a* précis; exact.

preclude, pri-cloude', *v* exclure; empêcher.

precocious*, pri-kau'-cheuce, *a* précoce.

predecessor, pri-di-sess'-eur, *n* prédécesseur *m.*

predicament, pri-dik'-a-mennte, *a* mauvaise passe *f;* situation difficile *f.*

predicate, predd'-i-quéte, *n* (gram) attribut *m.*

predict, pri-dicte', *v* prédire; **–ion**, *n* prédiction *f.*

predominant, pri-domm'-i-nannte, *a*

prédominant.

preface, preff'-ace, *n* préface *f.*

prefect, pri'-fecte, *n* préfet *m.*

prefer, pri-feur', *v* préférer.

preferable, preff'-eur-a-b'l, *a* préférable.

preference, preff'-eur-ennce, *n* préférence *f.*

prefix, prè'-fixe, *n* préfixe *m. v* mettre en tête.

pregnant, pregg'-nannte, *a* enceinte; (animals) pleine.

prejudice, prédj'-iou-dice, *n* préjugé *m;* préjudice *m. v* préjudicier; **–d**, *a* prévenu contre; **without –**, sans préjudice de.

prejudicial*, prédj-iou-dich'-'l, *a* préjudiciable.

prelate, prél'-éte, *n* prélat *m.*

preliminary, pri-limm'-i-na-ri, *a* préliminaire.

prelude, pré'-lioude, *n* prélude *m.*

premature*, pré'-ma-tioure, *a* prématuré.

premeditate, pri-medd'-i-téte, *v* préméditer.

premier, prî'-mi-eur, *n* (France) président du conseil (des ministres) *m. a* premier.

premises, premm'-i-cize, *npl* locaux *mpl.*

premium, prî'-mi-eume, *n* prime *f.*

preparation, prip-a-ré'-ch'n, *n* préparation *f.*

prepare, pri-pére', *v* préparer.

prepossessing, pri-pŏ-zess'-inng, *a* avenant.

preposterous*, pri-poss'-teur-euce, *a* absurde.

prerogative, pri-rog'-a-tive, *n* prérogative *f.*

prescription, pri-skrip'-ch'n, *n* (med) ordonnance *f.*

presence, préz'-ennce, *n* présence *f;* **–of mind**, présence d'esprit *f.*

present, pri-zennte', *v* présenter; (gift) offrir à.

present, préz'-ennte, *n* cadeau *m. a* présent; **–ation**, *n* présentation *f;* **–ly**, *adv* tout à l'heure.

presentiment, pri-zenn'-ti-mennte, *n* pressentiment *m.*

preservation, prèz-eur-vé'-ch'n, *n* protection *f;* (state, condition) conservation *f.*

preserve, pri-zeurve', *v* préserver; conserver; (candied) confire; **–s**, *npl* conserves *fpl.*

preside, pri-zâïde', *v* présider de.

president, préz'-i-dennte,

n président m.

press, presse, n presse f. v presser; appuyer; (clothes) repasser; **–ing,** a urgent.

pressure, préch´-eur, n pression f; urgence f.

presume, pri-zioume´, v présumer; (dare) oser.

presumption, pri-zomm´-ch'n, n présomption f.

pretend, pri-tennde´, v prétendre; (sham) feindre, faire semblant de.

pretense, pri-tennce´, n simulation f; prétexte m.

pretentious*, pri-tenn´-cheuce, a prétentieux.

pretext, prî´-texte, n prétexte m.

pretty, pritt´-i, a joli.

prevail, pri-véle, v prévaloir; **–upon,** persuader.

prevalent, prév´-a-lennte, a dominant; général.

prevent, pri-vennte, v empêcher; **–ion,** n prévention f; **–ive,** a* préventif.

previous, prî´-vi-euce, a précédent; préalable.

prey, pré, n proie f. v faire sa proie de.

price, prâïce, n prix m; **–less,** a hors de prix.

prick, prique, v piquer. n

piqûre f; **–le,** épine f; **–ly,** a épineux.

pride, prâïde, n orgueil m. v (to – oneself on) s'enorgueillir de.

priest, prîste, n prêtre m.

prim, prime, a collet monté; (dress) soigneux.

primary, prâï´-ma-ri, a primaire; fondamental.

primate, prâï´-méte, n primat m.

prime, prâïme, n (of life) fleur de l'âge f. a premier; de première qualité. v préparer; **–minister,** n (France) président du conseil m.

primer, prâï´-meur, n (school) livre élémentaire m.

primitive, primm´-i-tive, a primitif.

primrose, primm´-rauze, n primevère f.

prince, prinnce, n prince m; **–ly,** a princier; **–ss,** n princesse f.

principal, prinn´-ci-p'l, n directeur m; chef m; (funds) principal m. a* principal.

principle, prinn´-ci-p'l, n principe m.

print, prinnte, v imprimer. n impression f; (photo) épreuve f; **–er,** imprimeur m; **–ing,**

impression f; **–ing-works,** imprimerie f.

prior, prâï´-eur, n prieur m. a antérieur. adv avant de; **–ity,** n priorité f; **–y,** prieuré m.

prism, prizme, n prisme m; **–atic,** a prismatique.

prison, priz´-'n, n prison f; **–er,** prisonnier, -ère m & f.

privacy, prâï´-va-ci, n retraite f; intimité f.

private, prâï´-véte, a* privé; personnel; particulier. n (soldier) simple soldat m.

privation, prâï-vé´-ch'n, n privation f.

privilege, priv´-i-lidje, n privilège m. v privilégier.

privy, priv´-i, a privé; secret.

prize, prâïze, n prix m; (ship) prise f. v évaluer.

probable, prob´-a-b'l, a probable.

probate, pro´-béte, n vérification d'un testament f.

probation, pro-bé´-ch'n, n épreuve f; essai m; **–er,** stagiaire m & f; (eccl) novice m & f.

probe, praube, v sonder; explorer. n sonde f.

problem, prob´-lemme, n problème m.

procedure, prŏ-cîd´-ioure, n procédé m; (law) procédure f.

proceed, prŏ-cîde´, v procéder; continuer; **–ings,** npl mesures fpl; (law) poursuites fpl.

proceeds, prau´-cîdze, npl produit m; bénéfices mpl.

process, prau´-cesse, n cours m; (manufacture) procédé m.

procession, prŏ-cé-ch´n, n procession f.

proclaim, prŏ-cléme´, v proclamer; publier.

proclamation, prŏc-là-mé´-ch´n, n proclamation f.

procure, prŏ-kioure´, v se procurer; procurer.

prod, prŏde, v piquer; pousser.

prodigal*, prod´-i-g'l, a prodigue.

prodigious*, prŏ-di´-djeuce, a prodigieux.

prodigy, prod´-i-dji, n prodige m.

produce, prŏ-diouce´, v produire. n produit m; denrées fpl; **–r,** producteur, -trice m & f; (stage) metteur en scène m.

product, prod´-eucte, n produit m; **–ion,**

production f; (stage) représentation f.

profane, prŏ-féne´, v profaner. a* profane.

profess, prŏ-fesse´, v professer; déclarer; **–ion,** n profession f; carrière f; **–ional*,** a professionnel.

professor, prŏ-fess´-'r, n professeur m.

proficiency, prŏ-fi´-chenn-ci, n capacité f; compétence f.

proficient, prŏ-fi´-ch'nt, a avancé; versé.

profile, prau´-fâïle, n profil m.

profit, prof´-itte, n bénéfice m. v profiter; **–able,** a avantageux; **–eer,** n profiteur, -euse m & f.

profound*, prŏ-fâ'ounnde´, a profond.

profuse, prŏ-fiouce´, a prodigue; abondant.

program, prau´-grämme, n programme m.

progress, prau-gresse´, v faire des progrès; avancer.

progress, prau´-gresse, n progrès m.

prohibit, prŏ-hib´-itte, v interdire à; défendre.

project, prŏd-jecte´, v projeter; dépasser; déborder. n projet m;

–ile, projectile m; **–ion,** saillie f; **–or,** projecteur m.

proletarian, prau-lè-té´-ri-anne, n & a prolétaire m.

prologue, prau´-logue, n prologue m.

prolong, prau-lonng´, v prolonger.

promenade, promm-eu-nâde´, v se promener. n promenade (en grande toilette) f.

prominent, promm´-i-nennte, a proéminent.

promise, promm´-iss, n promesse f. v promettre.

promissory note, promm´-iss-o-ri naute, n billet à ordre m.

promote, prŏ-maute´, v promouvoir; (business) lancer; **–r,** n promoteur m; **company –r,** lanceur d'affaires m.

promotion, prau-mau´-ch'n, n avancement m; promotion f.

prompt, prommpte, a* prompt. v suggérer; (stage) souffler; **–er,** n souffleur m.

prone, praune, a étendu; (fig) enclin à; (bent) courbé.

prong, pronng, n dent f; pointe f.

pronoun, prau´-nâ'ounne, n pronom m.

pronounce, prŏnâ'ounnce´, v prononcer.

pronunciation, prŏ-nonnci-é´-ch'n, n prononciation f.

proof, proufe, n preuve f. a – against, à l'épreuve de.

prop, proppe, n (fig) soutien m, support m. v étayer; supporter.

propaganda, prop-a-gănn´-da, n propagande f.

propagate, prop´-a-guéte, v propager.

propel, prŏ-pelle´, v faire mouvoir.

propeller, prŏ-pell´-eur, n hélice f.

proper*, prop´-'r, a propre; (fit) convenable.

property, prop´-eur-ti, n propriété f; biens mpl.

prophecy, prof´-i-si, n prophétie f.

prophesy, prof´-i-sâï, v prédire.

prophet, prof´-ette, n prophète m.

propitious*, pro-pich´-euce, a propice.

proportion, pro-paur´-ch'n, n proportion f.

proposal, pro-pauz´-'l, n proposition f.

propose, pro-pauze´, v proposer; offrir.

proposition, pro-pauzich´-'n, n proposition f.

proprietor, pro-prâï-è-teur, n propriétaire m.

proprietress, pro-prâï-è-tresse, n propriétaire f.

propriety, pro-prâï-è-ti, n convenances fpl.

prose, prauze, n prose f.

prosecute, pross´-i-kioute, v (law) poursuivre.

prosecution, pross-i-kioue´-ch'n, n poursuites fpl.

prosecutor, pross´-i-kioue-teur, n plaignant m.

prospect, pross´-pecte, n vue f; (future) avenir m. v explorer; –ive, a futur.

prospectus, pross-pec´-teuce, n prospectus m.

prosper, pross´-p'r, v prospérer; –ity, n prospérité f; –ous*, a prospère.

prostitute, pross´-ti-tioute, n prostituée f.

prostrate, pross-tréte, v se prosterner; (fig) accabler. a posterné; accablé; prostré; abattu.

prostration, pross-tré´-ch'n, n prostration f.

protect, pro-tecte´, v protéger.

protection, pro-tec´-ch'n,

n protection f.

protest, pro-tesste´, v protester. n protestation f.

protract, pro-tracte´, v prolonger.

protrude, pro-troude´, v faire saillie; déborder.

proud*, prâ'oude, a fier; orgueilleux.

prove, prouve, v prouver; vérifier (a will, etc.).

proverb, prov´-eurbe, n proverbe m.

provide, prŏ-vâide´, v pourvoir; fournir.

Providence, prov´-i-dennce, n providence f.

provident, prov´-i-dennte, a prévoyant.

province, prov´-innce, n province f.

provision, prŏ-vi´-j'n, n provision f; stipulation f; –al*, a provisoire; –s, npl comestibles mpl.

provocation, prŏv-ô-qué´-ch'n, n provocation f.

provoke, prŏ-vauke´, v provoquer; irriter.

prowl, prâ'oule, v rôder.

proximity, prok-simm´-i-ti, n proximité f.

proxy, prok´-ci, n fondé de pouvoir m; **by –,** par procuration.

prude, proude, n prude f; –nce, prudence f; –nt*,

a prudent; **–ry,** *n* pruderie *f*.

prudish, prou´-diche, *a* prude.

prune, proune, *n* pruneau *m*. *v* (trees, etc) tailler.

pry, praï, *v* fureter; fourrer son nez dans . . .

psalm, sâme, *n* psaume *m*.

pseudonym, sioue´-dô-nimme, *n* pseudonyme *m*.

psychiatry, sâï-kâï´-a-tri, *n* psychiatrie *f*.

psychology, sâï-col-´ŏdj-i, *n* psychologie *f*.

public, pobb´-lique, *n* & *a* public *m*; **–an,** *n* aubergiste *m*; **–house,** auberge *f*.

publication, pobb-li-qué´-ch'n, *n* publication *f*.

publish, pobb´-liche, *v* publier; (books, etc) éditer.

publisher, pobb´-lich-*eur*, *n* éditeur *m*.

pucker, pok-´-'r, *v* rider; plisser (the brows, etc.); froncer.

pudding, poudd´-inng, *n* pudding *m*.

puddle, podd-´-'l, *n* flaque *f*.

puerile, pioue´-*eur*-âïl, *a* puéril.

puff, pof, *v* souffler; (swell) boursoufler. *n*

(breath) souffle *m*; (wind, etc) bouffée *f*; **powder –,** houppe à poudrer *f*; **–y,** *a* boursouflé.

pug, pogg, *n* (dog) carlin *m*; **–nacious,** *a* batailleur; **–-nosed,** qui a le nez épaté.

pugilist, pioue´-djil-ist, *n* pugiliste *m*.

pull, poull, *n* coup (d'aviron) *m*. *v* tirer; **–down,** abattre; démolir; (lower) baisser; **–out,** (draw) arracher; **–up,** remonter; hisser.

pullet, poull´-ette, *n* poulette *f*.

pulley, poull´-i, *n* poulie *f*.

pulp, polpe, *n* pulpe *m*; **wood –,** pâte de bois *f*.

pulpit, poull´-pitte, *n* chaire *f*.

pulse, pollse, *n* pouls *m*.

pulverize, poll´-*veur*-âïze, *v* pulvériser.

pumice, pomm´-ice staune, *n* pierre ponce *f*.

pump, pommpe, *n* pompe *f*. *v* pomper.

pun, ponne, *n* jeu de mots *m*.

punch, ponntche, *n* (blow) coup de poing *m*; (tool) poinçon *m*; (drink) punch *m*; (to hit) *v* donner un coup

de poing à; percer.

punctilious*, ponngk-til´-i-*euce*, *a* pointilleux.

punctual*, ponngk´-tiou-*eul*, *a* ponctuel.

punctuate, ponngk´-tiou-éte, *v* ponctuer.

punctuation, ponngk-tiou-é´-ch'n, *n* ponctuation *f*.

puncture, ponngk´-tioure, *n* (med) ponction *f*; (tire) crevaison *f*. *v* crever.

pungency, ponn´-djenn-si, *n* âcreté *f*; aigreur *f*.

pungent, ponn´-djennte, *a* âcre; piquant.

punish, ponn´-iche, *v* punir; **–able,** *a* punissable.

punishment, ponn´-iche-mennte, *n* punition *f*.

punitive, pioue´-ni-tive, *a* punitif.

punt, ponnte, *n* bateau plat *m*.

puny, pioue´-ni, *a* chétif; faible.

pupil, pioue´-pile, *n* élève *m* & *f*; (eye) pupille *f*.

puppet, popp´-ette, *n* marionnette *f*; poupée *f*.

puppy, popp´-i, *n* jeune chien *m*.

purchase, por´-tchiss, *v* acheter. *n* achat *m*.

purchaser, por´-tché-*seur*,

n acheteur, *-euse m & f.*

pure*, pioure, *a* pur; vierge.

purgative, peur´-*ga*-tive, *n & a* purgatif *m.*

purgatory, peur´-*ga*-tŏ-ri, *n* purgatoire *m.*

purge, peurdje, *v* purger. *n* purge *f.*

purify, pioue´-ri-fâï, *v* purifier.

purity, pioue´-ri-ti, *n* pureté *f.*

purloin, peur´-lô´ine, *v* dérober.

purple, peur´-p'l, *n & a* pourpre *m.*

purpose, peur´-*peuce,* *n* but *m;* **–ly,** *adv* exprès.

purr, peur, *v* ronronner.

purse, peurce, *n* porte-monnaie *m;* (prize) bourse *f.*

purser, peur´-*ceur,* *n* (ship's) commissaire *m.*

pursue, peur-sioue´, *v* poursuivre.

pursuit, peur-sioute´, *n* poursuite *f.*

purveyor, peur-vé´-*eur,* *n* fournisseur *m.*

pus, poss, *n* pus *m;* humeur *f.*

push, pouche, *v* pousser. *n* poussée *f.*

pushing, pouch´-inng, *a* (keen) entreprenant.

put, poutt, *v* mettre; placer; poser; **–off,** remettre; **–on,** mettre.

putrefy, pioue´-tri-fâï, *v* se putréfier; pourrir.

putrid, pioue´-tride, *a* putride.

putty, pott´-i, *n* mastic *m.*

puzzle, pozz-z'l, *v* embarrasser; intriguer. *n* embarras *m;* (toy) casse-tête *m;* puzzle *m;* **crossword –,** mots croisés *mpl.*

pyramid, pir´-*a*-mide, *n* pyramide *f.*

python, pâï-*t*sonn, *n* python *m.*

quack, couâque, *v* cancaner. *n* charlatan *m*; **-ery,** charlatanisme *m*.

quadrille, couodd´rile, *n* quadrille *m*.

quadruped, couodd´-roupedde, *n* quadrupède *m*.

quadruple, couodd´-roup´l, *a* quadruple.

quagmire, couâgue´-mâïre, *n* marécage *m*.

quail, couéle, *n* caille *f*. *v* trembler.

quaint*, couénnte, *a* bizarre; étrange.

quaintness, couénnte´-nesse, *n* bizarrerie *f*.

quake, couéque, *v* trembler; **earth–,** *n* tremblement de terre *m*.

Quaker, coué´-keur, *n* (sect) Quaker *m*.

qualification, couoll-i-fiqué´-ch'n, *n* aptitude *f*.

qualified, couoll´-i-fâïd, *a* diplômé.

qualify, couoll´-i-fâï, *v* qualifier; acquérir les qualités requises.

quality, couoll´i-ti, *n* qualité *f*.

quandary, couonn´-da-ri, *n* perplexité *f*.

quantity, couonn´-ti-ti, *n* quantité *f*.

quarantine, couor´-anntîne, *n* quarantaine *f*.

quarrel, couor´-elle, *n* dispute *f*. *v* se disputer.

quarrelsome, couor´-ell-*se*ume, *a* querelleur.

quarry, couor´-i, *n* carrière *f*; (prey) proie *f*.

quarter, couôr´-t'r, *v* (to lodge) loger; diviser en quatre. *n* quart *m*; (period) trimestre *m*; (district) quartier *m*; **–ly,** *a* trimestriel.

quartet, couôr-tette´, *n* quatuor *m*.

quartz, couortze, *n* quartz *m*.

quash, couoche, *v* subjuguer; réprimer; (law) annuler.

quaver, coué-v´r, *v* chevroter. *n* (*mus*) croche *f*.

quay, quî, *n* quai *m*.

queen, couîne, *n* reine *f*.

queer*, couire, *a* bizarre; étrange; drôle.

quell, couelle, *v* réprimer; dompter.

quench, couenntche, *v* éteindre; (thirst) apaiser sa soif.

querulous*, couèr´-ouleuce, *a* plaintif.

query, coui´ri, *v* mettre en doute. *n* question *f*.

quest, coueste, *n* recherche *f*; enquête *f*.

question, couess´-tieune, *v* questionner; douter. *n*

question f; –**able,** a
contestable; –**mark,** n
point d'interrogation m.
queue, kioue, n queue f.
quibble, couib´-b'l, v
ergoter. n chicane f.
quick*, couique, a rapide;
(hurry) vite; (wit, etc)
vif; –**en,** v accélérer;
animer; –**lime,** n chaux
vive f; –**ness,** vitesse f;
vivacité f; –**sand,** sables
mouvants mpl.
quiet, couâî´-ette, v
calmer. a* tranquille.
quill, couille, n (pen)
plume d'oie f.
quilt, couillte, n couvre-
pieds m; édredon
américain m.
quince, couinnce, n coing
m.
quinine, couinn´-âïne, n
quinine f.
quit, couitte, v quitter; –**s,**
adv quitte.
quite, couâîte, adv tout à
fait; entièrement; assez.
quiver, couiv´-'r, n
carquois m. v trembler; n
tremblement m.
quiz, couiz, n jeu-concours
m; devinette f;
interrogation f. v
interroger; questionner;
n test m; (game) jeu-
concours m.
quota, cou'au´ta, n quote-

part f; quota m.
quotation, cou'au-té´-
ch'n, n citation f;
(price) devis m; (shares,
etc) cote f.
quote, cou'aute, v citer;
coter; faire un prix.

rabbi, răb´-bâï, n rabbin
m.

rabbit, răb´-itte, n lapin
m.

rabble, rabb´-'l, n
populace f; (riffraff)
canaille f.

rabid, răb´-ide, a enragé.

rabies, ré´-bi-ize, n rage f.

race, réce, v courir; courir
vite; faire la course. n
(breed) race f; (contest)
course f; **—course,**
champ de courses m; **—
horse,** cheval de course
m; **-s,** courses fpl.

racism, ré´-si-z'm, n
racisme m.

racist, ré´-ssiste, a, n
raciste.

rack, răque, n (torture)
roue f; (luggage) filet m.

racket, răque´-ette, n
(sports) raquette f.

radar, ré-dâre, n radar m.

radiant*, ré´-di-annte, a
rayonnant (de); (fig)
radieux.

radiate, ré´-di-éte, v
rayonner (de); (heat)
émettre des rayons.

radiation, ré-di-é-ch'n, n
rayonnement m.

radiator, ré-di-é-teur, n
radiateur m.

radio, ré´-di-o, n radio f.

radioactive, ré-di-o-ăc´-
tive, a radioactif.

radio station, ré-di-o-stă-
ch'n, n station de radio
f.

radish, răd´-iche, n radis
m; horse- –, raifort m.

radium, ré´-di-omme, n
radium m.

radius, ré´-di-euce, n

rayon m.

raffle, ră?´-'l, n loterie f. v
mettre en loterie.

raft, râfte, n radeau n.

rafter, râf´-t'r, n chevron
m. poutre f.

rag, răgue, n chiffon m;
–ged, a en loques.

rage, rédje, n rage f. v être
furieux.

raid, réde, n incursion f;
(air –) raid m; (police –)
descente de police f.

rail, réle, v railler. n
(railroad) rail m; (stair)
barreau m; **–lery,**
raillerie f; **–road,**
chemin de fer m.

rain, réne, v pleuvoir. n
pluie f; **–bow,** arc-en-
ciel m; **–coat,**
imperméable m; **–fall,**
quantité de pluie f; **—
water,** eau de pluie f; **–y,**
a pluvieux.

raise, réze, v (courage)
lever; (to lift, etc.)
relever; soulever;
(increase) augmenter;
(heighten) rehausser;
(crops) cultiver.

raisin, ré-z'n, n raisin sec
m.

rake, réque, n râteau m;
(person) roué m. v
(mech) râtisser; (fire)
secouer.

rally, răl´-i, v rallier;

rassembler; n rallye m.

ram, rămme, n bélier m. v enfoncer; (ship) aborder.

rampant, rămm´-pannte, a rampant; exubérant.

rampart, rămm´-pârte, n rempart m.

rancid, rănn´-cide, a rance.

rancor, rănng´-keur, n rancune f.

random, rănn´-d'm, **at** –,adv au hasard.

range, réne´-dje, n série f; (kitchen) fourneau m; (extent) étendue f; (mountain) chaîne f; (practice) champ de tir m; (projectile) portée f. v ranger.

ranger, réne´-djeur, n garde-forestier m.

rank, rain-nk, a (taste, smell) rance. n rang m; (mil) grade m; (row) rangée f.

ransack, rănn´-săque, v saccager; fouiller.

ransom, rănn´-seume, n rançon f. v rançonner.

rap, răppe, n coup m. v frapper.

rape, répe, v violer; enlever. n viol m.

rapid*, răp´-ide, a rapide; –s, npl rapides mpl.

rapture, răp´-tioure, n

ravissement m.

rare*, raire, a rare; –**fy,** v raréfier.

rarity, ré´-ri-ti, n rareté f.

rascal, râsse´-c'l, n coquin m; fripon m.

rash*, răche, n (skin) éruption f. a* téméraire; –**er,** n tranche de lard f; –**ness,** témérité f.

rasp, râsse, n râpe f; grincement m. v râper; grincer.

raspberry, râze´-beur-i, n framboise f.

rat, rătte, n rat m; –**trap,** ratière f.

rate, réte, n proportion f; (tax; exchange; charge) taux m; (speed) vitesse f. v évaluer.

rather, râdz´-'r, adv plutôt; (somewhat) assez.

ratify, răt´-i-faï, v ratifier.

ratio, ré´-chi-au, n proportion f.

ration, ră-ch'n, n ration f. v rationner.

rational*, răch´-eunn-'l, a rationnel; raisonnable.

rattle, răt´-t'l, n (instrument) crécelle f; (toy) hochet m; (noise) tapage m; (death) râle de la mort m.

rattlesnake, răt´-t'l-snéke, n serpent à sonnettes m.

ravage, răv´-idj, v ravager.

n ravage m.

rave, réve, v délirer; –**about,** s'extasier sur.

raven, ré´-v'n, n corbeau m.

ravenous, răv´-'n-euce, a vorace.

ravine, ră-vine´, n ravin m.

raving, ré´-vinng, a en délire; (fig) furieux.

ravish, ră´-viche, v ravir; –**ing,** a ravissant.

raw, roa, a cru; (wound) à vif.

ray, ré, n rayon m.

raze, réze, v raser; abattre.

razor, ré´-z'r, n rasoir m; **safety–,**rasoir mécanique m; –**blade,** lame de rasoir f.

reach, rîtche, v atteindre; (arrive) parvenir à.

react, ri-acte´, réagir; –**ion,** n réaction f.

read, rîde, v lire; (for exam) étudier; –**er,** n lecteur m; (print) correcteur m; –**ing,** n lecture f.

readily, redd´-i-li, adv promptement; (willingly) volontiers.

ready, redd´-i, a prêt; –**made,** tout fait; (clothes) le prêt à porter.

real*, ri-´-l, a réel;

véritable.

reality, rî-ă´-li-tî, n réalité f.

realize, ri´-al-âïze, v se rendre compte de; (sell) réaliser.

realm, relme, n royaume n.

reap, rîpe, v moissonner; récolter; **–er,** moissonneur m; **–ing machine,** moissonneuse f.

rear, rire, v élever; (prance) se cabrer. n (mil) arrière-garde f; (back) arrière m.

reason, rî´-z'n, v raisonner. n raison f.

reasonable, rî´-z'n-a-b'l, a raisonnable.

reassure, ri´-a-choure´, v rassurer.

rebate, ri-béte´, v rabattre.

rebel, rebb´-'l, n & a rebelle m & f.

rebel, ri-bel´, v se révolter; **–lion,** n rébellion f.

rebound, ri-bâ´ounnde´, v rebondir. n rebond m; ricochet m; remontee f.

rebuff, ri-boffe´, v rebuter. n rebuffade f.

rebuke, ri-biouke´, v réprimander. n réprimande f.

recall, ri-coale´, v rappeler; (retract)

retirer.

recapitulate, ri-ca-pit´-iou-léte, v récapituler.

recede, ri-cîde´, v reculer.

receipt, ri-cîte´, n reçu m. v acquitter.

receipts, ri-cîtse´, npl (com) recettes fpl.

receive, ri-cîve´, v recevoir; **–r,** n receveur m; (bankruptcy) syndic de faillite m.

recent*, rî´-cennte, a récent.

receptacle, ri-sèpe´-ta-k'l, n réceptacle m.

reception, ri-sèpe-ch'n, n réception f.

recess, ri-cesse´, n (space) renfoncement m; (of a bed) alcôve f.

recipe, ress´-i-pi, n recette f.

reciprocate, ri-cip´-rŏ-quéte, v rendre la pareille.

recital, ri-sâï´-t'l, n récit m; récitation f; (mus, etc) récital m.

recite, ri-sâïte´, v réciter.

reckless*, rèque´-lesse, a imprudent.

reckon, rèque´-'n, v compter; calculer.

reclaim, ri-cléme´, v réclamer; (land) défricher.

recline, ri-clâïne´, v se

pencher; s'appuyer.

recluse, ri-clouce´, n & a reclus, -e m & f.

recognition, rèk-ŏgue-niche´-'n, n reconnaissance f.

recognize, rèk-ŏgue-nâïze, v reconnaître.

recoil, ri-coa'ile´, v reculer. n recul m.

recollect, rèk-ŏl-lecte´, v se rappeler; se souvenir de.

recollection, rèk-ŏl-lèque´-ch'n, n souvenir m.

recommence, ri-cŏmm-ennce´, v recommencer.

recommend, rè-cŏmm-ennde´, v recommander; **–ation,** n recommandation f.

recompense, rèk´-ŏmm-pennce, v récompenser. n récompense f.

reconcile, rèk-ŏnn-sâïle, v réconcilier (avec); concilier.

reconnoiter, rèk-ŏnn-no'i´-tr, v faire une reconnaissance.

reconsider, ri-cŏnn-cid´-'r, v considérer de nouveau.

record, ri-coarde´, v enregistrer; (in history) mentionner.

record, rèk´-oarde, n

registre *m*; archives *fpl*;
(phonograph) disque *m*;
––player, *n* tourne-
disques *m*.

recoup, ri-coupe´, *v*
dédommager (de).

recourse, ri-caurse´, *n*
recours *m*.

recover, rî-cov´-'r, *v*
recouvrer; (health) se
rétablir; **–y,** *n*
recouvrement *m*;
rétablissement *m*.

recover, ri-cov´-'r, *v*
recouvrir.

recreation, rèk-ri-é´-ch'n,
n divertissement *m*.

recruit, ri-croute´, *n*
recrue *f*. *v* recruter.

rectangular, rèk-tănng´-
guiou-l'r, *a*
rectangulaire.

rectify, rèk´-ti-fâï, *v*
rectifier.

rector, rèk´-t'r, *n* recteur
m; **–y,** presbytère *m*.

recumbent, ri-comm´-
bennte, *a* étendu;
couché.

recuperate, ri-kiou´-peur-
éte, *v* se remettre.

recur, ri-keur´, *v* (to
happen again) se
reproduire; se répéter.

red, red, *n* & *a* rouge *m*;
–breast, *n* rouge-gorge
m; **–den,** *v* rougir; **–dish,**
a rougeâtre; **––hot,**
chauffé au rouge; **–ness,**
n rougeur *f*.

redeem, ri-dîme´, *v*
(promise) accomplir une
promesse; (bonds, etc)
rembourser; (pledge)
dégager; (soul) délivrer.

redemption, ri-demmp´-
ch'n, *n* (com) rachat *m*.

red-light district, rèd-lâït-
diss-tricte, *n* quartier des
prostituées *m*.

redouble, ri-dob´-'l, *v*
redoubler.

redress, ri-dresse´, *v*
réparer. *n* réparation *f*.

reduce, ri-diouce´, *v*
réduire à ou en;
(disgrace) rétrograder.

reduction, ri-doque´-ch'n,
n réduction *f*; rabais *m*.

redundant, ri-donn´-
deunt, *a* licencié;
superflu.

reed, rîde, *n* roseau *m*.

reef, rîfe, *n* récif *m*; (sail)
ris *m*. *v* prendre un ris.

reek, rîque, *v* fumer;
exhaler; empester. *n*
odeur forte *f*.

reel, rîle, *n* (cotton; film)
bobine *f*; (angling)
moulinet, *m*. *v*
chanceler.

refer, ri-feur´, *v* se référer
(à); (apply) s'adresser à;
(to a book) consulter.

referee, rèf´-eur-î´, *n*
arbitre *m*.

reference, rèf´-eur-'nce, *n*
(allusion) allusion *f*;
(testimonial) référence
f; **with –to,** concernant.

referendum, rèf-eur-èn´-
deum, *n* référendum *m*.

refine, ri-fâïne´, *v* (sugar,
etc.) raffiner (liquids)
épurer; **–d,** *a* raffiné;
–ment, *n* raffinement *m*.

reflect, ri-flecte´, *v*
réfléchir; (lights, etc)
refléter; **–ion,** *n*
réflexion *f*; **–or,**
réflecteur *m*.

reform, ri-fôrme´, *v*
réformer; se réformer. *n*
réforme *f*; **–ation,**
réformation *f*.

refrain, ri-fréne´, *v*
s'abstenir de.

refresh, ri-frèche´, *v*
rafraîchir; se rafraîchir.

refreshment, ri-frèche´-
m'nt, *n* rafraîchissement
m.

refrigerator, ri-fridje´-eur-
é-*teur*, *n* frigidaire *m*.

refuge, rèf´-ioudje, *n*
refuge (contre) *m*;
(shelter) abri *m*.

refugee, rèf-iou-djî´, *n*
réfugié, -ée *m* & *f*.

refund, ri-fonnde´, *v*
rembourser. *n*
remboursement *m*.

refusal, ri-fiou-z'l, *n*

refus m.

refuse, ri-fiouze, v refuser.

refuse, rê´-iouce, n rebut m; (garbage) ordures fpl.

refute, ri-fioute´, v réfuter.

regain, ri-guéne´, v regagner; (health) récupérer.

regal*, rî´-g'l, a royal.

regale, ri-guéle, v régaler.

regard, ri-gârde´, v regarder; considérer. n regard m; (heed) égard (pour) m; **–less,** a sans égard; **–s,** npl amitiés fpl.

regatta, ri-găt´-ta, n régate f.

regenerate, ri-djenn´-eur-éte, v régénérer.

regent, rî´-djennte, n régent, -e m & f.

regiment, rèdj´-i-m'nt, n régiment m.

region, rî´-djeune, n région f.

register, rèdje´-iss-teur, v enregistrer; (letter) recommander. n registre m.

registrar, rèdge´-iss-trâre, n (births, etc) officier de l'état civil m; (court) greffier m.

registration, rèdge-iss-tré´-ch'n n enregistrement m; inscription f.

registry, rèdje´-iss-tri, n

bureau d'enregistrement m.

regret, ri-grette´, v regretter. n regret m.

regrettable, ri-grett´-a-b'l, a regrettable.

regular*, regg´-iou-l'r, a régulier.

regulate, regg´-iou-léte, v régler.

regulation, regg-iou-lé´-ch'n, n règlement m.

rehearsal, ri-heur´-s'l, n répétition f.

rehearse, ri-heurce´, v répéter.

reign, réne, n règne m. v régner.

reimburse, ri-imm-beurce´, v rembourser.

rein, réne, n rêne f.

reindeer, réne´-dire, n renne m.

reinforce, ri-inn-faurce´, v renforcer.

reinstate, ri-inn-stéte´, v réintégrer.

reject, ri-djecte´, v rejeter.

rejoice, ri-djoa'ice´, v réjouir.

rejoicings, ri-djoa'ice´-inngse, npl réjouissances fpl.

rejoin, ri-djô'ine´, v rejoindre.

rejuvenate, ri-djiou´-venn-éte, v rajeunir.

relapse, ri-lăpse´, n

rechute f. v retomber.

relate, ri-léte´, v raconter; **–d,** a apparenté à.

relation, ri-lé´-ch'n, n (a relative) parent, -e m & f; (com) rapport m; relation f.

relative, rèl´-a-tive, a parent, -e m & f. a* relatif; n (person) parent m.

relax, ri-lăxe´, v se détendre; **–ation,** n détente; relaxation f.

relay, ri-lé´, n (radio) relais m. v relayer.

release, ri-lice´, v relâcher; libérer. n (an obligation) décharge f.

relent, ri-lennte´, v se laisser fléchir.

relentless*, ri-lennte´-lesse, a implacable.

relevant, rèl´-i-vannte, a applicable (à); relatif.

reliable, ri-lâï´-a-b'l, a digne de confiance; sûr.

reliance, ri-lâï´-annce, n confiance f.

relic, rèl´-ique, n (of a saint or martyr) relique f; **–s,** pl restes mpl.

relief, ri-lîfe´, n (anxiety; pain) soulagement m; (help) secours m; (raised) relief m.

relieve, ri-lîve´, v soulager; secourir.

religion, ri-lidj´-onn, n
religion f.

religious*, ri-lidj´-euce, a
religieux.

relinquish, ri-linng´-
couiche, v abandonner.

relish, rèl´-iche, v
savourer. n saveur f.

reluctance, ri-loque´-
t'nce, n répugnance f.

reluctant, ri-loque´-
tannte, a peu disposé à.

rely, ri-lâï, v compter sur.

remain, ri-méne´, v rester;
–der, n reste m.

remand, ri-mânnde. v
(law) renvoyer à une
autre audience.

remark, ri-mârque´, n
remarque f. v remarquer.

remarkable, ri-mâr´-ka-
b'l, a remarquable.

remedy, remm´-i-di, n
remède m. v remédier á.

remember, ri-memm´-b'r,
v se souvenir de.

remembrance, ri-memm´-
brannce, n souvenir m.

remind, ri-mâïnnde, v
rappeler.

remit, ri-mitte´, v (a fine,
etc.) remettre; –tance, n
remise f.

remnant, remm´-nannte,
n reste m; –s, pl (fabrics)
coupons mpl.

remonstrate, ri-monn´-
stréte, v faire des

remontrances à.

remorse, ri-moarce´, n
remords m.

remote, ri-maute´, a
éloigné; (of time)
reculé; lointain.

removal, ri-moue´-v'l, n
(of furniture)
déménagement m.

remove, ri-mouve´, v
(furniture) déménager;
(shift) déplacer.

remunerate, ri-mioue´-
neur-éte, v rémunérer.

remunerative, ri-mioue´-
neur-a-tive, a
rémunérateur;
avantageux.

rend, rennde, v déchirer;
–er, rendre; (account)
présenter; –ering, n
traduction f.

renegade, renn´-i-guéde, n
renégat, -e m & f.

renew, ri-nioue´, v
renouveler; –al, n
renouvellement m.

renounce, ri-nâ'ounce´, v
renoncer.

renovate, renn´-ŏ-véte, v
renouveler.

renown, ri-nâ'oune´, n
renommée f; renom m.

rent, rennte, n (of houses
or rooms) loyer m; (tear)
déchirure f. v louer.

renunciation, ri-nonn-
ci-é´-ch'n, n

renonciation f.

repair, ri-paire´, v réparer;
(sewing, clothes, etc.)
raccommoder. n
réparation f.

reparation, rèp-a-ré´-ch'n,
n réparation f.

repartee, rèp-ar-tî´, n
repartie f.

repay, ri-pé´, v
rembourser.

repeal, ri-pîle´, v révoquer.
n révocation f.

repeat, ri-pîte´, v répéter.

repel, ri-pelle´, v
repousser; –lent, a
répulsif.

repent, ri-pennte´, v se
repentir (de).

repetition, rèp-i-tiche´-'n,
n répétition f.

replace, ri-pléce´, v (to
substitute) remplacer;
(put back) replacer.

replenish, ri-plenn´-iche,
v remplir (de).

reply, ri-plâï´, v répondre.
n réponse f.

report, ri-paurte´, n
rapport m; compte
rendu m; (news)
nouvelles fpl; (school)
bulletin m; (noise)
détonation f. v informer;
signaler.

reporter, ri-paur´-t'r, n
reporter m.

repose, ri-pauze´, n repos

m. v (se) reposer.

repository, ri-poz´-i-tŏ-ri, *n* dépôt *m*.

represent, rèp-ri-zennte´, *v* représenter; **–ation,** *n* représentation *f*; **–ative,** représentant *m*.

reprieve, ri-prîve´, *v* commuer (une peine), remettre.

reprimand, rèp-ri-mânnde´, *v* réprimander.

reprimand, rép´-ri-mânnde, *n* réprimande *f*.

reprint, ri-prinnte´, *v* réimprimer. *n* réimpression *f*; nouveau tirage *m*.

reprisal, ri-prâï´-z'l, *n* représaille *f*.

reproach, ri-prautche´, *v* reprocher à. *n* reproche *m*.

reprobate, rèp´-ro-béte, *n* vaurien *m*.

reproduce, ri-prŏ-diouce´, *v* reproduire.

reproduction, ri-prŏ-dock´-ch'n, *n* reproduction *f*.

reproof, ri-proufe´, *n* réprimande *f*.

reprove, ri-prouve´, *v* blâmer; censurer.

reptile, rèp´-tâïle, *n* reptile *m*.

republic, ri-pobb´-lique, *n* république *f*.

repudiate, ri-pioue´-di-éte, *v* répudier.

repugnant, ri-pog´-nannte, *a* répugnant.

repulse, ri-pollce´, *v* repousser. *n* échec *m*.

repulsive, ri-poll´-cive, *a* repoussant.

reputable, rèp´-ieu-tă-b'l, *a* de bonne réputation.

reputation, rèp´-iou-té´-ch'n, *n* réputation *f*.

repute, ri-pioute´, *n* renom *m*.

request, ri-couesste´, *n* demande *f. v* demander.

require, ri-couâïre´, *v* (to want) avoir besoin de; exiger; **–ment,** *n* besoin *m*; exigence *f*.

requisite, rèk´-oui-zitte, *a* requis; nécessaire.

rescue, ress´-kioue, *v* sauver. *n* sauvetage *m*.

research, ri-seurtche´, *n* recherche *f*.

resemble, ri-zemm´-b'l, *v* ressembler (à).

resent, ri-zennte´, *v* garder rancune; **–ful*,** *a* vindicatif; **–ment,** *n* ressentiment *m*.

reservation, rèz-eur-vé´-ch'n, *n* réservation *f*;(*doubt*) réserve *f*.

reserve, ri-zeurve´, *v* réserver. *n* réserve *f*.

reservoir, rèz´-eur-vo'ar, *n* réservoir *m*.

reside, ri-zâïde´, *v* résider; habiter; demeurer.

residence, rèz´-i-dennce, *n* résidence *f*; (stay) séjour *m*.

resident, rèz´-i-dennt, *n* habitant, -e *m & f*; pensionnaire *m & f. a* résidant.

resign, ri-zâïne´, *v* abandonner; (a post) démissionner (de); (oneself to) se résigner à.

resin, rèz´-inn, *n* résine *f*.

resist, ri-zisste´, *v* résister à; **–ance,** *n* résistance *f*.

resolute*, rèz´-o-lioute, *a* résolu; déterminé.

resolution, rèz´-o-lioue´-ch'n, *n* résolution *f*.

resolve, ri-zolve´, *v* résoudre; (of deliberate bodies) décider.

resort, ri-zoarte´, **–to,** *v* recourir à.

resound, ri-zâ´ounnde´, *v* retentir; résonner.

resource, ri-soarce´, *n* ressource *f*.

respect, riss-pecte´, *v* respecter. *n* respect *m*; égard *m*; **–ability** respectabilité *f*; **–able,** *a* respectable; **–ful*,** respectueux; **–ive*,** respectif.

respite, ress´-pâite, n répit m.

respond, riss-ponnde´, v répondre.

respondent, riss-ponn´-dennt, n (law) défendeur m.

response, riss-ponnce´, n réponse f.

responsible, riss-ponn´-ci-b'l, a responsable.

rest, reste, n repos m; (sleep) somme m; (remainder) reste m. v se reposer; –ful, a tranquille; –ive, rétif; –less, agité.

restaurant, ress´-to-rannte, n restaurant m; –car, wagon-restaurant m.

restore, ri-staure´, v restituer; (health) (to recover) rétablir.

restrain, ri-stréne´, v retenir; réprimer.

restraint, ri-strénnte, n contrainte f.

restrict, ri-stricte´, v restreindre.

restriction, ri-strick´-ch'n, n restriction f.

result, ri-zollte´, v résulter. n résultat m.

resume, ri-zioumme´, v reprendre; continuer.

resumption, ri-zomm´-ch'n, n reprise f.

resurrection, rèz-eur-rèque´-ch'n, n résurrection f.

retail, rî´-téle, v vendre au détail. n vente au détail f; –er, détaillant m.

retain, ri-téne´, v retenir; (keep) garder.

retaliate, ri-tăl´-i-éte, v user de représailles envers.

retard, ri-târde´, v retarder.

reticent, rètt´-i-sennte, a réservé; taciturne.

retinue, rètt´-i-nioue, n suite f; cortège m.

retire, ri-tâïre´, v se retirer; –ment, n retraite f.

retort, ri-toarte´, v riposter. n réplique f.

retract, ri-trăcte´, v rétracter.

retreat, ri-trîte´, v se retirer. n retraite f.

retrench, ri-trenntche´, v retrancher.

retribution, ri-tri-biu-shé-n, n châtiment m; récompense f.

retrieve, ri-trîve, v (to regain) recouvrer; (to repair) réparer.

return, ri-teurne´, v (come back) revenir; (go back) retourner; (give back) rendre. n retour m; –s, rendement m; –-ticket, (fam) billet d'aller et retour m.

reveal, ri-vîle´, v révéler.

revel, rèv´-'l, v faire bombance. n réjouissances fpl.

revenge, ri-venndje´, v venger de. n vengeance f.

revenue, rèv´-i-nioue, n revenu m; (state) fisc m.

reverse, ri-veurce´, v renverser; (engine) faire marche arrière. n revers m; contraire m. a inverse.

revert, ri-veurte´, v revenir (sur), (law) retourner à.

review, ri-vioue´, v examiner; (inspect) passer en revue; (books, etc) analyser. n revue f; (books) critique f.

revile, ri-vâïle´, v injurier.

revise, ri-vâïze´, v réviser.

revision, ri-vije´-'n, n révision f.

revive, ri-vâïve´, v ranimer; se ranimer.

revoke, ri-vauque´, v révoquer. n (cards) renonce f.

revolt, ri-volte´, n révolte f. v se révolter.

revolve, ri-volve´, v tourner.

revolver, ri-vole´-veur, n révolver m.

reward, ri-ouôrde´, n récompense f. v récompenser.

rheumatism, roue´-mă-tizme, n rhumatisme m.

rhinoceros, râï-noce´-i-rŏsse, n rhinocéros m.

rhubarb, rou´-bârbe, n rhubarbe f.

rhyme, râïme, n rime f. v rimer.

rib, ribbe, n côte f.

ribbon, ribb´-n, n ruban m.

rice, râïce, n riz m.

rich*, ritche, a riche; **–es**, n richesse f.

rickets, rik´-ètse, n rachitisme m.

rickety, rik´-ett-i, a (fig) branlant; (med) rachitique.

rid, ridde, v débarrasser; délivrer.

riddle, ridd´-l, n énigme f. v cribler de.

ride, râïde, v monter à cheval; aller en auto; aller à bicyclette. n promenade à cheval f, etc.

ridge, ridje, n (mountain) crête f.

ridicule, ridd´-i-kioule, v ridiculiser. n ridicule m.

ridiculous*, ri-dik´-iou-leuce, a ridicule.

rifle, râï-f'l, v piller. n fusil m.

rift, rifte, n fente f; fissure f.

rig, rigue, v (fig) (naut) gréer. n (ship) gréement m.

right, râïte, n droite f. v rétablir. a droit; juste; en règle.

rigid*, rid´-jide, a rigide; (stiff) raide.

rigor, rigg´-eur, n rigueur f.

rigorous*, rigg´-ŏr-euce, a rigoureux.

rim, rimme, n bord m; (brim) rebord m; (wheel) jante f.

rind, râïnnde, n (fruit) pelure f; (bacon) couenne f; (cheese) croûte f.

ring, rinng, n anneau m; (finger) bague f; (wedding) alliance f; (napkin) rond m; (circus) arène f; (of bell) coup de sonnette m. v sonner; (of the ears) tinter.

ringleader, rinng´-lî-d'r, n meneur m.

rinse, rinnse, v rincer. n rinçage m.

riot, râï´-ŏte, n émeute f. v faire une émeute.

rip, rippe, v fendre; (cloth) déchirer.

ripe, râïpe, a mûr; **–n**, v mûrir.

ripple, rip´-p'l, n action de rider f.

rise, râïze, v se lever; (revolt) se soulever; (river) (to ascend) monter; (prices) hausser. n (wages) augmentation f.

risk, risque, v risquer. n risque m.

rite, râïte, n rite m.

rival, râï´-v'l, n rival, -e m & f; (com) concurrent, -e m & f.

rivalry, râï´-val-ri, n rivalité f.

river, riv´-'r, n fleuve m; (small) rivière f.

rivet, riv´-ette, v river. n rivet m.

road, raude, n chemin m; route f; (street) rue f.

roam, raume, v rôder; errer.

roar, raure, v rugir (of the lion etc.); n rugissement m.

roast, rauste, v rôtir. n & a rôti m.

rob, robbe, v voler; dépouiller; **–ber**, n voleur, -euse m & f.

robbery, robb´-eur-i, n vol m.

robe, raube, n robe f;

(eccl) vêtements mpl.

robin, robb´-inn, n rouge-gorge m.

robust*, ro-bosste´, a robuste; vigoureux.

rock, roque, n rocher m. v (quake) secouer; (roll) rouler; (cradle) bercer; **–y,** a rocailleux; (sea) plein de rochers.

rock and roll, roque´-eun-raule´ n rock and roll m.

rocket, rok´-ette, n fusée f.

rod, rodde, n baguette f; (fishing) canne à pêche f; (curtain) triangle f.

roe, rau, n chevreuil m; biche f; (fish) laitance f.

rogue, raugue, n fripon m; **–ry,** friponnerie f.

roll, raule, v rouler; (– up) enrouler. n rouleau m; (bread, loaf) petit pain m; **–call,** appel m; **–er,** roulette f; (steam) rouleau m; **–er skate,** patin à roulettes f.

romance, rau-mănnce´, n roman dechevalerie m; (mus) romance f.

romantic, rau-mănne´-tique, a romantique; sentimental(e).

romp, rommpe, v jouer bruyamment.

roof, roufe, n toit m; (mouth) palais m.

rook, rouque, n

corneille f.

room, roumme, n pièce f; (bedroom) chambre f; **living –,** salon m; **dining –,** salle à manger f; **bath–,** salle de bains f; (public) salle f; (space) place f; **service–,** n service des chambres m.

roost, rouste, v percher. n perchoir m.

rooster, rous-teur, n coq m.

root, route, n racine f. v s'enraciner.

rope, raupe, n corde f; (naut) cordage m.

rosary, rau´-za-ri, n rosaire m.

rose, rauze, n rose f; **– bush,** rosier m.

rosemary, rauze´-mé-ri, n romarin m.

rosy, rauz´-i, a rosé; vermeil.

rot, rotte, n pourriture f. v pourrir.

rotate, rau´-téte, v tourner.

rouge, rouge, n rouge m.

rough*, roffe, a (manners) grossier; rude; (coarse) rugueux; rude; (sea) houleuse; (wind) tempêtueux; (bumpy) cahoteux.

roughness, roffe´-nesse, n rudesse f; grossièreté f.

round, râ´ounnde, a rond. v arrondir; **–about,** a détourné. n manège m; **–ness,** rondeur f.

rouse, râ´ouze, v (fig) exciter; (awaken) éveiller.

rout, râ´oute, v mettre en déroute. n déroute f.

route, route, n route f; itinéraire m.

routine, rou-tîne´, n routine f.

rove, rauve, v rôder; (fig) errer dans.

row, rau, n rangée f; (persons) file f; (boating) canotage m. v (scull) ramer.

row, râ´ou, n querelle f; (noise) vacarme m.

royal*, roa´i´-al, a royal; **–ty,** n royauté f; (payment) droits d'auteur mpl.

rub, robbe, v frotter; **–ber,** n caoutchouc m; (eraser) gomme à effacer f; **–off,** v effacer.

rubbish, robb´-iche, n ordures fpl; (trash) camelote f.

ruby, roue´-bi, n rubis m. a vermeil.

rucksack, roque´-săque, n sac à dos m.

rudder, rodd´-'r, n gouvernail m.

rude*, roude, *a* impoli;
(coarse) grossier.

rudiment, roue´-di-m'nt,
n rudiment *m.*

rue, roue, *v* déplorer;
–ful*, *a* lamentable.

ruffian, roffe´-iane, *n*
chenapan *m.*

ruffle, rof´-f'l, *v* déranger;
(*fig*) troubler.

rug, rogue, *n* couverture *f;*
(mat) tapis *m.*

rugby, rogg´-bî, *n* rugby *m.*

rugged, rogg´-ide, *a*
(scenery) accidenté.

ruin, roue´-inne, *v* ruiner.
n ruine *f.*

rule, roule, *v* gouverner;
(lines) régler. *n*
gouvernement *m;*
(regulation, etc) règle *f.*

ruler, roul´-'r, *n* (drawing)
règle *f.*

rum, romme, *n* rhum *m.*

rumble, romm´-b'l, *n*
grondement sourd *m.*

rummage, romm´-idj, *v*
fouiller. *n* fouillis *m.*

rumor, roue´-m'r, *n*
rumeur *f.*

run, ronne, *v* courir;
(colors) déteindre;
–away, fuir. *n* (horse)
cheval emballe *m.*

runway, ronn´-oué, *n* piste
f.

rupture, ropp´-tioure, *n*
rupture *f;* (*med*) hernie *f.*

rural, rou´-r'l, *a*
champêtre; rural.

rush, roche, *n* ruée *f;*
(water) torrent *m;*
(reed) jonc *m. v* se ruer;
se précipiter.

rust, rosste, *n* rouille *f. v*
rouiller; **–y,** *a* rouillé.

rustic, ross´-tique, *a*
rustique.

rustle, ross´-'l, *v* bruire. *n*
bruissement *m;* (silk, of
dresses) frou frou *m.*

rusty, ross´-tî, *a* rouillé(e).

rut, rotte, *n* (in a road)
ornière *f.*

ruthless, rots-lèss, *a* sans
pitie; cruel.

rye, râï, *n* seigle *m.*

sable, sé´-b'l, n (fur)
zibeline f.

sachet, să´-ché, n sachet
m.

sack, săque, n sac m. v
piller.

sacrament, săc´-ră-m'nt, n
sacrement m.

sacred, sé´-cridde, a sacré
(to); consacré à.

sacrifice, săc´-ri-făïce, n
sacrifice m. v sacrifier.

sacrilege, săc´-ri-lédje, n
sacrilége m.

sad*, sădde, a triste;
–ness, n tristesse f.

saddle, săd´-d'l, n selle f;
–r, sellier m.

safe, séfe, a sauf; sûr; n
(for money) coffre-fort
m; **–guard** sauvegarde f.
v protéger; **–ty,** n sûreté
f.

safety pin, séf-tî-pinne, n
épingle de sûreté f.

sag, săgue, v s'affaisser.

sagacious*, sa-gué´-
cheuce, a sagace.

sage, sédje, n sage m;
(herb) sauge f. a* sage.

sail, séle, n voile f. v
naviguer.

sailor, sé´-l'r, n matelot m;
marin m.

saint, sénnte, n saint, -e m
& f.

sake, séque, n cause f; (for
God's) égard m; (for the
love of God) amour m.

salad, săl´-ade, n salade f.

salad dressing, săl-ade-
drèss-inng n vinaigrette
f.

salary, săl´-a-ri, n

salaire m.

sale, séle, n vente f;
(shop) solde m; **–able,** a
vendable; **–sman,** n
vendeur m.

sales clerk, séle-s-clărque,
n vendeur, -se.

salient, sé´-li-ennte, n & a
(projecting) saillant m.

saliva, sa-lâï´-va, n salive
f.

sallow, săl´-au, a jaunâtre.

salmon, sămm´-'n, n
saumon m.

saloon, sa-loune´, n
(Grand) salon m; bar m.

salt, soalte, n sel m. a salé;
–cellar, n salière f.

salty, soal´-tî a salé.

salute, sa-lioute´, v saluer.
n salut m.

salvage, săl´-védje, n
sauvetage m. v sauver.

salvation, săl-vé´-ch'n, n
salut m; **–army,** Armée
du Salut f.

salver, sal´-v'r, n plateau
m.

same, séme, a même.

sample, sâmme´-p'l, n
échantillon m.

sanctify, sainnk´-ti-fâï, v
sanctifier.

sanction, sainnk´-ch'n, v
sanctionner. n sanction
f.

sanctuary, sainnk´-tiou-*a*-ri, n sanctuaire m.

sand, sännde, n sable m; **–y,** a sablonneux.

sandal, sänn´-d'l, n sandale f.

sandwich, sännde´-houitche, n sandwich m.

sane, séne, a sain d'esprit.

sanguine, saing´-gouine, a sanguin; confiant.

sanitary, sänn´-i-t*a*-ri, a sanitaire.

sanity, sänn´-i-ti, n bon sens m.

sap, säpe, n sève f. v saper.

sapper, säpp´-*eur*, n (mil) sapeur m.

sapphire, säf´-fâïre, n saphir m.

sarcasm, sâr´-căzme, n sarcasme m.

sarcastic, sâr-căs´-tique, a sarcastique.

sardine, sâr-dîne´, n sardine f.

sash, säche, n (belt) (mark of distinction) écharpe f.

satchel, sätt´-ch'l, n sacoche f; (school) cartable m.

satellite, satt´-i-lâïte, n satellite m.

satiate, sé´-chi-éte, v rassasier de.

satin, sätt´-inne, n satin m. a de satin.

satire, sätt´-âïre, n satire f.

satisfaction, sätt-iss-făk´-ch'n, n satisfaction f.

satisfactory, sätt-iss-făk´-teur-i, a satisfaisant.

satisfy, sätt´-iss-fâï, v satisfaire.

satsuma, sät-sou´-mä, n mandarine f.

saturate, sätt´-iou-réte, v saturer.

Saturday, sätt´-or-di, n samedi m.

satyr, sätt´-*eur*, n satyre m.

sauce, soace, n sauce f; **–pan,** casserole f.

saucer, soa´-seur, n soucoupe f.

sauna, soa´-nä, n sauna m.

saunter, soann´-t'r, v marcher en flânant.

sausage, soss´-idj, n (to be cooked) saucisse f; (preserved) saucisson m.

savage, säv´-idj, a* sauvage; féroce. n sauvage m & f.

save, séve, v (to spare) sauver; (economize) épargner (de); (keep) garder.

saving, sé´-vinng, a économe; frugal;

(things) économique. n économie f; **–s,** épargne f.

savior, sé´-v'*eur*, n sauveur m.

savor, sé´-v'r, v avoir le goût de; avoir l'odeur de. n saveur f; **–y,** a savoureux.

saw, soa, n scie f. v scier.

say, sé, v dire; **–ing,** n dicton m.

scabbard, scäbb´-'rd, n fourreau m.

scaffold, scäff´-ôlde, n échafaud m.

scaffolding, scäff´-ôldd-inng, n échafaudage m.

scald, scoalde, v échauder.

scale, skéle, n (fish) écaille f; (measure) échelle f; (mus) gamme f. v ecailler; (climb) escalader.

scales, skélze, npl balance f.

scallop, scäll´-oppe, n coquille Saint Jacques f.

scalp, scälpe, n cuir chevelu m.

scamper, scämm´-p'r, v déguerpir.

scan, scänne, v scruter; (verses) scander.

scandal, scänn´-d'l, n scandale m.

scandalous*, scănn´-dăl-euce, a scandaleux.

scanty, scănn´-ti, a insuffisant; (tight) étriqué.

scapegoat, sképe´-gaute, n bouc émissaire m.

scar, scâre, n cicatrice f. v cicatriser.

scarce*, skairce, a rare.

scarcity, skair´-ci-ti, n rareté f; (famine) disette f.

scare, skaire, n panique f. v effrayer; –**away**, épouvanter; –**crow**, n épouvantail m.

scarf, scărfe, n écharpe f; foulard m.

scarlet, scâre-lette, n & a écarlate f.

scarlet fever, scâre´-lette-fi´-veur, n scarlatine f.

scathing*, ské´-tsinng, a cinglant.

scatter, scătt´-’r, v disperser; éparpiller.

scavenger, scăv´-enn-dj’r, n boueur m.

scene, sîne, n scène f; –**ry**, (fig) vue f; paysage m; (theater) décors mpl.

scent, sennte, n parfum m; (trail) piste f. v parfumer de.

scepter, sepp´-t’r, n

sceptre m.

schedule, chedd´-ioule, n inventaire m; liste f.

scheme, skîme, n plan m, projet m; v projeter.

scholar, skol´-’r, n lettré, -e m & f; (pupil) élève m & f.

scholarship, skol´-’r-chippe, n (prize) bourse f.

school, skoul, n école f; –**teacher**, maître d’école m; maîtresse d’école f.

schooner, skoue´-n’r, n goëlette f.

sciatica, sâî-ătt´-i-ca, n sciatique f.

science, sâî´-ennce, n science f.

scientific, sâî-en-tiff´-ique, a scientifique.

scissors, siz´-eurze, npl ciseaux mpl.

scoff, skoffe, v se moquer de; railler.

scold, skaulde, v gronder.

scoop, skoupe, n (shovel) pelle à main f. v creuser.

scope, skaupe, n portée f; étendue f; place f.

scorch, skoartche, v roussir.

score, skaure, n (number) score m; marque f; partition f (mus); v

(win) gagner; (cut) faire des entailles; (keeping count) marquer.

scorn, skoarne, n dédain m. v dédaigner.

scornful*, skoarne´-foulle, a dédaigneux.

scoundrel, skâ´ounn´-dr’l, n coquin m; gredin m.

scour, skâ´oure, v récurer.

scourge, skeurdje, v fouetter. n fouet m; (fig) fléau m.

scout, skâ´oute, v aller en éclaireur. n éclaireur m; **boy**- –, boy-scout m.

scowl, skâ´oule, v froncer les sourcils. n regard menaçant m.

scraggy, skrăgg´-’i, a (thin) décharné.

scramble, skramm´-b’l (struggle) lutte f. v (climb) grimper; –**for**, se bousculer pour.

scrap, skrăppe, n fragment m; (cloth) morceau m.

scrape, skrépe, v gratter; (– mud off) (boots, etc.) décrotter.

scraper, skrépe´-’r, n grattoir m; (for shoes) décrottoir m.

scratch, skrătche, n égratignure f; (sport) ligne de départ f. v égratigner; (rub) gratter; (sports) retirer; (glass) (a smooth surface) rayer.

scream, skrîme, v crier; hurler. n cri m.

screen, skrîne, n (fire; cinema) écran m; (partition) paravent m. v protéger.

screw, skroue, n vis f. v visser.

screwdriver, skroue-drâï´-veur, n tournevis m.

scribble, skribb´-'l v griffonner. n griffonnage m.

scripture, skripp´-tioure, n Ecriture Sainte f.

scroll, skraule, n rouleau m.

scrounge, skrâ'oundje, m picue-assiette; que-assiette.

scrub, scrobbe, v laver à la brosse. n (bush) broussailles fpl.

scruple, scroue´-p'l, n scrupule m.

scrupulous*, scroue´-piou-leuce, a scrupuleux.

scrutinize, scroue-ti-nâïze, v scruter.

scuffle, scoff´-'l, n bagarre f. v se battre.

scull, scolle, n godille f. v godiller.

scullery, scoll´-eur-i, n laverie f.

sculptor, scolp´teur, n sculpteur m.

sculpture, scolp´-tioure, v sculpter. n sculpture f.

scum, scomme, v écumer. n écume f; (fig) lie f.

scurf, skeurfe, n pellicules fpl.

scurrilous*, skorr´-i-leuce, a grossier; injurieux.

scuttle, skott´-'l, n (coal) seau à charbon m. v (naut) saborder.

scythe, sâïdze, n faux f.

sea, sî, n mer f; –**man,** marin m; –**sickness,** mal de mer m; –**side,** bord de la mer m; –**weed,** algue f; –**worthy,** a navigable.

seal, sîle, n cachet m; (official) sceau m; (animal) phoque m. v cacheter; –**ingwax,** n cire à cacheter f; –**skin,** peau de phoque f.

seam, sîme, n (in sewing) couture f; (mine) veine f.

seamstress, sîme´-stresse, n couturière f.

sear, sîre, v (burn) brûler; (brand) marquer au fer.

search, seurtche, v (look

for) chercher; (people; luggage) fouiller. n recherche f.

searchlight, seurtche´-lâïte, n projecteur m.

season, sî´-z'n, v assaisonner de; (timber) sécher. m saison f; –**able,** a de saison; –**ing,** n assaisonnement m; –**ticket,** carte d'abonnement f.

seat, sîte, n siège m; place f; (bench) banc m; v asseoir; (to place) placer.

secluded, si-cloue´-dedde, a retiré.

seclusion, si-cloue´-j'n retraite f.

second, sèk´-õnnde, v (support) seconder. n (time) seconde f; (duel) témoin m. n & a* deuxième m & f; –**ary,** a secondaire; –**hand,** d'occasion.

secrecy, sî´-cri-ci, n secret m.

secret, sî´-crète, n secret m. a* secret.

secretary, sèk´-ri-ta-ri, n secrétaire m & f.

secrete, si-crîte´, v cacher; (gland) sécréter.

secretion, si-crî´-ch'n, n

sécrétion f.

sect, secte, n secte f.

section, sèk´-ch'n, n section f; (cross) coupe f.

secular, sèk´-iou-l'r, a (old) séculaire; (music) profane; (school) laïque.

secure, si-kioure´, v mettre en sûreté; (one's possession of) s'assurer (de); a sûr; à l'abri (de).

securities, si-kiour´-i-tize, npl valeurs; boursières fpl; titres mpl.

security, si-kiour´-i-ti, n sûreté f; garantie f.

sedate*, si-déte´, a posé, calme.

sedative, sedd´-a-tive, n & a sédatif m; calmant m.

sedentary, sedd´-enn-ta-ri, a sédentaire.

sediment, sedd´-i-mennte, n sédiment m.

sedition, si-diche´-'n, n sédition f.

seditious*, si-diche´-euce, a séditieux.

seduce, si-diouce´, v séduire.

see, sî, v voir; –**through,** voir à travers; (fig) pénétrer; –**to,** veiller à.

seed, sîde, n (of vegetables) graine f;

semence f.

seek, sîque, v chercher; (strive) s'efforcer de.

seem, sîme, v sembler; paraître; –**ly,** a convenable.

seethe, sîdz, v bouillonner; (fig) grouiller.

seize, sîze, v saisir; (take possession) s'emparer de.

seizure, sî´-j'r, n prise f; capture f; (stroke) attaque f; (law) saisie f.

seldom, sell´-d'm, adv rarement.

select, si-lecte´, v choisir. a choisi; d'élite.

selection, si-lec´-ch'n, n choix m.

self, selfe, one–,pron soi-même; se . . . ; –**ish,** a égoïste; –**ishness,** n égoïsme m; –**starter,** (motor) démarreur m.

self-catering, selfe-qué-teur-inng a (Brit) avec cuisine.

self-service, selfe-seur´-vice, a libre-service; self-service.

sell, selle, v vendre; –**er,** n vendeur, -euse m & f.

semblance, semm´-blannce, n semblant m.

semi, semm´-i, prefix semi;

demi; –**circle,** n demi-cercle m; –**colon,** point et virgule m.

seminary, semm´-i-na-ri, n séminaire m.

semolina, semm-ô-lî´-na, n semoule f.

senate, senn´-éte, n sénat m.

send, sennde, v envoyer; (goods) expédier; –**away,** –**back,** renvoyer; –**er,** n expéditeur, -trice m & f; –**for,** v envoyer; chercher; –**in advance,** envoyer à l'avance; –**on,** (letters, etc.) faire suivre.

senile, sî´-nâile, a sénile.

senior, sî´-ni-eur, a aîné; (rank) plus ancien; –**partner,** n associé principal m.

sensation, senn-sé´-ch'n, n sensation f.

sense, sennce, n sens m; –**less,** a dénué de sens.

sensible, senn´-si-b'l, a sensé.

sensitive*, senn´-si-tive, a sensible.

sensual*, senn´-chou-'l, a sensuel.

sentence, senn´-t'nce, n phrase f; (law) sentence f. v condamner.

sentiment, senn´-ti-m'nt, n sentiment m.

sentry, senn´-tri, n sentinelle f; **–box,** guérite f.

separate, sepp´-a-réte, v séparer. a* séparé.

separation, sepp-a-ré´-ch'n, n séparation f.

September, sepp-temm´-b'r, n septembre m.

septic, sepp´-tique, a septique.

sequel, sî´-couelle, n suite f; conséquence f.

sequence, sî´-couennce, n série f; succession f.

serene*, si-rîne´, a calme; serein.

serge, seurdje, n serge f.

sergeant, sâr´-dj'nt, n sergent m.

serial, sî´-ri-al, a en série; n feuilleton m.

series, si´-rîze, n série f.

serious*, si´-ri-euce, a sérieux.

sermon, seur´-m'n, n sermon m.

serpent, seur´-pennte, n serpent m.

servant, seur´-vannte, n domestique m & f.

serve, seurve, v servir.

service, seur´-vice, n service m; (eccl)

office m.

serviceable, seur´-viss-a-b'l, a utile (à).

servile, seur´-vâile, a servile.

servitude, seur´-vi-tioude, n servitude f; (penal) travaux forcés mpl.

session, sèch´-eune, n session f; (sitting) séance f.

set, sette, v (type) composer; (to music) mettre en ...; (fowls) couver; (clock) régler; (trap) tendre/dresser un piege(a); (task) imposer; (question) poser; (example) donner; (tools) affûter; (plants) planter; (fracture) réduire; (solidify) cailler; (jewels) monter. n collection f; série f; (china) service m; (buttons, etc) garniture f; **–on fire,** mettre le feu à.

settee, sett´-ie, n canapé m; divan m.

settle, sett´-'l, v (accounts) régler; (finish) mettre fin à; (decide) résoudre; (assign) assigner; (domicile) s'établir;

–ment, n colonie f; (dowry) dot f; (accounts) règlement m; (agreement) solution f; (foundation) tassement m.

seven, sèv´-'n, n & a sept m; **–teen,** dix-sept m; **–th,** septième m & f; **–ty,** soixante-dix m.

sever, sèv´-'r, v séparer; (cut) couper net.

several, sèv´-eur-'l, a plusieurs; divers.

severe*, si-vire´, a sévère; (of weather) rigoureux; (of pain) violent.

severity, si-vèr´-i-ti, n sévérité f.

sew, sau, v coudre; **–ing,** n couture f; **–ingthread,** coton à coudre m; **–ing machine,** machine à coudre f.

sewage, sioue´-idj, n eaux d'égout fpl.

sewer, sioue´-'r, n égout m.

sex, sexe, n sexe m; **–ual,** a sexuel.

sexist, sexe´-iste, a sexiste.

sexy, sexe´-î, a sexy.

shabby, chåbb´-i, a râpé; usé; (action) mesquin.

shackle, chåk´-'l, n chaînes fpl. v enchaîner.

shade, chéde, n ombre f;

(color) nuance f; (lamp) abat-jour m; (eyes) visière f. v protéger; (art) ombrer.

shadow, chăd´-au, n ombre f. v (follow) filer.

shady, ché´-di, a ombragé; (fig) (dishonest) louche.

shaft, châfte, n (arrow) flèche f; (mech) arbre m; (mine) puits m; **–s,** (vehicle) brancards mpl.

shaggy, chăgg´-i, a poilu, velu.

shake, chéque, v secouer; (nerves, etc) trembler de; (sway) ébranler; **–hands,** serrer la main.

shaky, ché´-ki, a branlant; tremblotant.

shall, chăle, v aux I s. do je ferai. we s. do nous ferons.

shallow, chăl´-au, a peu profond.

sham, chămme, n feinte f. a simulé. v feindre.

shame, chéme, n honte f. v faire honte à; **–ful*,** a honteux; **–less,** éhonté.

shampoo, chămm´-poue, n shampooing m.

shamrock, chămm´-roque, n (d'Irlande) trèfle m.

shape, chépe, n forme f. v former; modeler (sur).

share, chére, n part f; (stock) action f. v partager; participer à; **–holder,** n actionnaire m & f.

shark, chârque, n requin m.

sharp, chârpe, a (blade) tranchant; (point) pointu; (edge) coupant; (taste) piquant; (mind) dégourdi. n (music) dièse m; **–en,** v aiguiser; **–ness,** n acuité f.

shatter, chătt´-'r, v briser en pièces; fracasser; renverser.

shave, chéve, v raser; se raser.

shaving, ché´-vinng, **–brush,** n blaireau m.

shavings, ché´-vinngze, npl (of wood) copeaux mpl.

shawl, choale, n châle m.

she, chî, pron elle.

sheaf, chîfe, n (corn, etc) gerbe f; (papers) liasse f.

shear, chîre, v tondre; **–s,** npl (for metal) cisailles fpl.

sheath, chîts, n (scabbard) fourreau m.

shed, chedde, n hangar m. v (tears, blood) verser; (hair, leaves, feathers)

perdre.

sheen, chîne, n lustre m.

sheep, chîpe, n mouton m.

sheer, chîre, a pur; (steep) perpendiculaire.

sheet, chîte, n drap m; (paper, metal) feuille f; **–lightning,** éclair de chaleur m.

shelf, chelfe, n planche f; (of a bookcase) rayon m; (a set) étagère f.

shell, chelle, n (hard) (empty egg) coquille f; (soft) (peas, etc.) cosse f; (projectile) (mil) obus m; v (peas, etc) écosser; (shrapnel) bombarder; **–-fish** n mollusque m; crustacé m.

shelter, chel´-t'r, n abri m. v abriter; protéger.

shepherd, chepp´-eurde, n berger m; pâtre m.

sheriff, chè´-rife, n shérif m.

sherry, chèr´-i, n Xérès m.

shield, chîlde, n bouclier m. v protéger.

shift, chifte, n (working) équipe f; changement de vitesse m; v (to change place) changer de place.

shin, chine, n tibia m.

shine, châîne, v luire; briller. n lustre m;

éclat m.

shingle, chinng´-g'l, n
galet m.

shingles, chinng´-g'lz, n
zona m.

ship, chippe, n vaisseau m;
navire m; bateau m. v
embarquer; (goods)
expédier; –**ment,**
(cargo) chargement m;
–**owner,** armateur m;
–**wreck,** naufrage m.

shirk, cheurque, v éviter;
éluder.

shirker, cheur´-keur, n
flémard m.

shirt, cheurte, n chemise
f.

shiver, chiv´-'r, v
frissonner. n frisson m.

shoal, choale, n
(multitude) foule f;
(fish) banc m; (shallow)
haut-fond m.

shock, choque, n (elec)
secousse f; (fright) choc
m. v (disgust) choquer;
–**absorber,** n
amortisseur m; –**ing,** a
révoltant; choquant.

shoddy, chodd´-i, a
(goods) camelote;
(persons) râpé.

shoe, choue, n chaussure f;
soulier m; (horse) fer à;
cheval m; v (horse)

ferrer; –**horn,** chausse-
pied m; –**lace,** lacet m;
–**maker,** cordonnier m;
–**polish,** cirage m.

shoot, choutte, v tirer;
(kill) tuer d'un coup de
feu; (execute) fusiller;
(grow) (to push forth)
pousser. n chasse f;
(growth) (plant) pousse
f; –**ing,** (of firearms) tir
m; –**ing star,** étoile
filante f.

shop, choppe, n boutique
f; (stores) magasin m. v
faire des achats;
–**keeper,** n marchand, -e
m & f.

shoplifting, choppe´-lift-
inng, n vol à l'étalage m.

shore, chaure, n côte f;
(beach) rivage m; (land)
terre f; (support) étai m.
v étayer.

shorn, chorne, a tondu.

short, choarte, a court;
(persons) petit; (need)
dénué de; –**age,** n
insuffisance f; –**circuit,**
courtcircuit m; –**en,** v
raccourcir; abréger;
–**hand,** sténographie f;
–**ly,** adv sous peu; –
sighted, a myope.

shot, chotte, n (noise)
coup de feu m; (score,

etc) coup m;
(marksman) (shooter)
tireur m; (pellet) plomb
de chasse m.

should, choude, v aux
devoir.?

shoulder, chaule´-d'r, n
épaule f. v porter sur
l'épaule.

shout, châ-oute, n cri m. v
crier.

shovel, chov´-'l, n pelle f.
v ramasser à la pelle.

show, chau, n spectacle m;
(exhibition) exposition
f; (prize –) concours m. v
montrer; (teach)
enseigner; –**room,** n
salle d'exposition f; –**y,** a
voyant.

shower, châ-ou´-eur, n
(copious) averse f;
(bath) douche f; –**y,** a
pluvieux.

shred, chredde, n (tatter)
lambeau m. v
déchiqueter.

shrew, chroue, n mégère f.

shrewd, chroude, a malin;
(cunning) rusé; sagace.

shriek, chrîque, v pousser
des cris. n cri perçant m.

shrill, chrille, a perçant.

shrimp, chrimmpe, n
crevette f.

shrine, chrâine, n châsse f;

sanctuaire m.

shrink, chrinnque, v rétrécir; n psychiatre mf; psychanaliste mf.

shrivel, chriv´-'l, v ratatiner.

shroud, chrâ'oude, n linceul m.

Shrove Tuesday, chrôve-tiouze´-dé, n mardi gras m.

shrub, chrobbe, n arbuste m.

shrug, chrogue, v hausser les épaules.

shudder, chodd´-'r, n frémissement m. v frémir (de).

shuffle, choff´-'l, v (gait) traîner les pieds; (cards) battre.

shun, chonne, v éviter.

shunt, chonnte, v changer de voie; faire la manœuvre.

shut, chotte, v fermer.

shutter, chott´-'r, n volet m; (camera) obturateur m.

shuttle, chott´-'l, n navette f.

shy, châï, a timide; réservé. v se jeter de côté.

shyness, châï-nesse, n timidité f.

sick, sique, a malade; **–en,** v (fig) (to disgust) dégoûter; **–ly,** a maladif; **–ness,** n maladie f; **to be –,** vomir.

sickle, sik´-'l, n faucille f.

side, sâïde, n côté m; (mountain) versant m; (river) bord m; (of record) face f. v prendre parti; **–board,** n buffet m; **––car,** side-car m; **–ways,** adv de côté.

side effect, sâïd-î-fècte, n effet secondaire m.

siege, sîdje, n siège m.

sieve, sive, n (fine) tamis m; (coarse) crible m.

sift, sifte, v tamiser; cribler.

sigh, sâï, n soupir m. v soupirer.

sight, sâïte, v apercevoir. n (eye) vue f; (spectacle) spectacle m; (gun) guidon m; **at –,** adv à vue; **by –,** de vue.

sign, sâïne, v signer. n signe m; (board) enseigne f; **––post,** poteau indicateur m.

signal, sigue´-n'l, n signal m. v signaler.

signature, sigue´-na-tioure, n signature f.

significant*, sigue-nif´-i-

cannte, a significatif.

signify, sigue´-ni-fâï, v signifier.

silence, sâï´-lennce, n silence m. v faire taire.

silencer, sâï´-lenn-ceur, n (engine) silencieux m.

silent*, sâï´-lennt, a silencieux.

silk, silque, n soie f; **–en,** a de soie; **–worm,** n ver à soie m; **–y,** a soyeux.

sill, sile, n (door) seuil m; (window) rebord m.

silly, sill´-i, a sot, niais.

silver, sill´-v'r, n argent m. a d'argent. v argenter.

silversmith, sill´-v'r-smits, n orfèvre m.

similar*, simm´-i-l'r, a semblable.

similarity, simm-i-lar´-i-ti, n similitude f.

simile, simm´-i-li, n comparaison f.

simmer, simm´-'r, v mijoter.

simple, simm´-p'l, a simple; **–ton,** n nigaud, -e m & f.

simplicity, simm-pliss´-i-ti, n simplicité f.

simplify, simm´-pli-fâï, v simplifier.

simultaneous*, simm-eul-té´-ni-euce, a simultané.

sin, sine, *v* pécher. *n* péché *m*; **–ner**, pécheur *m*, pécheresse *f*.

since, sinnce, *prep* depuis. *adv* depuis lors. *conj* (cause) puisque; (time) depuis que.

sincere*, sinn-cire´, *a* sincère.

sinew, sinn´-ioue, *n* tendon *m*; (*fig*) nerf *m*.

sing, sinng, *v* chanter; **–er**, *n* chanteur *m*, chanteuse *f*; (star) (professional) cantatrice *f*; **–ing**, chant *m*.

singe, sinndje, (one's clothes, etc.) *v* roussir; (hair) brûler.

single, sinng´-g'l, *a* seul, (unmarried) célibataire; (ticket) simple; **– handed**, *adv* seul.

single room, sinng´-l- roumme, *n* chambre à un lit; pour une personne *f*.

singly, sinngue´-li, *adv* (individually) un à un.

singular*, sinng´-guiou-l'r, *a* singulier; unique.

sinister, sinn´-iss-*teur*, *a* sinistre.

sink, sinnque, *n* évier *m*. *v* enfoncer; couler; (ship) sombrer; (scuttle)

saborder; (shaft) creuser.

sip, sipe, *n* gorgée *f*. *v* boire à petites gorgées.

siphon, sâï´-f'n, *n* siphon *m*.

siren, sâï´-renn, *n* sirène *f*.

sirloin, seur-lô´ïne, *n* aloyau *m*.

sister, siss´-t'r, *n* sœur *f*; **– in-law**, belle-sœur *f*.

sit, sitte, *v* s'asseoir; (incubate) couver; **–ting**, *a* assis. *n* séance *f*.

site, sâïte, *n* site *m*; (building) emplacement *m*.

situated, sit´-iou-é-tedde, *a* situé.

situation, sit-iou-é´-ch'n, *n* situation *f*.

six, sixe, *n* & *a* six *m*; **–teen**, seize *m*; **–teenth**, seizième *m* & *f*; **–th**, sixième *m* & *f*; **–tieth**, soixantième *m* & *f*; **–ty**, soixante *m*.

size, sâïze, *n* dimension *f*; (measure) (of gloves, shoes, etc) pointure *f*; (persons) taille *f*; (glue) colle *f*. *v* coller.

skate, skéte, *v* patiner. *n* patin *m*; (fish) raie *f*.

skateboard, skétt´-baurde, *n* skateboard *m*.

skating, skétt´-inng, *n*

patinage *m*.

skating rink, skétt-inng- rinque, *n* patinoire *m*.

skeleton, skell´-*eu*-t'n, *n* squelette *m*.

skeptical*, skepp´-ti-c'l, *a* sceptique.

sketch, sketche, *v* esquisser. *n* esquisse *f*, croquis *m*.

skewer, skioue´-*eur*, *n* brochette *f*; broche *f v* embrocher.

ski, ski, *v* skier; faire du ski; *n* ski *m*; **lift**, *n* remonte-pente *m*; **–slope**, *n* piste de ski *f*.

skid, skidde, *v* déraper. *n* dérapage *m*.

skiff, ski?e, *n* esquif *m*, skiff *m*.

skiing, skî´-inng, *n* ski *m*.

skill, skille, *n* habileté *f*, adresse *f*; (natural) talent *m*.

skillful*, skill´-foull, *a* adroit, habile.

skim, skimme, *v* (*fig*) effleurer; écrémer; (scum) écumer.

skimmed milk, skimm'd- milque, *n* lait écrémé.

skin, skinne, *n* peau *f*; (hide) cuir *m*; (peel) écorce *f*; (thin peel) pelure *f*.

skip, skippe, v sauter; (with a rope) manquer; sauter à la corde.

skipper, skipp´-'r, n patron de bateau m.

skirmish, skeur´-miche, n escarmouche f.

skirt, skeurte, n (dress) jupe f. v border.

skull, skolle, n crâne m.

skunk, skonngk, n canaille f; (fur) putois m.

sky, skâï, n ciel m; **–light,** châssis vitre m; **–scraper,** gratte-ciel m.

slab, slâbbe, n dalle f; plaque f.

slack, slâque, n (small coal) menu charbon m. a (loose) lâche.

slacken, slâque´-'n, v relâcher; (pace) (to make slower) ralentir.

slander, slânne´-d'r, v calomnier. n calomnie f; (law) diffamation f; **–er,** calomniateur m.

slang, slain-ngue, n argot m.

slant, slânnte, v être en pente; incliner; n pente f; **–ing,** a oblique.

slap, slâppe, n gifle f. v gifler.

slash, slâche, v taillader; (gash) (the face) balafrer.

slate, sléte, n ardoise f. v couvrir d'ardoises.

slaughter, sloa´-t'r, v (animals) abattre; massacrer. n tuerie f; **–er,** tueur m; **–house,** abattoir m.

slave, sléve, n esclave m & f; **–ry,** esclavage m.

slay, slé, v tuer; massacrer.

sledge, slèdje, n traîneau m; **–hammer,** marteau de forgeron m.

sleek, slîque, a lisse; (manners) mielleux.

sleep, slîpe, v dormir. n sommeil m; **–ing car,** (railroad) wagon-lit m; **–less,** a sans sommeil; **–lessness,** n insomnie f; **–y,** a qui a sommeil.

sleeping bag, slîp-inng-bâgue n sac de couchage m.

sleeping pill, slîp-inng-pile, n somnifère m.

sleet, slîte, n grésil m.

sleeve, slîve, n manche f.

sleigh, slé, n traîneau m.

sleight, slâïte, n tour d'adresse m; **–of hand,** prestidigitation f.

slender, slenn´-d'r, a mince; (figure) svelte; (means) modeste.

slice, slâïce, n tranche f. v couper en tranches.

slide, slâïde, n glissade f; toboggan m; (microscopic) lamelle f; (photo) diapositive f; (lantern) verre m. v glisser.

slight, slâïte, n marque de mépris f. v traiter sans égards. a* mince; (mistake, etc) léger.

slim, slimme, a élancé. v se faire maigrir.

slime, slâïme, n vase f; limon m.

slimy, slâï´-mi, a vaseux; visqueux.

sling, slinng, n (med) (for a broken limb) écharpe f. v (throw) lancer.

slink, slinng-k, v s'esquiver.

slip, slippe, v glisser; **–pery,** a glissant.

slipper, slipp´-'r, n pantoufle f.

slit, slitte, v fendre. n fente f.

sloe, slau, n (bot) prunelle f.

slope, slaupe, v aller en pente. n pente f.

slot, slotte, n fente f; (box; machine) ouverture f.

sloth, slauts, n paresse f; indolence f.

slouch, slâ'outche, v marcher lourdement.

slovenly, slov´-'n-li, a sans soin.

slow*, slau, a lent; **to be –,** v (clock, etc) retarder.

slug, slogg, n limace f.

sluggish*, slogg´-iche, a lent; paresseux.

sluice, slouce, n écluse f; **--way,** vanne f.

slum, slomme, n bas quartier m; taudis m.

slumber, slomm´-b'r, v sommeiller. n sommeil m.

slump, slommpe, n effondrement des cours m.

slur, sleur, n tache f. v tacher; déprécier.

slush, sloche, n boue f; fange f; neige à moitié fondue f.

sly, slâï, a sournois; rusé.

smack, smâque, v (hand) (to slap) donner une claque à; (lips) faire claquer. n claque f; (boat) smack m.

small, smoal, a petit; **–ness,** n petitesse f.

smallpox, smoal´-poxe, n petite vérole f.

smart, smârte, a vif; (clever) spirituel; habile; (spruce) pimpant; chic. v (pain) cuire.

smash, smâche, n collision f; (com) krach m. v – **to pieces,** briser en morceaux; briser.

smattering, smätt´-eur-inng, n connaissance superficielle f.

smear, smire, v barbouiller (de); n barbouillage m.

smell, smelle, v sentir. n odeur f.

smelt, smelte, v fondre. n (fish) éperlan m.

smile, smâïle, v sourire. n sourire m.

smite, smâïte, v frapper; affliger.

smith, smits, n forgeron m; **–y,** forge f.

smoke, smauke, v fumer. n fumée f; **–less,** a sans fumée; **–r,** n fumeur m.

smoky, smau´-ki, a enfumé.

smolder, smaul´-d'r, v brûler sans flammes.

smooth, smoodz, a* lisse; v (the hair) lisser; (temper) apaiser.

smother, smodz´-'r, v étouffer; suffoquer.

smudge, smodje, v tacher. n tache f.

smuggle, smog´-g'l, v passer en contrebande.

smuggler, smog´-gleur, n contrebandier m.

snack, snăque, n casse-croûte m.

snail, snéle, n colimaçon m; (edible) escargot m.

snake, snéque, n serpent m.

snap, snăppe, n (noise) (of a whip,etc.) claquement m; (bite) coup de dent m. v fermer binet; (break) briser net; (fingers) claquer les doigts; (animal) happer.

snapshot, snăppe´-chotte, n instantané m.

snare, snère, n piège m. v prendre au piège.

snarl, snârle, v grogner. n grognement m.

snatch, snătche, v saisir; **–at,** v chercher à saisir; **–from,** arracher à.

sneak, snîque, n mouchard m. v (steal) chiper; **–away,** v s'esquiver furtivement.

sneer, snire, v ricaner. n ricanement m.

sneeze, snîze, v éternuer. n éternuement m.

sniff, sniffe, v renifler.

snip, snipe, n coup de ciseaux m. v couper avec des ciseaux.

snipe, snäïpe, n bécassine f; **-r,** tireur d'élite m.

snob, snobbe, n snob m; **-bish,** a poseur.

snore, snaure, v ronfler. n ronflement m.

snorkel, snoar´-k'l, n tuba m.

snort, snoarte, v renâcler. n renâclement m.

snout, snâ´oute, n museau m; (pig) groin m.

snow, snau, v neiger. n neige f; **-flake,** perce-neige m; **--storm,** tempête de neige f.

snub, snobbe, v dédaigner. n rebuffade f.

snuff, snoffe, n tabac à priser m; **-box,** tabatière f.

so, sau, adv (therefore) aussi; ainsi; comme cela; si.

soak, sauque, v tremper.

soap, saupe, n savon m.

soar, saure, v s'élever; **- over** planer sur.

sob, sobbe, v sangloter. n sanglot m.

sober*, sau´-b'r, a sobre; modéré.

sociable, sau´-cha-b'l, a sociable.

social, sau´-ch'l, a* social; **-ism,** n socialisme m; **-ist,** socialiste m & f.

society, sŏ-saï´-i-ti, n société f; compagnie f; grand monde m.

sock, soque, n chaussette f.

socket, sok´-ette, (eyes) orbite f; (teeth) alvéole m.

sod, sode, n motte de gazon f.

soda, sau´-da, n soude f; **-water,** eau de Seltz f.

sofa, sau´-fä, n sofa m; canapé m.

soft*, softe, a mou; doux; (tender) tendre; **-en,** v adoucir; (fig) attendrir; **-ness,** n douceur f.

soft drink, softe-drinnque, n boisson non alcoolisée f.

software, softe-ouère, n (comput) logiciel m; software m.

soil, soa´ile, v souiller; abîmer. n sol m, (land) terre f.

sojourn, sô´-djeurne, v séjourner. n séjour m.

solace, sol´-ace, n consolation f. v consoler (de).

solder, saule´-d'r, n soudure f. v souder.

soldier, saule´-dj'r, n soldat m.

sole, saule, n (shoes, etc) semelle f; (fish) sole f. v ressemeler. a* seul; unique.

solemn*, sol´-emme, a solennel.

solicit, sŏ-liss´-itte, v solliciter.

solicitor, sŏ-liss´-itt-'r, n avoué m; notaire m.

solicitude, sol-i´-ci-tioude, n sollicitude f.

solid*, sol´-ide, a solide; massif; **-ify,** v solidifier.

solitary, sol´-i-ta-ri, a solitaire; seul.

solitude, sol´-i-tioude, n solitude f.

soluble, sol´-iou-b'l, a soluble.

solution, so-lioue´-ch'n, n solution f.

solve, solve, v résoudre.

solvency, sol´-venn-ci, n solvabilité f.

solvent, sol´-vennte, a dissolvant; (com) solvable.

somber, somme´-beur, a sombre.

some, somme, art a & pron

du *m*; de la *f*; des *pl*;
quelques *pl*; en; **–body,** *n*
quelqu'un *m*; **–how,** *adv*
d'un façon ou d'une
autre; **–one,** *n* quelqu'un
m; **–thing,** quelque
chose *m*; **–times,** *adv*
quelquefois; **–what,**
quelque peu; **–where,**
quelquepart.

somersault, somm´-eur-
solte, *n* saut périlleux *m*;
culbute *f*.

somnambulist, somme-
nămm´-bioue-liste, *n*
somnambule *m* & *f*.

son, sonne, *n* fils *m*; **–in-
law,** gendre *m*.

sonata, sŏ-nâ´-ta, *n* sonate
f.

song, sonng, *n* (ballad)
chanson *f*; (hymn)
chant *m*.

soon, soune, *adv* bientôt;
as –as, aussitôt que; **how
–?** quand?

soot, soute, *n* suie *f*.

soothe, soudz, *v* adoucir;
(pacify) calmer.

sophisticated, sau-fis´-tî-
qué-téde, *a* sophistiqué.

sorcerer, saur´-ceur-eur,
n sorcier *m*.

sorcery, saur´-ceur-i, *n*
sorcellerie *f*.

sordid*, sôr´-dide, *a*

sordide; vil.

sore, saure, *n* plaie *f*; mal
m. *a** mal à; douloureux.

sorrel, sorr´-'l, *n* oseille *f*.

sorrow, sor´-au, *n* chagrin
m; affliction *f*; *v*
s'affliger; **–ful,** *a*
affligeant; triste.

sorry, sor´-i, *a* fâché de;
désolé; **I am –,** je
regrette; pardon!

sort, sôrte, *n* espèce *f*;
genre *m*; sorte *f*. *v* trier.

soul, saule, *n* âme *f*.

sound, sâ'ounnde, *v*
sonner; (naut) sonder. *a*
(health) robuste;
(character) droit;
(sleep) profond. *n* son
m; (bells) son *m*;
(channel) détroit *m*;
–proof, *a* insonore;
–track, *n* bande sonore
f; **–ing,** (naut) sondage
m.

soup, soupe, *n* potage *m*;
soupe *f*.

soup tureen, soupe-tioue-
rîne´, *n* soupière *f*.

sour*, sâ'oueur, *a* sur;
aigre.

source, saurce, *n* source *f*.

south, sâ'outs, *n* sud *m*;
–of France, le midi *m*.

southerly, seudz´-eur-li, *a*
du sud; méridional.

souvenir, sou-vi-nîre´, *n*
souvenir *m*.

sovereign, sov´-eur-ine, *n*
& *a* souverain *m*.

sow, sau, *v* semer; **–er,** *n*
semeur *m*; semailles *fpl*.

sow, sâ'ou, *n* truie *f*.

soya bean, soa'ï-a-bîne, *n*
graine de soja *f*.

space, spéce, *n* espace *m*;
(time) période *f*.

spacious*, spé´-cheuce, *a*
spacieux.

spade, spéde, *n* bêche *f*;
(cards) pique *m*.

span, spănne, *n* empan *m*;
envergure *f*;
(architecture) ouverture
f; (fig) durée *f*. *v* (to
cross) traverser.

spangle, spân´-g'l, *v*
pailleter de; *n* paillette *f*.

spaniel, spănn´-ieule, *n*
épagneul *m*.

spar, spâre, *v* s'exercer à la
boxe.

spare, spére, *a* (naut) de
rechange. *v* (forbear)
épargner; **can you –this?**
pouvez-vous vous en
passer?

sparing*, spére´-inng, *a*
frugal; économe.

spark, spârke, *n* étincelle
f; *v* étinceler.

sparkle, spăr´-k'l, *v*

étinceler; (wine) pétiller.

sparrow, spăr´-au, n moineau m.

spasm, spăzme, n spasme m.

spasmodic, spăz-mod´-ique, a spasmodique.

spats, spăttse, npl guêtres fpl.

spatter, spătt´-'r, v éclabousser.

spawn, spoanne, v frayer.

speak, spîke, v parler; **–er**, n orateur m.

spear, spîre, v percer d'un coup de lance. n lance f.

special*, spè´-ch'l, a spécial; (of correspondence, etc.) particulier.

speciality, spèch-i-al´-i-ti, n spécialité f.

specie, spî´-chî, n espèces fpl.

species, spî´-chîze, n espèce f; (fig) sorte f.

specific, speu-si´-fique, a précis(e); particulier(ère); (chem etc) spécifique.

specification, spess-i-fi-qué´-ch'n, n description f; (of a patent, etc,) précise f; (schedule) devis; descriptif m.

specify, spess´-i-fâï, v spécifier.

specimen, spess´-i-menn, n spécimen m; modèle m.

specious*, spî-cheuce, a spécieux; fallacieux.

speck, spèque, n petite tache f.

spectacle, spèk´-ta-k'l, n spectacle m.

spectacles, spèk´-ta-k'lse, npl lunettes fpl.

spectator, spèk-té´-t'r, n spectateur, -trice m & f.

specter, spèk´-t'r, n spectre m.

speculate, spèk´-iou-léte, v spéculer (sur); méditer (sur).

speech, spîtche, n parole f; (discourse) discours m; **–less**, a muet; (fig) interdit.

speed, spîde, n vitesse f; **–y**, a prompt; rapide.

speed limit, spîde-limm-itte, n limit de vitesse; vitesse maximale permise f.

speedometer, spî-domm-it'r, n indicateur de vitesse m.

spell, spelle, v épeler. n charme m.

spend, spennde, v

dépenser; **–thrift**, n dépensier, -ère m & f.

sphere, sfire, n sphère f.

spice, spâïce, n épice f. v épicer.

spicy, spâï´-ci, a épicé; (fig) piquant.

spider, spâï-d'r, n araignée f.

spike, spâïke, n piquant m; pointe f. v clouer.

spill, spille, v répandre; renverser.

spin, spinne, v filer; faire tourner; **–ning**, n (process) filage m.

spinach, spinn´-idj, n épinards mpl.

spinal, spâïne´-'l, a spinal; vertébral.

spindle, spinn-d'l, n fuseau m; (tech) axe m.

spine, spâïne, n épine dorsale f.

spinster, spinn´-st'r, n femme non mariée f.

spiral, spâï´-r'l, a spiral. n spirale f.

spire, spâïre, n flèche f.

spirit, spir´-itte, n esprit m; (alcohol) alcool m; (animation) entrain m; **–ed**, a animé; **–ual**, spirituel; **–ualist**, n (Phil) spiritualiste m.

spit, spitte, v cracher. n

crachat *m*; (roasting) broche *f*; –**toon**, crachoir *m*.

spite, spâîte, *v* dépiter. *n* dépit *m*; –**ful,** *a* vindicatif; **in –of,** *prep* malgré.

splash, splâche, *v* éclabousser; (play) patauger.

splendid*, splenn´-dide, *a* splendide.

splendor, splenn´-d´r, *n* splendeur *f*.

splint, splinnte, *n* (surgical) attelle *f*.

splinter, splinn´-t'r, *n* (in the hand) écharde *f*. *v* voler en éclats.

split, splitte, *v* fendre. *n* fente *f*.

spoil, spoa'ile, *v* gâter; (damage) abîmer.

spoke, spauke, *n* rayon d'une roue *m*.

spokesman, spaukce´-mănne, *n* porte-parole *m*.

sponge, sponndje, *n* éponge *f*. *v* éponger.

sponsor, sponn´-sor, *n* (surety) garant *m*; (baptism) parrain *m*; marraine *f*.

spontaneous*, sponn-té´-ni-euce, *a* spontané.

spool, spoule, *n* bobine *f*.

spoon, spoune, *n* cuiller *f*; –**ful,** cuillerée *f*.

sport, spaurte, *n* sport *m*; –**ing,** *a* sportif; –**ive,** *a* gai.

spot, spotte, *v* tacher. *n* tache *f*; (place) endroit *m*; –**less,** *a* sans tache.

spout, spâ'oute, *n* (gutter) gouttière *f*; (jug or pot) bec *m*. *v* jaillir.

sprain, spréne, *v* se fouler. *n* entorse *f*.

sprawl, sproale, *v* s'étaler; se vautrer.

spray, spré, *n* (water) embrun *m*. *v* arroser; pulvériser; atomiser.

sprayer, spré´-*eur*, *n* vaporisateur *m*; atomiseur.

spread, spredde, *v* étendre; (on bread, etc) étaler; (news) répandre; –**out,** déployer.

sprig, sprigue, *n* brin *m*; brindille *f*.

sprightly, sprâîte´-li, *a* enjoué; vif; gai.

spring, sprinng, *n* (season) printemps *m*; (leap) saut *m*; (water) source *f*; (metal) ressort *m*. *v – at,* sauter à la gorge de; –**y,** *a* élastique.

sprinkle, sprinng´-k'l, *v* asperger de; saupoudrer (with holy water).

sprout, sprâ'oute, *v* germer; *n* pousse *f*.

spruce, sprouce, *n* sapin *f*. *a* pimpant.

spur, speur, *n* éperon *m*. *v* éperonner.

spurious*, spiou´-ri-*euce*, *a* faux.

spurn, speurne, *v* dédaigner; (to treat with disdain) mépriser.

spy, spâî, *n* espion, -onne *m* & *f*. *v* espionner.

squabble, scouob´-b'l, *v* se chamailler; *n* dispute *f*.

squad, scouodde, *n* (mil) escouade *f*; –**ron,** (mil) escadron *m*; (naval, air) escadre *f*.

squalid*, scouoll´-ide, *a* sale; abject.

squall, scouoale; *n* (wind) rafale *f*. *v* (scream) brailler.

squalor, scouoll-*eur*, *n* abjection *f*.

squander, scouonn´-d'r, *v* dissiper; gaspiller.

square, scouère, *n* & *a* carré *m*; (public) place *f*.

squash, scouoche, *v* écraser. *n* écrasement *m*.

squat, scouotte, *v*

s'accroupir. *a* (*fig*) trapu.

squeak, scouîke, *v* crier; (bearings, etc) grincer.

squeeze, scouîze, *v* serrer; (cuddle) étreindre; (lemon, etc) presser.

squid, scouide, *n* calmar *m.*

squint, scouinnte, *v* loucher. *n* regard louche *m.*

squirrel, scouir´-'l, *n* écureuil *m.*

squirt, scoueurte, *n* seringue *f. v* seringuer; faire gicler.

stab, stăbbe, *v* poignarder. *n* coup de poignard *m.*

stability, stă-bil´-i-ti, *n* stabilité *f.*

stable, sté´-b'l, *n* écurie *f*; (cattle) étable *f. a* (for horses) stable.

stack, stăque, *n* pile *f*; (hay) meule *f*; (chimney) cheminée *f. v* empiler.

stadium, sté´-di-*e*um, *n* stade *m.*

staff, stăffe, *n* bâton *m*; (employees) personnel *m*; (*mil*) état-major *m*; **flag- –,**hampe *f.*

stag, stăgue, *n* cerf *m.*

stage, stédje, *n* (theater) scène *f*; (hall) estrade *f*;

(period) phase *f. v* mettre en scène.

stagger, stagg´-'r, *v* chanceler; (*fig*) renverser.

stagnate, stagg´-néte, *v* stagner; croupir.

staid*, stéde, *a* posé; sérieux.

stain, sténe, *v* (dyeing) teindre; (soil) souiller. *n* teinture *f*; (soil) tache *f*; **–less,** *a* (metal) inoxydable.

stair, stére, *n* marche *f*; **–s,** *pl* escalier *m.*

stake, stéque, *v* (to defend with stakes) garnir de pieux; (bet) parier. *n* pieu *m*; (wager) enjeu *m*; **at the –,**sur le bûcher.

stale, stéle, *a* (bread, etc) rassis; (beer, etc) éventé.

stalk, stoake, *n* tige *f. v* chasser à l'affût.

stall, stoale, *n* (market) étalage *m*; (cattle) box *m. v* (of engine) caler.

stalwart, stoal´-oueurte, *a* fort; robuste.

stamina, stămm´-i-n*a*, *n* force de résistance *f.*

stammer, stămm´-'r, *v* bégayer.

stamp, stămmpe, *n*

(documents, letters, etc.) timbre *m. v* timbrer; (foot) frapper du pied.

stampede, stămm-pîdé´, *v* (of animals) fuir en panique; *n* débandade *f.*

stand, stănnde, *v* être debout; (place) mettre; (endure) supporter. *n* (*fig*) tribune *f*; (platform) résistance *f*; (pedestal) support *m*; (market) étalage *m*; (exhibition) stand *m*; **–ing,** *a* permanent; *n* (rank) rang *m*; **–ingroom,** place debout *f*; **–still,** arrêt *m.*

standard, stănn´-deurde, *n* étendard *m. n* & *a* (*fig*) modèle *m*; (weights, measures) étalon *m.*

staple, sté´-p'l, *n* crampon de fer à deux pointes *m*; agrafe *f. a* principal.

star, stârre, *n* étoile *f*; **–ry,** *a* étoilé.

starboard, stârre´-baurde, *n* tribord *m.*

starch, stârtche, *n* amidon *m. v* empeser.

stare, stére, *v* regarder fixement. *n* regard fixe *m.*

starling, stăr´-linng, *n*

étourneau m.

start, stârte, n (beginning) commencement m; v (to begin) commencer; (machinery) mettre en marche; (leave) partir.

startle, stâr´-t'l, v (to become startled) sursauter; effrayer.

starvation, stâr-vé´-ch'n, n inanition f.

starve, stârve, v mourir de faim; (deprive) affamer.

state, stéte, v déclarer. n état m; (pomp) apparat m; **–ly,** a majestueux; **–ment,** n déclaration f; (account) relevé de compte m.

statesman, stéts´-mănne, n homme d'Etat m.

station, sté-ch'n, n position f; (railroad) gare f; (fire, police) poste m. v poster.

stationary, sté´-chŏnn-a-ri, a stationnaire.

stationer, sté´-cheunn-*eur*, n papetier m.

stationery, sté´-cheunn-eur-i, n papeterie f.

statistics, sta-tiss´-tiks, n statistique f.

statue, stă´-tiou, n statue f.

statute, stă´-tioute, n

statut m; loi f.

staunch, stânnche, v étancher. a ferme.

stave, stéve, n portée f **–off,** v conjurer; éviter.

stay, sté, n séjour m. v séjourner; rester.

stays, stéze, npl corset m.

stead, stedde, n place f; **in –of,** au lieu de.

steadfast, stedd´-fâsste, a solide; constant.

steady, stedd´-i, a ferme; (reliable) sérieux; (market) ferme.

steak, stéque, n bifteck m.

steal, stîle, v voler; dérober.

stealth, stèlts, **by –,** à la dérobée.

steam, stîme, n vapeur f; **–er,** bateau à vapeur m.

steel, stîle, n acier m.

steep, stîpe, a escarpé. v (soak) tremper.

steeple, stî´-p'l, n clocher m.

steer, stîre, v (naut) gouverner; (aero) diriger; (motor) conduire. n (ox) bouvillon m.

steerage, stîre´-idj, n entrepont m.

stem, stemme, n tige f; (glass) pied m; (tobacco-

pipe) tuyau m; (a current) v refouler.

stench, stenntche, n infection f; puanteur f.

step, steppe, v marcher; aller. n pas m; (stair) marche f; (ladder) échelon m; **–brother,** n demi-frère m; **–father,** beau-père m; **–mother,** belle-mère f; **–sister,** n demi-sœur f;**–ladder,** échelle double f.

stereo, stè´-rî-au, n stéréo f.

stereophonic, stér-io-fon´-ique, a stéréophonique.

sterile, stér-il, a stérile.

sterilize, stér´-i-lâïze, v stériliser.

sterling, steur´-linng, a sterling; pur; (fig) de bon aloi.

stern, steurne, n arrière m. a* sévère; (cross) rébarbatif.

stew, stioue, n (of meat) ragoût m. v mettre en ragoût.

steward, stioue´-eurde, n (estate) intendant m; (ship) garçon de cabine m; **–ess,** femme de chambre (de bord) f; n hôtesse (de l'air) f; **wine –,** sommelier m.

stick, stique, v (affix) coller. n bâton m; (walking) canne f; **-y,** a collant.

stiff*, stife, a raide; **-en,** v raidir; (linen) empeser.

stifle, stâï-f'l, v étouffer; suffoquer.

stigmatize, stigg´-ma-tâïze, v stigmatiser.

stile, stâïle, n barrière f; **turn -,** tourniquet m.

still, stille, n (distill) alambic m. v calmer. a tranquille; adv encore; toujours. conj (nevertheless) néanmoins.

stimulate, stimm´-iou-léte, v stimuler.

sting, stinng, v piquer. n piqûre f.

stink, stinng-k, v puer. n puanteur f.

stint, stinnte, v restreindre; rogner.

stipend, stâï´-pennde, n traitement m.

stipulate, stip´-iou-léte, v stipuler.

stipulation, stip-iou-lé-ch'n, n stipulation f.

stir, steur, v remuer; (fig) agiter; bouger. n émoi m.

stirrup, stirr´-eupe, n étrier m.

stitch, stitche, v coudre. n point m.

stock, stoque, v avoir en magasin; stocker; n (tree) tronc m; (gun) fût m; (flower) giroflée f; (goods) stock m; (live) animaux vivants mpl; (meat, etc) bouillon m; **-broker,** agent de change m; **-exchange,** bourse f; **-s,** (securities) valeurs fpl; (pillory) pilori m; **-taking,** inventaire m.

stocking, stok´-inng, n bas m.

stoke, stauque, v chauffer; **-r,** n chauffeur m.

stolid, stol´-id, a lourd.

stomach, stomm´-aque, n estomac m; **-ache,** mal à l'estomac m; mal au ventre m.

stone, staune, n pierre f; (pebble) caillou m; (med) calcul m; v lapider; (fruit) enlever les noyaux.

stool, stoule, n tabouret m; (med) selle f.

stoop, stoupe, v se baisser.

stop, stoppe, n arrêt m; (interruption) pause f; (punctuation) point m; v arrêter; s'arrêter;

(payment) suspendre; (teeth) plomber; (cease) (of trains, vessels, etc.) cesser; **-up,** boucher.

stopper, stopp´-'r, n bouchon m.

storage, staur´-idj, n magasinage m.

store, staure, n (shop) magasin m.

stores, staur´ze, npl approvisionnements mpl.

stork, stoarque, n cigogne f.

storm, stoarme, n tempête f. v donner l'assaut à.

stormy, stoar´-mi, a orageux.

story, stau-ri, n histoire f; (untruth) mensonge m; (floor) étage m.

stout, stâ´oute, a gros; (strong) fort.

stove, stauve, n poêle m; (cooking) cuisinière f.

stow, stau, v (naut) arrimer; (away) ranger.

stowaway, stau´-a-oué, n voyageur clandestin m.

straggle, strägg´-'l, v s'écarter de; (lag) traîner.

straight, stréte, a droit; direct; **-en,** v redresser; **-forward*,** a honorable;

franc.

strain, stréne, n effort m; (music) air m; (pull) tension f. v s'efforcer; (stretch) tendre; (tendon) fouler; (liquid) filtrer.

strainer, stré´-neur, n passoire f; filtre m.

straits, strétse, npl (channel) détroit m.

strand, strännde, v (naut) échouer. n plage f; (rope) brin m.

strange*, stréne'dje, a étrange; –r, n étranger, -ère m & f.

strangle, strain´-ng'l, v étrangler.

strap, sträppe, v attacher avec une courroie; n courroie f.

strategy, strä´-ta-djî, n stratégie f.

straw, stroa, n paille f; –berry, fraise f.

stray, stré, v s'égarer; s'éloigner. a égaré, perdu.

streak, strîke, n raie f; rayon m. v rayer.

streaky, strîk´-i, a rayé; (meat) entrelardé.

stream, strîme, n (brook) ruisseau m; courant m. v couler; –lined, a

aérodynamique.

street, strîte, n rue f.

strength, strenng-ts, n force f; –en, v renforcer.

strenuous*, strenn´-iou-euce, a ardu.

stress, stresse, n accent m; (pressure) pression f; tension f; (urge) urgence f. v accentuer; souligner.

stretch, stretche, v (widen) élargir; (oneself) s'étirer; (pull) tirer; –er, n (med) brancard m.

strew, stroue, v répandre; parsemer.

strict*, stricte, a exact; strict; rigoureux.

stride, strâïde, n enjambée f. v enjamber.

strife, strâïfe, n dispute f; contestation f.

strike, strâïke, v (work) se mettre en grève; (lightning; smite) frapper; (match) allumer; n (of workmen) grève f; –off, –out, v effacer; (disqualify) rayer; –r, n gréviste m & f.

string, strinng, v (beads) enfiler. n ficelle f; (music) corde f.

stringent, strinn´-djennte,

a rigoureux.

strip, strippe, v dénuder. n bande f.

stripe, strâïpe, n raie f; (mil) galon m. v rayer.

strive, strâïve, v s'efforcer de.

stroke, strauke, n (med) attaque f; (pen) trait de plume m; (blow) coup m; (piston) course f. v caresser.

stroll, straule, v flâner; faire un tour. n tour m.

strong*, stronng, a fort; solide.

structure, strok´-tioure, n structure f.

struggle, strogg´-'l, v lutter. n lutte f.

strut, strotte, v se pavaner. n (brace) étai m.

stubborn, stobb´-eurne, a obstiné; opiniâtre.

stud, stodde, n (nail) clou à grosse tête m; (collar) bouton m; (breeding) haras m. v garnir de clous.

student, stioue´-dennte, n étudiant, -e m & f, élève m & f.

studio, stioue´-di-ô, n atelier m; studio m.

studious*, stioue´-di-euce, a studieux.

study, stodd´-i, *v* étudier. *n*
étude *f;* (room) cabinet
de travail *m;* bureau *m.*

stuff, stoffe, *v* rembourrer;
(preserve) empailler;
(cookery) farcir. *n* (*fig*)
matière *f;* **–ing,**
(cookery) farce *f.*

stumble, stomm´-b'l, *v*
trébucher.

stump, stommpe, *n*
tronçon *m;* (arm, leg)
moignon *m;* (tooth)
racine *f.*

stun, stonne, *v* étourdir.

stunning, stonn´-inng, *a*
(*fig*) étourdissant.

stunt, stonnte, *n* tour de
force *m;* acrobatie *f;*
–man, cascadeur *m.*

stunted, stonn´-tedde, *a*
rabougri.

stupefy, stioue´-pi-fâï, *v*
stupéfier.

stupendous*, stiou-penn´-
deuce, *a* prodigieux.

stupid*, stioue´-pide, *a*
stupide; **–ity,** *n* stupidité
f.

stupor, stioue´-peur, *n*
stupeur *f.*

sturdy, steur´-di, *a*
vigoureux; hardi.

sturgeon, steur´-dj'n, *n*
esturgeon *m.*

stutter, stott´-'r, *v* bégayer;
balbutier.

sty, stâï, *n* porcherie *f;*
(med) orgelet *m.*

style, stâïle, *n* mode *f;*
(manner) style *m.*

stylish, stâïl´-iche, *a* à la
mode; élégant.

subdue, seub-dioue´, *v*
subjuguer; (tame)
dompter.

subject, sobb-djecte´, *v*
assujétir; exposer à.

subject, sobb´-djecte, *n*
sujet *m.*

subjection, sobb-djèque´-
ch'n, *n* dépendance *f;*
soumission *f.*

subjunctive, sobb-
djonngk´-tive, *n*
subjonctif *m.*

sublime*, seub-lâïme´, *a*
sublime.

submarine, sob´-ma-rine,
n & a sous-marin *m.*

submerge, seub-meurdje´,
v submerger.

submission, seub-mich´-
'n, *n* soumission *f.*

submit, seub-mitte´, *v*
soumettre à; se
soumettre à.

subordinate, seub-or´-di-
néte, *a* subordonné.

subpœna, seub-pî´-na, *n*
assignation *f. v* assigner.

subscribe, seub-scrâïbe´, *v*

souscrire (à or pour);
(papers) s'abonner; **–r,** *n*
souscripteur *m;* abonné,
-ée *m & f.*

subscription, seub-scrip´-
ch'n, *n* souscription *f;*
(papers, library, etc)
abonnement *m.*

subsequent*, seub´-sî-
couennte, *a* subséquent.

subservient, seub-seur´-vi-
ennte, *a* subordonné à.

subside, seub-sâïde´, *v* (to
sink) s'affaisser; (water)
baisser.

subsidiary, seub-side´-i-a-
ri, *a* subsidiaire.

subsidy, seub´-si-di, *n*
(grant) subvention *f.*

subsist, seub-cisste´, *v*
subsister; **–on,** vivre de.

substance, seub´-st'nce, *n*
substance *f;* (meaning)
fond *m.*

substantial*, seub-stänn´-
cheul, *a* substantiel.

substantiate, seub-stänn´-
chi-éte, *v* établir.

substantive, seub´-stänn-
tive, *n* substantif *m.*

substitute, seub´-sti-
tioute, *v* remplacer. *n*
(proxy) remplaçant, -e
m & f; **as a –,** à la place
de.

subterranean, seub-tèrré´-ni-ann, *a* souterrain.

subtitle, sob´-tî-tl, *n* (*cinema*) sous-titre *m*.

subtle, seutt´-'l, *a* subtil; adroit.

subtract, seub-trăcte´, *v* soustraire.

suburb, seub´-eurbe, *n* banlieue *f*.

subway, seub´-oué, *n* passage souterrain *m*; métro *m*.

succeed, seuk-cîde´, *v* succéder à; (achieve) réussir.

success, seuk-cesse´, *n* succès *m*; **–ful,** *a* couronné de succés; (person) heureux; **–ion,** *n* succession *f*; **–or,** successeur *m*.

succor, seuk´-'r, *n* secours *m*. *v* secourir.

succumb, seuk-komme´, *v* succomber.

such, sotche, *a* pareil; semblable.

suck, soque, *v* sucer; (baby) téter; **–le,** allaiter.

suction, soque´-ch'n, *n* succion *f*.

sudden*, sod´-'n, *a* soudain; imprévu.

sue, sioue, *v* poursuivre en justice.

suede, souéde, *n* daim *m*.

suet, sioue´-ette, *n* graisse de rognon *f*.

suffer, so?´-'r, *v* souffrir; supporter; **–ing,** *n* souffrance *f*. *a* patient. **on –ance,** par tolérance.

suffice, seuf-fâïce´, *v* suffire à.

sufficient*, seuf-fi´-chennte, *a* suffisant.

suffocate, sof´-ŏ-quéte, *v* suffoquer.

suffrage, seuf´-frédje, *n* suffrage *m*.

sugar, chou´-gueur, *n* sucre *m*.

suggest, seudd-jeste´, *v* suggérer; (advice) conseiller; **–ion,** *n* suggestion *f*; **–ive,** *a* suggestif.

suicide, siou´-i-sâïde, *n* suicide *m*.

suit, sioute, *v* convenir; (dress) aller bien. *n* complet *m*; costume *m*; (law) procès *m*; (cards) couleur *f*; **–able,** *a* convenable; **–case,** *n* valise *f*; **–or,** (wooer) prétendant *m*.

suite, souîte, *n* (retinue) suite *f*; (rooms) appartement *m*; (furniture) ameublement *m*.

sulfur, soll´-f'r, *n* soufre *m*.

sulk, sollque, *v* bouder; **–y,** *a* boudeur.

sullen*, soll´-'n, *a* maussade; morose.

sultry, soll´-tri, *a* lourd; accablant.

sum, somme, *n* somme *f*; **–up,** *v* résumer.

summary, somm´-a-ri, *n* résumé *m*. *a* sommaire.

summer, somm´-'r, *n* été *m*.

summit, somm´-itte, *n* sommet *m*.

summon, somm´-'n, *v* appeler; (call) convoquer.

summons, somm´-eunnze, *n* (to surrender, etc.) sommation *f*.

sumptuous*, sommp´-tiou-euce, *a* somptueux.

sun, sonne, *n* soleil *m*; **–bathe,** *v* prendre un bain de soleil; **–beam,** rayon de soleil *m*; **–burn,** *n* coup de soleil *m*; **–dial,** cadran solaire *m*; **–glasses,** *n* lunettes de soleil *fpl*; **–light,** sonn´-lâïte, *n* soleil *m*; **–ny,** *a* ensoleillé; **–rise,** *n* lever du soleil *m*; **–set,** coucher du soleil *m*;

–**stroke,** coup de soleil *m*; insolation *m*; –**tan,** *n* bronzage *m*.

Sunday, sonn´-dé, *n* dimanche *m*.

sundries, sonn´-drize, *npl* articles divers *mpl*.

sundry, sonn´-dri, *a* divers.

sunken, sonng´-k'n, *a* enfoncé;coulé.

suntan lotion, sonn´-tanne-lau-ch'n, *a* crème solaire.

sup, soppe, *v* souper; –**per,** *n* souper *m*.

super, sioue´-peur, *n* (theatrical) figurant *m*; –**abundant,** *a* surabondant; –**annuation,** *n* retraite *f*; –**cilious,** *a* hautain; dédaigneux; –**ficial,** superficiel; –**fine,** surfin; –**intend,** *v* surveiller; –**intendent,** *n* contrôleur *m*; –**market,** *n* supermarché *m*; –**natural,** *a* surnaturel; –**sede,** *v* supplanter; –**vise,** surveiller; –**vision,** *n* surveillance *f*.

superb*, sioue-peurbe´, *a* superbe.

superfluous, sioue-peur´-flou-*euce*, *a* superflu.

superior, sioue-pi´-ri-eur, *a* supérieur.

superlative, sioue-peur´-la-tive, *n* & *a* superlatif *m*.

superstitious*, sioue-peur-stich´-euce, *a* superstitieux.

supplant, seup-plânnte´, *v* supplanter.

supple, sopp´-l, *a* souple.

supplement, sopp´-li-m'nt, *n* supplément *m*.

supplier, seup-plâï´-eur, *n* fournisseur *m*.

supply, seup-plâï´, *v* fournir. *n* fourniture *f*.

support, seup-paurte´, *n* (prop) support *m*; (moral) appui *m*; (maintenance) entretien *m*. *v* supporter; entretenir; (morally) soutenir.

suppose, seup-pauze´, *v* supposer.

supposition, seup-pau-ziche´-'n, *n* supposition *f*.

suppress, seup-press´, *v* (to check) supprimer; (conceal) cacher.

supremacy, sioue-premm´-a-ci, *n* suprématie *f*.

supreme*, sioue-prîme´, *a* suprême.

surcharge, seur´-tchârdje, *n* surcharge *f*. *v* surcharger.

sure*, choueur, *a* sûr, certain.

surety, choueur´-ti, *n* (bail, etc) caution *f*.

surf, seurfe, *n* ressac *m*.

surface, seur´-féce, *n* surface *f*.

surfboard, seurf´-baurde, *n* planche de surf *f*.

surfing, seurf´-inng, *n* surf *m*.

surge, seurdje, *v* s'enfler. *n* houle *f*.

surgeon, seur´-djeune, *n* chirurgien *m*.

surgery, seur´-djeur-i, *n* chirurgie *f*.

surgical, seur´-dji-c'l, *a* chirurgical.

surly, seur´-li, *a* bourru; (dog) hargneux.

surmise, seur-mâïze´, *v* conjecturer. *n* conjecture *f*.

surmount, seur-mâ´ounnte´, *v* surmonter.

surname, seur´-néme, *n* nom de famille *m*.

surpass, seur-pâsse´, *v* surpasser; l'emporter sur.

surplus, seur´-pleuce, *n* excédent *m*; surplus *m*.

surprise, *seur*-prâïze´, *v* surprendre. *n* surprise *f*.

surrender, *seur*-renn´-d´r, *n* (*mil*) reddition *f*. *v* se rendre; (cede) céder.

surround, *seur*-râ´ounnde, *v* entourer; (*mil*) cerner; **–ings,** *npl* environs *mpl*.

survey, *seur*-vé´, *n* (land) arpentage *m*; enquête *f*; *v* (of land) mesurer; (look at) inspecter; **–or,** *n* (overseer) arpenteur *m*; architecte *m*; inspecteur *m*.

survival, *seur*-vâï´-v'l, *n* survivance *f*.

survive, *seur*-vâïve´, *v* survivre.

survivor, *seur*-vâï´-v'r, *n* survivant, -e *m* & *f*.

susceptible, *seuss*-cepp´-ti-b'l, *a* susceptible.

suspect, *seuss*-pecte´, *v* soupçonner. *n* & *a* suspect, -e *m* & *f*.

suspend, *seuss*-pennde´, *v* suspendre; (defer) ajourner; **–ers,** *npl* bretelles *fpl*.

suspense, *seuss*-pennce´, *n* suspens *m*; incertitude *f*.

suspension, *seuss*-penn´-ch'n, *n* suspension *f*; **–bridge,** pont suspendu *m*.

suspicion, *seuss*-pich´-'n, *n* soupçon *m*.

suspicious*, *seuss*-pich´-euce, *a* méfiant; suspect.

sustain, *seuss*-téne´, *v* soutenir; supporter.

swagger, sou´ägg´-'r, *v* faire le fanfaron.

swallow, sou´oll´-au, *v* avaler. *n* (bird) hirondelle *f*.

swamp, sou´ommpe, *n* marécage *m*. *v* submerger.

swan, sou´onne, *n* cygne *m*.

swarm, sou´oarme, *n* (bees, etc) essaim *m*; (people) multitude *f*. *v* essaimer; (crowd) pulluler.

sway, soué, *v* (to bias) influencer; osciller; (totter) chanceler. *n* influence *f*; (power) pouvoir *m*.

swear, sou´aire, *v* jurer de; (law) prêter serment.

sweat, sou´ète, *n* sueur *f*. *v* suer; transpirer.

sweep, sou´ïpe, *v* balayer; (chimney) ramoner. *n* (chimney) ramoneur *m*; **–er,** balayeur *m*.

sweet, sou´îte, *a* sucré; (*fig*) doux. *n*

(confection) bonbon *m*; (meals) entremets *m*; **– bread,** ris de veau ou d'agneau *m*; **–en,** *v* sucrer; **–heart,** *n* amoureux, -euse *m* & *f*; **–ness,** douceur *f*; **–pea,** pois de senteur *m*.

swell, sou´elle, *v* enfler; **–ing,** *n* (*med*) enflure.

swerve, sou´eurve, *v* dévier; (skid) déraper.

swift, sou´ifte, *a** rapide. *n* martinet *m*.

swim, sou´imme, *v* nager. *n* nage *f*; **–mer,** nageur, -euse *m* & *f*; **–ming,** *n* natation *f*; **–ming pool,** piscine *f*; **–ming trunks,** *n* maillot de bain *m*; **–suit,** *n* maillot (de bain) *m*.

swindle, sou´inn´-d'l, *v* escroquer; rouler; *n* escro querie *f*; **–r,** escroc *m*.

swine, sou-âïne, *n* cochon *m*; porc *m*.

swing, sou´inng, *n* oscillation *f*; (child's) balançoire *f*. *v* osciller; se balancer; (whirl) tournoyer.

switch, sou´itche, *n* (riding) cravache *f*; (electric) commutateur *m*.

m. v (train) aiguiller;
–off, (light) éteindre;
–on, (light) allumer.
swivel, sou'ive´-'l, *n*
tourniquet *m*; pivot *m*.
swoon, swoune, *v* se
pâmer en pâmoison *m*.
swoop, swoupe, *v* fondre
sur.
sword, saurde, *n* épée *f*;
(sabre) sabre *m*.
sworn, sou'aurne, *a* (law)
assermenté.
syllable, sil´-la-b'l, *n*
syllabe *f*.
syllabus, sil´-la-beuce, *n*
programme *m*.
symbol, simm´-b'l, *n*
symbole *m*.
symmetry, simm´-èt-ri, *n*
symétrie *f*.
sympathetic, simm´-pa-
tsèt´-ique, *a*
sympathique.
sympathize, simm´-pa-
tsâîze, *v* sympathiser.
sympathy, simm´-pa-tsi, *n*
sympathie *f*.
symptom, simmp´-t'm, *n*
symptôme *m*.
synchronize, sinn´-cronn-
âîze, *v* synchroniser.
syndicate, sinn´-di-kéte, *n*
syndicat *m*.
synonymous, si-nonn´-i-
meuce, *a* synonyme.

syringe, sir´-inndje, *n*
seringue *f*. *v* seringuer.
syrup, sir´-oppe, *n* sirop *m*.
system, siss´-t'm *n* système
m.

table, té-'b'l, n table f; —**cloth,** nappe f; —**land,** plateau m; —**spoon,** cuiller à bouche f.

table tennis, té-b'l-tenn-ice, n ping-pong f.

tablet, tăb´-lette, n tablette f; plaque f; comprimé m.

tack, tăque, n (nail) semence f. v clouer; (sew) faufiler; (naut) courir une bordée.

tackle, tăque´-'l, n (fishing) articles de pêche mpl; (naut) apparaux mpl; v (work, etc.) attaquer.

tact, tăkt, n tact m; —**ful,** a qui a du tact; —**ics,** n tactique f; —**less,** a sans tact.

tadpole, tăde´-pôle, n têtard m.

tail, téle, n queue f; (coat, short, etc) pan m.

tailor, té-'l'r, n tailleur m.

taint, ténnte, v souiller; infecter. n souillure f.

take, téque, v prendre; accepter; —**away,** (carry away) emporter; (clear away) enlever; (lead away) emmener; —**care of,** prendre soin de, avoir soin de; —**off,** enlever.

takings, té´-kinngse, npl recettes fpl.

talcum powder, tăl-qeum-pâ'ou-d'r, n talc m.

tale, téle, n récit m; (fairy) conte m.

talent, tăl´-ennte, n talent m.

talk, toak, v parler; causer.

n conversation f.

talkative, toak´-a-tive, a bavard.

tall, toal, a (of persons) grand; (of things) haut.

tallow, tăl´-au, n suif m.

tally, tăl´-i, v concorder; correspondre.

talon, tăl´-onne, n serre f.

tame, téme, a apprivoisé; domestique. v apprivoiser; (beasts) dompter; **taming,** n apprivoisement m; —**r,** dompteur m.

tamper, tămm´-p'r, —**with,** v attérer; falsifier.

tampon, tămm´-ponne, n med tampon hygiénique m.

tan, tănne, v (leather) tanner; (sun) bronzer.

tangerine, tănn´-dje-rinne, n mandarine f.

tangible, tănn´-dji-b'l, a tangible; palpable.

tangle, tain-ng'l, n emmêlement m. v embrouiller; emmêler.

tank, tain-ngk, n citerne f; (mil) char d'assaut m.

tantalize, tănn´-ta-lăïze, v tenter; torturer.

tap, tăppe, n tape f; (knock at door etc.) petit coup m; (cock) robinet m; v taper; (knock) frapper; (tree)

4 7 5

inciser.

tape, tépe, n bande f; **– measure,** mètre en ruban m; **–recorder,** n magnétophone m; **–worm,** ver solitaire m; **red –,**(*fig*) bureaucratie f.

taper, tépe´-'r, v effiler.

tapestry, tăp´-'s-tri, n tapisserie f.

tar, târe, n goudron m. v goudronner.

tardy, târe´-di, a lent; (late) tardif.

target, târe´-guette, n cible f.

tariff, tăre´-if, n tarif m.

tarnish, târe´-niche, v ternir.

tarpaulin, târe-poa´-linne, n bâche f.

tart, târte, n tarte f; tourte f. a* acide.

task, tâssque, n tâche f.

tassel, tăss´-'l, n gland m.

taste, téste, v goûter. n goût m; **–ful,** a de bon goût; **–less,** sans goût, insipide.

tasty, tést´-i, a savoureux.

tatter, tătt´-'r, n haillon m; lambeau m; **–ed,** a déguenillé.

tattle, tătt´-'l, v jaser. n bavardage m.

tattoo, ta-toue´, v (skin) tatouer. n tatouage m;

(*mil*) retraite aux flambeaux f.

taunt, toannte, v railler; persifler; n sarcasme m; raillerie f.

tavern, tăv´-eurne, n taverne f.

tawdry, toa´-dri, a clinquant.

tax, tăxe, v taxer. n impôt m; **–payer,** contribuable m & f.

taxi, tăk´-si, n taxi m.

tea, tî, n thé m; **–pot,** théière f.

teach, tîtche, v enseigner; **–er,** n professeur m; (primary) maître, -tresse m & f.

teaching, tîtch´-inng, n enseignement m.

team, tîme, n (sport) équipe f; (horses, etc) attelage m.

tear, tère, v (rend) déchirer. n déchirure f.

tear, tîre, n larme f.

tease, tîze, v taquiner; (annoy) agacer.

teat, tîte, n mamelon m; (dummy) tétine f.

technical*, tèque´-ni-c'l, a technique.

tedious*, tî´-di-*euce*, a ennuyeux; fatigant.

tedium, tî´-di-omme, n ennui m.

teem, tîme, **–with,** v

fourmiller de.

teenager, tîné-dje'r, n addescent,-e m & f.

teeny, tî-ni, a minuscule.

teething, tîdz´-inng, n dentition f.

teetotaler, tî-tŏ´-t'leur, n abstinent, -ente m & f.

telegram, tell´-i-grămme, n télégramme m.

telegraph, tell´-i-grăfe, v télégraphier.

telephone, tell´-i-faune, v téléphoner. n téléphone m.

telephone booth, tell-i-faune-boudz, n cabine téléphonique f.

telephone call, telle-i-faune-coal, n coup de téléphone m.

telephone number, telle-i-faune-nomm-b'r, n numéro de téléphone m.

telescope, tell´-i-scaupe, n télescope m; longue-vue f.

television, tell-i-vij´-'n, n télévision f; **– set,** n poste de télévision m.

tell, tell, v dire; (narrate) raconter.

temper, temm´-p'r, n (humor) humeur f; (anger) colère f; (steel) trempe f. v tremper; **–ance,** n tempérance f; sobriété f. a de

tempérance; –ate*, modéré; sobre; **–ature,** n température f; fièvre f.

tempest, temm´-peste, n tempête f.

temple, temm´-p'l, n temple m; (head) tempe f.

temporary, temm´-pŏ-ra-ri, a temporaire.

tempt, temmpte, v tenter; **–ing,** a tentant.

temptation, temmp-té´-ch'n, n tentation f.

ten, tenne, n & a dix m; **–th,** dixième m & f.

tenable, tenn´-a-b'l, a soutenable; (mil) tenable.

tenacious*, ti-né´-cheuce, a tenace.

tenacity, ti-nǎss´-i-ti, n ténacité f.

tenancy, tenn´-ann-ci, n location f.

tenant, tenn´-annte, n locataire m & f.

tend, tennde, v soigner.

tendency, tenn´-denn-ci, n tendance f.

tender, tenn´-d'r, v offrir; (contract) soumissionner pour; n offre f; soumission f. a* tendre; (painful) sensible; **–-hearted,** compatissant; **–ness,** n tendresse f; sensibilité f.

tenement, tenn´-i-m'nt, n habitation f; logement m.

tennis, tenn´-ice, n tennis m; **– court,** n court de tennis m; **– racket,** n raquette de tennis f.

tenor, tenn´-'r, n (mus) ténor m; (purport) teneur f.

tense, tennce, n (grammar) temps m. a* tendu.

tension, tenn´-ch'n, n tension f.

tent, tennte, n tente f.

tentative, tenn´-ta-tive, a expérimental.

tenure, tenn´-ioure, n jouissance f.

tepid, tepp´-idde, a tiède.

term, teurme, n terme m; (school) trimestre m; (time) durée f; **–inate,** v terminer; se terminer; **–inus,** n terminus m; **–s,** pl conditions fpl; (installments) à tempérament; **–inal,** a terminale, final; med en phase terminale; terminal (computer, oil) m; n terminus (rail) m.

terrace, terr´-ice, n terrasse f.

terrible, terr´-i-b'l, a terrible.

terrific, terr-i-´fique, a formidable.

terrify, terr´-i-fâi, v terrifier.

territory, terr´-i-tŏr-i, n territoire m.

terror, terr´-'r, n terreur f; effroi m; **–ist,** n terroriste m/f; **–ize,** v terroriser.

terse*, teurse, a sec; net.

test, tesste, v mettre à l'épreuve; essayer; n épreuve f, f, essai m; examen m; **–ify,** v attester; **–imonial,** n certificat m; (presentation) témoignage de reconnaissance m.

Testament, tess´-ta-m'nt, n Testament m.

testicle, tess´-ti-k'l, n testicule m.

testimony, tess´-ti-mo-ni, n témoignage m.

tether, tèdʒ´-'r, n longe f. v mettre à l'attache.

text, texte, n texte m; **– book,** manuel m

textile, tex´-tâïle, a textile.

texture, tex´-tioure, n tissu m; texture f.

than, dzǎnne, conj que; de (between more or less and a number).

thank, tsain-ngk, v remercier; **–you!** interj

merci! **-ful,** *a* reconnaissant; **-less,** *ingrat;* **-s,** *npl* remerciements *mpl;* **-s to,** *prep* grâce à.

thanksgiving, tsainngkse´-guiv-inng, *n* actions de grâces *fpl.*

that, dzätte, *pron rel* lequel; laquelle; lesquels; lesquelles; cela; *a* ce; cet; cette; *conj* que; afin que; **-one,** *pron dem* celui-là; celle-là.

thatch, tsätche, *n* chaume *m. v* couvrir de chaume.

thaw, ts oa, *n* dégel *m. v* dégeler.

the, dze, *art* le; la; les.

theater, tsî´-a-t'r, *n* théâtre *m.*

theft, tsefte, *n* vol *m;* (petty) larcin *m.*

their, dzère, *poss a* leur; leurs.

theirs, dzèrze, *poss pron* le leur; la leur; les leurs.

them, dzemme, *pron* eux; elles; les; **to -,**leur; **-selves,** eux-mêmes; elles-mêmes; (refl.) se.

theme, tsîme, *n* thème *m;* texte *m.*

then, dzenne, *adv* alors; ensuite; *conj* donc.

thence, dzennce, *adv* de là; **-forth,** désormais.

theology, tsî-ol´-ŏdj-i, *n*

théologie *f.*

theoretical*, tsî-ŏ-rett´-i-c'l, *a* théorique.

theory, tsî´-ŏ-ri, *n* théorie *f.*

therapy, tsè´-ra-pî, *n* thérapie *f.*

there, dzair, *adv* là; **-by,** *adv* par là; **-fore,** donc; **-upon,** là-dessus; sur ce.

thermal, tseur´-m'l, *a* thermal.

thermometer, tseur-momm´-i-t'r, *n* thermomètre *m.*

these, dzîze, *pron* ceux-ci; celles-ci; *a* ces; ces ... -ci.

thesis, tsî-sisse, *n* thèse *f.*

they, dzé, *pron* ils; elles; eux.

thick, tsique, *a** épais; (big) gros; **-en,** *v* épaissir; **-et,** *n* taillis *m;* **-ness,** épaisseur *f.*

thief, tsîfe, *n* voleur, -euse *m & f.*

thigh, tsäï, *n* cuisse *f.*

thimble, tsimm´-b'l, *n* dé à coudre *m.*

thin, tsinne, *a* mince; (lean) maigre; (sparse) clairsemé. *v* amincir; (trees, etc) élaguer; **-ness,** *n* minceur *f;* maigreur *f.*

thing, tsinng, *n* chose *f.*

think, tsinnque, *v* penser; (believe) croire; **-about,**

(of), penser à, (de); **-over,** réfléchir.

third, tseurde, *n & a** troisième *m & f;* (one-third) tiers *m.*

thirst, tseurste, *n* soif *f;* **to -y,** *v* avoir soif.

thirteen, tseur´-tîne, *n & a* treize *m;* **-th,** treizième *m & f.*

thirtieth, tseur´-ti-its, *n & a* trentième *m & f.*

thirty, tseur´-ti, *n & a* trente *m.*

this, dzice, *pron* ceci; ce; *a* ce; cet; cette.

thistle, tsiss´-'l, *n* chardon *m.*

thong, tsonng, *n* lanière *f.*

thorn, ts oarne, *n* épine *f;* **-y,** *a* épineux.

thorough*, tsor´-ŏ, *a* entier; (perfect) parfait; profond; **-bred,** *n & a* pur sang *m. a* (dog) de race; **-fare,** *n* voie *f;* (main) grande artère *f;* **no -fare,** rue barrée.

those, dzauze, *pron* ceux-là; celles-là. *a* ces; ces ... -là.

though, dzau, *conj* quoique; bien que.

thought, ts oate, *n* pensée *f;* **-ful*,** *a* pensif; attentif; **-less*,** étourdi; inattentif.

thousand, tsâ'ou´-z'nd,

& *a* mille *m*. *a* (date) mil.

thousandth, tsâ'ouz´-anndts, *n* & *a* millième *m* & *f*.

thrash, tsrâche, *v* battre; (flog) foutter; **–ing,** *n* raclée *f*.

thread, tsredde, *n* fil *m*. *v* enfiler; **–bare,** *a* râpé.

threat, tsrette, *n* menace *f*; **–en,** *v* menacer.

threatening*, tsrett´-ninng, *a* menaçant.

three, tsrie, *n* & *a* trois *m*.

threshold, tsrèch´-aulde, *n* seuil *m*.

thrift, tsrifte, *n* économie *f*; **–less,** *a* prodigue.

thrifty, tsrif´-ti, *a* économe.

thrill, tsrill, *v* émouvoir. *n* saisissement *m*.

thrive, tsrâïve, *v* prospérer.

throat, tsraute, *n* gorge *f*.

throb, tsrobbe, *v* vibrer; (heart) battre.

throes, tsrose, *npl* douleurs *fpl*; (fig) angoisses *fpl*.

throne, tsraune, *n* trône *m*.

throng, tsronng, *v* (together) venir en foule; *n* foule *f*.

throttle, tsrot´-t'l, *n* larynx *m*; (mech) étrangleur *m*

through, tsroue, *prep* (passage, conveyances, etc.) par; à travers; pour cause de; **–out,** *adv* partout; **–train,** *n* train direct *m*.

throw, tsrau, *v* jeter; lancer. *n* coup *m*.

thrush, tsroche, *n* grive *f*.

thrust, tsrosste, *v* pousser; (sword) porter un coup d'épée. *n* poussée *f*; coup d'épée *m*.

thud, tsodde, *n* bruit sourd *m*.

thumb, tsomme, *n* pouce *m*.

thump, tsommpe, *v* frapper du poing. *n* coup de poing *m*.

thunder, tsonn´-d'r, *v* tonner. *n* tonnerre *m*; **–bolt,** foudre *f*; **–storm,** orage *m*.

Thursday, tseurz´-dé, *n* jeudi *m*.

thus, dzosse, *adv* ainsi.

thwart, tsouoarte, *v* (fig) contrarier; frustrer.

thyme, tâïme, *n* thym *m*.

tick, tique, *v* (clock) faire tic-tac; (check) pointer. *n* (cattle) tique *f*; (cover) toile à matelas *f*.

ticket, tik´-ette, *n* billet *m*; (price, etc) étiquette *f*; **– office,** *n* guichet *m*; **season –,**carte d'abonnement *f*.

tickle, tik´-'l, *v* chatouiller.

ticklish, tik´-liche, *a* chatouilleux.

tidal, tâï´-d'l, *a* de marée.

tide, tâïde, *n* marée *f*; **high –,**marée haute *f*; **low –,**marée basse *f*.

tidings, tâï´-inngze, *npl* nouvelles *fpl*.

tidy, tâï´-di, *a* en ordre; (neat) rangé. *v* mettre en ordre.

tie, tâï, *n* (bow) nœud *m*; (neck) cravate *f*. *v* ficeler; (a knot) nouer; (together) attacher; (surgical) bander.

tier, tire, *n* rangée *f*; gradin *m*; rang *m*.

tiger, tâï´-gueur, *n* tigre *m*.

tight, tâïte, *a* serré; (tension) tendu; **–en,** *v* serrer; (tension) tendre; **–s,** *n* collant *m*.

tile, tâïle, *n* carreau *m*; (roof) tuile *f*; (slate) ardoise *f*. *v* carreler; couvrir de tuiles.

till, til, *n* tiroir caisse *m*. *v* (land) labourer. *conj* jusqu'à ce que. *prep* jusqu'à.

tiller, till´-*eur*, *n* (rudder) barre du gouvernail *f*.

tilt, tilte, *v* pencher; incliner.

timber, timm´-b'r, *n* bois de construction *m*.

time, tâïme, v contrôler; (engine) régler; n temps m; (occasion) fois f; (hour) heure f; (music) mesure f; (step) pas m; **–limit,** délai m; **–ly,** a & adv opportun; **––table,** n horaire m.

timid*, timm´-ide, a timide.

tin, tinne, n (sheet iron coated with tin) fer-blanc m; (pure metal) étain m; v étamer; **–box,** n boîte en fer-blanc f; **––foil,** feuille d'étain f; **––plate,** fer blanc m.

tincture, tinng´-ktioure, n teinture f.

tinge, tinndje, n teinte f; nuance f; (fig) soupcon m; v teinter.

tingle, tinng´-g'l, v picoter.

tinkle, tinng´-k'l, v tinter; faire tinter; n tintement m.

tinsel, tinn´-s'l, n clinquant m.

tint, tinnte, n teinte f; v teinter.

tiny, tâï´-ni, a tout petit, minuscule.

tip, tippe, v (give) donner un pourboire; (cart, etc) faire basculer. n pourboire m; (hint) tuyau m; (point) pointe

f; **on –toe,** adv sur la pointe des pieds.

tire, tâïeure, v fatiguer; se fatiguer; **–of,** se lasser de; **–some,** a fatigant; (fig) ennuyeux; n (auto) bande f; (pneumatic) pneu m.

tissue, ti´-chiou, n tissu m; mouchoir m.

tissue paper, ti´-chiou-pé´-p'r, n papier de soie m.

tithe, tâïdz, n dîme f.

title, tâî´-t'l, n titre m; **––deed,** titre de propriéte'e m; **–page,** page du titre f.

titter, titt´-'r, v ricaner. n ricanement m.

to, tou, prep à; (before name of countries) en; (toward) vers.

toad, taude, n crapaud m.

toast, tauste, n pain grillé m; toast m; v griller, rôtir.

toast, tauste, n (drink) toast m. v porter un toast à.

tobacco, to-bǎk´-au, n tabac m; **–nist,** marchand de tabac m; **––pouch,** blague à tabac f.

toboggan, tô-bogue´-an, n luge f.

today, tou-dé´, adv aujourd'hui.

toddler, tod´-l'r, n tout(e)

petit(e) enfant m/f.

toe, tau, n orteil m; doigt de pied m.

toffee, tof´-i, n caramel m.

together, tou-guèdz´-'r, adv ensemble.

toil, toa-ile, v peiner. n labeur m; **–er,** travailleur m

toilet, toa-il´-ette, n toilette f; toilettes mpl; **–paper,** n papier hygiénique m.

token, tau´-k'n, n marque f; symbole m; jeton m.

tolerable, tol´-eur-a-b'l, a tolérable.

tolerance, tol´-eur-'nce, n tolérance f.

tolerant*, tol´-eur-'nt, a tolérant.

tolerate, tol´-eur-éte, v tolérer.

toll, taule, n (knell) glas m; (highway) péage m. v sonner le glas.

tomato, tǒ-mâ´-tau, n tomate f.

tomb, toum, n tombeau m; **–stone,** pierre tombale f.

tomorrow, tou-morr´-au, adv demain.

tomtit, tomme´-tite, n mésange f.

ton, tonne, n tonne f; **–nage,** tonnage m.

tone, taune, n ton m; accent m; (voice)

timbre m.

tongs, tonngze, npl pincettes f.

tongue, tonng n langue f.

tonic, tonn´-ique, n & a tonique m. a fortifiant.

tonight, tou-nâîte´, adv cette nuit; ce soir.

tonsil, tonn´-s'l, n amygdale f.

tonsillitis, tonn-sil-aî´-tice, n amygdalite f.

too, toue, adv trop; (also) aussi; **–much,** trop.

tool, toule, n outil m.

tooth, tout s, n dent f; **–ache,** mal de dents m; **–brush,** brosse à dents f; **–paste,** pâte dentifrice f; **–pick,** cure-dents m; **–powder,** poudre dentrifice f.

top, toppe, n (upper part) haut m; (mountain) sommet m; (of tree) cime f; (spinning) toupie f; **–hat,** chapeau haut de forme m; **–less,** a aux seins nus; **on –,** adv par dessus; au-dessus.

topic, top´-ique, n sujet m.

topple, topp´-'l, **–over,** v culbuter; (car) verser.

topsy-turvy, topp´-ci-teur´-vi, adv sens dessus dessous.

torch, tôrtche, n torche f; (flaming) flambeau m;

(electric) lampe de poche f.

torment, tôr´-mennte, n tourment m. v tourmenter.

torpedo, tôr-pî´-dau, n torpille f.

torpedo boat, tôr-pî´-dau-baute, n torpilleur m.

torpid, tôr´-pidde, a engourdi; inerte.

torpor, tôr´-peur, n torpeur f.

torrent, tôr´-ennte, n torrent m.

torrid, tôr´-ride, a torride.

tortoise, tôr´-teuce, n tortue f; **–shell,** écaille f.

torture, tôr´-tioure, v torturer. n torture f.

toss, tosse, v lancer en l'air; (coin) tirer à pile ou face; **–about,** s'agiter; (naut) ballotter.

total, tau´-t'l, n total m; a total; complet; v totaliser.

totter, tott´-'r, v chanceler; **–ing,** a chancelant.

touch, totche, n contact m; (talent) doigté m; (sense) toucher m. v toucher.

touching, totch´-innng, a (emotion) touchant.

tough, toffe, a dur;

résistant.

tour, toueur, n tour m; excursion f; **–ist,** touriste m & f; **–nament,** tournoi m.

tourist office, toueur-iste-of-ice, n syndicat d'initiative m.

tout, taoute, v racoler. n racoleur m.

tow, tau, v (haul) remorquer. n (flax) étoupe f; **–age,** remorquage m (canal) halage m; **–line,** corde de remorque f.

towards, tŏ-ouôrdze´, prep envers; (direction) vers.

towel, tâ'ou´-elle, n serviette de toilette f.

tower, tâ'ou´-eur, n tour f.

town, tâ'oune, n ville f; **–center,** tâ'oune-senn-t'r, m centre de la ville; centre-ville; **–hall,** hôtel de ville m.

toy, toa'i, n jouet m. v jouer.

trace, tréce, n trace f; (trail) piste f; (harness) trait m. v suivre; suivre la piste; (draw) calquer; (origin) rechercher.

tracing, tréce´-inng, n calque m; **–paper,** papier décalque m.

track, trăque, n trace f; (race) piste f; (railroad)

voie *f. v* suivre la piste.

tract, trăkt, *n* étendue *f*;
(religious) opuscule *m*.

traction, trăk´-ch'n, *n*
traction *f*.

tractor, trăk´-t'r, *n*
tracteur *m*.

trade, tréde, *v* faire le
commerce. *n* commerce
m; (craft) métier *m*; – **mark,** marque de
fabrique *f*; –**sman,**
fournisseur *m*; –**s union,**
syndicat ouvrier *m*.

tradition, tră-dich´-eu_n_,
n tradition *f*.

traditional*, tră-dich´-eu_n_-al, *a* traditionnel.

traffic, trăf´-ique, *n* (going
and coming) circulation
f; (trade) trafic *m*; – **jam,**
n embouteillage *m*; –
lights, tră-fique-lâïtsse,
npl feux (de circulation)
mpl.

tragedian, tra-djî´-di-anne, *n* tragédien *m*.

tragedy, trădj´-i-di, *n*
tragédie *f*.

tragic, trădj´-ique, *a*
tragique.

trail, tréle, *v* suivre à la
piste; (drag) traîner; *n*
piste *f*; –**er,** (van)
remorque *f*.

train, tréne, *n* train *m*;
(dress) traîne *f*;
(retinue) suite *f. v*

instruire; éduquer;
(sport; *mil*) entraîner;
(animals) dresser.

training, tré´-ninng, *n*
éducation *f*;
entraînement *m*.

traitor, tré´-t'r, *n* traître *m*.

tram, trămme, *n* tramway
m.

tramp, trămmpe, *n*
clochard;
-e *m* & *f*; *v* aller à pied.

trample, trămm´-p'l, *v*
piétiner.

trance, trânnce, *n* extase *f*;
(*med*) catalepsie *f*.

tranquil, trănng´-kouill, *a*
tranquille; –**izer,** *n*
tranquilisant *m*.

transact, trănn-săcte´, *v*
traiter; faire.

transaction, trănn-săc´-ch'n, *n* affaire *f*.

transcribe, trănn-scrâïbe´,
v transcrire.

transfer, trănnss-feur´, *v*
(law) transférer;
transporter; *n* transport
m; billet de
correspondance *m*;
(shares) transfert *m*.

transform, trănnss-fôrme´,
v transformer.

transgress, trănnss-grèsse´, *v* transgresser.

transit, trănn´-citte, *n*
transit *m*.

translate, trănnss-léte´, *v*

traduire.

translation, trănnss-lé´-ch'n, *n* traduction *f*.

translator, trănnss-lé´-t'r,
n traducteur, -trice *m* &
f.

transmit, trănnss-mitte´, *v*
transmettre.

transparent, trănnss-pă-rennte, *a* transparent.

transpire, trănnss-pâïre´, *v*
transpirer.

transport, trănnss-pôrte´,
v transporter; *n*
transport *m*.

transpose, trănnss-pause´,
v transposer.

transship, trănn-chippe´,
v transborder.

trap, trăppe, *n* piège *m*; *v*
prendre au piège.

trash, trăche, *n* camelote
f; ordure *f*; –**y,** *a* de
camelote.

travel, trăv´-'l, *v* voyager;
–**er,** *n* voyageur, -euse *m*
& *f*; – **agent,** *n* agent de
voyages *m*; – **sickness,** *n*
mal de la route *m*.

traveler's check, trăv-leurz-tchèque, *n* chèque
de voyage *m*.

traverse, trăv´-eurse, *v*
traverser.

trawler, troa´-leur, *n*
chalutier *m*.

tray, tré, *n* plateau *m*; **ash-**

–, cendrier *m*.

treacherous*, trett´-cheur-euce, *a* traître; perfide.

treachery, trett´-cheur-i, *n* traîtrise *f*; perfidie *f*.

tread, tredde, *n* pas *m*; (stair) marche *f*. *v* poser le pied; (accidental) marcher sur.

treason, trî´-z'n, *n* trahison *f*.

treasure, tréj´-eur, *n* trésor *m*. *v* garder précieusement.

treasurer, tréj´-eur-eur, *n* trésorier *m*.

treasury, tréj´-eur-i, *n* trésor *m*.

treat, trîte, *n* (outing) partie de plaisir *f*. *v* traiter; (fig) régaler; (med) soigner; **–ment**, *n* traitement *m*.

treatise, trî´-tize, *n* traité *m*.

treaty, trî´-ti, *n* traité *m*.

treble, tréb´-'l, *v* tripler. *n* & *a* triple *m*.

tree, trî, *n* arbre *m*.

trellis, trell´-ice, *n* treillis *m*.

tremble, tremm´-b'l, *v* trembler.

tremendous*, tri-menn´-deuce, *a* prodigieux.

tremor, tremm´-'r, *n* tremblement *m*.

tremulous*, tremm´-iou-leuce, *a* (fig) craintif.

trench, trenntche, *n* fossé *m*; (mil) tranchée *f*.

trend, trennde, *n* tendance *f*.

trespass, tress´-pass, *v* empiéter sur.

trespasser, tress´-pass-'r, *n* intrus *m*.

trestle, tress´-'l, *n* tréteau *m*.

trial, traï´-al, *n* épreuve *f*; essai *m*; (law) procès *m*.

triangle, traï´-ănng-g'l, *n* triangle *m*.

triangular, traï-ănng´-guiou-lar, *a* triangulaire.

tribe, traïbe, *n* tribu *f*.

tribunal, traï-bioue´-n'l, *n* tribunal *m*.

tributary, trib´-iou-ta-ri, *n* affluent *m*.

tribute, trib´-ioute, *n* tribut *m*.

trick, trique, *n* (fraud) ruse *f*; truc *m*; (dexterity) tour *m*; (cards) levée *f*; *v* duper; **–ery**, *n* duperie *f*; **–ster**, fourbe *m*.

trickle, trique´-'l, *v* dégoutter; (flow) suinter.

trifle, traï´-f'l, *v* jouer; badiner; *n* bagatelle *f*.

trifling, traï´-flinng, *a* insignifiant.

trigger, trigg´-'r, *n* détente *f*; gachette *f*.

trim, trime, *v* (hat, dress) garnir; (hair) tailler; égaliser; *a* soigné; **–ming**, *n* garniture *f*.

trinity, trinn´-i-ti, *n* trinité *f*.

trinket, trinng´-kitte, *n* colifichet *m*; breloque *f*.

trio, trî´-au, *n* trio *m*.

trip, trippe, *n* excursion *f*. *v* (stumble) trébucher; **–up**, *v* donner un croc-en-jambe.

tripe, trâïpe, *n* tripes *fpl*.

triple, tripp´-'l, *a* triple.

triplets, tripp´-lètse, *npl* trois triplets *mpl*.

tripod, traï´-pode, *n* trépied *m*.

triumph, traï´-eummf, *n* triomphe *m*. *v* triompher.

trivial, triv´-i-al, *a* trivial; insignifiant.

trolley, troll´-i, *n* chariot *m*.

trombone, tromm´-bône, *n* trombone *m*.

troop, troupe, *n* troupe *f*; **–ship**, transport *m*.

trooper, troup´-eur, *n* (mil) cavalier *m*.

trophy, trau´-fi, *n* trophée *m*.

tropical, tropp´-i-c'l, *a* tropical.

tropics, tropp´-ikse, *npl* tropiques *mpl*.

trot, trotte, *v* trotter. *n* trot *m*; **–ter,** trotteur *m*; (pig) pied de cochon *m*.

trouble, trobb´-'l, *v* chagriner; (disturb) déranger. *n* (cares) soucis *mpl*; (inconvenience) dérangement *m*; (disturbance) trouble *m*; (difficulty) difficulté *f*; **–some,** *a* ennuyeux; difficile.

trough, troffe, *n* (kneading trough) pétrin *m*; (cattle, etc) abreuvoir *m*.

trousers, trâ´ou-zeurce, *npl* pantalon *m*.

trout, trâ´oute, *n* truite *f*.

trowel, trâ´ou-'l, *n* (mason's) truelle *f*.

T-shirt, tî´-cheurte, *n* tee-shirt *m*.

truant, troue´-annte, **play –,** *v* faire l'école buissonnière.

truce, trouce, *n* trève *f*.

truck, troque, *n* (rail) wagon *m*; (hand) voiture à bras *f*.

truculent*, trok´-iou-lennte, *a* brutal; féroce.

trudge, trodje, *v* marcher péniblement.

true, troue, *a* vrai; (faithful) fidèle.

truffle, troff´-'l, *n* truffe *f*.

truism, troue´-izme, *n* truisme *m*.

trump, trommpe, *n* atout *m*. *v* couper.

trumpet, trommp´-itte, *n* trompette *f*.

truncheon, tronn´-ch'n, *n* bâton *m*.

trunk, tronng-k, *n* (tree; body) tronc *m*; (elephant) trompe *f*; (traveling) malle *f*.

truss, trosse, *n* (hay, etc) botte *f*; (surgical) bandage herniaire *m*. *v* (poultry) trousser.

trust, trosste, *n* confiance *f*; (combine) trust *m*. *v* se fier à; (rely) compter sur.

trustee, tross-tî´, *n* dépositaire *m*; (public) curateur *m*; (liquidation) syndic de faillite *m*; administrateur *m*.

trustworthy, trosst´-oueurdz-i, *a* digne de confiance.

truth, trouts, *n* vérité *f*; **–ful*,** *a* véridique.

try, trâï, *v* essayer; (taste) goûter; (law) juger; **–ing,** *a* pénible; **–on,** *v* essayer.

tub, tobbe, *n* baquet *m*; (bath) baignoire *f*.

tube, tioube, *n* tube *m*; (railway) métro *m*.

tuck, toque, *n* pli *m*. *v* faire des plis; **–in,** (rug, etc) border; **–up,** retrousser.

Tuesday, tiouze´-dé, *n* mardi *m*.

tuft, tofte, *n* (grass) touffe *f*; (hair) houppe *f*.

tug, togue, *v* tirer; (boat) remorquer.

tugboat, togue´-baute, *n* remorqueur *m*.

tuition, tiou-i´-ch'n, *n* enseignement *m*; frais de scolarité *m*.

tulip, tioue´-lippe, *n* tulipe *f*.

tumble, tomm´-b'l, *v* (fall) dégringoler.

tumbler, tomm´-bl'r, *n* (glass) grand verre *m*.

tumor, tioue´-m'r, *n* tumeur *f*.

tumult, tioue´-meulte, *n* tumulte *m*; (riot) émeute *f*.

tuna, tioue´-nä, *n* thon *m*.

tune, tioune, *n* air *m*. *v* accorder.

tuneful, tioune´-foull, *a* mélodieux.

tunic, tioue´-nique, *n* tunique *f*.

tuning-fork, tioue´-ninng forque, *n* diapason *m*.

tunnel, tonn´-'l, n tunnel
m. v percer un tunnel.

turbine, teur´-bâïne, n
turbine f.

turbot, teur´-*beute*, n
turbot m.

turbulence, teur´-bioul´nce, n turbulence m.

turbulent, teur´-bioulennte, a turbulent.

tureen, tiou-rîne´, n
soupière f; (sauce)
saucière f.

turf, teurfe, n (grass)
gazon m; (peat) tourbe f.

turkey, teur´-ki, n dinde f;
dindon m.

turkish, teur´-quiche, a
turc.

turmoil, teur´-moa´ile, n
tumulte m; désordre m.

turn, teurne, n tour m. v
tourner; **–about,** se
tourner; **–aside,**
détourner; **–back,**
revenir sur ses pas; **–er,**
n (artisan) tourneur m;
–ing, (corner) tournant
m; **–ing-point,** point
décisif m; **–into,** v se
changer en; **–off,**
fermer; **–on,** ouvrir;
–out, (expel) renvoyer;
(light) éteindre; **–over,**
se retourner. n (com)
chiffre d'affaires m;
–stile, tourniquet m;
–to, v recourir à.

turnip, teur´-nipe, n navet
m.

turpentine, teur´-penntâïne, n térébenthine f.

turret, teur´-ette, n
tourelle f.

turtle, teur´-t'l, n tortue
de mer f; **–dove,** n
tourterelle f.

tusk, tossque, n (long)
défense f; (short) croc
m.

tussle, toss´-'l, v lutter. n
bagarre f.

tutor, tioue´-t'r, n
précepteur m, professeur
m. v instruire.

TV, tî-vi, n abbr télé f.

twang, touain-ng, n
nasillement m; (sound)
son m.

tweezers, touî´-zeurze, npl
pinces fpl.

twelfth, tou'elfts, n & a
douzième m & f.

twelve, tou'elve, n & a
douze m.

twentieth, tou'enn´-ti-its,
n & a vingtième m & f.

twenty, tou'enn´-ti, n & a
vingt m.

twice, tou'âïce, adv deux
fois.

twig, tou'igue, n brindille
f.

twilight, tou'âï´-lâïte, n
crépuscule m.

twin, tou'inne, n & a

jumeau m; jumelle f; **–bedded room,** n
chambre à deux lits f.

twine, tou'âïne, n
cordonnet m. v
s'enrouler.

twinge, tou'inndje, n
élancement m; (fig)
tourment m.

twinkle, tou'inng´-k'l, v
scintiller; (eyes) cligner.

twirl, tou'eurle, v
tournoyer; tourner. n
tour m.

twist, tou'iste, v tordre;
tourner; contourner.

twitch, tou'itche, v se
crisper. n crispation f; tic
m.

twitter, tou'itt´-'r, v
gazouiller; gazouillement
m.

two, toue, n & a deux m;
–fold, a double.

type, tâïpe, n type m;
(print) caractère m. v
taper à. la machine;
–writer, n machine à
écrire f.

typhoid, tâï´-fo'ide, n
fièvre typhoïde f.

typhoon, tâï-foune´, n
typhon m.

typical*, tip´-i-c'l, a
typique.

typist, tâïp´-iste, n
dactylographe m & f.

typography, ti-pogue´-ra-fi, *n* typographie *f.*

tyrannical*, ti-rănn´-i-c'l, *a* tyrannique.

tyrannize, ti´-*ra*-nâïze, *v* tyranniser.

tyrant, tâï´-r'nt, *n* tyran *m.*

ubiquitous, ioue-bik´-oui-teuce, *a* omniprésent.

udder, odd´-'r, n pis *m*.

ugliness, ogg´-li-nesse, n laideur *f*.

ugly, ogg´-li, *a* laid; vilain.

ulcer, ol´-ceur, n ulcère *m*; **–ate,** *v* ulcérer.

ulterior, ol-ti´-ri-*eur*, *a* ultérieur.

ultimate*, ol´-ti-méte, *a* définitif; final.

ultimatum, ol-ti-mé´-tomm, n ultimatum *m*.

umbrella, omm-brell´-*a*, n parapluie *m*; **–stand,** porte-parapluies *m*.

umpire, omm´-pâïre, n arbitre *m*. *v* arbitrer.

unabashed, onn-a-băshte´, *a* sans honte.

unabated, onn-*a*-bé´-tedde, *a* continu;

soutenu.

unable, onn-é´-b'l, **to be –,** *v* être incapable de; ne pas pouvoir.

unacceptable, onn-ăx-ep´-ta-b'l, *a* inacceptable.

unaccountable, onn-a-câ'ounn´-ta-b'l, *a* inexplicable.

unacquainted, onn-a-couénn´-tedde, *a* (person) étranger à; (subject) être ignorant de.

unaffected*, onn-a-fèque´-tedde, *a* naturel; (unmoved) impassible.

unaided, onn-é´-dedde, *a* sans aide.

unalterable, onn-oal´-teur-a-b'l, *a* immuable.

unaltered, onn-oal´-teurde, *a* pas changé.

unanimous*, ioue-nănn´-i-*meuce*, *a* unanime.

unapproachable, onn-a-prautch´-*a*-b'l, *a* inabordable; inaccessible.

unarmed, onn´-ârmde, *a* sans armes.

unassailable, onn-a-cél´-a-b'l, *a* inattaquable.

unassuming, onn-a-sioue´-minng, *a* modeste.

unattainable, onn-a-tén´-a-b'l, *a* inaccessible.

unavoidable, onn-a-vô'ï´-da-b'l, *a* inévitable.

unaware, onn-a-ouère´, *a* ignorant.

unawares, onn-a-ouèrze´, *adv* à l'improviste.

unbalanced, onn-băl´-'nsste, *a* déséquilibré.

unbearable, onn-bèr´-a-b'l, *a* insupportable.

unbelievable, onn-bî-lîve´-a-b'l, *a* incroyable.

unbending, onn-benn´-dinng, *a* inflexible.

unbiased, onn-bâï´-*asste*, *a* impartial.

unbleached, onn-blîtchte´, *a* écru; non décoloré.

unblemished, onn-blèm´-ichte, *a* sans tache.

unbounded, onn-bâ'ounn´-dedde, *a*

illimité.

unbreakable, onn-bréque´-*a*-b'l, *a* incassable.

unburden, onn-beur´-d'n, *v* décharger.

unbutton, onn-bot´-'n, *v* déboutonner.

uncalled for, onn-coalde´ fôr, *a* déplacé.

uncanny, onn-cănn´-i, *a* surnaturel; étrange.

uncared for, onn-cairde´ fôr, *a* négligé.

unceasing*, onn-sî´-cinng, *a* incessant.

uncertain*, onn-seur´-tinne, *a* incertain.

unchangeable, onn-tchéne´-dja-b'l, *a* invariable.

unclaimed, onn-clémde´, *a* non réclamé.

uncle, onn´-k'l, *n* oncle *m*.

unclean, onn-clîne´, *a* malpropre; impur.

uncomfortable, onn-comm´-*feur*-*ta*-b'l, *a* incommode; (not at ease) mal à l'aise.

uncommon, onn-comm´-'n, *a* peu commun; rare.

unconcern, onn-cŏnn-seurne´, *n* indifférence *f*.

unconditional*, onn-cŏnn-di-´ch'n-al, *a* sans condition.

unconscious*, onn-

conn´-cheuce, *a* sans connaissance; (*fig*) inconscient.

uncontrollable, onn-cŏnn-traul´-*a*-b'l, *a* incontrôlable.

uncork, onn-corque´, *v* déboucher.

uncouth*, onn-coûts, *a* (manners) grossier.

uncover, onn-cov´-*eur*, *v* découvrir.

uncultivated, onn-col´-ti-vé-tedde, *a* inculte.

undaunted, onn-doann´-tedde, *a* intrépide.

undeceive, onn-di-cîve´, *v* détromper.

undecided, onn-di-sâï´-dedde, *a* indécis.

undelivered, onn-di-liv´-'rde, *a* non livré.

undeniable, onn-di-nâï´-*a*-b'l, *a* incontestable.

under, onn´-d'r, *prep* sous; au-dessous de; *adv* dessous; **–age,** *a* mineur; **–done,** *a* peu cuit; (beef) saignant; **–estimate,** *v* sous-estimer; **–fed,** *a* mal nourri; **–go,** *v* endurer; **–ground,** *a* souterrain. *n* (railroad) métro *m*; **–hand,** *a* clandestin; **–line,** *v* souligner; **–mine,** *v* miner; **–neath,** *adv* audessous; **–rate,** *v* estimer trop bas; **–sell,** *v*

vendre à plus bas prix; **–signed,** *n* & *a* soussigné, -ée *m* & *f*; **–stand,** *v* comprendre; **–standing,** *n* entente *f*; compréhension *f*; **–study,** *n* doublure *f*; **–take,** *v* entreprendre; **–taker,** *n* entrepreneur de pompes funèbres *m*; **–taking,** *n* entreprise *f*; engagement *m*; **–tone,** *adv* à voix basse; **–wear,** *n* (men) vêtements de dessous *mpl*; (ladies) dessous *mpl*; **–writer,** *n* assureur *m*.

undeserved, onn-di-zeurvde´, *a* immérité.

undesirable, onn-di-zâï´-ra-b'l, *a* indésirable.

undignified, onn-dig´-ni-fâïde, *a* sans dignité.

undismayed, onn-diss-méde´, *a* sans peur.

undo, onn-doue´, *v* défaire; (untie) délier.

undoing, onn-dou´-inng, *n* (downfall) déchéance *f*.

undoubted*, onn-dâ´outt´-edde, *a* indubitable.

undress, onn-dresse´, *v* déshabiller; se déshabiller.

undulating, onn´-diou-lé-ting, *a* ondulé.

unduly, onn-dioue´-li, *adv*
indûment; à l'excès.

unearned, onn-eurnde´, *a*
non gagné; immérité.

unearthly, onn-eurts´-li, *a*
surnaturel.

uneasy, onn-î´-zi, *a*
inquiet; mal à l'aise.

uneducated, onn-éd´iou-
qué-tedde, *a* sans
éducation.

unemployed, onn-emm-
ploa'i´, *a* sans travail.
n les chômeurs *mpl*.

unemployment, onn-
emm-ploa'i´-m'nt, *n*
chômage *m*.

unequal*, onn-î´-coual, *a*
inégal; –ed, sans égal.

uneven*, onn-î´-v'n, *a*
irrégulier; rugueux;
(number) impair.

unexpected*, onn-ex-
pec´-tedde, *a* inattendu.

unfailing, onn-fél´-inng, *a*
infaillible.

unfair*, onn-fère´, *a*
injuste.

unfaithful, onn-féts´-foull,
a infidèle.

unfasten, onn-fâs´-s'n, *v*
défaire; ouvrir.

unfavorable, onn-fé´-veur-
a-b'l, *a* défavorable.

unfeeling, onn-fî´-linng,
a insensible.

unfit, onn-fite´, *a*
impropre à.

unflagging, onn-flăgue´-
inng, *a* soutenu.

unflinching, onn-
flinntch´-inng, *a* ferme,
résolu.

unfold, onn-faulde´, *v*
déplier; (reveal)
dévoiler.

unforeseen, onn-fore-
cîne´, *a* imprévu.

unfortunate*, onn-fôr´-
tiou-néte, *a* malheureux.

unfounded, onn-fâ'ounn´-
dedde, *a* sans
fondement.

unfriendly, onn-frennde´-
li, *a* peu amical; hostile.

unfulfilled, onn-foull-
fillde´, *a* inaccompli.

unfurl, onn-feurle´, *v*
déployer.

unfurnished, onn-feur´-
nichte, *a* non meublé.

ungrateful, onn-gréte´-
foull, *a* ingrat.

unguarded, onn-gâre´-
dedde, *a* (fig)
inconsidéré.

unhappy, onn-hăpp´-i, *a*
malheureux.

unhealthy, onn-hêltz´-i, *a*
malsain; (sick) maladif.

unheard, onn-heurde´,
–of, *a* inconnu; inouï.

unheeded, onn-hî´-dedde,
a inaperçu.

unhinge, onn-hinndje´, *v*
démonter; déranger.

unhurt, onn-heurte´, *a*
sain et sauf.

uniform*, ioue´-ni-fôrme,
n & *a* uniforme *m*.

uniformity, ioue-ni-fôr´-
mi-ti, *n* uniformité *f*.

unimaginable, onn-i-
mâdj´-i-na-b'l, *a*
inimaginable.

unimpaired, onn-imm-
pairde´, *a* intact.

unimportant, onn-imm-
por´-t'nt, *a* sans
importance.

uninhabitable, onn-inn-
hăb´-i-ta-b'l, *a*
inhabitable.

uninhabited, onn-inn-
hăb´-i-tedde, *a* inhabité.

unintelligible, onn-inn-
tel´-i-dji-b'l, *a*
inintelligible.

unintentional*, onn-inn-
tenn´-ch'n-al, *a*
involontaire.

uninviting, onn-inn-vâï´-
tinng, *a* peu attrayant.

union, ioue´-ni-eune, *n*
union *f*.

unique*, iou-nique´, *a*
unique.

unit, ioue´-nitte, *n* unité *f*.

unite, iou-nâïte´, *v* unir;
s'unir.

unity, ioue´-ni-ti, *n* unité
f; concorde *f*.

universal*, iou-ni-veur´-
s'l, *a* universel.

universe, ioue´-ni-ve*urce*, n univers m.

university, iou-ni-veur´-ci-ti, n université f.

unjust*, onn-djosse´, a injuste.

unkind*, onn-kâïnnde´, a pas gentil; peu aimable.

unknown, onn-naune´, a inconnu.

unlawful*, onn-loa´-foull, a illégal; illicite.

unleaded, onn-lèdd´-id, a sans plomb (gasoline, fuel).

unless, onn-lesse´, conj à moins que; à moins de.

unlike, onn-lâïque´, a différent; –ly, improbable.

unlimited, onn-limm´-i-tedde, a illimité.

unload, onn-laude´, v décharger.

unlock, onn-loque´, v ouvrir; (fig) révéler.

unlucky, onn-loque´-i, a malheureux; (ill-omened) de mauvais augure; qui porte malheur.

unmanageable, onn-männ´-idj-a-b'l, a ingouvernable; intraitable.

unmannerly, onn-männ´-'r-li, a grossier; mal élevé.

unmarried, onn-mär´-idde, a non marié; célibataire.

unmerciful*, onn-meur´-ci-foull, a impitoyable.

unmistakable, onn-mice-téque´-a-b'l, a évident.

unmoved, onn-mouvde´, a impassible.

unnatural, onn-nät´-tiou-r'l, a (hard) dénaturé.

unnecessary, onn-nèss´-ess-a-ri, a inutile.

unnerve, onn-neurve´, v effrayer; démonter.

unnoticed, onn-nau´-tisste, a inaperçu.

unoccupied, onn-ok´-kiou-pâïde, a inoccupé; libre.

unopposed, onn-ŏp-auzde´, a sans opposition.

unpack, onn-pâque´, v défaire; (case) déballer.

unparalleled, onn-pä´-ral-lelde, a sans pareil.

unpardonable, onn-pär´-donn-a-b'l, a impardonnable.

unpleasant*, onn-plè´-zannte, a déplaisant.

unpopular, onn-pop´-iou-lar, a impopulaire.

unprecedented, onn-pré´-sid-enn-tedde, a sans précédent.

unprepared, onn-pri-

pérde´, a à l'improviste.

unproductive, onn-pro-de*uc*´-tive, a improductif.

unprofitable, onn-prof´-i-ta-b'l, a peu profitable.

unprotected, onn-pro-tec´-tedde, a sans protection; sans défense.

unprovided, onn-prŏ-vâï´-dedde, a dépourvu de.

unpunctual, onn-ponngk´-tiou-al, a inexact.

unqualified, onn-couoll´-i-fâïde, a non qualifié; incapable de.

unquestionable, onn-couess´-tie*u*nn-a-b'l, a incontestable.

unravel, onn-räv´-'l, v démêler.

unreadable, onn-rî´-da-b'l, a illisible.

unreasonable, onn-rî´-z'n-a-b'l, a déraisonnable.

unrelenting, onn-ri-lenn´-tinng, a implacable.

unreliable, onn-ri-lâï´-a-b'l, a sur lequel on ne peut pas compter.

unreserved, onn-ri-zeurvde´, a non réservé; libre; sans réserve.

unrest, onn-reste´, n inquiétude f; agitation f.

unrestrained, onn-ri-strénnde, a sans

contrainte; (unruly) désordonné.

unrestricted, onn-ri-stric´-tedde, *a* sans restriction.

unripe, onn-râïpe´, *a* pas mûr; vert.

unroll, onn-raule´, *v* dérouler.

unruly, onn-roue´-li, *a* indiscipliné.

unsafe, onn-séfe´, *a* peu sûr; dangereux.

unsatisfactory, onn-sätt-iss-fâque´-t'ri, *a* peu satisfaisant.

unscrew, onn-scroue´, *v* dévisser.

unscrupulous, onn-scroue´-piou-*l*euce, *a* sans scrupule.

unseasonable, onn-sî´-z'n-a-b'l, *a* hors de saison.

unseemly, onn-sîme´-li, *a* inconvenant.

unseen, onn-sîne´, *a* inaperçu.

unselfish, onn-self´-iche, *a* désintéressé.

unsettled, onn-sett´-'lde, *a* incertain; troublé; (accounts) en suspens.

unshaken, onn-chéque´-'n, *a* inébranlable.

unshrinkable, onn-chrinng´-*k*a-b'l, *a* irrétrécissable.

unsightly, onn-sâïte´-li, *a* déplaisant; laid.

unskilled, onn-skillde, *a* inexpérimenté (dans).

unsociable, onn-sau´-cha-b'l, *a* insociable.

unsold, onn-saulde´, *a* invendu.

unsolicited, onn´sŏ-liss´-i-tedde, *a* spontané.

unsound, onn-sâ'ounnde´, *a* défectueux; (mind) dément.

unsparing*, onn-spére´-inng, *a* prodigue; (not merciful) impitoyable.

unsteady, onn-stedd´-i, *a* instable.

unsuccessful, onn-seuk-cess´-foull, *a* (person) sans succès; (undertaking) infructueux.

unsuitable, onn-sioue´-ta b'l, *a* déplacé; impropre.

unsupported, onn-seup-paur´-tedde, *a* (fig) sans appui.

unsurpassed, onn-seur-pâsse´, *a* sans égal.

unsuspecting, onn-seuss-pèque´-tinng, *a* confiant.

untamed, onn-témmde´, *a* indompté; sauvage.

untarnished, onn-târe´-nichte, *a* sans tache.

untenable, onn-tenn´-*a*-b'l, *a* insoutenable.

untidy, onn-tâï´-di, *a* en

désordre; (person) négligé.

untie, onn-tâï´, *v* délier; (a knot) défaire; dénouer.

until, onn-til´, *prep* jusqu'à; jusque. *conj* jusqu'à ce que.

untold, onn-taulde´, *a* non raconté; passé sous silence; (fig) inouï.

untouched, onn-tochte´, *a* intact; non ému.

untranslatable, onn-trännss-lé-*t*a-b'l, *a* intraduisible.

untried, onn-trâïde´, *a* non essayé.

untrodden, onn-trode-'n, *a* non frayé; vierge.

untrue, onn-troue´, *a* faux; pas vrai.

untrustworthy, onn-trosst´-oueudz-i, *a* indigne de confiance.

untruth, onn-trouts´, *n* mensonge *m*.

untwist, onn-tou'isste´, *v* détordre.

unusual*, onn-ioue´-joue*u*l, *a* rare; peu commun.

unvaried, onn-vair´-idde, *a* uniforme; constant.

unveil, onn-vaile´, *v* dévoiler; inaugurer.

unwarrantable, onn-ouor´-*a*nn-ta-b'l, *a* injustifiable;

inexcusable.

unwary, onn-ouè´-ri, *a*
imprudent.

unwelcome, onn-ouel´-
k'm, *a* importun;
indésirable.

unwell, onn-ouell´, *a*
indisposé; souffrant.

unwholesome, onn-
haule´-somme, *a*
malsain; insalubre.

unwieldy, onn-ouîld´-i, *a*
lourd; pesant.

unwilling, onn-ouil´-inng,
a de mauvaise volonté.

unwind, onn-ouâînnde´, *v*
dérouler; se relaxer.

unwise, onn-ouâîze´, *a*
peu sage, imprudent.

unwittingly, onn-ouitt´-
inng-li, *adv* sans y
penser.

unworthy, onn-oueurdz´-i,
a indigne.

unwrap, onn-răppe´, *v*
défaire.

unwritten, onn-ritt´-'n, *a*
non écrit; (*fig*)
traditionnel.

unyielding, onn-yîld´-
inng, *a* rigide; inflexible.

up, op, *adv* en haut; en
l'air; (stand up) debout;
(prices) en hausse;
(risen) levé; **–and down,**
de haut en bas; **–here,**
ici; **–side down,** sens
dessus dessous; à

l'envers; **–there,** là-haut;
–to, *prep* jusqu'à.

upbraid, op-bréde´, *v*
reprocher à.

upheaval, op-hî´-v'l, *n*
(geological)
soulèvement *m*.

uphill, op´-hill, *a* en
montant; (*fig*) ardu.

uphold, op-haulde´, *v*
soutenir; maintenir.

upholsterer, op-haule´-
steur-'r, *n* tapissier *m*.

upkeep, op´-kîpe, *n*
entretien *m*; soutien *m*.

upland, op´-lânnde, *n* pays
élevé *m*.

uplift, op-lifte´, *v* élever.

upon, op-onne´, *prep* sur.

upper, op´-'r, *a* supérieur;
de dessus; **–hand,** *n*
avantage *m*, dessus *m*;
–most, *a* dominant.

upright, op´-râïte, *a* droit;
honorable; (erect)
debout.

uprising, op-râï´-zinng, *n*
soulèvement *m*.

uproar, op´-raure, *n*
tumulte *m*; vacarme *m*.

uproot, op-route´, *v*
déraciner.

upset, op-cette´, *v*
renverser; **to be –,** être
bouleversé.

upstairs, op´-stèrze, *adv* en
haut; **to go –,** *v* aller en
haut.

upstart, op´-stärte, *n*
parvenu, -e *m & f*;
nouveau riche *m*.

upwards, op´-oueurdse,
adv en haut; en
montant.

urban, eur-'b'n, *a* urbain.

urchin, eur´-tchinne, *n*
(child) gamin, -e *m & f*.

urge, eurdje, *n* désir
ardent *m*. *v* pousser.

urgency, eur´-djenn-ci, *n*
urgence *f*.

urgent, eur´-djennte, *a*
urgent; pressant.

urine, iou´-râïne, *n* urine
f.

urinate, iou-ri-néte, *v*
uriner.

urn, eurne, *n* urne *f*.

us, osse, *pron* nous.

use, iouze, *v* user de; se
servir de; employer. *n*
usage *m*; utilité *f*; **–ful*,**
a utile; **–less*,** inutile;
–up, *v* consommer.

usher, och-'r, *n* (in a
court) huissier *m*; **–in,** *v*
annoncer.

usherette, och-'orette´, *n*
ouvreuse *f*.

usual*, iou-´jou'eul, *a*
usuel; habituel;
ordinaire; **–ly,** *a*
d'habitude; d'ordinaire.

usurer, iou-´jeu-r'r, *n*
usurier,
-ère *m & f*.

usurp, iou-zeurpe´, *v*
usurper.

usury, iou´-*jeu*-ri, *n* usure
f.

utensil, iou-tenn´-cil, *n*
ustensile *m.*

utility, iou-til´-i-ti, *n*
utilité *f.*

utilize, ioue´-til-âïze, *v*
utiliser.

utmost, ott´-mauste, *a*
extrême; dernier; *n*
comble *m;* tout son
possible *m.*

utter, ott´-'r, *v* (words)
prononcer; (sound, coin,
etc) émettre; (cry)
pousser. *a** entier;
absolu; total.

utterance, ott´-*eur*-'nce, *n*
expression *f;* émission *f.*

uttermost, (see **utmost**).

vacancy, vé´-k'n-ci, *n* vacance *f*; place vacante *f*; (emptiness) vide *m*.

vacant*, vé´-k'nt, *a* (empty) vide; (free) libre; (mind) distrait.

vacate, va-quéte´, *v* (law) vider; évacuer; quitter.

vacation, va-qué´-ch'n, *n* vacances *fpl*; congé *m*.

vaccinate, văque´-ci-néte, *v* vacciner.

vacillate, văss´-il-léte, *v* vaciller.

vacuum, văque´-iou-'m, *n* vide *m*; **–cleaner,** aspirateur *m*; **—flask,** thermos *m*.

vagabond, văgue´-a-bonnde, *n* vagabond, -e *m & f*.

vagina, va-dji´-na, *n* vagin *m*

vague*, végue, *a* vague.

vain*, véne, *a* vain; vaniteux; **in –,** *adv* en vain.

vale, véle, *n* vallée *f*; vallon *m*.

valet, văl´-ette, *n* valet de chambre *m*.

valiant*, văl´-i-annte, *a* vaillant; brave.

valid, văl´-ide, *a* valable; valide.

valley, văl´-i, *n* vallée *f*.

valor, văl´-'r, *n* bravoure *f*.

valuable, văl´-iou-a-b'l, *a* précieux; de valeur.

valuables, văl´-iou-a-b'lze, *n* objets de valeur *mpl*.

valuation, văl-iou-é´-ch'n, *n* évaluation *f*.

value, văl´-iou, *v* évaluer; priser. *n* valeur *f*.

valuer, văl´-iou-'r, *n*

(official) commissaire-priseur *m*.

valve, vălve, *n* (bot.) valve *f*; soupape *f*; (radio) lampe *f*.

vampire, văm´-pâïre, *n* vampire *m*.

van, vănne, *n* camion *m*; camionnette *f*; (train) fourgon *m*.

vane, véne, *n* girouette *f*; (windmill) aile *f*.

vanilla, va-nil´-a, *n* vanille *f*.

vanish, vănn´-iche, *v* disparaître.

vanity, vănn´-i-ti, *n* vanité *f*.

vanquish, vaing´-kouiche, *v* vaincre.

vapor, vé´-p'r, *n* vapeur *f*.

vaporize, vé´-por-âïze, *v* vaporiser.

variable, vé´-ri-a-b'l, *a* variable; (*fig*) inconstant.

variation, vé-ri-é´-ch'n, *n* variation *f*; différence *f*.

varicose vein, văr´-i-kôze véne, *n* varice *f*.

varied, vé´-ride, *a* varié; divers.

variegated, vé´-ri-i-gué-tedde, *a* (bot.) panaché; bigarré.

variety, va-râï´-i-ti, *n* variété *f*, choix *m*; **–theater,** music-hall *m*.

various, vè´-ri-*euce, a* divers, différent.

varnish, vâre´-niche, *n* vernis *m. v* vernir.

vary, vé´-ri, *v* varier; changer; dévier.

vase, vâze, *n* vase *m*; (oriental) potiche *f*.

vast, vâsste, *a* vaste; immense.

vat, vätte, *n* cuve *f*; cuvier *m*.

Vatican, vät´-i-k'n, *n* Vatican *m*.

vault, voalte, *n* voûte *f*; (church, etc) crypte *f*; (burial) caveau *m*; (cellar) cave *f. v* (jump) sauter.

veal, vîle, *n* veau *m*.

veer, vi´-*eur, v* tourner; (wind) changer.

vegetable, vedj´-i-*ta*-b'l, *n* (food) légume *m; a* végétal.

vegetarian, vedj-i-té´-ri-an, *n* végétarien, -ne *m* & *f*.

vegetation, vedj-i-té´-ch'n, *n* végétation *f*.

vehement, vî´-hi-m'nt, *a* véhément.

vehicle, vî´-i-k'l, *n* véhicule *m*.

veil, véle, *n* voile *m. v* voiler.

vein, véne, *n* veine *f*; (geological) filon *m*.

vellum, vell´-'m, *n* vélin *m*.

velocity, vi-loss´-i-ti, *n* vélocité *f*; (mech) vitesse *f*.

velvet, vell´-vett, *n* velours *m*.

velveteen, vell-vè-tine´, *n* velours de coton *m*.

vending machine, vennd-inng-ma-chîne, *n* distributeur automatique *m*.

vendor, venn´-d'r, *n* vendeur, -euse *m* & *f*.

veneer, vi-ni*eur´, n* placage *m. v* plaquer.

venerable, venn´-*eur-a*-b'l, *a* vénérable.

veneration, venn-*eur*-é´-ch'n, *n* vénération *f*.

venereal, vi-ni´-ri-*al, a* vénérien.

vengeance, venn´-dj'nce, *n* vengeance *f*.

venial*, vî´-ni-*al, a* véniel.

venison, venn´-i-z'n, *n* venaison *f*.

venom, venn´-'m, *n* venin *m*; **-ous,** *a* venimeux.

vent, vennte, *n* issue *f*; (cask) trou de fausset *m*; **give -to,** *v* donner cours à.

ventilate, venn´-ti-léte, *v* aérer.

ventilator, venn´-ti-lé-t'r,

n ventilateur *m*.

ventriloquist, venn-tril´-ŏ-couiste, *n* ventriloque *m* & *f*.

venture, venn´-tioure, *v* aventurer; risquer; (dare) oser. *n* aventure *f*; entreprise *f*; **-some,** *a* aventureux; (daring) osé.

veracity, vi-răss´-i-ti, *n* authenticité *f*; véracité *f*.

veranda, vi-rănn´-da, *n* véranda *f*.

verb, veurbe, *n* verbe *m*; **-al*,** *a* verbal; **-atim,** *adv* & *a* mot pour mot.

verbose, veur-bauce´, *a* verbeux; diffus.

verdant, veur´-dannte, *a* verdoyant.

verdict, veur´-dicte, *n* verdict *m*.

verdigris, veur´-di-gri, *n* vert-de-gris *m*.

verge, veurdje, *v* pencher vers. *n* (brink) bord *m*.

verify, vair´-i-fâï, *v* vérifier.

vermilion, veur-mil´-yonne, *n* & *a* vermillon *m*.

vermin, veur´-minne, *n* vermine *f*.

vernacular, veur-năk´-iou-l'r, *n* & *a* vernaculaire *m*.

versatile, veur´-*sa*-tâîle, *a*

versatile; apte à tout.

verse, veurce, n vers m;
(song) couplet m;
(Bible) verset m.

versed, veursste, a versé.

version, veur´-ch'n, n
version f.

versus, veur´-ceusse, prep
contre.

vertical*, veur´-ti-k'l, a
vertical.

vertigo, veur´-ti-gau, n
vertige m,
étourdissement m.

very, vèr´-i, adv très; fort;
bien; a même.

vessel, vess´-'l, n vase m;
récipient m; (naut)
vaisseau m.

vest, veste, n gilet m;
(under) tricot de corps
m.

vested, vess´-tedde, a
(interest; rights) acquis.

vestige, vess´-tidje, n
vestige m.

vestment, vesst´-m'nt, n
vêtement m.

vestry, vess´-tri, n (place)
sacristie f.

vet, vette, n vétérinaire
m/f.

veteran, vett´-e-rănn, n
vétéran m.

veterinarian, vett´-eur-i-
na-ri-an, n (pop. bet)
vétérinaire m.

veterinary, vett´-eur-i-na-

ri, a vétérinaire.

veto, vî´-tau, n veto m. v
mettre le veto à.

vex, vexe, v vexer;
contrarier.

vexatious, vex-é´-cheuce,
a vexant; contrariant;
irritant; (law) vexatoire.

via, vâï´-a, prep via, par.

viaduct, vâï´-a-docte, n
viaduc m.

vibrate, vâï´-bréte, v
vibrer.

vibration, vâï´-bré´-ch'n,
n vibration f.

vicar, vik´-'r, n (of a
parish) curé m;
(protestant) pasteur m.

vicarage, vik´-'r-idj, n
presbytère m.

vice, vâïce, n vice m;
(mech) étau m.

vice admiral, vâïce-ăd´-
mi-ral, n vice-amiral m.

vice president, vâïce-
prèz´-i-dennte, n vice-
president m.

viceroy, vâïce´-roa'i, n
vice-roi m.

vice versa, vâïce-veur-să,
adv vice versa.

vicinity, vi-cinn´-i-ti, n
voisinage m; proximité f.

vicious*, vich´-euce, a
vicieux.

viciousness, vich´-euce-
nesse, n nature vicieuse
f.

victim, vic´-time, n
victime f.

victimize, vic´-timm-âïze,
v rendre victime.

victor, vic´-t'r, n
vainqueur m.

victorious*, vic-tau´-ri-
euce, a victorieux.

victory, vic´-tŏr-i, n
victoire f.

victual, vitt´-'l, v
ravitailler; –s, npl vivres
mpl.

video, vi´-dî-ô n vidéo, f
(film); n vidéo-cassette
(videocassette) f; n
magnétoscope
(recorder) m.

vie, vâï, v rivaliser; faire
assaut de.

view, vioue, n vue f;
opinion f. v visiter;
examiner.

vigil, vidj´-il, n veille f;
(eccl) vigile f.

vigilance, vidj´-i-l'nce, n
vigilance f.

vigilant, vidj´-i-l'nt, a
vigilant.

vigor, vigg´-'r, n vigueur f;
force f.

vigorous*, vigg´-eur-euce,
a vigoureux; fort.

vile*, vâïle, a vil; abject.

vilify, vil´-i-fâï, v diffamer;
avilir.

villain, vil´-inne, n
scélérat m; gredin m.

villainous, vil´-*a*-neuce, *a* vil; infâme.

villainy, vil´-*a*-ni, *n* infamie *f*.

vindicate, vinn´-dik-éte, *v* défendre; justifier.

vindication, vinn-di-ké´-ch'n, *n* justification *f*; défense *f*.

vindictive*, vinn-dic´-tive, *a* vindicatif; rancunier.

vindictiveness, vinn-dic´-tive-nesse, *n* rancune *f*.

vine, vâîne, *n* vigne *f*.

vinegar, vinn´-i-gueur, *n* vinaigre *m*.

vineyard, vinn´-*ieur*de, *n* vignoble *m*.

vintage, vinn´-tidje, *n* vendange *f*; (year) année *f*.

viola, vi-au´-la, *n* alto *m*.

violate, vâî´-ŏ-léte, *v* violer.

violence, vâî´-ŏ-l'nce *n* violence *f*.

violent*, vâî´-ŏ-lennte, *a* violent.

violet, vâî´-ŏ-lette, *n* violette *f*. *n* & *a* violet *m*.

violin, vâî-ŏ-linne´, *n* violon *m*.

violinist, vâî-ŏ-linn´-ist, *n* violoniste *m* & *f*.

viper, vâî´-p'r, *n* vipère *f*.

virgin, veur´-djinne, *n* & *a* vierge *f*.

virile, vi´-râîle, *a* viril.

virtual*, veur´-tiou-al, *a* virtuel.

virtue, veur´-tioue, *n* vertu *f*.

virtuous*, veur´-tiou-euce, *a* vertueux.

virulent*, vir´-iou-lennte, *a* virulent.

virus, vî´-reusse, *n* virus *m*.

visa, vî´-za, *n* visa *m*.

viscount, vâî´-câ'ounnte, *n* vicomte *m*.

viscountess, vâî´-câ'ounn-tesse, *n* vicomtesse *f*.

visibility, viz-i-bile´-i-ti, *n* visibilité *f*.

visible, viz´-i-b'l, *a* visible.

visibly, viz´-i-bli, *adv* visiblement.

vision, vij´-'n, *n* vision *f*.

visit, viz´-itte, *v* visiter; aller voir; (a person) rendre visit à. *n* visite *f*.

visitor, viz´-itt-'r, *n* visiteur, -euse *m* & *f*.

visual, vij´-iou-'l, *a* visuel.

vital*, vâî´-t'l, *a* essentiel; vital; –s, *npl* organes essentiels *mpl*.

vitality, vâî-tăl´-i-ti, *n* vitalité *f*.

vitamin, vit´-*a*-minn, *n* vitamine *f*.

vitriol, vite´-ri-ŏle, *n* vitriol *m*.

vivacious*, vi-vé´-cheuce, *a* vif; animé.

vivacity, vi-văss´-i-ti, *n* vivacité *f*.

vivid, viv´-ide, *a* vif; frappant; (color) éclatant.

vixen, vic´-senn, *n* (female fox) renarde *f*; (fig) mégère *f*.

vocabulary, vau-căb´-iou-la-ri, *n* vocabulaire *m*.

vocal*, vau´-c'l, *a* vocal; –**chords,** *npl* cordes vocales *fpl*.

vocalist, vau´-cal-ist, *n* chanteur *m*; cantatrice *f*.

vocation, vau-qué´-ch'n, *n* vocation *f*; profession *f*.

vociferous*, vŏ-ci´-feur-euce, *a* bruyant.

vogue, vaugue, *n* vogue *f*; mode *f*.

voice, voa'ice, *n* voix *f*.

void, voa'ide, *a* vide; nul; dénué de. *n* vide *m*.

volatile, vol´-*a*-tâîle, *a* volatil; (fig) gai.

volcano, vol-qué´-nau, *n* volcan *m*.

volley, vol´-i, *n* (of cannon) volée *f*; (salute) salve *f*.

volt, volte, *n* (electric) volt *m*; –**age,** tension *f*.

voluble, vol´-iou-b'l, *a* volubile; loquace.

volume, vol´-ioume, *n*
volume *m*.
voluminous*, vol-ioue´-
mi-*neuce*, *a*
volumineux.
voluntary, vol´-*eunn*-ta-ri,
a volontaire; spontané.
volunteer, vol-*eunn*-tîre´,
n volontaire *m* & *f*. *v*
s'offrir.
voluptuous*, vol-op´-
tiou-*euce*, *a* voluptueux.
vomit, vomm´-itte, *v*
vomir.
voracious, vŏ-ré´-*cheuce*,
a vorace; dévorant.
vortex, voar´-texe, *n*
tourbillon *m*.
vote, vaute, *n* vote *m*;
scrutin *m*; voix *f*. *v*
voter; **–r,** *n* électeur, -
trice *m* & *f*.
vouch, vâ'outche, *v*
attester; (persons)
répondre de.
voucher, vâ'outch´-'r, *n*
pièce justificative *f*; bon
m.
vow, vâ'ou, *n* vœu *m*. *v*
faire vœu de; jurer.
vowel, vâ'ou´-'l, *n* voyelle
f.
voyage, voa'i´-idj, *n*
voyage par mer *m*.
vulgar, vol´-gueur, *a*
vulgaire; commun.
vulnerable, vol´-*neur*-a-
b'l, *a* vulnérable.

vulture, vol´-tioure, *n*
vautour *m*.

wad, ouode, n (for fire arms, etc.) bourre f; (surgical) tampon m.

wadding, ouodd´-inng, n coton-hydrophile m; (padding) ouate f.

waddle, ouodd´-'l, v se dandiner.

wade, ouéde, v marcher dans.

wafer, oué´-f'r, n (thin biscuit) gaufrette f; (eccl) hostie f.

wag, ouăgue, v remuer; secouer. n farceur m.

wage, ouédje, v (war) faire la guerre à.

wager, oué´-dj'r, n gageure f; pari m. v parier.

wages, oué´-djize, npl (servants) gages mpl; (workmen) salaire m.

waggle, ouăgg´-'l, v remuer; –about, v frétiller.

wagon, ouăgg´-'n, n chariot m.

waif, ouéfe, n épave f.

wail, ouéle, v se lamenter. n lamentation f.

waist, ouéste, n taille f; ceinture f.

wait, ouéte, v attendre; (at table) servir; –er, n serveur m; –for, v attendre; –ing, n attente f; (service) service m; –ing room, salle d'attente f; –ress, serveuse f; –upon, v servir.

waive, ouéve, v abandonner; renoncer à.

wake, ouéke, v (to awake) se réveiller; (to be called) réveiller. n (ship's) sillage m.

walk, ou'oak, v aller à pied; marcher; (stroll) se promener. n promenade f.

wall, ou'oal, n mur m; –flower, giroflée f; –paper, papier peint m.

wallet, ouol´-ite, n portefeuille m.

wallow, ouol´-au, v se vautrer.

walnut, ouôl´-notte, n noix f; (tree) noyer m.

walrus, ouôl´-reuce, n morse m.

waltz, ouôlts, v valser. n valse f.

wan, ou'oanne, a pâle; blême.

wander, ou'oann-d'r, v errer; (mentally) délirer.

wane, ouéne, (of the moon) v décroître. n déclin m.

want, ou'oannte, n (lack) manque m; (distress) dénuement m; **for –of,** faute de; v vouloir; avoir besoin de; avoir envie de.

wanton, ou'onne´-t'n, a (lustful) licencieux; (wicked) criminel; (waste) de gaieté de cœur.

war, ou'oar, v faire la guerre à; n guerre f;

–like, *a* belliqueux; **––office,** ministère de la guerre *m;* **––ship,** vaisseau de guerre *m.*

warble, ou'oar´-b'l, *v* gazouiller.

warbler, ou'oar´-bleur, *n* fauvette *f.*

ward, ou'oarde, *n* (minor) pupille *m* & *f;* (hospital) salle *f;* **–en,** (guard) gardien *m;* **–off,** *v* parer; **–ress,** *n* gardienne *f;* **–robe,** armoire *f;* **––room,** (naval) carré des officiers *m.*

ware, ouère, *n* marchandise *f.*

warehouse, ouère´-hâ'ouce, *n* entrepôt *m;* magasin *m. v* emmagasiner; (furniture, etc) entreposer.

warm, ou'oarme, *a** chaud. *v* chauffer; se chauffer; **–th,** *n* chaleur *f;* (fig) ardeur *f.*

warn, ou'oarne, *v* avertir; notifier à; **–ing,** *n* avertissement *m;* (caution) avis *m.*

warp, ou'oarpe, *v* (wood) jouer; (mind) fausser.

warrant, ouor´-'nte, *n* (authority) autorisation *f;* (for arrest) mandat d'arrêt *m;* (voucher) mandat *m;* **–y,**

garantie *f.*

warrior, ouor´-ieur, *n* guerrier *m.*

wart, ou'oarte, *n* verrue *f.*

wary, oué´-ri, *a* circonspect, prudent.

wash, ou'oache, *v* laver; se laver; **–basin,** *n* cuvette *f;* **–up,** *v* faire la vaisselle; **–erwoman,** laveuse *f;* **–ing,** blanchissage *m;* **–ing machine,** *n* lave-linge *m;* **–stand,** table de toilette *f.*

washer, ou'oache´-'r, *n* (mech) joint *m;* rondelle *f.*

washing machine, ou'oache´-inng-ma-chîne, *m* machine à laver *f.*

wasp, ou'oaspe, *n* guêpe *f.*

waste, ouéste, *n* gaspillage *m;* (refuse) rebut *m;* déchets *mpl* (land) terrain vague *m. v* gaspiller; **–away,** dépérir; **–ful,** *a* gaspilleur; prodigue.

watch, ouotche, *v* (not to sleep) veiller; observer; (vigilance) surveiller. *n* montre *f;* (wrist) montre-bracelet *f;* (naut) quart *m;* **––dog,** chien de garde *m;* **–maker,** horloger *m;*

–man, veilleur de nuit *m;* **–over,** *v* veiller sur; **–word,** *n* mot d'ordre *m.*

water, ou'oa´-t'r, *v* arroser; (cattle, etc) abreuver. *n* eau *f;* **hot –bottle,** bouillotte *f;* **–color,** aquarelle *f;* **–cress,** cresson *m;* **–fall,** chute d'eau *f;* **–jug,** cruche *f;* **–lily,** nénuphar *m;* **–line,** ligne de flottaison *f;* **–logged,** *a* plein d'eau; **–mark,** *n* niveau des eaux *m;* (paper) filigrane *m;* **–proof,** *a* imperméable; **–tank,** *n* réservoir *m;* **–tight,** *a* étanche; **–skiing,** *n* ski nautique *m;* **–works,** *npl* ouvrages hydrauliques *mpl.*

watering, ou'oa-teur-inng, *n* (of plants, etc.) arrosage *m;* abreuvage *m;* **–can,** arrosoir *m.*

wave, ouéve, *n* (sea, etc) vague *f;* (radio, etc) onde *f. v* (flags, etc) flotter; agiter; (to somebody) faire signe; (sway) se balancer; (hair) onduler; **–length,** *n* longueur d'onde *f.*

waver, ouéve´-'r, *v* hésiter; être indécis.

wavering, ouéve´-eur-inng, *a* indécis; irrésolu.

wavy, ouéve´-i, *a* onduleux; (hair) ondulé.

wax, ouâxe, *v* cirer. *n* cire *f;* **--works,** musée de figures de cire *m.*

way, oué, *n* chemin *m;* manière *f;* façon *f;* **–in,** entrée *f;* **–lay,** *v* dresser un guet-apens; **–out,** *n* sortie *f;* **–through,** passage *m;* **–ward,** *a* entêté; capricieux.

we, oui, *pron* nous.

weak, ouíque, *a** faible; infirme; débile; **–en,** *v* affaiblir; **–ening,** *a* débilitant; **–ling,** *n* être faible *m;* **–ness,** faiblesse *f.*

weal, ouíle, *n* bien-être *m;* (mark) marque *f.*

wealth, ouèl*t*s, *n* richesse *f;* opulence *f.*

wealthy, ouèl*t*s´-i, *a* riche; opulent.

wean, ouíne, *v* sevrer; (*fig*) détacher de.

weapon, ouèp´-'n, *n* arme *f.*

wear, ouère, *n* (by use) usage *m. v* (carry) porter; (last) durer; **–able,** *a* mettable; **–out** (away), *v* user; (fatigue) épuiser.

weariness, ouí-ri-nesse, *n* lassitude *f;* (*fig*) ennui *m.*

weary, ouí-ri, *a* las;

ennuyé. *v* fatiguer; **–of,** se lasser de.

weasel, ouí-z'l, *n* belette *f.*

weather, ouèdz´-'r, *n* temps *m. v* surmonter; **--bound,** *a* retenu par le mauvais temps; **–cock,** *n* girouette *f;* **–report,** bulletin météorologique *m.*

weave, ouíve, *v* tisser; **–r,** *n* tisserand *m.*

web, ouèbe, *n* (spider) toile *f.*

webbing, ouèbe´-inng, *n* (of a chair, bed, etc.) sangle *f.*

web-footed, ouèbe-foutt´-èdde, *a* palmé.

wed, ouède, *v* se marier avec; épouser; (perform ceremony) marier.

wedding, ouède´-inng, *n* mariage *m;* **–ring,** alliance *f.*

wedge, ouèdje, *n* coin *m;* (for fixing) cale *f. v* caler; **–in,** serrer; presser.

wedlock, ouède´-loque, *n* mariage *m.*

Wednesday, ou'ennze´-dé, *n* mercredi *m.*

weed, ouíde, *n* mauvaise herbe *f. v* sarcler.

week, ouíque, *n* semaine *f;* **--day,** jour de semaine *m;* **--end,** fin de semaine

f; week-end *m;* **–ly,** *a* (of newspapers) hebdomadaire.

weep, ouîpe *v* pleurer.

weevil, ouí-v'l, *n* charançon *m.*

weigh, oué, *v* peser; (mentally) considérer.

weight, ouéte, *n* poids *m;* **–y,** *a* pesant; (*fig*) grave.

weir, ouire, *n* barrage *m.*

weird, ouirde, *a* étrange; fantastique.

welcome, ouell´-*k*eume, *n* bienvenue *f. a* bienvenu. *v* bien recevoir; accueillir.

weld, ouelde, *v* souder.

welfare, ouell´-fére, *n* bien-être *m;* prospérité *f.*

well, ouell, *n* puits *m. adv* bien. *a* bon; **--being,** *n* bien-être *m;* **--bred,** *a* bien élevé; **–done,** (meat, etc) bien cuit; **--known,** *a* (bien) connu.

wend, ouennde, *v* aller; se diriger vers.

west, ouesste, *n* ouest *m;* occident *m.*

westerly, ouess´-*t*eur-li, *a* d'ouest; occidental.

wet, ouette, *n* humidité *f. a* humide; mouillé; (weather) pluvieux. *v* mouiller; **–suit,** *n* combinaison de plongée *f.*

whack, houâque, *v* rosser; battre.

whale, houéle, *n* baleine *f*; **—bone,** baleine *f*.

whaler, houél´-*eur*, *n* baleinier *m*.

wharf, hou'oarfe, *n* quai *m*; embarcadère *m*.

what, houotte, *pron* ce qui; ce que; que; quoi; qu'est-ce qui; qu'est-ce que. *a* quel; quelle; quels; quelles.

whatever, houotte-èv´-'r, *pron* & *a* tout ce qui; tout ce que; quel que soit; quelque ... que.

wheat, houîte, *n* froment *m*; blé *m*.

wheedle, houîdd´-'l, *v* cajoler; câliner.

wheel, houîle, *n* roue *f*. *v* faire rouler; **spinning- —,** *n* rouet *m*; **—barrow,** brouette *f*; **—wright,** charron *m*; **—chair,** *n* fauteuil roulant *m*.

wheezy, houîz´-i, *a* poussif.

when, houenne, *adv* quand; lorsque; où; que; **—ce,** d'où; **—ever,** chaque fois que.

where, houère, *adv* où; **—about(s),** où; **—as,** *conj* tandis que; **—** (law) vu que; **—at,** *adv* sur quoi; *conj* **—by,** par quoi; **—fore,** c'est pourquoi;

—in, dans lequel; **—on,** sur lequel.

wherever, houère-èv´-'r, *adv* partout où.

whet, houette, *v* aiguiser.

whether, houèdz´-'r, *conj* si; soit que; que.

which, houitche, *pron* qui; que; lequel; laquelle; lesquels; lesquelles.

whichever, houitch-èv´-'r, *pron* lequel; laquelle; lesquels; lesquelles.

while, houâîle, *v* passer. *conj* pendant que.

whim, houimme, *n* lubie *f*; caprice *f*; **—sical,** *a* capricieux.

whimper, houimm´-p'r, *v* pleurnicher.

whine, houâîne, *v* gémir; (fig) pleurnicher.

whip, houippe, *n* fouet *m*. *v* fouetter; (riding whip) cravacher; (cream) fouetter.

whirl, hou'eurle, *v* faire tourner; **—pool,** *n* tourbillon (d'eau) *m*; **—wind,** tourbillon *m*.

whisk, houisske, *n* (cooking) fouet *m*. *v* (eggs) battre; (cream) fouetter.

whiskers, houissk´-*eur*ze, *npl* favoris *mpl*; (cat) moustaches *fpl*.

whiskey, houiss´-ki, *n* whisky *m*.

whisper, houiss´-p'r, *v* chuchoter. *n* chuchotement *m*.

whistle, houiss´-'l, *n* sifflet *m*. *v* siffler.

whistling, houiss´-linng, *n* sifflement *m*.

white, houâîte, *n* & *a* blanc *m*; **—ness,** blancheur *f*; **—of egg,** blanc d'œuf *m*; **—wash,** *v* (lime) blanchir à la chaux.

whither, houidz´-'r, *adv* où.

whiting, houâîte´-inng, *n* (fish) merlan *m*.

whiz, houize, *v* siffler.

who, houe, *pron* qui.

whoever, houe-èv´-'r, *pron* quiconque.

whole, haule, *n* tout *m*; total. *a* tout; entier; **—sale,** *n* vente en gros *f*. *a* en gross; **—some*,** sain; salubre.

wholewheat bread, haule-houîte-brède, *a* pain complet *m*.

wholly, haul´-li, *adv* entièrement.

whom, houme, *pron* que; qui; lequel; laquelle; lesquels; lesquelles.

whoop, houpe, *v* huer. *n* cri (de guerre) *m*.

whooping cough, houpe´-

inng-coaf, n coqueluche f.

whose, houze, *pron* dont.

whosoever, (see **whoever**).

why, houâî, *adv* pourquoi.

wick, ouique, n mèche f.

wicked*, ouik´-ide, a méchant; mauvais; criminel.

wickedness, ouik´-ide-ness, n méchanceté f.

wicker, ouik´-´r, n osier m.

wide, ouâïde, a large; vaste; étendu; **–awake,** bien éveillé; (*fig*) vif; sur ses gardes; **–ly,** *adv* largement; très; **–spread,** a répandu.

widen,´ ouâïde´-´n, v élargir; s'élargir.

widow, ouid´-au, n veuve f.

widower, ouid´-au-´r, n veuf m.

width, ouidts, n largeur f; (extent) étendue f.

wield, ouilde, v manier; (power) détenir.

wife, ouâîfe, n femme f; femme mariée f; épouse f.

wig, ouigue, n perruque f.

wild*, ouâïlde, a sauvage; farouche; (*fig*) furieux; **–life,** n faune f.

wilderness, ouil´-d´r-ness, n désert m; (*fig*)

solitude f.

wile, ou'âîle, n ruse f; artifice m.

will, ouil, n volonté f; testament m. v vouloir; (bequeath) léguer; **good- –,**n (*com*) clientèle f.

willful*, ouil´-foull, a volontaire; (act) prémédité.

willing, ouil´-inng, a consentant; complaisant; **–ly,** *adv* volontiers; **–ness,** n bonne volonté f.

will-o'-the-wisp, ouil-ŏ-dzi-ouispe´, n feu follet m.

willow, ouil´-au, n saule m; **weeping- –,**saule pleureur m.

wily, ou'âï´-li, a astucieux; malin.

win, ouinne, v gagner; (victory) remporter; **–ner,** n gagnant, -e m & f; **–ning,** a (manners) engageant; but m; **–nings,** gain m.

wince, ouinnce, v (*fig*) reculer; tressaillir.

winch, ouinntche, n treuil m.

wind, ouâïnnde, v enrouler; (road, river, etc) serpenter; **–ing,** a sinueux; (stairs) en colimaçon; **–up,** v

rouler; (clock) remonter; (*com*) liquider.

wind, ouinnde, n vent m; flatulence f; **–fall,** (luck) aubaine f; **–mill,** moulin à vent m; **–pipe,** trachée- artère f; **–ward,** côté du vent m; **to be –y,** v (weather) faire du vent.

windlass, ouinnde´-lasse, n cabestan m.

window, ouinn´-dau, n fenêtre f, (car, etc) glace f; (shop) vitrine f; **–shopping,** n lèchevitrines m.

windshield, ouinnde´-chîlde, n pare-brise m.

windshield wiper, ouinnde-chîlde-ouâïpeu, n essuie-glace m.

wine, ouâîne, n vin m; **–list,** n carte des vins f.

wineglass, ouâîne´-glâce, n verre à vin m.

wing, ouinng, n aile f; (theatre) coulisse f.

wink, ouinnque, v cligner de l'œil. n clin d'œil m.

winkle, ouinnque´-'l, n bigorneau m.

winter, ouinn´-t'r, n hiver m. v passer l'hiver à; hiverner; **– sports,** npl sports d'hiver mpl.

wipe, ouâïpe, v essuyer;

–off, v effacer.

wire, ouâîre, n fil de fer m; **–less,** sans fil; n (radio) radio; T.S.F.

wisdom, ouiz´-d'm, n sagesse f; prudence f.

wise*, ouâîze, a sage; prudent.

wish, ouiche, n souhait m; vœu m; désir m. v souhaiter; désirer; vouloir.

wishful, ouiche´-foull, a désireux.

wisp, ouissppe, n touffe f; (straw) bouchon de paille m; (hair) mèche f.

wisteria, ouiss-terr´-i'a, n glycine f.

wistful*, ouisst´-foull, a pensif; d'envie de regret.

wit, ouitte, n esprit m; **to –,** à savoir; c'est-à-dire.

witch, ouitche, n sorcière f.

witchcraft, ouitche´-crâfte, n sorcellerie f.

with, ouidz, prep avec; (among) chez; de.

withdraw, ouidz-droa´, v retirer; se retirer.

wither, ouidz´-'r, v se faner; se flétrir.

withhold, ouidz-haulde´, v retenir; (sanction) refuser.

within, ouidz-inne´, prep dans; en. adv à l'intérieur.

without, ouidz-â'oute´, prep (not having) sans; adv (outside) dehors.

withstand, ouidz-stânnde´, v résister à.

witness, ouitt´-nesse, n témoin m. v témoigner.

wits, ouittse, npl jugement m; **to live by one's –,** vivre d'expédients.

witticism, ouitt´-i-cizme, n trait d'esprit m.

witty, ouitt´-i, a spirituel.

wizard, ouiz´-eurde, n sorcier m; magicien m.

wobble, ou'obbe´-'l, v branler; vaciller.

woe, ou'au, n malheur m; (fig) peine f.

woeful*, ou'au´-foull, a triste; affligé.

wolf, ou'oulf, n loup m; **female –,** louve f.

woman, ou'oum´-m'n, n femme f.

womanhood, ou'oum´-m'n-houdde, n état de femme m.

womanly, ou'oum´-m'n-li, a féminin.

womb, ou'oumme, n utérus m; matrice f; (fig) sein m.

wonder, ouonn´-d'r, n merveille f. v s'émerveiller de;

s'étonner de; (doubt) se demander.

wonderful, ouonn´-d'r-foull, a merveilleux; étonnant.

woo, ou'ou, v faire la cour â; **–er,** n prétendant m.

wood, ou'oude, n bois m.

woodcock, ou'oude´-coque, n bécasse f.

wooden, ou'oude´-'n, a de bois.

woodpecker, ou'oude-pèque´-'r, n pivert m.

woody, ou'oud´-i, a (trees) boisé.

wool, ou'oul, n laine f.

woolen, ou'oul´-'n, a de laine.

woolly, ou'oul´-i, a laineux.

word, oueurde, n mot m; parole f; (news) nouvelles fpl. v (verbal) exprimer; (written) rédiger; **–of honor,** n parole d'honneur f.

wording, oueurde´-inng, n termes mpl; style m; rédaction f.

work, oueurque, v travailler; (mine) exploiter; (mech) fonctionner; marcher. n travail m; ouvrage m; (literary) œuvre f.

worker, oueurque´-'r, n travailleur, -euse m & f.

working, oueurque´-inng, n (*mech*) fonctionnement m; marche f; (mine) exploitation f; (handling) manœuvre f; **–expenses,** frais d'exploitation mpl.

workman, oueurque´-m'n, n ouvrier m; **–ship,** exécution f; façon f.

works, oueurque'se, npl usine f; (*mech*) mécanisme m.

workshop, oueurque´-choppe, n atelier m.

world, oueurlde, n monde m; univers m.

worldly, oueurlde´-li, a mondain.

worm, oueurme, n ver m; (screw) filet m.

worm-eaten, oueurme´-îtt-'n, a vermoulu.

worry, ouorr´-i, n tracas m; (anxiety) tourment m. v s'inquiéter; se tracasser; se tourmenter; (bother) ennuyer.

worse, oueurse, adv pis. a pire.

worship, oueur´-chippe, v adorer. n adoration f; (divine) culte m.

worst, oueurste, a le pire. n le pis m.

worsted, ou'ouss´-tèdde, n (yarn) fil de laine m.

worth, oueurts, n valeur f; mérite m. a qui vaut; **to be –,** v valoir; mériter; **to be –while,** valoir la peine.

worthily, oueurdz´-i-li, adv dignement.

worthless, oueurts´-lesse, a sans valeur.

worthy, oueurdz´-i, a digne; méritant.

would, ou'oude, aux v he w. do (*conditional tense*) il ferait; **he w. have done** il aurait fait; **I w. come every day** (*used to*) je venais chaque jour; **I w. like some tea** je voudrais du thé; **w. you come here?** voulez-vous venir ice? **he w.n't come** il a refusé de venir.

would-be, ou'oude´-bî, a soi-disant; prétendu.

wound, ou'ounde, n blessure f; plaie f. v blesser.

wrangle, rain´-ng'l, v se disputer. n querelle f.

wrap, răppe, n sortie de bal f. v envelopper; **–up,** (oneself) s'emmitoufler.

wrapper, răppe´-'r, n enveloppe f; (postal) bande f; (book) couverture f.

wrapping paper, răppe-

inng-pé-p'r, n papier d'emballage m.

wrath, roats, n courroux m; colère f.

wreath, rits, n couronne f.

wreathe, ridz, v entrelacer.

wreck, rèque, n naufrage m; (*fig*) ruine f. v faire naufrage; (*fig*) ruiner; **–age,** n (pieces of ship, etc) épaves fpl.

wrecked, rèkte, a naufragé; ruiné.

wren, rène, n roitelet m.

wrench, renntche, n arrachement violent m; (sprain) entorse f; (tool) clé anglaise f. v tordre; (pull) arracher (à or de).

wrestle, ress´-l'l, v lutter.

wrestler, ress´-l'r, n lutteur m.

wretch, rètche, n misérable m & f.

wretched, rétch´-edde, a triste; (person) misérable.

wretchedness, rétch´-edde-ness, n misère f.

wriggle, rigg´-l'l, v se tortiller; **–through,** se faufiler.

wring, rinng, v tordre; (washing) essorer.

wrinkle, rinng´-k'l, n ride f. v rider; (brow) froncer.

wrist, risste, n poignet m.

writ, rite, n assignation f;

commandement *m*.

write, râîte, *v* écrire.

writer, râîte´-'r, *n* auteur *m*; écrivain *m*.

writhe, râîd*z*, *v* se tordre (de douleur).

writing, râîte´-inng, *n* écriture *f*; inscription *f*; **hand–,**écriture *f*; **in–,** *adv* par écrit.

writing paper, râîte´-inng-pé´-pr, *n* papier à lettres.

written, ritt´-'n, *a* écrit.

wrong, ron-ng, *n* tort *m*; injustice *f*. *v* faire tort à. *a** faux; mauvais; mal; injuste; illégal; **–side,** *n* mauvais côté *m*; (material) envers *m*; **to be –,** avoir tort.

wrought iron, roat âî´-*eu*rne, *n* fer forgé *m*.

wry, râï, *a* désabusé; **–face,** *n* grimace *f*.

Xmas (Christmas), criss´-meusse, *n* Noël *m*.

x-rays, èkce-réze, *npl* rayons X *mpl*; (X-ray photograph) radiographie *f*. *v* radiographier.

xylophone, sâï´-lo-faune, *n* xylophone *m*.

yacht, i'ŏte, *n* yacht *m.*

yachting, i'ote´-inng, *n* yachting *m.*

yard, i'ârde, *n* cour *f;* (measure) yard *m;* (ship, timber, etc) chantier *m.*

yarn, i'ârne, *n* fil *m;* (story) histoire *f.*

yawn, i'oanne, *v* bâiller. *n* bâillement *m.*

yawning, i'oann´-inng, *n* bâillement *m. a* (*fig*) béant.

year, i'îre, *n* an *m;* année *f.*

yearly, i'îre´-li, *a* annuel. *adv* annuellement.

yearn, i'eurne, *v* soupirer après; languir pour.

yearning, i'eurne´-inng, *n* désir *m;* aspiration *f.*

yearningly, i'eurne´-inng-li, *adv* ardemment.

yeast, yi'îste, *n* levure *f;* levain *m.*

yell, c'ell, *n* hurlement *m;* cri *m. v* hurler; crier.

yellow, i'ell´-au, *n* & *a* jaune *m.*

yelp, i'elpe, *v* glapir, japper. *n* glapissement *m.*

yes, i'ess, *adv* oui; (after negative question) si.

yesterday, i'ess´-t'r-dé, *adv* & *n* hier *m.*

yet, i'ette, *adv* encore; déjà. *conj* cependant.

yew, i'oue, *n* (*bot*) if *m.*

yield, yi'île, *v* céder; produire; (bring in) rapporter. *n* rapport *m;* produit *m;* revenu *m.*

yogurt, i'ŏg´-eurte, *n* yaourt *m.*

yoke, i'auke, *n* joug *m;* (*fig*) sujétion *f. v* mettre au joug; subjuguer.

yokel, i'au´-k'l, *n* rustre *m.*

yolk, i'auke, *n* jaune d'œuf *m.*

yonder, i'onn´-d'r, *adv* là-bas. *a* ce . . . là.

you, i'oue, *pron* vous; (*fam*) tu; te; toi.

young, i'onng, *a* jeune. *n* (animals) petits *mpl.*

youngster, i'onng´-st'r, *n* jeune garçon; fille.

your, i'our, *poss a* votre; vos.

yours, i'ourze, *poss pron* le vôtre; la vôtre; les vôtres.

youth, i'outs, *n* jeunesse *f;* (lad) jeune homme *m;* – **hostel,** *n* auberge de jeunesse *f*

youthful, i'outs´-foull, *a* jeune; juvénile.

youthfulness, i'outs´-foull-nesse, *n* jeunesse *f.*

yuletide, i'oule´-tâïde, *n* temps de Noël *m.*

zap, zap, *v* bombarder, détruire; (TV) changer de chaîne.

zeal, zîle, *n* zéle *m.*

zealous, zèl´-euce, *a* zélé; ardent.

zebra, zî´-bra, *n* zèbre *m.*

zenith, zenn´-its, *n* zénith *m.*

zephyr, zèf´-'r, *n* zéphyr *m.*

zero, zi´-rau, *n* zéro *m.*

zest, zeste, *n* (*fig*) ardeur *f*; (relish) saveur *f.*

zinc, zinnque, *n* zinc *m. v* zinguer.

zipper, zip-ar, *n* fermeture-éclair *f.*

zone, zaune, *n* zone *f.*

zoo, zoue, *n* zoo *m.*

zoological, zau-ŏl-odj´-i-c'l, *a* zoologique.

zoology, zau-ol´-odj-i, *n* zoologie *f.*

zoom, zoum, *n* vombrissement *m*; zoom *m. v* vombrir; passer en trombe.